W9-DEZ-973

Case Problems in Finance

Case Problems in Finance

Edited by

J. KEITH BUTTERS, Ph.D.
Professor of Business Administration

WILLIAM E. FRUHAN, JR., D.B.A.
Assistant Professor of Business Administration

THOMAS R. PIPER, D.B.A.
Assistant Professor of Business Administration

All of the
Graduate School of Business Administration
Harvard University

1972 • SIXTH EDITION

RICHARD D. IRWIN, INC. *Homewood, Illinois 60430*
IRWIN-DORSEY LIMITED *Georgetown, Ontario*

Sixth Edition

First Printing, May 1972

Case material of the Harvard Graduate School of Business Administration is made possible by the cooperation of business firms who may wish to remain anonymous by having names, quantities, and other identifying details disguised while basic relationships are maintained. Cases are prepared as the basis for class discussion rather than to illustrate either effective or ineffective handling of administrative situations.

Library of Congress Catalog Card No. 71–190538

Printed in the United States of America

Acknowledgments

To the businessmen who contributed the material for the cases in this volume we express our sincere gratitude. In the development of these cases they gave liberally of their time and, in most instances, they made available to us facts about their businesses normally held confidential.

We wish to acknowledge our debt to Pearson Hunt, Charles M. Williams, James T. S. Porterfield, Leonard C. R. Langer, Alan B. Coleman, Frank L. Tucker, James E. Walter, Erich A. Helfert, and Victor L. Andrews, whose names have appeared as editors of the first four editions of this book. Their influence on the organization and objectives of the current edition will be obvious to anyone who has used the early editions of *Case Problems in Finance.*

The cases in this edition have been written by 25 different individuals under the supervision of 15 different members of the senior faculty of the Harvard Graduate School of Business Administration. Most of the cases appearing for the first time in this edition have been written by one of the editors of this volume.

In addition to the editors of earlier editions of this volume we wish to thank Professors Robert N. Anthony, Lee Bodenhamer, Gordon Donaldson, Bertrand Fox, Fred K. Foulkes, Samuel L. Hayes III, Warren A. Law, Leonard Marks, Jr., Robert L. Masson, John H. McArthur, Robert W. Merry, Powell Niland, William W. Sihler, Lawrence E. Thompson, Richard F. Vancil, and William L. White for permission to use cases for which they are responsible as author or supervisor. We also wish to express our appreciation to the Stanford University Press for permission to reprint the Phoenix Aircraft Company case in this volume.

We also extend our thanks to the many instructors and research assistants of the Harvard Graduate School of Business Administration who wrote many of the cases in this volume under the supervision of senior members of the faculty.

Most of all we should like to express our special appreciation to Miss Carolyn Stubbs and Miss Hedwig Pocius for their invaluable editorial assistance in the preparation of this volume and the accompanying Teacher's Manual. To the extent that errors and inconsistencies have been avoided, they deserve much of the credit.

The editors assume full responsibility for the contents of this edition, but they are keenly aware of their obligation to their predecessors and associates.

Graduate School of Business Administration
Harvard University
April 1972

J. KEITH BUTTERS
WILLIAM E. FRUHAN, JR.
THOMAS R. PIPER

Contents

LONG-TERM CAPITAL STRUCTURE AND COST OF CAPITAL

APPENDIXES

INDEX

Introduction

Many readers may be meeting the case method of instruction for the first time. More often than not the experience is a frustrating one, for cases typically end at the critical point—in the words of some, "just when they seem to be getting some place." At that point the reader is left to make his own way. It may be helpful, therefore, to know from the outset what case problems are and what advantages we believe can be gained from their use.

The heart of the case method of instruction is the use of problems to train the student to discover, and then to fix in his mind, *ways of thinking that are productive in the subject area.* Appropriate use of theory and the acquisition of factual material and procedural skills are also important goals, but the main objective is an ability to handle different types of managerial problems intelligently.

The word "decisional" is sometimes used to contrast the case method with "expository" teaching. The reader will find, for example, that most of the cases in this book are essentially descriptions of actual business situations. The facts are those which were known to some businessman; in total they present an immediate financial problem which that person had to decide. Some cases emphasize the preliminaries of decision making—the difficulty of isolating and defining the crucial problem or of determining whether enough information is at hand to make an intelligent decision. The great majority of cases, however, are "issue" cases; these present reasonable alternative courses of action which might have been followed in the given situation. Sufficient information is given for the reader to place himself in the businessman's position. From this vantage point he is challenged to analyze the problem and to decide upon the course of action to be taken.

The cases themselves depict a wide variety of financial problems and business situations. Reference to the Table of Contents will show that problems have been drawn from most of the major areas covered in financial courses. Cases have been selected from a wide variety of industries and from different time periods. Cases are also included which illustrate different phases in the life cycle of business firms and problems of cyclical decline as well as of prosperity.

Twenty cases appear in this edition for the first time. The early portion of the book consists of well-tested cases that provide an opportunity for drill on fundamental techniques of analysis. This material has been carried over largely unchanged from the fifth edition.

The latter portion of the book has been substantially revised. Three new cases are added to the section on capital structure and debt capacity. The dividend section is completely new. Major changes have been made in the capital budgeting section. Two new cases have been added in the new venture section. One of these, a case on the Polaroid Corporation, traces the development of a very interesting company from its formation through the year 1970. A new series of cases emphasizes the impact of the chaotic conditions of the capital markets in 1969 and 1970 on corporate financial policy. Several cases in the section on public issues and one comprehensive case are new in this edition. In general, fresh material has been added to the sections of the book where topical developments are of most importance.

In order to keep the book of manageable length, many of the older cases appearing in the fifth edition have been dropped. Inevitably, some instructors will find that a few cases that they regard as valuable have been omitted from this edition. If an instructor is especially anxious to use one or more of these older cases, they can be ordered separately from the Case Clearing House of the Harvard Business School.

All of these cases are designed to provide a basis for class discussion; as such they are not intended to present either correct or incorrect illustrations of the solution of management problems. It need hardly be added that the discussion which they provoke will move along more realistic lines if students also have a standard finance text or reference book available and use it freely for background information not provided by this casebook. In addition, students will need to acquire proficiency in a number of analytical techniques useful in handling the quantitative aspects of cases.

Case problems confront students with the necessity of making decisions, and this is perhaps their greatest value. The student cannot stop with an understanding of the facts and a listing of items that deserve consideration. Mastery of these matters is merely the jumping-off point for class discussion. To be effective, the student must actually think the problem through to a decision, explain his analysis to his classmates, and defend it against their ideas. The need to choose among balanced alternatives and to discuss the decision intelligently is a great force in learning. It helps to provide that elusive quality of judgment that is often missed when learning is restricted to memorization of fact and views which others have codified.

Since the cases present business situations that pose debatable alternatives of action, they contain problems which can be narrowed but not settled by the usual techniques of financial analysis. Judgment must enter into the process of decision making, and therefore unanimous agreement as to the best decision is neither an expected nor a desired result of class meetings. This end result also contributes to the initial frustration of many students who have been working with scientific and technical problems; in the beginning phases of study in these areas a mechanistic approach can usually be counted on to yield a single "right" conclusion.

In developing a logical approach toward case problems, the reader should not overlook intangible human factors. The choice between financial alternatives in many, if not all, of the cases depends in part upon the principal's disposition for risk taking and other matters of judgment and taste.

In some instances, work with cases may require more of the student's time than would normal textbook reading assignments; however, the satisfaction of handling problems that bridge the gap between classroom study and business action, and the zest of independent thinking are usually adequate recompense for any extra time employed.

Part I

financing current operations

THE CASE OF THE UNIDENTIFIED INDUSTRIES

^^

Despite variations in operational and financial policies and practices and in operating results between firms in the same industry, the nature of the industry has an important impact on the general patterns of the need for funds (asset allocation), the methods of meeting these needs, and the financial results of most firms in the industry. Presented in Exhibit 1 are balance sheets, in percentage form, and selected ratios drawn from the balance sheets and operating statements of 10 firms in 10 different industries. Recognizing the fact of certain differences between firms in the same industry, each firm whose figures are summarized is broadly typical of those in its industry.

See if you can identify the industry represented. Then, be prepared as best you can to explain the distinctive asset structures and ratios of each industry.

1. Basic chemical company.
2. Electric and gas utility.
3. Supermarket chain.
4. Hotel chain.
5. Maker of name-brand, quality women's apparel.
6. Meat-packer.
7. Retail jewelry chain.
8. Coal-carrying railroad.
9. Automobile manufacturer.
10. Tobacco manufacturer.

Exhibit 1

THE CASE OF THE UNIDENTIFIED INDUSTRIES

*Balance Sheet Percentages**	*A*	*B*	*C*	*D*	*E*	*F*	*G*	*H*	*I*	*J*
ASSETS										
Cash and marketable securities	8.1	13.9	8.2	15.1	2.3	1.7	1.9	17.4	4.1	6.1
Receivables	2.8	11.7	16.2	21.6	53.7	4.6	6.5	2.9	36.6	7.6
Inventories	1.1	22.4	14.8	28.6	32.7	2.1	79.4	35.8	39.1	3.0
Other current assets	1.3	1.0	—	0.3	0.6	0.4	—	1.2	0.5	—
Plant and equipment (net)	78.2	40.1	49.0	34.0	6.8	89.9	10.9	40.0	19.1	78.4
Other assets	8.5	10.9	11.8	0.4	3.9	1.3	1.3	2.7	0.6	4.9
Total assets	100.0	100.0	100.0	100.0	100.0	100.0	100.0	100.0	100.0	100.0
LIABILITIES										
Notes payable	—	—	7.1	—	23.0	—	3.4	0.3	17.2	6.5
Accounts payable	3.5	14.6	5.3	28.5	6.9	2.9	1.6	22.7	21.0	5.7
Accrued taxes	3.8	5.6	4.8	4.3	4.2	3.5	6.5	4.0	5.2	0.2
Other current liabilities	2.1	10.5	3.4	0.5	1.3	3.3	2.5	9.1	8.5	3.5
Long-term debt	25.0	3.5	18.8	—	14.9	46.5	8.3	8.3	6.6	61.6
Other liabilities	4.1	1.2	—	—	10.1	1.3	0.2	7.9	0.4	1.0
Preferred stock	1.2	—	—	—	—	4.7	6.4	4.8	—	0.6
Capital stock and capital surplus	17.3	10.7	47.8	13.7	33.6	30.2	24.8	10.9	13.1	16.9
Retained earnings and surplus reserves	43.0	53.9	12.8	53.0	6.0	7.6	46.3	32.0	28.0	4.0
Total liabilities and stockholders' equity	100.0	100.0	100.0	100.0	100.0	100.0	100.0	100.0	100.0	100.0
Selected Ratios										
Current assets/current liabilities	1.64	1.59	1.89	1.98	2.52	0.93	6.38	1.57	1.55	1.05
Cash, marketable securities, and receivables/current liabilities	1.16	0.83	1.18	1.10	1.58	0.66	0.62	0.57	0.78	0.86
Total debt/total assets	0.393	0.382	0.399	0.333	0.601	0.573	0.224	0.526	0.581	0.885
Long-term debt/capitalization	0.290	0.051	0.237	—	0.274	0.523	0.097	0.148	0.165	0.740
Net sales/total assets	0.28	1.50	0.85	5.20	1.11	0.35	1.46	4.69	2.22	0.88
Net profits/total assets	0.051	0.078	0.074	0.072	0.024	0.044	0.089	0.056	0.090	0.015
Net profits/total net worth	0.083	0.126	0.123	0.108	0.061	0.103	0.115	0.119	0.218	0.068
Net profits/net sales	0.182	0.052	0.087	0.014	0.022	0.128	0.061	0.012	0.041	0.017

* Without adjustment for lease obligations and other items not generally shown on the balance sheet.

THE HINTZ COMPANY

On May 10, 1967, Mr. Samuel Hintz, president of The Hintz Company, noted that the company's accounts receivable balance had increased to $93,000 as of April 30, 1967. Since this was $19,000 higher than it had been on March 31, 1967, Mr. Hintz decided to investigate the reasons for the increase to see whether it might have significance in determining the company's future plans.

The Hintz Company, located in New York City, manufactured baseball, basketball, and other athletic uniforms. The company's 20 employees cut and sewed fabrics to color and size specifications. The uniforms were sold directly to retail sporting goods shops in the New York metropolitan area. As there were several other small manufacturers of uniforms in New York City, competition for the business of these retail outlets was keen.

Since Hintz's founding in 1959 it had operated profitably, and sales volume had reached a peak of $350,000 in 1964. In the fall of 1965, sales failed to recover from the seasonal low of the summer months. In July, 1966, when a new sales manager, Mr. Katz, was employed, sales volume began improving. By May, 1967, Mr. Katz had secured 50 new accounts for the company.

After reading trade papers, Mr. Hintz believed that the prospects of the athletic uniform market looked promising for the remainder of 1967. It was reported that there were a large number of newly organized athletic teams in the New York area and that schools and other regular purchasers were buying new uniforms more frequently. Since Mr. Katz's more detailed experience in the market tended to confirm this information, Mr. Hintz was looking forward to the best year in the company's history. On this basis, he projected sales and profits by months for the remainder of 1967 as follows:

	Sales	*Profit before Taxes*
May	$ 50,000	$ 4,000
June	40,000	2,000
July	40,000	2,000
August	40,000	2,000
September	50,000	4,000
October	55,000	5,000
November	60,000	6,000
December	60,000	6,000
Total	$395,000	$31,000

Hintz's customers were for the most part small sporting goods stores. Of 450 accounts, only six purchased more than $10,000 worth of uniforms in a year. Most of the remainder made periodic purchases of approximately $100 per order. Hintz sold on terms of net 30, but only the large stores paid consistently within 60 days of billing. Bad debt losses were 2% of sales in 1966. A substantial portion of the retail stores' sales of athletic uniforms was made to schools that paid their accounts slowly, and Hintz's collections also tended to be slow. Mr. Hintz believed that many of the smaller stores were operated without adequate capital investment.

Mr. Katz received a salary of $10,000 and a 2% commission on his personal sales. He sold one third of the company's accounts as well as supervised the company's two other salesmen. Each salesman was paid a straight commission of 5%. No attempt was made to charge a salesman for bad debt losses resulting from his sales efforts.

Neither Mr. Hintz nor the company's bookkeeper, Mr. Stein, had abundant time to devote to credit management. As a result, the following general policies had been established for guidance in credit matters. Before selling to a new account, a company salesman was expected to appraise the storekeeper's character and abilities on the basis of his observations at the store, and to judge the financial condition of the store as best he could. If these appeared satisfactory, a line of credit of $200 was extended to the store. After a year, a salesman was authorized to increase the line of credit to $500 if the store had made all its payments within 90 days of billing. After two years of satisfactory credit experience, open lines of credit were granted when necessary. If a specific case warranted exception to these rules, Mr. Hintz reviewed the information available and made the final decision.

Billings were prepared by Mr. Stein when shipment was made. If payment was not received within 60 days, a form letter was sent to the customer calling his attention to this omission. After 90 days, a warning letter was sent, requesting payment within 10 days. Mr. Hintz telephoned all store owners who had not made payment within 100 days of billing; and unless he received a firm promise for immediate remittance, he threatened to turn the account over to his lawyer. If payment was not received after 120 days, the receivables were given to a law firm for collection, and the account was written off as a bad debt.

On April 30, 1967, $2,200 in outstanding receivables were in the hands of lawyers pending settlement. Legal fees on these collections amounted to 25% of the amount collected or $50, whichever was the larger. Mr. Hintz considered the company fortunate if it received as much as 50% on a receivable after it had been turned over to a law firm. In several instances, final settlement took as long as one year.

Although sales tended to fluctuate from month to month, Mr. Hintz maintained raw material and finished goods inventories at even levels. Since the company's production facilities were adequate to support a substantial increase in sales volume, no additions to fixed assets were contemplated. Mr.

Hintz noted that with the exception of the bank loan, current liabilities tended to remain relatively constant.

On May 10, 1967, when Mr. Hintz received the April 30, 1967, balance sheet shown in Exhibit 1, he was disturbed by the sharp increase in accounts receivable. He thought several questions important: (1) whether the increase indicated larger bad debt losses might be incurred in the future; (2) whether the current policies of credit administration needed alteration; and (3) whether the receivables balance might increase in the future to the point where the company would require more funds from the bank. To help answer these questions, he requested Mr. Stein to prepare the information contained in Exhibits 2 and 3. Profit and loss statements are given in Exhibit 4.

Exhibit 1

THE HINTZ COMPANY

BALANCE SHEETS, DECEMBER 31, 1965–66; APRIL 30, 1966–67

CHANGES IN BALANCE SHEET AMOUNTS, SELECTED PERIODS

(Dollar figures in thousands)

	Balance Sheets				*Changes*	
ASSETS	*Dec. 31, 1965*	*April 30, 1966*	*Dec. 31, 1966*	*April 30, 1967*	*Dec. to April, 1966–67*	*April to April, 1966–67*
Cash	$10	$10	$ 10	$ 4	$ −6	$ −6
Accounts receivable (net)	41	37	68	93	+25	+56
Inventory	23	22	25	22	−3	—
Total current assets	$74	$69	$103	$119	$+16	$+50
Machinery and equipment (net)	20	20	19	19	—	−1
Other assets	4	3	4	3	−1	—
Total assets	$98	$92	$126	$141	$+15	$+49
LIABILITIES						
Accounts payable	$20	$19	$ 21	$ 21	$ —	$ +2
Taxes payable	4	—	4	5	+1	+5
Accrued payroll	6	8	5	8	+3	—
Bank loan	—	—	25	32	+7	+32
Total current liabilities	$30	$27	$ 55	$ 66	$+11	$+39
Common stock	35	35	35	35	—	—
Surplus	33	30	36	40	+4	+10
Total liabilities and net worth	$98	$92	$126	$141	$+15	$+49

Exhibit 2

THE HINTZ COMPANY

SUMMARY OF TRANSACTIONS IN ACCOUNTS RECEIVABLE, JANUARY, 1966–APRIL, 1967

(Dollar figures in thousands)

1966	*Accounts Receivable Beginning*	*Sales* (+)	*Collections* (−)	*Bad Debts* (−)	*Accounts Receivable Ending*	*Collection Period* (*Days*)
January	$41.5	$ 30.6	$ 30.7	$0.5	$40.9	
February	40.9	32.4	37.1	0.6	35.6	34*
March	35.6	24.1	21.4	0.6	37.7	40*
April	37.7	26.3	26.4	0.6	37.0	44*
May	37.0	25.4	24.7	0.6	37.1	43*
June	37.1	22.0	28.0	0.7	30.4	38*
July	30.4	24.6	22.7	0.5	31.8	41*
August	31.8	27.6	17.7	0.5	41.2	47*
September	41.2	24.6	23.1	0.5	42.2	49*
October	42.2	31.7	28.0	0.4	45.5	48*
November	45.5	30.1	13.3	0.5	61.8	60*
December	61.8	38.2	31.2	0.5	68.3	60*
Total	$41.5	$337.4	$304.3	$6.3	$68.3	73†
1967						
January	$68.3	$ 33.7	$ 40.8	$0.5	$60.7	51*
February	60.7	38.1	28.4	0.6	69.8	58*
March	69.8	45.8	41.0	0.5	74.1	53*
April	74.1	54.9	35.1	0.6	93.3	56*
Total 1967 to date	$68.3	$172.5	$145.3	$2.2	$93.3	65†

* Based on most recent 60-day sales period.
† Based on year, or year to date.

Exhibit 3

THE HINTZ COMPANY

ANALYSIS OF COLLECTIONS, APRIL, 1966–67, AND ACCOUNTS RECEIVABLE, APRIL 30, 1966–67

(Dollar figures in thousands)

Month of Sale	*Age April 30 (Days)*	*Amount of Sales* 1966	*Amount of Sales* 1967	*Amount Collected in April* 1966	*Amount Collected in April* 1967
Collections in April:					
April	0–30	$26.3	$54.9	$ 1.0	$ 2.7
March	31–60	24.1	45.8	2.1	5.5
February	61–90	32.4	38.1	22.7	26.3
January	91–120	30.6	33.7	0.6	0.5
Earlier	121+	....	....	0.0*	0.1*
				$26.4	$35.1
				Amount of Outstanding Receivables by Month of Sale	
Age of accounts receivable on April 30:					
April	0–30	26.3	54.9	$25.3	$52.2
March	31–60	24.1	45.8	9.5	37.7
February	61–90	32.4	38.1	2.0	2.7
January	91–120	30.6	33.7	0.2	0.7
Earlier	....	....	....	0.0*	0.0*
				$37.0	$93.3

* Charged off, in hands of attorneys.

Exhibit 4

THE HINTZ COMPANY

PROFIT AND LOSS STATEMENTS

(Dollar figures in thousands)

	Year 1965	*Year* 1966	*Four Months Jan.–Apr.* 1966	*Four Months Jan.–Apr.* 1967
Sales	$335	$338	$114	$173
Cost of goods sold	213	215	75	120
Gross profit	$122	$123	$ 39	$ 53
General selling and administrative expenses	101	103	36	40
Bad debt loss	3	3	1	1
Operating profit	$ 18	$ 17	$ 2	$ 12
Provision for taxes	4	4	0	3
Net profit	$ 14	$ 13	$ 2	$ 9
Dividends	10	10	5	5
Retained earnings	$ 4	$ 3	$ (3)	$ 4

THE COLLAPSIBLE LAWN CHAIR COMPANY

In early August, 1968, Mr. R. R. Doister, president of The Collapsible Lawn Chair Company, thought he saw an alarming trend in the pattern of payments by the company's customers. Although the absolute level of accounts receivable had declined as payments on the heavy sales made during the spring had been received, the number of days' sales in accounts receivable (based on the most current 30-day sales period) had risen significantly. The figures that caused Mr. Doister's alarm are shown in Exhibit 1.

Mr. Doister asked the treasurer, Mr. Udall, to prepare an aging of the balances in accounts receivable for April and July and to prepare a similar comparison for the collections received during those months. The resulting figures, which are shown in Exhibit 2, increased Mr. Doister's sense of unease. Only 51% of the receivables balance in July was 30 days old or less, compared with 97% in April. Likewise, only 7% of the collections in July represented payments on the current month's sales, compared with 73% of the collections in April.

Mr. Udall was asked to determine whether the company was suddenly making sales to less reliable accounts. He reported, however, that the pattern of payments had so far remained current for the entire year. Approximately 20% of the sales were paid for before the end of the month of sale. Half of the sales were paid for during the first month following sale. An additional 27% was paid for between 61 and 90 days following sale. Finally, the 3% of the volume that took longest to collect was paid during the fourth month. Mr. Udall said that virtually no bad accounts had been experienced.

Mr. Doister was not completely convinced, but on the advice of the treasurer and the sales manager decided not to take any drastic action. He watched the level of receivables and was pleased to see them decline by year-end to a level with which he was more comfortable.

After the end of the year, Mr. Udall prepared an analysis of the receivables to explain to Mr. Doister why there had been no cause for alarm. Mr. Doister found the explanation to be most satisfactory. Mr. Udall's figures are reproduced in Exhibit 3.

Exhibit 1

THE COLLAPSIBLE LAWN CHAIR COMPANY

SALES AND ACCOUNTS RECEIVABLE

(Dollar figures in thousands)

Month	*Sales*	*Balance in Accounts Receivable*	*Number of Days' Sales in Accounts Receivable—Based on Most Recent 30-Day Sales*
March	$ 20	$ 21	31 days
April	200	166	25
May	400	380	28
June	150	246	49
July	75	117	47

Exhibit 2

THE COLLAPSIBLE LAWN CHAIR COMPANY

AGE OF RECEIVABLES AND COLLECTIONS

(Dollar figures in thousands)

	Age of Receivables in Accounts Receivable Balance as of:				*Age of Collections during:*			
Period	*April*		*July*		*April*		*July*	
0–30	$160	97%	$ 60	51%	$40	73%	$ 15	7%
31–60	6	3	45	39	10	18	75	37
61–90	*	...	12	10	5	9	108	53
91–120	...	...	...	...	*	...	6	3
	$166	100%	$117	100%	$55	100%	$204	100%

* Less than $1,000.

Exhibit 3

THE COLLAPSIBLE LAWN CHAIR COMPANY

RECEIVABLES AT MONTH END LISTED BY MONTH OF ORIGIN

(Dollar figures in thousands)

Month	*Sales*	*Jan.*	*Feb.*	*Mar.*	*Apr.*	*May*	*June*	*July*	*Aug.*	*Sept.*	*Oct.*	*Nov.*	*Dec.*
January	$ 10	8	3	*									
February	15		12	5	*								
March	20			16	6	*							
April	200				160	60	6						
May	400					320	120	12					
June	150						120	45	5				
July	75							60	23	2			
August	50								40	15	2		
September	30									24	9	1	
October	20										16	6	*
November	15											12	5
December	15												12
	$1,000												
Total receivables		†	†	21	166	380	246	117	68	41	27	19	17
Average day's annual sales in A/R		†	†	8	61	139	90	43	25	15	10	7	6
Average day's sales to date in A/R		†	†	42	81	89	56	28	18	12	8	6	6
Average day's sale in most recent 30-day period in A/R		†	†	31	25	28	49	47	41	41	40	38	34

* Less than $1,000.
† Not calculated because includes receivables from prior year.

JERVIS TOY COMPANY

In January, 1958, Mr. Horace Nelson, president of Jervis Toy Company, was considering a proposal to change to level monthly production for the coming year. The company's production schedules had always been highly seasonal, reflecting the seasonal pattern of sales. Mr. Nelson could appreciate the improvement in production efficiency that the proposal promised, but he was uncertain of its impact on other phases of the business.

Jervis Toy Company was a manufacturer of plastic toys for children. These included tea sets, billiard sets, space helmets, earth satellites, guns, automobiles, trucks, and a wide variety of other items. Exhibit 1 shows the company's product mix for the years 1953–57.

The manufacture of plastic toys was a highly competitive business with many producers, most of which were not strongly financed. Capital requirements were not large, and technology was relatively simple, so that a number of new firms entered the business each year. On the other hand, competition was severe with respect to both price and design, resulting in a relatively high failure rate. There was sometimes a significant, temporary advantage in designing a popular new toy of the "fad" type. Margins tended to be high on such an item, until competitors were able to offer a similar product. For example, the successful introduction by Jervis Toy Company of plastic toy billiard sets had contributed significantly to profits in 1956. In 1957, 11 competitors had offered a similar item, and the wholesale price of Jervis billiard sets had been nearly halved.

Jervis Toy Company had been founded in 1946 by Mr. John Jervis after his release from naval service. Before World War II, Mr. Jervis had been employed as production manager by a large manufacturer of plastic toys. Mr. Jervis and his former assistant, Mr. Horace Nelson, established Jervis Toy Company with their savings in 1946. Originally a partnership, the firm had been incorporated in 1947, with Mr. Jervis taking 75% of the capital stock and Mr. Nelson, 25%. The latter served as production manager, and Mr. Jervis, as president, was responsible for overall direction of the company's affairs. After a series of illnesses, Mr. Jervis' health had broken down in 1956 and he had been forced to retire from active participation in the business. Mr. Nelson had assumed the presidency at this time. In 1957, he had hired Mr. James Hardy, a recent graduate of a prominent eastern technical institute, as production manager. Mr. Hardy had worked during summers in the plastics plant of a large diversified chemical company and thus had a basic familiarity with plastics production processes.

Jervis Toy Company had experienced relatively rapid growth since its founding and had enjoyed profitable operations each year since 1949. Sales were $840,000 in 1957 and were projected at $1,000,000 in 1958. Net profits had reached $127,000 in 1957 and were estimated at $152,000 in 1958, under seasonal production, after taxes of 50%. Exhibits 2 and 3 present the latest financial statements for the company. The cost of goods sold had averaged 60% of sales in the past and was expected to maintain approximately that proportion in 1958 under seasonal production. In keeping with the company's experience, operating expenses were considered likely to be incurred evenly throughout each month of 1958 under either seasonal or level production.

Expanding operations had resulted in a somewhat strained working capital position for Jervis Toy Company. The year-end cash balance of $86,000 in 1957 was regarded as the minimum necessary for the operations of the business. The company had occasionally borrowed from its bank of account, Hood Trust Company, on an unsecured line of credit. A loan of $40,000 was outstanding at the end of 1957. Mr. Nelson had been assured that the bank would be willing to extend a credit line of up to $150,000 in 1958, with the understanding that the loan would be completely repaid and "off the books" for at least a 30-day period during the year. Interest would be charged at a rate of 6%, and any advances in excess of $150,000 would be subject to further negotiations.

The company's sales were highly seasonal. Over 80% of annual dollar volume usually was sold during August–November. Exhibit 4 shows sales by months for 1957 and projected monthly sales for 1958. Sales were made principally to variety store chains and toy brokers on net 30-day terms. Large variety store chains were becoming increasingly important customers of Jervis Toy Company, accounting for over 65% of sales in 1957.

The company's production processes were not complex. Plastic molding powder, the principal raw material, was processed by injection molding presses and formed into the shapes desired. The plastic shapes were next painted at "merry-go-round" painting machines. The final steps in the process were assembly of the toy sets and packaging in cardboard cartons or plastic bags. Typically, all runs begun were completed in the same day so that there was virtually no work in process at the end of the day. Purchases on net 30-day terms were made weekly in amounts necessary for estimated production in the forthcoming week. Total purchases in 1958 were forecast at $300,000.

Jervis Toy Company's practice was to produce in response to orders. This meant production at a small fraction of capacity for about the first seven months of the year in order to take care of the restricted demand during this period. Only one of the five injection presses was customarily in use at one time during this period.

The first sizable orders for Christmas business were usually received from variety store chains early in August. For the next four months all equipment was utilized for 12 hours per day. The work force was greatly increased and also put on a 12-hour day. In 1957, overtime premiums had amounted to $53,000. Shipments were made whenever possible on the day that an order was produced. Hence, production and sales amounts in each month tended to be equivalent. A small inventory of representative finished goods, averaging $32,000 in 1957, was maintained in a nearby public warehouse, owing to lack of space in the plant. Storage costs of $800 had been incurred in this connection.

As in the past, pro forma balance sheets and income statements based on an assumption of seasonal production had been prepared for 1958 and presented to Mr. Nelson for his examination. These appear in Exhibits 5 and 6.

Since coming to work at Jervis Toy Company, Mr. Hardy had been impressed by the many problems arising from this method of scheduling production. Overtime premiums reduced profits. Seasonal expansion of the work force brought difficulties in recruitment and training. Machinery was largely unused during eight months of the year and was subjected to heavy usage during the remaining four months. Accelerated production schedules during the peak season necessitated frequent setup changes on the presses and painting machines. Some seeming unavoidable confusion in scheduling runs resulted. Relatively short runs and frequent setup changes caused inefficiencies in the manual assembly and packaging operations as workers encountered difficulties in relearning their operations.

For these reasons, Mr. Hardy had urged upon Mr. Nelson adoption of a policy of level monthly production in 1958. He pointed out that estimates of sales volume had usually proved to be reliable in the past. Purchase terms would not be affected by the rescheduling of purchases. The elimination of overtime wage premiums would result in substantial savings, estimated at $60,000 in 1958. Moreover, Mr. Hardy firmly believed that significant additional direct labor savings, amounting to about $47,000, would result from orderly production. Mr. Nelson speculated upon the effect that level production might have on the company's funds requirements in 1958. He assumed that except for profits, tax payments, and fluctuations in the levels of inventories, accounts receivable, and accounts payable, funds inflows and outflows would be approximately in balance. To simplify the problem, Mr. Nelson decided to assume that gross margin percentages would not vary significantly by months under either method of production.

Exhibit 1

JERVIS TOY COMPANY

SALES BY PRODUCTS, 1953–57

(As percentages of total sales)

	1953	*1954*	*1955*	*1956*	*1957*
Trucks and autos	18%	15%	15%	14%	15%
Space helmets	..	3	15	8	2
Guns (conventional)	10	9	2	3	3
Guns (ray)	..	..	6	9	4
Tea sets	44	49	50	43	44
Earth satellites	..	..	..	..	11
Space ships	..	..	2	6	7
Airplanes	16	12	2	1	3
Billiard sets	..	..	..	9	1
Miscellaneous	12	12	8	7	10
	100%	100%	100%	100%	100%

Exhibit 2

JERVIS TOY COMPANY

BALANCE SHEET, DECEMBER 31, 1957

(Dollar figures in thousands)

ASSETS	
Cash	$ 86
Accounts receivable	96
Inventory	31
Total current assets	$213
Plant and equipment, net	186
Prepaid items	78
Total assets	$477

LIABILITIES	
Accounts payable	$ 29
Notes payable—bank	40
Reserve for federal income taxes	88*
Total current liabilities	$157
Capital stock (1,000 shares)	100
Surplus	220
Total liabilities	$477

* Taxes payable on 1957 income; due in equal installments on March 15 and June 15, 1958. On September 15 and December 15, 1958, payments of 20% each of the estimated tax on 1958 income were due.

Exhibit 3

JERVIS TOY COMPANY

CONDENSED INCOME STATEMENTS, 1955–57

(Dollar figures in thousands)

	1955	*1956*	*1957*
Net sales	$634	$710	$840
Cost of goods sold	340	400	504
Gross profit	$294	$310	$336
Operating expenses	50	74	82
Profit before taxes	$244	$236	$254
Federal income taxes	102	105	127
Net profit	$142	$131	$127

Exhibit 4

JERVIS TOY COMPANY

MONTHLY SALES, 1957

(Dollar figures in thousands)

Month	Sales	Month	Sales
January	$ 8	July	$ 11
February	10	August	132
March	11	September	157
April	10	October	183
May	10	November	201
June	10	December	96

PROJECTED MONTHLY SALES, 1958

(Dollar figures in thousands)

Month	Sales	Month	Sales
January	$12	July	$ 16
February	14	August	162
March	16	September	184
April	14	October	214
May	14	November	228
June	14	December	112

Exhibit 5

JERVIS TOY COMPANY

PRO FORMA BALANCE SHEETS, 1958 (SEASONAL PRODUCTION)

(Dollar figures in thousands)

	Actual Dec. 31, 1957	Jan. 31, 1958	Feb. 28, 1958	March 31, 1958	April 30, 1958	May 31, 1958	June 30, 1958	July 31, 1958	August 31, 1958	Sept. 30, 1958	Oct. 31, 1958	Nov. 30, 1958	Dec. 31, 1958
ASSETS													
Cash (*a*)	$ 86	$102	$ 98	$ 86	$ 86	$ 86	$ 86	$ 86	$ 86	$ 86	$ 86	$104	$191
Accounts receivable (*b*)	96	12	14	16	14	14	14	16	162	184	214	228	112
Inventory (*c*)	31	31	31	31	31	31	31	31	31	31	31	31	31
Total current assets	$213	$145	$143	$133	$131	$131	$131	$133	$279	$301	$331	$363	$334
Plant and equipment (*d*)	186	186	186	186	186	186	186	186	186	186	186	186	186
Prepaid items (*d*)	78	78	78	78	78	78	78	78	78	78	78	78	78
Total assets	$477	$409	$407	$397	$395	$395	$395	$397	$543	$565	$595	$627	$598
LIABILITIES													
Accounts payable (*e*)	$ 29	$ 4	$ 4	$ 5	$ 4	$ 4	$ 4	$ 5	$ 49	$ 55	$ 64	$ 69	$ 34
Notes payable (bank) (*f*)	40	..	..	35	36	38	84	87	132	112	56	..	..
Accrued taxes (*g*)	88	87	86	41	40	39	(6)	(7)	21	24	63	104	92
Total current liabilities	$157	$ 91	$ 90	$ 81	$ 80	$ 81	$ 82	$ 85	$202	$191	$183	$173	$126
Capital stock	100	100	100	100	100	100	100	100	100	100	100	100	100
Surplus (*h*)	220	218	217	216	215	214	213	212	241	274	312	354	372
Total liabilities and net worth	$477	$409	$407	$397	$395	$395	$395	$397	$543	$565	$595	$627	$598

a) Assumes maintenance of minimum $86,000 balance and includes excess cash in months when company is out of debt.
b) Assumes 30-day collection period.
c) Assumes inventories maintained at December 31, 1957, level for all of 1958.
d) Assumes equipment purchase equal to depreciation, and that prepaid items do not change.
e) Assumed equal to 30% of month's sales and relates to material purchases of $300,000 for year as against sales of $1,000,000. Since inventories are level, purchases will follow seasonal production and sales pattern.
f) Plug figure.
g) Adjusted for tax payments of $44,000 in March and June, $30,000 in September and December (20% of $152,000 each); negative figures in June and July represent tax credits.
h) Adjusted for net profit from current month's operations, as per attached pro forma income statements.

Exhibit 6

JERVIS TOY COMPANY

PRO FORMA INCOME STATEMENTS, 1958 (SEASONAL PRODUCTION)

(Dollar figures in thousands)

	January	*February*	*March*	*April*	*May*	*June*	*July*	*August*	*September*	*October*	*November*	*December*	*Total*
Net sales	$12	$14	$16	$14	$14	$14	$16	$162	$184	$214	$228	$112	$1,000
Cost of goods sold (*a*)	7	8	10	8	8	8	10	97	110	129	137	68	600
Gross profit	$ 5	$ 6	$ 6	$ 6	$ 6	$ 6	$ 6	$ 65	$ 74	$ 85	$ 91	$ 44	$ 400
Operating expenses (*b*)	8	8	8	8	8	8	8	8	8	8	8	8	96
Profit before taxes	$(3)	$(2)	$(2)	$(2)	$(2)	$(2)	$(2)	$ 57	$ 66	$ 77	$ 83	$ 36	$ 304
Federal income taxes (*c*)	(1)	(1)	(1)	(1)	(1)	(1)	(1)	28	33	39	41	18	152
Net profit	$(2)	$(1)	$(1)	$(1)	$(1)	$(1)	$(1)	$ 29	$ 33	$ 38	$ 42	$ 18	$ 152

a) Assumes cost of goods sold equal to 60% of sales.
b) Assumed to be same for each month throughout the year.
c) Negative figures are tax credits from operating losses, and reduce accrued taxes shown on balance sheets.

JAMES W. SAXTON COMPANY

^^

The James W. Saxton Company, manufacturer of fine home furniture in Rocky Mount, North Carolina, distributed its products directly to department stores, independent home furnishing retailers, and a few small regional furniture chains. Early in April, 1951, the credit manager of the Saxton company, Mr. Frank Preston, received from his assistant, Mr. Richard Rossi, pertinent information on two accounts in Missouri—Bauman's, Inc., of St. Louis, and Vardon's Emporium of Kansas City. Mr. Rossi believed changes in these companies warranted Mr. Preston's attention.

Bauman's retailed quality home furnishings from four locations, one in the downtown section of St. Louis and the others in nearby suburban areas. The company also manufactured custom upholstered furniture on special order. Since Bauman's handled a complete line of home furnishings, sales were fairly steady throughout the year and were approximately 75% for cash and 25% by 30-day charge or 12-month installment terms. Installment terms called for 25% down and the balance in equal monthly payments over a 12-month period.

The store had been established in 1915 as a partnership and was incorporated in 1946. In June, 1950, two of the four original partners sold their shares in the company to the two remaining owners.

Bauman's had been a customer of the Saxton company since 1918 and had previously handled its affairs in a most satisfactory manner. Vardon's Emporium was a comparatively new customer of Saxton's, having been sold since 1946. A medium-sized department store in downtown Kansas City, it was well known for its extensive lines of home furnishings. Its account with Saxton had been satisfactory through 1950.

Both accounts were sold on terms of 1/10, net 30 and, although not discounting, had been paying invoices promptly until December, 1950. Mr. Preston had previously established a $10,000 limit on Bauman's and a $15,000 limit on Vardon's.

The Saxton company advertised its lines nationally and attempted to maintain intensive coverage of trading areas by distributing through stores strategically located within a particular marketing area. Beginning in 1949, activity in the furniture market had become sufficiently spotty that quality of product and service were not the only bases for competition among manufacturers for outlets. Credit terms and financing of dealers became equally important; thus, the Saxton company, in Mr. Preston's words, was "backed into the position of supporting numerous customers in order to maintain adequate distribution for its products."

Because of this requirement for the extension of fairly liberal credit, Mr. Preston had since 1949 adhered strictly to a policy of obtaining current reports on the financial status of customers. These reports, obtained as annual balance sheets and profit and loss statements for customers that were considered satisfactory risks, were supplied directly by the customers. Under certain circumstances, wherein Saxton was working very closely with a particular customer who was trading actively on a small investment, Mr. Preston received quarterly and at times monthly statements in order to keep on top of the credit situation.

In early April, 1951, Mr. Richard Rossi, assistant credit manager of the James W. Saxton Company, received the annual reports of Bauman's, Inc., and Vardon's Emporium. After reviewing these statements and checking the accounts receivable ledger for both customers, Mr. Rossi felt that the accounts should be reviewed by Mr. Preston. Accordingly, he furnished Mr. Preston with the information found in Exhibits 1 through 5.

When reviewing the accounts, Mr. Rossi kept in mind that 1950 had not been a particularly good year for retail furniture stores. It was generally known that stores such as Vardon's, carrying low-priced furniture lines, were the first to suffer the declines that had come in the late summer and early fall. This situation was followed by signs of a relaxing demand for furniture of higher quality and higher price toward the end of 1950. The drop in volume and the subsequent price cutting hit the profit margins of some retailers to such an extent that their losses in the latter part of the year equaled or more than offset profits gained in the earlier part of the year.

In the early months of 1951 the softness of the furniture business continued. Although there was no severe drop in the buying of furniture at the retail level, there was an indication that scare buying and purchasing in anticipation of potential shortages had been curtailed. Accordingly, retail stores reduced orders of new lines and reorders of established lines in February, March, and April. Throughout the country, orders for shipment in April were down about 30% from March; March had itself shown a drop of about 10% from February. Thus, credit managers among furniture manufacturing concerns were placed in the unhappy position of trying to please sales managers who wanted to maintain volume, while they were aware that the shipment of furniture to customers who had already overextended their financial positions was potentially dangerous in such a period.

Exhibit 1

JAMES W. SAXTON COMPANY

BAUMAN'S, INC.—BALANCE SHEETS AS OF JANUARY 31, 1949–51
(Dollar figures in thousands)

ASSETS	*1/31/49*	*1/31/50*	*1/31/51*
Cash	$ 14	$ 11	$ 8
Accounts receivable, net	231	261	268
Inventory	304	303	304
Total current assets	$549	$575	$580
Land	$ 59	$ 59	$ 59
Buildings, fixtures, and equipment	$225	$228	$263
Less: Reserve for depreciation	31	48	66
Net buildings, fixtures, and equipment	$194	$180	$197
Investment	11	11	11
Due from stockholders	...	36	48
Deferred charges	7	4	3
Total assets	$820	$865	$898
LIABILITIES			
Accounts payable	$144	$145	$154
Notes payable—employees	12	13	13
Estimated federal income tax	11	...	...
Current maturities on long-term debts	26	60	37
Miscellaneous accruals	36	34	11
Total current liabilities	$229	$252	$215
Notes payable—bank*	91	150	145
Mortgage notes payable	376	375	438
Preferred stock—5% noncumulative	32	32	32
Common stock	60	60	60
Capital surplus	...	...	19
Earned surplus (deficit)	32	(5)	(11)
Total liabilities	$820	$865	$898

* Secured by pledged accounts receivable.

Exhibit 2

JAMES W. SAXTON COMPANY

BAUMAN'S, INC.—INCOME STATEMENTS FOR YEARS ENDING JANUARY 31, 1949–51

(Dollar figures in thousands)

	1/31/49	*1/31/50*	*1/31/51*
Sales	$1,945	$1,583	$1,502
Less: Returns and allowances	175	186	122
Net sales	$1,770	$1,397	$1,380
Cost of goods sold	1,077	854	859
Gross profit	$ 693	$ 543	$ 521
Less: Operating expenses	595	515	498
Operating profit	$ 98	$ 28	$ 23
Other income	67	11	14
Net after other income	$ 165	$ 39	$ 37
Other deductions	40	41	43
Net profit (loss) before tax	$ 125	$ (2)*	$ (6)
Dividends paid	35	35	....
Net to surplus	$ 90	$ (37)	$ (6)

* Parentheses denote losses.

Exhibit 3

JAMES W. SAXTON COMPANY

VARDON'S EMPORIUM—BALANCE SHEETS AS OF JANUARY 31, 1950–51

(Dollar figures in thousands)

ASSETS	*1/31/50*	*1/31/51*
Cash	$ 123	$ 79
Notes and accounts receivable[p]	917	884
Inventory	895	821
Tax carryback claim	.....	74
Total current assets	$1,935	$1,858
Fixed assets, net	244	221
Leasehold improvements, net	598	577
Cash value life insurance[p]	47	46
Investments	9	9
Notes receivable—officers and employees[p]	18	23
Prepaid and deferred items	25	26
Total assets	$2,876	$2,760
LIABILITIES		
Notes payable—Industrial Finance Corporation	$ 885	$ 717
Accounts payable	407	443
Miscellaneous accruals	98	113
Total current liabilities	$1,390	$1,273
Common stock	570	570
Surplus	916	917
Total liabilities	$2,876	$2,760

[p] Pledged to secure 30-day renewable notes to Industrial Finance Corporation.

Exhibit 4

JAMES W. SAXTON COMPANY

VARDON'S EMPORIUM—INCOME STATEMENTS FOR YEARS ENDING JANUARY 31, 1950–51

(Dollar figures in thousands)

	1/31/50	*1/31/51*
Gross sales	$5,210	$4,828
Less: Returns and allowances	478	369
Net sales	$4,732	$4,459
Cost of goods sold	2,975	3,064
Gross profit	$1,757	$1,395
Operating expenses	1,499	1,630
Operating profit (loss)	$ 258	$ (235)
Adjustments:		
Elimination—reserves for inventory losses	...	145
Reduction—bad debt reserve	...	18
Tax carryback	...	74
Federal income tax	108	...
Net before dividends	$ 150	$ 2
Dividends paid	100	1
Net to surplus	$ 50	$ 1

Exhibit 5

JAMES W. SAXTON COMPANY

AGING OF ACCOUNTS RECEIVABLE BALANCES AS OF MARCH 31, 1951

Due from	*Prior*	*Dec.*	*Jan.*	*Feb.*	*Mar.*	*Totals*
Bauman's, Inc.	......	$5,803.14	$ 913.30	$3,524.37	$1,028.01	$11,268.82
Vardon's Emporium	$380.84*	4,883.96	1,025.55	4,352.00	9,124.77	19,767.12

* Represents invoice on disputed shipment in October; customer claimed damaged merchandise.

SPRAGUE MACHINE TOOL COMPANY

On September 20, 1951, Mr. Harry Greenwood, vice president of the Wolverine National Bank of Detroit, was examining the company's credit file on Sprague Machine Tool Company, a customer located in a nearby small city. Renewal of a $350,000 loan made to that company was to be considered by the loan committee the next day, and Mr. Greenwood was reviewing what had happened since the bank had taken on Sprague's account, so that he could decide what action he should recommend to the committee. The note had originally been a nine-month loan made in December, 1950, but the Sprague management was requesting a 90-day extension.

Since its establishment in 1900, Sprague had successfully weathered the cyclical fluctuations characteristic of the machine tool manufacturing business. Its peak production had been achieved during World War II—sales reaching $7.3 million in 1943. From that year, however, sales had declined, reaching a low of $1,765,000 in 1947, and the sales volume had been below $3 million in each subsequent year through 1948. Sprague had come out of World War II with a strong working capital position; with volume reduced in subsequent years, it had had no need to borrow prior to December, 1950.

Mr. Greenwood recalled that in December, 1950, Mr. Robert G. Murray, president of Sprague, requested a loan of $350,000 to assist in purchasing the stock interests of several dissident stockholders. While Sprague Machine Tool Company at that time had some excess cash over that required for normal operations, even more cash was required for the stock purchase, and Mr. Murray had, therefore, requested the Wolverine National Bank to lend Sprague Machine Tool Company $350,000 for a period of nine months. To justify the credit, Mr. Murray had submitted a monthly forecast of shipments for 1951 (Exhibit 1) and a balance sheet dated November 30, 1950 (shown in the first column of Exhibit 2). The Wolverine National Bank had agreed to make the loan, and in December, 1950, the company had retired 24,300 shares of its $10 par value stock purchased from its stockholders at an aggregate cost of $936,100. After this, there remained several hundred stockholders.

After the loan was made, Mr. Murray regularly sent the bank profit and loss statements and balance sheets. Mr. Greenwood selected the figures given on Exhibits 2 and 3 for use in his analysis.

The company manufactured machine tools, which were sold to several metalworking industries but principally to automobile manufacturers and some aircraft manufacturers. These products were largely made to order; their sales prices ranged from $20,000 to $500,000 per installation. Sprague's selling terms were 30 days net. Occasionally, a customer placing a large order would make Sprague an advance payment to help finance the construction of the machines involved, which covered periods up to five or six months for some of the more complex types of machines. Upon completion and shipment of orders against which advances had been obtained, Sprague deducted the amount of the advance from the amount billed the customer.

On September 19, 1951, Mr. Greenwood had received a letter from Mr. Murray requesting a 90-day extension of Sprague Machine Tool Company's note. Mr. Murray's letter commented at some length on the company's financial condition and stated that the management expected to be able to pay off the note in full within 90 days. Mr. Murray's letter is presented in Exhibit 4.

Exhibit 1

SPRAGUE MACHINE TOOL COMPANY

SHIPMENTS AT SELLING PRICE

(Dollar figures in thousands)

1951	*As Forecast December, 1950*	*Actual*	*As Forecast September, 1951*
January	$434	$287	
February	624	224	
March	545	622	
April	351	522	
May	431	291	
June	493	540	
July	496	241	
August	599	169	
Eight months' total	$3,973	$2,896	
September	433		$721
October	449		435
November	437		468
December	766		655

Exhibit 2

SPRAGUE MACHINE TOOL COMPANY

BALANCE SHEETS

(Dollar figures in thousands)

ASSETS	*11/30/50*	*12/31/50*	*3/31/51*	*6/30/51*	*7/31/51*	*8/31/51*
Cash	$ 855	$ 155	$ 214	$ 507	$ 652	$ 602
Accounts receivable, net	415	664	657	631	423	228
Inventories	867	883	1,158	1,092	1,208	1,588
Total current assets	$2,137	$1,702	$2,029	$2,230	$2,283	$2,418
Fixed assets	$1,301	$1,301	$1,301	$1,302	$1,302	$1,308
Less: Reserve for depreciation	998	1,002	1,011	1,018	1,018	1,022
Net fixed assets	$ 303	$ 299	$ 290	$ 284	$ 284	$ 286
Prepaid expenses	21	20	13	8	8	14
Total assets	$2,461	$2,021	$2,332	$2,522	$2,575	$2,718
LIABILITIES						
Notes payable—bank	...	$ 350	$ 350	$ 350	$ 350	$ 350
Accounts payable	$ 116	117	227	133	207	316
Accruals	140	249	283	179	148	137
Reserve for federal taxes*—1950	138	154	108	63	63	63
—1951	...	...	112	218	242	277
Customer advance payments	280	280	280	522	522	522
Total current liabilities	$ 674	$1,150	$1,360	$1,465	$1,532	$1,665
Common stock	380	137	137	137	137	137
Surplus	1,407	734	835	920	906	916
Total liabilities	$2,461	$2,021	$2,332	$2,522	$2,575	$2,718

* 1950 Federal Income Taxes Payable in 1951: 30% of total on each of March 15 and June 15; 20% of total on each of September 15 and December 15.

1951 Federal Income Taxes Payable in 1952: 35% of total on each of March 15 and June 15; 15% of total on each of September 15 and December 15.

Exhibit 3

SPRAGUE MACHINE TOOL COMPANY

INCOME STATEMENT

(Dollar figures in thousands)

	Year Ending 12/31/50	*1950 Dec.*	*1951 Jan.*	*Feb.*	*March*	*April*	*May*	*June*	*July*	*August*	*Eight Months Ending 8/31/51*
Net sales	$2,618	$517	$287	$224	$622	$522	$291	$540	$241	$169	$2,896
Cost of sales*	1,684	374	158	123	454	379	189	399	170	92	1,964
Gross profit	$ 934	$143	$129	$101	$168	$143	$102	$141	$ 71	$ 77	$ 932
Selling and administration expenses	564	107	49	32	97	83	47	68	40	31	447
Net profit before taxes	$ 370	$ 36	$ 80	$ 69	$ 71	$ 60	$ 55	$ 73	$ 31	$ 46	$ 485
Provision for federal and state taxes	154	16	41	35	36	29	28	46	24	36	275
Net profit	$ 216	$ 20	$ 39	$ 34	$ 35	$ 31	$ 27	$ 27	$ 7	$ 10	$ 210
Dividends paid	$ 14	....	$ 7	....	....	....	....	....	$ 21	....	$ 28

* Includes depreciation charges of $28,000 in 1950, $4,000 in December, and $3,000 per month in 1951.

Exhibit 4

SPRAGUE MACHINE TOOL COMPANY

DEARBORN, MICHIGAN

September 18, 1951

Mr. Harry Greenwood, Vice-President
Wolverine National Bank
Detroit, Michigan

DEAR MR. GREENWOOD:

I enclose the company's August 31 financial statements. While our cash balance currently is $602,000, you will note that we have an obligation to a customer for cash advances of $522,000, and we expect to ship this order over the next two months. With respect to our note for $350,000 due September 25, we request that you renew our loan for another 90 days. At the end of that period, as you can see for yourself, we expect to be able to have enough cash on hand to retire our obligation in full.

For the past month or more, we have been producing at capacity and expect to continue at that rate through the end of the year. On August 31, our backlog of unfilled orders amounted to about $5,500,000. Our shipment schedule has been upset, particularly the last month or two, because we have had to wait on our suppliers for shipment of electrical control mechanisms; at August 31, we had seven machines with an accumulated cost of about $440,000 completed except for the installation of these electrical components. The components were finally received last week and will enable us to complete a number of machines in the next few days. The remainder of our work in process will probably stay at present levels for the foreseeable future because of our capacity rate of production. Our finished goods inventories are negligible at all times, since we ship machines within a day of completion.

We bought raw materials beyond our current needs in July and August to be assured of completing our orders scheduled to be shipped by December 31. Our purchases were $220,000 in July and $330,000 in August. We have, therefore, accumulated about $140,000 worth of scarcer components above our normal raw material inventories. The extra $140,000 will be used up by the end of the year, bringing our raw material inventories back to normal levels for capacity production. Because we have bought ahead this way, we expect to cut our purchases to about $200,000 a month in each of the four remaining months of 1951.

Our revised shipment estimates are as follows:

	(at selling prices)
September	$ 721,000
October	435,000
November	468,000
December	655,000
	$2,279,000

The shipment estimates include the $700,000 order for the Giant Automobile Company. We are now scheduled to ship against this order as follows: September, $280,000; October, $280,000; November, $140,000. Since we obtained a $522,000 advance from Giant on this order, we will be due nothing on these shipments until their $522,000 credit with us is exhausted.

You will probably note the decline in our accrued expenses. As I mentioned to you last month when you visited us, we have been paying off commissions due our two principal salesmen (who are also large stockholders in the company). Last year when we needed funds to redeem part of our capital stock, these men agreed to defer their commissions until the funds could more easily be spared. In August, we paid off the last of these back commissions. This has been the principal cause of the decline in this item, which normally does not change much from month to month. Our outlay each month for all expenses other than materials should be around $136,000. This assumes that accruals will stay about the same as on August 31.

The business which we expect to ship in the next four months is on our books on profitable terms. While our profit, as you know, varies with the item involved, our engineering estimates indicate we will probably make a net profit (before taxes) of about 15% of sales on these items. Unfortunately, we shall be working mostly for Uncle Sam—we have already exceeded our excess profits tax credit and as a result our profits earned during the next four months will be taxed at 77% (normal tax plus excess profits tax).

We have spent very little on new equipment in the last eight months. We will avoid buying new equipment in the next four months, unless breakdowns make it necessary to replace existing equipment.

Our profits for the year to date have been quite satisfactory, and toward the end of December we plan to pay a dividend to our stockholders. Our dividend disbursements in 1951 have been quite modest so far, and we want to be sure that those stockholders who stood by us last December have no cause to regret their action. Under the circumstances, we feel that a $50,000 dividend payable in December is the least we can do in view of our high earnings.

If there is anything further you need to know, please do not hesitate to write or phone.

Sincerely yours,
ROBERT G. MURRAY
President

THE CUNNINGHAM COMPANY

In early September, 1967, Mr. Thomas Carr, assistant vice president and loan officer of the Farmers Union Bank of Kansas City, Missouri, was reviewing a loan request of $60,000 from Mr. Harry Cunningham, president of The Cunningham Company.

The Cunningham Company manufactured medical research and diagnostic equipment, and highly technical scientific instruments for industrial use. Its plant, located in rented space in a downtown area of Topeka, Kansas, was fully equipped with the latest type of electrically driven machinery.

The company, founded in 1947 by Mr. Cunningham, started as a small wholesaler of electrical appliances. Although this business was moderately successful, Mr. Cunningham showed more interest in experimenting with electronic equipment than in running the business. He devoted a substantial portion of his time to experimentation, and by 1956 had developed several electronic instruments, which appeared to have wide application in industry. When these models were sold successfully in 1957, Mr. Cunningham decided to manufacture them himself. Although demand for these instruments exceeded the limited production facilities from the start, Mr. Cunningham continued to spend much of his time experimenting with new equipment. All of the company's subsequent products were designed and developed by him.

In 1959 the company was incorporated with an initial capital of $34,000. Sales volume, which had grown continuously from the start, was always large in relation to the available capital, and as a result, there had always been heavy reliance on short-term credit to supply the expanding working capital requirements. Since incorporation, the company had never incurred a loss and all earnings had been retained in the business. Mr. Cunningham, the company's only officer, was 52 years old and drew a salary of $15,000.

On August 25, 1967, at the suggestion of his public accountant, Mr. Cunningham visited the Farmers Union Bank to discuss the possibility of securing a line of credit. He met with Mr. Carr, assistant vice president and loan officer of the bank. Mr. Carr explained that although he was unfamiliar with Cunningham's products, he had handled the accounts of several similar types of manufacturing companies. Exhibits 1 and 2 present the financial statements Mr. Cunningham had brought to the bank.

Mr. Cunningham was thoroughly dissatisfied with the company's current loan arrangement with the Topeka City Trust Company, from which it had been borrowing between $25,000 and $35,000 at an annual interest rate of 8% (7% interest fee plus 1% service charge) with accounts receivable pledged as security. He thought that Mr. Heath, the loan officer at the Topeka bank who handled the Cunningham account, made no effort to understand the company's problems, although he was constantly making suggestions that seemed inappropriate. Mr. Cunningham felt the bank had been quite arbitrary in selecting the receivables it would accept as collateral so that he never knew from one day to the next whether there would be sufficient funds to operate the company.

Mr. Cunningham thought that this restrictive attitude on the bank's part limited the company's ability to expand its sales volume. In the last few years the company had been unable to solicit new customers because of insufficient funds. Thus, increased sales volume, which had been financed internally, had come solely from expansion of existing accounts. Since Mr. Cunningham thought operations were currently just above the break-even point (he believed general, selling, and administrative expenses would remain fixed at an annual level of $130,000), any further increase in sales volume would increase profits before taxes by the amount of the gross margin, which was 36% in 1966. Because the plant was being operated at only 60% of capacity, Mr. Cunningham was eager to increase sales.

Mr. Cunningham was perfectly willing to pledge the company's accounts receivable or anything else that the bank thought would be desirable security so long as the arrangement was fair to the company and specific enough so that he could count on having the funds available when he needed them.

Mr. Carr explained that the bank was "pretty well loaned up" at the moment but that it was always interested in sound loan proposals from companies that showed promise of developing into good accounts. Mr. Carr promised to look into Mr. Cunningham's request and said he would plan to visit the company on August 28, 1967. He suggested Mr. Cunningham prepare an estimate of his cash requirements by that time. Mr. Cunningham seemed pleased with this arrangement; he said that although the Topeka bank was only 10 blocks from his plant, Mr. Heath had never visited the company.

Before going to the company, Mr. Carr telephoned Mr. Heath and learned that his experience with Cunningham had been thoroughly unsatisfactory. According to Mr. Heath, the company had maintained extremely low balances and on numerous occasions had overdrawn its account. The receivables pledged as security did not always measure up to the bank's standards of acceptable collateral. Although Mr. Cunningham seemed entirely competent from a technical standpoint, Mr. Heath thought he lacked financial and administrative ability. Mr. Cunningham had been promising for several years "to get his house in order" but had never accomplished it to the satisfaction of the bank. However, Mr. Heath believed that the company's products were well received by the trade and that with better management, Cunningham had good possibilities of developing into a sound business.

Upon visiting the Cunningham plant, Mr. Carr noted that although the production process included some fabricating, it was primarily an assembly operation. The instruments sold to the medical profession were all standard models and were produced in small lots. There was no apparent orderly flow of work, and a number of partially completed units were in storage awaiting further processing. It took an average of eight weeks to complete the processing of medical instruments. Industrial products, however, were manufactured on an individual basis and generally were designed to meet specific requirements of a customer. Because each unit required individual engineering modifications by Mr. Cunningham, the company accepted orders on a four-month delivery basis. Sales volume was equally divided between these two product lines. Mr. Carr was impressed with the company's products and thought that the company could increase its sales volume substantially without much difficulty.

Since the inventory of $168,000 on July 31, 1967, seemed excessive in relation to sales volume, Mr. Carr inquired into its composition. Finished goods inventory, which included only medical instruments, totaled $18,000; there were $30,000 of medical instruments and $36,000 of industrial equipment in process; the remaining $84,000 represented raw materials. Mr. Carr noted that the raw material inventory consisted of a large number of electronic and mechanical parts, ranging in value from a few cents each to several hundred dollars.

Mr. Cunningham agreed with Mr. Carr's comment that inventory was probably too large and said that he planned to reduce it to a total of $120,000 by the end of the year. Most of this reduction would be in raw materials inventory and would result from a recently installed inventory control system whereby all purchases were channeled through one man. Mr. Cunningham believed this action had already proved beneficial since purchases had dropped from an average of $14,000 per month at the beginning of the year to $6,000 in recent months despite a steady increase in sales volume. Terms of these purchases ranged from C.O.D. to net 30.

Sales to the medical profession were made through 120 surgical supply houses and doctors' equipment houses as well as directly to the Armed Service Medical Procurement Agency, a few hospitals, and, on occasion, individual doctors. These accounts had all been extended open lines of credit on net 30 terms without investigation, and in several instances credit balances ran as high as $8,000. Most accounts, however, purchased infrequently with orders ranging from $200 to $1,000. Although Mr. Cunningham believed that some wholesalers might be considered poor credit risks since they tended to be undercapitalized, he had never experienced a bad debt loss in the five or more years he had dealt with them.

Cunningham sold its industrial products directly to 20 large corporations, including General Motors, whose credit standings were above question. Orders by these companies, although infrequent, usually ranged between $2,000 and $10,000, and in all instances payments were made within the company's sales terms of net 30.

Accounts receivable on Cunningham's books as of July 31, 1967, were aged as follows:

Shipment	*Age*	*Outstanding Receivables*	*Sales*
July	0– 30 days	$36,000	$37,100
June	31– 60 days	12,000	43,600
May	61– 90 days	6,000	33,600
April	91–120 days	7,000	36,200
Total		$61,000	

Of the $7,000 representing accounts over 90 days old, $6,000 was due from the Armed Service Medical Procurement Agency, which was often slow in paying its accounts. The other $1,000 was owed by two surgical supply houses and one hospital. The remaining $18,000 in receivables over 30 days old were due from 28 other wholesalers. Mr. Carr noted that by August 28, 1967, collection had been made of all shipments prior to June and that only $8,000 of June shipments remained uncollected.

In investigating several disturbing aspects of the July 31, 1967, balance sheet, Mr. Carr learned that the accounts payable balance of $49,000 compared with total purchases of $70,000 during the first seven months of 1967. To ascertain the company's credit picture, Mr. Carr aged the trade debt on the company's books as of August 28, 1967, as shown below:

Purchase Month	*Purchases*	*Trade Debt Payable*
August	$ 6,100	$ 4,800
July	4,900	3,000
June	7,800	4,800
May	10,400	9,500
Prior		23,500
Total		$45,600

Mr. Cunningham said that the prior accounts included $3,000 in dispute and $3,500 payable to friendly creditors to whom payment could be postponed indefinitely.

The accrued taxes payable account on July 31 included delinquent withholding taxes totaling $22,000. Federal income taxes had been paid in March and June, 1967. Mr. Cunningham said the tax collector had been "after him" in August and all but $9,800 of these delinquent taxes were paid. Although no penalty was imposed on the company, a tax lien of $9,800 was filed against the company and Cunningham was put on a "pay as you collect" withholding tax basis. By arrangement with the tax collector, weekly payments of $350 were being made against the tax lien. After learning this, Mr. Carr said the bank would not consider making a loan unless the delinquent taxes were paid in full and maintained on a current basis in the future.

The company's public accountant, acting as trustee for a group of investors, had loaned Cunningham $35,000 at 17% interest secured by a chattel mortgage on the company's machinery and equipment. The note was payable on demand with no definite repayment schedule set, although it was originally intended that $1,500 be repaid monthly.

Mr. Cunningham estimated that sales in the last five months of 1967 would average $42,000, and his goal for 1968 was a monthly average of $50,000. Since a number of medical wholesaling houses had expressed continued interest in carrying Cunningham's instruments, and since the company's industrial products were almost without competition, Mr. Cunningham thought that with bank support there would be little difficulty in achieving these goals. In this respect, he estimated his needs as follows:

Repayment of present bank loan..........	$29,000
Additional working capital..............	31,000
Total requirement....................	$60,000

As the company had recently modernized its production facilities, no further expenditures for fixed assets were planned. Depreciation charges amounted to $400 per month. Mr. Cunningham did not expect the balances in the deferred asset account and the miscellaneous accrual account would change much in the next few months. In addition, he planned to maintain a cash balance of $3,000 in the future.

When Mr. Carr returned to Kansas City, he sent out letters of inquiry to a random list of Cunningham's suppliers. (Excerpts from the responses received by the bank are shown in Exhibit 3.) He also obtained a copy of the Dun & Bradstreet report on the company. Since the report was almost a year old and related to financial statements prior to 1966, it contained no additional information that was helpful to Mr. Carr. However, he noted that the company's credit rating was in the lowest category and that Mr. Cunningham had withheld from the Dun & Bradstreet reporter general financial information and in particular had declined to give information on payables and sales.

On September 1, 1967, Mr. Cunningham returned to the Farmers Union Bank to discuss the loan proposal further. He reported that the accounts receivable balance on August 31 was $67,000 (August sales totaled $41,000), and of this, $60,000 represented accounts less than 60 days old. Mr. Cunningham said he would invest an additional $2,000, the last of his personal resources, in subordinated debt and would agree not to pay dividends, increase his salary, or repay the loan he had made to the company until the bank debt had been cleared. Finally, Mr. Cunningham said he had discussed the chattel mortgage with his public accountant who suggested that his group might be willing to subordinate the chattel mortgage to the bank loan. On September 1, the company was borrowing $29,000 from the Topeka bank.

Mr. Carr agreed to consider this proposal further and promised to let Mr. Cunningham know the bank's decision within a few days.

Exhibit 1

THE CUNNINGHAM COMPANY

BALANCE SHEETS, DECEMBER 31, 1962–66, JULY 31, 1967

(Dollar figures in thousands)

ASSETS	12/31/62	12/31/63	12/31/64	12/31/65	12/31/66	7/31/67
Cash	..	..	$ 1	$ 5	$ 4	$ 1
Accounts receivable	$ 50	$ 36	38	43	71	61
Inventory	75	72	100	130	164	168
Total current assets	$125	$108	$139	$178	$239	$230
Fixed assets, net	22	20	18	21	22	45
Deferred assets	7	6	6	7	14	14
Total assets	$154	$134	$163	$206	$275	$289
LIABILITIES						
Overdraft—bank	$ 5	$ 4	..	..	..	..
Notes payable—bank	26	18	$ 31	$ 28	$ 37	$ 26
Notes payable—chattel mortgage	7	..	..	..	18	35
Accounts payable	21	17	17	44	47	49
Taxes payable	7	7	16	13	25	22
Miscellaneous accruals	6	7	8	10	19	20
Total current liabilities	$ 72	$ 53	$ 72	$ 95	$146	$152
Subordinated loan from officers	25	20	12	19	26	26
Total liabilities	$ 97	$ 73	$ 84	$114	$172	$178
Common stock	34	34	34	34	34	34
Surplus	23	27	45	58	69	77
Total liabilities and net worth	$154	$134	$163	$206	$275	$289

Exhibit 2

THE CUNNINGHAM COMPANY

INCOME STATEMENTS, 1962–66, JANUARY–JULY, 1967
(Dollar figures in thousands)

	1962	*1963*	*1964*	*1965*	*1966*	*Jan.–July, 1967*
Net sales	$206	$223	$259	$372	$396	$228
Less cost of goods sold:						
Material	67	71	77	120	127	75
Labor	31	32	36	59	63	41
Overhead	36	39	42	58	59	30
Depreciation	3	2	2	2	4	3
Total cost of goods sold	$137	$144	$157	$239	$253	$149
Gross profit	$ 69	$ 79	$102	$133	$143	$ 79
General, selling, and administrative expenses	63	74	78	115	127	71
Net profit before taxes	$ 6	$ 5	$ 24	$ 18	$ 16	$ 8
Taxes	1	1	6	5	5	
Net after taxes	$ 5	$ 4	$ 18	$ 13	$ 11	

Exhibit 3

THE CUNNINGHAM COMPANY

EXCERPTS FROM RESPONSES TO LETTERS OF CREDIT INQUIRY SENT OUT BY MR. CARR

. . . The firm in question is definitely undercapitalized but apparently has a good market for its products as they seem to be quite busy. Their available capital has always been small resulting in slow payments to their suppliers. From time to time we have had to hold orders pending a payment on account as is true at this writing. . . .

. . . . .

At times they are slow paying, but all amounts are paid. They are fine people to do business with.

. . . . .

At the present time the company owes us a low four-figure amount. In the past payments have all been met in approximately 60 to 90 days. The company appears to be a small, progressive, and expanding concern which we hope to develop into a good customer.

. . . . .

. . . We used to extend them credit, but their payments were so slow we now sell them only on C.O.D.

. . . . .

We have sold the company for several years. We have given credit up to a medium four-figure amount, but their payments have been continuously six months or more slow.

LASTMORE SHEARS, INC.

^^^

On April 28, 1958, Mr. Hamilton, senior loan officer at the Fulton National Bank of New York, was reviewing the credit file of Lastmore Shears, Inc., in preparation for a luncheon meeting with the company's president and treasurer. Mr. Shultz, treasurer of Lastmore, had recently informed Mr. Hamilton that the company would be unable to liquidate its outstanding seasonal loan as initially anticipated. Mr. Hamilton, while agreeing to extend the outstanding $500,000 loan, had suggested that he would like to stop by and discuss the company's recent progress when he was next in the vicinity of Savannah, Georgia, where Lastmore's home plant and offices were located.

Lastmore Shears, Inc., manufactured a complete line of household scissors and shears. Its quality lines were distributed through jobbers to specialty, hardware, and department stores located throughout the country. Cheaper products were sold directly to large variety chains. Although competition, particularly from companies in foreign countries, was severe, Lastmore had made profits in each year since 1934. Sales and profits had grown fairly steadily, if not dramatically, throughout the postwar period.

Fulton National Bank had been actively soliciting the Lastmore account for several years before early 1957. After several unsuccessful calls, Mr. Hamilton finally convinced the officers of Lastmore that association with a large New York bank offered several advantages not to be found with local banks. Mr. Hamilton was particularly pleased with the success of his efforts because Lastmore historically held fairly sizable deposit balances in its principal banks.

The company had sufficient capital to cover its permanent requirements over the immediate foreseeable future. Its short-term borrowings from banks were typically confined to the period July through December of each year, when additional working capital was needed to support a seasonal sales peak. As a matter of policy the company attempted to produce at an even rate throughout the year, and this accounted in good part for the sizable need for seasonal funds.

In June, 1957, Mr. Shultz arranged a line of credit of $1,200,000 with the Fulton National Bank to cover requirements for the fall. At the time, Mr. Shultz anticipated that the loan would be completely paid off by January, 1958. He gave Mr. Hamilton a pro forma estimate of the company's funds requirements over the forthcoming 12-month period to support his request. (These estimates are shown in Exhibits 1 and 2.) In addition to the above requirements, the forecast showed a need for a new loan of approximately $600,000 by June, 1958. Mr. Shultz attributed this increase in funds requirements (no funds were needed in June, 1957) to a plant modernization program. He explained that the program, requiring expenditures of $2,000,000, was approximately half completed and would be finished by August, 1957. Efficiencies resulting from the modernization program, once completed, were expected to effect savings in manufacturing costs of about $300,000 per year before taxes.

Mr. Shultz called Mr. Hamilton in early September, 1957, to let him know that the company would require $100,000 more than had been initially requested to cover peak seasonal needs. Mr. Shultz explained that the principal reason for the larger requirements was higher expenditures for modernization than had initially been estimated. Mr. Hamilton informed Mr. Shultz that the bank would be happy to accommodate the additional loan requirements.

In January, 1958, Mr. Shultz again called Mr. Hamilton. Mr. Shultz noted that sales had slackened considerably since his previous call. He attributed this decline largely to the economic recession then in progress, not to any special conditions affecting his company or the shear industry. Slackening in sales demand, however, had created a need for additional short-term borrowing. Mr. Shultz believed more funds than initially forecast would be required until the company adjusted to the new economic conditions. He envisioned that this adjustment probably would not occur until mid-April, 1958, or thereabouts. Once more, Mr. Hamilton agreed to extend necessary loan funds to Lastmore.

In early April, 1958, Mr. Shultz telephoned Mr. Hamilton a third time to inform him that Lastmore would probably not be able to repay its outstanding short-term loan of $500,000 before the seasonal upturn in funds requirements in June. Mr. Shultz explained that a further sales decline, occasioned by the recession, was largely responsible for the company's inability to liquidate the loan as anticipated. Mr. Hamilton in reply noted that the bank preferred seasonal loans to be "off the books" for at least two months of the year but saw no reason why he would not be willing to renew Lastmore's outstanding loan. He nevertheless thought it advisable to explore whether or not the inability to repay the seasonal loan in 1958 might be caused by a permanent change in the nature of the company's loan needs, such as might be occasioned by the modernization program. Consequently, he suggested a meeting for April 29 to discuss the company's recent progress.

In preparing for this meeting, Mr. Hamilton examined carefully the various profit and loss statements and balance sheets (Exhibits 3 and 4) that Mr. Shultz had submitted to the bank over the course of the last nine months. He hoped this analysis might uncover the reasons for Lastmore's inability to repay its loan in accordance with original estimates.

Exhibit 1

LASTMORE SHEARS, INC.

PRO FORMA INCOME STATEMENTS BY MONTHS—FISCAL YEAR ENDING JUNE 30, 1958

(Dollar figures in thousands)

	Year Ending June 30, 1957	*July*	*Aug.*	*Sept.*	*Oct.*	*Nov.*	*Dec.*	*Jan.*	*Feb.*	*March*	*April*	*May*	*June*
Net sales	$10,079	$700	$900	$1,100	$1,500	$1,300	$1,100	$700	$700	$600	$500	$400	$ 500
Less cost of goods sold: materials and labor @ 60% of sales	6,184	420	540	660	900	780	660	420	420	360	300	240	300
Overhead (includes depreciation of $50 per month)	1,191	100	100	100	100	100	100	100	100	100	100	100	100
Total	$ 7,375	$520	$640	$ 760	$1,000	$ 880	$ 760	$520	$520	$460	$400	$340	$ 400
Gross profit	2,704	180	260	340	500	420	340	180	180	140	100	60	100
Selling and administrative expenses	1,083	90	90	90	90	90	90	90	90	90	90	90	90
Profit before taxes	$ 1,621	$ 90	$170	$ 250	$ 410	$ 330	$ 250	$ 90	$ 90	$ 50	$ 10	$(30)	$ 10
Taxes at 50%	811	45	85	125	205	165	125	45	45	25	5	(15)	5
Profits after taxes	$ 810	$ 45	$ 85	$ 125	$ 205	$ 165	$ 125	$ 45	$ 45	$ 25	$ 5	$(15)	$ 5
Dividends	500			100			100			100			200
Retained earnings	$ 310	$ 45	$ 85	$ 25	$ 205	$ 165	$ 25	$ 45	$ 45	$(75)	$ 5	$(15)	$(195)

Exhibit 2

LASTMORE SHEARS, INC.

PRO FORMA BALANCE SHEETS BY MONTHS, FISCAL 1958

(Dollar figures in thousands)

ASSETS	*Actual June 30, 1957*	*July 31*	*Aug. 31*	*Sept. 30*	*Oct. 31*	*Nov. 30*	*Dec. 31*	*Jan. 31*	*Feb. 28*	*Mar. 31*	*Apr. 30*	*May 31*	*June 30*
Cash	$ 988	$ 400	$ 400	$ 400	$ 400	$ 400	$ 400	$ 770	$ 960	$ 721	$ 661	$ 501	$ 400
Accounts receivable*	697	950	1,250	1,550	2,050	2,050	1,750	1,250	1,050	950	800	650	700
Inventories (see below)	2,711	2,800	2,780	2,640	2,260	2,000	1,860	1,960	2,060	2,220	2,440	2,720	2,940
Total current assets	$ 4,396	$ 4,150	$ 4,430	$ 4,590	$ 4,710	$ 4,450	$ 4,010	$ 3,980	$ 4,070	$ 3,891	$ 3,901	$ 3,871	$ 4,040
Net plant	8,215	8,715	9,215	9,215	9,215	9,215	9,215	9,215	9,215	9,215	9,215	9,215	9,215
Total assets	$12,611	$12,865	$13,645	$13,805	$13,925	$13,665	$13,225	$13,195	$13,285	$13,106	$13,116	$13,086	$13,255
LIABILITIES AND NET WORTH													
Bank loans payable	......	$ 203	$ 802	$ 1,151	$ 861	$ 271	$ 120	......	......	......	......	......	$ 588
Accounts payable—trade†	$ 288	249	260	260	260	260	260	$ 260	$ 260	$ 260	$ 260	$ 260	260
Taxes payable‡	678	723	808	594	799	964	750	795	840	736	741	726	602
Miscellaneous other	90	90	90	90	90	90	90	90	90	90	90	90	90
Total current liabilities	$ 1,056	$ 1,265	$ 1,960	$ 2,095	$ 2,010	$ 1,585	$ 1,220	$ 1,145	$ 1,190	$ 1,086	$ 1,091	$ 1,076	$ 1,540
Mortgage, 4%	4,000	4,000	4,000	4,000	4,000	4,000	3,900	3,900	3,900	3,900	3,900	3,900	3,800
Common stock	4,000	4,000	4,000	4,000	4,000	4,000	4,000	4,000	4,000	4,000	4,000	4,000	4,000
Earned surplus	3,555	3,600	3,685	3,710	3,915	4,080	4,105	4,150	4,195	4,120	4,125	4,110	3,915
Total liabilities and net worth	$12,611	$12,865	$13,645	$13,805	$13,925	$13,665	$13,225	$13,195	$13,285	$13,106	$13,116	$13,086	$13,255

Inventory Subsidiary Data (Fifo)	*July*	*August*	*September*	*October*	*November*	*December*	*January*	*February*	*March*	*April*	*May*	*June*
Raw Materials:												
Opening balance	$ 271	$ 260	$ 260	$ 260	$ 260	$ 260	$ 260	$ 260	$ 260	$ 260	$ 260	$ 260
Plus purchases	249	260	260	260	260	260	260	260	260	260	260	260
Less transfers to work in process	260	260	260	260	260	260	260	260	260	260	260	260
Closing balance	$ 260	$ 260	$ 260	$ 260	$ 260	$ 260	$ 260	$ 260	$ 260	$ 260	$ 260	$ 260
Work in Process:												
Opening balance	1,040	1,040	1,040	1,040	1,040	1,040	1,040	1,040	1,040	1,040	1,040	1,040
Plus raw material additions	260	260	260	260	260	260	260	260	260	260	260	260
Plus labor additions	260	260	260	260	260	260	260	260	260	260	260	260
Transfers to finished goods	520	520	520	520	520	520	520	520	520	520	520	520
Closing balance	$ 1,040	$ 1,040	$ 1,040	$ 1,040	$ 1,040	$ 1,040	$ 1,040	$ 1,040	$ 1,040	$ 1,040	$ 1,040	$ 1,040
Finished Goods:												
Opening balance	1,400	1,500	1,480	1,340	960	700	560	660	760	920	1,140	1,420
Plus additions from work in process	520	520	520	520	520	520	520	520	520	520	520	520
Less cost of goods sold	420	540	660	900	780	660	420	420	360	300	240	300
Closing balance	$ 1,500	$ 1,480	$ 1,340	$ 960	$ 700	$ 560	$ 660	$ 760	$ 920	$ 1,140	$ 1,420	$ 1,640
Total closing inventory	2,800	2,780	2,640	2,260	2,000	1,860	1,960	2,060	2,220	2,440	2,720	2,940

* Assumes collections lag sales by 45 days.

† Assumes 30-day payment period, in accordance with trade terms.

‡ Outstanding tax liability of $678,000 was due in two installments in September and December, 1957; estimated payments on fiscal 1958 taxes were $129,000, payable in both March and June.

Exhibit 3

LASTMORE SHEARS, INC.

INCOME STATEMENTS BY MONTHS, JULY, 1957–MARCH, 1958

(Dollar figures in thousands)

	July	*August*	*September*	*October*	*November*	*December*	*January*	*February*	*March*
Net sales	$692	$871	$1,030	$1,360	$1,128	$936	$588	$581	$ 501
Less cost of goods sold:									
Materials and labor	$436	$549	$ 652	$ 816	$ 677	$562	$353	$366	$ 321
Overhead (includes depreciation of $50 per month)	99	97	114	104	101	96	98	125*	108*
Total	$535	$646	$ 766	$ 920	$ 778	$658	$451	$491	$ 429
Gross profit	$157	$225	$ 264	$ 440	$ 350	$278	$137	$ 90	$ 72
Selling and administrative expenses	91	93	98	93	92	90	87	86	86
Profit before taxes	$ 66	$132	$ 166	$ 347	$ 258	$188	$ 50	$ 4	$ (14)
Taxes at 50%	33	66	83	174	129	94	25	2	(7)
Profits after taxes	$ 33	$ 66	$ 83	$ 173	$ 129	$ 94	$ 25	$ 2	$ (7)
Dividends	...	...	100	.....	.....	100	...	...	100
Retained earnings	$ 33	$ 66	$ (17)	$ 173	$ 129	$ (6)	$ 25	$ 2	$(107)

* Includes special costs for laying off personnel.

Exhibit 4

LASTMORE SHEARS, INC.

BALANCE SHEETS BY MONTHS, JULY 31, 1957–MARCH 31, 1958

(Dollar figures in thousands)

ASSETS	*July 31*	*Aug. 31*	*Sept. 30*	*Oct. 31*	*Nov. 30*	*Dec. 31*	*Jan. 31*	*Feb. 28*	*Mar. 31*
Cash	$ 474	$ 345	$ 388	$ 387	$ 432	$ 367	$ 533	$ 514	$ 385
Accounts receivable	949	1,219	1,470	1,890	1,848	1,864	1,324	1,060	882
Inventories	2,802	2,777	2,663	2,401	2,242	2,174	2,316	2,398	2,466
Total current assets	$ 4,225	$ 4,341	$ 4,521	$ 4,678	$ 4,522	$ 4,405	$ 4,173	$ 3,972	$ 3,733
Net plant	8,730	9,255	9,314	9,317	9,312	9,326	9,312	9,301	9,287
Total assets	$12,955	$13,596	$13,835	$13,995	$13,834	$13,731	$13,485	$13,273	$13,020
LIABILITIES AND NET WORTH									
Bank loans payable	$ 300	$ 800	$ 1,300	$ 1,100	$ 700	$ 1,000	$ 700	$ 500	$ 500
Accounts payable—trade	264	259	282	293	279	229	234	220	172
Taxes payable	711	777	521	695	824	579	604	606	509
Miscellaneous other	92	106	95	97	92	90	89	87	86
Total current liabilities	$ 1,367	$ 1,942	$ 2,198	$ 2,185	$ 1,895	$ 1,898	$ 1,627	$ 1,413	$ 1,267
Mortgage, 4%	4,000	4,000	4,000	4,000	4,000	3,900	3,900	3,900	3,900
Common stock	4,000	4,000	4,000	4,000	4,000	4,000	4,000	4,000	4,000
Earned surplus	3,588	3,654	3,637	3,810	3,939	3,933	3,958	3,960	3,853
Total liabilities and net worth	$12,955	$13,596	$13,835	$13,995	$13,834	$13,731	$13,485	$13,273	$13,020

Exhibit 4—Continued

Inventory Subsidiary Data (Fifo)	*July*	*August*	*September*	*October*	*November*	*December*	*January*	*February*	*March*
Raw Materials:									
Opening balance	$ 271	$ 272	$ 253	$ 254	$ 265	$ 275	$ 260	$ 255	$ 252
Plus purchases	263	260	280	290	268	230	231	218	173
Less transfers to work in process	262	279	279	279	258	245	236	221	201
Closing balance	$ 272	$ 253	$ 254	$ 265	$ 275	$ 260	$ 255	$ 252	$ 224
Work in Process:									
Opening balance	1,040	1,047	1,069	1,077	1,078	1,049	1,015	987	929
Plus raw material additions	262	279	279	279	258	245	236	221	201
Plus labor additions	264	264	258	264	250	264	264	230	216
Transfers to finished goods	519	521	529	542	537	543	528	509	500
Closing balance	$ 1,047	$ 1,069	$ 1,077	$ 1,078	$ 1,049	$ 1,015	$ 987	$ 929	$ 846
Finished Goods:									
Opening balance	1,400	1,483	1,455	1,332	1,058	918	899	1,074	1,217
Plus additions from work in process	519	521	529	542	537	543	528	509	500
Less cost of goods sold	436	549	652	816	677	562	353	366	321
Closing balance	$ 1,483	$ 1,455	$ 1,332	$ 1,058	$ 918	$ 899	$ 1,074	$ 1,217	$ 1,396
Total closing inventory	2,802	2,777	2,663	2,401	2,242	2,174	2,316	2,398	2,466

CLARKSON LUMBER COMPANY

After a rapid growth in its business during recent years, the Clarkson Lumber Company in the spring of 1968 anticipated a further substantial increase in sales. Despite good profits, which were largely retained in the business, the company had experienced a shortage of cash and had found it necessary to borrow $48,000 from the Suburban National Bank. In the spring of 1968, additional borrowing seemed necessary if sales were to be increased and purchase discounts taken. Since $48,000 was the maximum amount that Suburban National would lend to any borrower, it was necessary for Mr. Paul Clarkson, proprietor of the Clarkson Lumber Company, to look elsewhere for additional credit.

Through a personal friend who was well acquainted with one of the officers of a large metropolitan bank, the Northrup National Bank, Mr. Clarkson obtained an introduction to the officer and presented a request for an additional bank loan of $80,000. Consequently, the credit department of the Northrup National Bank made its usual investigation of the company for the information of the loan officers of the bank.

The Clarkson Lumber Company was founded in 1958 as a partnership of Mr. Clarkson and his brother-in-law, Mr. Henry Stark. Six years later Mr. Clarkson bought out Mr. Stark's interest and continued the business as sole proprietor.

The business was located in a suburb of a large midwestern city. Land and a siding were leased from a railroad. Two portable sheet metal storage buildings had been erected by the company. Operations were limited to the wholesale distribution of plywood, moldings, and sash and door products to lumber dealers in the local area. Quantity discounts and credit terms of net 30 days and net 60 days on open account were usually offered customers.

Sales volume had been built up largely on the basis of successful price competition made possible through careful control of operating expenses and by quantity purchases of materials at substantial discounts. Almost all of the moldings and sash and door products, which amounted to 40% and 20% of sales, respectively, were used for repair work. About 55% of total sales were made in the six months from March through August. No sales representatives were employed, orders being taken exclusively over the telephone. Annual sales of $313,646 in 1963 and of $476,275 in 1964 gave net profits of $32,494 and of $34,131, respectively. Comparative operating statements for the years

1965 through 1967 and for the three months ending March 31, 1968, are given in Exhibit 1.

Mr. Clarkson was an energetic man, 39 years of age, who worked long hours on the job, not only handling management matters but also performing a large amount of the clerical work. Help was afforded by an assistant who, in the words of the investigator of the Northrup National Bank, "has been doing and can do about everything that Mr. Clarkson does in the organization."

Other employees numbered 9, of whom 7 worked in the yard and 2 drove trucks. Mr. Clarkson had adopted the practice of paying union dues and all social security taxes for his employees; in addition, bonuses were distributed to them at the end of each year. Mr. Clarkson was planning to incorporate the business in the near future and to sell stock to certain employees.

As a part of its customary investigation of prospective borrowers, the Northrup National Bank sent inquiries concerning Mr. Clarkson to a number of firms that had business dealings with him. The manager of one of his large suppliers, the Barker Company, wrote in answer:

> The conservative operation of his business appeals to us. He has not wasted his money in disproportionate plant investment. His operating expenses are as low as they could possibly be. He has personal control over every feature of his business, and he possesses sound judgment and a willingness to work harder than anyone I have ever known. This, with a good personality, gives him an excellent turnover; and from my personal experience in watching him work, I know that he keeps close check on his own credits.

All of the other trade letters received by the bank bore out the statements quoted above.

In addition to the ownership of his lumber business, Mr. Clarkson held jointly with his wife an equity in their home, which was mortgaged for $12,000 and cost $25,000 to build in 1955. He also held a $16,000 life insurance policy, payable to Mrs. Clarkson. Mrs. Clarkson owned independently a half interest in a home worth about $20,000.

The bank gave particular attention to the debt position and current ratio of the business. It noted the ready market for the company's products at all times and the fact that sales prospects were particularly favorable. The bank's investigator reported: ". . . it is estimated sales may run from $1,280,000 to $1,600,000 in 1968." The rate of inventory turnover was high, and losses on bad debts in past years had been quite small. Comparative balance sheets as of December 31, 1965–67, are given in Exhibit 2. A detailed balance sheet drawn up for the bank as of March 31, 1968, and the change in proprietorship for the first quarter of 1968 appear as Exhibits 3 and 4.

The bank learned through inquiry of another wholesale lumber company that the usual terms of purchase in the trade were 2%, 10 days after arrival. Suppliers took 60-day notes when requested but did this somewhat unwillingly.

Exhibit 1

CLARKSON LUMBER COMPANY

OPERATING STATEMENTS FOR THE YEARS ENDING DECEMBER 31, 1965, THROUGH 1967 AND FOR THE THREE MONTHS ENDING MARCH 31, 1968
(Dollar figures in thousands)

	1965	*1966*	*1967*	*1st Quarter, 1968*
Net sales	$740	$880	$1,179	$310*
Cost of goods sold:				
Beginning inventory	$111	$ 97	$ 141	$180
Purchases	611	846	1,069	336
	$722	$943	$1,210	$516
Ending inventory	97	141	180	244
Cost of goods sold	$625	$802	$1,030	$272
Gross profit	$115	$ 78	$ 149	$ 38
Operating expenses	38	48	73	20
Net operating profit	$ 77	$ 30	$ 76	$ 18
Add: Purchase discounts taken	5	5	5	0.6
	$ 82	$ 35	$ 81	$ 19
Deduct: Sales discounts allowed†	16	18	28	8
Net profit‡	$ 66	$ 17	$ 53	$ 11*
Drawings by proprietor	...	...	$ 28	$ 6

* In the first quarter of 1967, net sales were $252,000 and net profit was $13,000.
† Quantity discounts.
‡ This item is stated before any provision for federal income tax liabilities. As distinct from corporations, no federal income taxes are levied on the profits of proprietorships and partnerships, as such. The owners of a proprietorship or partnership, however, must include in their personal income their proportionate share of such profits and must pay taxes on them at the regular personal income tax rates.

Exhibit 2

CLARKSON LUMBER COMPANY

COMPARATIVE BALANCE SHEETS AS OF DECEMBER 31, 1965–67

ASSETS	*1965*	*1966*	*1967*
Cash	$ 56	$ 282	$ 3,560
Accounts receivable—net of reserve for bad debts	57,322	89,387	109,686
Inventory	97,005	141,416	179,557
Total current assets	$154,383	$231,085	$292,803
Property—net of reserve for depreciation	5,963	7,608	11,430
Deferred charges	......	......	......
Total assets	$160,346	$238,693	$304,233
LIABILITIES			
Notes payable—bank	......	......	......
Notes payable—employees for bonuses	......	......	......
Notes payable—Henry Stark	$ 32,000	......	......
Notes payable—trade	......	......	......
Accounts payable	57,460	$136,723	$173,439
Accrued expenses	......	3,440	7,194
Total current liabilities	$ 89,460	$140,163	$180,633
Net worth	70,886	98,530*	123,600
Total liabilities	$160,346	$238,693	$304,233

*Mr. Clarkson invested $10,500 of his own money in the business in 1966. This investment accounts for the fact that the net worth account in 1966 shows a larger increase than the retained earnings for 1966.

Exhibit 3

CLARKSON LUMBER COMPANY

Balance Sheet as of March 31, 1968

ASSETS			
Cash			$ 1,338
Notes receivable			4,211*
Accounts receivable		$126,282	
Less reserve		1,600	
Accounts receivable—net			124,682
Inventory			243,658
Total current assets			$373,889
Buildings	$20,736		
Less reserve	14,821		
Buildings—net		$ 5,915	
Trucks and automobiles	$ 4,920		
Less reserve	474		
Trucks and automobiles—net		4,446	10,361
Deferred charges			2,594
Total assets			$386,844
LIABILITIES			
Notes payable—bank			$ 48,000
Notes payable—trade			65,767
Notes payable employees†			4,840
Accounts payable			138,336
Accruals			902
Total current liabilities			$257,845
Proprietorship, March 31, 1968			128,999
Total liabilities			$386,844

* Assigned to Barker Company.
† For bonuses.

Exhibit 4

CLARKSON LUMBER COMPANY

Change in Proprietorship, First Quarter, 1968

Proprietorship, January 1, 1968		$123,600
Net profit first quarter	$11,271	
Drawings by proprietor	5,872	
Balance		5,399
Proprietorship, March 31, 1968		$128,999

NATIONAL MOTOR CAR COMPANY

During the summer of 1963, Mr. Otto Carr, manager of National Motor Car Company's cash management activities, was preparing recommendations to the treasurer regarding both the company's cash management policies and the basic investment strategy the company should follow in investing surplus cash during the coming months. In his review Mr. Carr expected to cover three main areas: the effectiveness of the company's scheduling and handling of cash inflows and outflows; company bank relations; and the investment of temporary excess cash balances. Recent changes in National's business, as well as in prospective short-term investment opportunities in marketable securities, prompted the treasurer to request the review.

The National Motor Car Company was one of the largest manufacturers of automobiles and automotive parts in the world. In addition to these automotive activities, the company also manufactured engines for industrial and marine use; heating, cooling, and air conditioning equipment; powdered metal products; as well as guided missiles and other defense products. These nonautomotive lines represented between 10% and 15% of annual sales. Operating results and financial condition over the eight years ending in 1962 are shown in Exhibit 1. Exhibits 2 and 3 show the results of operations during the first six months of 1963.

Automobile sales, as demonstrated by Exhibit 4, were relatively cyclical throughout the postwar period, although there had been some secular growth as well. National's share of market also varied quite widely from year to year, which tended to magnify the underlying cyclical and seasonal changes otherwise inherent in the industry.

These demand characteristics of the automobile industry, coupled with the objectives, operating policies and practices, and competitive position of National in the industry, strongly influenced the general pattern and level of funds movements through the company. This is shown by Exhibits 5 and 6. Exhibit 5 shows the principal funds movements through the business each year between 1954 and 1962. Exhibit 6 shows the same information on a selected quarterly basis. From this information it is evident that National was subject to very wide movements in both its sources and uses of funds. It is also clear from the so-called closing liquid asset balances that these variations in funds flows were absorbed largely by corresponding changes in the company's liquid asset holdings.

An important characteristic of the automobile industry was that all of the major manufacturers maintained large liquid balances, i.e., cash and marketable securities, to provide for operations and protect against the kind of widely fluctuating funds movements mentioned above. In the case of National, a number of factors influenced the size of its cash and marketable securities balances. First, there was a desire to maintain sufficient cash deposits in banks to compensate them fairly for services rendered. As explained below, this amounted to about $60 million in 1963. Second, it was necessary to provide for the day-to-day changes in operating cash requirements that were incident to the normal functioning of the company's domestic and international operations. Third, it was the company's policy to fund its peak seasonal and cyclical funds requirements internally insofar as possible rather than borrow such amounts externally as they were required. This policy involved several hundred million dollars. To give just one example of what this meant, the annual retooling and model changeover resulted in a period of weeks each summer during which there were no cash receipts from automobile sales and sharply increased payments to suppliers and outside contractors. The cash deficit during this one short period often ranged up to $200 million. Given the policy of funding these requirements internally, it was necessary to have this much liquid assets available throughout the year so as to have adequate cash on hand when needed. Fourth, and in addition to funding operating cash requirements, it was thought desirable to maintain a reserve fund sufficient to meet unforeseen requirements arising from the unpredictable nature of the company's funds requirements. Finally, management desired enough liquidity to maintain a high degree of flexibility to take advantage of major investment opportunities as they presented themselves at home and abroad.

Largely in response to these policies and objectives, National's liquidity increased sharply during the 1950's. Between 1953 and 1957, for example, the company's investment in cash and marketable securities increased from $120 million to over $530 million. This represented a big increase in terms of cash and securities as a percent of sales and as a percent of total assets. The increase was financed largely from internally generated sources of funds and from a long-term loan of $250 million.[1] This is reflected in Exhibit 5.

At about the same time as National's liquid balances were being supplemented in the mid-1950's, yields on short-term marketable securities also increased significantly. These factors, i.e., increasing cash balances and in-

---

[1] In 1954, National negotiated a $250 million loan at 3¾% with a large insurance company, taken down at the rate of $62.5 million annually in 1954, 1955, 1956, and 1957. This loan represented the first time National had borrowed money in almost 20 years. The loan agreement specified a lump-sum principal repayment at the end of 100 years, although the whole loan was convertible at the option of either party beginning in 1962 into a 3½% 20-year loan to be amortized in equal annual installments of $12.5 million. In accordance with the insurance company's subsequent handling of all similar loans, the option to convert was exercised by the insurance company in 1962.

creasing short-term interest rates, encouraged even greater efforts than had been true in the past to invest excess cash more fully and systematically. The result was that by the end of the decade a very large proportion of National's cash was kept continuously invested in U.S. Treasury obligations, U.S. agencies, repurchase agreements, municipals, finance and other commercial paper, bankers' and export acceptances, and certificates of deposit. In June, 1963, for example, National had almost $500 million of excess cash so invested.

Thus Mr. Carr's job as manager of National's cash management activities had evolved rather recently in response to these changes in both company liquidity and external short-term investment opportunities. The essence of his work was to gather as much cash as possible from throughout the entire organization and then, after allowing for appropriate bank balances, to invest all remaining cash so as to earn the greatest possible returns given certain investment policy guidelines that had been formulated by management.

The job of marshalling the company's cash resources focused on the efficient scheduling and handling of cash inflows and outflows. What Mr. Carr and his associates tried to do was speed the flow of cash collections into the company's investable cash pool and to hold them there until disbursements were required. It is easiest to understand how this was accomplished by focusing on collections and disbursements separately.

All of National's automobile sales were made on a cash basis to its dealers. To accomplish this outcome, its cash collection procedures were arranged so that National received collected or investable funds on the scheduled delivery dates of automobile shipments to its dealers. The cash transfers involved in this process were effected either directly through the banking system or through a sales finance company. All of the company's dealers had established working relationships with a local bank or a sales finance company for wholesale financing of their automobiles. In the case of a bank, payments for the automobiles were made from the dealer's bank account or from a line of credit established with the bank. The credit line typically was secured by the automobiles actually involved, so that title passed from National to the local bank rather than to the dealer. Each dealer sent a "letter of authorization" to National authorizing the company to collect directly from the dealer's local bank or finance company. The local bank or finance company, in turn, sent a "letter of commitment" to National stating that it would pay for the automobiles delivered to the dealer involved.

About half of National's cash receipts were handled through a cash draft system. A cash draft is a deposit instrument similar to a regular check except that it is initiated by the payee, in this case, National Motor Car Company. Simulating a simple transaction, the system worked as follows: On Monday, June 3, National shipped an automobile to ABC dealer in Jacksonville, Florida, with a normal in-transit delivery time of three days. ABC dealer had a line of credit with XYZ bank. On Tuesday, June 4, National sent an invoice for the automobile directly to the person or department in XYZ bank designated in its letter of commitment. Also on Tuesday, June 4, a check-type cash draft drawn on XYZ bank was prepared and coded with the three-day in-transit delivery time. A "nonnegotiable" copy of the draft was sent with the invoice to XYZ bank to facilitate matching with the draft when it was presented for payment.

On the day before the automobile was scheduled to arrive, in this example Wednesday, June 5, National deposited the bank draft in its local bank, which credited National's account with uncollected funds in the amount involved. National's bank immediately sent the draft to the XYZ bank through the banking system. One or two business days later, in accordance with a standardized collection procedure followed throughout the banking system, the uncollected funds originally credited to National's account would become collected. In this example, because Jacksonville was a Federal Reserve city, funds were collected one day after deposit by National or on Thursday, June 6, the day the automobile was scheduled to arrive at ABC dealer. It took two days to collect funds through commercial banks located outside Federal Reserve cities. In these cities, cash drafts for collections were deposited in National's bank two days prior to the scheduled delivery date so that funds would become collected when the automobile was scheduled to be delivered.

The next most important method of collection was through large finance companies, which made collected funds available to the company on the scheduled delivery date. In these instances, the assembly plant making shipment would teletype the amount of the billings to a dealer to Mr. Carr's office. One of his assistants would notify the finance company of the total amount of all shipments scheduled for delivery that day to dealers all over the country with whom the finance company had a wholesale financing arrangement. The finance company, in turn, immediately notified its bank to wire transfer the amount involved from its account to National's account. Since the funds were transferred over the wire transfer system of the banks, they were collected funds and could be invested or disbursed immediately. More than a third of National's receipts were handled this way.

Government checks for defense sales were the only major source of domestic receipts that fell outside the above procedures. In this area, because the checks involved often amounted to several million dollars, special efforts were made to expedite collection. Each morning government checks were sorted out of the mail and delivered to National's bank by special messenger. The bank, in turn, would rush the checks to the local Federal Reserve bank and have them cleared. These cleared or collected funds were then transferred to National's account, from which they could be invested or paid out the same day.

While the company, in effect, operated a centralized cash drawer as far as collections were concerned, it followed a policy of decentralization with respect to disbursements. Each afternoon the financial managers of National's plants and offices around the country wired or telephoned one of Mr. Carr's assistants and advised him as to the amount of cash required to cover large local cash expenditures the following day. Then, the next day, the branch financial manager would write the necessary checks, usually drawn on the branch's local bank, and inform Mr. Carr's assistant before noon of the exact amount involved. National would then ask one of its central banks to wire federal funds in like amount to the banks and accounts of its local branches. This bank wire system made possible the instantaneous transfer of collected funds from bank to bank throughout the country. The effect of these cash disbursement procedures was that while National's geographically scattered managers maintained disbursement authority on a decentralized basis, it was not also necessary for National to maintain additional cash balances for this specific purpose in a lot of local banks.

The company's underlying liquidity, coupled with the above collection and disbursement practices aimed at maintaining the greatest possible collected cash balances for the longest time, determined the amount of funds available for short-term investment. However, this pool of available funds was reduced by the amount of National's compensating cash balances with its banks. In 1963 these compensating balances amounted to about $60 million.

Because National's banks played a prominent role in both the management of cash flows and the investment of excess cash, the question of compensating balances and bank relations was closely related to Mr. Carr's cash management activities. The services rendered by the company's 133 domestic commercial banks were manifold. Apart from providing normal banking services, many of the company's banks offered the special handling of drafts and checks that was required to expedite their conversion into collected balances. Use of the bank wire system facilitated the rapid transfer of collected balances from bank to bank. The banks involved in the company's disbursement activities also undertook to reconcile their various accounts with the company. As a part of this service these banks rendered special monthly statements of account, and they performed semiannual account-by-account analyses for the company. At the local level, the banks often gave important assistance to National's dealers and employees. With the dealers this assistance usually took the form of credit to finance both dealer inventories and consumer sales of new and used automobiles. Another important consideration was that National maintained lines of credit totaling $150 million with a group of more than 100 banks. Although the company had never had occasion to use these lines, management considered the insurance they provided of value. A final important intangible factor taken into account was the size, location, and general ability of a given bank to help the company in unusual situations.

In addition to the above banking services, some 15 of the company's largest banks helped in connection with its cash investment activities. They would hold in safekeeping securities purchased by National, physically transfer securities bought and sold between buyer and seller, expedite cash transfers in connection with securities transactions and cash coupons due. Five of the banks were dealer banks; i.e., they operated in the money market on their own account and stood ready at any time to buy or sell securities with

National. Three of these five also acted, through different departments, as agents for National in its money market operations. In this capacity they would advise Mr. Carr and his associates and keep them abreast of market developments, as well as negotiate securities purchases and sales with third parties and present National's tenders at the weekly Treasury bill auctions held in New York.

While many of these extra services might have been purchased on a fee-for-service-rendered basis, Mr. Carr and his associates felt that much of the help they got from their banks was intangible and difficult to measure and in the final analysis depended upon maintaining good bank relations. This meant giving the banks compensating balances on which they could earn income rather than periodic cash payments for services rendered.

The question of how large these balances should be had been more difficult to answer. The company's basic philosophy was that it should compensate its banks fairly for real services performed. For some years, National attempted to get at this amount by first trying to decide what each individual bank balance should be and then summing the parts to get an overall total. More recently, this approach had been augmented by starting from a judgment as to what the total amount should be, and then adjusting individual accounts within the total.

This amount might be increased if studies showed it failed to fairly compensate a particular bank for the cost of services rendered. Several such studies suggested that an allowance of five cents per item (check, draft, deposit, etc.) should cover normal bank costs. Thus the total annual allowed transactions cost in any given account was calculated by multiplying five cents times the number of items per year. National also required that each of its banks submit semiannually a statement of earnings from the company's business with the bank. If either of these steps showed that the balances of any bank were out of line, adjustments in the outstanding compensating balance might then be made in either direction. In addition to balances required to cover normal bank costs and a reasonable margin of profit, National kept balances to compensate its banks for the intangible services they rendered. These additional balances were a matter of judgment and could not be mathematically determined. In this category, the most difficult to determine were the proper balances to maintain with National's key banks to pay for general, high-level financial advice as well as assistance in the international field. It was also important to anticipate the lead role these key banks would play in any future external financing.

The control figure used for each bank was the average collected balance per the bank's books. In other words, the planned balance took into consideration the float caused by check activity and the uncollected funds from deposits. Since the control figure was the average balance, Mr. Carr's department adjusted its individual bank balances each month to bring the cumulative average daily bank balance into line.

As mentioned above, National maintained a constant cash balance of $60 million per its books and invested all remaining cash in marketable securities. To keep fully invested and at the same time maintain the planned balances, Mr. Carr's staff had to calculate the net effects of daily cash receipts and disbursements early each day and take appropriate action immediately to maintain the fixed cash balance. For example, inflows from receipts and maturing or previously sold investments would be added and disbursements and previously purchased securities subtracted in estimating required daily securities purchases or sales as follows:

	Millions of Dollars	
	A	*B*
Portfolio securities maturing today	$10	$ 5
Plus: Forecast collected funds available today after any adjustments to the planned balances	5	5
Plus: Securities sold for delivery today	2	..
	$17	$10
Less: Forecast disbursements today	15	5
Less: Securities previously purchased for delivery today	..	8
Balance to invest (sell) today	$ 2	$(3)

In Case A, therefore, $2 million would be added to the portfolio, while in Case B, $3 million would be provided by selling securities.

Excluding repurchase agreements, over 80% of National's portfolio transactions were arranged prior to the actual delivery date. There were two reasons: First, experience showed that better deals could be made (both purchases and sales) on a "regular delivery" basis wherein the actual delivery of a security was made from one to four business days after the transaction date. Second, the new issues of many types of securities, e.g., Treasury bills, U.S. agencies, municipals, were auctioned or sold well in advance of their actual delivery dates.

Having thereby determined the amount of change to be made in the portfolio, Mr. Carr's staff then had to determine what to buy or sell to meet the requirements of the day. Mr. Carr had several objectives in dealing with the marketable securities portfolio. Complicated by the large swings in liquidity inherent in National's operation, he saw it as the main function of his securities staff to keep these funds invested so as to earn for the firm the highest yield possible within the limits imposed by the following guidelines:

1. Funds could be invested only in securities with a maturity of one year or less.
2. Funds were invested solely in the various short-term government obligations, agencies, municipals, repurchase agreements, finance and other commercial paper, acceptances, certificates of deposit, and foreign securities. No funds were invested in corporate obligations or securities of any kind, other than as just mentioned.
3. The maturity pattern of the company's securities portfolio was determined by estimated future funds requirements, rather than by any attempt to take into account a forecast of changes in future interest rates.

In particular, preference was often given to maturities due on dates of anticipated funds requirements.

4. The breakdown of the company's portfolio between the various security types was shaped more by the firm's forecast of funds requirements and the yields afforded by the several types of securities available to the company than by any preconceived concept of what a "good" portfolio breakdown should be.
5. The day-to-day operating decisions regarding what to buy and sell were delegated to one of Mr. Carr's assistants. The portfolio manager needed flexibility and freedom to act quickly within the company's policy guidelines in order to negotiate effectively with the various security dealers.

In addition, there were other factors which Mr. Carr and his associates took into account. Although he was guided mainly by the pattern of major cash needs resulting from the timing and size of payrolls, accounts payable, dividend payments, tax payments, the model changeover period, the expected level of sales and production, and large scheduled investments, some additional diversification among security types and maturities was desired. Since there were often significant differences among the many security types as to liquidity, marketability, and after-tax yields to maturity, diversification was expected to reduce the risk of loss due to peculiar demand and supply influences acting on particular security types and maturities. And, because yields tended to be higher with longer maturities, Mr. Carr tried to keep that portion of his portfolio which was in excess of amounts needed for major predicted needs invested in longer term issues. In this way, he felt he could maintain a maximum rate of return on the portfolio as a whole. Some securities (i.e., Treasury bills) were more marketable than others (i.e., commercial paper); therefore he tried to keep a portion of the portfolio in more marketable, although perhaps lower yielding, securities in order to retain flexibility in case unexpected cash needs or opportunities to purchase higher yielding securities arose later. Since interest rates paid by the large finance companies were usually comparable to those available elsewhere, Mr. Carr tried to allocate his investments in finance company paper in accordance with the level of wholesale dealer financing done for the company's dealers by particular finance companies. Finance companies would often arrange the maturities of their securities to suit National's needs. Although the composition of the portfolio varied widely from time to time, a sample breakdown of the portfolio by maturities and security types in July, 1959, and 1963 is shown in Exhibit 7.

Since the maturity pattern of National's marketable securities portfolio was so strongly influenced by the company's projected cash requirements, cash forecasting was another important element of the investment decision. Several different forecasts of funds movements and requirements were prepared within the company. These included a five-year forecast of year-end liquid assets (revised annually); a one-year forecast of quarter-ending cash and security totals (revised monthly); a three-month forecast of monthly receipts, disbursements, and month-end balances (revised monthly); a one-month forecast of daily receipts, disbursements, and closing balances (revised weekly); and, finally, a one-day forecast of receipts, payments, and end-of-day closing balances. In addition, Mr. Carr knew for the next year the dates when many large disbursements would be made, even though he did not know how large the actual disbursements would be. Because of the great swings in cash flows through the business, as was shown in Exhibit 5, Mr. Carr had found only the one-day and one-month forecasts of real value in setting the maturity pattern of his portfolio at any given time. Although the one-month forecasts were usually fairly accurate, the forecast amounts could be off by as much as $100 million in either direction in a very few days as shown in Exhibit 8. Apart from these forecasts, and in view of the degree of forecast uncertainty involved, Mr. Carr relied very heavily upon his generalized knowledge of the business in structuring the maturity pattern and in selecting security types.

As Mr. Carr reviewed the cash management program in July, 1963, he had two things in mind. First, in view of the recent sharp improvement in the company's business, the treasurer had asked that a careful study be made of all aspects of the company's cash management program. It was anticipated that this review might well lead to changes in either operating policies or procedures. Second, it was necessary for the cash management group to formulate a basic investment strategy for investing excess cash over the coming weeks and months. This strategy would have to reflect both forecasted August cash balances as shown in Exhibits 9 and 10, and expected interest rate trends as discussed in Exhibit 11. Money market conditions were quite unsettled because only recently the Federal Reserve Board had raised the discount rate from 3% to 3½%.

Exhibit 1

NATIONAL MOTOR CAR COMPANY

SELECTED FINANCIAL DATA, YEARS ENDING DECEMBER 31, 1955–62
(Dollar figures in millions)

	1955	*1956*	*1957*	*1958*	*1959*	*1960*	*1961*	*1962*
Operating results:								
Net sales	$3,466	$2,676	$3,565	$2,165	$2,643	$3,007	$2,127	$2,378
Net earnings (loss)	100	20	120	(34)	(5)	32	11	65
Earned per share	11.49	2.29	13.75	(3.88)	(0.62)	3.61	1.24	7.24
Dividends paid	35	26	35	13	9	13	9	9
Dividends per share	4.00	3.00	4.00	1.50	1.00	1.50	1.00	1.00
Price range	101–66⅛	87–60	82¼–52¼	59⅛–44	72⅝–50⅝	71⅞–38	57⅝–37⅜	75¼–38½
Financial position—year-end:								
Current assets	$ 891	$ 669	$ 940	$ 756	$ 690	$ 802	$ 892	$1,007
Current liabilities	586	461	514	392	415	371	386	445
Net current assets	305	208	426	364	275	431	506	562
Property, plant, equipment, and tools—less accumulated depreciation	458	614	546	548	633	510	439	399
Total assets	1,363	1,295	1,497	1,338	1,375	1,369	1,399	1,525
Long-term debt	125	188	250	250	250	250	250	238
Shareholders' investment	652	646	732	691	679	704	712	770
Analysis of operations:								
Net sales	100.00%	100.00%	100.00%	100.00%	100.00%	100.00%	100.00%	100.00%
Cost of goods sold	84.76	86.63	81.82	85.77	86.97	86.40	84.48	81.04
Selling, general, and other expense	8.77	11.79	11.49	17.45	13.25	11.24	14.26	13.58
Operating profit (loss)	6.47	1.58	6.69	(3.22)	(0.22)	2.36	1.26	5.38
Other income	0.12	0.22	0.41	0.46	0.40	0.32	0.45	0.52
Net income (loss) before income taxes	6.49	1.58	7.07	(3.38)	(0.38)	2.19	1.01	5.30
Net income (loss)	2.89	0.74	3.36	(1.56)	(0.21)	1.07	0.52	2.75
Financial and operating ratios—year-end:								
Current assets ÷ current liabilities	1.52	1.45	1.83	1.93	1.66	2.16	2.31	2.26
% cash and securities to current assets	39.27	30.58	56.62	32.41	28.15	41.10	51.29	55.29
Capitalization:								
% long-term debt	16.09	22.49	25.45	26.56	26.92	26.20	26.00	23.58
% common stock and surplus	83.91	77.51	74.55	73.44	73.08	73.80	74.00	76.42
% net income to net worth	15.34	3.09	16.38	d4.89	d0.80	4.56	1.57	8.50

Source: *Moody's Industrial Manual.*

Exhibit 2

NATIONAL MOTOR CAR COMPANY

INCOME STATEMENT
SIX MONTHS ENDING JUNE 30, 1963
(Dollar figures in millions)

Net sales	$ 1,551.0
Other income and deductions	9.5
	$ 1,560.5
Less:	
Cost of products sold	$ 1,273.2
Selling and administrative expenses	131.4
Interest on long-term debt	4.2
Taxes on income—United States and other countries	73.8
	$ 1,482.6
Net earnings	$ 77.9
Net earnings per share	$ 4.22
Number of shares outstanding (in thousands)	18,447
Depreciation charged to cost of products sold and expenses in the amount of	$ 24.1

Exhibit 3

NATIONAL MOTOR CAR COMPANY

BALANCE SHEET AS OF JUNE 30, 1963
(Dollar figures in millions)

ASSETS

Cash and marketable securities	$ 578.7
Accounts receivable	174.0
Inventories	308.2
Prepaid expenses	16.9
Total current assets	$1,077.8
Property, plant, and equipment (after accumulated depreciation of $633.0 at June 30, 1963)	381.9
Investments and other assets	230.5
Total assets	$1,690.2

LIABILITIES

Current liabilities	$ 585.9
Long-term debt	225.0
Total debt	$ 810.9
Net worth	879.3
Total liabilities and net worth	$1,690.2

Exhibit 4

NATIONAL MOTOR CAR COMPANY

CHART SHOWING TOTAL INDUSTRY UNIT SALES OF AUTOMOBILES AND NATIONAL'S SHARE OF MARKET, 1947 TO 1962

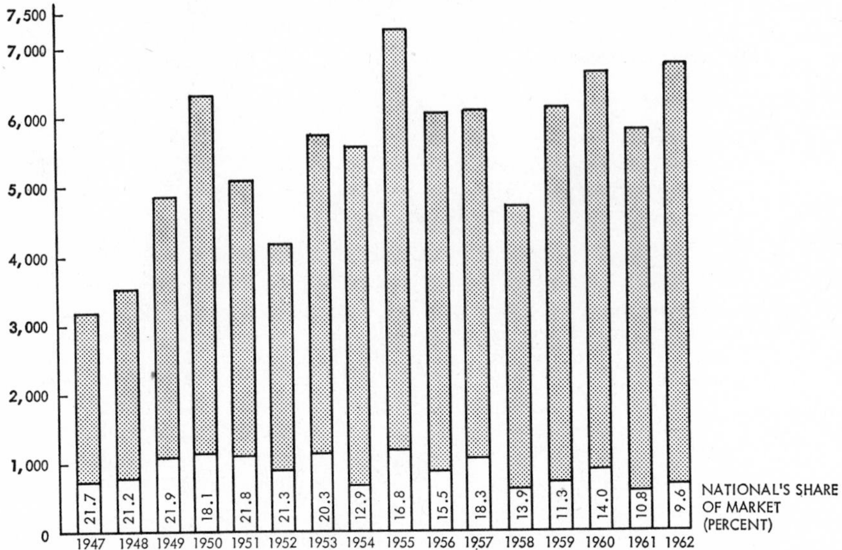

Source: *Automotive News* (1963 Almanac issue).

Exhibit 7

NATIONAL MOTOR CAR COMPANY

ANALYSIS OF MARKETABLE SECURITIES PORTFOLIO ON JULY 21, 1959

Portfolio Breakdown July 21, 1959	*July 21– July 31*	*Aug. 1– Aug. 15*	*Aug. 16– Aug. 31*	*Sept. 1– Sept. 15*	*Sept. 16– Oct. 15*	*Oct. 16– Nov. 15*	*Other*	*Total**	*% of Total Port-folio*	*Number of Lots*	*Smallest Lot Size ($)*	*Average Lot Size ($)*
Repurchase agreements...	$78,117,500							$ 78,117,500	24.54%	17	$1,960,000	$4,595,147
Bills....................		$ 6,960,787	$15,908,644	$29,272,110	$ 78,372,929	.....	$4,897,333	135,411,803	42.55	29	495,880	4,669,373
U.S. certificates..........		997,344				$4,997,500		5,994,844	1.88	2	997,344	2,997,422
Agencies................		10,425,000	7,360,000	4,099,234	5,297,688			27,181,922	8.54	29	100,000	937,308
Finance companies.......	1,483,517	9,908,368	990,837		40,578,132	246,986		53,207,840	16.72	21	245,601	2,533,707
Bankers' acceptances.....	3,632,181	2,026,606	1,683,131	3,033,143	1,984,250			12,359,311	3.88	15	31,518	823,954
Export acceptances.......				43,368		23,160	44,468	110,996	0.04	3	23,160	36,999
State and local...........	399,974		497,636	2,999,625	1,499,760	500,000		5,896,995	1.85	8	299,625	737,124
Total.............	$83,633,172	$30,318,105	$26,440,248	$39,447,480	$127,732,759	$5,767,646	$4,941,801	$318,281,211	100.00%	124		$2,566,784
% to total.........	26.28%	9.53%	8.31%	12.39%	40.13%	1.81%	1.55%	100.00%				
Accumulative......	26.28%	35.81%	44.12%	56.51%	96.64%	98.45%	100.00%					

* Book value.

Exhibit 7—Continued

NATIONAL MOTOR CAR COMPANY

Short-Term Marketable Securities
By Month of Maturity
As of July 15, 1963
(000)

	Aug., 1963	*Sept., 1963*	*Oct., 1963*	*Nov., 1963*	*Dec., 1963*	*Jan., 1964*	*Feb., 1964*	*Mar., 1964*	*Apr., 1964*	*May, 1964*	*June, 1964*	*July, 1964*	Total *Amount*	Total *Percent*	*Number of Lots*	*Smallest Lot Size ($)*	*Average Lot Size ($)*
Repurchase agreements	$ 24,200	$	$	$	$	$	$	$	$	$	$	$	$ 24,200	4.9%	11	$ 500	$2,200
U.S. Treasury Bills	700	5,700	53,550	2,000									61,950	12.5	30	200	2,065
U.S. agencies	3,875	1,000	12,300	9,100	15,700	15,300	13,750	7,500	17,750		9,500		105,775	21.3	21	500	5,037
Certificates of deposit								3,000	1,000		5,000	1,000	10,000	2.0	10	1,000	1,000
Tax exempts	35,537	8,000	5,596	9,900	400		3,000	15,000	1,230	1,000		20.561	100,224	20.2	31	400	3,233
Automobile finance company paper	21,000	15,500	23,000	500									60,000	12.1	19	250	3,158
Other commercial paper	17,500	35,500	13,500	7,500	9,500								83,500	16.9	43	1,000	1,942
Canadian and other foreign securities	10,000	5,000	5,510	4,075		10,000	500						35,085	7.1	16	500	2,193
Bankers acceptances	9,848	2,903	1,000	1,000									14,751	3.0	19	100	776
Total	$122,660	$73,603	$114,456	$34,075	$25,600	$25,300	$17,250	$25,500	$19,980	$1,000	$14,500	$21,561	$495,485	100.0%	200		$2,477
Percent maturing in month	24.7	14.9	23.0	6.9	5.2	5.1	3.5	5.1	4.0	.2	3.0	4.4	100.0%				
Cumulative percent	24.7	39.6	62.6	69.5	74.7	79.8	83.3	88.4	92.4	92.6	95.6	100.0%					

Exhibit 8

NATIONAL MOTOR CAR COMPANY

Forecasted and Actual Receipts (Cash and Securities) for Month of January, 1963, by Day

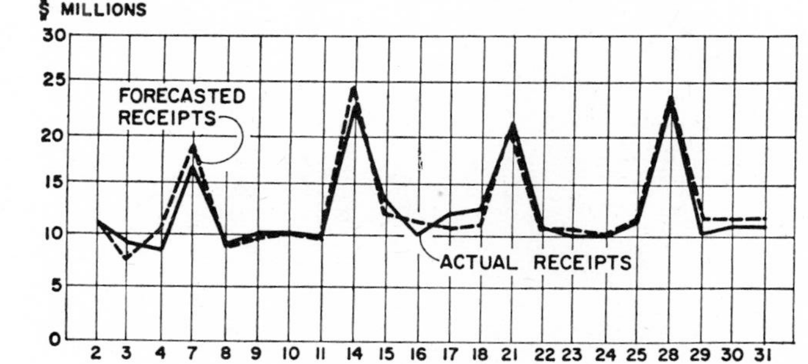

Forecasted and Actual Ending Balances (Cash and Securities for Month of January, 1963, by Day

FORECASTED ENDING BALANCES
ACTUAL ENDING BALANCES
650
600
550
500
450
31 2 3 4 7 8 9 10 11 14 15 16 17 18 21 22 23 24 25 28 29 30 31
(Dec.) JANUARY

Forecasted and Actual Disbursements (Cash and Securities) for Month of January, 1963, by Day

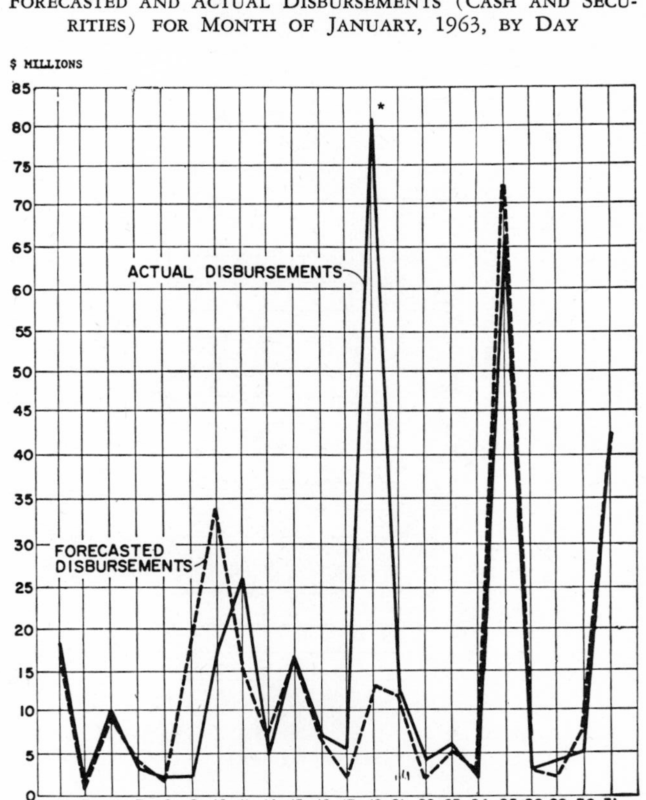

* Reflects cash required for an acquisition.

Exhibit 9

NATIONAL MOTOR CAR COMPANY

FORECASTED AND ACTUAL ENDING BALANCES (CASH AND SECURITIES) FOR MONTH OF AUGUST, 1962, BY DAY

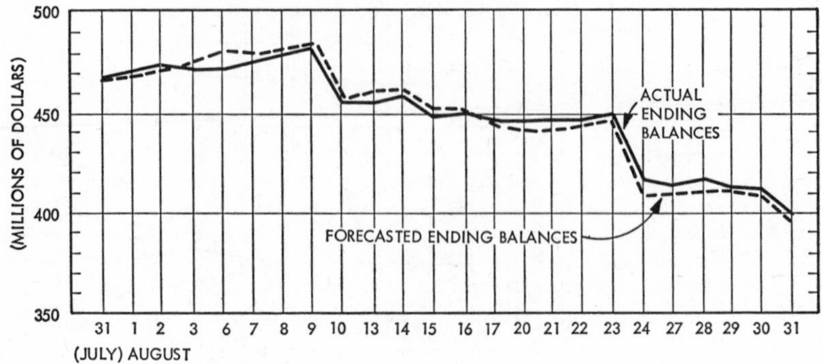

FORECASTED ENDING BALANCES (CASH AND SECURITIES) FOR MONTH OF AUGUST, 1963, BY DAY

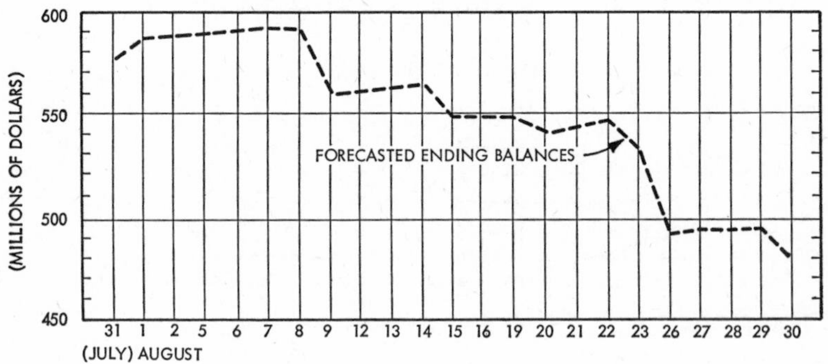

Exhibit 10

NATIONAL MOTOR CAR COMPANY

FORECAST RECEIPTS, DISBURSEMENTS, AND ENDING BALANCES FOR AUGUST, SEPTEMBER, AND OCTOBER, 1963

(Dollar figures in thousands)

	August	*September*	*October*
Cash and securities—beginning	$578,700	$482,700	$550,500
Receipts during month	110,000	343,300	350,000
Disbursements during month	206,000	275,500	278,100
Cash and securities—ending	$482,700	$550,500	$622,400

Exhibit 11

NATIONAL MOTOR CAR COMPANY

EXCERPT FROM THE *New York Times,* JULY 9, 1963*

Rise in Interest on Loans Hinted

Secretary of the Treasury Douglas Dillon indicated strongly today that steps might be taken soon to increase interest rates on short-term borrowings.

Such a move would have little or no immediate effect on the interest paid by individuals on personal loans or mortgages, but it would immediately raise the cost of many types of business and commercial borrowings.

Action to increase short-term interest rates would have to come from the Federal Reserve Board, rather than the Treasury. But Mr. Dillon made it clear that any such move on the part of the Board would have full Treasury approval.

In testimony before the Joint Economic Committee of Congress, Secretary Dillon argued at length that a rise in short-term interest rates would contribute greatly to a reduction in the United States balance of payments deficit.

He said that a recent study by the Federal Reserve Bank of New York, which may be made public later this week, indicated that a rise in short-term interest rates in this country would reduce the balance of payments deficit by $500,000,000 or more. This reduction would occur because more funds would remain in and come to this country, rather than being sent abroad in search of a higher rate of return.

. . . . .

An increase in short-term interest rates has been anticipated in financial circles for about two months. The Federal Reserve Board, in May, began taking certain steps which frequently herald an impending change in the basic short-term rate that the Federal Reserve controls—the so-called rediscount rate, which is the interest charge the Federal Reserve makes to banks which borrow from it.

Mr. Dillon's statement today, however, marked the first time that any member of the Kennedy Administration had publicly indicated approval of a move toward higher interest rates.

Whether Mr. Dillon's endorsement of such a move is shared unanimously within the Administration was not made clear. The President's Council of Economic Advisors has generally, in the past, felt that interest rates should not be increased so long as unemployment remains essentially unchanged at its present level of more than 5.5 per cent of the work force.

Mr. Dillon, however, expressed the view that no damage would be done to the American economy by an increase in short-term rates alone.

. . . . .

Mr. Dillon at no point in his statement, nor in his answers to the questions of committee members, indicated how large an increase in short-term interest rates was contemplated. He spoke merely of a change that would bring about "a reasonable reduction of the current differential in short-term interest rates" here and abroad. . . .

* P. 39, col. 1, and p. 41, col. 1.

ALLEN DISTRIBUTION COMPANY

^^^

On June 16, 1967, Mr. William McConnell of the mid-Atlantic office of the Allen Distribution Company was considering whether his company should extend a credit limit of $1,000 to the Morse Photo Company of Harrisburg, Pennsylvania. Mr. McConnell had recently transferred from his job as credit representative in one of the company's western branch offices to become credit manager of the mid-Atlantic branch office, where he assumed full responsibility for initiating and supervising the branch's credit policies. When he assumed this position, Mr. McConnell had asked the five credit representatives who had been handling the branch's accounts on their own to submit to him for review a few borderline credit accounts waiting the establishment of credit limits. Mr. McConnell believed that his decision and method of analysis might prove helpful in setting the tone of future operations in the credit department. Therefore, he planned to write out his analysis and decision so that it could be circulated.

The Allen Distribution Company, a subsidiary of the Allen Electric Company, one of the nation's largest manufacturers of electrical appliances and lighting equipment, was a national wholesale distributor of the parent company's products. Merchandise sold by the Allen Distribution Company ranged from refrigerators and television sets to electric light bulbs. Its competition included other nationally known wholesalers and small regional wholesalers of the Allen line as well as wholesalers of a number of competing product lines.

The parent company sold goods to the Allen Distribution Company on the same terms as to independent wholesalers. Allen Distribution in turn usually sold its merchandise at the wholesale prices and on the terms suggested by the parent company, as did most other wholesalers of the Allen line. However, Allen Distribution maintained the right to set its own prices, and occasionally, when price competition developed in local areas, prices were reduced for short periods.

Since wholesale prices for competing products tended to be uniform, the intense competition for retail outlets and intermediary wholesale houses handling the Allen line caused the company to give major attention to the services offered these customers, including cooperative advertising, store displays, inventory control, and credit arrangements. However, the slight differences in the quality of services rendered by the large wholesalers of Allen products were not fully appreciated by customers, and sales often depended more on the personal relationships developed between the customer and company salesmen. For this reason, Allen Distribution's salesmen tended to concentrate on maintaining current accounts and on expanding sales by securing outlets carrying competing product lines where brand differentials could be emphasized.

These salesmen were paid a straight commission of 1% for net sales in their territory. An additional 1% commission was given salesmen on net sales to new accounts during the first year. Salesmen were not held responsible for bad debt losses resulting from their sales efforts, although they sometimes helped in collecting overdue receivables.

Sales during the first four months of 1967 for the entire company, as well as the mid-Atlantic branch, had decreased 2% in comparison with the similar period in 1966 even though the number of customers serviced remained relatively unchanged. In late May, 1967, the president of Allen Distribution had called together the branch managers and announced an intensified sales campaign for new outlets to offset the sales decline. Sales quotas by branch and by salesmen were established, and a prize system was devised to reward sales personnel for successful efforts. Mr. McConnell knew that the mid-Atlantic branch manager was actively supporting the program and that he wanted the branch to make a good showing.

The mid-Atlantic branch office of Allen Distribution had net sales of $78 million in 1966. A percentage analysis of the branch's 1966 income statement is shown below:

Net sales	100.0%	
Cost of merchandise	92.0	(All costs variable)
Gross profit	8.0%	
Operating and other expenses:		
Warehouse	4.1	(Variable portion: 1.2% of sales)
Selling	1.4	(Variable portion: 1.1% of sales)
Administrative	1.1	(Variable portion: 0.1% of sales)
Bad debt loss	0.13	
Interest expense	0.27	
Total	7.0%	
Net profit before taxes	1.0%	

Mr. McConnell found that throughout 1966 the branch's outstanding receivables had averaged $5.6 million, of which approximately $150,000 represented overdue amounts. The active accounts, numbering 15,000, were turning over approximately every 25 days. Twelve people were employed in the credit department, and its operating expenses (included in the administrative expenses above) were $150,000 per year. This did not include bad debt losses, which were 0.13% of sales in 1966 and had averaged 0.14% of sales in recent years. These bad debt losses derived principally from the marginal accounts and were, therefore, approximately 1.4% of sales to the marginal accounts.

In Mr. McConnell's belief, a credit department should have little difficulty in approving good accounts and rejecting the bad ones. The real core of the credit department's operation rested in the evaluation of marginal accounts. Although Mr. McConnell had not made a study of the branch's operation, it was his opinion that the good accounts covered Allen Distribution's total operating and overhead costs, whereas the selection and handling of marginal accounts made the difference between profit and loss. Furthermore, Mr. McConnell believed that the purpose of a credit department was not to minimize credit losses but rather to maximize profits. He thought it was significant to recognize that an increase in sales volume for Allen Distribution usually meant increased sales for the parent company.

In evaluating a marginal account, Mr. McConnell considered the cost of handling the account, the current and potential profitability of the account, and the inherent risks. Although Mr. McConnell did not know how much more it cost a credit department to maintain a marginal account, he knew the credit department spent at least twice as much time maintaining credit files and collecting overdue amounts on marginal accounts as on good accounts. He estimated that 20% of the branch's accounts, representing nearly 10% of sales, were marginal firms. Nevertheless, collections from these companies tended to be on the average only 5 to 10 days slower than collections from good accounts. Mr. McConnell had not determined an appropriate basis for distributing these costs to marginal firms, but he thought they should bear a substantial portion of the credit department's operating expenses. He also believed that the 7% interest charge on bank loans, which roughly paralleled the size of the accounts receivable balance, was a cost factor chargeable to his department. Although Mr. McConnell was not certain how it might apply, he knew that management of the parent company expected new investments to promise returns of 20% or more (before taxes) before the investment was considered acceptable.

Although Mr. McConnell hesitated to define a good account in specific terms, he generally considered that companies with a two-to-one current ratio and with an equity investment greater than outstanding debt fitted into this category. He also examined, when appropriate, acid test ratios, net working capital, inventory turnover, and other balance sheet and income statement relationships, but found it difficult to establish rules to cover every situation. Unsatisfactory credit requests were also difficult to define in terms of specific ratios. With experience, a good credit analyst was able to handle good and bad accounts in a routine manner. Real judgment, however, was required to select from the marginal applications those worthy of credit. In evaluating a marginal account, Mr. McConnell thought the principal's character, although difficult to ascertain, was as important as the company's financial status. In an analysis of a credit application, two factors were considered important: (1) the risk of losing all or part of the outstanding receivable balance through bankruptcy; and (2) the cost of having to carry the amount due beyond the net period. Since the credit department screened almost 1,000 new requests for credit annually, Mr. McConnell knew that the evaluative procedures would have to be streamlined.

Mr. McConnell thought that the most difficult aspect of his new job would be translating any changes in credit policy into appropriate action by the credit representatives. Consequently, he planned to analyze a few selected marginal accounts so he might set forth the reasons for accepting or rejecting the accounts as a step toward establishing new credit standards. The Morse Photo Company was the first situation he had decided to review.

A credit file on the Morse Photo Company had been established on the basis of the following memorandum, dated May 16, 1967, from the company's Harrisburg salesman:

> Have sold Mr. Anthony W. Morse, president of Morse Photo Company, 280 Carlisle Avenue, Harrisburg, Pennsylvania, on the idea of switching from Oliver Electric Company's flash bulbs to ours. Sales would be $5,000 a year on current volume, and the Morse company is a real grower. Tony Morse is a terrific salesman and should sell a whale of a lot of bulbs for us. He wants $1,000 worth (net cost to him) of bulbs as a starter.

Photographic flash bulbs were not a major product item and for statistical purposes were grouped with electric lighting equipment, which accounted for 25% of Allen Distribution's sales volume. These electrical lighting supplies normally carried gross margins of 7% to 10% for Allen Distribution, but photo bulbs, one of the highest profit items sold by the company, had a gross margin of 17% after cash discounts. In addition, the parent company earned a "contribution" profit margin of 20% (before taxes) on its sales of photo bulbs.

The Morse Photo Company was similar to a number of Allen Distribution's customers. Almost half of Allen Distribution's 15,000 credit accounts purchased only lighting supplies from the company. Many of these accounts were small wholesale houses or regional chain stores whose annual purchases were in the $5,000 to $20,000 range.

Largely in order to control the retail price, photo bulbs were sold only on a consignment basis, but the practice had possible financial significance. Although a supply of bulbs was delivered to a customer, Allen Distribution remained the owner until the bulbs were sold by the consignee and, hence, was entitled to recover its bulbs at any time from the consignee's stock. To insure recovery, segregation of inventory was agreed to by the customer. This meant that his stock of Allen bulbs should be plainly marked and physically separated from the remainder of his inventory.

After a sale of bulbs, the consignee was supposed to keep the resulting receivables or cash separate from its other accounts or funds until payment was made to Allen Distribution. Therefore, if the prescribed procedures were followed, it was possible to identify, as Allen Distribution's, the total value of a consignment, either in inventory, receivables, or cash. Thus, in the event of liquidation, no other creditor could make claim against these items.

Owing to the inconvenience of keeping separate stocks, accounts, and funds, the safeguards associated with these consignment shipments were not often observed in practice. Allen Distribution made little effort to verify whether a separate inventory was actually maintained by its photo bulb customers. Nevertheless, it was believed that the company might have some protection in recovering consigned merchandise in the event of a customer's bankruptcy, since the bulbs carried the Allen brand name. More significantly, Allen Distribution made no effort to enforce segregation of funds after bulb sales were made by the customer. In consequence, it stood in the same general position as other creditors from the time the bulbs were sold by the consignee until remittance was made. Mr. McConnell, therefore, concluded that the consignment method afforded little financial protection in practice and appraised these accounts in the same way as open accounts.

At each month's end, the consignee inventoried the bulb supply and made payment in the amount of actual sales, less its 25% trade discount. Credit terms were 5% 10 E. O. M. All photo bulb consignees were on a one-year contract basis, whereby the customer agreed to sell Allen bulbs exclusively, and Allen Distribution agreed to supply the customer's needs up to a predetermined limit ($1,000 in the case of Morse Photo Company), provided payments were made within terms.

In the credit file Mr. McConnell found a credit report containing balance sheets and income statements of the Morse Photo Company (Exhibit 1) and four letters in reply to credit inquiries sent out by a branch credit representative (Exhibit 2).

Exhibit 1

ASSOCIATED CREDIT AGENCY REPORT, MAY 27, 1967

Company: Morse Photo Company, 280 Carlisle Avenue, Harrisburg, Pennsylvania.

Rating: Limited (unchanged from previous report).

Business: Commercial developing and photographic finishing. Also does a small volume of wholesaling films and camera supplies. Its distribution includes about 300 drug and periodical stores within a 130-mile radius of Harrisburg.

Management: Anthony W. Morse, president and principal stockholder.

History: Business started as proprietorship in May, 1961, with limited capital. On November 12, 1962, present owner purchased the assets but did not assume the liabilities for a reported $11,000; $2,000 was derived from savings and the balance was financed through a bank loan. On April 30, 1965, the proprietorship was succeeded by the present corporation, which corporation took over assets and assumed liabilities of the predecessor business.

Sales terms: 2% 10 days, net 30.

Employees: Twelve individuals of which three are salesmen.

Exhibit 1—Continued

BALANCE SHEETS FOR THE PERIOD ENDED APRIL 30, 1966, AND 1967
(Figured in even dollars)

ASSETS	*April 30, 1966*	*April 30, 1967*
Cash	$ 320	$ 439
Accounts receivable, net	11,503	16,201
Inventory at cost	12,712	12,681
Total current assets	$ 24,535	$ 29,321
Fixed assets:		
Cost	$ 58,331	$ 93,574
Depreciation	12,573	21,492
Net	$ 45,758	$ 72,082
Other assets	2,839	9,641
Total assets	$ 73,132	$111,044
LIABILITIES		
Accounts payable	$ 9,953	$ 22,311
Note payable—bank	5,136	9,360
Notes payable—other	9,127	15,158
Income tax	198	373
Other tax	3,123	2,546
Interest payable	...	96
Payroll payable	...	1,514
Total current liabilities	$ 27,537	$ 51,358
Other liabilities:		
Notes payable—officers	2,648	2,648
Notes payable—bank	764	...
Notes payable—other	...	810
Bond payable	...	14,000
Total liabilities	$ 30,949	$ 68,816
Net worth:		
Preferred stock	$ 10,000	$ 10,000
Common stock	32,100	32,100
Earned surplus	83	128
Total net worth	$ 42,183	$ 42,228
Total liabilities and net worth	$ 73,132	$111,044

Exhibit 1—Continued

INCOME STATEMENT FOR FISCAL YEARS 1966 AND 1967
(Figured in even dollars)

	April 30, 1966	*April 30, 1967*
Net sales	$162,898	$269,461
Less cost of goods sold:		
Material	$ 58,453	$ 88,079
Wages	33,963	65,263
Other	28,841	44,049
Total cost of goods sold	$121,257	$197,391
Gross profit	$ 41,641	$ 72,070
Administrative and selling expense:		
Officers' salaries	$ 12,000	$ 22,000
Office salaries	5,733	10,000
Sales commissions	...	3,568
Depreciation	7,848	10,071
Other	15,779	25,613
Total administrative and selling expense	$ 41,360	$ 71,252
Net earnings before tax	$ 281	$ 818
Income tax	198	373
Earnings	$ 83	$ 445
Dividends	nil	400
Earnings transferred to surplus	$ 83	$ 45

Analysis of Financial Statements:

This seven-year old concern has expanded rapidly since its founding. This has been accomplished by expanding from a local territory to a radius of 130 miles and by giving 24-hour service to its customers. In order to accomplish this, there has been a substantial increase in fixed assets and approximately a 60% increase during the last year under review. This has been made possible in part by acquiring the Meade Photo Company in September, 1966. While the net earnings transferred to surplus have been small, there has been an increase in capital. During 1965 an 8% preferred stock issue of $10,000 was made, and in 1967 bonds were issued for $14,000. In connection with the acquisition of the Meade Photo Company for $24,000, $7,000 was borrowed from the Harrisburg Fidelity and Trust Company and the seller was given a chattel mortgage for $17,000, payable $180 a week. In addition Meade receives a payment of 10% of the net sales which are transacted from their former customers for a period of five years. During the year more equipment was purchased with money obtained in the form of notes from the bank. The amount due the bank is made up of five installment notes, secured by various pieces of equipment. Other notes payable consist of $5,500 payable to a large film manufacturer; $8,500 payable to Meade Photo; and the balance to others. Notes payable after one year are due to Meade Photo. Mr. Morse, the president, estimates that sales during the fiscal year, 1968, will be $320,000.

Exhibit 1—Continued

CREDIT RECORD, MAY 15, 1967

High Credit	*Owes Currently*	*Past Due*	*Terms*	*Payments*
3,000	0	0	Net 30	Prompt
2,693	0	0	2% 10 E.O.M.	Prompt
2,740	245	127	Net 30	Slow 8 months
582	0	0	2% 10	Prompt to slow 60 days
108	108	108	Net 10	Slow
2,518	2,518	0	Net 30	Prompt
582	61	0	2% 10	Prompt
9,308	8,854	4,601	2% 10, net 30	Slow 30 to 60 days
5,000	4,800	4,800	2% 10 E.O.M.	Slow 90 to 120 days
4,492	3,452	3,452	2% 10 E.O.M.	Slow 90 to 120 days
167	0	0	Net 30	Slow 60 days
118	118	118	Net 15	Slow 60 to 90 days

Exhibit 2

ALLEN DISTRIBUTION COMPANY

LETTER FROM THE HARRISBURG FIDELITY AND TRUST COMPANY

June 6, 1967

Allen Distribution Company
Philadelphia, Pennsylvania

Attention: Credit Manager

GENTLEMEN:

Morse Photo Company has maintained a satisfactory account with us for a number of years and such accommodation as we have extended them is cared for as agreed. It is our feeling that they are entitled to their reasonable trade requirements.

Yours very truly,

(*Signed*) GEORGE GRUBB
Assistant Vice-President
Harrisburg Fidelity and Trust Company

LETTER FROM A LARGE FILM MANUFACTURER

June 5, 1967

Allen Distribution Company
Philadelphia, Pennsylvania

Attention: Credit Manager

GENTLEMEN:

Re: Morse Photo Company

With reference to your inquiry regarding the above account, we wish to advise that we have been doing business with them since 1961.

Recently we have had a fair amount of trouble with them because of overexpansion in relation to their net worth. In the past, customer's promises for payment could not be depended upon, although there has been a decided improvement in the last six months. Around the first of the year we had to take notes totaling $7,500 for the past-due accounts. At the present time $2,500 is still outstanding, but the notes are not in default. In April, we extended them $2,700 worth of credit, $2,600 of which was under the term

Exhibit 2—Continued

⅓ payable every ten days. The last payment was not received until June 1, whereas it was due May 22. At the present time the concern owes us outside of the notes $115 of which $76.70 represents the April charge which is past due in our books.

To sum the whole thing up we are willing to extend credit up to $5,000 but must watch the account carefully.

Yours very truly.

(*Signed*) ALFRED WHITTIER
Credit Manager

LETTER FROM A LARGE CHEMICAL COMPANY

Allen Distribution Company
Philadelphia, Pennsylvania

June 7, 1967

Attention: Credit Manager

GENTLEMEN:

The following summary is the information you requested with respect to Morse Photo Company:

How Long Sold—May, 1965
Last Sale—June, 1967
Highest Credit—$700
Amount Owing—$700
Past Due—0
Terms—2% 10 days
Amount Secured—None
Manner of Payment—Previous sales C.O.D.

This is a trial order on restricted credit terms. Future policy will be determined by payment record.

Yours very truly,

(*Signed*) ARNOLD HEAD
Credit Manager

LETTER FROM OLIVER ELECTRIC COMPANY

Allen Distribution Company
Philadelphia, Pennsylvania

June 9, 1967

Attention: Credit Manager

GENTLEMEN:

Re: Morse Photo Company
How Long Sold—July, 1962
Date of Last Sale—April, 1967
High Credit—$1,600
Amount Owing—$630
Past Due—$630
Terms—2% 10 End of the Month

Other comments:

We would suggest watching this account carefully. It has been up to nine months slow with us.

Yours very truly,

(*Signed*) J. E. STEWART
Credit Manager

THE O. M. SCOTT & SONS COMPANY

Between 1955 and 1961, management of The O. M. Scott & Sons Company launched a number of new programs aimed at maintaining and increasing the company's past success and growth. Largely in response to these activities, Scott's field sales force grew from 6 to 150 men, several entirely new and expanded production facilities went on stream, and the number of products in the company's product line tripled. Sales increased from about $10 million to $43 million. In late 1961, company officials were preparing to review the results of all these changes to ascertain how, if at all, Scott's plans and financial policies should be changed.

The O. M. Scott & Sons Company commenced operations in 1868, when it began processing the country's first clean, weed-free grass seed. Scott's early business came from a small but rapidly growing local market in central Ohio. Later, however, the company went through several stages in its growth. At about the turn of the century the company turned from supplying its local market to selling grass and other farm seeds over a wider geographic area by mail. As its success with its mail-order business increased, the company began to advertise extensively and in 1927 added a free magazine called *Lawn Care,* which has been widely distributed ever since. In all of these early promotional activities, the company sought to sell the Scott name and products as well as the idea of improved care of lawns. In the 1920's a special lawn fertilizer developed for home use was added to the company's product line. During the 1930's the company began to distribute its products on a small scale through selected retail stores and garden centers. Sales and profits grew steadily throughout these years. Scott continued to grow along these same general lines until 1945, by which time sales reached $2.7 million and net profits after taxes were about $30,000.

Over the decade immediately following the war, pioneering research by Scott led to the development and introduction of a wide range of new chemical weed and garden pest controls and special-purpose lawn fertilizers. In addition, the company's grass seed lines were upgraded and supplemented. Largely in response to the success of this research, sales increased to $11.4 million and profits to over $210,000 in fiscal 1955.

By 1955, however, despite the company's impressive postwar record of growth in sales and profits, management was convinced that neither Scott nor its competitors had begun to develop and tap the potential inherent in the national lawn care market. In Scott's own case this failure to develop and tap the national market was attributed to the fact that Scott's customers could not buy its products easily where and when they expected to find them. The company's distribution system had not evolved adequately in response to developing market opportunities, and in many instances the company's dealers either were poorly stocked or were not the right kind of dealer for the company's products.

Thus began a new stage in Scott's development. Early in 1955 the company launched a program to build a national field sales organization with the objective of increasing the number, quality, and performance of its distributors so as to capitalize more fully on the success of its product research and development efforts. When this program started, the company had six field salesmen. By 1960 Scott had a field sales force of 150 men serving almost 10,000 retail dealers across the country. These dealers were mainly department stores and small hardware stores and garden supply centers. The company's salesmen spent most of their time training the dealers how to do a better selling job with Scott products and were paid a salary plus a bonus based on factory shipments to dealers.

Scott's product development program continued apace with the buildup in the direct selling force so that by the end of the 1950's the company was engaged in the purchase, processing, and sale of grass seed, and the manufacture and sale of fertilizers, weed and pest control products, mechanical spreaders, and electric lawn mowers. In 1959 sales increased to $30.6 million and profits to $1.5 million. A large proportion of these sales comprised new products that had been developed and patented by the company within the past few years.

Reviewing the company's progress again in early 1959, management was still not satisfied that the company was marketing its products as effectively as possible. For one thing, it was estimated that an annual market potential of at least $100 million existed for Scott products. Another important consideration was that several nationally known chemical firms had either begun or were expected to begin competing against Scott in certain lines. These facts led management to conclude that the most effective way for Scott to preserve its preeminent market position would be to push for immediate further market penetration. If successful, such a strategy would enable Scott to eclipse competition as completely as possible before its competitors could establish a firm market position against the company. In this context an annual growth rate in sales and profits of up to 25% was thought to be a reasonable goal for the company over the next few years.

Apart from the need to continue strengthening the company's field sales force and dealer organization, management thought in early 1959 that the most important factor standing in the way of further rapid growth and market penetration was the inability of the typical Scott dealer to carry an adequate inventory of Scott products. Because of the highly seasonal character of sales at retail of the company's products, it was essential that dealers have enough inventory on hand to meet local sales peaks when they came. Experience showed that in many parts of the country a large percentage of dealer sales were made on a few weekends each season. Failure to supply this demand when it materialized most often resulted in a sale lost to a competitor, although sometimes a customer simply postponed buying anything. The problem of assuring adequate dealer inventories had become more of a problem in recent years. The effectiveness of Scott's product development program meant that the dealer was expected to carry many more products than in the past. In addition, Scott had shifted its marketing emphasis from selling individual products to one of selling complete lawn and garden programs. And in order to sell a full lawn maintenance program it was necessary that the dealer carry the complete Scott line and have it on hand when needed by the consumer.

Because of their small size and often weak working capital position, most of Scott's dealers could not realistically be expected to increase their inventory investment in Scott products. This meant that any desired buildup in dealer inventory levels would have to be financed in some way by Scott itself. In the past the company had extended generous seasonal datings to its dealers, as was industry practice. As a normal pattern, winter and early spring shipments became due at the end of April or May, depending on the geographical area. Shipments during the summer months were due in October or November. The purpose of these seasonal datings was to enable and encourage as many dealers as possible to be well stocked in advance of seasonal sales peaks. Anticipation at the rate of 0.6% a month was offered on payments made in advance of these seasonal dates, although few dealers availed themselves of this opportunity. With purchases made outside the two main selling seasons, dealers were expected to pay on the tenth of the second month following shipment.

The company's past experience with seasonal datings suggested certain changes in the event Scott proceeded to finance a higher level of dealer inventories. Because of the seasonal nature of the business and the fact that most dealers were thinly capitalized, payment was not often received by Scott until the merchandise involved was sold, irrespective of the terms of sale. This meant that many dealers were continually asking for credit extensions. Another problem inherent in the seasonal dating policy was that Scott retained little or no effective security interest in the goods involved. A final problem was that in the past Scott had followed a policy of not selling to dealers that could not be relied upon to maintain prices at reasonable levels. It was thought that widespread selling at discount prices would undermine the company and the market image it was trying to project. Thus, in any decision to expand dealer inventories, management hoped to contrive a procedure whereby Scott would retain the right to reclaim goods from third parties in the event any of its dealers began selling at wholesale to a discounter.

After considerable study it was decided to continue the traditional seasonal dating plan and to introduce a new trust receipt plan as well. This combination was thought to fulfill all of the requirements outlined in the previous paragraph. As the particular trust receipt plan adopted by Scott worked, a trust receipt dealer was required to sign a trust receipt that provided for (1) immediate transfer to the dealer of title to any Scott products shipped in response to a dealer order, (2) retention of a security interest by Scott in merchandise so shipped until sold by the dealer acting in his capacity as a retailer, and (3) segregation of a sufficient proportion of the funds received from such sales to provide for payment to Scott as billed. Among other things, these provisions made it possible for Scott to move in and reclaim any inventory held by third parties that had been sold by a trust receipt dealer acting illegally as a wholesaler. Exhibit 5 shows the trust receipt form used by Scott. In addition to obtaining the trust receipt from its dealers, the company also was required to file a statement of trust receipt financing with the secretary of state in each state where a trust receipt plan dealer was domiciled. Such a statement is shown in Exhibit 6. Dealers using the trust receipt plan were charged an extra 3% on the cost of purchases from Scott. They also had to place all purchase orders directly through Scott's field salesmen, inasmuch as these account executives were held responsible by the company for controlling dealer inventories in connection with the trust receipt plan.

This last-mentioned role of Scott's sales force was absolutely central to the proper functioning of the trust receipt plan. Apart from simply policing the level and character of dealer inventories, the account executives also periodically inventoried the trust receipt dealers so that Scott could bill the dealers for merchandise sold. During the two peak retail selling seasons these physical inventories were taken once a month, and even oftener in the case of large dealers. In the off seasons the inspections occurred much less frequently. In any event, the terms of payment associated with the trust receipt plan required that the dealer pay Scott within 10 days of receipt of an invoice from the company for goods sold since the last physical inventory date.

After introduction of the two payment plans in 1960, about half of Scott's sales were by seasonal dating and half by trust receipt. The trust receipt dealers were for the most part local garden centers and hardware stores, whereas the seasonal dating dealers were the larger chain garden centers and department stores. The company's overall collection experience with both plans was that about 75% of receivables were collected in the month due, another 16% in the following month, an additional 6% in the next month after that, and the balance thereafter.

The rapid growth in outstanding receivables resulting from the trust receipt program was financed largely by a combination of subordinated notes, a revolving line of bank credit, and increased use of supplier credit arising out of special deferred payment terms extended by the company's chemical suppliers. The company also retained almost all of its earnings each year as had been its policy in the past.

At the end of fiscal 1961 Scott and its subsidiaries had $16.2 million of long-term debt outstanding, of which $12 million comprised renewable five-year subordinated notes of the parent company held by four insurance companies and a trustee and $4.2 million was publicly held bonds owed by Scotts Chemical Plant, Inc., a wholly owned subsidiary. The key terms associated with the $12 million of subordinated notes are summarized in the footnotes to Exhibits 1 and 2. The governing loan indenture limited the unconsolidated parent company's maximum outstanding debt at any time to an amount not greater than three times what was termed the company's "equity working capital" as of the preceding March 31. What was meant by equity working capital and the calculation of maximum allowed debt are shown in Exhibit 7. The note indenture restricted outstanding subordinated notes to only 60% of maximum allowed debt as determined by the above equity working capital formula. The agreement also required that Scott be out of bank debt for 60 consecutive days each year and that the company earn before taxes 1½ times its fixed financial charges including interest on funded and unfunded debt, amortization of debt discount, and rentals on leased properties.

In addition to the long-term debt just described, Scott also had a $12.5 million line of credit at the end of fiscal 1961 with a group of seven commercial banks. The purpose of this line was to provide for seasonal funds needs, and in recent years the maximum line had been used at some point during each year. An informal understanding covering this seasonal financing arrangement required that Scott maintain average compensating balances with the banks involved of 15% of the line of credit.

As far as accounts payable were concerned, Scott had negotiated an arrangement with its principal chemical suppliers whereby the company settled with these suppliers just once or twice a year. It had been possible to negotiate these favorable terms because the suppliers were persuaded that it was in their best interests to help Scott develop and expand the home lawn market. Generally, no interest or other charges were levied on these amounts.

As fiscal 1961 drew to a close, management was generally pleased with what appeared to have been the results of the trust receipt program, although final figures for the year just ending were not yet available. Company sales had increased from $31 million in 1959 to over $43 million in 1961. At this level of operations the company's break-even point was estimated at between $27.5 million and $30 million.

By the end of 1961, when company officials were reviewing the results of fiscal 1961 and preparing plans for the 1962 selling season, the audited statements shown in Exhibits 1 and 2 were available, as well as the unaudited and unconsolidated quarterly statements in Exhibits 3 and 4. In addition, on the basis of a physical inventory taken by the company's sales force, combined standard and trust receipt plan dealer inventories were estimated to be at a level of about $28 million at the end of calendar 1961. This compared with roughly $17 million at the end of 1960. On the basis of these and other data, Scott's sales department estimated that in terms of cost of sales, dealer sales in fiscal 1961 reached an all-time high of over $30 million. The recent record of earnings, dividends, and market price range is shown in Exhibit 8.

It was against this background that company officials began their review and evaluation of recent operations and current financial position. They were particularly anxious to formulate any indicated changes in company plans and financial policies before the new production and selling seasons were upon the company.

Exhibit 1

THE O. M. SCOTT & SONS COMPANY AND SUBSIDIARY COMPANIES

CONSOLIDATED BALANCE SHEETS AS OF SEPTEMBER 30, 1957–61

(Dollar amounts in thousands)

	1957	*1958*	*1959*	*1960(a)*	*1961(e)*
Cash	$ 533.9	$ 1,232.0	$ 1,736.4	$ 2,328.7	$ 1,454.3
Accounts receivable	2,640.0	4,686.5	5,788.4	15,749.7	21,500.5(f)
Inventories	2,340.3	3,379.8	6,993.2	3,914.3	5,590.5
Total current assets	$5,514.2	$ 9,298.3	$14,518.0	$21,992.7	$28,545.3
Land, buildings, equipment	$2,253.5	$ 2,439.5	$ 7,364.6	$ 8,003.4	$ 8,370.2
Less: Accumulated depreciation	544.0	650.0	1,211.3	1,687.1	2,247.1
Net fixed assets	$1,709.5	$ 1,789.5	$ 6,153.3	$ 6,316.3	$ 6,123.1
Investment in and advances to affiliates	1,165.6	28.9	232.3	462.0	133.6
Other assets	488.5	376.6	837.5	1,132.0	937.8
Total assets	$8,877.8	$11,493.3	$21,741.1	$29,903.0	$35,739.8
Accounts payable	$1,540.8	$ 2,134.6	$ 4,140.2	$ 2,791.0	$ 6,239.2
Notes payable—banks	300.0	...	1,000.0	...	...
Accrued taxes, interest, and other expenses	674.3	1,437.7	1,900.7	1,941.2	1,207.7
Current sinking fund requirements	77.0	173.9	324.3	382.5	512.5
Total current liabilities	$2,592.1	$ 3,746.2	$ 7,365.2	$ 5,114.7	$ 7,959.4
Long-term debt:					
Of parent company (c) (h)	2,186.7	2,059.7	1,777.2	9,000.0	12,000.0
Of subsidiary (c) (h)	...	...	5,162.6	4,649.5	4,170.4
Total liabilities (d)	$4,778.8	$ 5,805.9	$14,305.0	$18,764.2	$24,129.8
Preferred stock (i)	1,757.2	2,432.2	2,392.5	2,347.5	2,254.3
Common stock and surplus	2,341.8	3,255.2	5,043.6	8,791.3 (b) (g)	9,355.7
Total liabilities and net worth	$8,877.8	$11,493.3	$21,741.1	$29,903.0	$35,739.8

See notes beginning p. 86.

Exhibit 2

THE O. M. SCOTT & SONS COMPANY AND SUBSIDIARY COMPANIES

CONSOLIDATED INCOME STATEMENTS FOR THE YEARS ENDING SEPTEMBER 30, 1957–61

(Dollar amounts in thousands)

	1957	*1958*	*1959*	*1960(a)*	*1961(e)*
Net sales (*b*) (*g*)	$18,675.9	$23,400.2	$30,563.7	$38,396.4	$43,140.1
Cost of sales and operating expenses:					
Cost of products sold including processing, warehousing, delivery and merchandising (including lease rentals)	$15,500.9	$18,914.7	$24,119.5	$30,416.8(*d*)	$34,331.7
General and administrative, research and development expenses	1,817.2	2,134.1	2,499.3	2,853.6	3,850.7
Depreciation and amortization	263.2	185.9	377.6	584.2	589.6
Interest charges	199.8	212.7	410.6	881.6	1,131.5
Total cost of sales	$17,781.1	$21,447.4	$27,407.0	$34,736.2	$39,903.5
Earnings before taxes on income	$ 894.8	$ 1,952.7	$ 3,156.7	$ 3,660.2	$ 3,236.6
Federal and state taxes on income	443.5	1,051.6	1,671.2	1,875.2	1,665.9
Net income after taxes	$ 451.3	$ 901.1	$ 1,485.5	$ 1,785.0	$ 1,570.7

See notes following.

Exhibits 1 and 2—Continued

THE O. M. SCOTT & SONS COMPANY

NOTES TO FINANCIAL STATEMENTS

a) *1960 Auditor's Statement*

The Board of Directors
The O. M. Scott & Sons Company

We have examined the statement of consolidated financial position of The O. M. Scott & Sons Company and its subsidiaries as of September 30, 1960, the related consolidated statements of operations, capital surplus and retained earnings for the fiscal year then ended, and accompanying notes to financial statements. Our examination was made in accordance with generally accepted auditing standards, and accordingly included such tests of the accounting records and such other auditing procedures as we considered necessary in the circumstances.

In our opinion, the accompanying statements, together with the explanatory notes, present fairly the consolidated financial position of The O. M. Scott & Sons Company and its subsidiaries at September 30, 1960, and the results of their operations for the year then ended, in conformity with generally accepted accounting principles, except as described in note (*b*), applied on a basis consistent with that of the preceding year.

PEAT, MARWICK, MITCHELL & CO.

Columbus, Ohio
November 23, 1960

Exhibits 1 and 2—Continued

b) *Sales*

For several years the company has followed a prebilling system to obtain more efficient and economical control of production through the medium of unappropriated inventory. Under this system, the invoicing of customers predates shipment. Consequently, both fiscal 1960 and 1959 sales stated in the operating statement include firm orders received, billed, and costed-out in late September which were shipped early in the immediately following October. Prior to September 30, 1960, the amounts involved were not significant, but toward the end of that month shipment was delayed by the company to facilitate the taking of physical inventories at storage warehouses as of the month end. The result of the foregoing is to include an additional amount of approximately $343,000 in net earnings for the year 1960. In management's opinion, the earnings on these sales are properly earnings of the year 1960.

c) *Long-Term Debt*

All long-term obligations of the parent company at September 30, 1959, were retired prior to December 31, 1959.

In fiscal 1960, the parent company sold five-year subordinated promissory notes, principally to certain insurance companies, at the principal amount of $9 million, maturing October 13, 1964. The notes bear interest to October 10, 1960, at 6½% per annum and thereafter to maturity at (*a*) 6% per annum, or (*b*) the New York prime commercial rate plus 1½%, whichever is higher.

The loan agreement provides, among other things, that (*a*) payment of principal and interest on the notes is subordinated to repayment of bank loans due within one year, (*b*) new or additional notes may be sold on October 28th of each future year, and (*c*) any holder of the notes may, before October 15th of each year, require payment by October 10th of the immediately ensuing year of all or part of the notes held.*

All holders of the notes at September 30, 1960, surrendered the notes then held in exchange for new notes having exactly the same terms but maturing October 28, 1965, at an interest rate of 6% per annum to October 10, 1961. Interest after October 10, 1961, accrues at the rate determinable under the provisions of the loan agreement.

Long-term obligations of subsidiary outstanding on September 30, 1960:

20-year 5¾% first mortgage bonds due March 15, 1977	$1,026,000
18-year 6% secured sinking fund debentures due Feb. 1, 1977	2,840,500
10-year 6% sinking fund notes due March 15, 1967	178,000
10-year 6% subordinated debentures due Dec. 15, 1967	950,000
	$4,994,500
Less: Current sinking fund provision	345,000
	$4,649,500

* Such payments were to be made in four equal annual installments beginning on October 10 of the immediately ensuing year.

Exhibits 1 and 2—Continued

The above obligations of a subsidiary are secured by property mortgages, and/or assignment of lease rentals payable by the parent company.

d) *Long-Term Leases*

The main production, warehousing, and office facilities used by the company are leased from affiliated interests not consolidated, namely, the company's Pension and Profit Sharing Trusts, and also from a consolidated subsidiary, Scotts Chemical Plant, Inc. These leases, all having over 10 years to run, required minimum annual rentals in fiscal 1960 of $872,577. This represented less than 17% of net taxable profit before deduction for rentals, depreciation, and expenses based on net profits. It is anticipated that in fiscal 1961, the fixed rentals under these leases will approximate the same amount.

e) *1961 Auditor's Statement*

Board of Directors
The O. M. Scott & Sons Company
Marysville, Ohio

We have examined the statement of consolidated financial position of The O. M. Scott & Sons Company and its subsidiaries as of September 30, 1961, and the related statements of consolidated operations, capital surplus, and retained earnings for the year then ended. Our examination was made in accordance with generally accepted auditing standards, and accordingly included such tests of the accounting records and such other auditing procedures as we considered necessary in the circumstances.

In our opinion, the accompanying statements of financial position, operations, capital surplus, and retained earnings present fairly the consolidated financial position of The O. M. Scott & Sons Company and its subsidiaries at September 30, 1961, and the consolidated results of their operations for the year then ended, in conformity with generally accepted accounting principles which, except for the changes (in which we concur) referred to in Notes (*f*) and (*g*), have been applied on a basis consistent with that of the preceding year.

ERNST & ERNST

Dayton, Ohio
January 6, 1962

f) *Accounts Receivable*

Accounts receivable are stated net after reserve of $740,000 for dealer adjustments, allowances, and doubtful accounts.

In 1959 the company adopted a plan of deferred payments for certain retail dealers. Accounts receivable include $16,033,093 for shipments under this plan which are secured by trust receipts executed by the dealers. The trust receipt arrangements provide for (1) immediate transfer to the dealers of title to the merchandise shipped in response to the dealers' orders, (2) retention by the company of a security interest in the merchandise until sold by the dealers, and (3) payment by the dealers to the company as the merchandise

Exhibits 1 and 2—Continued

is sold at retail. The dealers, whether trust receipt or other, do not have the right to return any part of merchandise ordered by them and delivered in salable condition, but they may tender merchandise in full or part payment of their accounts in the event of termination by the company of their dealerships. To provide for possible adjustments and allowances in the liquidation of dealer accounts receivable, the company has provided an increase in reserve by a charge to net earnings of the current year of $150,000 and a charge to retained earnings at October 1, 1960, of $530,000.

g) *Sales*

In the financial statements for the year ended September 30, 1960, attention was directed to the company's policy of including in the operating statement firm orders received, billed, and costed out in late September which were shipped early in the immediately following October. During 1961, this policy was discontinued. In order to reflect this change in policy prebilled sales at September 30, 1960, together with related costs and expenses included in operations of the year then ended, have been carried forward and included in the operating statement for the year ended September 30, 1961, with a resulting charge to retained earnings at October 1, 1960, of $429,600. This change in accounting principle did not have a material effect on net earnings for the year ended September 30, 1961.

h) *Long-Term Debt: Five-Year Subordinated Promissory Notes*

The notes bear interest to October 10, 1961, at 6% per annum and thereafter to maturity at a rate which is the higher of (*a*) 6% per annum, or (*b*) the New York prime commercial rate plus 1½%. The loan agreement provides, among other things, that (*a*) payment of principal and interest on the notes is subordinated to repayment of bank loans due within one year, and (*b*) elections may be exercised annually by the holders to (1) exchange the notes currently held for new notes having a maturity extended by one year, (2) purchase additional notes if offered for sale by the company, or (3) require payment of all or part of the notes held, such payments to be made in four equal annual installments beginning on October 10 of the immediately ensuing year.

All holders of the notes at September 30, 1961, except for $1 million, surrendered the notes then held in exchange for new notes having exactly the same terms but maturing October 28, 1966, at an interest rate of 6% per annum to October 10, 1962. Subsequent to September 30, 1961, arrangements have been made for the note for $1 million not exchanged to mature September 1, 1962, and to issue a note for $1 million to another lender maturing October 28, 1966.

Exhibits 1 and 2—Continued

Obligations of Subsidiaries:

$5\frac{3}{4}$% first mortgage bonds, due March 15, 1977	$ 964,000	
6% sinking fund notes, due March 15, 1967	147,500	
6% subordinated debentures, due December 15, 1967	819,000	
6% secured sinking fund debentures due February 1, 1977	2,620,500	
	$4,551,000	
Less classified as current liability	414,000	$4,137,000
Real estate mortgage notes ($252 payable monthly for interest at 6% per annum and amortization of principal)	$ 34,383	
Less classified as current liabilities	1,000	33,383
		$4,170,383

The above long-term obligations of subsidiaries are secured by mortgages on property, plant, and equipment, and/or assignment of lease rentals payable by the parent company.

i) Preferred Stock

Preferred stock is 5% cumulative, $100 par value.

Exhibit 3

THE O. M. SCOTT & SONS COMPANY

UNCONSOLIDATED QUARTERLY BALANCE SHEETS OF PARENT COMPANY FOR FISCAL YEAR 1961*

(Dollar amounts in thousands)

	12/31/60	*3/31/61*	*6/30/61*	*9/30/61*
Cash	$ 1,810	$ 2,140	$ 1,760	$ 2,070
Accounts receivable:				
Standard plan	$ 1,500	$ 6,540	$ 3,110	$ 4,400
Trust receipt plan	8,660	15,880	11,890	16,830
Total receivables	$10,160	$22,420	$15,000	$21,230
Inventories:				
Finished goods	$ 7,390	$ 5,850	$ 6,420	$ 4,040
Raw materials and supplies	2,380	2,520	1,890	1,460
Total inventories	$ 9,770	$ 8,370	$ 8,310	$ 5,500
Total current assets	$21,740	$32,930	$25,070	$28,800
Land, buildings, equipment	$ 2,130	$ 2,190	$ 2,270	$ 2,290
Less: Accumulated depreciation	800	830	870	910
Net fixed assets	$ 1,330	$ 1,360	$ 1,400	$ 1,380
Other assets	$ 1,990	$ 1,730	$ 1,720	$ 1,240
Total assets	$25,060	$36,020	$28,190	$31,420
Accounts payable	$ 1,390	$ 3,680	$ 3,150	$ 7,040
Notes payable—bank	6,250	12,000	5,750	—
Accrued taxes, interest, and other expenses	(390)	950	110	1,170
Total current liabilities	$ 7,250	$16,630	$ 9,010	$ 8,210
Subordinated promissory notes	9,000	9,000	9,000	12,000
Total liabilities	$16,250	$25,630	$18,010	$20,210
Net worth:				
Preferred stock	2,380	2,380	2,350	2,250
Common stock and surplus	6,430	8,010	7,830	8,960
Total liabilities and net worth	$25,060	$36,020	$28,190	$31,420

* Excluding items relating to certain nonoperating subsidiaries. Unaudited and unpublished. For these reasons Exhibit 3 does not correspond exactly with Exhibit 1. In particular, the cash account in Exhibit 3 is not consistent with that in Exhibit 1.

Exhibit 4

THE O. M. SCOTT & SONS COMPANY

UNCONSOLIDATED QUARTERLY INCOME STATEMENTS OF PARENT COMPANY FOR THE YEAR ENDING SEPTEMBER 30, 1961*

(Dollar amounts in thousands)

	Quarter Ending 12/31/60	*Quarter Ending 3/31/61*	*Quarter Ending 6/30/61*	*Quarter Ending 9/30/61*	*Year*
Net sales	$ 1,300	$15,780	$9,570	$14,740	$41,390
Cost of sales and operating expenses:					
Cost of products sold including processing, depreciation, warehousing, delivery and merchandising	$ 3,250	$11,730	$8,670	$10,790	$34,440
General and administrative, research and development expenses	660	800	940	1,000	3,400
Interest charges	150	240	260	200	850
Total cost of sales	$ 4,060	$12,770	$9,870	$11,990	$38,690
Earnings (losses) before taxes on income	$(2,760)	$ 3,010	$ (300)	$ 2,750	$ 2,700
Federal taxes on income	(1,440)	1,570	(160)	1,390	1,360
Net income (loss) after taxes	$(1,320)	$ 1,440	$ (140)	$ 1,360	$ 1,340

* Excluding items relating to the operations of certain nonoperating subsidiaries. Unaudited and unpublished.

Exhibit 5

THE O. M. SCOTT & SONS COMPANY

TRUST RECEIPT

The undersigned Dealer, as Trustee, and Entruster agree to engage in Trust Receipt financing of the acquisition by Trustees of seed, fertilizer, weed controls, pest controls, applicators, mowers and other lawn and garden products, all bearing the brands and trade marks of The O. M. Scott & Sons Company. Entruster will direct said company to deliver said products from time to time as ordered by Dealer.

a) Dealer agrees to hold said products in trust for the sole purpose ot making sales to consumers, functioning as a retailer and not as a wholesaler.

b) Dealer agrees to hold a sufficient proportion of the funds received from such sales for payment to Entruster as billed.

c) Either party may terminate this Trust Receipt on notice. In such event Dealer will surrender to Entruster his complete stock of The O. M. Scott & Sons Company products, proceeds thereof to be credited to Dealer.*

Official Business Name of Dealer as Trustee:	Accepted at Marysville, Ohio
________________________	________________________, 19__
Street & No.________________	
City__________Zone____State______	THE O. M. SCOTT & SONS COMPANY (Entruster)
Authorized Signature________________.	
Date__________Title__________	President

* This statement differs from the statement quoted in footnote (*f*) to Exhibits 1 and 2. Presumably the statement in Exhibit 5 is correct.

Exhibit 6

THE O. M. SCOTT & SONS COMPANY

Statement of Trust Receipt Financing

The Entruster, The O. M. Scott & Sons Company, whose chief place of business is at Marysville, Ohio, and who has no place of business within this state, is or expects to be engaged in financing under trust receipt transactions, the acquisition by the Trustee whose name and chief place of business within this state is:

of seed, fertilizers, weed controls, pest controls, applicators, mowers and other lawn and garden products, all bearing the brands and trade marks of The O. M. Scott & Sons Company.

Entruster: The O. M. Scott & Sons Company — Date________________, 19__

For the Trustee (Dealer)

By:________________ President — By:________________

Exhibit 7

THE O. M. SCOTT & SONS COMPANY

EXAMPLE SHOWING CALCULATION OF EQUITY WORKING CAPITAL AND MAXIMUM ALLOWED DEBT OF PARENT COMPANY FOR THE TWELVE MONTHS FOLLOWING MARCH 31, 1961*

(Dollar amounts in millions)

Calculation of equity working capital:		
Current assets		$32.9
Current liabilities	$16.6	
Long-term debt	9.0	
Total debt	$25.6	25.6
Equity working capital		$ 7.3
Calculation of maximum allowed parent company debt:		
300% of equity working capital		$21.9
Actual parent borrowings—March 31, 1961		21.0
Available debt capacity		$ .9
Calculation of maximum allowed subordinated debt of parent:		
60% of maximum allowed total debt ($21.9 million × 60%)		$13.1

* Calculations based on figures taken from Exhibit 3.

Exhibit 8

THE O. M. SCOTT & SONS COMPANY

RECORD OF EARNINGS, DIVIDENDS, AND MARKET PRICE RANGE, 1958–61

Fiscal Year	*Earnings per Share*	*Dividends per Share*	*Market Price Range**
1958	$0.69	10% stk.	6⅛– 1½
1959	1.15	10% stk.	32⅞– 6⅛
1960	1.21	10% stk.	51 –31⅞
1961	0.99	10¢ + 5% stk.	58¾–30

* Calendar year; bid prices. Closing prices September 29 and December 29, 1961 were $49 and $32¼ respectively. Stock first sold publicly in 1958 and has traded over-the-counter since then. The company had about 4,100 common shareholders in 1961.

KOEHRING COMPANY

^^

The Koehring Company is a Milwaukee-based manufacturer of heavy non-electrical industrial equipment, primarily construction machinery. Koehring is known as the most widely diversified company in its industry. Early in 1958 it comprised seven manufacturing divisions; two nonmanufacturing divisions, which constituted Koehring's world-wide marketing apparatus handling products of all the manufacturing divisions; and still another division, which was essentially a field servicing organization for the western states. Plants were located in four midwestern states and one Canadian province. An illustrative product listing included "commercial-sized"[1] power cranes, trench diggers, small motorized concrete mixers, concrete handling equipment used at mass pouring installations such as the St. Lawrence Seaway, road rollers and compactors, pulp and paper making machinery, hydraulic presses, plastic injection molding machinery, mining machinery, and water well drilling rigs. Of these products, earthmoving and excavating equipment were the primary revenue producers. Replacement parts typically amounted to about one fourth of annual sales.

Substantial growth had taken place during the 1950's by acquisition of existing companies. Waterous Ltd., a Canadian producer, was added in 1952 as Koehring-Waterous Ltd., a subsidiary, and in 1956 the Buffalo-Springfield Roller Company and Hydraulic Press Manufacturing Company were acquired, and subsequently operated as divisions. Other manufacturing divisions had been a part of the company since at least the early 1930's.

In January, 1958, Koehring's vice president–finance, Mr. Orville Mertz, was pondering a proposal from the marketing department for the institution of a schedule of terms on installment sales and a policy declaration of credit practices. Until then, divisional credit managers had evaluated each request for installment sales financing individually. No company-wide policy on down payments, length of payment period, and financing charge had been employed, and final decisions on these terms were made at the divisional level. In essence, special terms had been granted in each instance. Bad debts had never exceeded 2/100 of 1% in a single year after World War II. During the capital

[1] Up to three cubic yards capacity when used as a shovel and up to four cubic yards when used as the power for a dragline. Giant shovels, not produced by Koehring, have capacity as high as 60 cubic yards.

goods boom of 1955 through 1957, the number of requests for deferred payment sales contracts increased in number, and requests for more liberal terms grew increasingly common. The combination threatened to dangerously weaken managerial control of both marketing policy and, in turn, financial policy through its indirect impact on the length and size of notes receivable. If the vice president–finance concurred with marketing's proposal, a series of meetings were to be held with the general, sales, and credit managers of each of the divisions, and the new policy on terms quickly implemented. Administration was to remain in the hands of divisional credit managers.

A few days previously the company's president had issued a letter to the vice presidents of marketing and finance relating in part to this subject (Exhibit 1). Consequently, Mr. Mertz welcomed a review of procedure and an establishment of policy; but because of its possible effects on company financing, he held serious reservations about the advisability of a loosening of credit terms. His apprehension about the impact of the proposed installment sales program arose partly because recent rapid asset expansion had occasioned resort to substantial amounts of debt and preferred stock, and partly because the company's liquidity was low. Rapidly expanding receivables would force the firm to use outside fund sources. More debt, he feared, would raise risk in the firm through the fixed cash drain it would add to the existing fixed interest, sinking fund, and preferred stock dividend cash outflows. (See footnotes to the balance sheets in Exhibit 4.) He was also unsure of his banks' and long-term creditors' reaction. Although his company's relations were secure with both of these classes of its creditors, Mr. Mertz was aware that the cyclical variability of capital goods sales led to a preference on the part of institutional lenders for moderate use of debt by heavy equipment makers. Although no more mergers were contemplated presently, a policy of expansion by this means inclined Mr. Mertz to hedge against commitments that might make the company's capital structure inflexible in the face of unforeseeable demands for funds.

Market structure

While many of its competitors concentrated in relatively narrower product lines, diversification internally and through acquisition had led Koehring to straddle a broad segment of the nonelectrical machinery market. Because of this great diversity Koehring probably faced a broader array of product competitors than any other single firm. A representative cross-classification of Koehring's major competitors with its major construction machinery lines appears in Exhibit 2.

A substantial part of the marketing apparatus for these equipment lines was the domestic and foreign distributorship network. Since low unit volume prevailed, most of the industry's sales were made directly through distributors, and few retail outlets were maintained. Most distributors handled more than one manufacturer's product line, and many handled several. It was common, however, for individual distributors to market only part of a single manufacturer's product line. Koehring distributed through 450 distributors, for example, but only 70 handled equipment produced by all of its manufacturing divisions. Competition among manufacturers was intense for priority in inventory stocking and in the sales efforts by distributors.

Koehring customarily made some sales on special order directly from its factory to ultimate purchasers, but much the greater part of sales was made via the company's distributors, who sold mostly off the shelf. Open account sales, possibly with a discount for short-term payment but net 30 days, were the dominant type of distributor sales. In the few years preceding 1958, however, installment sales had grown relatively. These were financed (1) by the dealer, who carried the resulting installment receivable on his own books; or (2) by a lender such as a sales finance company or local commercial bank with or without the endorsement of the distributor; or (3) by Koehring, which absorbed the installment receivable and carried it for the life of the sales contract. Installment receivables resulting from sales to ultimate purchasers were known as "retail financing." Also, distributors frequently required assistance in financing inventories. Thus, for many years Koehring had made a practice of lending to its distributors through inventory-secured loans, known as "wholesale financing" or "floor planning." Koehring's product competitors typically extended this kind of financing to distributors. In part, the readiness of the manufacturers to extend wholesale financing stemmed from a desire on the part of each company to have its product line prominent among the offerings of distributors at point of sale. Manufacturers competed too in another sense. Individual distributors possessed a limited capacity to finance receivables from deferred payment retail sales, and there was a strong tendency for each to allocate it to what he considered his prime product line. Installment sales of other manufacturers would be financed as the distributors or buyers could find available funds elsewhere.

Competition in Koehring's product lines in recent years had centered at least as much around the terms of financing offered dealers and buyers by manufacturers as around equipment prices. After sharp rises in the post–World War II decade, prices had stabilized and been virtually uniform for machines of comparable capacity.

Proposed schedule of terms of sale

The schedule of terms of sales and credit policies proposed by the marketing department essentially constituted a four-point statement of company policy with respect to retail and wholesale financing. After a reiteration of the desirability of cash and open account sales, the draft document presented to Mr. Mertz addressed itself to the following points:

1. The Koehring "Buy-Back" Plan.
2. Retail financing through notes and rental purchase plans.
3. Special retail financing through distributors.
4. Floor planning.

The proposed Buy-Back Plan would essentially be Koehring's guarantee of a bank-financed installment sale. If a distributor negotiated bank financing and endorsed the sale contract upon which the buyer ultimately defaulted, Koehring guaranteed to repurchase the repossessed machine from the distributor. Similarly, if the buyer negotiated a bank loan directly, Koehring would guarantee repurchase from the bank. In both types of transactions the agreed repurchase price scaled downward with time to parallel loss of value.

Repurchase agreements would be offered on bank-financed sales, but not on sales financed by commercial or sales finance companies.

The retail financing and rental purchase plans would commit Koehring's financial resources. If neither a distributor nor banks and finance companies could or would finance a deferred payment sale when more than enough machines were available for cash or open account sales, Koehring would accept a note signed by the purchaser under the installment sale plan, or, alternatively, the rental purchase plan would allow a customer to, in effect, rent machinery with a purchase option. The two plans differed primarily in the terms of payment, length of contract, and interest rate. The terms to be offered were as follows:

Plan	*Down Payment*	*Interest Rate*	*Maximum Time*
Retail note	25% of purchase price	4½% per annum add-on*	24 months, 12 months preferred with equal monthly payments
Rental purchase plan	One monthly payment for each year the loan is to run	5% per annum add-on	36 months maximum with equal monthly payments

*The draft document explained computation of payment terms with add-on interest in this way. For example if a 24-month deal had been made with the amount to be financed $10,000, the payments would be:

Amount to be financed	$10,000.00
4½% add-on per year	900.00
Total	$10,900.00
24 monthly payments of	$ 454.17

Incentive prepayment terms were to be offered with both plans. It was anticipated that the retail note financing would be the more heavily used of the two plans.

The special retail financing through distributors scheme was envisaged as an exception program applying only "when inventory liquidation is considered necessary" and was "to be limited to good credit risks." It would have no-down-payment provisions and enable the customer to defer monthly payments in slack periods. It would be "in effect only when specifically so stated by the division management and then only for the products or models designated."

The floor planning arrangement would continue the distributor inventory financing policy of the past. Terms proposed were:

1. The distributor takes a 2% cash discount in paying for the machine 10 days after he sells it, net 30 days after the sale or 90 days after shipment from Koehring Company, whichever comes first.

2. If he has not paid by then, he may defer payment of the total amount, plus 6% simple interest, for up to an additional 90 days.

During the financing period inventory was secured by a trust receipt, chattel mortgage, or other title retention device.

Sales situation in December, 1957

When Mr. E. B. Hill, vice president–marketing, had first presented a draft of the new sales financing policies, he emphasized several conditions current in industry competition. He pointed to what he thought were signs of imminent recession in the economy generally and more particularly in the capital goods industries. Mr. Hill's research staff maintained a chart of the Department of Commerce's monthly data on inventories, sales, new orders, and order backlogs in the nonelectrical machinery industry. It appears as presented to Mr. Mertz in Exhibit 3. Mr. Hill pointed out that monthly sales for the industry had been falling off steadily in the latter half of 1957, and new orders had dropped behind sales. He compared this situation with that of late 1953, which had preceded the 1953 to 1954 recession. In support of his argument for a liberalization of credit terms, Mr. Hill said that competition in the industry would be worsened by a sales decline during the recession he felt "was in the cards." He was even more certain about "the near term prospects for dog-eat-dog sales competition" because he felt the industry had added greatly to its productive capacity during the 1955 through 1957 period, and he feared there would be strong efforts by individual companies to maintain sales above the resulting higher break-even points. By 1957 annual expenditures on new plant and equipment by the nonelectrical machinery industry had almost doubled at a yearly rate from the total of $694 million compiled in the recession year 1954. Mr. Hill "had a hunch" that the expansion of capacity may have been more excessive in the construction machinery industry than elsewhere because of rosy anticipations about the Federal Highway Program, which had not been met.

Though sympathetic with Mr. Hill's view about the likelihood of a recession and its probable effects on the industry, Mr. Mertz had questioned the need for liberalized sales terms. In reply, Mr. Hill had said that although he could not produce figures to buttress the point, he was certain that Koehring's competitors had been using progressively liberalized payment terms as a sales weapon in the last few years. This feeling came from field feedback, but also from Mr. Hill's observation that a number of the competitors had formed and had begun operating captive finance companies. He pointed out that these captives had been used to absorb the growing installment receivables produced by looser credit rationing and longer payment terms.[1] Moreover, it was

---

[1] The receivables accounts of Koehring's largest competitors consolidated with their captive company receivables are shown in Exhibit 6 with the exception of Euclid Division of General Motors, which used the facilities of Yellow Manufacturing Acceptance Corporation, a captive of General Motors.

common knowledge that many commercial banks had become loaned up in the tight money period of 1956 and 1957. This had placed a premium on manufacturer financing of installment sales. If Koehring failed to meet its competitors' deferred sales terms in the intense competition during the recession and beyond, Mr. Hill said, "sales will be 15% to 20% below" the level otherwise attainable.

At the conclusion of their conversation Mr. Mertz promised to return his views on the proposal within a few days.

Effects upon company financing

After this conversation, Mr. Mertz retained a number of doubts about the need for liberalization of sales terms, and also held reservations about Koehring's ability to meet the financial demands implied by such a program. On the other hand, he found the prospect of supporting sales at a high level to be most attractive because of its presumably beneficial effects on profits and cash flows (see Exhibits 4 and 5). Under the stimulus of booming sales, Koehring had participated in the industry's fixed asset expansion, and now a falling volume of production might prove awkward.

He asked a staff assistant to gather information on the credit terms currently offered by Koehring's competitors. Although confidential treatment by many companies made it impossible to assemble these data directly, the assistant returned the information in Exhibit 6 relating to a sample of competitors' accounts and notes receivable. Mr. Mertz noted some contrasts in sales results and receivables behavior between size classes of firm, product types, and time periods. These disparities reinforced his ambivalence about lengthening payment terms.

In view of these uncertainties Mr. Mertz reflected on a counter suggestion that would play upon the interest rates offered on installment financing and deemphasize the time period. If a competitive interest rate concession could be substituted for lengthy deferred sales contracts, it would minimize the cash committed to receivables. By the same token, however, the rate of return on the investment in installment receivables would be sliced, and Mr. Mertz noted that the add-on interest rates hypothesized in the proposed sales terms already were not high by industrial standards for cutoff rates of return applied to investment projects. Also, a reduction in interest rates below market was tantamount to a price cut, and to him not patently better than a forthright reduction of a gross margin. Also, since the company's president had recently voiced the need for intensified surveillance of the credit worthiness of Koehring's accounts, Mr. Mertz wondered whether the investment of funds in data processing equipment for centralized credit management might not be more profitable than investment in longer receivables.

A worrisome facet of the program was its effect on the company during the business recovery that would follow the recession. Even with liberalized terms, it was unlikely that the effect of the recession on sales could be stemmed altogether. Falling sales would result in liquidation of inventory and generation of cash, but commitment of this block of funds to a portfolio of lengthening receivables during the recession would pose a problem of financing inventory expansion in the ensuing upswing. The modest sales decline of 1954 had led to more than proportionate inventory reduction, but resurgent sales in 1955 resulted in considerable absorption of cash into inventory. With this experience fresh in mind, Mr. Mertz was particularly concerned about the problems of cash management entailed by the program over the next two years.

Exhibit 1

KOEHRING COMPANY

January 4, 1958

E. B. Hill
O. R. Mertz

SUBJECT: CREDIT

Dear Ed and Orville:

The recent experience with [name withheld] emphasizes what we have known for some time, namely that the low profit situation prevailing in the contracting industry will inevitably lead to some distributor failures and has already resulted in an extraordinary high level of contractor bankruptcies. At the same time these conditions make it necessary for us to engage in an increasing amount of credit business if we are to maintain anything like a normal level of market penetration and anything like the sales volume that is necessary to support our fixed overhead. We need, therefore, to take every precaution in our granting of credit to protect ourselves through title retention and other means against the contingency of customers or distributors failing financially.

One of the fundamental procedures that we need to follow is a greater degree of liaison between our divisions on credit matters. The way we have operated in the past it has been entirely possible, and in fact has happened, that one division would grant credit to a distributor who was currently in financial difficulties and not meeting payments to another division. We could reduce the possibility of this happening by having the various division credit managers check with all other divisions before granting credit. The time and expense involved in such a precedure would be substantial and the method quite cumbersome.

While we want to avoid as much as possible having reports sent here to the Central Office, I believe the circumstances make it necessary for us to require each division to make up a monthly credit report and send it to the Central Office where the various reports will be collated and danger spots pinpointed and reported back to the various divisions.

In addition we should undertake to set out for the divisional credit managers (many of whom operate in this capacity on a part-time basis only) those procedures which will minimize our possibilities of loss even in the event of a distributor or customer bankruptcy.

Exhibit 1—Continued

I would like to emphasize the responsibility for credit determination will still rest with the division but we must undertake to give them every assistance possible and see to it that they can carry out this responsibility with maximum effectiveness.

Yours truly,
KOEHRING COMPANY
(*Signed*) JULIEN
President

JRS/dz
cc: All Gen. Mgrs.

Exhibit 2

KOEHRING COMPANY

CROSS-CLASSIFICATION OF PRODUCERS AND PRODUCTS IN CONSTRUCTION EQUIPMENT MANUFACTURING
1958

	Commercial-Sized Power Shovels and Cranes	*Earthmoving and Other Construction Equipment**	*Concrete Handling Equipment†*
Large companies			
(Sales over $500 million)			
International Harvester		x	
Caterpillar		x	
Allis-Chalmers		x	
Euclid Division of General Motors		x	
Le Tourneau-Westinghouse		x	
Medium-sized companies			
(Sales $100–500 million)			
Baldwin-Lima-Hamilton	x	x	x
Worthington			x
Blaw-Knox			
Link-Belt	x	x	
Clark Equipment	x	x	
Small-sized companies			
(Sales less than $100 million)			
Harnischfeger	x		
Bucyrus-Erie	x	x	
Chain Belt		x	x
Thew Shovel	x	x	
Universal Marion	x		
American Hoist & Derrick	x		
Northwest Engineering	x	x	
Jaeger Machine			x
Unit Crane and Shovel	x		
Schield Bantam	x		
Gar Wood Industries	x	x	
Manitowoc Shipbuilding & Engin.	x		
Pettibone Mulliken		x	
Koehring	x	x	x

* Includes trench diggers, tandem road rollers, compactors, conveyor loaders, smaller earth dumpers, and other off-highway construction equipment.
† Includes primarily mixers, pavers, and spreaders.

Exhibit 3

KOEHRING COMPANY

SALES, NEW ORDERS, INVENTORIES, AND ORDER BACKLOGS IN NONELECTRICAL MACHINERY MANUFACTURING, 1953–57

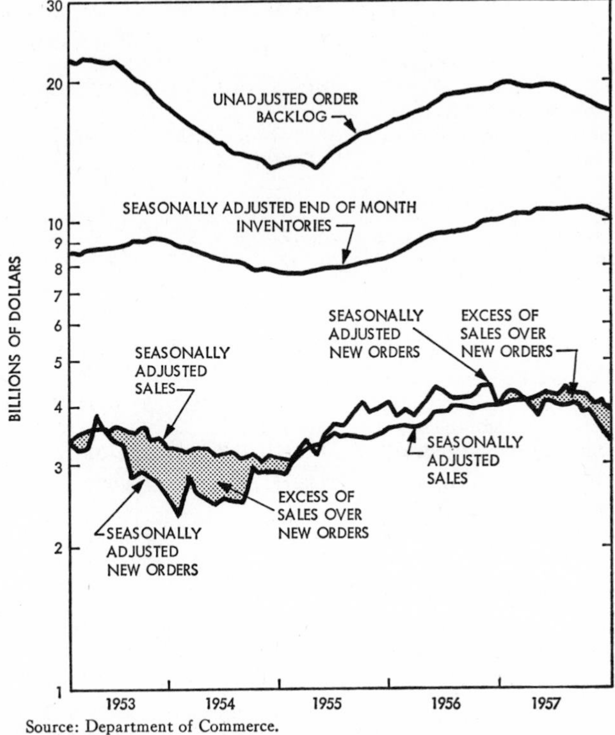

Source: Department of Commerce.

Exhibit 4

KOEHRING COMPANY

CONDENSED BALANCE SHEETS, 1953–57

(Dollar figures in thousands)

	Nov. 30, 1953	*Nov. 30, 1954*	*Nov. 30, 1955*	*Nov. 30, 1956*	*Nov. 30, 1957*
Current assets:					
Cash	$ 1,323	$ 1,024	$ 1,546	$ 1,412	$ 2,288
Notes and accounts receivable:					
Installment and deferred notes*	520	1,382	1,434	2,676	3,921
Trade accounts	1,661	2,070	2,435	3,718	4,075
Miscellaneous	28	46	82	86	152
Less: Allowance for doubtful accounts	(92)	(101)	(99)	(160)	(178)
Net receivables	$ 2,117	$ 3,397	$ 3,852	$ 6,320	$ 7,970
Inventories	11,385	9,707	12,991	22,510	26,259
Other	434	350	437	578	572
Total current assets	$15,259	$14,478	$18,826	$30,820	$37,089
Investments	$ 67	$ 44	$ 41	$ 267	$ 187
Property, plant, and equipment:					
Land	$ 538	$ 327	$ 335	$ 408	$ 504
Buildings, machinery and equipment, and construction in progress	11,339	11,388	12,210	19,019	22,087
Gross fixed assets	$11,877	$11,715	$12,545	$19,427	$22,591
Less: Accumulated depreciation	(6,009)	(5,770)	(6,577)	(10,049)	(11,407)
Net fixed assets	$ 5,868	$ 5,945	$ 5,968	$ 9,378	$11,184
Other assets	$ 39	$ 50	$ 46	$ 14	$ 13
Total assets	$21,233	$20,517	$24,881	$40,479	$48,473
* Including installment notes due after one year:	n.a.	$ 168	$ 188	$ 241	$ 460

NOTES FOR BALANCE SHEET

A. Of the $4\frac{1}{4}$% notes payable to insurance companies, $2,728,000 are payable in quarterly installments of $62,500 and the remaining $812,000 are payable in annual installments of $83,000. In addition, the conformed loan agreements covering these notes provide for annual sinking fund payments equal to 25% of the excess of consolidated net income, as defined, over $500,000, provided that such payments shall not exceed a calculated amount approximating $129,000 in any year.

The $5\frac{1}{4}$% notes payable to insurance companies are payable $250,000 on December 1, 1965, and $500,000 annually thereafter to December 1, 1973, when the remainder is due.

Among other provisions, the various loan agreements and amendments offered by the insurance companies covering the foregoing notes contain certain restrictions and requirements, which are summarized as follows: (1) the company is required to maintain consolidated net working capital of $20,000,000; (2) additional long-term borrowings are restricted to purchase money borrowings up to $200,000; (3) short-term borrowings are limited to $12,000,000 with the further requirement that the company be free of such borrowings for a period of 90 days annually.

The $4\frac{3}{4}$% first mortgage sinking fund bonds issued by the Canadian subsidiary, Koehring-Waterous Ltd., mature June 30, 1974, but the subsidiary is to provide a sinking fund sufficient to redeem $25,000 principal amount of the bonds annually beginning June 30, 1956.

Exhibit 4—Continued

	Nov. 30, 1953	*Nov. 30, 1954*	*Nov. 30, 1955*	*Nov. 30, 1956*	*Nov. 30, 1957*
Current liabilities:					
Notes payable: Secured	$ 1,177	$ 910	$ 841	$ 1,153	0
Unsecured	1,600	0	1,900	6,550	$ 6,990
Long-term debt due within one year	300	272	376	489	488
Trade accounts payable	937	885	1,705	2,115	1,289
Other accounts payable	0	0	0	1,127	830
Accrued payments to employees	515	527	546	1,084	854
Taxes on income	1,465	871	1,844	3,047	1,701
Miscellaneous	519	519	789	721	605
Total current liabilities	$ 6,513	$ 3,984	$ 8,001	$16,286	$12,757
Long-term debt—Note A:					
4¼% notes payable insurance companies	$ 1,800	$ 3,078	$ 2,928	$ 3,540	$ 3,078
5¼% notes payable insurance companies	0	0	0	0	4,500
3½% notes payable bank	550	350	150	0	0
4¾% first mortgage bonds	0	513	487	461	436
Total long-term debt	$ 2,350	$ 3,941	$ 3,565	$ 4,001	$ 8,014
Stockholders' investment:					
5% cumulative convertible preferred:* Series A	0	0	0	$ 2,639	$ 2,618
Series B	0	0	0	0	1,699
Common stock† and paid-in capital	$ 5,372	$ 5,374	$ 5,398	$ 6,527	$12,124
Retained earnings	6,998	7,218	7,917	11,026	11,261
Total net worth	$12,370	$12,592	$13,315	$20,192	$27,702
Total liabilities and net worth	$21,233	$20,517	$24,881	$40,479	$48,473

Common stock price trading range‡	*1953*	*1954*	*1955*	*1956*	*1957*
High	10	9⅞	14¾	25	25¼
Low	7⅞	7½	9¾	14½	13½

		Series A ($50 par)	*Series B ($50 par)*
* Preferred shares outstanding at year-end:	1956	52,777	0
	1957	52,369	33,987

Basic conversion price per share of common stock:

Prior to July 1, 1958	$23.06	$38.92
July 1, 1958 to June 30, 1961	24.51	46.13
After June 30, 1961	25.95	60.54

† Common shares outstanding at year-end:

1953	348,719
1954	348,761
1955	349,624
1956	1,206,290
1957	1,481,740

‡ Adjusted for splits and stock dividends.

Exhibit 5

KOEHRING COMPANY

CONDENSED OPERATING STATEMENTS, 1953–57

(Dollar figures in thousands)

	Year Ending				
	Nov. 30, 1953	*Nov. 30, 1954*	*Nov. 30, 1955*	*Nov. 30, 1956*	*Nov. 30, 1957*
Income					
Net shipments	$26,157	$25,197	$30,181	$51,765	$55,668
Royalties and service fees	226	234	283	401	377
Interest income	41	51	70	131	177
Other income	23	73	38	86	172
Total	$26,447	$25,555	$30,572	$52,383	$56,394
Expenses					
Cost of product sold	$22,962*	$23,123*	$26,154*	$39,385	$43,101
Selling, administrative, and general expenses				5,255	6,582
Depreciation	633	812	893	1,472	1,657
Interest expense	161	271	237	536	660
On long-term borrowings				196	290
Other				340	370
Employee profit sharing and retirement trusts	119	38	147	303	227
Income taxes	1,342	526	1,673	2,883	2,230
Other expenses	32	0	0	0	0
Total expenses	$25,249	$24,770	$29,104	$49,834	$54,457
Net earnings	$ 1,198	$ 785	$ 1,468	$ 2,549	$ 1,937
Dividends paid: Common†	$ 657	$ 767	$ 768	$ 900	$ 1,480
Preferred				66	222

* Including selling, general, and administrative expenses.
† Dividends per share were $0.72 in 1953–56 and $1.00 in 1957.

Exhibit 6

KOEHRING COMPANY

RELATIONSHIP OF RECEIVABLES TO SALES IN THE CONSTRUCTION MACHINERY MANUFACTURING INDUSTRY, 1955–57

(Dollar figures in millions)

	Finance Subsidiary	Net Sales to Dealers			Accounts and Notes Receivable*			Accounts and Notes Receivable as % of Net Sales		
		1955	1956	1957	1955	1956	1957	1955	1956	1957
Large										
International Harvester	1949	$947.2	$1,008.5	$969.9	$251.1	$332.9	$380.9	26.5%	33.1%	39.3%
Caterpillar	1954	523.9	685.9	649.9	51.4	64.5	63.5	9.8	9.4	9.8
Allis-Chalmers	1956	535.1	547.4	534.1	118.6	133.5	145.7	22.2	24.4	27.3
Medium										
Worthington	no	140.9	170.2	191.5	27.0	35.1	41.2	19.2	20.4	21.5
Baldwin-Lima-Hamilton	no	160.3	195.3	184.4	31.3	38.9	38.9	19.5	19.7	21.0
Blaw-Knox	no	109.2	167.0	182.7	17.9	25.9	26.5	16.3	15.5	14.5
Link-Belt	no	129.5	163.9	163.5	19.4	20.6	21.2	15.0	12.6	13.0
Clark Equipment	1954	131.3	145.4	143.1	35.4	44.8	44.6	26.9	30.8	31.2
Small										
Harnischfeger	1956	66.3	81.1	87.5	9.7	10.0	11.2	14.7	12.2	12.9
Bucyrus-Erie	no	71.7	86.6	87.5	8.0	10.8	8.9	11.1	12.5	10.1
Chain Belt	no	45.2	56.8	59.6	5.7	7.1	7.8	12.6	12.5	13.1
Koehring	no	30.2	51.8	55.7	3.9	6.3	8.0	12.7	12.2	14.3
Gar Wood Industries	no	29.9	41.0	43.4	4.5	4.9	3.2	15.0	12.0	7.4
Pettibone Mulliken	no	24.0	34.5	41.8	3.6	4.9	5.9	15.0	14.2	14.1
Thew Shovel	no	34.7	46.3	36.4	3.8	3.8	2.3	11.1	8.3	6.3
American Hoist & Derrick	1955	21.4	30.8	35.6	2.9	4.3	6.3	13.5	13.9	17.7
Jaeger Machine	no	12.6	16.5	15.9	1.7	1.7	1.8	13.5	10.5	11.5
Schield Bantam	no	9.3	10.2	7.9	0.7	0.9	0.9	7.5	9.0	11.5

* The accounts and notes receivable figures reflect the consolidation of a finance subsidiary where this is appropriate, except for Harnischfeger and American Hoist & Derrick, whose finance subsidiary balance sheets were unavailable. Accounts and notes receivable carried net of reserves and unearned finance charges.

TRIDENT KNITTING CORPORATION

Late in November, 1963, Mr. Robert Winston, loan officer at the Great Eastern National Bank of Providence, Rhode Island, was reviewing the progress of the Trident Knitting Corporation (Tri-Knit), a manufacturer of knitted sweaters and other clothing, in preparation for the November meeting of a banking syndicate. This syndicate of six banks had been organized formally earlier in the year to grant a special loan to help finance a major broadening of Tri-Knit's product line. Evidence of lagging sales in the sweater industry had prompted the various loan officers representing banks in the syndicate to take a new look at the Tri-Knit loan.

Tri-Knit, founded in 1900, was a leader in the children's knitted clothing industry. For many years the company, located in Westerly, R.I., had specialized in quality garments for young girls and boys, such as sweaters, caps, and gloves. Sales in recent years had averaged about $13.0 million, and except for a loss in fiscal year 1963, the company had always earned a profit. (Exhibit 1 presents income statements for fiscal years 1960 through 1963. Exhibit 2 provides comparative balance sheets for six-month intervals between January 31, 1962, and July 31, 1963. Note that the company's fiscal year ended in January.) The sales decline in fiscal years 1961 and 1962 was said to have been caused by the business recession and a loss of market share.

Short-term borrowing had been required annually by Tri-Knit because of a combination of a highly seasonal sales pattern and management's desire to maintain level production throughout the year. Ordinarily, about 75% of yearly sales was made between July and January, whereas 60% of anticipated production requirements was scheduled for completion by July 31. As a matter of company policy, any garments left in inventory at the end of a selling season were sold to discount jobbers at 65% of Tri-Knit's normal selling price.

The company's credit policy was designed to reduce the amount of space required to store finished inventory by encouraging customers to accept early delivery. Customers who took shipments between July and October could delay payment until November 2 without losing the normal 8% trade discount. Although this credit policy helped minimize the storage problem, it merely substituted receivables for inventory without reducing the aggregate need for short-term funds, which had been met by seasonal bank financing.

The loans had been repaid as accounts receivable were collected, and the company usually had been free of bank debt for three or four months each year.

The short-term credit needs of Tri-Knit had been provided over the years by credit lines the company had negotiated with six banks in the eastern part of the country. Tri-Knit, for example, had maintained banking relations with Great Eastern since 1943, and in recent years the company's cash balances had averaged about $500,000 annually. Great Eastern was also trustee for the company's pension funds, which totaled more than $1.0 million. Relations between the banks and the company had been cordial, and the annual granting of lines of credit had developed into somewhat of a formality. The company typically sent each of the participating banks a copy of its annual report and an estimate of its required line of credit from that bank for the coming year. Each bank would then notify the company treasurer that a line of credit had been set up for the amount requested. When the company desired to use the credit, the treasurer would forward a signed note to one of the banks, and the bank would then credit the amount to the company's account. Tri-Knit had always borrowed at the prime rate. Coordination between the banks in former years had been at a minimum, although Great Eastern had accepted an informal role as Tri-Knit's primary bank. Under these informal arrangements the company's high credit at Great Eastern had reached $1.0 million in 1960.

In February, 1962, the Rapallo Corporation purchased a 52% controlling interest in Tri-Knit from Mr. Horatio Thomas, son of the founder. Mr. Thomas remained as chairman of the board of directors, but the new owners appointed a man from outside the company as president and chief operating officer. They also appointed a new vice president for marketing. These men had consumer sales experience but not in the knitted goods industry. The Tri-Knit acquisition was typical of recent purchases made by the Rapallo Corporation in that very little cash was involved in the initial transaction. Of the $4 million price, only 30% was paid in cash. The remainder was to be paid over an extended period of time by Rapallo. The Rapallo Corporation controlled several subsidiaries in the entertainment field and was well known to one of the other banks in the syndicate.

Shortly after the sale to Rapallo had been completed, Tri-Knit embarked on a major expansion program. The program was planned to take effect in fiscal year ending January 31, 1964, and was calculated to increase sales to a level of $24.0 million, more than double the fiscal year 1962 total of $11.6 million. The sales increase was to come principally as the result of entry into the adult knitted goods (primarily high-fashion and ski goods) market for the first time. Major manufacturers in the women's market, for example, were Evan-Picone, Garland, Villager, and Darlene. Tri-Knit officials thought that Tri-Knit could enter the market by designing high-fashion and ski sweaters that could be given extensive advertising in regional editions of national magazines.

The plan represented a major departure from Tri-Knit's historical strategy of slowly developing a few knit items at a time and conducting lengthy market tests before officially adding a new item to its established line. In the clothing industry, the mortality rate on new fashion designs was extremely high, and it was difficult to predict which, if any, new item would be a big seller. In Tri-Knit's traditional market, however, a successful item could be sold for many years.

Management anticipated that with the new sales program, Tri-Knit would require total short-term financing of $11.0 million. Of this amount, approximately $1.9 million would be used for advertising and design fees. The latter costs would be a net addition to normal administrative and selling expenses, which were virtually fixed at $3.0 million, regardless of sales volume. The remaining proceeds of a loan would be used to finance increased inventories and accounts receivable. An additional $1.7 million was required for plant expansion, but these funds would be furnished out of general company resources. The $11.0 million loan requirement was substantially larger than the $4.7 million loan taken down to finance working capital for fiscal year 1963.

This request was turned down by the banks in late 1962 because they thought the company's expansion program was too ambitious and speculative to be financed by short-term borrowing. Instead, they offered to provide up to $6.0 million on an unsecured basis and recommended that the company raise the remaining $5.0 million through new equity capital.

The company in turn objected to this proposal because management believed that equity capital would be too expensive to raise at the time. As an alternative, the banks then offered to agree to guarantee Tri-Knit a loan of up to $7.5 million for one year if the company could obtain a $3 million secured term loan from a finance company. As a condition of the loan, the banks stated that they would require a written loan agreement for the first time and a ½ of 1% interest premium above the usual prime rate. Monthly statements would be required by the banks, and all future borrowing (other than the $3 million) would have to be subordinated to the bank loans. In addition, the company would have to agree not to:

1. Merge, consolidate, liquidate, or acquire the assets of other companies without bank approval.
2. Undertake any purchase contracts or leases that amounted to installment purchases.
3. Create any contingent liabilities.
4. Further encumber or dispose of any assets.
5. Retire or repurchase any company stock.
6. Pay any dividends.
7. Make any loans or advances to officers or other companies.

A final provision would permit a combination of banks holding more than 51% of the outstanding loans to secure their loans with accounts receivable and inventories if they deemed it necessary. (Appendix A contains information on the mechanics of loaning against receivables and inventory.) The company agreed to accept these terms and conditions.

Management thereupon entered into negotiations with the Holdman Company, a large national finance company, and finally worked out a $3 million term loan at an interest rate of 8%. The company's existing term debt of $970,000 was to be repaid from the proceeds. The Holdman loan was secured by a first mortgage or lien on all real estate, fixed assets, patents, and trademarks. The banks agreed that in the event they exercised their option to secure their loan against Tri-Knit's receivables and inventory, Holdman would receive a secondary claim on these assets, contingent upon satisfaction of the claims of the banks. The agreement called for annual repayments of $600,000 commencing in March, 1964, and for the company to maintain net working capital of at least $3.0 million. There was no penalty for prepayment, except through refinancing.

The new loan agreement between the banking syndicate and Tri-Knit was signed in April, 1963, with each bank taking a pro rata share based on its relative asset position. Great Eastern was committed for 22% of the credit line, about $1.6 million. Because the amount of the loan represented a sizable increase over prior years, officers of Great Eastern, and of the other banks as well, began to watch industry and company developments much more closely. Mr. Robert Winston was assigned primary responsibility for the account at Great Eastern.

In July and August it became evident to Mr. Winston, through industry reports, that sweater sales were lagging for the year. The industry consensus was that clothing buyers were waiting to see which garments would sell before placing large orders and committing themselves. The company, however, continued to assure the banks that everything was proceeding according to plan. In a letter written to Great Eastern in August, the president of Tri-Knit emphasized that the company was controlling inventories very carefully and that production schedules were revised weekly. He claimed that this production flexibility would continue until September 31, after which production and other expenses would become relatively fixed. The president estimated in the same letter that fiscal 1964 sales would be $22.3 million including sales of $3.0 million through discount stores.

This reference to discount store sales was the first time the banks became aware that discount outlets were being used as retailers by Tri-Knit. The company had traditionally sold through department and children's specialty stores. Further investigation disclosed that discount sales were on a consignment basis. A company spokesman indicated that these sales would consist exclusively of the old-line, children's knit goods, and he estimated that up to 20% of consignment sales might be returned. One of the company's principal competitors was already active in the discount area, but no information was available on its sales or profits from this business. The competitor's clothing was generally lower priced than similar Tri-Knit items.

In order to obtain additional information about discount sales, Mr. Winston wrote to several of the large chains participating in Tri-Knit's program. Their responses were much the same—that they were eager to do business with Tri-Knit because of its reputation for quality. While they did not feel that they could estimate possible sales volume precisely because such an estimate depended so much on customer acceptance, they did anticipate that the Tri-Knit program would ultimately prove profitable for all concerned.

In October, the company raised its discount store sales estimate to $4.9 million out of total sales, which were still expected to be about $22.3 million. They also sent a copy of a confidential research report written for the company by Dr. Randolph Wood, a noted researcher and statistician. Dr. Wood, who had helped prepare the initial company sales estimates, concluded that although knit goods sales were lagging, final sales would be within $1.0 million of the original company estimate of $24.0 million total sales. The report estimated that store buyers as of October 13 had purchased only 81% of their requirements of Tri-Knit's traditional line and 70% of their requirements for the new Tri-Knit products.

On November 7, 1963, Tri-Knit executives submitted their final pro forma statements for the fiscal year to Mr. Winston and indicated that operations were in order and under control. Sales were now projected at $20.5 million, with profit estimates ranging from $311,000 to $408,000 depending on returns from the discounters. To meet competition, however, extended billing until February 10 had been offered on all orders shipped during November and December. Company officials indicated that they expected the most likely profit figure to be about $380,000. Exhibit 3 shows the pro forma 1964 income statements prepared by the company using various assumptions of discount store returns. Exhibit 4 is the pro forma balance sheet Tri-Knit submitted for January 31, 1964, assuming a profit of $382,000.

Tri-Knit also provided production and sales information to supplement that which had previously been sent to Mr. Winston. Exhibit 5 shows the estimate of sales, actual orders, and production scheduled by product lines based on an estimated sales volume of $20.5 million. Exhibit 6 shows how production had been committed by months compared with sales forecasts.

In spite of these assurances, Mr. Winston was disturbed by two newspaper articles he had read in the last two weeks. The first quoted a knitted clothing manufacturer as stating that the late buying habits of the trade were causing some stores to request delivery dates that manufacturers would be unable to meet. As a result, the manufacturer feared sales would be lost by both the retailers and the manufacturers. The other article reported that sales of Tri-Knit for the first nine months were $14.0 million. Mr. Winston knew that actual company sales (exclusive of discount store sales) for the period were only $7.5 million. The article also reported that sales were twice fiscal 1963 levels; whereas, Mr. Winston knew that actual sales so far in fiscal 1964 were lower than actual sales of the previous year.

In view of these developments, Mr. Winston decided that he should review the Tri-Knit situation very carefully. The time of year was approaching when the company had normally repaid its seasonal bank financing and the account would almost surely be reviewed as a matter of course by the bank's loan committee within the next few weeks. Mr. Winston noted that the pro forma balance sheet indicated that Tri-Knit expected to be using a line of $3.6 million at the end of January. He suspected this point would be questioned by the committee. He therefore wanted to have an appraisal and recommendation prepared before the meeting. Given the long, satisfactory banking relations with Tri-Knit, Mr. Winston also wanted to be of whatever help he could to the company.

In preparing for the November meeting of the syndicate and for prospective internal review of the loan within Great Eastern, Mr. Winston obtained additional information from his files. He prepared an extract, which is shown in Exhibit 7, of cumulative quarterly sales and income data for Tri-Knit over the period of fiscal year 1961 through the middle of fiscal year 1964. Exhibit 8 presents the company's forecast of sales and orders for the latter part of fiscal year 1964 along with a record of sales and orders received through October, 1963. Mr. Winston also obtained a record of sales and orders received by Tri-Knit during the fiscal years 1961–63. This is reproduced as part of Exhibit 8. Finally, Mr. Winston obtained the figures on Tri-Knit's outstanding loans and deposit account balances with Great Eastern from 1960 to November, 1963. These are listed in Exhibit 9.

Exhibit 1

TRIDENT KNITTING CORPORATION

COMPARATIVE INCOME STATEMENTS

(Dollar figures in thousands)

	Fiscal Year Ending			
	January 31, 1960	*January 31, 1961*	*January 31, 1962*	*January 31, 1963*
Net sales	$14,100	$12,598	$11,563	$10,907
Cost of goods sold*	9,800	8,694	8,432	7,798
Gross profit	$ 4,300	$ 3,904	$ 3,131	$ 3,109
General and selling expense	3,000	2,901	2,821	3,513
Net operating income	$ 1,300	$ 1,003	$ 310	$ (404)
Other income†	.....	.....	74	.....
Other expenses‡	150	219	472	159
Federal income tax§	480	405	(108)	(282)
Net income	$ 670	$ 379	$ 20	$ (281)
* Includes depreciation of	$ 480	$ 480	$ 502	$ 583

† Gain on life insurance.
‡ Includes $344,000 bad debt loss in fiscal year 1962, mostly on one account.
§ In fiscal year 1962 includes $47,000 in prior year's tax adjustment.

Exhibit 2

TRIDENT KNITTING CORPORATION

COMPARATIVE BALANCE SHEETS

(Dollar figures in thousands)

ASSETS	*January 31, 1962*	*July 31, 1962*	*January 31, 1963*	*July 31, 1963*
Cash	$2,716	$ 775	$1,145	$ 504
Accounts receivable	1,348	2,868	1,264	1,152
Inventory	1,883	4,069	2,954	6,864
Federal tax claim	40	685	299	787
Total current assets	$5,988	$ 8,397	$5,662	$ 9,307
Fixed assets (net)*	3,045	2,928	3,068	3,472
Investments	....	....	....	1
Prepaid—deferred	250	664	854	248
Life insurance (cash surrender value)	27	31	32	35
Other†	10	16	....	954
Total assets	$9,320	$12,036	$9,616	$14,017
LIABILITIES				
Accounts payable	$ 255	$ 168	$ 398	$ 481
Bank loans	....	2,550	....	2,900
Accruals	255	1,250	713	1,062
Local taxes	222	177	258	....
Federal taxes	....	....	....	....
Long-term debt, current	145	145	145	600
Total current liabilities	$ 877	$ 4,290	$1,514	$ 5,043
Long-term debt	840	695	695	2,527
Common stock	1,510	1,560	1,560	1,560
Capital surplus	35	70	70	70
Earned surplus	6,057	5,421	5,776	4,817
Total liabilities and stockholders' equity	$9,320	$12,036	$9,616	$14,017

* Depreciation reserve............$ 3,631 $ 3,705 $ 3,650 $ 3,532

† At July 31, 1963, includes advanced royalty payments, design fees, and advance advertising expenses.

Exhibit 3

TRIDENT KNITTING CORPORATION

OPERATING FORECASTS SUBMITTED ON NOVEMBER 7, 1963, FOR THE FISCAL YEAR ENDING JANUARY 31, 1964

(Dollar figures in thousands)

	A	*B*	*C*	*D*
Sales	$20,468	$20,468	$20,468	$20,468
Less: Returns and allowances	1,158	1,082	1,006	949
Net sales	$19,310	$19,386	$19,462	$19,520
Less: Cost of sales*	12,615	12,615	12,615	12,615
Gross margin	$ 6,694	$ 6,771	$ 6,847	$ 6,905
Less: General and administrative expense	5,710	5,710	5,710	5,710
Operating income	$ 984	$ 1,061	$ 1,137	$ 1,195
Other income and expenses:				
Purchase discounts	$ (60)	Same as Alternative A		
Commissions	(24)			
Interest expense	370			
Inventory obsolescence	150			
Total other	$ 436	$ 436	$ 436	$ 436
Income before tax	$ 548	$ 624	$ 701	$ 758
Federal income tax	237	278	319	350
Net income after tax	$ 311	$ 346	$ 382	$ 408
Returns and allowances assumed:				
Returns and allowances, regular sales	4.5%	4.5%	4.5%	4.5%
Returns from discount store consignments	16.0%	12.0%	8.0%	5.0%

* Includes depreciation.

Exhibit 4

TRIDENT KNITTING CORPORATION

PRO FORMA BALANCE SHEET FOR JANUARY 31, 1964, SUBMITTED ON NOVEMBER 7, 1963

(Dollar figures in thousands)

ASSETS			
Cash*			$ 864
Accounts receivable (net)			7,072
Inventories:			
Raw materials and supplies		$ 336	
Work in process		1,189	
Finished goods		2,229	
		$3,754	
Less: Allowance for obsolescence		150	3,604
Prepaid items			683
Total current assets			$12,223
Plant and property		$7,700	
Less: Accumulated depreciation		4,352	3,349
Investments			1
Deferred license agreements			145
Goodwill and deferred charges			12
Total assets			$15,729
LIABILITIES AND STOCKHOLDERS' EQUITY			
Notes payable to banks			$ 3,579
Current installment, long-term debt and accrued interest			662
Accounts payable			389
Accruals			165
Federal and state taxes			319
Other			281
Total current liabilities			$ 5,395
Long-term notes			2,400
Accrued royalties			146
Common stock, 311,976 shares at par		$1,560	
Capital surplus		70	
Earned surplus, January 31, 1963	$5,776		
Add: Net 1963 profit	382		
Balance, January 31, 1964		6,158	
Total stockholders' equity			7,788
Total liabilities and stockholders' equity			$15,729

Earnings per share: $1.23 Book value per share: $24.96
Working capital, net: $6,828 Current ratio: 2.27

* Assumes life insurance had been surrendered for cash value.

Exhibit 5

TRIDENT KNITTING CORPORATION

TOTAL ESTIMATED FISCAL YEAR 1964 SALES, ACTUAL ORDERS RECEIVED AS OF NOVEMBER 6, 1963, AND THE TOTAL VALUE OF GOODS SHIPPED, IN INVENTORY, AND SCHEDULED FOR PRODUCTION AS OF NOVEMBER 6, 1963

(Dollar figures in thousands)

	Total Fiscal Year 1964 Estimated Sales	*As of November 6, 1963* — *Actual Orders Received*	*As of November 6, 1963* — *Goods Shipped, in Inventory, and Scheduled for Production**
Traditional line—normal channels	$11,965	$ 7,983	$13,511
Traditional line—discount stores	$ 4,890	$ 4,888	$ 4,890
New line—normal channels only:			
Children's high-fashion sweaters	$ 300	$ 210	$ 740
Men's ski sweaters	620	126	620
Men's ordinary sweaters	317	97	317
Women's skiing sweaters	884	192	884
Women's gloves	45	5	45
Scarves	250	155	573
Miscellaneous caps, gloves, etc.	445	95	463
Women's ordinary sweaters	756	183	755
Subtotal, new line	$ 3,617	$ 1,063	$ 4,397
Total sales	$20,472	$13,934	$22,798

* All valued at sales price.

Exhibit 6

TRIDENT KNITTING CORPORATION

CUMULATIVE PRODUCTION COMMITMENTS COMPARED WITH FORECASTS OF ANNUAL SALES

(Dollar figures in thousands)

	Sales Forecasts for Fiscal Year 1964 as Revised in Specified Month	*Production Committed in Dollars**	*Production Committed as Percentage of Appropriate Forecasts*
April, 1963	$21,600	$11,147	51.6%
May	21,600	13,191	61.1
June	20,896	17,345	83.0
July	22,381	18,590	83.1
August	22,287	19,735	88.5
September	22,281	20,502	92.0
October	22,281	n.a.	n.a.
November 6	20,472	22,798	111.4

* Expressed at selling price.

Exhibit 7

TRIDENT KNITTING CORPORATION

COMPARATIVE INCOME STATEMENTS

(Dollar figures in thousands)

	Three Months Ending April	*Six Months Ending July*	*Nine Months Ending October*	*Twelve Months Ending January*
Fiscal year 1961:				
Sales	$ 446	$ 3,251	$ 8,007	$12,598
Net operating income	(946)	(927)	(119)	1,003
Net income after tax	(454)	(445)	(57)	379
Fiscal year 1962:				
Sales	288	1,844	6,700	11,563
Net operating income	(1,201)	(1,759)	(1,147)	310
Net income after tax	(511)	(734)	(437)	20
Fiscal year 1963:				
Sales	336	3,430	7,642	10,907
Net operating income	(1,159)	(1,327)	(727)	(404)
Net income after tax	(557)	(637)	(349)	(281)
Fiscal year 1964:				
Sales	684	2,007		
Net operating income	(1,213)	(1,520)		
Net income after tax	(582)	(729)		

Exhibit 8

TRIDENT KNITTING CORPORATION

CUMULATIVE PERCENTAGE BY MONTHS OF SALES AND ORDERS RECEIVED (AVERAGE OF FISCAL YEARS 1961–63), SALES AND ORDERS RECEIVED IN FEBRUARY THROUGH SEPTEMBER, 1963, AS A PERCENTAGE OF ESTIMATED FISCAL YEAR 1964 SALES, AND FORECAST OCCURRENCE OF SALES FOR JULY, 1963, THROUGH JANUARY, 1964

	Average Percentage of Sales and Orders Received by Months in Fiscal Years 1961–63 (Cumulative)	*Sales and Orders Received in Fiscal Year 1964, Expressed as a Percentage of the Sales Estimate Provided by Tri-Knit in November, $20.5 million (Cumulative)*	*Tri-Knit's June Estimate of Sales and Orders Expected in July, 1963, through January 1964, Expressed as Percentages of Estimated Sales as of June, 1963, $20.9 million (Cumulative)*
February	0.6%	1.2%	....
March	1.0	3.4	....
April	8.2	7.0	....
May	20.5	11.6	....
June	33.3	20.6	19.0%
July	53.9	37.3	35.5
August	68.4	52.0	55.5
September	77.5	67.4	73.5
October	85.8	n.a.	87.0
November	91.3	69.0*	94.0
December	96.3	....	98.0
January	100.0	....	100.0

* As of November 7, 1963.

Exhibit 9

TRIDENT KNITTING CORPORATION

AMOUNT OF CREDIT USED AND COMPENSATING BALANCES MAINTAINED WITH GREAT EASTERN NATIONAL BANK

(Dollar figures in thousands)

	Loan Outstanding	Account Balance	Loan Outstanding	Account Balance
	1960		1961	
February	...	$792	...	$927
March	...	386	...	300
April	$ 750	720	...	525
May	750	191	$ 250	201
June	750	641	500	595
July	750	272	500	132
August	750	604	500	672
September	1,000	181	750	232
October	1,000	663	750	476
November	250	324	750	182
December	...	618	750	723
January	...	196	...	481
	1962		1963	
February	...	$980	...	$550
March	...	729	...	83
April	...	633	...	82
May	$ 500	176	$ 126	87
June	500	698	357	504
July	500	136	609	50
August	500	755	903	34
September	750	242	1,155	20
October	750	550	966	202
November	750	149	1,260*	57*
December	500	586	...	...
January	...	127	...	...

* As of November 7, 1963.

APPENDIX A

A BRIEF NOTE ON THE MANAGEMENT OF LOANS SECURED BY ACCOUNTS RECEIVABLE AND INVENTORIES

In those states that have adopted the Uniform Commercial Code, of which Rhode Island is one, the first step in securing a loan with the accounts receivable, the inventory, or both, requires the lender to file notice with the state government that he is taking such action. The purpose of this requirement is to alert other creditors of the borrower that some of the assets of the borrower have been attached. Such information may be of use, for example, to trade creditors in determining how large an amount to grant to the borrower in accounts payable.

An assignment is not valid if the borrower becomes bankrupt within a given time following the assignment (four months in Rhode Island). Prior creditors might be able to force bankruptcy and void the assignment during the four-month period by calling for the money due them. If the assignment is voided, the pledged assets will be returned to the pool from which general creditors would draw payment and the secured lender will find his claim without priority to those claims of other creditors.

When a bank decides to secure its loan with the accounts receivable or inventory, it must determine what percentage it will be willing to advance against the collateral. For example, a bank might decide to allow the borrowing company 85% against invoices less than 45 days old. A tabulation is made at the time the security is taken to find the amount of invoices in this category. Eighty-five percent of this amount is the maximum loan the bank would advance at the beginning. The borrower, of course, could take down less than the full amount if he wished to. The bank will establish a "loan account" to record the amount advanced the borrower.

Under a normal accounts receivable financing arrangement, customers continue to make payment directly to the company. The borrowing firm, however, forwards these payments to the bank, where they are used to *reduce* the *loan* account rather than to increase the deposit account. Once the loan has been repaid, the remittances will, of course, be deposited in the borrower's checking account. As long as a loan is outstanding, however, the borrowing company must forward more valid invoices to the bank or request an advance against an unutilized borrowing potential in order to get money into its checking account. In practice, the company will periodically forward its receipts and invoices (covering recent shipments) to the bank, along with a request for the bank to release additional funds to the company's checking account. If, by any chance, the company's request brings the advance to more than 85% of the valid receivables (for example, a large invoice might have grown older than 45 days), the bank will release only up to the 85% figure and notify the company of the reason why the advance was smaller than requested.

When a syndicate of banks secures its loan with the accounts receivable of a borrowing company, it is customary to appoint one of the syndicate to watch the account and perform the bookkeeping. The borrower's deposit accounts with other syndicate members are transferred to the bank managing the secured arrangement. As the borrower draws money from the managing bank, the managing bank requests each syndicate member to deposit a pro rata amount in the managing bank's accounts with it. When the borrower reduces his loan account with the managing bank, the managing bank makes corresponding pro rata deposits to the accounts of each of the syndicate members at the managing bank. The computations and deposit transactions are made as often as the balance in the loan account changes.

The cost of handling a secured loan generally varies with the number and size of the customer's shipments. The cost is usually passed on to the borrower in the form of a direct fee rather than by increasing the interest rate on the loan. (The effective interest rate of such an arrangement normally runs to about 7% or 8%.) Mr. Winston estimated that it would probably cost Great Eastern about $1,750 a month to operate Tri-Knit's loan if it was secured with the accounts receivable. Because the loan agreement did not permit a change of the interest rate, this fee would be passed directly to the company.

As a general rule, Great Eastern was reluctant to become involved in securing a loan against inventory. Field warehousing, which involves segregating the inventory used as collateral and releasing it to the company only upon cash payment, is an extremely expensive way to obtain collateral. In the absence of field warehouse arrangements, it is difficult to keep track of the security. Nevertheless, Great Eastern did often make loans against inventory and receivables without insisting on a physical separation of the collateral. In some conditions and in some states this arrangement does not mean the bank would lose its priority in the event of liquidation.

Another disadvantage of a loan against inventory is that inventory frequently loses much of its value when it is sold under distressed conditions. It is generally difficult to sell an inventory as such for more than 50% of cost; frequently the figure falls as low as 30%.

Part II

long-term financing

BURKE CANDY COMPANY

In October, 1949, after a dispute between stockholders of the Burke Candy Company, Mr. A. K. Martin, a St. Louis businessman, agreed to act as chairman of a committee to establish a value for 1,000 shares of the common stock. At the time, there were 10,000 shares of common stock outstanding; these were owned by various descendants of Jeremiah Burke, who had founded the company in 1860. A majority of the shares were held by three grandsons of Jeremiah Burke, each of whom was active in the management of the company. The board of directors of the company included the grandsons, the company's lawyer, and a commercial banker.

A cousin, Mrs. Richard Wilson, who owned 1,000 shares, over a period of time had expressed sharp dissatisfaction with the policies and results of the majority's management. After protracted discussion the majority stockholders agreed to buy Mrs. Wilson's shares at "a fair price." However, the ideas of the management group and Mrs. Wilson and her lawyer as to "fair value" were very different. Finally, each group agreed to the appointment of a three-man committee to establish the value of the shares. Each group named one man to the committee, and the two nominees together selected Mr. Martin as the third member and chairman of the committee.

Realizing that his views as to the value of the stock might well prove decisive, Mr. Martin undertook an inquiry into the affairs and financial status of the company.

He learned that the Burke Candy Company had long operated as a "general-line house," that is, it manufactured a wide variety of candies with no one type of candy predominating. While most candy houses had started in this way, by 1948 most confectionery manufacturers had specialized in one or more lines, so that general-line houses accounted for only some 11% of total industry sales. Burke products included five-and-ten-cent specialty items, such as packages of mints and caramels; package goods, chiefly in the less than one dollar per pound retail category; bulk goods, such as hard "Christmas candy" and unpackaged chocolates; penny goods, such as small marshmallow eggs; and candy bars. The company was generally acknowledged as the first American manufacturer of one of the popular types of chocolate bars. This candy was first marketed about 1900 in the form of large blocks, which the retailer cut apart to sell. The Burke company then furnished the retailer with small glassine bags in each box of blocks so the retailer could cut the bar from the block and slip it into a bag as he gave it to the customer. A change in manufacturing was next introduced so that each bar was a separate piece of candy. This change was enthusiastically received, and the company then decided to wrap each bar separately and label each wrapper "Burke's Best-Bet Bar."

Despite its early success with the Best-Bet Bar the company did not go along with a general tendency in the industry toward specialization in bar goods or other types of candy, and sales of Best-Bet Bar did not grow relatively to competitive products. During World War II, however, the company did sell large quantities of Best-Bet Bar and other bar items to the Army and Navy for sale in PX's and Ships' Stores. As military demand fell off, postwar sales returned to the prewar pattern of wide distribution among product lines.

Like most candy manufacturers, Burke owned no retail outlets. The company's products were marketed through brokers and by the company's own sales force. Direct sales effort was concentrated in Missouri and adjoining states and primarily on candy and tobacco jobbers and on grocery, variety, and drug chains. Sales through brokers were primarily made to candy jobbers. In an effort to compensate for declining military sales, the sales manager in 1946 and 1947 had expended substantial amounts in national magazines and in trade-paper advertising and other efforts to gain national distribution through brokers. Almost half of 1948 sales had been through brokers, many in distant areas. One broker in Texas had been particularly effective in producing volume. On the other hand, the advertising expense involved had been substantial, and the company was forced to absorb almost all the freight in order to compete successfully in distant states. Further, the brokers, who operated on a 5% commission, appeared to concentrate their efforts on standard product items, which were easy to sell but carried a very low margin to the manufacturer.

In general, competition among manufacturing confectioners was keen, except during World War II when sugar rationing limited production and demand was strong. Competition was particularly keen in unbranded candies, and with the exception of its candy bars, most of the Burke products were unbranded or had brands that meant very little to buyers. Two other candy manufacturers located in St. Louis competed directly with the company in the metropolitan area, and manufacturers in Chicago and Indianapolis also competed strongly in the St. Louis market area.

Reviewing the financial records of the company, Mr. Martin found that operations had been profitable during the 1920's. Severe competition had developed during the 1930's, and recurring losses were suffered owing to declining sales and an apparent tendency to change too slowly with the times. The company had entered the depression in strong financial condition, however, and had successfully withstood the drain of cash caused by unprofitable operations. Operations proved profitable in 1939, and the development of a sellers' market during World War II contributed to very profitable years. Management officials pointed out, however, that the lack of profits during prewar years had given the company an unfavorably low base of "normal" earnings for purposes of excess profits taxation. Consequently, Burke's excess profits taxes were higher than those of its competitors with similar earnings *before* taxes. As is indicated in Exhibit 2, postwar operations were also profitable until 1948.

Mr. Martin talked at length with the management regarding the large losses suffered in 1948 and in the first eight months of 1949. The management explained that a large portion of the losses in 1948 had resulted from a very sharp and unexpected decline in the market prices for chocolate, sugar, and other major raw materials. The cost of raw materials accounted for almost 80% of total cost of sales, and the purchasing officer had made heavy forward commitments at fixed prices during 1947 and early 1948. At the same time that the market prices of these commodities were falling rapidly, a decline in the company's own physical volume of sales set in. For competitive reasons it was necessary to reduce the company's selling prices substantially. Further, management at first had diagnosed the decline in sales as a temporary development. Consequently, appropriate retrenchment measures were not taken for some months after sales declined.

By August, 1949, a number of steps had been taken to remedy the situation, and operations in August were profitable for the first time in many months. Purchasing methods had been revised so as to minimize the risks of further inventory price decline. Steps had also been taken to strengthen the management of the company through employment of a young and aggressive man with an excellent educational background, who had been highly successful during a business career of some 10 years. This man, the son of one of the majority stockholders, had been established as executive vice president and given substantial responsibilities for the overall direction of the company. In addition, major changes had been made in the company's sales methods and personnel. The sales force had been strengthened and major efforts had been made to improve the company's sales effort in the home St. Louis area.

Painstaking analysis had been made of the profitability of various product items and lines. As a result, a number of unprofitable items were dropped and sales effort was shifted to particularly promising and profitable items. New product development was also being pushed aggressively.

In general, management officials were convinced that the new policies were well advised and would produce results.

In the summer of 1948 the board of directors voted to suspend the dividend payments. It was then that Mrs. Wilson, whose only income from the company was in the form of dividends, expressed particular concern and sought the advice of her lawyer, Mr. L. K. Eagle, regarding her investment. Dividend payments since 1938 are shown in Exhibit 2.

Since the stock was held only by members of the Burke family and all transfers had been among various members of the family, no market for the shares of the company existed. Investigation showed that there was no active market in the shares of any confectionery manufacturing company of comparable size and nature in the Midwest, so that no closely comparable market quotations were available as guides to the value of the Burke stock.

Acting in anticipation of difficulty in arriving at a satisfactory valuation, Mr. Roger Burke, the new executive vice president of the company, in September requested the Midwestern Company, local investment bankers, to undertake an appraisal of the value of the stock. Largely on the basis of the summary data given in Exhibits 1 and 2, along with personal discussion of the firm's affairs and policies with its officers, the Midwestern Company had arrived at a maximum valuation of $12 per share. Their report took the form of a letter, attached as Exhibit 3.

Mr. Martin talked at some length with officials of the Burke company regarding the financial statements as of August 31, shown in Exhibits 1 and 2. He first sought to establish the validity of the book value of the stock as shown on the balance sheet. He was told that the accounts receivable consisted entirely of receivables from the trade for merchandise sold. The amount of receivables shown was net of a reserve for bad debts of $30,000. This reserve had been accumulated over several years and was considered more than ample to cover expected bad debt losses. The raw material inventory consisted primarily of cornstarch and syrup, chocolate, sugar, and nuts. Mr. Martin satisfied himself that the company maintained accurate inventory records and that the material concerned was in good physical condition. Inventories were valued at the lower of cost or market. Prepaid expenses consisted largely of prepaid insurance premiums. Company officials explained that the large investment in United States bonds represented a temporary investment of funds earmarked to pay for machinery soon to be ordered. This machinery was needed to modernize several of the company's manufacturing operations, and management believed that the machines would pay for themselves in a few years by lowering costs.

In the opinion of company officials the fixed assets of the company were very conservatively valued. Operations were carried on in a multistory concrete building, which with an annex building occupied an entire city block in the center of an industrial area. Advanced construction ideas had been incorporated in the construction of the main building in 1909, and the building was considered in excellent condition and entirely adequate for the needs of the company. With the land it stood on, the annex building, carried in the balance sheet at $182,914 (net of the reserve for depreciation), was also of concrete construction and of multipurpose type. This building had housed certain operations of the company discontinued in 1938. At that time the building was leased to a bakery company that was expanding its operations. When the 10-year lease expired in 1948 a shortage of factory buildings in the area existed, and the company was able to lease the 84,000 square foot building for one year at $0.55 a square foot, or $46,200. The lessee assumed all costs of the building except property taxes, which were about $10,000 a year. In September, 1949, it was expected that a five-year lease would be signed at about $0.45 a square foot per annum, or $37,800 before taxes.

The multistory building in which the operations of the company were conducted provided a total floor area of 133,400 square feet. Current construction costs of similar buildings were approximately $8 a square foot. The management believed that with an unhurried sale of the main building, it could realize approximately $3.50 a square foot or approximately $466,900 for the building. The newer annex building was thought to have a normal resale value of about $4.50 a square foot.

The equipment of the company was considered fairly efficient, although much of it had been in use for many years. It was believed that depreciation rates had been appropriate, so that the balance sheet values represented reasonable values from the accounting point of view.

When Mr. Martin raised the question of realizable values in the event the company was liquidated, the officials of the company appeared reluctant to discuss the subject. They commented that many of the 175 employees of the company had been with the concern for many years, that they had faith in the business, and that management had no intention of terminating the business. Finally, they did agree to discuss the value in liquidation of each major asset. It was believed that the net value of receivables could be collected completely, with perhaps a 10% excess of collections over the amount shown net of the unusually large reserve. The liquidating value of the inventory was regarded as hinging on the speed of liquidation. It was felt that in an unhurried liquidation the inventory could be completely worked off at between 60% and 80% of its book value. Much of the value of prepaid expenses would be lost in liquidation, so that an estimate of 25% was given as the realizable value. The value of the fixed assets in liquidation was regarded as particularly problematical. If a willing buyer was available, as indicated above, the two buildings probably could be sold at approximately $3.50 and $4.50 per square foot. If no buyer was anxious to have the space for immediate use, distress sale could be expected to attract buyers only at a very much lower price. Currently, the market for industrial real estate in the area was active, and it was thought that a willing buyer could be found within a few months.

The value of the equipment in liquidation was highly uncertain. It was thought of most value to a candy manufacturer who would take over the entire plant. In 1947, the company had received and rejected informal inquiries from two large manufacturers regarding the possibility of sale of the company to them for operation as a branch plant. No inquiries had been received since that time. Much of the equipment would be next to valueless in a hurried liquidation, and the total proceeds from equipment under such circumstances would probably be no more than 30% of the book value.

Exhibit 1

BURKE CANDY COMPANY

BALANCE SHEET, AUGUST 31, 1949

ASSETS		
Cash		$ 13,396
Accounts receivable, net		32,673
Inventory:		
Raw materials	$101,665	
Candies in process	13,833	
Finished candies	84,209	
Packaging materials	32,002	
Other supplies	8,183	239,892
Prepaid expenses		25,606
U.S. bonds		145,172
Total current assets		$456,739
Factory building and land, net		61,868
Annex building and land, net		182,914
Equipment, net		200,072
Total assets		$901,593
LIABILITIES		
Accounts payable—trade and commissions		$ 51,944
Notes payable—bank		75,000
Accrued expense		28,080
Total current liabilities		$155,024
Common stock ($11.50 par)		115,000
Reserve for contingencies		65,856
Paid-in surplus		562,092
Earned surplus January 1, 1949	$ 14,060	
Plus tax refund to company	108,844	
Less loss since January 1, 1949	119,283	
Earned surplus August 31, 1949		3,621
Net worth August 31, 1949		$746,569
Total liabilities		$901,593

Exhibit 2

BURKE CANDY COMPANY

SELECTED DATA

	Net Sales	*Net Profit or (Loss) before Taxes*	*Net Profit or (Loss) after Taxes*	*Dividends*
1938	$ 975,714	$ (38,934)	$ (38,934)	.....
1939	930,942	(27,493)	(27,493)	.....
1940	956,425	(25,647)	(25,647)	.....
1941	1,175,383	27,007	27,007	.....
1942	1,423,455	136,456	86,027	$23,000
1943	1,679,869	220,755	76,002	34,500
1944	1,917,260	193,343	45,169	40,250
1945	1,914,799	216,427	61,464	40,250
1946	2,073,594	201,531	89,915	46,000
1947	2,636,122	316,302	143,802	80,500
1948	1,769,103	(212,806)	(117,791)	23,000
1949—8 months	700,495	(119,283)	(119,283)†	.....

Exhibit 2—Continued

	Net Profit or (Loss) after Taxes as Percentage of Net Sales — Industry*	Burke	Net Profit or (Loss) after Taxes as Percentage of Net Worth — Industry*	Burke
1938	1.5%	(4.0)%	3.8%	(5.5)%
1939	2.1	(3.0)	5.9	(4.0)
1940	2.2	(2.7)	6.5	(4.0)
1941	2.8	2.3	8.6	4.0
1942	4.1	6.0	15.8	11.5
1943	4.7	4.5	16.0	9.7
1944	5.2	2.4	20.1	5.8
1945	2.9	3.2	13.5	7.5
1946	7.9	4.3	11.8	9.7
1947	7.0	5.5	19.2	15.7
1948	6.5	(12.0)†	13.9	(28.1)†

Comparison of Selected Ratios, 1948

	Industry*	Burke
Turnover of net worth	2.68	2.34
Turnover of working capital	5.32	4.92
Average collection period	15 days	15 days
Current ratio	3.48	2.50
Fixed assets to net worth	41.5%	58.6%
Total debt to net worth	35.8%	27.6%

* Figures are the median figures reported by 45 firms.
† Before tax refund credit, which can be carried back against prior year's earnings.

Exhibit 3

BURKE CANDY COMPANY

LETTER FROM THE MIDWESTERN COMPANY

September 20, 1949

Mr. Roger Burke
Burke Candy Company
203 West Illinois Street
St. Louis 6, Missouri

DEAR MR. BURKE

We have made an examination of the Burke Candy Company based principally upon financial statements furnished us by you, and other information which you have given us; and we have also examined the markets of stocks and financial statements of other companies in similar lines of business, so as to arrive at an opinion as to a fair value for the stock of the Burke Candy Company.

As I told you over the phone today, this is a very difficult question for us to answer, principally because the pattern of sales and earnings of your company does not justify its comparison with the history of the other companies with which you compete. These other companies in general have profits for most of the years, if not all of the years, under review; while your company has made money only during the war and the first year or two after the war, and during 1948 and the first eight months of 1949 has lost a substantial amount of money. The stock of the Burke Candy Company, therefore, could not be valued on the same basis as the other stocks, being intrinsically more speculative.

Exhibit 3—Continued

The speculative aspects of the stock are increased by the fact that your company is now evidently changing its type of business and has not yet indicated any earnings possibilities from the new type of business. In addition, the change-over requires a relatively substantial capital expenditure which has depleted and will probably continue to deplete your working capital position.

The company has some real estate holdings which might be used as a source of additional working capital if sold; but you have not indicated any such intention, and therefore I assume that the company will have to get along for capital expenditures and current operations on its present working capital position, augmented by profits in the future, if any.

As I told you, there is usually no relationship between market value and book value when valuing common stocks; in fact, any study of such relationship leads to such wide disparities that the only conclusion from such a study can be that there is no connection between market value and book value.

I believe the only likely buyer of stock of your company would be some person familiar with the type of business you are in, who would be willing to buy control at a sacrifice price and take over the management of the company in the hopes of making operations profitable and therefore of making himself a substantial profit by entering into the management. I do not believe it would be possible to sell the stock to investors in this area, because the company's record does not justify such an offering.

We are of the opinion that the stock of the Burke Candy Company, based largely on the previous comments, is not worth over $12.00 per share.

I am sure that you will appreciate that the comments made above are not in any way a reflection on the management of the company, but are made from the point of view of an outsider looking at the figures and the company's course of business in an effort to arrive at an impartial valuation of the stock.

Very truly yours,
MIDWESTERN COMPANY

(Signed) JOHN K. GRIMES

Vice President

UPSTATE CANNING COMPANY, INC.

During the period following his graduation from a business school in 1950, Mr. Nelson Shields had attempted to prepare himself for the opportunity of becoming the manager and sole or part owner of a company with real growth possibilities. Because he lacked financial resources, he had sought employment offering substantial immediate income as well as managerial experience that would be useful in later years. This search led him successively through positions in three distinctly different businesses, in each of which experience was largely concentrated in the sales and sales management areas. By 1956 he had accumulated personal savings of $15,000, which added to some family money placed at his disposal gave him an investment fund of $35,000.

At this point, Mr. Shields had begun an active search for opportunities to purchase an existing business. In the course of the year he looked into about 25 possibilities that came to his attention. Some of these were quickly rejected; others involved the expenditure of considerable time and some money before a negative decision was reached. While looking for business possibilities, Mr. Shields also sought to develop contacts with business and professional men who might be induced to invest equity capital in an attractive opportunity, should one be found requiring more capital than he possessed. By the end of 1956 he was still investigating business leads, but with no real prospect in sight. Meanwhile, the pressure to settle on a business was increasing. He had given up employment in October in order to devote full time to his search, and he realized that he could not afford many months of unemployment without eating into the sum set aside for investment.

In February, 1957, a business broker called Mr. Shields to advise him that a small cannery had just come up for sale. The property consisted of two plants, equipped for the canning of fruits and vegetables, which were located close to the source of supply in rural towns in New York State. The business, known as the Upstate Canning Company, Inc., was owned and managed by Mr. A. C. Fordham. Mr. Fordham's health was uncertain and at 55 he had decided to sell out because he had no relatives to take his place in the business. The broker urged Mr. Shields to investigate this opportunity because it looked as though it might fit his circumstances.

Mr. Shields immediately set out to learn what he could about the fruit and vegetable canning industry in general and this business in particular. The broker arranged a meeting with Mr. Fordham; and from this and subsequent meetings and telephone conversations, Mr. Shields assembled a picture of the business.

In general, Mr. Fordham was very cooperative in providing the information requested from him. He was reluctant, however, to disclose the financial details of operations for the three years prior to 1956. During 1952 Mr. Fordham had brought in a general manager on a three-year employment contract as a means of easing himself out of the day-to-day responsibilities of the business. The new man had not worked out well, and sales and profits had suffered as a result. Upon the termination of this contract, Mr. Fordham had again assumed full management responsibilities, and results in 1956 improved substantially over those of 1953, 1954, and 1955. Mr. Fordham argued that these years were not representative of the earnings potential of the business and that 1956 should be taken as the most accurate measure of its possibilities. From what Mr. Shields had been able to find out about the business from other sources, he was inclined to accept Mr. Fordham's explanation and to base his estimates on the figures for 1956.

The physical plant of the business appeared to be in very good condition. The two buildings had been kept in excellent repair, and the canning equipment was modern. The combined plant and equipment had recently been appraised for insurance purposes, and their value had been placed at $200,000. Mr. Shields was assured that no major repairs would be necessary over the next few years.

Mr. Fordham had been accustomed to operating the plants only during the limited harvest season for the fruits and vegetables that he canned. The season lasted for four months, from July through October, with August and September normally accounting for two thirds of the company's total production. At times, Mr. Fordham had considered stretching out the production period with other canning operations, but he had never taken any action on the idea. During the 1956 season Upstate had produced canned fruits and vegetables with a total value of $850,000 (valued at Upstate's selling price). This production represented only about 50% of combined productive capacity of the plants during the production season. Excess capacity was attributed to the substantial expansion of facilities that had been undertaken to meet wartime demands.

The vegetables and fruits canned by Upstate were bought on a contract basis from farmers in the surrounding area; farmers were paid cash on delivery on the basis of prevailing market prices at the time of delivery. The quantities canned by Upstate varied to some extent with the crop conditions from year to year; normally, output could be increased considerably, however, by noncontract purchases if good marketing opportunities existed. The production process was almost entirely mechanical, and the towns and surrounding areas offered an ample supply of seasonal labor sufficiently skilled to perform the various operations in the plant. Labor was paid on a weekly basis.

The products of the Upstate Canning Company were marketed primarily under the Upstate brand through jobbers. It was the normal practice to sell the entire season's pack before the next canning season began, so that little inventory would be carried over from one year to the next. Sales tended to be concentrated during and immediately following the production period. Mr. Fordham indicated that about 50% of the pack would normally be sold by the end of the canning season (October) and 70% by the end of December. The rest of the sales were customarily spread rather evenly over the remaining months through June.

Mr. Shields was particularly attracted by the marketing opportunities of the business. It was his impression that Mr. Fordham had not been aggressive in sales promotion—that much better use could be made of the company's productive capacity. Mr. Shields believed that he could greatly increase the scale of operations by undertaking an active but relatively inexpensive sales program. He had in mind direct sales to supermarket chains of both Upstate and private brands, to be obtained largely through his own efforts with no significant increase in present selling costs.

Relying on these expectations, Mr. Shields prepared a five-year sales program (see Exhibit 1) which he planned to use as the basis of his estimates of profits and working capital requirements. He was informed by Mr. Fordham that collections on accounts receivable caused little trouble in this business; bad-debt losses were rare, and accounts were normally collected within 30 days. Mr. Shields expected that the planned expansion would not affect this collection period and might even improve it, because he would be increasing direct sales to large accounts.

In examining the cost aspects of the business, Mr. Shields soon became aware of the high proportion of variable costs. The principal items were the fruits and vegetables and other ingredients, cans, and direct labor. As previously indicated, fruits and vegetables were bought on a cash basis, labor was paid weekly at fixed hourly rates, and cans and "other ingredients" were purchased on normal terms of 2/10, net 30 days. The details of revenues and costs for 1956 are shown in Exhibits 2 and 3.

As negotiations proceeded, it became evident that Mr. Fordham was anxious to sell the business as soon as possible. The new crop season was coming on; and Mr. Fordham felt that if he were to operate the business for another year, it would soon be necessary to sign contracts with farmers for the year's production. After three weeks, during which Mr. Shields was gathering and studying information and talking to bankers, can company officials, government agencies, and others, Mr. Fordham came forward with a specific proposal for the sale of the business (see Exhibit 4).

The plan anticipated that Mr. Shields would organize a new company and purchase certain Upstate assets, namely, its plant and equipment, a small amount of finished goods inventory, and the right to use the Upstate brand names. Current assets (other than the inventory mentioned above) and liabilities of the old company would not pass to the new company. It was apparent from the plan that Mr. Fordham had guessed that Mr. Shields had very limited resources and, accordingly, had provided for an installment purchase of Upstate assets through the gradual redemption of $300,000 of income bonds to be issued to Mr. Fordham. By this time, Mr. Shields had become convinced that this business was sufficiently promising to justify a full and detailed study of Mr. Fordham's proposal.

Before accepting the proposal or making a counterproposal, it was necessary for Mr. Shields to determine how the new company was to be financed. His best lead for additional equity capital was a professional man who had indicated that he was prepared to invest as much as $100,000 if the right opportunity came along. This man was 50 years of age, and his investment goal appeared to be capital appreciation over the years rather than immediate income.

Mr. Shields was determined that the plan for the new company would include a means by which he could become the owner of 51% of the voting stock as soon as possible. More specifically, he hoped to obtain control within five years, and hence was intent on arranging a compensation plan for himself as manager that would enable him to accomplish this objective. Mr. Shields's plan, as tentatively formulated, provided for a basic salary of $15,000 plus 5% of profits before taxes; these figures took account of his estimate that roughly 60% of his annual income would be absorbed by living expenses and tax payments. His plan also included an option to buy enough additional shares—either new shares to be issued by the company or outstanding shares held by his associate(s)—to raise Mr. Shields's holdings to 51% of all outstanding voting stock. It was clear, however, that the exact details of the final plan would have to be worked out with the other shareholder or shareholders before arrangements could be completed with Mr. Fordham.

As part of his program to assure an adequate supply of capital, Mr. Shields obtained an introduction, through a mutual friend, to one of the officers of a medium-sized bank in a nearby city. This officer indicated that it was the bank's normal policy to avoid substantial loans to new enterprises, but that exceptions were occasionally made where there was adequate security. Canning operations were important to the surrounding area, and he suggested that the bank might consider a secured loan to the new company if it looked promising on closer examination. From further conversation, Mr. Shields concluded that the best possibility would be a loan of up to 75% of the cost of finished goods inventory under a field warehousing arrangement. The cost of this kind of financing, including field warehousing expenses, which would not otherwise have been incurred, would be about 6% per annum. In addition to the bank loan, Mr. Shields also believed that it might be possible to stretch the payment period on cans to 60 days without creating serious credit problems.

In considering his preliminary calculations, Mr. Shields planned to make a detailed study of the year 1957–58 and to use this as a basis for approximating the necessary figures for the fiscal years 1958–59 through 1961–62. He had in mind a fiscal year beginning July 1.

Mr. Shields was aware that the next move was up to him. As he saw it, there were three obvious courses of action: (1) accept Mr. Fordham's proposal as presented; (2) reject the proposal and look for another business; or (3) propose a compromise plan that would have a reasonable prospect of meeting the objectives of all interested parties.

Exhibit 1

UPSTATE CANNING COMPANY, INC.

PLANNED SALES VOLUME, 1957–62

1957–58	$ 850,000
1958–59	1,050,000
1959–60	1,250,000
1960–61	1,450,000
1961–62	1,650,000

Exhibit 2

UPSTATE CANNING COMPANY, INC.

INCOME STATEMENT FOR YEAR ENDED DECEMBER 31, 1956
(Dollar figures in thousands)

		Amount	*Percent of Sales*
Sales (net after returns and allowances)		$850	100%
Less: Cost of goods sold			
Beginning inventory, January 1, 1956	$257		
Add: Cost of goods manufactured	630		
	$887		
Ending inventory, December 31, 1956	254	633	74
Gross profit on sales		$217	
Less: Selling and administrative expense			
Selling and delivery	$ 64		8
Administrative and general (including salary to Mr. Fordham of $20,000)	56	120	7
Profit before taxes		$ 97	
Less: Federal income tax*		45	5
Net profit after taxes		$ 52	6

* Federal income tax was computed on the basis of 30% of the first $25,000 of taxable income plus 52% of income in excess of $25,000. For companies of this size the tax was payable in the succeeding fiscal year as follows: 50% on the 15th day of the 3d month following the end of the tax year and 50% on the 15th day of the 6th month following.

Exhibit 3

UPSTATE CANNING COMPANY, INC.

STATEMENT OF COST OF GOODS MANUFACTURED FOR YEAR ENDED DECEMBER 31, 1956
(Dollar figures in thousands)

		Amount	*Percent of Total Cost of Goods Manufactured*
Direct costs:			
Vegetables and fruit	$232		
Labor	138		
Cans	112		
Other ingredients	36	$518	82%
Variable overhead:			
Fuel oil	$ 17		
Electricity and water	7		
Factory supplies	5		
Payroll taxes	7		
Truck and auto expenses	2		
Gas and oil	5	43	7
Fixed overhead:			
Repairs and maintenance	$ 18		
Insurance	12		
Property taxes	10		
Depreciation—plant and equipment	24		
Machinery rental	5	$ 69	11
Total cost of goods manufactured		$630	100%

Exhibit 4

UPSTATE CANNING COMPANY, INC.

INITIAL PROPOSAL BY MR. FORDHAM FOR THE PURCHASE OF CERTAIN ASSETS OF THE UPSTATE CANNING COMPANY, INC., BY MR. SHIELDS AND ASSOCIATE(S)

1. New corporation to be formed with capitalization of $400,000 and with a capital structure as follows:
   a) $100,000 of common stock, $1 par, one vote per share, to be issued to Shields and associate(s) for $100,000 cash. Cash to be retained in new corporation.
   b) $300,000 of income bonds due on June 30, 1967; 3% interest per annum, payable semiannually (June 30 and December 31) if and when earned, cumulative, to be issued to Fordham in exchange for all plant and equipment of Upstate Canning Company, $50,000 of salable finished goods inventory, and the right to use the brand names of the Upstate Canning Company. (Prior to the exchange, the Upstate Canning Company will be liquidated and the assets distributed to Fordham as sole owner.)
2. Repayment provisions of income bonds:
   a) Company to repurchase $50,000 of income bonds on or before June 30, 1958.
   b) In succeeding years, company to repurchase income bonds equivalent in par value to 50% of the net profit after taxes, provided that the amount in any year will be no less than $15,000. The $15,000 will be due on June 30, and any balance within 30 days after the close of the fiscal year.
   c) Company to have the option of purchasing any amount of income bonds in excess of the minimum requirements according to a schedule of discounted prices as follows: in the first year at 80% of par, in the second year at 82½% of par, in the third year at 85% of par, and so on.

Exhibit 4—Continued

3. No fixed assets to be sold or encumbered in any way without the consent of the income bondholders.
4. Control of the company to be divided equally between the income bondholders and the common shareholders until the income bonds have been completely retired. Each group will elect two directors to a four-man board.
5. Fordham to act as chairman of the board and receive compensation for whatever time he spends on operating matters, beyond board meetings, on a basis to be determined in further negotiations.
6. Shields to act as president and general manager.
7. New company to be incorporated and assets of Upstate to be acquired on or about June 30, 1957. In the meantime, it is to be understood that Fordham and Shields will work together in negotiating contracts with farmers and arranging for an orderly transfer of ownership.

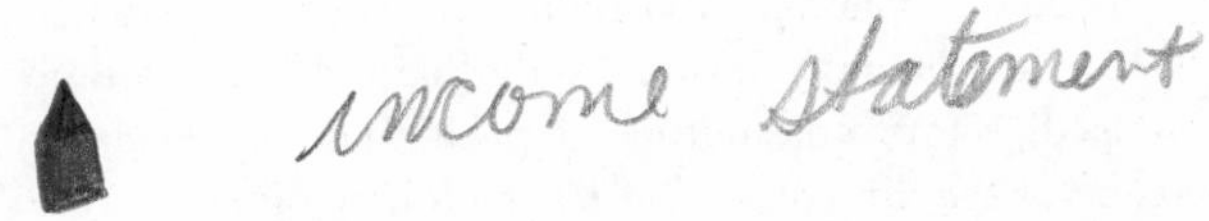

THE SABBATH CONTAINER COMPANY

In November, 1952, Mr. Callahan, treasurer of The Sabbath Container Company, was considering the question of how best to determine the relative costs and advantages of two alternative methods of financing the company's expansion program, the sale of bonds or common stock. The question had been precipitated by a disagreement among the company's directors at a recent meeting. After the meeting, Mr. Callahan had been asked by Mr. Rocco, the president of the company, to assess the logic of the arguments presented by the various directors and outline a position to be taken by the company's management at the directors meeting the following month.

The Sabbath company manufactured containers for industrial and commercial use. Although the level of sales and profits fluctuated considerably with the level of business activity, the company's operations had been profitable in almost all years. Originally founded in 1896 to manufacture kerosene cans, the company had changed its product line considerably over the years; metal snuffboxes, cigarette "flat 50" tins, and a variety of other containers had proved profitable. During World War II, the company had concentrated its efforts in the manufacture of first-aid kit containers for the armed forces. Currently a considerable volume of sales was being obtained from the manufacture of small aluminum cans for the shipment of delicate instruments, particularly those used in aircraft. The company also had contracts to supply several pharmaceutical firms with tins for pills and small bandages. The latter line had contributed a needed element of stability to demand.

Management had customarily followed the policy of avoiding long-term debt. Apart from war periods, when working capital requirements had been unusually heavy, the company had met its needs by retained earnings, supplemented from time to time by short-term bank loans. In 1952 the capitalization of the company consisted of common stock and surplus, with no fixed indebtedness of any sort.

Although descendants of the founders still retained sizable holdings, ownership of the stock was widely distributed; there was no dominant interest, and the shares, which were traded over the counter, were transferred infrequently.

Late in 1952 the management of the Sabbath company decided that a small plant in Los Angeles, which had been acquired in 1932, should be modernized and enlarged. In recent years this plant had proved inadequate to meet the rising demand for aluminum containers for aircraft instrument firms, and it had become clear that fundamental changes were required. Management estimated that the larger plant and additional working capital needed to finance expanded operations would require $10 million in new funds. Originally it had been planned to provide these funds from retained earnings, but a general increase in working capital requirements and a lowered balance of earnings after higher income and excess profits taxes made this plan inadvisable. It was, therefore, planned to seek capital from outside sources.

The proposed investment was expected to net $2 million in annual earnings before interest and taxes as soon as the plant was in operation. The added investment would increase the tax base of the corporation for purposes of excess profits tax computation, so that it was assumed that the 1951 overall tax rate of 58% would apply also to the added income from the new investment. Consequently, the net incremental income after taxes was forecast at 8.4%, or $840,000.

A preliminary investigation of the price record of Sabbath common stock led Mr. Callahan to the opinion that barring a general market decline, common stock could be sold to the public through investment bankers at $26.50 per share. After underwriting expenses and other fees, net proceeds to the company would be $25 per share. Thus, if common stock was used, the proposed financing would require the issuance of 400,000 shares.

For some years, both Mr. Rocco and Mr. Callahan had been disappointed in the market prices of Sabbath common stock (see Exhibit 1). For this reason, they had decided to reexamine the company's established policy of avoiding long-term debt. Circumstances had changed, and they believed that a new policy might be justified by the prospect of more stable future earnings. Inquiry in financial circles established the likelihood that the company could raise $10 million through the sale of bonds. It appeared that the interest rate on a 15-year issue would be 4%. If such securities were sold directly to insurance companies or other institutional investors, they undoubtedly would insist upon some sinking fund arrangement. It seemed likely that they would require retirement of at least $500,000 of the issue annually, leaving $2.5 million outstanding at maturity. While such terms would create a sizable annual requirement for cash, they were regarded by the company's management as about as good as could be expected.

In view of the tax deductibility of bond interest and the current income tax experience of 58%, the 4% rate was regarded by Mr. Callahan as the equivalent of 1.68%. In contrast, he considered that the stock at $25 per share and a $2 dividend rate would cost the company 8%. This comparison made the bond issue seem very desirable to Mr. Rocco.

Early in November, 1952, Mr. Rocco decided to submit the expansion proposal to the Sabbath board of directors for its formal approval. The proposal to increase the Los Angeles plant had been discussed previously by the board; after reconsidering it briefly, the board voted unanimously to authorize the president to go forward with the project, assuming satisfactory financing could be arranged. At this point, Mr. Rocco decided to sound out board sentiment to see if the possibility of debt financing as an alternative to common stock financing should be explored further. He presented the cost comparison given above. Somewhat to his surprise and concern, an active and at times acrimonious discussion developed in which all of the directors participated.

Mr. Rocco was immediately challenged as to the cost of the bond issue, since his figure did not include the annual payment to the sinking fund. One director figured this as 8% of the average size of the bond issue over its 15-year life; to him, the cost of the stock issue was less than that of the bonds. Furthermore, he emphasized the cash outlay called for in the bond program and the $2.5 million maturity. The use of debt thus added risks to the company, and he argued that this would make the common stock more speculative and cause greater variation in its market price.

Another director argued for a stock issue because "simple arithmetic" showed that the company could net 8.4%, or $840,000, per year after taxes on the new investment. Yet if 400,000 shares of common stock were sold, the dividend requirements at the current rate of $2 per share would equal only $800,000 per year. Since there was no thought that the $2 dividend rate should be changed, he could not see how the sale of the new common stock would hurt the interest of present stockholders. Further, if there were any immediate sacrifice, he argued that it would be overcome shortly as the expansion of the company continued. Under such circumstances, there could be no thought of the bond issue, for it would place much greater obligations on the company.

On the other hand, one director argued vigorously that common stock was a "giveaway" at $25. He pointed out that the retention of a substantial percentage of past profits in the business had built up the book value of the stock to roughly $45 last December and $47 in November. Moreover, this value substantially understated the true worth of the business, because at today's prices the company could not begin to replace properties and inventories at balance sheet cost. He concluded that the sale of common stock at $25 would give new buyers a substantial part of the value held by the company's present stockholders.

Two other directors agreed that the sale of stock at this price would dilute the value of the stock, but they measured the dilution in terms of earnings per share rather than book or market value. At the level of earnings currently anticipated, about $13 million before interest or income taxes, they maintained that income per share of existing common stock would be diluted to $3.03 per share if common stock was sold to net $25. In contrast, these directors asserted that the sale of bonds would raise earnings per share to $3.78. These directors said it was unimportant that the annual sinking fund would amount to $0.36 per share.

As discussion of these and other arguments related to cost of financing continued well past the usual hour for adjournment with no signs of developing agreement, Mr. Rocco finally interrupted the discussion to explain that he had not expected the board to go this far into the matter at this meeting. "Obviously," he said, "management must do more thinking about this matter of the costs of the two financing methods." He promised that a careful review of the costs aspects, including all those raised by the directors, would be prepared before the next meeting of the board and asked that decision on the matter be held over. The directors agreed to this proposal, and the meeting was thereupon adjourned.

Exhibit 1

THE SABBATH CONTAINER COMPANY

SELECTED INCOME, DIVIDEND, AND MARKET PRICE DATA, 1945–52

	*Net Sales**	*Income before Taxes**	*Income after Taxes**	*Income per Share*	*Dividends per Share*	*Market Prices per Share of Common Stock* High	Low
1945	$ 83,562	$ 9,150	$2,366	$1.69	$1.20	$29⅝	$19⅜
1946	51,434	4,742	2,802	2.00	1.20	40	21¾
1947	81,503	7,225	3,844	2.75	1.20	27⅛	18¼
1948	89,822	9,560	5,071	3.62	1.20	25¼	16¾
1949	70,662	4,100	3,109	2.22	1.20	19⅛	15½
1950	77,736	5,802	3,495	2.50	1.20	22½	17
1951	105,640	10,790	4,464	3.19	2.00	26¾	24
1952	.....	....	....	...	2.00†	28½‡	23⅞‡

* In thousands of dollars.
† Annual rate.
‡ To November 6 (November 5 prices were 28⅜–28¼).

Exhibit 2

THE SABBATH CONTAINER COMPANY

SUMMARY BALANCE SHEET

DECEMBER 31, 1951

(In thousands of dollars)

ASSETS	
Cash	$ 8,924
Accounts receivable	15,146
Inventory	32,492
	$56,562
Plant	18,821
Goodwill	5,000
Other	3,676
Total assets	$84,059
LIABILITIES	
Accounts payable	$ 8,888
Accrued federal taxes	5,831
Accrued expenses	5,995
	$20,714
Common stock ($10 par)	14,000
Surplus	49,345
Total liabilities	$84,059

WESTERN FABRICATING CORPORATION

In January, 1954, Mr. Rhodes, vice president and treasurer of the Western Fabricating Corporation, was preparing a report for the company's board of directors. At their last meeting the directors had discussed several methods of financing the first $3 million of a long-term expansion program and had narrowed the choice to two alternatives: (1) an offering of common stock to the public, and (2) private placement of a bond issue with an insurance company. The meeting had been adjourned at this point, with a request that Mr. Rhodes analyze these alternatives and recommend a course of action for the board to consider at its next meeting.

Western Fabricating Corporation (Westfab) was a medium-sized manufacturer of aircraft components and substructures. The company had originally been organized in 1925 to produce automotive parts and had operated successfully in this field until the depression. In 1932 most of the company's subcontracts with major auto manufacturers were lost, with the result that the company had been forced into a search for new products. Losses experienced between 1932 and 1936 drained off nearly half of the company's accumulated capital, but with miscellaneous sales to a variety of industries and recovery of a part of its automotive parts business the company had managed to weather the depression.

The search for new products was continued during the recovery period, and in 1939 the company entered its first successful bid to subcontract parts for a leading aircraft manufacturer. During the next four years of rearmament and war, aircraft production doubled each year, and Westfab grew with the industry. The company was awarded the Navy E in three successive years and by the end of World War II had established a reputation as a reliable fabricator of a wide variety of airframe subassemblies. These products accounted for 95% of the company's total sales of $29 million in 1945.

In the immediate postwar period, sales declined abruptly to $7 million, and a small loss was experienced in 1947. Although sales remained roughly constant at this level in 1948 and 1949, the company was able to report a profit of approximately $350 thousand in each year. Government orders for aircraft were greatly increased in 1950 as a result of the Korean crisis, and by 1953 Westfab's sales and profits had climbed to record levels of $48 million and $3 million, respectively. Selected data from the company's postwar operating statements are shown in Exhibit 1.

The 1950–53 increase in sales created extremely heavy working capital requirements. Cost and inventory controls were tightened to conserve funds, and from time to time the company was able to secure advances from prime contractors; in spite of such measures, however, the company was forced to rely heavily on short-term bank loans and a large increase in tax accruals to meet its increased requirements. By the end of 1953 the bank loans had been repaid, but the tax liability (income and excess profits tax) had increased to $9.1 million, an amount slightly less than the company's entire net worth. Comparative balance sheets for these years are shown in Exhibit 2.

Westfab's financial plight was further complicated during the postwar period by its plant and equipment requirements. At the end of World War II the company's officers had concluded that extensive equipment replacements were needed if the company was to retain its efficiency and reputation for quality output in the coming period of costlier, more complex aircraft. Equally important, it was thought that an effort should be made to diversify the company's production and decrease its dependence on the aircraft industry. Funds were invested in new equipment between 1946 and 1950, as they could be spared, but the profits of this period had not permitted modernization of the company's aircraft plant to the extent visualized or the hoped-for entry into new markets. Larger capital expenditures became imperative after the Korean war began, but the working capital squeeze limited plant and equipment additions to items that were considered essential for the company's immediate military contracts.

By the end of 1953, management had become convinced that its reequipment and diversification plans should be delayed no longer. The cost of the full program, it was estimated, might run as high as $10 million. This was more, however, than the company could either finance or absorb at one time, and consequently a decision was made to undertake the program in two phases.

The first half of the program, budgeted at $5.25 million, was limited to projects that would directly increase the company's efficiency as an aircraft parts manufacturer. The largest single item, for example, was an expansion of the tool and die shop.

Under its contracts with aircraft manufacturers, Westfab had been obliged to change dies and machine setups at frequent intervals, and its own shop was neither large enough nor adequately equipped to supply the company's needs. The problems created by the shop's limited capacity had not been serious in the immediate postwar period, but experience during recent years of high demand had persuaded management to enlarge the shop at the earliest opportunity. Since 1950, Westfab had found that the cost of purchasing dies and carbide tools of suitable quality had increased tremendously and, also, that it was difficult if not impossible to get deliveries on schedule. Delays were apt to be critical because the company's contracts with aircraft manufacturers often contained severe penalty clauses for the protection of the prime contractor against subcontractor delays. The new shop was expected to support a sales volume of roughly $30 million.

Other projects included in the first part of the program were regarded as equally important. In total the projects were expected to produce annual savings of $1.2 million before taxes assuming Westfab was able to maintain an annual sales volume of $30 million or more after completion of the projects in early 1955.

Diversification projects made up a large part of the second half of the program. Though their immediate return was more problematical, they too were considered highly important.

Westfab's immediate sales outlook was favorable, judged by past standards, but Mr. Rhodes knew that a substantial portion of the estimated sales for 1954 represented carry-forward orders. With the return of peacetime conditions, it was expected that defense spending would be cut, perhaps drastically, and this in turn would affect Westfab's sales. When aircraft production declined, prime contractors often undertook many of the manufacturing operations previously awarded to subcontractors. This invariably created more intense competition among subcontractors for new orders, and both volume and profit margins tended to suffer.

To reduce Westfab's vulnerability to this cycle, management planned to diversify into new products for other industries. Several products with more stable earnings prospects had been investigated, but expenditures of at least $4.75 million appeared necessary to purchase new equipment and adapt current facilities to their production requirements. Mr. Rhodes did not believe that the diversification program could be started much before early 1955, even if the financing were completed before then, since the program would require the new tool and die shop and other facilities scheduled for purchase in 1954.

The decision to raise $3 million externally for the initial part of the program was based on the belief that the company could provide no more than $2.25 million from internal sources. This figure reflected estimates of $1.65 million for retained earnings in 1954 and $600 thousand for depreciation.

The directors were aware that it had been impossible in the past to predict Westfab's net earnings with much accuracy beyond a one-year period. For this reason they had been unwilling to look beyond 1954 earnings and depreciation for funds to finance the first stage of the program. Estimates for 1954 indicated that sales would probably decline to about $37 million and profits (before tax) to $6.9 million. However, with the repeal of the excess profits tax (effective for tax years beginning January 1, 1954) the company's effective tax rate would drop from approximately 75% to 52%, leaving a net profit of about $3.3 million. In view of the variable nature of the company's earnings, the directors had followed the policy of paying substantial dividends during favorable years. With a 50% dividend planned for 1954, retained earnings would amount to approximately $1.65 million. Depreciation of $600 thousand would make up the balance of the $2.25 million to be secured from operations.

At the end of 1953 the company held substantial liquid assets, including almost $1.2 million of tax anticipation notes and short-term government securities and $3.5 million of cash. These funds, above a minimum working balance of $2.0 million, plus funds released by an adjustment of inventories and accounts receivable to a $37 million sales level, would be needed for tax payments in 1954 and hence were not considered available for the expansion program.

As the first step in his investigation of the financing alternatives, Mr. Rhodes had attempted to determine the approximate terms under which each issue could be sold. After discussions with representatives of several investment banking houses and insurance companies, it appeared that the possibilities were approximately as follows:

1. *Common Stock.* An underwriter had indicated to Mr. Rhodes that the company could probably float an issue of common stock to the public at a price 6.7% below the market price existing a few days before the date of the offering. In Westfab's case, this relatively large discount appeared necessary to assure the successful sale of such a large block of stock relative to shares currently outstanding. Thus, if the present market price of $22.50 held, the issuing price would be set at $21 per share. At a price of $21 Mr. Rhodes planned to issue 150,000 shares to gross $3,150,000 before underwriting fees of 2% or $63,000. Westfab would also incur legal and other similar expenses of approximately $50,000, so that net proceeds to the company would amount to $3,037,000. These estimates were all subject to revision in the event market conditions changed significantly during the three-month period preceding final registration of the issue with the Securities and Exchange Commission.

2. *Debentures.* Unsecured debentures placed with an insurance company would have to carry an interest rate of 4.5% and be amortized in equal installments over a 10-year period. It also appeared that any lender who bought the issue would insist on an acceleration clause which would make the full loan due and payable within one month of default on any one of the following restrictions:

a) A minimum net working capital limit of $4.5 million.

b) A maximum limit of approximately $5 million on bank loans and long-term debt, including the present debentures.

c) A ban against the creation of senior long-term debt.

d) Restriction of dividend payments to earnings accumulated after the date of issuance of the debentures plus $150,000.

While the terms of the debt issue seemed fairly definite, Mr. Rhodes had thought it necessary to collect additional information on the market behavior of the company's common stock, since the price of the issue would be a crucial consideration. This information—annual price ranges, per share earnings and dividends, and volume of shares traded in recent years—is shown in Exhibit 3. Mr. Rhodes attributed much of the recent rise in the market price to the fact that the company had increased its regular quarterly dividend from $0.50 to $0.75 in December, 1953. In announcing the increase, the directors had stated that it was their intention to maintain the $0.75 quarterly payment insofar as future earnings permitted.

The figures in Exhibit 3 have been adjusted for a 2 for 1 stock split in late 1952. The stock, which was listed on the American Stock Exchange, had been split at that time to increase the number of shares available for trading and, also, to bring the price into a range where it might interest a broader group of investors. In the following year the volume of trading increased, as did the number of individual shareholders and joint accounts (currently 2,700). On the other hand, the percentage of shares registered in the name of individuals and joint accounts decreased, and the percentage registered in the name of stockbrokers, security dealers, and nominees increased; by the end of 1953 the holdings of the latter group amounted to almost one third of the 550,000 shares outstanding (Exhibit 3). Heavy purchases (25,000 shares) by two dealers who had never before been interested in Westfab's stock had given rise to rumors that some group might be seeking control of the company, but the principals of such a group, if any, were still unknown to Mr. Rhodes and the directors. At the current time Westfab's management owned or controlled beneficially approximately 10% of the shares outstanding.

Exhibit 1

WESTERN FABRICATING CORPORATION

SELECTED OPERATING DATA

(Thousands of dollars)

Year	*Net Sales*	*Operating Profit*	*Net Income (after Taxes and Provision for Renegotiation)*
1945	$29,211	$ 3,468	$ 943
1946	10,068	275	236
1947	7,011	(258)	(64)
1948	6,642	622	326
1949	7,416	717	391
1950	9,419	1,263	657
1951	24,545	5,379	1,149
1952	42,876	12,350	1,839
1953	48,464	13,947	3,003

Exhibit 2

WESTERN FABRICATING CORPORATION

COMPARATIVE BALANCE SHEETS, AS OF DECEMBER 31

(Thousands of dollars)

ASSETS	*1950*	*1951*	*1952*	*1953*
Cash	$ 551	$ 2,515	$ 5,160	$ 3,528
U.S. government securities	177	182	188	1,185
Accounts receivable	1,514	3,981	5,630	5,699
Inventories	4,225	7,527	9,432	8,761
Prepaid expenses	145	212	353	378
Total current assets	$6,612	$14,417	$20,763	$19,551
Net plant and equipment	3,052	3,495	3,692	4,358
Total assets	$9,664	$17,912	$24,455	$23,909
LIABILITIES				
Accounts payable	$ 378	$ 969	$ 1,606	$ 1,070
Notes payable	1,275	2,925	1,500	...
Customers' deposits	88	1,471	701	182
Reserve for federal income taxes and renegotiation	606	4,230	10,511	10,944
Other accruals	450	848	1,716	1,591
Total current liabilities	$2,797	$10,443	$16,034	$13,787
Reserve for employees' benefits	433	404	343	283
Common stock*	2,750	2,750	2,750	2,750
Earned surplus	3,684	4,315	5,328	7,089
Total liabilities and net worth	$9,664	$17,912	$24,455	$23,909

* Common stock—$5 par, 550,000 shares currently outstanding. In September, 1952, the previous $10 par stock was split 2 for 1.

Exhibit 3

WESTERN FABRICATING CORPORATION
SELECTED FINANCIAL DATA*

	Common Stock Price Range High	Low	Number of Shares Traded (000's)	Earnings per Share	Dividends
1945	14¾	7	110	$1.71	$0.85
1946	17⅝	7	114	0.43	0.55
1947	8⅞	5⅜	97	(0.12)	nil
1948	8⅛	4¾	107	0.59	0.20
1949	7	4⅝	105	0.71	0.65
1950	11⅛	6⅞	103	1.19	0.65
1951	12	8⅞	113	2.09	0.95
1952	15	12½	390	3.34	1.45
1953	23⅞	13⅛	650	5.46	2.25
1953—BY QUARTERS					
1st	18⅞	13⅛	174		0.50
2d	18⅛	14¾	86		0.50
3d	19¼	14¼	176		0.50
4th	23⅞	18¾	214		0.75
Jan. 1–10, 1954	23⅛	22			

DISTRIBUTION OF STOCK OWNERSHIP, DECEMBER 31, 1953

	Number of Shareowners	Number of Shares Owned
By type of owner:		
Individuals and joint accounts	2,682	361,542
Stock brokers, security dealers, and nominees	170	176,213
Fiduciaries, institutions, foundations, and others	45	12,245
Total	2,897	550,000
By size of holding:		
1 to 99 shares	1,960	94,372
100 to 999 shares	892	282,619
1000 or more shares	45	173,009
Total	2,897	550,000

* Adjusted for 2 for 1 split in 1952.

FISCHER PHARMACEUTICAL COMPANY

In January, 1955, Mr. Patrick O'Conner, treasurer of the Fischer Pharmaceutical Company, decided to issue $30 million in common stock to provide funds for meeting a term-loan balloon maturity payable in June, 1955, and for expanding the company's product line. When Mr. O'Conner discussed the proposed issue with an underwriting firm, the underwriter pointed out that successful issuance of common stock depended on future stock market developments. The underwriter argued that the stock market was in a state of flux and might be subject to radical downward pressures. In view of this Mr. O'Conner decided to consider a privately placed issue of debentures as an alternative method of raising the required funds. Fischer's December 31, 1954, balance sheet and selected income statement information for the years 1948–54 are shown in Exhibits 1 and 2.

Fischer Pharmaceutical Company was one of the largest companies engaged in the development, manufacture, and distribution of quality chemicals, which it sold chiefly for medicinal, nutritional, industrial, and laboratory purposes. Approximately 25% of the company's sales were made directly to pharmaceutical houses, food processors, and other industrial users. The remainder of its sales, including prescription chemicals and ethical drugs for medicinal and household use, were made directly to wholesale and retail distributors. The ethical drug industry was a highly competitive and constantly changing field in sales of existing products as well as research for new and improved products.

The discovery of new wonder drugs beginning in the late 1930's, together with the large requirement for drugs resulting from World War II and later the Korean conflict, encouraged a rapid expansion of production facilities in the ethical drug industry. In late 1950 and 1951, distributors, fearing a wartime drug shortage, had heavily stocked their inventories. Unaware of this false layer of demand, the industry continued expanding its productive capacity. Suddenly, in late 1951, a condition of general oversupply became evident, and ethical drug manufacturers undertook drastic competitive action. Prices on all major products were cut substantially, some as much as 40%, and profit margins were reduced to postwar lows. After three years of depressed earnings there were some indications in early 1955 that profit margins were stronger and that demand was increasing.

Fischer's dollar sales volume had increased fivefold from 1941 to 1950. This rapid expansion had been financed primarily through equity sources. During this period, $20 million or nearly 50% of earnings after taxes was retained in the business, and three stock issues were successfully floated: an $8 million common stock issue in 1942; a $9 million issue of $3.50 cumulative preferred stock in 1944; and a $10 million issue of $4 cumulative convertible preferred stock in early 1947. Nine months after the issuance of the convertible preferred stock, the market price of the common had risen to a level where the company was able to call the issue and successfully force conversion.

In June, 1950, Fischer negotiated a five-year $20 million term loan with the Broad Street National Bank of New York. The loan, carrying a 3% interest rate, was repayable in semiannual installments of $1 million with a balloon maturity of $11 million due in June, 1955. Under the provisions of the term loan, the company, without the prior written consent of the bank, could not declare or pay any dividend on its outstanding stock or purchase or redeem any shares of its outstanding stock if these expenditures amounted in the aggregate to more than net additions to earned surplus accruing from net earnings after December 31, 1949, plus $3 million.

In October, 1951, Fischer successfully sold a 200,000 share issue of $4 cumulative convertible preferred stock at $100 per share. It was convertible into common stock in the ratio of four shares of common for each share of preferred and was callable at $106 per share. At the time of the offering, Mr. O'Conner believed the market value of the common stock would appreciate sufficiently within a two-year period to enable the company to force conversion. However, with adverse developments affecting the ethical drug industry's profits, the market price of Fischer's common fell below the point where conversion could be forced. (Market prices for 1948–54 for Fischer convertible preferred and common stock are shown in Exhibit 3.)

The company's inability to force the convertible stock conversion was a matter of serious concern to Mr. O'Conner. He believed that sophisticated investors would regard the issue as unsuccessful and would be less receptive to future stock offerings made by the company. This, in turn, put pressure on the company to make certain that its next public offering would be favorably accepted. The "frozen" convertible preferred stock issue, in Mr. O'Conner's opinion, eliminated a preferred issue as an alternative method of financing new capital requirements because the company's proportion of preferred capital was substantially larger than that of other companies in its industry, as shown below:

Capital Structure	*Fischer, December 31, 1954*	*Average of Nine Other Leading Drug Companies, December 31, 1953*
Debt	11%	2%
Preferred stock	28	10
Common stock and earned surplus	61	88
	100%	100%

Because the company had no intention of ever passing a preferred dividend payment, Mr. O'Conner regarded preferred stock as a form of subordinated debt. From this standpoint, he considered the company's debt ratio too high and hoped it would be reduced as the term loan was repaid. He believed that the "top should be kept open" for emergency use, and that the company's financial position could not bear more debt without a substantial increase in equity.

Thus, Mr. O'Conner had made strenuous efforts to "keep the bottom open" for favorable issuance of common stock. Despite the fact that earnings had fallen off sharply after 1951, the dividend rate was maintained at $0.60 per share in order to lend maximum support to the common stock's market price. However, depreciation and the small amount of retained earnings did not cover the necessary capital replacement costs and the maturities of the term loan. As a result, the company's cash balance was reduced to a minimum level of $10 million by December 31, 1954.

In looking to the future, Mr. O'Conner foresaw the need for additional cash by June, 1955. With lifesaving drugs pouring out of laboratories in bewildering numbers, old "new wonder drugs" rapidly became obsolete. In order to hedge against possible declines in demand for any of its major specialty drug products, Fischer had decided to begin a $19 million expansion program in the summer of 1955 aimed at widening the company's product line of consumer drugs. The final maturity of the term loan, $11 million, was also to be repaid in June, thus bringing the company's total fund requirements to $30 million.

In Fischer's laboratories, several promising new antibiotics were nearing the final stage of development. Although it was not expected that commercial production could be begun until early 1956, an additional $15 million would be required to purchase processing equipment. When these products were developed, it would be necessary to move rapidly in order to establish a market before competitors could develop substitutes. Consequently, Mr. O'Conner was expected to have outside sources of capital readily available for this purpose. Mr. O'Conner had not projected capital requirements beyond early 1956 but was certain that additional external financings would be required for future expansion programs.

Mr. O'Conner believed a new common stock issue would be the most desirable method of raising the required $30 million but, as previously indicated, he decided in January, 1955, to investigate other possible alternatives. After discussing Fischer's fund requirements with several banks and insurance companies, Mr. O'Conner concluded that only a privately placed debenture issue merited further consideration. The Municipal Life Insurance Company expressed a willingness to accept a $30 million, 15-year debenture issue at 4% interest. The debentures would carry an annual sinking fund provision of $2 million. The first sinking fund payment would not be scheduled until two years after the loan agreement was completed, thus leaving a $4 million balloon maturity at the end of 15 years. Approximately one month's time would be required to complete negotiations. Although restrictions were not discussed in detail, Mr. O'Conner gathered the impression that the insurance company would insist on a provision limiting dividend payments and stock retirements to future net earnings after providing for sinking fund requirements. He had also discussed the possibility of a smaller 15-year loan but found that the insurance company would require the same general sinking fund repayment schedules and restrictions. Mr. O'Conner had rejected this alternative because he believed the sinking fund requirement would prove burdensome during a period of expansion.

In February, 1955, when he discussed a $30 million common stock issue with a large underwriting firm in New York, Mr. O'Conner learned that an issue of this size would require a substantial discount from market price in order to insure acceptance. Although Fischer's common stock was selling at $19 a share at the time, the underwriter doubted if the company would net more than $15 per share after all expenses even though the company's stock was widely held and well known. On this basis, approximately 2 million shares would have to be issued. The underwriters indicated that the arrangements for issuing common stock, including registering with the SEC, would take about three months. During this period, the final issuing price would be subject to modifications necessitated by changes in stock market conditions affecting the market price of Fischer's stock. The underwriter pointed out that after a strong advance in November and December, 1954, the stock market had taken an erratic course. Opinion of market experts was sharply divided between those who anticipated a sharp downward readjustment and those who expected a continued upward trend after a short period of instability. In any event, Fischer common appeared to be relatively vulnerable to a decline, if it came, since the stock was "priced high in relation to its current earnings." (Weekly Standard and Poor's Industrial Averages from November 1, 1954, to March 18, 1955, are shown in Exhibit 4.)

Although the market price of Fischer's common had been relatively stable since early February, 1955, trading in a range between 18½–19½, Mr. O'Conner believed there was a substantial degree of uncertainty involved in issuing stock. Consequently he decided on March 18, 1955, to review other considerations relative to a new common stock issue. Since he expected to maintain the common stock dividend at $0.60 per share, an additional cash drain of $1.2 million would be imposed on the company. This represented a 4% cost after taxes on the money received or approximately 8% before taxes based on a 50% tax rate. Since the new funds would not expand the company's earning power immediately, the new stock issue would cause a dilution of stockholders' earnings per share, and this in turn might adversely affect future opportunities for common stock marketings. A further complication was the existence of the unconverted preferred stock. This stock contained the provision that in the event of a new issue of stock the conversion ratio had to be adjusted upward so as not to dilute the preferred stockholders' rights to acquire common. Mr. O'Conner felt that the possibility of conversion might adversely affect the market price of the common during the period of the offering. Finally, Mr. O'Conner believed that Fischer's current market price was temporarily depressed by the recent unfavorable developments in the pharmaceutical industry. If earnings recovered as expected, it might be possible to issue common stock at some future date on more favorable terms.

On the basis of this analysis, Mr. O'Conner thought it would be desirable to continue active consideration of a private issue of debentures to the Municipal Life Insurance Company. If he decided to issue common stock, he thought it would be important to make the decision within a week's time, so the issue could be marketed before the end of June, 1955. He planned to defer consideration of other factors of a common stock issuance, including whether rights would be used, until a later stage of the arrangements.

Mr. O'Conner estimated that profits before taxes would approximate $15 million in 1955 and expected this to increase an average of $1 million per year in the future. Future taxes were estimated at 50% of profits. Depreciation would contribute about $4 million to available cash, but necessary capital replacements would absorb about $2.5 million of these funds. Preferred dividend requirements were $1,115,000 per year, and there were no sinking funds on the outstanding preferred issues. Mr. O'Conner had projected a statement of source and application of funds (see Exhibit 5) through June, 1957, based on the assumption that 2 million shares of common stock would be sold in June, 1955. After modifying this projection to reflect the $300,000 quarterly interest payments on the debentures, and the $2 million annual sinking fund, payable beginning June, 1957, Mr. O'Conner planned to compare the effects of the two alternative methods of financing the required $30 million on future financial needs.

Exhibit 1

FISCHER PHARMACEUTICAL COMPANY

BALANCE SHEET, DECEMBER 31, 1954

(Dollar figures in millions)

ASSETS		LIABILITIES	
Cash	$ 10.7	Accounts payable	$ 5.2
Accounts receivable	10.3	Accruals	2.0
Inventory	32.9	Taxes payable	9.3
Total current assets	$ 53.9	*Total current liabilities*	$ 16.5
Fixed assets, net	59.0	Term loan (due June, 1955)	11.0
Investment in subsidiaries	4.6	$3.50 cumulative preferred ($100 par)	9.0
Deferred charges	1.5	$4.00 convertible preferred ($100 par)	20.0
		Common stock ($5 par)	36.5
		Earned surplus	26.0
Total assets	$119.0	*Total liabilities and net worth*	$119.0

Exhibit 2

FISCHER PHARMACEUTICAL COMPANY

SELECTED INCOME STATEMENT INFORMATION, 1948–54
(Dollar figures in thousands)

Year	*Net Sales*	*Gross Operating Profits*	*Interest*	*Net Profit before Tax*	*Provision for Tax*	*Net Income*
1948	$51,390	$19,590	nil	$ 9,904	$ 3,749	$6,155
1949	51,886	18,674	nil	8,452	3,319	5,133
1950	71,177	28,174	$300	17,226	8,735*	8,491
1951	90,519	41,588	540	28,189	18,768*	9,421
1952	78,898	30,343	480	14,386	8,015*	6,371
1953	82,515	31,219	420	12,624	6,983	5,641
1954	71,551	29,570	360	13,792	7,202	6,590

Year	*Preferred Dividends*	*Income Applicable to Common Stock*	*Common Shares Outstanding*	*Earnings per Share*	*Dividends per Share*
1948	$ 315	$5,840	7,300,000	$0.80	$0.40
1949	315	4,818	7,300,000	0.66	0.40
1950	315	8,176	7,300,000	1.12	0.40
1951	515	8,906	7,300,000	1.22	0.60
1952	1,115	5,256	7,300,000	0.72	0.60
1953	1,115	4,526	7,300,000	0.62	0.60
1954	1,115	5,475	7,300,000	0.75	0.60

* Includes excess profits tax.

Exhibit 3

FISCHER PHARMACEUTICAL COMPANY

COMPARATIVE NEW YORK STOCK EXCHANGE MARKET PRICES, 1948–MARCH 18, 1955

Year	*Fischer Common Stock* *High*	*Low*	*Yield on Common Stock: Range*	*Price-Earnings Ratio: Range*	*Fischer $4 Convertible Preferred* *High Low*
1948	$ 7 7/8	$ 5 5/8	5.1%–7.1%	9.8– 7.0	
1949	10 7/8	6 3/4	3.7 –5.9	16.5–10.2	
1950	16 1/2	10 1/8	2.4 –4.0	14.7– 9.0	
1951	29 7/8	15	2.0 –4.0	24.5–12.3	122 1/2–113
1952	26 1/4	16 7/8	2.3 –3.6	36.5–23.4	121 –104
1953	19 7/8	13 1/2	3.0 –4.4	32.1–21.8	104 1/2–101
1954	17 1/4	12 1/2	3.5 –4.8	23.0–16.7	109 –102 3/4
Through March 18, 1955	19 3/4	16 1/2			109 –105 3/4
Closing price March 18, 1955	19 3/8				108 1/2

Exhibit 4

FISCHER PHARMACEUTICAL COMPANY

STANDARD AND POOR'S INDUSTRIAL AVERAGES (50 STOCKS) BY WEEKS, NOVEMBER 1, 1954–MARCH 18, 1955

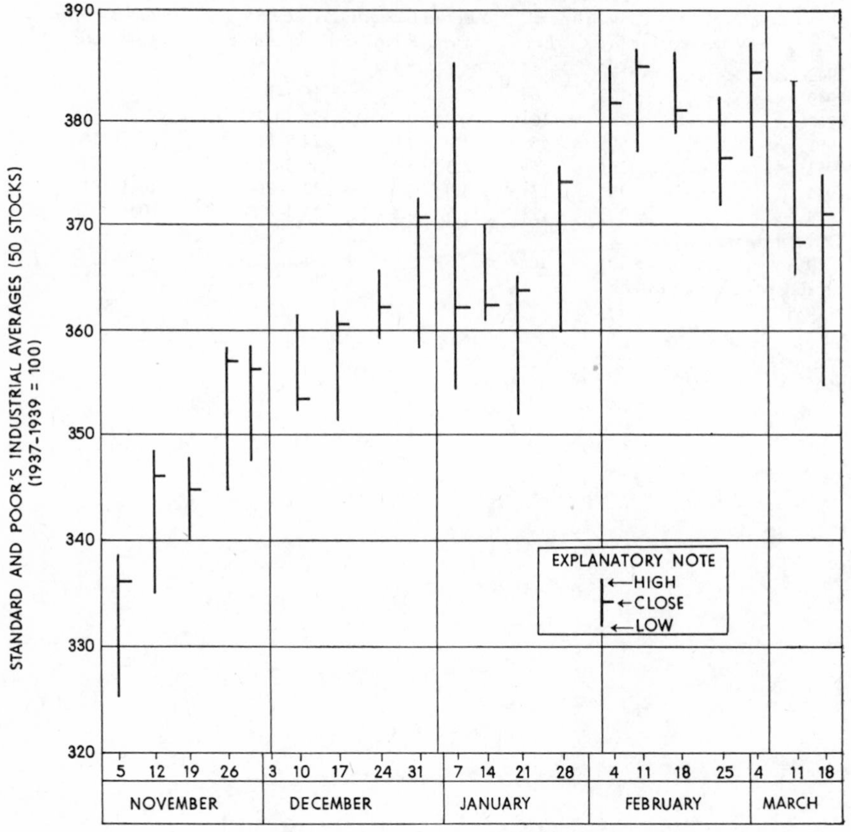

Source: Standard and Poor's Statistical Survey.

Exhibit 5

FISCHER PHARMACEUTICAL COMPANY

PROJECTED SOURCE AND APPLICATION OF FUNDS, BY SIX-MONTH PERIODS JANUARY, 1955–JUNE, 1957

(Dollar figures in thousands)

	January–June 1955	*July–December 1955*	*January–June 1956*	*July–December 1956*	*January–June 1957*
Projected profits before taxes	$ 7,500	$ 7,500	$ 8,000	$ 8,000	$ 8,500
Estimated taxes	3,750	3,750	4,000	4,000	4,250
Sources:					
Profit after taxes	$ 3,750	$ 3,750	$ 4,000	$ 4,000	$ 4,250
Depreciation, amortization, etc.	2,000	2,000	2,000	2,000	2,000
Outside financing	30,000	......	15,000	......	......
Total sources	$35,750	$ 5,750	$21,000	$ 6,000	$ 6,250
Applications:					
Preferred dividends	$ 557	$ 558	$ 557	$ 558	$ 557
Common dividends	2,190	2,790	2,790	2,790	2,790
Maturity term loan	11,000	......	......	......	......
Capital expansion program	......	19,000	15,000	*	*
Capital replacements	1,250	1,250	1,250	1,250	1,250
Total applications	$14,997	$23,598	$19,597	$ 4,598	$ 4,597
Opening cash balance	$10,700	$31,453	$13,605	$15,008	$16,410
Plus sources	35,750	5,750	21,000	6,000	6,250
	$46,450	$37,203	$34,605	$21,008	$22,660
Less applications	14,997	23,598	19,597	4,598	4,597
Closing cash balance	$31,453	$13,605	$15,008	$16,410	$18,063

* Not projected after June, 1956.

PHOENIX AIRCRAFT COMPANY*

In May, 1966, Mr. John Larson, president of Phoenix Aircraft Company, was preparing a proposal to present at the June meeting of the board of directors concerning how to finance $40 million in long-term funds needed for working capital, plant expansion, and other purposes over the next several years. After conferring with his senior vice president of finance, he had narrowed the possible sources of funds down to debt instruments, but the questions of what form this debt should take and the date of issue were yet to be decided.

The past three years had brought spectacular growth to Phoenix, with dollar sales doubling in the period from 1963 to 1966 (estimated), thereby creating pressing new needs for additional funds. A larger pool of long-term money was needed to support rising working capital requirements. This would allow the retirement of substantial short-term bank borrowing. Outstanding short-term bank loans had risen to $8.4 million as of the fiscal year ended September 30, 1965, and the combination of short-term bank loans and commercial paper had risen to $16 million by March 31, 1966 (Exhibit 1). The company was also engaged in an expansion program to enlarge the plant and equipment needed to meet increased sales demands and to introduce new production models. Expansion plan commitments for 1966 and 1967 alone entailed the addition of nearly one million square feet of plant space to existing facilities in Columbus at a cost of $11 million, in addition to new machinery and equipment costing about $12 million. Part of these funds would be provided from profits (profits had nearly tripled in four years, going from $5.1 million in 1963 to an estimated $14 million in 1966, as shown in Exhibits 2 to 4), but outside sources were needed to supplement flows into retained earnings. In his latest evaluation of these needs, Mr. Larson had decided that a total of $40 million of long-term capital within two years would be adequate to finance this growth.

Management believed that the company's outlook for the future was bright. The company's main thrust was in the general aviation market, which included all civil flying except that of public air carriers. The total time ac-

* Reprinted from Stanford Business Cases 1969 with the permission of the publishers, Stanford University Graduate School of Business, © 1969 by the Board of Trustees of the Leland Stanford Junior University.

cumulated in general aviation flying in the United States had grown very rapidly in the postwar years, to the point that general aviation averaged nearly four times the total scheduled flying time each year of domestic airline transports. Total industry sales of general aircraft had spurted in recent years, rising from $125 million in 1961 to nearly $320 million in 1965, with projections pointed steadily upward. Phoenix officers foresaw in the future a continued strong economy, with rising discretionary incomes and increased leisure time, all of which would contribute to expanding demands for business and pleasure flying.

In 1966, Phoenix was one of the top three manufacturers of general aviation aircraft for the 21st consecutive year. Out of all the light aircraft flying in the United States in 1966, Phoenix claimed nearly one fourth of the total small aircraft. Phoenix had first been incorporated in Ohio in the 1920's. Prior to World War II the company had manufactured several types of small aircraft, principally the Skychief, a single-engine, four-place cantilever-wing plane. During World War II, the company produced twin-engine trainer aircraft for the United States government. After the war, Phoenix reentered the private and business aircraft fields, retaining some government business while at the same time starting to diversify.

The company's marketing strategy was to maintain a balanced mix of commercial and military business to hedge against any downturn in defense expenditures. The company had also been able to diversify through acquisitions of existing companies. For example, Phoenix had acquired manufacturers of aircraft accessories, airborne communication and navigation equipment, and fluid power components for industrial equipment. By 1965, two thirds of sales resulted from commercial aircraft, 15% were in government business, and the rest came from other lines of manufacture.

In looking at its future business mix the Phoenix management foresaw a continued rapid increase in government orders due to the war in Vietnam. The company's policy in the past with respect to government contracts had been to bid only on work that could be performed with existing engineering and manufacturing facilities. As a result, sales to the United States government and to foreign governments over the past few years, which had been substantial, were regular commercial aircraft models. By May, 1966, the backlog on government work had grown to $21 million and was rising rapidly, with approximately 75% of this backlog in prime contracts and 25% in subcontracts.

Phoenix maintained a centralized manufacturing center, producing all its aircraft in company plants near Columbus, Ohio. Most component parts of the aircraft were fabricated by Phoenix. Those components that were not company-produced were purchased from independent sources.

Phoenix maintained a separate marketing division for commercial aircraft. Made up of 300 employees, the division conducted marketing research and established sales promotion and advertising programs for the network of distributors and dealers. Generally, sales were made directly to franchised distributors who had developed some 460 dealers in the United States and 110 in foreign countries. These dealers sold aircraft as well as providing flight instruction, servicing, and other ground support services. The company's capable marketing organization, which had conducted such successful promotional campaigns as the $5 first flight lesson, helped Phoenix meet active competition in the production and sale of general aviation aircraft. In addition to this strong network of distributors and dealers, the company had developed a reputation for producing quality products, with good engineering and design, all of which contributed to maintaining its prominent position in the industry.

From 1962 to 1966, Phoenix produced about one third of the industry's total unit output and dollar value. The other two large competitors together accounted for one half of unit output and one half of dollar volume for the industry. Phoenix also encountered strong competition in government business, where many of its competitors were corporations with total sales and resources far in excess of those of Phoenix. These competitors were at the same time customers buying various Phoenix products.

In order to assist dealers in financing its inventory and to provide retail financing, Phoenix established in 1957 a wholly owned unconsolidated finance subsidiary, Phoenix Finance Company, Inc. P.F.C. contributed greatly to Phoenix's aircraft sales and was growing rapidly. At fiscal year-end 1965, P.F.C.'s net notes receivable were $14.9 million, up 45% from the prior year (Exhibit 5). By the spring of 1966 these notes receivable had risen to about $25 million. Phoenix's investment in P.F.C., stated at cost plus undistributed earnings, totaled $3.3 million on September 30, 1965, and was expected to rise by more than $2 million by September 30, 1966, to support P.F.C.'s rapid rate of growth. In late 1965, after the close of the 1965 fiscal year, P.F.C. had negotiated with two insurance companies a 12-year $5.5 million unsecured loan, which was not guaranteed by Phoenix. In 1965, P.F.C.'s net earnings rose by 40% to $180,000. P.F.C.'s earnings growth in 1966 was expected to be interrupted because of a temporary lag in realizing the benefits from increased rates charged by P.F.C. and from the higher level of receivables as compared with the more immediate effect of recent high money costs to P.F.C. and greater acquisition costs.

In the examination of alternative methods of financing the $40 million long-term capital needs a new issue of common stock was considered, but it was generally agreed that at existing stock prices the dilution of earnings per share would be prohibitively high. The two most promising alternatives remaining were some form of long-term debt, either straight debt or convertible debt.

After discussion of these issues with Kidder, Peabody & Co., Incorporated, the investment bankers with whom the Phoenix management had built up a close relationship over the years, the following possibilities stood out as the best alternatives for the board of directors to consider:

A. The sale in 1966 of either:
   1. A straight debt issue of $20 million taking the form of:
      a) A private placement with a New York insurance company, or
      b) A public issue underwritten by a syndicate headed by Kidder, Peabody & Co.
   2. A $20 million public issue of convertible debt, convertible into common stock at a price 20% above the common price at the time of the offering, to be sold by the syndicate.

B. An issue next year for $20 million in the form of the instrument not used this year.

Members of the Phoenix management appreciated the possible advantages of these different financial methods, and it was planned to present the alternatives to the board of directors for their consideration. Several persons who had studied this problem and discussed the alternatives with Kidder, Peabody & Co. felt that a $20 million straight debt issue should be sold immediately, to be followed by a $20 million convertible issue to be sold approximately one year later. Other company officers, backed by the opinion of a different investment banking house, believed the company should reverse the order. That is, Phoenix should sell the convertible debt now and wait one year before issuing the $20 million of straight debt. Another possibility raised was to issue the entire $40 million package in one bundle, either immediately or in one year.

Several points of speculation about future conditions concerned Mr. Larson as he grappled with these strategic timing questions. Sales and earnings had grown rapidly over the past few years, with profits after taxes projected to increase more than 250% over 1963 profits. In projecting these sales and earnings into the future, Mr. Larson was trying to determine whether the slope of the earnings line would be a straight extension of the trend, would increase faster than the recent past performance, or would increase less rapidly. As president of the company, his outlook for the future was generally very optimistic, with continued increases foreseen in sales demand. But Phoenix would encounter several special operating problems in the near future. The company was planning to introduce three new small aircraft models over the next two years, possibly involving high start-up production and marketing costs. Capacity production levels were being approached in nearly every facility, causing increases in overtime hours and shortages in strategic components. Moreover, the completion of the new Columbus plant was slated for the coming year, possibly involving high moving expenses and initial costs. On the other hand, aggregate disposable income within the economy had continued to post strong gains in the past few months, which normally would mean higher demand for Phoenix airplanes. Government orders due to the Vietnam War were also being stepped up, thus expanding Phoenix's sales of trainers and light observation aircraft.

Exhibit 4 presents management's projected increase in sales through 1968.

In this exhibit earnings were projected to expand in proportion to sales. As a first approximation, changes in current assets and liabilities were also projected to increase proportionately to sales. The other items shown seemed reasonable in the light of management plans. For the reasons indicated in the preceding paragraph there was considerably more uncertainty with respect to the earnings estimates than to the anticipated increase in sales and consequent changes in current assets and current liabilities.

Mr. Larson was also concerned about whether the price of the company's common stock would increase in proportion to the anticipated rise in earnings. He did not know the degree to which the current stock price already reflected the outlook for improved earnings. Recent stock prices and price-earnings ratios are given in Exhibit 6. In any event, Mr. Larson knew that continued increases in stock prices would be essential to the success of a convertible issue. A higher market price for the common stock at the time the convertible was issued would mean less dilution when the bonds were ultimately exchanged for stock, as is illustrated by Exhibit 7. Moreover, a further increase in the common stock price after the convertible issue would permit early retirement of the outstanding debt, thereby reducing interest payments by Phoenix and, more importantly, lowering the relatively high debt ratio. Mr. Larson tried to consider all these factors and their implications in determining the timing and sequence in which to issue the straight and the convertible debt.

Phoenix's debt policy had been discussed many times before by the board of directors, and Mr. Larson knew that several questions concerning the new capital proposal would be raised at the coming meeting. The outstanding long-term debt had never exceeded $10 million. The projected $40 million in new debt issues would therefore represent a major shift in capital structure policy. As additional information, Kidder, Peabody & Co. had provided the ratios of similar companies that had recently sold new debt issues (Exhibit 8). The high debt position of the unconsolidated finance subsidiary, P.F.C., made the burden of the proposed $40 million of new debt financing seem even heavier. As of September 30, 1965, P.F.C. had $11 million of bank debt and commercial paper outstanding (Exhibit 5). These obligations had grown somewhat during 1966; and in addition, P.F.C. had negotiated the $5.5 million term loan, previously described, in late 1965.

In the light of these facts Mr. Larson knew that he would be called upon to demonstrate the need for the planned large increase in external capital and to justify the reasons for raising it in the form of debt. He planned to emphasize the rapid past and projected increase in sales, which would have the effect of raising the sales-to-debt ratio and of diminishing the relative burden of the proposed debt issues in comparison with historical figures. Mr. Larson could see no other means of meeting the financial needs created by expanding sales without a very large dilution of earnings per share. More plant and equipment and a greater working capital base clearly were required. Mr. Larson also knew that the stockholders would expect dividends on the common stock to be maintained at their present level of $1.15 per share and to be increased if earnings rose as projected.

The additional leverage provided by debt in raising future earnings per share seemed attractive to Mr. Larson. Nonetheless, he remained concerned about the question of excessive risk due to high debt obligations and the burden of mandatory interest and sinking fund payments. This risk was further compounded by the possibility of a "frozen convertible" if the stock price failed to perform as hoped.

The crucial nature of timing the company's entry into the bond market brought up the question of future interest rates. The total dollar interest cost of the proposed debt over the next 20 to 25 years would vary depending upon the rate demanded in the money markets at time of issue. (See Exhibit 9.) Interest rates on a convertible debenture normally ran about 1% less than the rate paid on straight debt. Since interest costs would affect company earnings up until conversion, thereby affecting the company's stock price, the Phoenix management was attempting to anticipate the direction and movement of interest rates in the relatively near term future. Corporate bond yields were rising steadily in the months preceding May, 1966, and were approaching record levels. Whether interest rates would continue to climb or had already reached their peak seemed uncertain. A survey of capital spending plans reported in *The Monthly Economic Letter* of the First National City Bank of New York showed that business outlays were slated to increase on new plant and equipment in the near future and that backlogs of unfilled orders for durable goods were lengthening. These pressures had tended to reverse the decline in interest rates that occurred in mid-March of 1966, causing rates to climb during April. Mr. Larson was well aware that the current rate of about 5.8% on corporate bonds of a quality similar to the prospective Phoenix issue was the highest he had encountered in the last 35 years, but the prospect of still higher rates in the future made the postponement of the debt issue seem even less attractive.

In addressing himself to the remaining question of whether the straight debt issue should be publicly or privately placed, Mr. Larson outlined the differences in terms of the two debt issues. Since the analysts at Kidder, Peabody & Co. were most familiar with the acceptable design of debt instruments under the latest market conditions, Mr. Larson asked for an appraisal of the most important differing features between a public offering of senior debentures and a private placement of senior notes. Assuming that both these debt issues would be for the same amount, i.e., $20 million, the maturity of the private placement would probably be 20 years, whereas the maturity date of the public offering of senior debentures would be 25 years. The coupon interest rates would be nearly the same, about 5¾%, plus or minus ⅛%–¼%, depending on the immediate market conditions, with the slight possibility that the public offering might be somewhat less than the private placement. The spread by the investment banker would be ⅜% on the private placement and 1¼% on the public issue. The length of nonrefundability at a lower interest cost on the debentures would be 5 years, whereas the privately placed notes would be nonrefundable for 10 years. The private issue with a financial institution might involve some restrictions on the amount of subordinated debt and on working capital balances, whereas the public issue would not carry such restrictions.

Several other relevant considerations were raised by Mr. Larson in deciding between the private placement and the public debt. Since the company was considering two separate issues of $20 million each, the prospectus covering an initial public offering of debt would be made available to analysts, allowing them to become familiar with the company's current situation and thereby helping to prepare the investment community for a later security offering. Sinking fund payments on the debentures would be set at $800,000 per year starting at the end of the fifth year. Debt retirement on the private placement would be at the rate of $1.2 million per year beginning at the end of the fourth year. Credit against mandatory sinking fund requirements for debentures acquired by the company on the open market in advance of the specified date would be permitted under the public issue, but this same flexibility would not be available under the private placement. In the case of the public issue Phoenix would probably be able to buy its own debentures on the open market at less than par if interest rates continued to rise, thereby realizing savings on its debt retirement. The timing of the issue was extremely important since the period was one of rapidly changing interest rates. In this respect the private placement had the advantage in that it could be consummated one month sooner than the public issue.

The debt retirement provisions of the convertible debentures would be considerably more lenient than those of either form of straight debt. Under the convertible issue it was proposed that debt retirement start at the end of the 11th year at the rate of 5.9% of the amount of the issue, or $1,180,000 annually. Credit would be given for converted debentures or for debentures acquired on the open market.

With these data before him, Mr. Larson was preparing to present his conclusions to the board of directors, recommending a specific course of action and asking for prompt board ratification so that the financing decision could be promptly implemented.

The following quotation summarized key economic trends at this time:

> The economy continues to push ahead into high ground with undiminished vigor. While the physical volume of goods and services produced and consumed has expanded—and will no doubt continue to expand—this expansion has been accompanied increasingly by price advances, as pressures on the economy's resources have mounted. . . . The rate of growth in spending for business fixed investment continued to exceed the rate of increase in over-all GNP in the first quarter. The latest survey of business plans by McGraw-Hill clearly supports earlier indications that the remainder of this year will see further strong advances in outlays for new plant and equipment.

Exhibit 1

PHOENIX AIRCRAFT COMPANY
COMPARATIVE STATEMENTS OF FINANCIAL POSITION AS OF SEPTEMBER 30, 1961–65, AND MARCH 31, 1966
(In millions of dollars)

	September 30					*March 31,*
	1961	*1962*	*1963*	*1964*	*1965*	*1966*
ASSETS						
Cash	$ 2.6	$ 1.7	$ 1.9	$ 2.4	$ 2.1	$ 4.5
Notes and accounts receivable	8.2	7.9	9.2	10.6	12.6	17.8
Inventories	26.6	28.0	30.4	36.8	53.7	55.1
Prepaid expenses	0.2	0.2	0.3	0.2	0.2	0.4
Total current assets	$37.6	$37.8	$41.8	$50.0	$68.6	$ 77.8
Investments and other assets	$ 5.7	$ 6.1	$ 5.4	$ 4.9	$ 5.4	$ 5.5
Property, plant, and equipment	$30.1	$29.3	$31.5	$33.2	$37.1	$ 40.8
Less: Accumulated depreciation	17.8	18.0	19.2	20.6	22.9	24.0
Net fixed assets	$12.3	$11.3	$12.3	$12.6	$14.2	$ 16.8
Deferred charges	3.5	4.1	3.4	4.0	3.5	3.4
Total assets	$59.1	$59.3	$62.9	$71.5	$91.7	$103.5
LIABILITIES						
Accounts payable	$ 3.8	$ 3.2	$ 4.4	$ 5.3	$ 7.7	$ 6.2
Federal income taxes	3.4	3.1	2.9	5.3	6.7	7.0
Other taxes	0.6	0.6	0.7	0.8	1.1	0.8
Accrued and other liabilities	1.7	1.5	1.9	3.1	4.0	4.5
Bank notes payable	4.1	5.1	—	0.5	8.4	16.0*
Long-term debt—current portion	0.5	0.5	0.4	0.4	0.4	—
Total current liabilities	$14.1	$14.0	$10.3	$15.4	$28.3	$ 34.5
Long-term debt	4.3	3.3	9.6	8.8	8.4	8.4
Stockholders' equity	40.7	42.0	43.0	47.3	55.0	60.6
Total liabilities and net worth	$59.1	$59.3	$62.9	$71.5	$91.7	$103.5

* Includes $5 million of commercial paper outstanding.

Exhibit 2

PHOENIX AIRCRAFT COMPANY

COMPARATIVE STATEMENTS OF OPERATIONS FOR YEARS ENDED SEPTEMBER 30, 1961–65

(Dollar figures in millions)

	1961	*1962*	*1963*	*1964*	*1965*
Sales	$87.7	$89.8	$96.4	$122.9	$148.4
Other income	0.5	0.5	0.6	0.6	0.7
	$88.2	$90.3	$97.0	$123.5	$149.1
Manufacturing and engineering costs	$67.1	$69.8	$75.4	$ 94.4	$110.5
Depreciation	2.1	1.8	1.6	1.6	2.4
Sales and administrative expenses	6.4	6.8	6.9	9.2	11.2
Taxes other than federal income	1.6	1.8	2.1	2.6	2.9
Interest	0.3	0.5	0.5	0.5	0.6
	$77.5	$80.7	$86.5	$108.3	$127.6
Earnings before taxes	$10.7	$ 9.6	$10.5*	$ 15.2	$ 21.5
Provision for federal taxes	5.5	4.9	5.4	7.7	10.5
Earnings after taxes	$ 5.2	$ 4.7	$ 5.1*	$ 7.5	$ 11.0

(As percentage of net sales)

	1961	*1962*	*1963*	*1964*	*1965*
Sales	100.0%	100.0%	100.0%	100.0%	100.0%
Other income	0.6	0.5	0.5	0.4	0.4
	100.6%	100.5%	100.5%	100.4%	100.4%
Manufacturing and engineering costs	76.5%	77.7%	78.2%	76.8%	74.5%
Depreciation	2.4	2.0	1.6	1.3	1.7
Sales and administrative expenses	7.3	7.6	7.2	7.5	7.5
Taxes other than federal income	1.8	2.0	2.2	2.1	1.9
Interest	0.4	0.5	0.5	0.4	0.4
	88.4%	89.8%	89.7%	88.1%	86.0%
Earnings before taxes	12.2%	10.7%	10.8%*	12.3%	14.4%
Provision for federal taxes	6.2	5.5	5.5	6.2	7.0
Earnings after taxes	6.0%	5.2%	5.3%*	6.1%	7.4%

* Before special charge of $900,000 (after taxes) from discontinuance of helicopter program in 1963.
Note: Figures may not add due to rounding.

Exhibit 3

PHOENIX AIRCRAFT COMPANY

COMPARATIVE STATEMENT OF OPERATIONS FOR THE SIX MONTHS ENDED MARCH 31, 1965, AND 1966

(In millions of dollars)

	1965	*1966*
Sales	$70.5	$ 99.4
Other income	0.5	0.7
	$71.0	$100.1
Manufacturing and engineering costs	$53.9	$ 76.9
Depreciation	0.8	1.2
Sales and administrative expenses	5.3	6.9
Interest	0.3	0.5
	$60.3	$ 85.5
Earnings before taxes	$10.7	$ 14.6
Provision for income taxes	5.4	7.1
Earnings after taxes	$ 5.3	$ 7.5

Exhibit 4

PHOENIX AIRCRAFT COMPANY

PROJECTIONS AS OF MAY, 1966, OF SELECTED FINANCIAL ACCOUNTS FOR YEARS ENDED SEPTEMBER 30

(In millions of dollars)

	Actual		Projected		
	1964	*1965*	*1966*	*1967*	*1968*
Sales	$122.9	$148.4	$189.0	$225.0	$252.0
Depreciation	1.6	2.4	2.5	3.6	3.9
Net profit after taxes*	7.5	11.0	14.0	16.7	18.6
Dividends	3.3	3.8	4.9	5.8	6.5
Retained earnings	4.2	7.2	9.1	10.9	12.1
Increase in current assets			19.2	16.7	12.5
Increase in investments and other assets†			5.7	3.5	—
Outlays on fixed assets			11.5	11.5	6.0
Increase in current liabilities‡			5.9	4.8	3.6
Reduction of long-term debt			0.4	0.7	0.7

* In this projection, allowance is made for interest payments on the outstanding bank loans, estimated at $8.4 million (the September 30, 1965, level) and for the existing long-term debt of $8.4 million, less the scheduled reduction of the existing long-term debt. As a crude approximation these interest payments on existing indebtedness are estimated at $1.0 million a year. No allowance is made for any new borrowing that may be needed to finance the projected expansion during the years 1966–68.

† This item consists primarily of an allowance for anticipated investments in Phoenix Finance Company and in unconsolidated foreign subsidiaries.

‡ Increases in current liabilities as shown here are for all current liabilities *except* short-term bank loans. One of the decisions confronting the Phoenix management was whether to replace its short-term bank loans with long-term debt.

Exhibit 5

PHOENIX FINANCE COMPANY, INC.

FINANCIAL STATEMENTS, 1964–65
(In thousands of dollars)

STATEMENT OF FINANCIAL POSITION
(As of September 30)

	1964	*1965*
ASSETS		
Cash	$ 319	$ 1,018
Notes and contracts receivable	10,272	14,889
Accrued interest and other receivables	129	203
Repossessed aircraft, at estimated realizable value	—	4
Prepaid expenses	37	83
Depreciable assets—net	44	29
Total assets	$10,801	$16,226
LIABILITIES		
Short-term notes payable:		
Banks and commercial paper	$ 6,400	$11,000
Phoenix Aircraft Company	900	750
Accounts payable:		
Phoenix Aircraft Company	49	675
Other	107	186
Federal income tax	100	148
Other	144	187
Total liabilities	$ 7,700	$12,946
Stockholders' equity	3,101	3,280
Total liabilities and net worth	$10,801	$16,226

STATEMENT OF OPERATIONS AND EARNINGS REINVESTED IN BUSINESS
(Years ended September 30)

	1964	*1965*
Income:		
Interest	$ 765	$ 1,072
Service	23	31
	$ 788	$ 1,103
Expenses:		
Interest	$ 318	$ 458
General and administrative	170	211
Provision for doubtful items	34	83
Depreciation	10	10
Other	3	2
	$ 535	$ 764
Earnings before federal income tax	$ 253	$ 339
Provision for federal income tax	125	159
Net earnings	$ 128	$ 180
Earnings reinvested in business at beginning of year	722	850
Earnings reinvested in business at end of year	$ 850	$ 1,030

Exhibit 6

PHOENIX AIRCRAFT COMPANY
PRICES OF COMMON STOCK, EARNINGS PER SHARE, AND PRICE-EARNINGS RATIOS, 1959–66

Year Ended September 30	*Stock Prices** *High*	*Low*	*Close*	*Earnings per Share*	*Price-Earnings Ratio†*
1959	$30	$13	$26	$2.47	10.5
1960	35	28	29	2.24	12.9
1961	46	26	37	1.58	23.4
1962	38	16	18	1.41	12.7
1963	26	16	21	1.55	13.5
1964	31	21	29	2.27	12.8
Period Indicated					
October–December, 1964	32	28	32		14.1
January–March, 1965	35	31	32		14.1
April–June, 1965	36	29	32		14.1
July–September, 1965	43	31	41	3.30‡	18.1
October–December, 1965	51	37	50		15.2
January–March, 1966	57	44	49		14.8
April, 1966	58	49	53		16.1
May, 1966	54	42	49		14.8

* Stock prices are rounded to the nearest dollar.

† Price-earnings ratios for annual data are computed on the basis of closing prices and earnings per share for the current year. Price-earnings ratios for quarterly and monthly intervals are computed on the basis of the earnings per share of the preceding fiscal year.

‡ Earnings per share for the year ended September 30, 1965.

Exhibit 7

PHOENIX AIRCRAFT COMPANY
POTENTIAL EFFECT OF DELAYED CONVERTIBLE OFFERING ON NUMBER OF SHARES OF COMMON STOCK ISSUED

Price of Common Stock	*Price-Earnings Ratio**	*Conversion Price†*	*Total Common Shares Issuable‡ (In Thousands)*	*Net Savings in Number of Shares Issuable§* *Number (In Thousands)*	*Percentage*
May, 1966:					
$46	13.9	$55.20	362		
May, 1967:					
$42	10.0	50.40	397	−35	−9.7%
46	11.0	55.20	362	0	0.0
50	12.0	60.00	333	29	8.0
54	12.9	64.80	309	53	14.6
58	13.9	69.60	287	75	20.7
66	15.8	79.20	253	109	30.1
74	17.7	88.80	225	137	37.8
82	19.6	98.40	203	159	43.9

* The price-earnings ratio in May, 1966, was computed on the basis of the earnings per share of $3.30 for the year ended September 30, 1965. The price-earnings ratio for May, 1967, was based on earnings per share of $4.18, computed from the figure for net profit after taxes projected in Exhibit 4 for the year ended September 30, 1966.

† Computed at a 20% premium over the price of the common stock.

‡ $20 million divided by the conversion price.

§ Amount by which the total number of shares issuable if the convertible was offered in 1967 at indicated prices differs from the 362,000 shares issuable if the convertible was issued immediately.

Exhibit 8

PHOENIX AIRCRAFT COMPANY
COMPARATIVE CAPITALIZATION RATIOS

	Senior Debt	*Subordinated Debt*	*Preferred Stock*	*Minority Interest*	*Common and Surplus*
*Certain companies recently offering convertible debentures by rights offerings:**					
Stauffer Chemical	18.3%	11.4%	1.1%	–%	69.2%
R. H. Macy	10.7	12.6	13.4	—	63.3
American Airlines	49.0	16.9	0.5	—	33.6
International Silver	8.2	18.5	2.3	—	71.0
Celanese Corporation	37.1	8.9	10.9	—	43.1
United Air Lines	41.2	12.9	2.7	—	43.2
W. R. Grace	34.5	13.4	1.6	2.4	48.1
Cluett, Peabody	27.0	11.7	2.1	—	59.2
*Certain companies recently offering convertible debentures directly to the public:**					
Great Northern Paper	38.8%	5.6%	9.4%	–%	46.2%
Reynolds Metals	41.5	7.2	8.7	—	42.6
Chicago Musical Instrument	10.0	29.5	—	1.2	59.3
Rockwell-Standard	17.4	16.7	—	1.0	64.9
Reeves Brothers	17.3	20.6	—	—	62.1
International Minerals & Chem.	37.0	15.0	3.0	—	45.0
General Instrument	1.5	25.5	—	—	73.0
United Merchants & Mfrs.	20.9	14.4	—	—	64.7
Beaunit	27.5 (*a*)	18.1	—	—	54.4
W. T. Grant	15.0	15.0	6.4	—	63.6
J. P. Stevens	24.3	7.6	—	—	68.1
*Certain companies recently offering senior debentures publicly:**					
Weyerhaeuser	23.8%	—%	—%	0.3%	75.9%
Allied Chemical	35.6	—	—	—	64.4
Anheuser-Busch	35.1	—	—	—	64.9
Rockwell-Standard	17.4	16.7	—	1.0	64.9
Hooker Chemical	29.5	—	3.8	—	66.7
Sun Oil	15.3	1.2	—	0.4	83.1
Texas Instruments	29.3	—	—	—	70.7
Magnavox	28.5	—	—	—	71.5
General Mills	35.8	—	—	—	64.2
Lone Star Cement	31.9	—	—	—	68.1
Burlington Industries	33.2	3.5	—	0.9	62.4
Champion Papers	27.4	7.5	3.8	—	61.3
Times Mirror	37.7	—	—	—	62.3
Deere	21.7	8.4	—	—	69.9
Ralston Purina	22.6	0.9	—	—	76.5
Honeywell	27.0	—	7.2	—	65.8
Firestone Tire & Rubber	17.8	—	—	0.3	81.9

* Based on pro forma capitalization in prospectus.
a) Includes commitment.

Exhibit 9

PHOENIX AIRCRAFT COMPANY
Effect of Decline in Interest Rate
(Based on Projected Net Income for 1968)
(In thousands except for per share data)

	Financing Alternative *No. 1*	*No. 2*
Net income	$18,600	$18,600
Less: After-tax interest cost	575	475
	$18,025	$18,125
Common shares now outstanding	3,350	3,350
Plus: Common shares issued in conversion	315	378
Pro forma common shares	3,665	3,728
Pro forma earnings per share	$4.92	$4.87

Financing Alternative No. 1:

Direct offering of $20 million of senior debentures at 5¾% now, and $20 million of subordinated debentures convertible at $63.40 (120% × $52.90—projected 1967 common price) in one year.

Financing Alternative No. 2:

Rights offering of $20 million of subordinated debentures convertible at $52.90 (115% × $46—approximate current price) now and $20 million of senior debt at 4¾% in one year.

NATIONAL LIGHT AND ELECTRIC COMPANY

In February, 1953, Regional Utilities, Inc., was a wholly owned subsidiary of National Light and Electric Company. Both organizations were subject to the jurisdiction of the Securities and Exchange Commission, which had ordered National Light and Electric Company to divest itself of its interest in Regional Utilities. The SEC had issued this order under the "death sentence" provisions of the Public Utility Holding Company Act of 1935.

As of February, 1953, Regional had one class of securities outstanding, common stock, all of which was owned by National. The management of National, however, did not believe that National could obtain the most attractive return on its investment in Regional simply by selling the existing common stock of Regional to the public. It was decided, instead, to have Regional create a new package of securities designed specifically for sale to the public. Regional would then exchange the newly designed package of securities for its outstanding common stock, now owned by National. After this exchange had taken place, National would arrange for a public sale of the newly issued Regional securities. Mr. Johnson, chairman of the Finance Committee of National and a member of the board of directors of both National and Regional, was asked to supervise the design and execution of this plan.

In considering the proportions of the various securities that would form the new capital structure of Regional, Mr. Johnson had to contend with two conflicting interests. On the one hand, it was to the interest of National to have the securities designed so that National would receive the largest possible net sales price for the package of new securities. On the other hand, the new capitalization had to take into account the long-run interests of the future owners of Regional; the new capital structure would have to be designed so that it would not restrict the operations or subsequent financing of Regional. Mr. Johnson thought that the needed flexibility would be assured if Regional's requirements for external funds (as distinguished from reinvested earnings) could be met by floating securities that would be considered "high grade" on the basis of current levels of earnings plus a reasonable return on new assets.

The Securities and Exchange Commission held overall supervisory powers regarding new capitalizations resulting from a "death sentence" proceeding. Decisions relating to individual cases were made largely on an *ad hoc* basis, but it had been generally held that bonds and preferred stocks, treated as a group, should constitute no more than 70% to 75% of the total book capitalization. In the case of Regional Utilities, Inc., the Commission had indicated that it would not approve a proportion of over 70%.

It should be emphasized that while the proportion of bonds, preferred stock, and common stock in Regional's new capital structure could be varied within the constraints imposed by the marketplace and by the Securities and Exchange Commission, the book value of Regional's total capitalization, that is, its net worth plus long-term debt, was fixed at $193.3 million as of December 31, 1952 (Exhibit 1). In other words, National would not be allowed arbitrarily either to write up the book value of Regional's assets or to write down liabilities before selling Regional's securities to the public. National would not, however, have to sell the newly issued securities of Regional at book value but rather at what the market would pay for them.

Regional Utilities, Inc., had enjoyed profitable operations since its inception in 1923. In addition, it served a fast-growing community and had a reputation for progressive management policies. For these reasons, Mr. Johnson felt quite sure that its securities, when offered to the public, would be rated "high grade" by the market, provided that the proportion of debt to equity in the revised capitalization was reasonable.

Regional had been organized to serve the needs of an expanding eastern area with a population, according to the 1950 census, of 885,000. For the past few years the company's earnings, before income taxes, had stabilized at approximately 13% of its capitalization, and the management had used this rate of return as a basis for plans up to five years in the future. The company's financial condition and earnings record are summarized in Exhibits 1 and 2.

The Bureau of the Census had predicted, in 1950, a population of 1,425,000 in 1960 in the area served by Regional. The directors, with this growth in mind, had recently approved a sizable expansion program for 1953–55, covering increased capacity in electric generating, transmitting, and distributing facilities. Though a part of the funds required for this program would be generated internally through retained earnings and depreciation allowances, it was estimated that a substantial portion of the new money would have to be obtained through new financing during the period. The program would have a minimal effect on sales and earnings until after 1953.

In the latter part of 1952 all litigation in connection with the divestiture had been resolved. Mr. Johnson had noted that the securities market had become actively interested in utility issues, and he believed that the time was appropriate to undertake the refinancing program.

Mr. Johnson knew that there had been a great deal of activity in utility financing since the end of World War II and that at present the market for all utility securities was active and rising. He felt that he could predict with some accuracy the terms which the company could obtain for newly issued securities.

Public utilities were characteristically financed with a substantial proportion of fixed debt, since their earnings were relatively stable and little risk to investors was involved. Further, the sale of debt securities represented the lowest cost form of financing and was attractive to utilities for this reason. Mr. Johnson thought that under present market conditions it would be possible to sell a large first mortgage bond issue to the public. The utilities industry had not suffered a truly "poor year" since 1938, when the earnings of Regional had dropped 23% under the level of the previous year.

Mr. Johnson believed that savings banks and insurance companies would be large purchasers of Regional's bonds. Although state banking and insurance company statutes placed numerous restrictions on the eligibility of securities for investment by banks and insurance companies, Mr. Johnson knew that a Moody's "Aaa" rating would qualify the Regional bonds as legal investments for these institutions in most states.

In the analysis of corporate bonds for rating purposes, Moody's took into consideration a wide variety of factors including the nature of the business, the importance of its products in the economy, the history of the company, past record, significant statistical ratios, indenture provisions, and intangible factors. In connection with statistics, however, Moody's did not attempt to reduce such ratios to any simple form of measurement that would quickly identify an issue with a specific rating group. "Aaa" was assigned only to those issues where protection was strong, where future changes were likely to be small, and where the element of long-term risk was at a minimum.

Mr. Johnson thought that Regional should follow a conservative financial policy and that such a policy would require that income before interest and taxes exceed the interest payments on any bond issue by at least six times in good years such as 1952–53. The bonds should have a senior lien on fixed assets with a book value well in excess of the amount of the issue and should represent no more than 50% of the company's capitalization. If a sinking fund requirement existed, profits after taxes and before preferred dividends should cover the sinking fund by at least three times in good years. This degree of coverage of interest and sinking fund payments in good years would insure investors adequate protection in poor years because of the basic stability in Regional's operations.

The cost to the company of issuing Aaa bonds would be about 3⅝% on an annual basis after usual fees and expenses of issue. Any interest payment would be considered as an expense for tax purposes. Mr. Johnson thought that purchasers would require a sinking fund arrangement; for planning purposes he projected an annual sinking fund requirement equal to 2% of the face value of the issue. With a 40-year bond maturity, this sinking fund would leave 20% of the issue outstanding at maturity. This balance could be refunded by the sale of an appropriate security issue at that time.

A number of preferred stock issues of utilities had been placed in recent months, and Mr. Johnson thought that some preferred stock could be included in the revised capitalization. For the purposes of planning, he used the figure of 4.5% dividend cost after expenses of issue. Under current market conditions he thought that an annual retirement fund of about 2% of the original issue would be necessary. The principal buyers of such an issue would be trusts and insurance companies.

Mr. Johnson knew that bonds and preferred stock, treated as a group, could not exceed 70% of total capitalization. He felt, furthermore, that sound financial practice would require that bond interest and preferred dividends should not exceed 65% of net earnings after taxes in a good year.

Market demand for the common stock of utilities had been encouraging for some time; a number of important state utility regulatory commissions had started what appeared to be a nationwide trend in allowing rate increases, thus foreshadowing more generous common stock earnings. National had already begun negotiations with underwriters for the sale of the proposed issue of newly created common stock. The underwriters had suggested that a price to the public of $29.75 a share with proceeds to the company of $29.20 a share would be appropriate, provided that senior securities did not exceed the limits stated above and that general market conditions did not change significantly before the offering date. It was planned to assign no-par value to the stock. This was common practice in the state in which Regional was incorporated. An annual cash dividend rate of $2.00 a share, which would yield 6.7% at a price of $29.75, was planned. Mr. Johnson thought that common stock dividends could equal 75% of the earnings available to the common stock after deducting the sinking fund payments and still have the common stock dividends considered reasonably safe. The underwriters had indicated that a very large issue of common stock could be sold to the public without prejudicing further issues during the following three-year period. Such a stock would be bought by many individuals seeking income, as well as by trusts and certain insurance companies.

With this information at hand, Mr. Johnson began the task of designing the precise terms of the newly created package of securities for Regional. As already indicated, these securities would first be given to National in exchange for Regional's existing common stock. National would then sell these securities to the public. Mr. Johnson's tentative plan was to sell first the newly created common stock of Regional. Shortly thereafter he planned to sell the senior securities of Regional. Separate sales were planned because the respective securities would be sold largely to segmented markets, and the prior sale of the new common stock would give added protection and strength to the senior securities, thus facilitating their distribution.

Exhibit 1

NATIONAL LIGHT AND ELECTRIC COMPANY
CONDENSED BALANCE SHEET OF REGIONAL UTILITIES, INC. AS OF DECEMBER 31, 1952

ASSETS	
Current assets	$ 19,308,656
Fixed assets (net)	208,893,866
Total assets	$228,202,522
LIABILITIES	
Current liabilities	$ 34,919,820
Capitalization	193,282,702
Total liabilities	$228,202,522

Exhibit 2

NATIONAL LIGHT AND ELECTRIC COMPANY
CONDENSED INCOME STATEMENTS OF REGIONAL UTILITIES, INC., 1947–53
(In millions)

	1947	*1948*	*1949*	*1950*	*1951*	*1952*	*1953**
Gross sales	$36.6	$40.1	$51.1	$57.9	$60.0	$64.2	$68.6
Operating expenses	20.1	23.9	31.3	35.1	37.3	39.2	41.4
Operating income	$16.5	$16.2	$19.8	$22.8	$22.7	$25.0	$27.2
Other income	0.4	0.2	0.3	0.3	0.5	0.6	1.0
Net income before income taxes†	$16.9	$16.4	$20.1	$23.1	$23.2	$25.6	$28.2
Income taxes‡	8.1	7.9	9.7	12.7	13.9	14.8	14.1
Net income	$ 8.8	$ 8.5	$10.4	$10.4	$ 9.3	$10.8	$14.1

* Estimated without allowance for expansion program.

† As stated in the case, Regional Utilities as a subsidiary of National was capitalized with only common stock outstanding. Interest expense therefore was negligible under Regional's existing all-equity capital structure.

‡ Includes excess profits taxes during the Korean war.

LIQUIGAS, INC.

^^^

In the fall of 1952, Mr. Bayard, treasurer of the Liquigas corporation, was studying a list of projects that had been proposed for capital investment in 1953. At the next meeting of the company's directors, to be held late in October, Mr. Bayard would be asked to make recommendations as to which projects should be adopted and how they should be financed.

The Liquigas corporation, located in Hillandale, New Jersey, was a large producer of diversified industrial and commercial chemicals and allied products. Organized in 1926 to manufacture certain chemical compounds used in the oil refining industry, the company's sales volume expanded rapidly until 1931. During the depression years, operations were so successfully cut back that despite the poor position of the industry, the company showed a small profit in every year from 1931 to 1935. Interest payments were met on bank loans and on a mortgage bond issue, and cash dividends, though on a greatly reduced basis, were paid to shareholders each year.

In the latter thirties, the company continued to expand its product line, and during World War II it reached a position of prominence in the industry. The resurgence of demand for chemicals in the postwar period pushed the industry's and the company's sales to record levels.

In 1952 the company remained a leading producer of chemical compounds for the petroleum refining industry, and in addition had diversified its product line through the manufacture of polyethylene and polyvinyl plastics, soil conditioners, anhydrous ammonia for agricultural use, and a range of commercial and household chemicals. The company's directors had recently approved participation in a government-industry project leading to the improvement of synthetic rubber manufacture, and they were considering the advisability of taking part in certain aspects of nuclear chemical development at the request of a government agency.

Sales volume for the entire year 1952 was estimated on the basis of the current rate of sales to be approximately $27,500,000; a net profit of $2,800,000 after taxes was predicted.

The company's management had adopted a system of capital budgeting which required that each individual department submit the capital construction projects desired for the coming year; these programs contained an estimate of the funds required and an estimate of the average annual rate of return on the initial amount of the investment, after allowance for costs, including depreciation and amortization sufficient to maintain the earning power of the project by replacements, but before consideration of taxes. Estimates of the rate of return were made very carefully, and in recent years had been proved reliable. The most promising proposals for calendar 1953 which had been submitted to Mr. Bayard are summarized as follows:

Nature of Proposal	*Amount*	*Annual Rate of Return before Income Taxes*
Mechanization of accounting and inventory control system	$ 118,000	25%
Acquisition of additional chemical storage tanks	1,750,000	20
Purchase of railroad tank cars and loading equipment	240,000	20
Purchase of leased space and facilities—Arkansas	800,000	15
Additions for plastics division, including machinery	1,100,000	14
Replacement of power facilities—New Jersey plant	620,000	12
Construction of new materials handling system	460,000	10–15
Construction of facilities for loading and transfer of explosives to barges—New Jersey	900,000	10
Purchase of New Jersey affiliate to handle export sales and relations	400,000	8
Modernization of New Jersey office building—relocation of functional departments	150,000	4
Purchase of adjacent office building offered for sale	1,000,000	4
	$7,538,000	

The company's expansion policies were based on a desire to satisfy only those demands that seemed to be of a permanent nature, and to avoid speculative prospects, however attractive they might appear. On the basis of this policy, Mr. Bayard did not feel that any of the above proposals would compromise the long-range interests of the company; each one would be a desirable addition to the company's assets. Sales prospects for 1953 and 1954 were very promising; sales of plastics products had far exceeded expectations and export sales had continued above the expected rate. The management had informed the company's stockholders in a midyear letter that they could look forward to a continued increase in sales volume and a corresponding expansion of facilities for at least the next two years.

Mr. Bayard knew that the proposed projects would have to be financed largely through new funds obtained outside the company. The level of earnings remaining after dividends was insufficient to supply all desirable projects, so Mr. Bayard planned to count on no more than $1,750,000 as being available through internally generated sources for the 1953 projects as listed.

Mr. Bayard knew that new financing could be accomplished in several ways. The probable terms attending the sale of additional securities had been discussed with underwriters and bankers from time to time during recent months. Reviewing the possibilities of obtaining funds from outside sources, Mr. Bayard contemplated the following alternatives:

1. *Bonds*

Mr. Bayard knew from conversations with underwriters that it would be possible to sell mortgage bonds on the present market. Such a sale could be made to the public or could be privately placed with institutional investors. Bonds would be of 20–30 year maturity and would carry a sinking fund provision. The cost to the company would be approximately 3% annually after usual expenses.

Unsecured debentures with a shorter maturity were also possible and would cost the company between 3 and 3½% annually.

2. *Preferred Stock*

Underwriters had told Mr. Bayard that it would be possible to sell a large issue of preferred stock on the present market at an attractive price. Such an issue would be cumulative and convertible and would carry with it a sinking fund or retirement provision. After expenses but before consideration of income taxes, the cost to the company would be between 5% and 5½%. The company's outstanding 4½% preferred stock was currently selling at about 100.

3. *Common Stock*

The company's postwar growth had been financed largely through the sale of common stock; an issue sold in 1948 had been very successful and underwriters thought that a large issue, covering the present requirements, could be sold without difficulty at a return to the company, after all costs, of $41 per share. The stock currently outstanding yielded 5 6% on the present market price of 44½ and the cash dividend rate of $2.50; shares were listed on a national exchange and were actively traded. Since 1946, the price-earnings ratio of the common stock had varied from 6.5 to 10.1: the ratio was currently 6.7.

In 1951, the company had paid federal income taxes of 52%, and in 1952 it expected to pay this same rate as well as excess profits taxes of 8%. Mr. Bayard decided to use an overall figure of 60% in computing the future impact of taxes on earnings. He also decided to use the above costs of financing for the various alternatives, in determining the costs of obtaining outside capital.

In considering the profitability of financing a given new project, with a determinable rate of return, through the use of new money, Mr. Bayard had always in the past used a weighted average cost of capital—that is, the cost of the various types of equity and debt capital weighted by the proportion of each type in the company's current capital structure. The present cost of capital computed by this method was 7.7%, reached as follows:

Type of Capital	*Earnings Required to Cover Cost, before Taxes*	*Stated Amount (Millions)*	*Weights*	*Weighted Average Calculation*
Fixed debt	3%	$ 8.0	32	96
Preferred stock* $\frac{5\%‡}{0.4}$	13	2.4	10	130
Common stock† $\frac{5.6\%‡}{0.4}$	14	9.6	39	546
Surplus	No cost	4.8	19	0
		$24.8	100	772 = 7.7

* 24,000 shares, $100 par.
† 411,428 shares, no par, book value $35 per share on 12/31/51.
‡ Current yield = $\frac{\text{Dividend}}{\text{Price}}$.

The "Surplus" account was carried at no cost, since it was available and would not have to be raised outside the company.

Mr. Bayard had recently attended a businessmen's "round table" discussion, at which the cost of financing in relation to rates of return had been the chief topic. At this meeting, an economist had advanced several interesting arguments in favor of using the "marginal cost" of capital as the criterion for determining to what extent additional funds should be invested in productive capacity. On this basis, after allowances for depreciation and after consideration of taxes, any project that would return more than the cost of the least expensive method of financing, again after tax considerations, was a legitimate and desirable investment.

In Mr. Bayard's opinion, employment of the "marginal rate" computation would make all the projects appear desirable, since it was possible to finance the total requirements in part with mortgage bonds, costing only 3%, and in part with reinvested earnings, costing nothing.

AMERICAN TELEPHONE AND TELEGRAPH COMPANY

^^

In late 1959, the treasurer of the American Telephone and Telegraph Company began a review of the company's major financial policy guidelines. The decision to undertake this review was made in response to both increasing outside criticism of the company's financial policies and to a recognized need to reexamine these policies in the context of evolving and anticipated economic, competitive, and regulatory conditions.

The American Telephone and Telegraph Company and its 20 principal operating telephone subsidiaries furnished local and long-distance telephone service to over 80% of all the telephones in service in the United States. It operated a network of wire and radio circuits and related equipment for communication between and through the territories of its own telephone affiliates and those of other telephone companies, and for interconnection between telephone systems in this country and abroad. A subsidiary, the Western Electric Company, Inc., manufactured telephone equipment and apparatus for the company and its telephone subsidiaries. Another affiliate, the Bell Telephone Laboratories, Inc., conducted scientific research, development. and engineering work on behalf of both A. T. & T. and Western Electric.

Exhibit 1 summarizes a number of statistics indicating the extent and pattern of A. T. & T.'s growth between 1945 and 1959. Annual consolidated operating revenues are shown to have increased from $1.9 billion to $7.4 billion, and gross plant investment from $5.7 billion to $22.2 billion over the period. The amount and financing of this plant expansion program are summarized by years in Exhibit 2 for the years between 1955 and 1959. Exhibit 2 shows that annual capital expenditures ranged from $1.6 billion to $2.2 billion and totaled almost $10.9 billion over the five-year period. The sources of the funds used to finance these expenditures are shown to have been depreciation, capital stock, long-term debt, and retained earnings in that order. Additional comparative financial statistics of A. T. & T. for the years from 1949 to 1959 are summarized in Exhibit 3. Exhibit 4 presents similar data for the General Telephone & Electronics Corporation. General Telephone was the second largest telephone and manufacturing holding company operating in the United States in 1959.

The company's external financing program made it one of the dominant factors in the postwar capital market. Between 1946 and 1959, for example, American Telephone and Telegraph Company and its affiliates issued about 23% of all new common stock. It also placed 6% of all corporate bonds.

An important difference between A. T. & T. and most other private enterprises was that both the size and the profitability of its investments were determined in large measure by exogenous forces not fully under the control of management. As regulated public utilities, the company and its telephone affiliates were typically required by law or regulatory fiat to provide whatever level of service the public demanded and was willing to pay for. As discussed below, the rate of return on these investments was regulated also. Because the company could not arbitrarily limit capital expenditures to internally generated sources of funds, or even to internally generated sources plus a certain amount of debt, the company's debt and dividend policies ultimately determined its overall capitalization.

Beginning in 1921, A. T. & T. followed virtually unchanging policies towards dividends and debt. From 1921 to 1959 the company maintained a constant $9 per share dividend policy, even during those years when it was necessary to use retained earnings to do so. This policy was based on a belief that the best way for a regulated utility such as A. T. & T. to attract and hold the goodwill and faith of a large number of small shareholders was through regular reasonable dividends coupled with the right to make further investments on favorable terms as the business required new funds. As far as debt policy was concerned, from 1921 on A. T. & T. maintained an average debt ratio of about one third. This was as much debt as management thought the company could have while at the same time protecting the long-run safety of the business.

Despite the apparent success of these policies over the years, critics of A. T. & T. argued that the company's financial policies were both ill conceived and poorly executed as far as the interests of both shareholders and ratepayers were concerned. These critics claimed management had overestimated the hazards inherent in the telephone business and that the company should have used more debt and paid out less of its earnings than it had. An important consequence of its past policies was said to be that despite the company's tremendous postwar growth in profits after taxes, earnings per share had shown only a modest increase and dividends per share none at all. Apart from these leverage considerations, however, the critics also saw what they considered to be significant cost of capital penalties inherent in the company's traditional financing policies. Debt was seen to be a lower cost source of funds than equity, as well as a deductible expense for income tax purposes. Along these lines it was argued that given its 1959 capital base, A. T. & T. could have saved up to $100 million in taxes and lower capital costs per year for every five percentage point increase in its debt ratio up to a 45% or 50% level of debt. The critics also contended that "the highly conservative and inflexible debt and dividend policies" of the company had led it to adopt a costly financing strategy during the 1950's as regards the timing of new capital issues. Instead of selling convertible debentures and retaining a small proportion of earnings in the early postwar years, it was argued by some that A. T. & T. should have sold medium-grade bonds in an effort both to save taxes and to put itself in a position to sell common stock cheaply in the subsequent bull market.

All of the above arguments relate primarily to what might be considered the stockholders' interest in the company. Being a regulated public utility, however, A. T. & T.'s financial policies were also subject to close scrutiny and regulation by numerous federal, state, and local government regulatory agencies. These various regulatory bodies were established to protect the interests of consumers and investors alike through regulation of rates, services, and competition. Although many factors were taken into account by these government agencies in determining allowed rates, the guiding principle was that rates be high enough to cover full operating expenses plus capital costs including debt service and dividends. As this principle had been interpreted in practice, a fair return was quite generally considered to be equal to a company's weighted average cost of capital. This being the case, numerous critics of A. T. & T.'s financial policies argued that the consumer's interest in low rates would be better served if the company adopted a higher target debt ratio and a lower dividend payout. In short, it was contended that A. T. & T.'s average cost of capital could be reduced over the long run by the adoption of less conservative financial policies and that the savings so obtained could in turn be passed along to telephone users in the form of lower rates.

As part of the company's continuing program of reviewing its financial policies, the treasurer of A. T. & T. requested in 1959 that his staff prepare a statistical comparison of several electric utilities, A. T. & T., and a group of selected manufacturing companies. It was his intention to use the results of this comparison to reevaluate A. T. & T.'s historical financial policies from the viewpoints of risk, credit, and cost of capital and particularly to think about these matters in the light of the arguments so often advanced by A. T. & T.'s critics. The results as well as a staff analysis of the statistical comparison requested by the treasurer are included in the following appendix.

Exhibit 1

AMERICAN TELEPHONE AND TELEGRAPH COMPANY

FACTS ABOUT THE BELL SYSTEM

	12/31/45	12/31/50	12/31/55	12/31/59
Telephones	22,445,519	35,343,440	46,218,233	57,944,404
Dial operated	14,504,851	26.700,319	40,041,368	55,478,225
Percent dial operated	64.6	75.5	86.6	95.7
Central offices	7,374	8,470	9,751	10,754
Average dial telephone conversations	90,548,000	140,782,000	168,936,000	208,042,000
Gross plant (000's)	$ 5,702,057	$ 10,101,522	$ 15,340,495	$ 22,205,475
Operating revenues (000's)	$ 1,930,889	$ 3,261,528	$ 5,297,043	$ 7,392,997
Profits after taxes (000's)	$ 177,057	$ 346,962	$ 664,244	$ 1,113,152
Employees:				
Bell System	387,300	523,251	615,895	582,860
Western Electric Company	80,029	73,458	120,054	134,867
Bell Tel. Laboratories	7,198	5,757	9,680	11,308
Total	474,527	602,466	745,629	729,035
A. T. & T. Co. shareowners	683,897	985,583	1,408,851	1,736,681
A. T. & T. Co. shares outstanding	60,498,753	85,847,868	162,347,880	214,630,257
Earnings per share	$ 2.92	$ 4.04	$ 4.09	$ 5.19

Source: *1959 Annual Report.*

Exhibit 2

AMERICAN TELEPHONE AND TELEGRAPH COMPANY

ANNUAL FUNDS FLOW ANALYSIS, 1955–59

(Dollar amounts in millions)

	1955		*1956*		*1957*		*1958*		*1959*		*Total 1955–59*	
	$	%	$	%	$	%	$	%	$	%	$	%
SOURCES OF FUNDS												
Depreciation charges	488	18.9	535	19.3	763	27.3	843	25.8	930	31.9	3,559	24.8
Increase in current liabilities	271	10.5	81	2.9	15	0.5	110	3.4	121	4.1	598	4.2
Increase in debt	375	14.6	242	8.7	1,070	38.3	354	10.9	390	13.4	2,431	17.0
Increase in capital stock	777	30.2	1,161	41.9	117	4.2	1,000	30.7	366	12.5	3,421	23.9
Net income	664	25.8	755	27.2	829	29.7	952	29.2	1,113	38.1	4,313	30.1
Total sources	2,575	100.0	2,774	100.0	2,794	100.0	3,259	100.0	2,920	100.0	14,322	100.0
USES OF FUNDS												
Increase in current assets	529	20.5	55	2.0	(456)	(16.3)	455	14.0	20	0.7	603	4.2
Expenditures on fixed assets, in unconsolidated subsidiaries, and minority interests	1,590	61.8	2,203	79.4	2,676	95.8	2,193	67.3	2,212	75.7	10,874	75.9
Dividends	456	17.7	516	18.6	574	20.5	611	18.7	688	23.6	2,845	19.9
Total uses	2,575	100.0	2,774	100.0	2,794	100.0	3,259	100.0	2,920	100.0	14,322	100.0

Source: Published financial statements.

Exhibit 3

AMERICAN TELEPHONE AND TELEGRAPH COMPANY

COMPARATIVE FINANCIAL STATISTICS, 1949–59

Year	Gross Revenues ($ Mill.)	% Op.* Inc. to Net Plt.	Gross for Com. %†	Net Income ($ Mill.)	Working Capital ($ Mill.)	Common Equity %	No. Shares Outstanding (000)‡	Earnings per Share $‡	Dividends per Share $‡	Dividend Payout %	Price Range‡	Price × Earnings	Average Yield %
1949	2,893	4.39	8.0	232.9	23.2	48.6	75,783	3.07	3.00	97	52^2–46	15.6	6.24
1950	3,262	5.88	10.6	347.0	0.1	51.9	85,848	4.04	3.00	74	53^7–48^6	12.7	5.84
1951	3,640	5.50	10.0	364.9	87.1	54.9	99,537	3.67	3.00	81	54^3–50	14.2	5.76
1952	4,040	5.47	10.0	406.7	223.2	58.4	116,937	3.48	3.00	86	53^6–50^2	15.0	5.76
1953	4,417	5.55	10.8	478.5	320.2	58.8	126,846	3.77	3.00	79	53^6–50^6	13.8	5.73
1954	4,784	5.88	11.4	549.9	266.3	63.3	144,483	3.81	3.00	78	59^3–52	14.6	5.38
1955	5,297	6.30	12.5	664.2	524.0	64.0	162,348	4.09	3.00	73	62^4–57^4	14.2	5.14
1956	5,825	6.10	13.0	755.9	497.5	66.2	188,682	4.01	3.00	75	62^3–55	14.6	5.11
1957	6,314	5.96	13.2	829.8	27.7	62.3	193,944	4.28	3.00	70	60 –53^3	13.2	5.30
1958	6,771	6.59	14.1	952.3	372.8	63.6	211,636	4.50	3.00	67	75^6–56	14.6	4.55
1959	7,393	7.08	15.1	1,113.2	271.0	63.8	214,630	5.19	3.15	61	89 –74^7	15.8	3.84

* Ratio of net operating income to net plant. Excludes income from nonconsolidated subsidiaries.
† Ratio between balance available for common equity and operating revenues.
‡ Adjusted for 3 for 1 split 4/59.

Background: American Telephone and Telegraph Company and its subsidiaries form the Bell System. They furnish telephone and other services, and own 60 million or about 82% of the total telephones in the country. Bell Telephone Laboratories, which engages in research, and Western Electric, which manufactures equipment, are wholly owned, but their accounts are not consolidated. . . . Expansion since the war has been rapid; gross plant has increased $16.4 billion and has required large amounts of new capital. Nearly 96% of system telephones are now dial operated. The 7/59 dividend increase, following 3 for 1 split in April, represented first change in policy since 1922. System management is top quality and aggressive in all phases of operation.

Source: *Moody's Handbook of Widely Held Common Stocks*, second 1960 edition.

Exhibit 4

AMERICAN TELEPHONE AND TELEGRAPH COMPANY

Comparative Financial Statistics of General Telephone & Electronics Corporation, 1949–59

Year	Gross* Revenues ($ Mill.)	% Op. Inc. to Net Plt.†	Gross for Com. %‡	Net Income ($000)	Working Capital ($ Mill.)	Common Equity %	No. Shares Outstanding (000)§	Earnings per Share $§	Dividends per Share $§	Dividend Payout %	Price Range§	Price × Earnings	Average Yield %
1949...	60.7	3.89	4.3	3,040	4.6	22	8,073	0.32	0.30	92	4^{5}–3^{3}	12.4	7.46
1950...	70.0	4.35	5.3	4,136	...	21	9,189	0.39	0.30	76	4^{4}–3^{5}	10.4	7.32
1951...	84.7	4.36	5.9	5,529	8.2	22	12,960	0.39	0.30	76	4^{6}–4	13.3	6.78
1952...	102.0	5.14	7.6	8,763	13.7	24	16,137	0.48	0.30	61	5^{2}–4^{3}	10.1	6.12
1953...	127.9	6.15	10.5	13,952	5.8	32	22,779	0.59	0.30	50	6^{6}–5^{1}	10.1	5.48
1954...	188.5	6.43	12.6	23,823	9.4	34.5	34,257	0.51	0.36	51	8^{2}–6^{5}	11.1	4.63
1955...	209.8	6.76	14.5	30,507	...	33.3	34,806	0.88	0.53	61	15^{1}–7^{6}	13.0	4.67
1956...	259.3	6.57	16.5	43,628	24.8	37.3	44,694	0.97	0.55	57	15 –12^{5}	14.4	3.92
1957...	289.0	5.90	15.6	45,733	6.1	33.7	44,592	1.01	0.62	61	15 –12^{1}	13.4	4.53
1958...	895.1	8.18	6.6	59,453	28.5	39.9	60,039	0.98	0.67	68	21 –13^{4}	17.6	3.86
1959...	1,081.0	8.38	6.6	72,253	207.2	43.1	66,027	1.08	0.70	65	28^{3}–20	21.4	2.88

* 1949–57 telephone only.
† Ratio of net operating income to net plant.
‡ Ratio between balance available for common equity and operating revenues.
§ Adjusted for 50% stock dividends in 1954 and 1955 and 3 for 1 split 5/60.

Background: Name of this telephone and manufacturing holding company was changed to its present form with the acquisition of Sylvania Electric Products in March 1959. Basically telephone, it has 3.8 mill. stations, over 90% dial operated. Under aggressive management, postwar expansion has been rapid. . . . Gross telephone plant 12/31/59 totaled $1,380 mill.; gross manufacturing plant, $209 mill. . . . But system revenue of $1.08 bill. in 1959 was divided $375 mill. telephone (34.7%) and $706 mill. manufacturing (65.3%) . . . 1960 capital expenditures will total about $280 mill. The company expects to spend $1 billion for expansion in the next five years.

Source: *Moody's Handbook of Widely Held Common Stocks*, second 1960 edition.

APPENDIX

CAPITAL STRUCTURE AS RELATED TO RISK AND CREDIT

I. Problem of Appropriate Capital Structure

A. A number of considerations are involved in determining appropriate capital structure for a particular business.

1. Appropriate capital structure for a particular enterprise is a matter of experience and sound business judgment.

a) No mathematical or statistical formula can determine proper capital structure.

2. Although debt-free capitalization is ideal from many points of view, in practice, companies having to obtain the major portion of new capital requirements from the public have found it advantageous to have some portion of debt in their capital structure.

a) Bond market offers a large source of capital not otherwise available.

(1) Many institutional investors can invest in common stocks to a limited degree only, and others limit investments largely to bonds as a matter of preference or policy.

b) It may be necessary to resort to borrowing at times when conditions are unfavorable for equity financing on reasonable terms.

3. Assuming an excessive debt burden is unwise if conditions are favorable for a more conservative policy.

a) It is necessary to maintain a margin of borrowing power to provide for financing at times when it is impossible to sell stock.

b) Debt in any amount carries with it the problem of refunding in the future under conditions which cannot be predicted.

4. Factors to be considered in determining an appropriate capital structure fall into two major categories.

a) Nature and overall risks of the business.

b) Necessity for maintaining high credit.

(1) Particularly important to a growing industry such as the Bell System, which must enter capital markets frequently, to raise new capital and refund existing obligations.

5. It is essential that the debt ratio be kept from rising to higher levels than these factors warrant, for capital structure is relatively inflexible. Errors of judgment in this regard cannot be readily corrected in periods of adversity.

II. Nature and Overall Risks of the Business

A. Certain basic risks are inherent in every business, and they vary considerably among industries.

1. In comparing different industries these risks are related essentially to:
   a) The nature of the demand existing for the industry's product, and
   b) The operating characteristics of the industry.
2. These basic risks are reflected in the earnings experience of the enterprise.
   a) The degree of movement that is apt to occur in the earnings under changing economic conditions is a major factor in determining the balance that is advisable between debt and equity capital in the business.
   b) A company facing risk of widely fluctuating earnings may face serious difficulties in periods of low earnings, and therefore, cannot carry as high a debt as a company with relatively stable earnings.

B. These differences in risk can be seen in a comparison of overall risks of Bell System, electric utilities, and manufacturing companies.
1. Comparison of demand for the product (Chart 1).
   a) Demand is reflected in revenues of the Bell System and electric power industry and in sales of manufacturing industry.
   b) Although general trend has been similar for the three groups, the electric industry's revenues have been most stable, while the manufacturing industry's sales have shown the widest fluctuations.
   c) Depression experience of 1930's also shows that users generally consider light and power more essential than telephone service in periods of economic stress.
      (1) From 1930 peak to the depression low, electric revenues declined less than 12%, while telephone revenues fell over 20%.
      (2) Number of electric customers declined less than 3%, as compared with 17% decline in Bell System subscribers.
   d) Changes in demand with changing economic conditions were also measured by comparing revenue changes with changes in Gross National Product, after adjustment for trend.
      (1) For every 10% change in Gross National Product there was a change of 5% in electric revenues, 8% in telephone revenues, and 11% in manufacturing sales, on the average.
      (2) On the basis of this measure, telephone revenues are more sensitive to changes in the general volume of business than electric revenues but are less sensitive than manufacturing sales.
2. Differences in operating characteristics are reflected in the operating ratio (Chart 2).
   a) Higher operating ratio involves greater risk of reduction of

income with a drop in revenues than a low operating ratio, since expenses are not susceptible of rigid control.

b) Relative risks shown by the operating ratios place the electric utilities, Bell System, and manufacturing industry in the same order as that shown by revenue stability.

(1) Over the period 1926 through 1958, electric utility operating ratio has averaged about 70%, Bell System about 84%, and manufacturing industry about 96%.

c) At present the operating ratio for electric utilities and Bell System is higher than the period average.

(1) Bell System ratio is at a level (84% in 1958) which results in a narrow margin of safety, particularly in view of the increased rigidity of expenses.

(2) The margin of safety of the electric utilities is nearly one-half greater than that of the Bell System, and indications are that their major expense factors are subject to a greater degree of contraction in the event of a business downturn.

(3) Wages are an important factor in Bell System's higher operating ratio, absorbing about 36% of total revenues, compared with about 18% for the electric utilities. (The lower wage ratio of the electric utilities is offset to some degree by fuel costs, but these are relatively flexible and can be reduced as business declines; fuel adjustment clauses in industrial and commercial contracts also offer some protection against rising fuel costs.)

C. Earnings experience reflects these basic risks.

1. When a high operating ratio is accompanied by volatile revenues, the earnings remaining for investors are subject to wide fluctuations, and it is therefore necessary to limit the debt carried by the business in order to insure adequate coverage of fixed charges at all times.

2. Comparative earnings experience measured by relative instability of rates earned on total capital, 1922–58 (Chart 3).

a) Comparison of data for Bell System, 20 large operating electric utilities, and 20 large manufacturing companies made by computing the degree of year-to-year fluctuation in earnings rates expressed as a percentage of the average rate earned.

b) Chart indicates that manufacturing company earnings fluctuate most widely, and electric earnings are most stable, while Bell System earnings fluctuate in the middle range.

(1) These results are in line with the other measures of basic risk.

c) Instability may also be measured by the degree of earnings decline that is apt to occur in periods of poor business.

(1) Bell System had considerably less stability than the

electric utilities during the severe depression of the early 1930's, when rate earned on total capital declined 51% for the Bell System and only 28% for the electrics.

(2) Similarly during the 1937–38 recession, the respective declines were 13% and 6%.

3. Comparison of debt ratios (Chart 4).

a) Debt ratios have conformed broadly to the respective instability measures for each industry.

(1) Electric utilities, with more stable earnings, have averaged about 46% debt, Bell System about 35%, and the less stable manufacturing companies about 13%.

(2) In recent years, the debt ratios of electric utility and manufacturing companies have remained close to their historical ranges.

(3) After the war, Bell System debt rose well above its previous prevailing range but in recent years has closely approached its long-term objective. This fluctuation in the debt ratio was brought about by the raising of large amounts of new capital in the postwar period in the face of inadequate earnings.

b) Close relationship exists between earnings instability and debt ratio (Chart 5).

(1) Electric utilities, with relatively stable earnings, maintain a high average debt ratio.

(2) Manufacturing companies, with relatively unstable earnings, maintain a low average debt ratio.

(3) Bell System has maintained its debt ratio in the middle ground between the two extremes, and this objective is supported by the experience of the other industries.

(4) It is clear from these studies that while the Bell System can safely maintain more debt than manufacturing industries, it would be inappropriate to incur an average debt burden anywhere near as high as the more stable electric utilities could carry.

D. Capital structure of the railroad industry.

1. Railroad industry furnishes a good example of dangers inherent in use of debt in excess of that warranted by basic risks and earnings stability of an industry.

a) Railroads over the years have relied too heavily on debt, as illustrated by data for the 20 largest roads for which data are available (Chart 6).

(1) Earnings instability measure approaches the average for the relatively unstable manufacturing companies.

(2) Debt ratio has averaged not far below the average for the relatively stable electric utilities.

b) Although none of the 20 railroads included on Chart 6 has gone through financial reorganization, a majority failed to earn debt charges at some time during the period studied.

(1) Only 7 roads were able to meet debt charges in all years; those had an average debt ratio of 31% as compared with 44% for the 13 which failed to earn charges in all years.

c) The railroads, on average, have had too large a burden of debt, and it is significant that they have been steadily reducing the proportion of debt in the capital structure, particularly in the last decade.

(1) The average debt ratio in the 20 railroads was down to 32.1% at the end of 1958.

III. NECESSITY FOR MAINTAINING CREDIT

A. A definite relationship exists between debt ratio and credit standing.

1. Study made of debt ratios and credit ratings assigned by Moody's Investors' Service (Chart 7).

a) Twenty-five largest operating electric utilities for which adequate data were available were classified as either high grade or medium grade on basis of Moody's rating of bonds. Debt ratios were then computed for each company and averaged for the two groups.

b) Debt ratio of the medium-grade group has exceeded the debt ratio of the high-grade group in every year of the period. Medium-grade group has averaged about 54% as compared with only 45% for the high-grade group.

c) Study clearly indicates that electric utilities should restrict their debt to the 45% level on the average, in order to maintain a high credit rating.

d) Because of its greater risks, the Bell System debt ratio must be lower than the electric utility level.

2. Maintenance of highest credit standing is necessary to obtain needed capital on most favorable terms.

a) Good credit means not only the ability to raise capital but also to raise it at reasonable costs.

(1) Almost any business can raise some capital at some prices.

(2) Real test of good credit is investor evaluation of a company's securities compared with high-grade competitive investment opportunities.

(3) One of the most important factors on which investors base their evaluation of a company's securities is the composition of its capital structure.

b) Capital costs vary with the credit of the company, and investors pay the highest prices for the best grade securities, at all times.

c) Price differentials between various grades of securities are subject to wide fluctuations with changes in business conditions and in the money markets.

(1) When business activity is at high levels, investors are apt to be less discriminating and to overlook, to some extent, flaws that may exist in the financial setup of a particular company.

(2) When business activity drops, investors lose their complacency and become much more demanding, with the results that price differentials between different grades of securities widen greatly.

(3) Companies that have maintained highest grade credit find they can continue to raise capital at reasonable costs, while companies with low-grade credit find that capital costs tend to increase as the economic climate worsens.

d) These cost differentials between securities of different grade are illustrated by Chart 8.

(1) Moody's public utility bond yield averages are plotted in percent of the Aaa utility average.

(2) Yields of the four highest grades of bonds spread apart in years of low business activity and come together in more prosperous years.

(3) Since 1920 the differential in yields between Baa bonds Aaa bonds has averaged 35%. Present differential is about 14%, which is below the average, as would be expected in a period of relatively good business such as the present. On the other hand, the differential went as high as 119% in the depression year 1933.

e) Conclusion inescapable that failure to maintain credit will not only cause higher capital costs at *all* times but also will raise these costs disproportionately high when business recessions occur.

B. Bell System must enter the capital markets repeatedly, not only for new capital to meet service demands but also to refund existing obligations as they mature.

1. Refunding needs alone are great, as shown by the fact that the Bell System has debt maturing in each year from 1970 through 1996, generally in large amounts (Chart 9).

a) It is important to maintain the highest credit standing to insure successful refunding operations at reasonable cost regardless of money market conditions.

2. Future financing needs make it unsafe to ignore the cost differentials caused by quality differences, merely because they happen to be low at the present time.

C. Relationship between Bell System debt ratio and credit rating (Chart 10).

1. Upper grid of chart shows that Bell System bonds sold at yields corresponding to those of high-grade public utility bonds from 1922 to 1946 and again from 1953 to 1958.

a) In 1920 and 1921, and again from 1947 to 1952, investors appraised Bell System bonds on a medium-grade basis.

2. The debt ratio plottings on the lower grid of the chart reveal the fact that investors appraised the System debt as high grade as long as the Bell System debt ratio remained below 40%. When the debt ratio exceeded 40%, investors regarded the bonds as medium grade.
3. Bell System experience clearly indicates that the debt ratio must be kept somewhat below 40% in order to maintain a high credit rating at all times. Long-term average debt ratio, allowing for a reserve borrowing margin, must be well below 40%.

IV. Conclusion as to Appropriate Debt Ratio for Bell System

A. Debt ratio average of one third is indicated as an appropriate objective by sound business judgment. Based upon:

1. Comparison of basic risks of telephone industry with other industries;
2. Indicated level required to maintain the high credit rating necessary to finance at lowest costs; and
3. Substantiation by the debt policies and views of a multitude of managements and investors.

B. Wisdom of Bell System objective of one-third debt has been proven by experience.

1. With this debt ratio the System has maintained a high investment standing for its securities, which has enabled it to raise the capital it needed.
2. Unlikely that System could have raised the capital needed in the postwar period at reasonable costs without the borrowing margin afforded by the one-third ratio at the outset.

V. Increasing Risks in the Telephone Business

A. Telephone business faces greater risks today than it has in the past.

1. This has resulted from several recent developments:
   a) Change in nature of the market for telephone service.
   b) Larger proportion of telephone revenues coming from more volatile forms of service.
   c) Changes tending to increase the rigidity of operating expenses.
2. These developments all tend to make telephone earnings more vulnerable to unfavorable changes in business conditions and must be recognized in considering the problem of an appropriate capital structure.

B. Changes in the market for telephone service are reflected in changed distribution of telephones among types of users, with an increase in proportion of those types which tend to be less permanent (Chart 11, first grid).

1. Residence telephones now about 71% of total telephones in service,

compared with prewar stable average of 60% (Chart 11, second grid).

a) In the past, residence telephones have been about 48% more volatile than business telephones, as measured by year-to-year changes.

b) In business declines, the market for residence telephones falls further than the market for business telephones.

(1) Residence telephones declined 18% during the depression of the thirties, while business telephones showed a 12% decrease.

2. Residence telephone market is now more saturated (Chart 11, third grid).

a) Percentage of households having telephones has more than doubled since 1940, increasing from 37% in 1940 to 78% in 1958.

b) Current higher proportion of subscribing households indicates that there is included among present customers an even greater proportion of those who are more likely to discontinue service in the event of a business decline.

C. Larger proportion of current revenues is derived from more volatile forms of service.

1. Toll revenues now constitute 37% of the total, compared with a consistent 30% average prior to 1940 (Chart 12, second grid).

a) Year-to-year changes have averaged about 65% greater for toll revenues than for local.

b) In depression of the thirties, toll revenues decreased 30%, while local revenues decreased 16%.

2. Greater proportion of toll revenues now derived from residence telephones, indicating a greater proportion of social calling. Customers are much more inclined to curtail social than business calling during periods of general business recession.

D. Increased rigidity of operating expenses.

1. Brought about by several factors, the most important of which is payroll expense.

a) Union contracts freeze wage rates, wage progression, and many personnel practices for the lives of the contracts, thus making it more difficult for the industry to adjust its operations quickly to changing economic conditions.

2. Greater rigidity of expenses is particularly significant in view of the reduced margin of operating income (Chart 12, third grid).

a) Ratio of net operating income to total revenues now 16%, as compared with 19% over long period prior to war.

E. Increased risks faced by the Bell System will result in greater volatility of earnings in the future than has been experienced in the past.

1. This makes it all the more imperative that the Bell System debt ratio be kept at its long-term level of approximately one third.

Chart 1

REVENUES

(Index 1930 = 100)

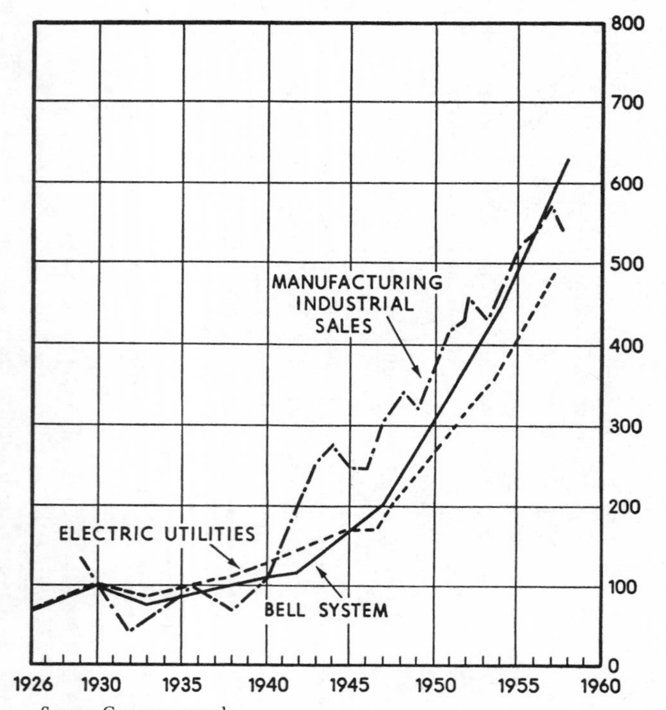

Source: Company records.

Chart 2

OPERATING RATIO

(Ratio of operating expenses including taxes to total revenues)

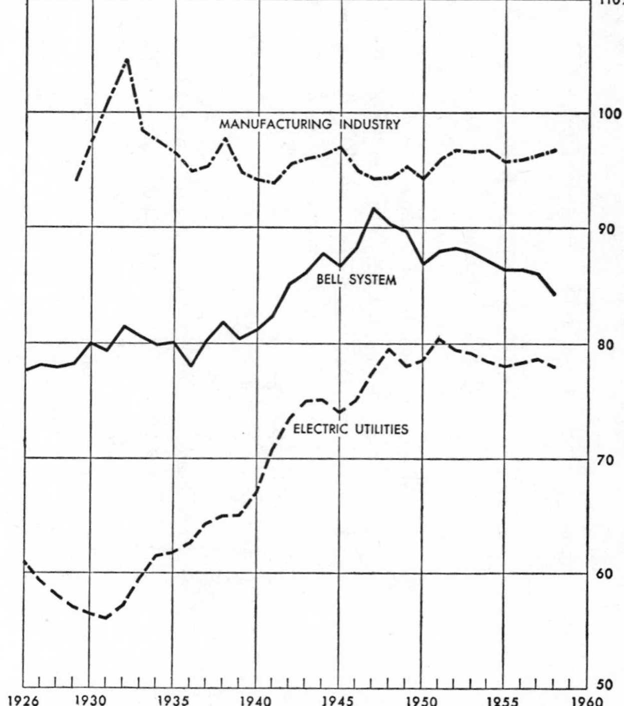

Chart 3

Instability of Rate Earned on Total Capital

(Measured by change from year to year)

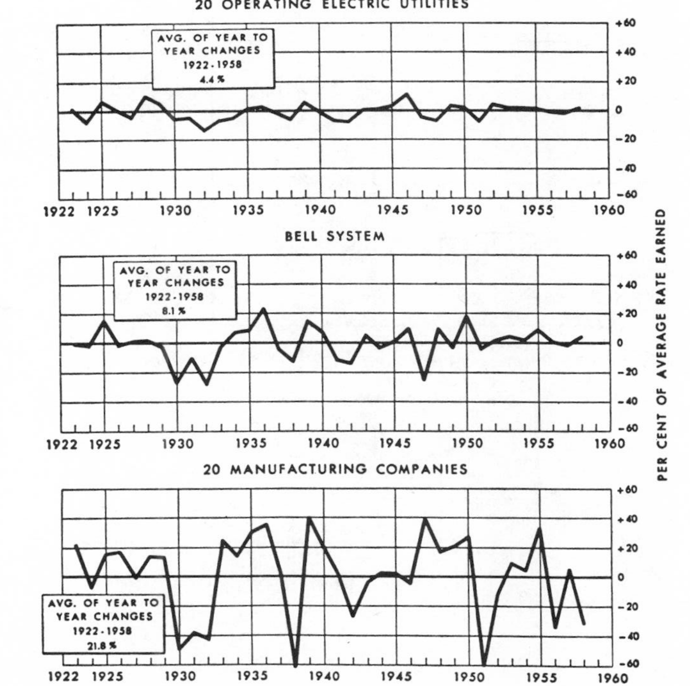

Chart 4

Debt Ratio

(Debt in percent of total capital)

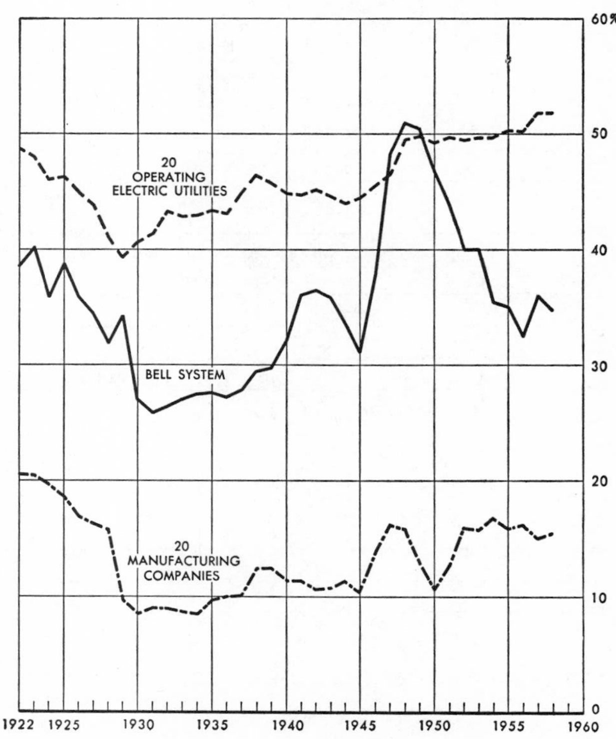

Chart 5

Earnings Instability and Debt Ratio

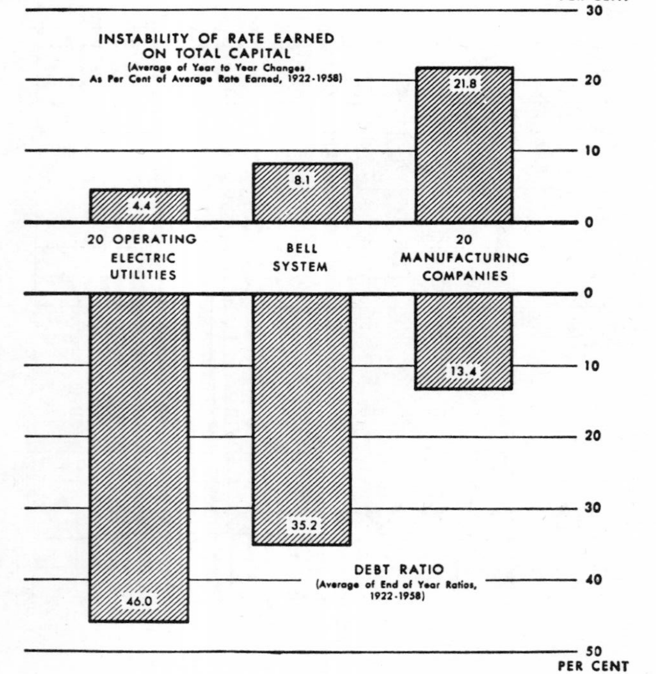

Chart 6

Earnings Instability and Debt Ratio for 20 Railroads

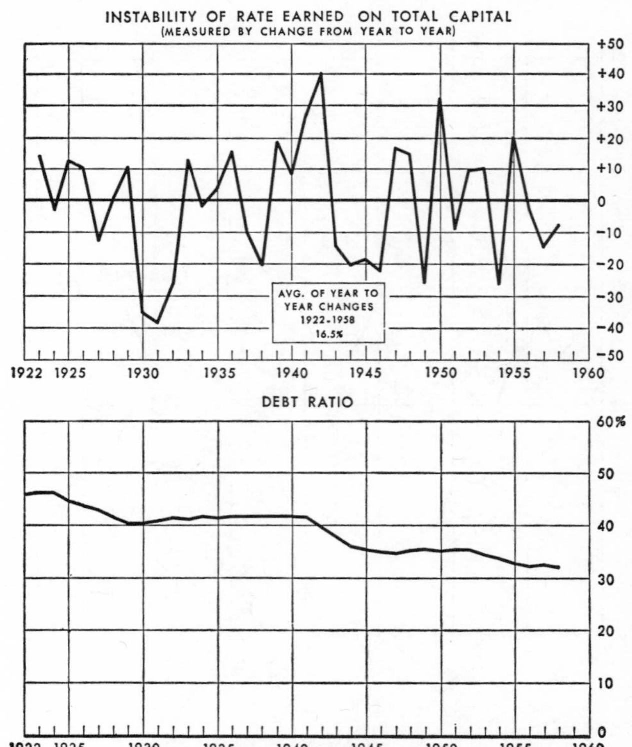

Chart 7

DEBT RATIO AND CREDIT RATING

(Twenty-five operating electric utilities grouped by Moody's bond ratings)

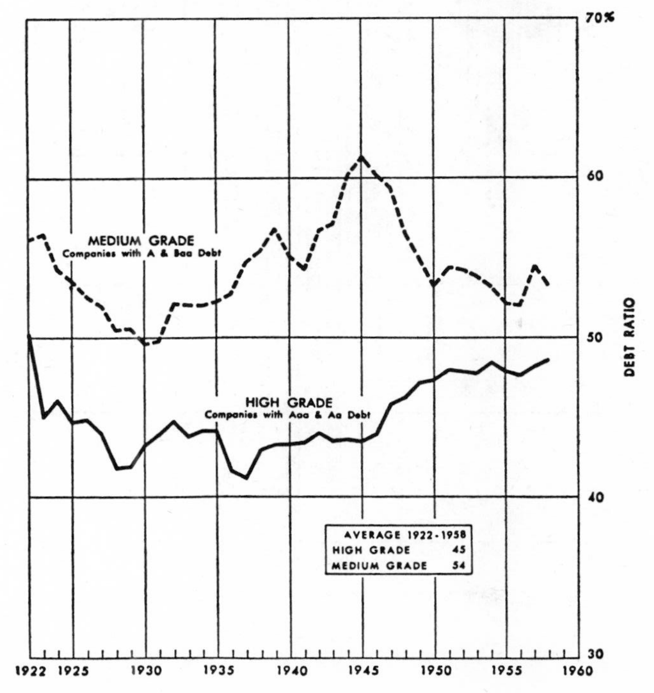

Chart 8

DEVIATIONS IN BOND YIELDS BY QUALITY GROUPS

(Moody's public utility averages in percent of Aaa utility average)

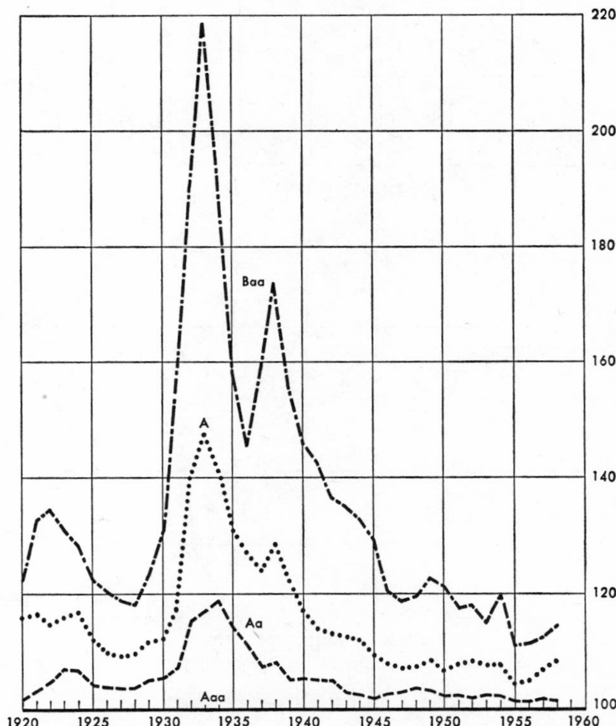

Chart 9

BELL SYSTEM DEBT* MATURING ANNUALLY, 1970–96

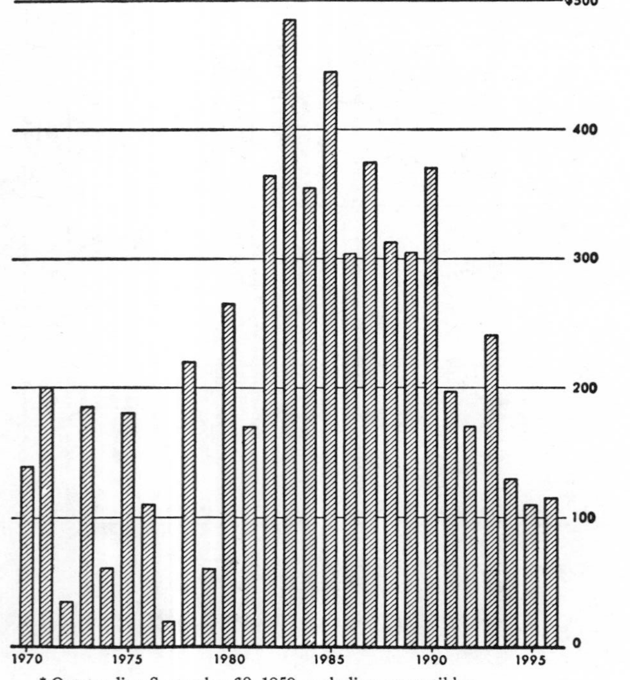

* Outstanding September 30, 1959, excluding convertibles.

Chart 10

DEVIATIONS IN BOND YIELDS*

Bell System and Moody's Aa Public Utility Averages in % of Aaa Utility Average

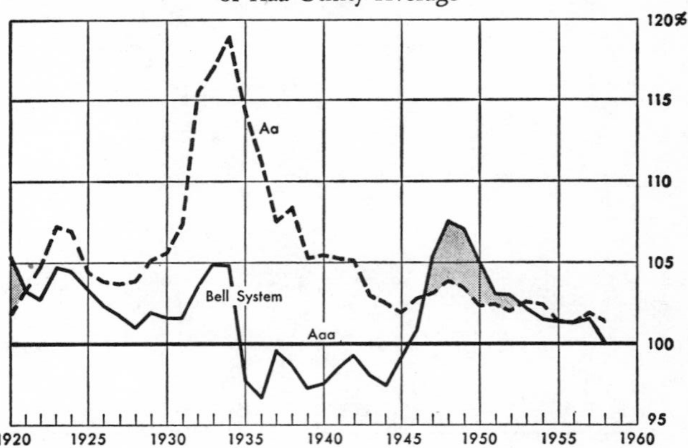

Bell System Debt Ratio

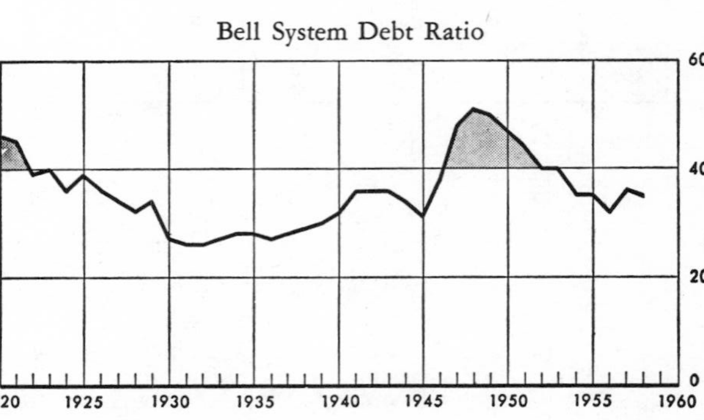

* End of year.

Chart 11

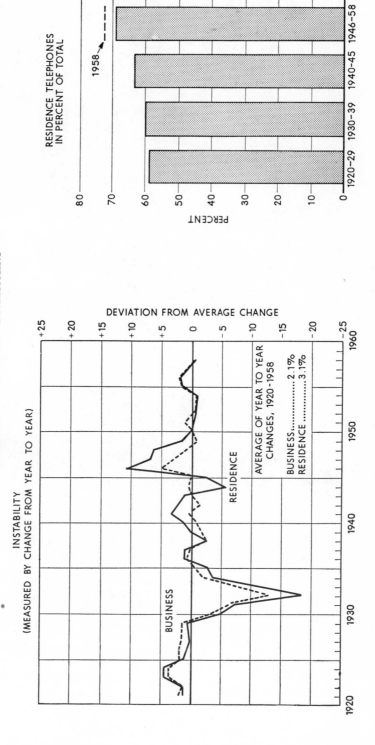

CHANGES IN TELEPHONE DEVELOPMENT

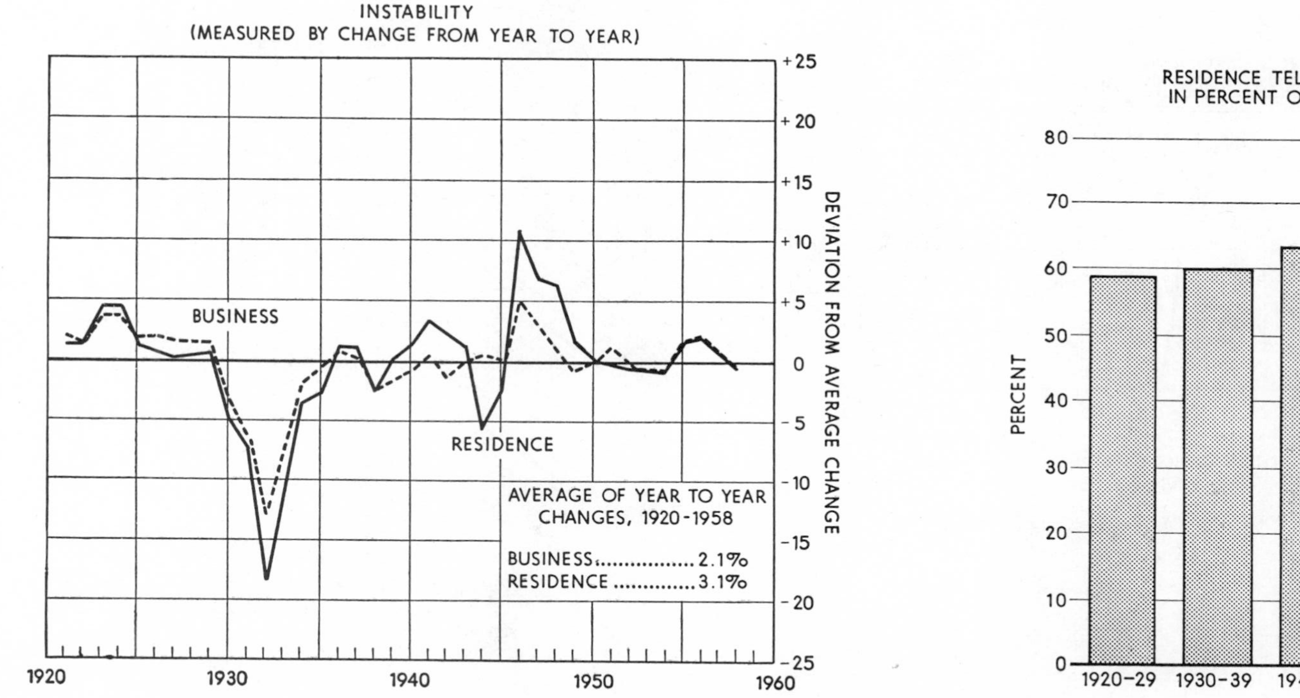

Chart 11—Concluded

PERCENT HOUSEHOLDS IN U.S.
WITH RESIDENCE TELEPHONES

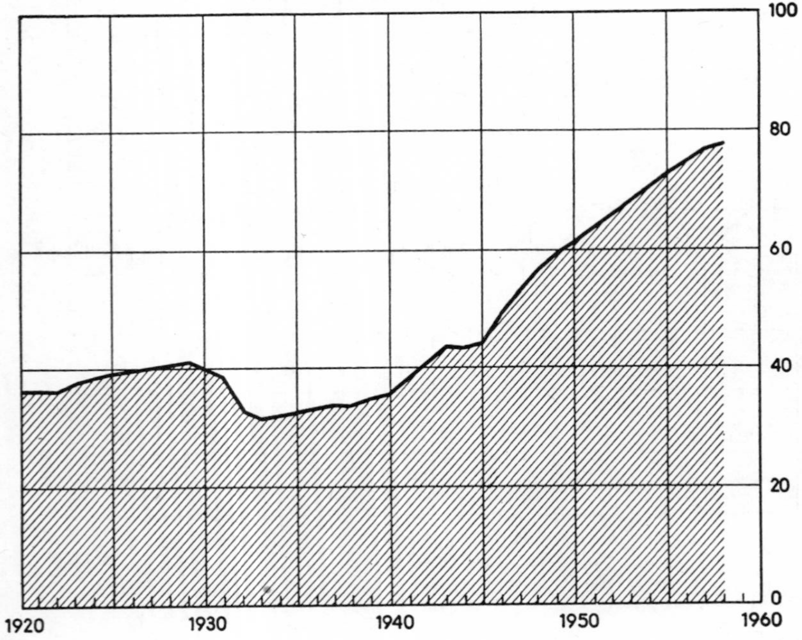

PERCENT

100
80
60
40
20
0

1920 1930 1940 1950 1960

Chart 12

CHANGES IN BELL SYSTEM REVENUES AND EARNINGS

INSTABILITY
(MEASURED BY CHANGE FROM YEAR TO YEAR)

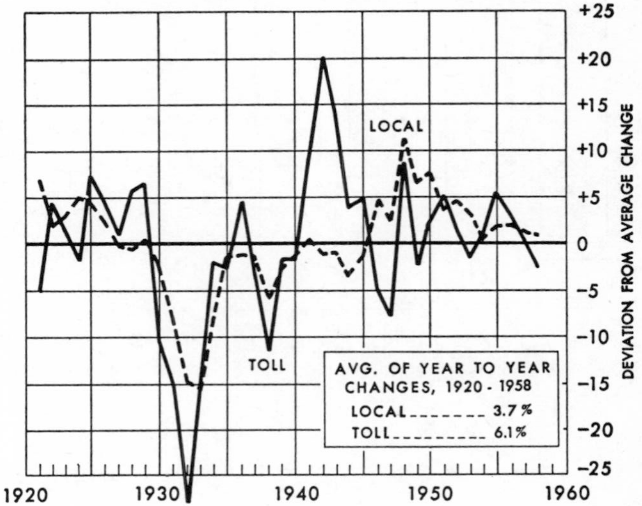

DEVIATION FROM AVERAGE CHANGE

+25
+20
+15
+10
+5
0
−5
−10
−15
−20
−25

LOCAL

TOLL

AVG. OF YEAR TO YEAR
CHANGES, 1920 - 1958
LOCAL ------- 3.7 %
TOLL --------- 6.1%

1920 1930 1940 1950 1960

Chart 12—Concluded

LIST OF COMPANIES*

25 Operating Electric Utilities

1. Baltimore Gas & Electric Co.
2. Boston Edison Co.
3. Cleveland Electric Illuminating Co.
4. Commonwealth Edison Co.
5. Consolidated Edison Co. of N.Y., Inc.
6. Consumers Power Co.
7. Detroit Edison Co.
8. Duke Power Co.
9. Duquesne Light Co.
10. Northern States Power Co.
11. Ohio Power Co.
12. Pacific Gas & Electric Co.
13. Pennsylvania Power & Light Co.
14. Philadelphia Electric Co.
15. Public Service Electric & Gas Co.
16. Southern California Edison Co.
17. Union Electric Co.
18. Virginia Electric & Power Co.
19. West Penn Power Co.
20. Wisconsin Electric Power Co.
21. Alabama Power Co.
22. Applachian Power Co.
23. Florida Power & Light Co.
24. Northern Indiana Public Service Co.
25. Public Service Co. of Colorado

20 Manufacturing Companies

1. Allied Chemical Corp.
2. American Tobacco Co.
3. Armour & Co. (Ill.)
4. Bethlehem Steel Corp.
5. Chrysler Corp.
6. E. I. du Pont de Nemours & Co.
7. Eastman Kodak Co.
8. General Electric Co.
9. General Motors Corp.
10. Goodyear Tire & Rubber Co.
11. International Harvester Co.
12. Jones & Laughlin Steel Corp.
13. Liggett & Myers Tobacco Co.
14. Republic Steel Corp.
15. R. J. Reynolds Tobacco Co.
16. Swift & Co.
17. Union Carbide Corp.
18. United States Steel Corp.
19. Westinghouse Electric Corp.
20. Youngstown Sheet & Tube Co.

20 Railroads

1. Atchison, Topeka & Santa Fe Ry. Co.
2. Atlantic Coast Line R.R. Co.
3 Baltimore & Ohio R.R. Co.
4. Chesapeake & Ohio Railway Co.
5. Chicago, Burlington & Quincy R.R. Co.
6. Delaware, Lackawanna & Western R.R. Co.
7. Great Northern Railway Co.
8. Illinois Central R.R. Co.
9. Louisville & Nashville R.R. Co.
10. New York Central R.R. Co.
11. New York, Chicago & St. Louis R.R. Co.
12. Norfolk & Western Railway Co.
13. Northern Pacific Railway Co.
14. Pennsylvania R.R. Co.
15. Reading Co.
16. Southern Pacific Co.
17. Southern Railway Co.
18. Texas & New Orleans R.R. Co.
19. Texas & Pacific Railway Co.
20. Union Pacific R.R. Co.

* The above companies were selected on the basis of size of assets at the end of 1949. They represent the largest companies in their respective fields for which adequate financial data are generally available since 1922.

Sources: Primarily Moody's Public Utility, Railroad, and Industrial Manuals. Also annual reports to stockholders and reports filed with such governmental agencies as ICC, FPC, and SEC.

CYCLOPS CEMENT COMPANY (Abridged)

On May 27, 1965, Mr. Clinton Howe, a director of the Cyclops Cement Company, received from the president of the company a copy of the consultant's report on cash flows in recession conditions, a summary of which is reproduced as an Appendix to this case. Mr. Howe had been present at the directors meeting on March 15, when the scope and methodology to be used in the study had been discussed. Therefore he knew that the consultant planned to use his analysis of recession cash flows as a basis for recommendations on the company's future debt policy. Mr. Howe also knew that the president, Mr. Patrick Dean, had a number of proposals for expansion (by acquisition as well as internally) under study, and that he was prepared to consider an increase in Cyclops' borrowing ratio rather than issue stock at its currently depressed level. Mr. Dean had assured the directors, however, that he would not consider a debt/capitalization ratio of over 50%.

The report was likely to be discussed at the next meeting of the board of directors on June 5, and Mr. Howe undertook a study of the consultant's recommendations.

The Cyclops Cement Company had been established in the upper Mississippi Valley area in the late 19th century, and approximately 50% of company sales still came from this area. The remaining sales were evenly distributed among three widely separated areas: the Southwest, the Southeast, and New England, which Cyclops had entered through mergers with three smaller companies. In terms of production volume, Cyclops ranked among the top 15 companies in the industry in 1965, with six plants and a total productive capacity of 18,200,000 barrels a year.

The cement industry

The broadly based use of cement and concrete products in most types of construction provides the industry with considerable stability. The historical record has demonstrated this. The only exceptions have been the major depression of the 1930's and World War II (see Chart I in the Appendix).

The production of cement is very capital intensive, utilizing a highly mechanized process involving very old, well-established, and well-known technology. Significant reductions in unit production costs are possible from the operation of large plants, since coordination requires no more effort for large- than for small-scale operations. The cost of a barrel of production capacity also declines with increased plant size.

Plant size is limited, however, by the high cost of transport of cement—a bulky, low-value product. Since the raw materials used in cement production are readily available in most regions of the country, it is generally less expensive to operate a number of regional plants close to cement users than to incur high transport costs by shipping cement long distances from a few very large plants. Ninety percent of total U.S. cement production is shipped less than 160 miles, with the primary exceptions being the output of some new and very large plants where ready access to low-cost water transportation permits competitive pricing in markets up to 1,300 miles away. Competition, therefore, is generally on a regional basis, with three or four producers operating plants in the region and accounting for the great majority of total cement sales. The plants are small, but the relatively high production costs are offset by low distribution expense.

The ruinous trade conditions of the 1930's produced chronic overcapacity in the cement industry and made most companies reluctant to expand their facilities.[1] The 10-year period ending in 1955 saw very little increase in productive capacity despite strong gains in construction activity and use of cement. The resulting rise in operating rates combined with firm product prices to yield profit rates considerably above the average for manufacturing as a whole. By 1955 the industry was operating at 94% of capacity and was earning almost 19% on net worth. This high return resulted in part from the use of fully depreciated plant. Exhibit 1 provides data on this period.

Exhibit 1

CYCLOPS CEMENT COMPANY

OPERATING RATES, PRICES, AND PROFITS IN THE CEMENT INDUSTRY, 1950–55

	1950	*1951*	*1952*	*1953*	*1954*	*1955*
Industry capacity (mil. bbls.)	268	282	284	292	298	315
Cement production (mil. bbls.)	226	246	249	264	272	297
Percent capacity utilization	84	87	88	90	91	94
Annual increase in capacity (mil. bbls.)		14	2	8	6	17
Annual increase in production (mil. bbls.)		20	3	15	8	25
Bureau of Mines cement price index (1950 = 100)	100	108	108	114	117	122
Profit after tax as % of net worth:						
All manufacturing companies	17.1	14.4	12.3	12.7	12.3	14.9
Cement industry	17.8	14.5	14.3	15.0	17.6	18.6

Source: Standard & Poor's *Trade and Securities Statistics*.

The prosperity was short-lived, however. A number of factors spurred companies to invest heavily in new capacity in the years 1955–62, most important of which were (*a*) the high operating rates and profits of the industry,

[1] Shipments of Portland cement fell from 170 million barrels in 1929 to 81 million barrels in 1932, while the average realized price of cement at the mills fell from $1.48 per barrel in 1929 to $1.01 in 1932.

(*b*) inauguration of the federal highway program, and (*c*) a favorable ruling on depletion allowance (reversed by legislation in 1960). Existing cement producers expanded their facilities and entered new regional markets both by acquisition and by construction of new plants. In addition, a number of new companies entered the cement business during this period. By 1962 the industry's operating rate had declined to 72% under the pressure of substantial additions to capacity and a slowdown in cement consumption (see Exhibit 2).

Exhibit 2

CYCLOPS CEMENT COMPANY

OPERATING RATES, PRICES, AND PROFITS IN THE CEMENT INDUSTRY, 1956–62

	1956	*1957*	*1958*	*1959*	*1960*	*1961*	*1962*
Industry capacity (mil. bbls.)	349	380	403	420	433	443	469
Cement production (mil. bbls.)	316	298	312	339	319	324	337
Percent capacity utilization	91	78	77	81	74	73	72
Annual increase in capacity (mil. bbls.)	34	31	23	17	13	10	26
Annual increase in production (mil. bbls.)	19	−18	14	27	−20	5	13
Bureau of Mines cement price index (1950 = 100)	130	135	138	140	143	141	140
Profit after tax as % of net worth:							
All manufacturing companies	13.8	12.9	9.8	11.7	10.6	9.9	10.9
Cement industry	18.5	14.2	14.7	14.3	11.2	10.2	9.8

Source: Standard & Poor's *Trade and Securities Statistics*.

Despite the decline in operating rates, product prices were reasonably well maintained until 1960. Typically, the largest producer in each regional market set the base price, subject to the right to meet any lower price quoted by a competitor. The base prices were announced quarterly and were generally followed by the other competitors.

The combination of excess capacity, high fixed costs, and new entrants eager to secure a share of the market eroded the oligopolistic competitive structure in the early 1960's and producers adopted several strategies to offset the heightened competition. Financial support was provided by some cement producers to ready-mixed concrete companies in the form of lengthened payment periods and guarantees of bank loans. Typically short on capital, the ready-mix companies accounted for 60% of the cement industry's sales, and their business was essential to the profitable operation of a cement plant.

"Off-list" price reductions in the form of larger discounts for prompt payment, special "competitive" discounts, and "phantom delivery point" billing increased sharply. The average realized mill price of cement, which had risen in each year since 1940, fell in each year from 1961 through 1964.

AVERAGE REALIZED MILL PRICE PER BARREL

1955	*1956*	*1957*	*1958*	*1959*	*1960*	*1961*	*1962*	*1963*	*1964*
$2.86	$3.05	$3.18	$3.25	$3.28	$3.35	$3.32	$3.29	$3.20	$3.19

Customer service was improved by the establishment of distribution terminals that could insure prompt delivery of cement to users, thereby reducing the importance *to the user* of buffer inventories. The terminals also permitted the adoption of separate pricing policies for each terminal, in place of the historical reliance on a single policy for an entire region.

NUMBER OF NEW DISTRIBUTION TERMINALS

1950–59	*1960–61*	*1962*	*1963*	*1964*
69	32	42	44	43

By 1964 profitability of the cement industry had fallen to a 15-year low as product prices continued to erode (see Exhibit 3). Heavy investments in

Exhibit 3

CYCLOPS CEMENT COMPANY

OPERATING RATES, PRICES, AND PROFITS IN THE CEMENT INDUSTRY, 1963–64

	1963	*1964*
Industry capacity (mil. bbls.)	478	479
Cement production (mil. bbls.)	353	369
Percent capacity utilization	74	77
Annual increase in capacity (mil. bbls.)	9	1
Annual increase in production (mil. bbls.)	16	16
Bureau of Mines cement price index (1950 = 100)	136	136
Profit after tax as % of net worth:		
All manufacturing companies	11.6	12.7
Cement industry	8.9	8.8

Source: Standard & Poor's *Trade and Securities Statistics.*

plant modernization and automation and in distribution terminals were widespread in the industry and resulted in little competitive advantage for any one company. Rather than being a source of higher reported earnings, the savings merely offset (and possibly contributed to) price cuts. There was, however, one encouraging sign; namely, industry investment in capacity additions was low in 1963 and 1964 and, on the basis of announced investment plans, it seemed likely that the low level of capacity additions would continue into 1966. Some industry observers hoped that rising operating rates might permit a firming of product prices and a recovery in profits.

Financial history of Cyclops Cement Company

Cyclops did not escape the industrywide competitive pressures. Earnings plummeted by 35% in the two-year period 1959–60 and then rebounded in 1962–64 (see Exhibit 4 for a summary of operations). Capital expenditures were very heavy, and the company sold an issue of $15 million 5% debentures in 1958. The restriction in this issue that funded debt was not to exceed 33⅓% of net tangible assets was suggested by the company's investment bankers, who stated that this was in line with recent issues by other firms in a variety of industries. At the time, the provision seemed to allow for a

Exhibit 4

CYCLOPS CEMENT COMPANY
SEVEN-YEAR STATISTICAL AND FINANCIAL SUMMARY
(Dollar figures in millions except per share data)

	1958	*1959*	*1960*	*1961*	*1962*	*1963*	*1964*
Sales	$44.2	$49.4	$45.3	$48.9	$55.5	$54.3	$53.1
Net earnings after tax	4.7	4.4	3.1	3.3	4.35	3.8	4.75
Capital expenditures	12.0	13.3	7.1	5.5	5.7	9.7	11.8
Net working capital	11.0	2.0	8.0	9.1	12.2	9.2	5.8
Total assets	70.5	74.5	85.2	79.6	83.4	88.9	88.0
Long-term debt	15.0	15.0	19.75	19.75	19.75	19.75	19.3
Preferred stock	4.5	4.5	9.2	9.2	9.2	9.2	9.0
Common stockholders' equity	38.6	39.7	39.8	41.0	43.4	44.9	47.3
Cement capacity (mil. bbls.)	13.9	15.9	15.9	16.8	16.8	16.8	18.1
Employees	1,457	1,503	1,491	1,470	1,498	1,489	1,421
Common shareholders	5,600	6,300	6,700	7,200	7,300	7,300	7,400
Earned per share	$2.75	$2.57	$1.81	$1.93	$2.54	$2.22	$2.77
Dividends per share	2.00	2.00	1.60	0.90	0.80	0.95	1.00

considerable increase in the company's funded debt and had been accepted without comment by the officers and directors of Cyclops.

In 1960, however, the company's large plant-rebuilding programs and an adverse tax ruling forced Cyclops to go to the market for additional long-term funds. The 33⅓% restriction limited borrowing to an issue of $4.75 million of 5% debentures, and it was necessary to raise an additional $4.7 million by means of 6% cumulative preferred stock. Both issues were placed privately with groups of insurance companies.

Exhibit 5 presents the capitalization ratios of several cement companies. Except for Cyclops the list is in the order of debt ratio, with the highest ratio at the top. Companies A, B, and C are "captives" of larger companies whose financial strength in a sense guarantees their solvency. Consequently, their very high debt ratios cannot be considered as typical of the industry. With the exception of these three companies Cyclops is near the median position in this listing.

Future financing needs

Cyclops had a number of proposals for expansion under study. Capital expenditures were expected to average $7–$7.5 million over the next few years, although technological changes in the industry might make major investments necessary at some stage if Cyclops was to remain cost competitive. The directors were also interested in further mergers and acquisitions including the possibility of diversifying outside the cement industry. They wished to develop financial policies that would give the company sufficient flexibility to take advantage of any opportunities that might arise.

However, it was clear that there would be considerable resistance from the board of directors to any reduction in the current dividend rate to finance

Exhibit 5

CYCLOPS CEMENT COMPANY

TYPICAL CAPITALIZATION RATIOS IN THE CEMENT INDUSTRY

	Total Capitalization 100%		
	Debt	*Preferred*	*Common*
Cyclops Cement Company	25%	13%	62%
A†	78	11*	11
B†	82	—	18
C†	79	—	21
D	33	18	49
E	33	30	37
F	31	—	69
G	30	—	70
H	27	12	61
I	24	—	76
J	24	—	76
K	22	3	75
L	20	—	80
M	11	—	89
N	11	20	69
O	—	—	100
P	—	—	100
Q	—	—	100

* Subordinated notes.

† These companies were captives of larger corporations so that their financial structures cannot be taken to be representative of independently owned companies in the cement industry.

the planned expansion. In Mr. Dean's words, "The board would take a hard and long look before cutting or omitting a dividend." Dividends had nevertheless been cut substantially in recent years from $2.00 a share in 1958 to $0.80 in 1962. The rate had been increased slightly to $1.00 in 1964. A recent study by the company had indicated that the stock prices of publicly owned cement companies were very closely correlated with dividend yields, and Mr. Dean had decided that the cash dividend should be increasd to $1.20 a share and had instructed the consultant to use this figure in his projections of future cash flows. It was hoped that the increased dividend rate would raise the stock price from its recent range of $25–$28.

APPENDIX

CYCLOPS CEMENT COMPANY SUMMARY OF CONSULTANT'S REPORT

Introduction

In this section we shall explain briefly the importance of cash flows in any appraisal of the risk of default in a recession period. We shall make use of the recent history of Cyclops to indicate the advantages of cash flow analysis over income statements and balance sheets in an analysis of this kind.

The ability of a firm to meet its financial obligations in any given period or set of circumstances can only be determined after a study of each and every one of the sources and uses of funds expected to arise during that period. Attention to income and expense is not enough. Many profitable firms suffer temporary shortages of funds. For example, in the year 1964 Cyclops reported a net profit of $4.750 million; yet the net cash gain available for common and preferred dividends was a *negative* figure of $3.604 million. The disparity between these figures alone is sufficient evidence that profitability by itself is no guarantee of solvency. Other firms remain safely solvent during periods in which losses are being experienced. Some firms have enjoyed an adequate cash flow to keep them solvent through long periods of unprofitability.

Financial obligations are undertaken in order to obtain funds to be used to create income (and therefore value) in the firm. Properly used, low-cost senior securities add to the value of the common stock equity position by increasing the earnings available per common share. But the degree to which the fixed-charge burden associated with these senior securities may be accepted depends not on income but on cash flows. If the sources of cash provide a flow sufficient to meet all uses, *including the demands of the financial obligations,* without exhausting the organization's cash balances, then solvency is assured. If not, even if profits are earned, then there will be default unless either new sources of cash are found or uses are reduced.

To determine what financial burden is acceptable, it is necessary to examine the flows likely to arise during a recession period, making a realistic assessment of these flows on the basis of the organization's past experience in recession conditions. Only then can a debt-financing policy safely be made part of the company's long-range plans. In this study, therefore, the sources and uses of funds in Cyclops Cement Company will be forecast under various sets of assumptions about business recession, and under each set of assumed conditions the total burden of proposed financial obligations will be compared with net funds changes arising from other activities. Where the difference is positive—that is, the net positive cash flow from all other sources exceeds the financial burden—then that burden will be safely covered, whatever the reported earnings may be.

This method may be illustrated by examining the experience of Cyclops during the period 1961–64 in terms of funds movements. These data are presented in Table 1. In terms of the method of analysis we are here introducing, solvency was in fact threatened in 1964, but the reserves available in the form of cash balances were more than adequate to overcome the threat.

It should be noted that the financial burden sections of the "uses" columns are further subdivided between "contractual" and "policy" burden. Contractual burden includes those financial obligations, like bond interest and sinking fund payments, that are matters of contract and so must not be defaulted. Policy burden is made up of those obligations, such as dividends, that are at the discretion of the board of directors. The annual retirement of $225,000 of the 6% cumulative preferred issue is considered discretionary in view of the mild penalties for failure to do so.

Table 1

CASH FLOWS, 1961–64
(Dollar figures in millions)

	1961	*1962*	*1963*	*1964*
Reported earnings after taxes	$ 3.3	$ 4.4	$ 3.8	$ 4.8
Sources of funds:				
Operations before lease payments, interest, noncash charges, and taxes	$ 12.1	$ 13.2	$ 12.8	$ 12.8
Working capital excluding cash	8.3*	—	3.6	—
Total sources	$ 20.4	$ 13.2	$ 16.4	$ 12.8
Uses of funds—operating:				
Working capital excluding cash and accrued taxes	—	$ (0.6)	—	$ (0.8)
Plant and equipment	$ (5.0)	(4.7)	$ (8.4)	(11.7
Other needs	(1.2)	—	(0.7)	(0.4)
Total operating uses	$ (6.2)	$ (5.3)	$ (9.1)	$(12.9)
Available for financial uses	$ 14.2	$ 7.9	$ 7.3	$ (0.1)
Uses of funds—financial:				
Income tax payments	$ (5.0)	$ (2.1)	$ (0.8)	$ (0.5)
Contractual burden:				
Lease payments	$ (0.5)	$ (0.6)	$ (0.7)	$ (0.7)
Interest	(1.2)	(0.9)	(1.0)	(1.0)
Debt reduction	(3.8)	—	(0.8)	(0.8)
Total contractual burden	$ (5.5)	$ (1.5)	$ (2.5)	$ (2.5)
Policy burden:				
Preferred dividends	$ (0.6)	$ (0.6)	$ (0.5)	$ (0.5)
Preferred redemption	—	—	(0.2)	(0.4)
Common dividends	(1.6)	(1.4)	(1.6)	(1.7)
Total policy burden	$ (2.2)	$ (2.0)	$ (2.3)	$ (2.6)
Total financial uses	$(12.7)	$ (5.6)	$ (5.6)	$ (5.6)
Balance—change in cash	$ 1.5	$ 2.3	$ 1.7	$ (5.7)

* Primarily reduction of receivables by use of new financing.

The choice of a recession to be studied

The risks arising from debt-servicing burden are often too vaguely presented. Any debt increases the risk of default by some degree, however small. The question should be not whether there is or is not some abstract risk but whether or not there is a real risk of cash inadequacy in any foreseeable depression. To answer this question it is necessary to specify, after study of the economic conditions of the industry, the dimensions that a depression might assume.

Volume. The cement industry trends shown in Chart 1 (which is drawn on a semilogarithmic scale to emphasize relative changes) demonstrate a generally stable upwards tendency in both consumption and cement prices. The only major interruptions in this trend occurred during the depression of the 1930's and in World War II. Only two declines in volume have been experienced since World War II, neither of them involving a drop of more than 7% from the previous peak or lasting more than three years. The recession of 1936–38 was of similar magnitude.

Cyclops Cement Company has experienced a greater fluctuation in post-war volume than that shown in the industry trends. No decrease experienced by the company has involved a decline of more than 17% from the previous peak, however, and no division has experienced a volume decline greater than 18%. It did take Cyclops five years to return to 1956 volumes after the 1957 decline. The author has concluded, therefore, that a recession of four years' duration with a return to previous volumes in the fifth year is for this company a conservative but not unrealistic basis for this study of recession cash flows. Volume levels during the five-year period are assumed to be:

Year preceding	100%
Year 1	90
Year 2	85
Year 3	80
Year 4	80
Year 5	100

Chart 1

CEMENT INDUSTRY TRENDS

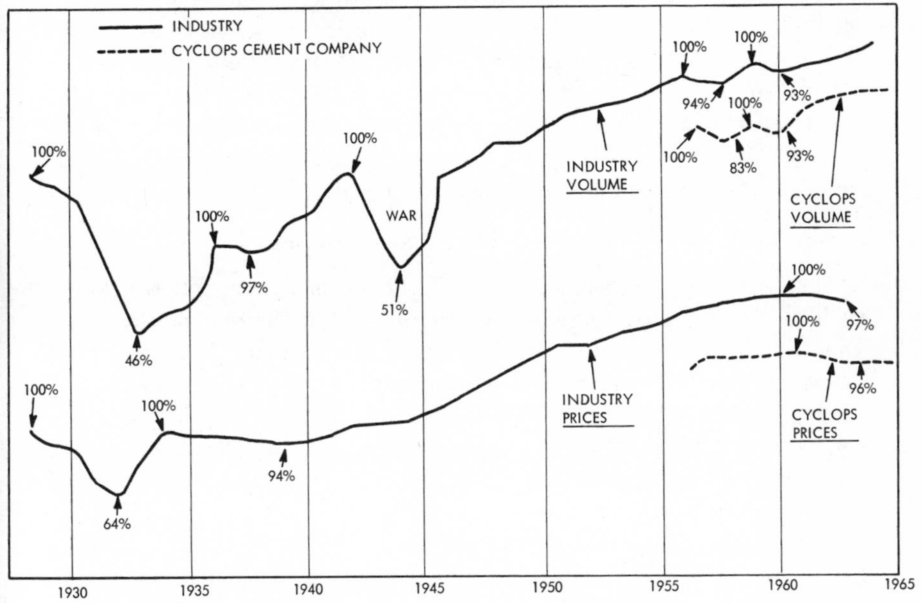

Note: The percentage figures show the peaks and troughs of the major declines.

In Chart 1 the upper long, unbroken line represents total industry volume plotted on a semilogarithmic scale and the lower unbroken line represents industry prices similarly plotted. The shorter dashed lines to the right of the chart represent Cyclops' actual volume and price performance for the years 1956–65. It is clear from these data that the author's assumptions concerning possible recession conditions and Cyclops' response to these conditions reflect more severe fluctuations than have actually been experienced since World War II.

Price. Cement prices have fallen surprisingly little in view of the severe competition in the industry in recent years. Certain areas have experienced marked fluctuations in prices, but the general pattern is one of considerable stability. The average industry price has fallen only twice since the 1930's: by 6% after 1934 and by 5% in the early 1960's. For the purposes of this study, however, since we are studying a particular company, a price decline of up to 10% of the prerecession price is assumed to be possible, distributed over the recession period as follows:

Year preceding	100%
Year 1	100
Year 2	95
Year 3	90
Year 4	90
Year 5	95

These assumptions as to the volume and price declines likely to be experienced in the recession period have been used as the basis for the analysis that follows. Although prices of delivered products were assumed to fall, there has been no adjustment for the reduction of prices of the elements of cost.

The recommendations concerning financial policy, which will be made in the final section of this study, will be designed to insure that the company is able to survive a recession of the dimensions specified above without appreciable danger of being unable to meet its contractual financial burdens and without contraction of the common stock dividends.

Forecast of cash movements related to operations

The information presented in Table 2 was obtained from detailed studies made by the divisions of Cyclops and coordinated by the headquarters staff. This table shows the cash receipts and expenditures arising from operations for each year of the recession as deliveries fall below 1965 levels. In each year except recession year 4 the assumption is made that this year is the first at that particular volume: the fourth-year column demonstrates the results of stabilizing volume for a second year at 80% of the 1965 level. Deliveries are assumed to return to their prerecession level in year 5.

Table 2 seeks to show the cash flow effects of changes in volume separately from those of changes in price. Thus, in the upper part of the table, cement prices are assumed to remain constant at their 1965 levels ($3.76 per barrel, delivered) so that the effect of volume changes may be seen in isolation. The slow decline in net operating inflow as a percentage of receipts is strikingly portrayed and demonstrates that the cash elements in the cost of production are dominated by variable costs. This fact is overlooked when one thinks of cost as including the heavy depreciation charges of a capital-intensive company such as Cyclops.

In the lower part of Table 2 the results of price declines of various

Table 2

FORECAST OF CASH FLOWS FROM OPERATIONS AT VARIOUS PRICE LEVELS
(Dollar figures in millions)

	Year Preceding Recession	*Recession Year* 1	2	3	4	5
Shipments (mil. bbls.)	13.7	12.3	11.6	11.0	11.0	13.7
As % of 1965 levels	100	90	85	80	80	100
As % of capacity	77	69	65	62	62	77
Receipts at 1965 prices	$ 51.43	$ 46.29	$ 43.22	$ 41.15	$ 41.15	$ 51.43
Other income	0.58	0.52	0.49	0.46	0.46	0.58
	$ 52.01	$ 46.81	$ 43.71	$ 41.61	$ 41.61	$ 52.01
Cash operating expenditures*	(35.17)	(33.60)	(31.37)	(30.27)	(28.51)	(35.17)
Net operating inflow:						
At 1965 prices	$ 16.84	$ 13.21	$ 12.34	$ 11.34	$ 13.10	$ 16.84
As % of receipts	32%	28%	28%	27%	31%	32%
Net operating inflow:						
Assuming 5% price decline	$ 14.24	$ 10.87	$ 10.18	$ 9.28	$ 11.04	$ 14.24
Assuming 10% price decline	11.64	8.53	8.02	7.22	8.98	11.64
Assuming 15% price decline	9.04	6.19	5.86	5.16	6.92	9.04
Net operating inflow under assumed recession volumes and price levels	$ 16.84	$ 13.21	$ 10.18	$ 7.22	$ 8.98	$ 14.24

* Does not include headquarters expenditures, pension fund contributions, interest and lease payments, and taxes.

magnitudes are superimposed on the volume changes and the effects on net operating inflows are shown. Whenever the consequences of a price change are being considered, it is necessary to take into account the change in income tax liability consequent on this reduction in revenues. Finally, the table shows the net operating inflows likely to be experienced under the combination of volume and price changes selected by this report as the dimensions of the recession to be studied. These inflow figures will be used in Table 5 below.

Forecast of other cash flows (excluding taxes on income and financial burden)

All nonoperating cash flows that may be expected under recession conditions, with the exception of changes in the company's cash balances, income taxes, and financial obligations, are set out in Table 3.

After discussion with company officers it was decided that it would be reasonable to assume that the onset of a recession would not bring about immediate adjustments in any items other than those directly related to volume. There are two reasons for this. First, it is unlikely that the recession will be recognized as such immediately, especially as short-term fluctuations of as much as 10% may be encountered in a normal year. Second, there will be considerable pressure to continue normal investment expenditures. The column representing the first year of the recession in Table 3 therefore uses "normal" levels of expenditure. Further columns depict the flows in years 2 and 3 and thereafter as investments are reduced in response to the continuing recession.

Table 3

FORECAST OF NONOPERATING FLOWS
(Dollar figures in millions)

	Year Preceding Recession	*Recession Year* 1	2	3	*Subsequent Severe Years*	*Recovery to Prerecession Volumes*
Headquarters expenditures*	$(1.97)	$(1.95)	$(1.83)	$(1.79)	$(1.33)	$(1.87)
Plant and equipment	(7.50)	(7.50)	(2.50)	(1.00)	(1.00)	(5.00)
Subtotal	$(9.47)	$(9.45)	$(4.33)	$(2.79)	$(2.33)	$(6.87)
In-house resources:						
Reduction in pension fund contributions	0	0	0.20	0.20	0.20	0
Reduction of cash balances	0	0.87	0	0	0	0
Special market expenditures.	0	0	(0.43)	0	0	0
Reduction (increase) in noncash working capital (below)	0	(1.00)	0.18	0.21	0	(0.80)
Total	$(9.47)	$(9.58)	$(4.38)	$(2.38)	$(2.13)	$(7.67)
DETAILS OF CHANGES IN NONCASH WORKING CAPITAL ACCOUNTS						
Volume as percentage of base (prerecession) year	100	90	85	80	80	100
Accounts receivable	$ 5.36	$ 6.04	$ 5.70	$ 5.36	$ 5.36	$ 6.77
Inventories (direct cost portion)	1.43	1.28	1.21	1.13	1.13	1.44
	$ 6.79	$ 7.32	$ 6.91	$ 6.49	$ 6.49	$ 8.21
Accounts payable	4.68	4.21	3.98	3.77	3.77	4.69
	$ 2.11	$ 3.11	$ 2.93	$ 2.72	$ 2.72	$ 3.52
Change in working capital account from previous year.		(1.00)	0.18	0.21	0	(0.80)

* Nonfinancial cash expenditures excluding leases.

It is clear that the dominant factors affecting these flows are, on the outflow side, the plant and capital equipment budget, and on the other side, the amount of liquid reserves that are quickly available. The December 31, 1964, cash level of $3.12 million is probably a minimum for the next several years, and even this figure is well in excess of management's comfortable assessment of minimum operating cash requirement of $2.25 million. It is assumed, therefore, that excess cash of $0.87 million is available and is used in year 1 of the recession.

The lower portion of Table 3 shows the amounts forecast for those working capital items that fluctuate with volume. An explanation of the amounts chosen and of other items in Table 3 follows.

Detailed discussion of Table 3

Headquarters expenses. An estimate was made by company officers of the needs to support the central office. They were made at four possible recession levels, keyed to earnings rather than to cash flow. Therefore, with a one-year lag, from the onset of the recession, the level of Headquarters Expense has been reduced according to plan.

Plant and equipment. At the beginning of 1965 the company projected $7.5 million for capital expenditures during the year. Although $11.7 million (net funds) was spent in 1964 and $8.5 million in 1963, management believes that no further major modernization expenditures will be required for several years and that an average of $7.5 million would be a generous allowance for normal years in the next decade. The five-year plan, already adopted, shows lower levels of expenditure than those in the last two years.

In recession, a much less ample program can be anticipated, but there will always be an important time lag before cutbacks can become a reality. Many projects require one to two years for construction, and it seems unlikely that they would be halted prior to completion in response to a recession. The author has been assured that the lower figures used in recession years are feasible, without any damage to the company's need to return to high levels of production in the recovery period. The figure of $5.0 million is used in the year of recovery, because it is believed that this is all that could be spent effectively in the first year following a period of retrenchment.

In-house resources. Most companies possess considerably more capacity to produce funds under the pressure of need than is apparent at first glance. The following in-house resources have been considered in picturing the funds flow of Cyclops Cement Company in a recession period.

Use of accumulated contributions to pension reserve: Since the company has built up $0.6 million above the legally required minimum, it is estimated by company officers that the present outflow of about $0.3 million annually could be reduced to $0.1 million for three years, without creating any need for higher levels of payment than previous levels when prosperity is restored. This estimate has been used with a one-year time lag. The saving appears in each of three years because the full pension charge was taken as an operating expense.

Liquidation of outside investments: Although there is a considerable investment in real estate that could be liquidated, the policy given to us by management is not to rely on this source of funds.

Use of cash reserves: The $3.12 million of cash funds shown at December 31, 1964, is well in excess of operating needs, which have been estimated at $1.3 million by a careful study recently made. A larger figure, $2.25 million, has been chosen on the authority of management, which feels that it is desirable to maintain liberal balances in the company's banks. So a reduction of only $0.87 million is taken.

Drawing down the liquid position as indicated would require the increased use of short-term credit to meet seasonal requirements. This credit is certainly available under present conditions, but the author's forecast that it would also be available under recession conditions should be checked.

Since the company manifests a large cash-generating capacity in normal years, the idea of recession use of the present cash reserves does not present the risk of permanent reduction of the firm's strength.

Special promotion fund: At the request of management, a special fund of

$0.43 million is appropriated in the second recession year, to permit special sales efforts and the absorption of bad debts beyond normal figures.

Working capital items related to sales volume. Significant changes would also occur in certain working capital items.

Accounts receivable: These are currently 10.3% of 1965 estimated sales volume. Since it is known that the granting of liberal credit terms is an important source of sales in a buyer's market, an increase of the collection period by 25% (about $1.5 million at current volume) is assumed.

Accounts payable: Since the maintenance of a strong credit position requires prompt payment, the "last ditch" resort to slowness on the part of Cyclops is rejected, and payables are maintained at 9% of sales, the recent average level.

Inventories: The nature of the production process and the present inventory control systems should permit the maintenance of inventories at approximately a constant relationship to shipments. This relationship is assumed here. Consistent with the objective of this analysis only the cash costs of production are reflected in Table 3.

Financial burdens

The year 1967 was chosen as the source of the figures for financing burden in the year preceding the recession, because in that year all the sinking fund requirements rise to their fullest amounts. They are presented in Table 4. The amounts are shown on a pretax basis. The tax deductibility of interest and lease payments is included in calculating the estimated tax payments shown in Table 5.

The "Contractual Burden," strictly defined, is the sum of interest and lease

Table 4

FINANCIAL BURDENS
(Dollar figures in millions)

	As in 1967	*Recession Year* 1	2	3	4	5
Contractual:						
Interest, debentures (5%)	$0.82	$0.76	$0.71	$0.67	$0.60	$0.54
Lease payments	0.56	0.56	0.56	0.56	0.56	0.56
	$1.38	$1.32	$1.27	$1.23	$1.16	$1.10
Debenture sinking funds	1.07	1.07	1.07	1.07	1.07	1.07
Total contractual	$2.45	$2.39	$2.34	$2.30	$2.23	$2.17
Policy:						
Preferred sinking fund*	$0.45	$0.23	$0.23	$0.23	$0.23	$0.23
Preferred dividend (6%)	0.49	0.47	0.46	0.44	0.43	0.42
	$0.94	$0.70	$0.69	$0.67	$0.66	$0.65
Total contractual and preferred burdens	$3.39	$3.09	$3.03	$2.97	$2.89	$2.82
Common dividend ($1.20)	2.07	2.07	2.07	2.07	2.07	2.07
Total burden	$5.46	$5.16	$5.10	$5.04	$4.96	$4.89

* It is assumed that Cyclops will exercise its option to retire an additional $225,000 of preferred stock in the year prior to the downturn.

payments and debenture sinking funds, but the author feels that Cyclops will always plan to meet the dividend and sinking fund requirements on the preferred stock. Not only is it in the spirit of a preferred stock agreement to pay dividends as long as possible, but also an accumulation of preferred dividends has disastrous effects on the value of the common stock. Therefore, the author proposes that the figures in Table 4 be interpreted to show a continuing burden of approximately $3.1 million, of which $1.3 million represents deductions due to sinking fund operations.

By making sinking fund payments, Cyclops is regularly restoring its borrowing power. Perhaps in recession this fact is not important, but it is a matter of long-run importance which will enter the final recommendations of this report. Debt of $5.36 million is scheduled for retirement in the five years shown.

A forecast of recession cash flows

Table 5 combines the cash flow patterns developed in Tables 2–4 and indicates the impact of the selected recession on the borrowing needs of Cyclops. The financial burdens are based on the present capital structure and on an increase to $1.20 in the dividend rate on the common stock.

The following conclusions seem important.

1. The pattern of changes in cash is very different from the pattern of reported earnings.[2] In contrast to net earnings, which decline through year 3, peak borrowing needs are reached in the first year of the recession.

2. Sharp curtailment in investment in plant and equipment by the second year of the recession is a key influence on the company's low borrowing needs during the recession. In view of the long construction period for many of Cyclops' projects, this assumes quick perception of, and response to, the onslaught of a recession.

3. Even at low levels of volume and price, and after maintaining the $1.20 annual dividend on the common stock, there is not a cash deficit after the volume of investment in new assets is reduced. Income tax carry-backs are important contributors to this result. [The tax calculations are not included in the report but are available from the vice president–finance.]

4. In interpreting Table 5 the reader should keep in mind that several additional elements of conservatism are built into the calculations. The cash balance is set at a level $1.0 million above operating needs. A four-year recession with declines in volume and in price below the experience of any recession since the 1930's has been assumed. While prices of delivered goods have been assumed to decline, no decline has been assumed in the prices of the elements of cost. Finally, Cyclops has an excellent credit standing. The

---

[2] The consultant and the Cyclops management elected to omit the earnings figures from the report to ensure that the board of directors would focus on the critical numbers —namely, the cash flow figures. The tax payment figures provide some insight, however, into the pattern of earnings. The differences between earnings and cash flow patterns are also shown in Table 1, which provides historical data for the 1961–64 period.

Table 5

A FORECAST OF RECESSION CASH FLOWS
(Dollar figures in millions)

Summary of Operations	*Year Preceding Recession*	*Recession Year* 1	2	3	4	5
Shipments (mil. bbls.)	13.7	12.3	11.6	11.0	11.0	13.7
Percent of base year	100	90	85	80	80	100
Percent of capacity	77	69	65	62	62	77
Price per barrel	$ 3.76	$ 3.76	$ 3.57	$ 3.38	$ 3.38	$ 3.57
Percent of base year	100	100	95	90	90	95
Summary of Cash Flows*						
Operating inflows (from Table 2)	$ 16.84	$ 13.21	$10.18	$ 7.22	$ 8.98	$ 14.24
Headquarters expenditures (from Table 3)	(1.97)	(1.95)	(1.83)	(1.79)	(1.33)	(1.87)
Investment in plant and equipment (from Table 3)	(7.50)	(7.50)	(2.50)	(1.00)	(1.00)	(5.00)
Reduction (increase) in working capital (from Table 3)	0	(0.13)	0.18	0.21	0	(0.80)
Reduction in pension fund contributions (from Table 3)	0	0	0.20	0.20	0.20	0
Special marketing expenditures (from Table 3)	0	0	(0.43)	0	0	0
Contractual financial burden (from Table 4)	(2.45)	(2.39)	(2.34)	(2.30)	(2.23)	(2.17)
Tax (payments) or refunds	(2.25)	(1.03)	(0.29)	1.02	0.46	(1.91)
Subtotal	$ 2.67	$ 0.21	$ 3.17	$ 3.56	$ 5.08	$ 2.49
Preferred burden (from Table 4)	(0.94)	(0.70)	(0.69)	(0.67)	(0.66)	(0.65)
Common dividend at $1.20	(2.07)	(2.07)	(2.07)	(2.07)	(2.07)	(2.07)
Total cash flow	$ (0.34)	$ (2.56)	$ 0.41	$ 0.82	$ 2.35	$ (0.23)
Effect on cash, excluding preferred burden and common dividend	2.67	0.21	3.17	3.56	5.08	2.49
Cumulative effect, excluding preferred burden and common dividend	2.67	2.88	6.05	9.61	14.69	17.18
Effect on cash, including preferred burden and common dividend	(0.34)	(2.56)	0.41	0.82	2.35	(0.23)
Cumulative effect, including preferred burden and common dividend†	(0.34)	(2.92)	(2.66)	(1.97)	0.28	0.05

* Figures in ( ) are cash outflows.
† The cumulative effect includes interest on the prior-year cash deficit.

company obviously has an untapped source of short-term funds not shown in Table 5.

Recession cash flows and various debt policies

It seems desirable to expand the recession cash flow analysis to include a range of possible capital structures. Three specific capital structures are considered:

1. The present capital structure, which includes debt, 25%; preferred stock, 12%; common stock, 63% (based on book values).

2. The capital structure that would result from refinancing the two preferred issues with a new debt issue and would include debt, 37%; common stock, 63%.
3. An increase in debt to 50% of total capitalization, with the balance as common stock.

The implications of each of the three capital structures for Cyclops' cash flows and cyclical borrowing needs are shown in Table 6 and are discussed in the recommendations that follow.

Table 6

CASH FLOWS UNDER VARIOUS CAPITAL STRUCTURES
(Dollar figures in millions)

	Year Preceding Decline	*Recession Year* 1	2	3	4	5
Current Policy: debt, 25%; preferred, 12%; common, 63%:						
Effect on cash, excluding preferred burdens and common dividend	$ 2.67	$ 0.21	$ 3.17	$ 3.56	$ 5.08	$ 2.49
Cumulative effect, excluding preferred burdens and common dividend	2.67	2.88	6.05	9.61	14.69	17.18
Effect on cash, including preferred burdens and common dividend	(0.34)	(2.56)	0.41	0.82	2.35	(0.23)
Cumulative effect, including preferred burdens and common dividend*	(0.34)	(2.92)	(2.66)	(1.97)	0.28	0.05
Capital Structure: debt, 37%; common, 63%:†						
Effect on cash, excluding common dividend	1.94	(0.51)	2.47	2.86	4.40	1.82
Cumulative effect, excluding common dividend	1.94	1.43	3.90	6.76	11.16	12.98
Effect on cash, including common dividend ($2.07 million)	(0.13)	(2.58)	0.40	0.79	2.33	(0.25)
Cumulative effect, including common dividend*	(0.13)	(2.72)	(2.46)	(1.79)	0.45	0.20
Capital Structure: debt, 50%; common, 50%‡ (and repurchase of common):						
Effect on cash, excluding common dividend	1.18	(1.24)	1.74	2.16	3.69	1.14
Cumulative effect, excluding common dividend	1.18	(0.06)	1.68	3.84	7.53	8.67
Effect on cash, including common dividend ($1.72 million)	(0.54)	(2.96)	0.02	0.44	1.97	(0.58)
Cumulative effect, including common dividend*	(0.54)	(3.53)	(3.64)	(3.38)	(1.58)	(2.24)

* The cumulative figures include interest on the prior year's deficit cash position. The preferred burden and common dividend in the year preceding the decline are $0.94 million and $2.07 million respectively.

† Assumes funding the retirement of the preferred issues with 20-year debt issue at 5½% on which sinking fund payments start immediately.

‡ Assumes a negotiated increase of ¼% in the rate on the existing debt in exchange for relaxation of the restriction on debt and issuance of an additional $18.6 million of 20-year debt at 5¾% (sinking fund payments start immediately). The proceeds from the $18.6 million debt issue are used to retire the preferred stock and to repurchase 300,000 shares of common stock at $30 per share. The common stock dividend in each year is $1.72 million. The reduction reflects the smaller number of shares outstanding as a result of recapitalizing the company. It is recognized that the company would probably not repurchase its stock but would use its newly discovered borrowing power in a series of steps through acquisitions to reach the desired goal over a period of years.

Recommendations

1. Since the first recession year shows large drains because of the continuation of expenditures for plant and equipment, it is recommended that the company maintain reserves in liquid funds or assured credit in amounts roughly equivalent to the capital commitments that are considered irreversible. Such an arrangement as a banker's commitment for a term loan might be considered and would bolster the certainty of the common dividend rate.

2. Since there appears to be no reason to pay the high cost of preferred stock, because the reduction of preferred dividends is not required to preserve solvency, it is recommended that this type of security be eliminated from the capital structure by the use of (*a*) funds generated in prosperous years and (*b*) increased long-term indebtedness.

On December 31, 1964, total long-term debt amounted to $19 million, or 25% of net tangible assets ($76 million). The ratio of 33⅓% imposed under the terms of the 5% debentures of 1958 permitted long-term debt of $25 million with net tangible assets at this level. Unused debt capacity of $6 million was therefore available without offending existing contracts. The extent of the funds available from operations for the retirement of the preferred stock was dependent upon the size of new capital investment projects being undertaken. In a year of normal sales volume in which investment in new plant and equipment did not exceed $5 million (e.g., 1961–62) approximately $2 million might be expected to be available for preferred retirement. The total sum required to accomplish the retirement of both preferred issues as of June 30, 1965, is $9 million.

3. Since dividend payments are an important key to value of the common stock of cement companies, it is recommended that the net savings of retiring preferred stock be passed on in the form of increased dividends on the common stock.

4. At present Cyclops Cement Company's flexibility in financial policy is greatly constrained by the existing indentures and preferred stock agreements. Thus, at the moment the only major available reductions in expenditures to meet recessions (other than in the control of operations) are in the budget for plant and equipment or the common dividend.

It is recommended that the company study its present indentures and consider how they might be changed to introduce needed flexibility. Raising the debt limit to make unnecessary the use of preferred stock is one goal. Another is to arrange an alternative to the sinking fund in the form of investment in approved types of assets. A third is the introduction of flexibility by specifically authorizing that advance payments could be made on sinking fund payments with the provision that an equal amount of later payments could be skipped over in times of stress if necessary. All these changes might be arranged by amendment of the existing indentures, and this step should be attempted first. But in the long run, if calling the present issues is necessary, it is a step worth taking.

WINN-DIXIE STORES, INC. (A)

In October, 1968, Mr. Stephen Darcie, a security analyst employed by a large mutual fund, was preparing to evaluate the dividend policy of Winn-Dixie Stores, Inc. The information about Winn-Dixie that he had assembled from his firm's research files is summarized below. Mr. Darcie realized that Winn-Dixie's long-standing policy of paying monthly cash dividends to stockholders and of increasing the dividend annually was unique among major American corporations.

Mr. Darcie decided to begin his analysis by considering the rationale for Winn-Dixie's unusual dividend policy. He wanted to determine the likely advantages and disadvantages of the dividend policy from the viewpoints of both the corporation and its stockholders. He then planned to try to anticipate Winn-Dixie's future dividend policy and the effect it might have on future common stock values.

The company

Winn-Dixie Stores, Inc., was a regional food chain located in the southeastern portion of the United States, with headquarters in Jacksonville, Florida. It operated a network of 746 modern retail supermarkets which dealt in all types of foods and other items usually sold in general retail food businesses. Winn-Dixie ranked seventh in the industry in terms of sales volume and number of stores operated.

Winn-Dixie had been incorporated in 1928 and had grown by expansion and acquisition from a sales level of about $10 million in 1939 to over $1 billion in fiscal 1968. In 1944 the company had operated 118 retail stores in Florida and southern Georgia with total sales of $35 million. From 1945 to 1964 Winn-Dixie had added, by acquisition, 406 retail grocery stores located in Kentucky, Florida, North Carolina, South Carolina, Louisiana, and Alabama. The acquisition of a chain of 35 stores in Alabama in 1962 had resulted in antitrust action by the Federal Trade Commission, and Winn-Dixie signed a consent order in 1966 giving up its acquisition rights for 10 years unless prior FTC approval could be obtained. No divestiture was required, however. During this period of growth by acquisition, the company had aggressively pursued a policy of internal expansion through the opening of new stores and the closing of older facilities. For example, of the 406 stores added by acquisition between 1945 and 1964, only 159 (accounting for 20% of the company's sales and net earnings) were in operation at the end of fiscal 1964. Average weekly sales per store increased by 175% between 1950 and 1960 as the company replaced older units with large, modern supermarkets. This transition was largely completed by 1960, and average sales per store had remained relatively constant since that time.

In recent fiscal years, changes in the number of stores were as follows:

	1962	*1963*	*1964*	*1965*	*1966*	*1967*	*1968*
New stores opened	40	41	31	55	44	38	40
Stores acquired	9	36	9	4	2	0	0
Less: Stores closed	−24	−29	−18	−22	−18	−13	−15
Net increase in number of stores	25	48	22	37	28	25	25

Fifty-four new stores were budgeted for opening during the 1969 fiscal year. Construction had begun on a new distribution center in metropolitan Atlanta which was scheduled to open in the spring of 1969. Contractual obligations for construction and purchase of plant and equipment at June 29, 1968, amounted to approximately $6,000,000.

Practically all retail stores and wholesale units were in leased premises. Winn-Dixie retained title to all movable equipment installed by it at leased locations. In most instances alterations or additions to the premises were made, and their costs were carried as leasehold improvements and amortized over the life of the particular lease.

Because of occasional shifts in population and traffic patterns, the company preferred to negotiate leases for terms of not more than 10 or 12 years, although it entered into longer term leases in some key locations and shopping centers. The relatively short lease period gave the company the flexibility to shift its store locations periodically to new facilities. As of June 29, 1968, leases were in effect on locations for 746 retail stores, 7 wholesale units, and 11 other facilities (warehousing and distribution centers, bakeries, and processing plants). Rent expense on long-term leases for 1968 totaled $15,949,073.

In addition to the marketing flexibility resulting from the company's policy of leasing its facilities, the company reported in 1965 that its leasing policy contributed greatly to its high rate of return (21%) on average invested capital (i.e., long-term debt and stockholders' equity).

The company competed in its trading area with a number of national and regional food chains, including Colonial Stores Incorporated, Food Fair Stores, Inc., The Grand Union Company, IGA stores, The Kroger Co., National Tea Co., and Safeway Stores, Incorporated. However, Winn-Dixie had a larger concentration of stores in the Southeast than any other retailer, and it ranked first or second in most of the market areas in which it operated.

The geographical scope of the company's operations proved to be a significant advantage. While disposable income per capita in the South and Southeast was still among the lowest in the nation, income levels had increased more rapidly in this geographical area during the past 15–20 years than in many other parts of the United States. Furthermore, the State of Florida had shown, in the previous 15 to 20 years, a higher percentage growth in population than any other state. Both of these factors contributed to making Winn-Dixie the most profitable and one of the fastest growing of the major food retailers.

Winn-Dixie was controlled by, and for many years operated under the leadership of, four brothers: Mr. A. D. Davis, vice chairman of the board; Mr. James E. Davis, chairman of the board; Mr. M. Austin Davis, senior vice president; and Mr. Tine W. Davis, senior vice president. In 1968, the Davis brothers were still active in the company's management, but three of them were devoting less than full time to their duties for reasons of health. Approximately 29% of the 12,568,907 outstanding shares of common stock was owned by the Davis family. Approximately 233,000 shares were held by institutional investors, and the remaining shares were owned by about 33,000 stockholders.

The company dealt with its employees directly rather than through labor unions, and avoided labor problems that plagued some other companies in the industry. In addition to paying competitive wage rates, the company provided employees with a number of fringe benefits, including a profit-sharing retirement plan, a stock purchase plan, a contributory group life and hospitalization insurance program for employees and their families, and a college scholarship program for children of employees.

The purpose of the stock purchase plan for employees was to promote increased interest among the company's employees in its affairs, growth, and development and to foster an identity of interest between employees and management. The first stock purchase plan was instituted in 1952; and by June 29, 1968, employees had purchased a total of 923,848 shares of the company's stock.[1] Under the plan in effect in 1968, eligible employees could buy stock at a price not less than 85% of the fair market value on the date when a specified number of shares were offered for sale under the plan. Such stock offerings in recent years had been substantially oversubscribed by employees, and about 40% of the company's 13,000 full-time employees were Winn-Dixie stockholders at the end of fiscal 1968.

Dividend policy

Mr. Darcie's research had indicated two major distinctive features of Winn-Dixie's dividend policy. First, fiscal 1968 was the 25th consecutive year in which cash dividends had been increased and the 36th consecutive year in which cash dividends had been paid. The long history of annual dividend increases was unusual among merchandising and industrial companies. Second, dividends had been paid on a monthly basis since January, 1953. Most dividend-paying American corporations pay dividends quarterly; only a handful make monthly payments.

The record of annual dividend increases was made possible by Winn-

[1] Winn-Dixie purchased treasury stock to offset the sale of stock to employees.

Dixie's earnings history and financial condition. The company had earned a profit in every year since its incorporation in 1928. With the exception of fiscal 1967, when earnings dipped slightly, per share earnings had increased each year since 1942. The company's sales increased every year from 1928. Sales surpassed the $1 billion level in 1967, a sales level never before achieved by a southern-based retailer.

At June 29, 1968, the company's net working capital was $81,832,206, and the ratio of current assets to current liabilities was 3.17 to 1. Cash and marketable securities exceeded current liabilities by $814,958. Long-term debt amounted to $5,400,000, and sinking fund requirements for fiscal 1969 had already been met. Indentures relating to the long-term debt imposed certain restrictions on the amount of cash dividends that might be paid; however, at June 29, 1968, $92,824,760 of retained earnings was not so restricted and was available for dividends. Cash dividends averaged 71% of net earnings in the five years ended June 29, 1968. Financial statements of the company appear in Exhibits 1, 2, and 3.

One of Winn-Dixie's main objectives, according to a brokerage house study which Mr. Darcie had reviewed, was to be a "blue-chip" growth company. The company's annual cash dividend payment since 1934 and annual cash dividend increases since 1944 appeared to be part of its plan to achieve this goal.

For many years, Winn-Dixie had had a policy of paying dividends on a month-to-month basis. Mr. Darcie understood that the purpose of monthly payments was to interest as many as possible of Winn-Dixie's employees and customers in becoming stockholders. The company believed that most stockholders favored the monthly dividend payments and that the monthly budget tie-in appealed to housewives and resulted in more stockholder-customers. A housewife who became a Winn-Dixie stockholder was expected to become a loyal customer. Furthermore, the monthly payments were believed to appeal to employees of the company; and the company believed that stock ownership helped bridge the gap between labor and management, provided other personnel policies were fair.

Winn-Dixie's 1968 annual report indicated that management expected record sales and profits in fiscal 1969 and that further dividend increases would be dependent upon the company's ability to overcome rising taxes and increasing operating costs. As he began to think about future dividend prospects, Mr. Darcie decided to assume that per share earnings would continue to grow at the rate experienced during the last five years.

Exhibit 4 shows a 20-year history of per share earnings and dividends. A record of market price changes in Winn-Dixie's stock for the same period appears in Exhibit 5. Selected financial data for Winn-Dixie and other companies in its industry are presented in Exhibit 6.

Exhibit 1

WINN-DIXIE STORES, INC. (A)
STATEMENT OF CONSOLIDATED EARNINGS, FISCAL YEARS 1964–68
(In millions)

	Fiscal Year Ended:				
	June 27, 1964	*June 26, 1965*	*June 25, 1966*	*July 1, 1967*	*June 29, 1968*
Net sales	$871.8	$915.3	$982.5	$1,020.3	$1,082.1
Cost of sales	700.4	731.7	780.5	813.4	860.6
Gross profit	$171.4	$183.6	$202.0	$ 206.9	$ 221.5
Operating and administrative expenses	137.0	146.8	162.0	168.1	178.8
Other income (net)	6.3	6.9	7.8	7.2	5.8
Income before taxes	$ 40.7	$ 43.7	$ 47.8	$ 46.0	$ 48.5
Federal income taxes	20.3	20.9	23.0	22.5	24.0
Net income	$ 20.4	$ 22.8	$ 24.8	$ 23.5	$ 24.5
Lease rental expense included above	$ 12.9	$ 13.9	$ 15.2	$ 15.9	$ 15.9

Exhibit 2

WINN-DIXIE STORES, INC. (A)
CONSOLIDATED BALANCE SHEETS, 1964–68
(In millions)

ASSETS	*June 27, 1964*	*June 26, 1965*	*June 25, 1966*	*July 1, 1967*	*June 29, 1968*
Cash and marketable securities	$ 30.5	$ 25.0	$ 32.2	$ 38.7	$ 38.5
Receivables	2.0	3.0	1.9	1.9	2.4
Inventories	62.8	67.9	67.5	69.3	74.9
Prepaid expenses	2.4	2.9	3.0	2.2	3.8
Total current assets	$ 97.7	$ 98.8	$104.6	$112.1	$119.6
Plant and equipment, at cost	$ 76.7	$ 85.4	$ 92.9	$ 97.0	$104.7
Less: Reserve for depreciation and amortization	48.4	50.6	53.5	58.0	64.4
Net plant and equipment	$ 28.3	$ 34.8	$ 39.4	$ 39.0	$ 40.3
Other assets	5.3	4.5	4.2	4.9	4.5
Total assets	$131.3	$138.1	$148.2	$156.0	$164.4
LIABILITIES AND STOCKHOLDERS' EQUITY					
Current liabilities	$ 25.7	$ 28.3	$ 29.6	$ 34.1	$ 37.7
Sinking fund debentures	9.6	6.6	6.6	5.8	5.4
Stockholders' equity	96.0	103.2	112.0	116.1	121.3
Total liabilities and stockholders' equity	$131.3	$138.1	$148.2	$156.0	$164.4

Exhibit 3

WINN-DIXIE STORES, INC. (A)
SOURCE AND APPLICATION OF FUNDS, 1964–68
(In millions)

	Fiscal Year Ended:				
	June 27, 1964	*June 26, 1965*	*June 25, 1966*	*July 1, 1967*	*June 29, 1968*
SOURCE OF FUNDS					
Net income	$20.4	$22.8	$24.8	$23.5	$24.5
Depreciation and amortization	9.5	9.1	9.9	10.6	11.3
	$29.9	$31.9	$34.7	$34.1	$35.8
APPLICATION OF FUNDS					
Cash dividends	$13.7	$15.2	$16.7	$18.1	$18.8
Expenditures for plant and equipment (net)	7.5	15.0	14.0	9.7	12.1
Reduction of long-term debt	2.2	3.0	—	0.8	0.4
Other	0.4	0.5	(0.5)	2.5	0.6
Increase (decrease) in working capital	6.1	(1.8)	4.5	3.0	3.9
	$29.9	$31.9	$34.7	$34.1	$35.8

Exhibit 4

WINN-DIXIE STORES, INC. (A)
SELECTED FINANCIAL DATA, 1949–68

Fiscal Year Ended	*Earnings per Share**	*Dividend per Share**	*Dividend Payout*
June 25, 1949	$0.12	$0.04	33%
June 24, 1950	0.19	0.05	26
June 30, 1951	0.20	0.08	40
June 28, 1952	0.23	0.10	43
June 27, 1953	0.25	0.13	52
June 26, 1954	0.31	0.14	45
June 25, 1955	0.41	0.22	54
June 30, 1956	0.73	0.35	48
June 29, 1957	0.85	0.42	49
June 28, 1958	0.98	0.48	49
June 27, 1959	1.11	0.54	49
June 25, 1960	1.26	0.60	48
July 1, 1961	1.36	0.71	52
June 30, 1962	1.39	0.85	61
June 29, 1963	1.49	0.97	65
June 27, 1964	1.62	1.08	67
June 26, 1965	1.81	1.21	67
June 25, 1966	1.98	1.32	67
July 1, 1967	1.87	1.44	77
June 29, 1968	1.95	1.50	77

* Based on shares outstanding (12,568,907) at end of fiscal 1968.

Exhibit 5

WINN-DIXIE STORES, INC. (A)
MARKET PRICES AND STOCK MARKET INDEXES, 1949–68

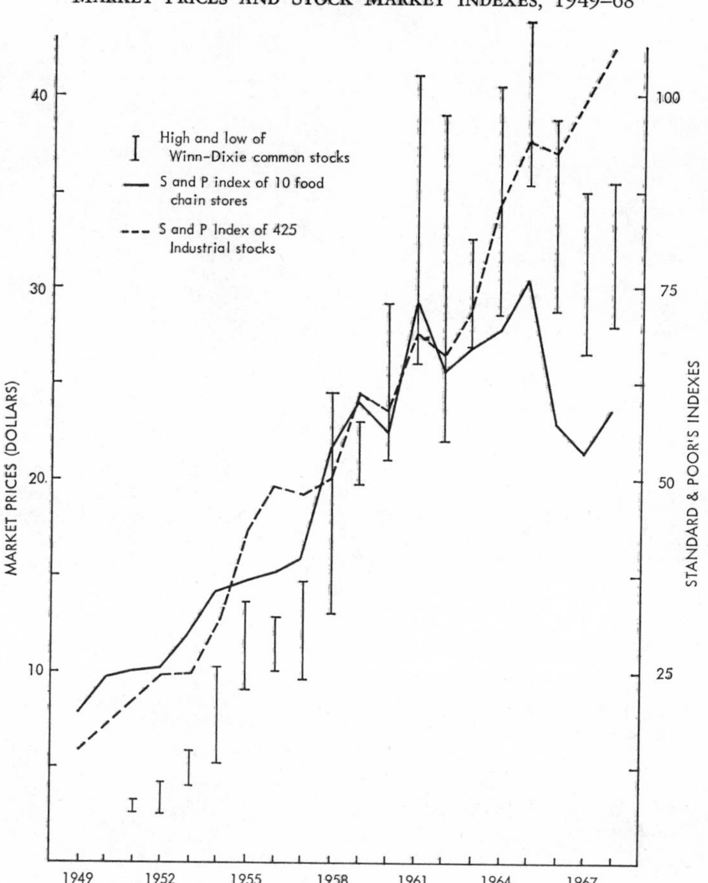

Exhibit 6

WINN-DIXIE STORES, INC. (A)

COMPARATIVE FINANCIAL DATA FOR LEADING GROCERY CHAINS

	Acme Markets, Inc.	*Allied Super-markets, Inc.*	*Colonial Stores, Inc.*	*First National Stores, Inc.*	*Food Fair Stores, Inc.*
Latest statement date	*4/1/68*	*6/29/68*	*12/31/67*	*3/30/68*	*4/27/68*
Total assets (in millions)	$275	$196	$104	$123	$291
Long-term debt as % of total capitalization	8%	65%	20%	5%	37%
Long-term debt + leases as % of adjusted capitalization[1]	58%	79%	65%	57%	73%
Profit after taxes as % of sales (latest year)	0.64%	0.48%	1.32%	[d]1.03%	0.79%
Return on common equity (latest year)	5.1%	7.0%	12.0%	[d]7.8%	9.2%
Book value per share	$55.11	$12.64	$20.64	$52.77	$15.82
Sales (latest year, in millions)	$1,294	$756	$552	$640	$1,372
Annual growth[2] of sales:					
Last 3 years	3.7%	19.7%	4.8%	−3.3%	7.0%
Last 7 years	3.2%	10.4%	3.1%	2.5%	7.3%
Earnings per share (latest year)	$2.81	$0.84	$2.48	[d]$4.14	$1.49
Annual growth[2] of e.p.s.:					
Last 3 years	−13.1%	−13.1%	7.0%	deficit	4.9%
Last 7 years	−5.6%	−5.5%	17.5%	deficit	−1.9%
Dividends per share (latest year)	$1.91	$0.60	$1.40	$1.00	$0.90
Annual growth[2] of d.p.s.:					
Last 3 years	5.0%	-0-	16.9%	−26.4%	-0-
Last 7 years	5.0%	2.7%	8.3%	−12.3%	1.7%
Dividend payout (latest year)	68%	71%[4]	57%	*	61%
Average annual payout:					
Last 3 years	59%	55%	53%	*	55%
Last 7 years	45%	51%	49%	*	59%
Average dividend yield (latest year)[3]	4.9%	3.2%	5.9%	3.9%	5.6%
Average dividend yield:					
Last 3 years	4.1%	3.4%	5.1%	5.9%	4.6%
Last 7 years	3.2%	4.0%	4.4%	5.1%	4.0%
Average price-earnings ratio (latest year)[3]	13.7	22.6[4]	9.6	†	10.7
Average price-earnings ratio:					
Last 3 years	14.2	15.6	10.6	†	12.2
Last 7 years	14.0	12.9	11.4	†	15.9

[d] Deficit.

[1] "Adjusted capitalization" consists of long-term debt, stockholders' equity, and capitalized value of lease obligations. The capitalized value of leases has been estimated, for purposes of this exhibit, by capitalizing annual lease rentals at a 10% rate.

[2] Growth rates shown are the compound average rate of increase from the beginning of the time period indicated to the current year. Negative figures represent compound rates of decline.

[3] Dividend yields and price-earnings ratios are based upon average market price (i.e., mean of high and low prices) for the year. Prices are New York Stock Exchange prices, with the exception of Colonial Stores, Inc., which is traded over-the-counter.

[4] High payout and price-earnings ratio for Allied Supermarkets, Inc., is the result of a 32% decline in e.p.s. in fiscal 1968 without a corresponding change in dividend payments and average market prices.

Grand Union Co. 3/2/68	*Great Atlantic & Pacific Tea Co.* 2/24/68	*Jewel Companies Inc.* 2/3/68	*The Kroger Co.* 12/31/67	*Lucky Stores, Inc.* 1/28/68	*National Tea Co.* 12/31/67	*Red Owl Stores, Inc.* 1/27/68	*Safeway Stores, Inc.* 12/31/67	*Von's Grocery Co.* 12/31/67	*Winn-Dixie Stores, Inc.* 6/29/68
$195	$884	$313	$548	$120	$205	$67	$654	$72	$164
12%	0	36%	10%	41%	15%	28%	8%	1%	4%
61%	60%	57%	58%	70%	61%	69%	65%	25%	58%
1.22%	1.02%	1.41%	0.92%	1.83%	0.81%	0.79%	1.51%	2.26%	2.26%
10.7%	8.9%	7.9%	10.1%	29.9%	7.6%	7.9%	12.6%	11.0%	20.2%
$17.12	$25.28	$20.86	$18.52	$7.49	$15.48	$19.65	$15.71	$17.19	$9.48
$936	$5,459	$1,244	$2,806	$627	$1,147	$313	$3,361	$268[5]	$1,082
8.1%	2.4%	16.5%	6.4%	26.5%	0.7%	1.0%	6.1%	1.3%	5.7%
6.5%	3.6%	13.6%	6.0%	18.6%	4.3%	1.9%	4.5%	5.8%	5.0%
$1.90	$2.25	$2.63	$1.98	$2.17	$1.18	$1.63	$2.00	$1.89[5]	$1.95
4.0%	2.3%	8.0%	−2.6%	31.3%	−1.9%	−7.2%	1.0%	-0-	2.5%
5.6%	−2.1%	9.1%	0.8%	21.4%	−0.6%	−0.2%	5.7%	7.6%	5.3%
$0.60	$1.60	$1.25	$1.30	$0.84	$0.80	$1.00	$1.10	$1.20	$1.50
4.9%	3.1%	5.3%	4.8%	30.3%	-0-	1.7%	5.8%	6.3%	7.4%
3.6%	8.6%	5.5%	2.4%	15.3%	-0-	3.2%	6.5%	17.8%	11.3%
32%	71%	48%	66%	38%	68%	61%	55%	63%	77%
30%	69%	48%	59%	45%	62%	69%	51%	55%	74%
34%	64%	52%	63%	52%	65%	55%	50%	56%	69%
3.4%	5.2%	4.1%	5.7%	3.4%	5.7%	5.5%	4.4%	4.7%	4.8%
2.9%	4.6%	3.5%	4.5%	3.8%	5.3%	5.1%	3.6%	4.0%	4.5%
2.8%	3.8%	3.0%	4.1%	3.7%	4.9%	4.1%	3.3%	3.7%	3.7%
9.2	13.6	11.7	11.6	11.3	11.9	11.2	12.4	13.5	16.0
10.3	15.3	14.2	13.5	12.0	11.8	14.4	14.4	14.2	16.5
13.4	17.4	17.8	15.7	13.8	13.5	14.7	15.6	15.5	19.2

[5] Sales of Von's Grocery Co. do not include $51.5 million sales of 40 supermarkets which were divested in 1967 pursuant to a decision of the U.S. Supreme Court. E.p.s. for 1967 is before an extraordinary gain (equivalent to $2.97 per share) on the sale of divested stores.

* Cash dividend payments exceeded net income for the time periods indicated.

† Price-earnings ratios not computed because of negative e.p.s. in the last two years.

Sources: *Moody's Industrial Manual* and *Moody's Handbook of Common Stocks.*

SCM CORPORATION (A)

In October, 1965, Mr. Paul Elicker, vice president and treasurer of SCM Corporation, was considering possible changes in SCM's dividend policy. He knew that this topic would be discussed at the December meeting of the board of directors, and he wanted to be adequately prepared to make a sound recommendation on this matter to Mr. Mead, president of SCM, and to the board of directors.

Earlier in October, Mr. Elicker had received a comprehensive report on dividend policy for SCM from the Corporate Services Division of Irving Trust Company (see Appendix). This report recommended that SCM resume paying cash dividends in December and eliminate its stock dividend at the same time. After reviewing this recommendation, Mr. Elicker had asked Mr. Anthony H. Meyer of Irving Trust Company for his opinion about the implications of deferring the resumption of cash dividend payments until a later time. Mr. Meyer's reply is contained in Exhibit 5.

SCM's business had been founded in 1903 to manufacture and sell typewriters. In the early 1950's the company, then known as the Smith-Corona Typewriter Company, had two main product lines. Office typewriters were expected to provide a fairly stable earnings base regardless of swings in the business cycle. Portable typewriters were thought to be more subject to consumer whims and economic conditions, and thus were expected to contribute to the company's profits primarily during periods of prosperity. On a cash basis, sales of office typewriters (with relatively short collection periods) were expected to provide a steady net inflow of cash throughout the year. Portables, on the other hand, were subject to a pronounced seasonal sales pattern, which required a seasonal buildup of inventories, and were sold through dealers who were often slow in paying SCM for the typewriters, necessitating a seasonal swing in receivables.

Because of the stability of the office typewriter line, and because many of the 300,000 shares of common stock then outstanding were held by a family group who had special dividend interests, the company had adopted what it considered to be a fairly liberal cash dividend policy in the early 1950's. For example, the dividend payout ratio ranged from 36% to 64% in the 1951–53 period.

During the 1950's, however, sales of manual office typewriters proved to be unstable for SCM, and as IBM electric typewriters began to command an increasing share of the office typewriter market, SCM's manual typewriter line began to generate large losses. Portable typewriter sales grew rapidly during this period and proved to be relatively insensitive to general business conditions. While SCM's share of the market for portables increased from 30% in 1953 to 35% in 1960, this growth of sales plus the seasonal pattern of inventories and receivables for this line created a growing need for funds at a time when losses on office typewriters were also consuming funds. By the late 1950's, these developments had created a severe cash shortage.

Despite the cash squeeze and the necessity for additional debt financing in the late 1950's, cash dividends were continued. Earnings declined to $0.30 per share in fiscal 1959, but SCM maintained its dividend payment of $0.85 per share in the hope that earnings would improve in the following year. In addition, the company planned to force conversion of its outstanding convertible debentures in fiscal 1959 to strengthen its equity base in anticipation of future debt financing, and an adverse market price reaction to a dividend cut could have made it impossible to force conversion of the debentures. In fiscal 1960, however, when SCM reported a loss of $0.24 per share, the directors voted—in a close vote—to eliminate the cash dividend payment entirely. Modest earnings of $301,747 (or $0.16 per share) were reported in fiscal 1961, but special charges and write-offs of $2,398,000 were made directly to Earned Surplus.

SCM's management had begun taking steps in the late 1950's to improve the company's long-range prospects. The acquisition of Kleinschmidt Laboratories (1956) and Marchant Company (1958) added teletype equipment and calculators to the product line; and by 1965 other product lines, such as office supplies, photocopy machines, peripheral data processing equipment, electronic calculators, adding machines, and accounting machines, had been developed or acquired.

This restructuring of SCM's business began to show results in fiscal 1962 as earnings improved to $2,592,000 ($1.35 per share), and a 2% stock dividend was paid. Management's rationale for the 2% stock dividend was that it should enable stockholders to benefit from the improving earnings outlook. Cash dividends were not considered appropriate at that time because of the company's continuing cash squeeze.

Earnings in 1963 and 1964 were somewhat below the 1962 level, but stock dividends of 3% were paid in each of these years. In fiscal 1965 earnings had increased to $3,815,477 ($1.47 per share) and management was very optimistic about the outlook for SCM's photocopy equipment, particularly a new model of the Coronastat electrostatic office copier scheduled for introduction in fiscal 1968. The directors had discussed resuming cash dividend payments during fiscal 1965; but the company's cash needs were still considerable, and additional external financing was planned to raise additional cash. As a result of the optimistic earnings outlook during a period of continuing cash stringency, the directors declared a 5% stock dividend during fiscal 1965.

As Mr. Elicker approached the study of the Irving Trust Company material in October, he had certain additional data available for consideration. SCM's annual report for fiscal 1965 had recently been sent to stockholders; so Mr. Elicker knew that investors were aware of the company's improved situation. (Exhibits 1 and 2 contain financial data about the company.) The cash situation was still tight in view of SCM's projected need for funds, but he felt that the worst part of the cash squeeze was past. (Exhibit 3 shows an historical record of sources and uses of funds; Exhibit 4 is the company's forecast of sources and uses of funds for a four-year period, based upon the assumption that SCM adopts Irving Trust Company's recommendation of a $0.10 cash dividend per quarter.)

Mr. Elicker's own research had suggested that "glamour companies" which paid modest cash dividends might have higher price-earnings ratios than those in the nondividend-paying group, but he was not sure whether the apparent difference in price-earnings ratios was due to dividend policy differences or to other factors. It was possible, but not certain, that a cash dividend might help maintain the current high market price of SCM's stock or push it up even further.

Since external financing was contemplated in the future, Mr. Elicker desired to take legitimate steps to create a better and more solid market value for the common stock. On the other hand, SCM had not paid a cash dividend for five years, the image of the company had changed significantly during that time, and SCM's stock was actively traded. The market price had risen from $25¾ to $51⅝ during September, and the shares had been trading in late October between $44 and $52 per share. Consequently, Mr. Elicker doubted whether SCM's present shareholders really cared very much about cash dividends.

Since Mr. Elicker expected dividend policy to be a main topic for discussion at the December meeting of directors, he planned to review the Irving Trust Company report again and then decide what type of dividend action he would recommend. If he decided that resumption of cash dividends was desirable, he would have to decide on a recommendation about the amount of the cash dividend as well as whether a stock dividend should also be declared.

Exhibit 1

SCM CORPORATION (A)
Consolidated Balance Sheets as of June 30, 1964–65
(In millions)

ASSETS	*1964*	*1965*
Current assets:		
Cash	$ 1.2	$ 2.1
Accounts receivable	25.0	28.0
Inventories	41.2	41.5
Total current assets	$67.4	$71.6
Fixed assets, net	22.5	23.9
Other assets	1.8	1.4
Total	$91.7	$96.9
LIABILITIES		
Current liabilities	$18.0	$20.7
Long-term debt	23.3	21.9
Deferred income taxes	0.5	1.4
Stockholders' equity	49.9	52.9
Total	$91.7	$96.9

Notes:

1. Under the provisions of the long-term debt, approximately $2.5 million of retained earnings was available for cash dividends at June 30, 1965.

2. In June, 1965, the company announced that it would redeem for cash any shares of its convertible preferred stock still outstanding on July 8, 1965. As a result of this announcement, over 99% of the outstanding preferred stock was converted into common stock in June and early July.

3. At June 30, 1965, 2,694,178 shares of common stock were issued and outstanding, and an additional 235,445 shares were reserved (and subsequently issued) for conversion of the preferred stock.

Exhibit 2

SCM CORPORATION (A)
EIGHT-YEAR STATISTICAL SUMMARY
FISCAL YEARS ENDED JUNE 30, 1958–65

	1958	*1959*	*1960*	*1961*	*1962*	*1963*	*1964*	*1965*
Net sales (in thousands)	$ 87,146	$ 90,411	$ 93,359	$ 96,476	$103,165	$117,343	$ 124,704	$ 149,657
Net income (loss) (in thousands)	2,244	482	(455)	302	2,592	1,656	2,437	3,815
Earnings per common share*	$ 1.22	$ 0.23	$ (0.21)	$ 0.14	$ 1.21	$ 0.57	$ 0.83	$ 1.47
Dividends paid on common stock:								
Cash dividends per share	$ 0.77	$ 0.75	—	—	—	—	—	—
Stock dividends	—	—	—	—	2%	3%	3%	5%
Market price of common stock (calendar years)	$13¼–20¼	$11–19½	$9⅞–16¼	$10¾–26⅞	$8⅞–24⅞	$9⅛–15	$12½–19⅛	$15⅞–52½†
Price-earnings ratio‡								
SCM Corporation	14.5	66.3	—	134.4	13.9	21.2	19.0	23.3
Dow-Jones Industrials	18.2	18.3	19.4	21.5	17.3	17.2	17.8	16.8

* 1965 on average shares outstanding after stock dividend; prior years adjusted for subsequent stock dividends.
† Range for year to October 25, 1965.
‡ Based on midpoint of price range.

Exhibit 3

SCM CORPORATION (A)
SOURCE AND USE OF FUNDS
FISCAL YEARS ENDED JUNE 30, 1958–65
(In millions)

	1958	*1959*	*1960*	*1961*	*1962*	*1963*	*1964*	*1965*
Beginning cash balance	$ 2.4	$ 4.2	$ 4.0	$ 3.2	$ 3.2	$ 2.3	$ 3.9	$ 1.0
Add:								
Income after taxes	2.2	0.5	(0.5)	0.3	2.6	1.7	2.4	3.8
Depreciation	1.2	1.6	2.0	2.0	2.3	2.7	2.4	2.5
Other increases (decreases) in current liabilities	1.0	(2.0)	(0.5)	1.5	1.7	(0.1)	1.9	1.9
Borrowings from (repayments to) banks	(3.1)	(6.7)	7.4	2.4	0.9	(10.7)	0.5	1.6
Debentures	4.2	7.4	—	—	—	—	—	—
Other long-term debt	9.7	6.0	—	—	—	—	—	—
Increases (decreases) in stockholders' equity	0.2	4.9†	(1.7)‡	(2.0)§	(0.6)¶	11.4**	0.1	0.1
Total available	$17.8	$15.9	$10.7	$ 7.4	$10.1	$ 7.3	$11.2	$10.9
Less:								
Increase (decrease) in accounts receivable	$ 5.0	$(4.0)	$ 3.0	$ 0.6	$ 1.1	$ 1.0	$ 1.1	$ 3.0
Increase (decrease) in inventories	1.0	4.8	(0.2)	2.8	2.2	(0.9)	4.8	0.3
Capital expenditures*	6.2	3.7	3.0	2.5	2.2	1.4	2.8	3.8
Long-term debt repayments	—	4.9†	1.5	1.1	2.6	1.4	1.5	1.4
Other increases (decreases) in assets	—	1.0	0.2	(2.8)‖	(0.3)	0.1	(0.7)	(0.4)
Cash dividends paid	1.4	1.5	—	—	—	0.4††	0.7††	0.7††
Total cash employed	$13.6	$11.9	$ 7.5	$ 4.2	$ 7.8	$ 3.4	$10.2	$ 8.8
Ending cash balance	$ 4.2	$ 4.0	$ 3.2	$ 3.2	$ 2.3	$ 3.9	$ 1.0	$ 2.1
Interest expense—long-term debt*	$ 1.2	$ 1.5	$ 2.0	$ 2.2	$ 2.0	$ 1.7	$ 1.4	$ 1.6

* Casewriter's estimate, based upon analysis of published financial statements.

† Increase in equity in 1959 represents conversion of outstanding 6% convertible subordinated debentures into 229,128 shares of common stock. An equivalent reduction in long-term debt is included in "debt repayments" for 1959.

‡ Net special charges to retained earnings amounted to $1,737,349 in 1960, and represented provision for nonrecurring costs and write-downs of assets (less estimated reduction in U.S. income taxes).

§ Reduction in equity in 1961 was due to special charges to retained earnings ($2,144,850), less proceeds from issuance of common stock for acquisitions and stock options.

‖ Includes write-offs and sales of assets.

¶ Due primarily to change in accounting method in one corporate division.

** Represents net proceeds from sale of $12,002,200 (par value) 5½% convertible preferred stock, after issuance and distribution expenses of $561,050.

†† Dividends paid on 5½% convertible preferred stock.

Exhibit 4

SCM CORPORATION (A)
SOURCE AND USE OF FUNDS FORECAST
FISCAL YEARS ENDED JUNE 30, 1966–69
(In millions)

	1966	*1967*	*1968*	*1969*	*Total*
Beginning cash balance	$ 2.1	$ 4.8	$ 4.7	$ 5.0	$ 2.1
Add:					
Income after taxes *	8.6	10.9	11.9	18.7	50.1
Depreciation	2.1	5.6	8.1	10.4	26.2
Borrowings—banks and payables	15.5	4.3	(20.5)	5.5	4.8
Debentures	—	—	33.0	—	33.0
Other long-term debt	—	10.0	—	—	10.0
Increase in equity†	1.9	5.5	—	—	7.4
Total available	$30.2	$41.1	$ 37.2	$39.6	$133.6
Less:					
Increase in accounts receivable	$ 6.0	$ 5.3	$ 5.7	$ 7.5	$ 24.5
Increase in inventories	6.1	7.5	8.0	10.5	32.1
Increase in lease inventories	1.3	6.7	7.0	9.2	24.9
Capital expenditures	5.0	8.5	6.7	3.9	24.1
Debt repayments†	3.0	6.9	1.9	1.9	13.7
Other increases in assets	3.4	0.2	0.8	0.2	4.6
Cash dividend‡	0.6	1.3	1.4	1.4	4.7
Total cash employed	$25.4	$36.4	$ 32.2	$34.6	$128.6
Ending cash balance	$ 4.8	$ 4.7	$ 5.0	$ 5.0	$ 5.0
Interest on long-term debt at 7%§	$ 1.4	$ 1.6	$ 3.1	$ 4.2	$ 10.3

* The reader may assume an income tax rate of 50% in his study of this exhibit.

† Increases in equity in 1966 and 1967 represent anticipated conversion of $7,441,900 of outstanding 5¼% convertible subordinated debentures for 377,378 shares of common stock. An equivalent reduction in long-term debt is included in "debt repayments" for 1966 and 1967.

‡ Assuming dividends of $0.10 per quarter (two quarters in fiscal 1966) on outstanding shares (including shares issued for conversion of convertible preferred stock in fiscal 1966 and shares expected to be issued for conversion of the 5¼% convertible subordinated debentures in fiscal 1966 and 1967).

§ Casewriter's estimate.

Exhibit 5

SCM CORPORATION (A)
IRVING TRUST COMPANY
ONE WALL STREET
NEW YORK, N.Y. 10015

Anthony H. Meyer
Assistant Vice President

Telephone: LL3–3283

October 20, 1965

Mr. Paul Elicker
Vice President and Treasurer
SCM Corporation
410 Park Avenue
New York, New York

Dear Paul:

You asked me to comment on our dividend policy recommendations for SCM with respect to what the results might be if you decide to defer the resumption of cash dividends for the time being.

Short range, we would not expect any very significant reaction. As we stated in our report, SCM's shareholders at this point are not likely to be dividend oriented. Even if they were, no reasonable dividend would provide a yield of any consequence.

However, you'll recall that Mr. Mead's remarks at the New York Society of Security Analysts last summer implied that the time to resume dividends was not too far distant. The market may be looking for a dividend declaration, not for yield but as an expression of management's confidence in the future, and may expect it to come when the

Exhibit 5—Continued

stock dividend is usually declared. To avoid any possible adverse reaction, SCM should make it clear if dividends are deferred that this decision is in no way a reflection of management's thinking about earnings prospects.

We would also have to recommend that you pay a stock dividend again this year if you don't reinstitute a cash payout. Again we are considering short-range market effect. As you know we don't believe there are any permanent market effects from stock dividends, but you could get an unfavorable temporary reaction by taking no dividend action whatever in December.

Long range, we are back in never-never land because of the difficulty of relating payout policy to price-earnings ratio. We do believe that the ultimate effect of a regular cash dividend policy is to enhance a stock's investment quality, thereby broadening its ownership base and improving both its price-earnings ratio and its price stability. If SCM defers the resumption of cash dividends, it is doing no more than deferring the time when it begins to acquire the improved investment quality a regular dividend record would give it.

If current cash needs merit a higher priority than enhancing your image a bit sooner, we would see no serious objection to delaying the dividend. At the same time, we would hate to see a "cash needs" argument marshaled against dividends year after year. There is a positive value to a cash dividend record, even if the dividend is modest. On the other side of the coin, the difference between retaining 75% of earnings and retaining them all is relatively minor in terms of helping to meet SCM's capital needs.

You sometimes hear people say that dividends can't matter for growth companies because there are nondividend-paying growth companies whose stocks sell at very fancy earnings multiples. What this argument overlooks is that there is no way of knowing where these stocks would sell if they did pay a dividend. Statistics can't tell us much, but just to take a couple of examples:

	Year	*% Increase in Earnings per Share over Prior Year*	*Average Price-Earnings Ratio*	*Payout Ratio*
Litton Industries	1962	56	34X	0
	1963	40	31X	0
	1964	25	25X	0
IBM	1962	19	40X	27%
	1963	19	34X	31
	1964	18	36X	39

There are a great many differences between Litton and IBM, and dividends aren't likely to be the most important one—but the devil can quote scripture to his purposes, and someone could argue from these figures that Litton should adopt a dividend policy like IBM's.

I hope some of these thoughts will be useful to you. Let me know if we can do anything more.

With best regards,

Sincerely,
(*Signed*) Tony

APPENDIX

SCM CORPORATION (A)
DIVIDEND POLICY FOR SCM CORPORATION[1]

I. Summary

In this report we set forth what we consider the underlying principles on which to base an effective dividend policy and then apply these criteria to

[1] A report prepared by Corporate Services Division, Irving Trust Co., Oct., 1965.

SCM. Briefly stated, we believe an effective dividend policy involves:

1. The establishment of a consistent dividend record on which investors can reasonably base their future dividend expectations; and
2. The selection of an appropriate dividend payout ratio based on earnings expectations, earnings volatility, the nature of investment interest in the company's stock, and in some cases credit considerations.

Applied to SCM, all criteria point to the resumption of cash dividends with a low payout target. Our recommendation is that the company resume cash dividends at an initial $0.40 annual rate and eliminate its stock dividend at the same time.

II. Introductory Comments

The ultimate goal of corporate financial policy is to maximize the stockholder's return on investment in the long run. Return on investment usually takes only two forms—dividends and capital appreciation. Dividend policy is an important aspect of overall financial policy because it influences, directly and significantly, both forms of return.

A simple example can be used to highlight the main elements in the dividend policy problem. Assume that two companies, A and B, both earn a steady 12% on equity. Equity in each case consists of one share of stock with a book value of $100. Company A elects to pay out 25% of its earnings in dividends, and Company B pays 75%. The results would be as follows:

Company A

Year	*Equity*	*Earnings at 12%*	*Dividends Paid (25%)*	*Earnings Retained (75%)*
1	$100.00	$12.00	$3.00	$ 9.00
2	109.00	13.08	3.27	9.81
3	118.81	14.26	3.56	10.70
4	129.51	15.54	3.89	11.65
5	141.16	16.94	4.24	12.70

Company B

Year	*Equity*	*Earnings at 12%*	*Dividends Paid (75%)*	*Earnings Retained (25%)*
1	$100.00	$12.00	$ 9.00	$3.00
2	103.00	12.36	9.27	3.09
3	106.09	12.73	9.55	3.18
4	109.27	13.11	9.83	3.28
5	112.55	13.51	10.13	3.38

Effect on dividend return

The differing dividend payout policies of A and B clearly result in radically differing dividend returns to their owners. B's dividend is initially three times as great as A's. As time goes on, however, A's dividend will overtake and pass B's, since A's dividend, in keeping with its earnings, is growing at 9% annually, whereas B's is growing at only 3%. The effect of any payout policy on future dividend returns is easily measurable to the extent that future earnings can be predicted.

Effect on appreciation return

The impact of dividend policy on future capital gains is more nebulous and more complex. On the one hand a cash dividend is a certain, current return compared with the uncertain, future return offered by potential capital gains. Therefore, investors like cash dividends, and a stock which pays a higher dividend, all other things being equal, will command a higher price.

However, all other things are not equal. The effect of dividend payout policy on earnings growth shows up very clearly in the Company A–Company B illustration. Simply stated, the higher the payout the slower the growth. More precisely, the rate of internal growth in earnings per share can be expressed as the percentage return on equity times the percentage of earnings retained. 12% return × 25% retained = 3% growth. 12% return × 75% retained = 9% growth. Since investors like earnings growth, they will pay a higher price for a stock if its earnings are growing more rapidly.

Moreover, a fast earnings growth obviously implies higher earnings per share in the future than slow earnings growth, starting from the same earnings base. Companies A and B each earned the same amount in the first year. In the fifth year A's earnings were 25% greater than B's. And earnings are a major determinant in stock market prices.

To summarize, payout policy affects appreciation return in three ways. Payout exerts pressure on the price-earnings ratio (the rate at which earnings are capitalized) in one direction because of investor interest in dividends. It exerts pressure in an opposite direction because of investor interest in earnings growth. Finally, it affects the future earnings to which the capitalization rate will be applied.

Combined effect on overall return

Clearly a low payout policy, because it accelerates earnings growth, will produce a higher stock price eventually. However, this does not necessarily argue for a low payout in all cases. A higher eventual capital gain return resulting from a low payout may be more than offset by a lower dividend return in the meanwhile.

Even if management can make a reasonably close estimate of future earning power, it is left with the problem of what capital gain returns would result from various payout policies. If a correlation between price-earnings ratio and payout ratio could be found, the capital gain question could be answered and the effect of dividend policy on overall return to investors could be determined with some fairly simple mathematics.

However, the market prices of industrial common stocks are a reflection of so many factors that the long-range effect of payout on price-earnings ratio is usually impossible to isolate. It is equally difficult to find the precise payout ratio which is sure to produce the highest overall return to investors. Nevertheless, careful evaluation of a number of relevant factors can direct a company toward a payout range appropriate to its particular circumstances.

III. Dividend Pattern

Before selecting a target payout ratio it is necessary to consider what constitutes an effective dividend pattern, since the company's goal with respect to pattern will influence its decision on payout.

The importance of dividend pattern cannot be overstressed. The company's dividend record influences the future dividend expectations of investors, and these expectations in turn affect the market price of the company's stock. Investors learn about a company's dividend policy primarily by looking at its dividend history. A regular pattern in the past implies a regular pattern in the future. A dividend cut in the past makes future payments less certain. And the more certain investors feel about future dividends, the more they will pay for them.

With this in mind, what is the most effective dividend pattern a company can hope to achieve?

A regular dividend increasing regularly would be highly effective, but a record like this can be established only by companies which enjoy extremely stable and predictable earnings growth. Many public utilities are in this category, but most industrial companies are not.

A regular dividend increasing irregularly as earnings permit is probably the best pattern which can be accomplished by typical industrial companies, subject as they are to fairly wide earnings fluctuations.

A regular dividend is somewhat less desirable, since it implies flat earnings. Unless a company suffers from a steadily declining return on equity, earnings retention should result in earnings and dividend growth.

Variable dividends offer an investor little on which to base his future dividend expectations, so they are unlikely to exert much influence on the market price of the stock.

The same is true of *irregular extra dividends.* As for *regular extras,* most analysts feel that companies which can pay them would do more for their stock by incorporating the extra amount into the regular dividend rate. Extra dividends may in some cases be a perfectly sound way of disposing of excess cash, but they probably have no appreciable effect on stock prices.

Stock dividends were the subject of an exhaustive and rigorous statistical analysis by C. Austin Barker, a partner at Hornblower & Weeks, Hemphill Noyes & Co. He reported on his work in a *Harvard Business Review* article, "Evaluation of Stock Dividends," which appeared in the July–August, 1958, issue. Barker's principal finding was that stock dividends have no lasting effect on stock prices. This being the case, and bearing in mind that stock dividends are costly[2] and tend to confuse a company's record, it is hard to

[2] Note also that stock dividend issuing costs are not deductible for tax purposes.

see much merit in a policy of paying stock dividends either to supplement or to replace cash dividends.

Credibility of pattern

No dividend record, however regular, will have a favorable long-run market effect if the dividend pattern is clearly unsustainable. To illustrate:

	Company A			*Company B*		
Year	*Earnings per Share*	*Dividend*	*Payout Ratio*	*Earnings per Share*	*Dividend*	*Payout Ratio*
1	$1.15	$0.60	52%	$1.05	$0.60	57%
2	1.35	0.60	44	0.92	0.60	65
3	1.60	0.80	50	1.10	0.80	73
4	1.73	0.80	46	0.93	0.80	86
5	2.05	1.00	49	1.00	1.00	100

Company A's dividend policy is right in line with its earnings growth. Investors will feel fairly certain about a continuation of orderly dividend increases if they believe the company has good prospects for continued earnings growth. For Company B, the same dividend record makes no sense in terms of its earnings record. If no earnings improvement is in sight, investors will expect no dividend increases in spite of the past pattern—in fact they will recognize that the future of the $1.00 dividend is in jeopardy. The future of A's dividend is therefore very much more valuable than the future of B's, even though the patterns are identical.

Payout ratio and pattern

Since corporate earnings tend to fluctuate from year to year around the line of their long-term trend, the maintenance of a precise payout ratio every year would result in a variable cash dividend. It is usually necessary, and entirely in order, to take liberties with the payout target in any given year in order to maintain an effective dividend pattern.

IV. Payout Ratio

The question of payout for most industrial companies can be approached by thinking in terms of three broad payout categories:

	Payout Percentage
Small payout	25
Average payout	50
Full payout	75

The factors which would govern the choice of one of these payout areas are discussed below.

Payout and return on equity

The rate of return a company earns on its equity investment is an extremely important element in the payout decision. A few mathematical relationships are worth reviewing to bring out the points involved:

1. *Return to investors through yield and growth.* If a stock is bought and later sold at the same price-earnings ratio and the dividend payout ratio remains constant, the total return to investors is the sum of the dividend yield when the stock is bought and the annual rate of growth in earnings per share. For example, suppose a stock's cash dividend yield on its market price is 3%, and earnings per share are growing at 7% annually. With a constant price-earnings ratio, the price of the stock will appreciate at 7% per year in keeping with earnings, thereby giving the investor a 7% appreciation return when he sells it. Meanwhile he will have been receiving another 3% return from dividends, or a total of 10%.
2. *Price-earnings ratio, payout, and yield on market value.* Dividend yield on market value is entirely unaffected by return on equity. It is a function of only two things—price-earnings ratio and payout ratio.
3. *Earnings retention, rate of return, and rate of growth.* Earnings growth is directly affected by return on equity. As we noted in the Introductory Comments, the rate of growth in earnings per share is the percentage return on equity times the percentage of earnings retained.

With these relationships in mind we can examine how varying rates of return on equity and varying payout ratios will tend to affect overall return to stockholders.

Table 1 illustrates the returns to investors which would result from various payout ratios at various rates of return on equity, assuming the investor buys and sells at the same price-earnings ratio. Appreciation return on this basis

Table 1

PAYOUT AND RETURNS TO INVESTORS

			Range of Percentage Returns to Investors				
				From Yield, Assuming Price-Earnings Ratios of		Overall	
Company	*% Return on Equity*	*Payout %*	*From Appreciation*	*10×*	*and 25×*	*At 10× Earnings*	*At 25× Earnings*
A	5	25	3.75	2.50	1.00	6.25	4.75
		50	2.50	5.00	2.00	7.50	4.50
		75	1.25	7.50	3.00	8.75	4.25
B	10	25	7.50	2.50	1.00	10.00	8.50
		50	5.00	5.00	2.00	10.00	7.00
		75	2.50	7.50	3.00	10.00	5.50
C	15	25	11.25	2.50	1.00	13.75	12.25
		50	7.50	5.00	2.00	12.50	9.50
		75	3.75	7.50	3.00	11.25	6.75

is always percentage earned on equity times percentage of earnings retained. Since yield return is affected by price-earnings ratio, we show a range of possible price-earnings ratios in the table, and the range of yields and overall returns these price-earnings ratios would produce.

Although it isn't possible to pinpoint price-earnings ratios, it is likely that Company A, whose earning power is low, would tend to sell at closer to 10 times earnings than 25. Company C, with its substantially greater earnings potential, would tend to sell at closer to 25 times earnings than 10. This being the case, high payout adds up to higher overall return for Company A, while low payout produces higher overall return for Company C. At 10 times earnings, A gains 5% in yield and loses only 2½% in appreciation if its payout is 75% rather than 25%.[3] At 25 times earnings, C gains 7½% in appreciation and loses only 2% in yield if its payout is 25% rather than 75%.

This seems to suggest that companies like A should pay out all their earnings in dividends, and companies like C should pay none. However, several factors are present which would make this unwise.

For low-earning, low price-earnings ratio companies like A, the higher the payout, the better, *provided* an effective pattern of well-protected dividends can be maintained. A payout of 75% pushes very hard at the upper limit of what would be considered well protected. Investors would have serious doubts about the company's ability to maintain a dividend rate which represented a higher payout. Moreover, investors might well be proved right. Several years of poorer earnings might force the company to cut its dividend, which would hurt its dividend record and the price of its stock.

For high-earning, high price-earnings ratio companies like C, the question of why pay dividends at all is a hard one to answer, but the major factor is the degree of uncertainty investors feel about appreciation return. Our illustrations have assumed steady earnings growth and a constant price-earnings ratio. However, investors are properly uncertain about both these assumptions. Earnings growth, particularly when it reflects a high return which will tend to attract competition, may decelerate. The future price-earnings ratio may decline, either because earnings fall short of expectations or because of a generally poorer stock market period. Moreover, investors recognize that stocks which sell at a high multiple of earnings are particularly vulnerable to market fluctuation. Cash dividends, on the other hand, are a more certain return to investors. Even a small one is to some extent an anchor to windward.

A final consideration is that some investors, particularly institutions and fiduciaries, restrict their common stock investments to dividend-paying securities.[4] Omitting cash dividends would deprive a company of this pool of potential investment interest in its stock.

Payout and stability of earnings

Because of the importance of dividend pattern, a company must choose a dividend rate which it can sustain. If earnings are volatile, a low target pay-

---

[3] Actually, A would be unlikely to sell as low as 10 times earnings with a 75% payout, since the resulting 7½% yield is extremely high. Analysts tend to think of a well-protected dividend yield of 4½ to 5% as quite attractive, and the market price of a stock with a higher yield would tend to rise until the yield declined to this level. With a 75% payout A's stock would probably sell at 15 times earnings so as to yield 5%. This tendency of dividends to put a floor on a stock's market price is a very significant consideration for companies which earn a low return on equity.

[4] For example, a stock which does not have a 10-year uninterrupted cash dividend record does not qualify as a legal investment for insurance companies under New York State insurance law.

out ratio is indicated, since this would produce a dividend rate which could be sustained even during a period of sharply reduced earnings. If earnings are stable, on the other hand, a high target payout ratio can be set if other factors make high payout desirable. Several factors influence earnings stability. The major ones are these:

Level of earnings. In our economy, a company which earns an abnormally high return tends to attract competition which will force earnings down to an average level sometime in the future. Conversely, when a company is earning a low return, chances are good that this condition will remain stable or improve as time goes on. New competition is unlikely to rush into an essentially unpromising area, and companies with poor earnings are likely to be very active in seeking ways to improve profits.

Nature of the business. By their nature some companies are far more stable than others. A company supplying parts to one auto manufacturer runs a higher risk of earnings fluctuation than a chain of department stores. Electronics companies are less predictable than electric utilities.

Debt leverage. The stability of a company's earnings is also affected by the percentage of debt in its capital structure. Debt leverage magnifies fluctuations in operating earnings into larger fluctuations in common stock earnings. For this reason, a decision on capital structure should normally be made before a decision is reached on dividend policy.

Payout and the nature of investment interest

Stockholders differ on the returns they seek on their investments. They may be seeking cash dividends, or growth in market price, or both. Each company must decide, in the light of the nature of its business, what sort of investment interest it is likely to attract. At one end of the spectrum is the investor in a new and speculative venture, hoping for market gain. He is not particularly interested in receiving dividends. He wants earnings to be plowed back into the business and feels that a large dividend would limit the company's internal growth rate. At the other end of the spectrum is the investor in a stable, low-growth company who plans on income from cash dividends.

The speculative investor is unlikely to pay a premium price for stock in consideration of its dividend, but the income-seeking investor probably will.

Summary—selection of a payout ratio

In selecting a payout ratio, we would suggest that potential return on retained earnings be used as a starting point. On this basis, a 25% payout would constitute a sound preliminary target for companies which visualize a future return of 15% or better on new investment. The payout target should move up toward the 50% area if future return expectations range down toward 10%. A payout of up to 75% would produce the best overall results if future earnings expectations are substantially lower than 10%.

The target area selected on the basis of potential earnings on equity should then be reviewed and perhaps modified in the light of (1) the earnings stability factor and (2) the probable nature of investment interest in the company's stock.

As a matter of interest, the average payout ratio of Moody's 125 Industrials during the 1960–64 period declined from 63% to 53%, averaging 59%. Return on equity during this period climbed from 11% to 14% and averaged 12%.

Special situations—nominal payout or none

Companies which are financially strong can consider their capital needs aside from their dividend policy, since strong companies can raise capital externally on a reasonable basis. Weaker companies are forced to subordinate dividend policy to their capital needs to the extent that avenues for raising capital externally on a satisfactory basis are closed to them.

Typically, new companies have a very thin equity base; their growth potential is high; and raising capital externally is a considerable problem for them. The success of these companies may well depend on the reinvestment of every dollar of earnings they can generate, and their stockholders are almost certain to have no interest whatever in dividends. Cash dividends would make no sense for these companies.

A policy of paying nominal cash dividends is one into which a young company might evolve temporarily. The company would presumably still need virtually all of its earnings for reinvestment in the business. However, a nominal dividend payout would establish a basis for eventual purchases of the company's stock by institutional investors who prefer or require a dividend record. Nominal payout would also accord recognition to the belief of many investors that a cash dividend is an indication of some measure of investment quality.

Payout and changing the dividend

Since investors know that most seasoned companies do in fact have a target payout ratio, a change in the dividend rate carries with it strong implications about management's future earnings expectations. In raising the rate, for example, management is saying that earnings will rise, or have risen already to a sustainable new plateau high enough to justify the increase. Holding the rate if earnings go off implies management's faith that previous earnings levels will be restored. Cutting the dividend implies a permanent downtrend. The market for the company's stock will react accordingly. Since one of the objectives of financial management is to minimize fluctuations in the price of a stock, it is important to change the dividend rate only when future expectations warrant such a change. Increasing the dividend capriciously can give the stock a short-term lift, but in the long run will tend to undermine investor confidence.

Payout and tax considerations

The personal income tax treatment of dividend income as distinguished from capital gains is well known to us all. Stated briefly, dividend income is taxed at full income tax rates, which range up to a current maximum of 70%, while capital gains are taxed at either half the income tax rate or 25%, whichever is less. Consequently, the argument is sometimes advanced that dividend payout should be minimized so as to permit investors to receive most of their return on a capital gains basis.

For companies with great earning capacity, selling at high price-earnings ratios, the personal income tax aspect reinforces other powerful arguments for a low payout. However, for companies with poor earnings the tax factor does not, on careful examination, justify disregarding other arguments for high payout. Consider what might happen to investors in Company A in Table 1 if it changed its payout from 75% to 25%. It will be recalled that Company A earned 5% on equity, and we suggested that a 75% payout might cause it to sell at 15 times earnings so as to yield 5%. We will assume a personal income tax rate of 40%, which would mean a capital gains rate of 20%.

		Percentage Gross Return			Percentage Return to Investors after Payment of Personal Income Taxes		
Payout %	*Price-Earnings Ratio*	*Yield*	*Appreciation*	*Total*	*Yield*	*Appreciation*	*Total*
75	15×	5.0	1.25	6.25	3.0	1.0	4.0
25	15×	1.67	3.75	5.42	1.0	3.0	4.0

In spite of tax savings, net return has not improved in amount. Moreover, it has declined in quality, since the return now has a larger component of appreciation, which is relatively uncertain, and a smaller component of dividends, which are relatively certain. Finally, a stock yielding 1⅔% and expected to grow in earnings at 3¾% is unlikely to sell at 15 times earnings. It might well drop to 10 times or below. At that level yield will be somewhat improved, but the stockholder will have sustained a capital loss of a third or more of his investment.

A final aspect of the personal income tax question is the fact that not all investors are taxed at the same rate. Speculative investors are likely to be in a higher bracket than income-seeking investors, and some income-seeking investors—charitable trusts, pension funds, etc.—are entirely tax-free. Differences in the extent to which investors are taxed will thus tend to coincide with other factors favoring high payout with low earnings and low payout with high earnings.

V. Dividend Policy for SCM

A review of SCM's present situation convinces us that a low payout target is the company's best dividend policy for the time being. Each factor in this decision is discussed below.

Return on common equity

SCM's historical return on common equity has been subnormal in recent years, but has shown marked improvement which the company expects to continue. The following returns for 1963–65 and an estimated return for 1966 are based on the company's equity at the beginning of each year and its net income for that year. Equity includes preferred equity in each year and net income has not been reduced by the preferred dividend. This gives us a good comparative performance measure.

Fiscal Year	*Return on Equity*
1963	4.6%
1964	5.1%
1965	7.6%
1966	9.0%–10.0% (est.)

Since these are overall returns which are partially a reflection of losses in the Data Processing Systems Division and unsatisfactory results in some other areas, opportunities clearly exist in the more profitable sectors of SCM's business to invest retained earnings at potential returns substantially greater than the 10% which is average for American industry. Moreover, SCM is currently selling at a high price-earnings ratio. Earnings retained might add considerably to future appreciation return; earnings paid out wouldn't constitute a very significant yield return. It is difficult to pin down SCM's price-earnings ratio because of the stock's recent market behavior; but our analysis suggests that a 20× price-earnings ratio is, on the average, a reasonable expectation for SCM. A price-earnings ratio of 20× would result in the following yields:[5]

Payout Ratio	*Yield*
25%	1.25%
50	2.50
75	3.75

On the basis of our return-on-equity criterion, a low payout appears to be indicated.

Earnings stability

SCM's management is in a better position than we are to judge how stable its business is, but we would be inclined to classify it as relatively unstable. Factors we would cite are strong competition in those sectors of its business which are actually or potentially highly profitable, a market demand subject to cyclical fluctuations, heavy dependence on continuously productive R & D, and the risks associated with capital commitments abroad and reliance on foreign sales.

---

[5] Yield on current market of about $44⅛ (October 5, 1965, closing price) would of course be somewhat lower.

Debt leverage is also present to a significant extent, and increases the potential for variance in earnings available for common. SCM's 1966 budgeted figures indicate interest coverages will be just under seven times pretax and just under four times after-tax—rather low, although they represent a substantial improvement over recent years' results.

All told, the stability factor also suggests a low payout policy.

Nature of investment interest in SCM

SCM's stock has been extremely volatile this year, ranging from $16¼ to $51⅝ so far. Most of the move occurred during the month of September, when the stock rose from $25¾ to $51⅝ and then backed off to $42. There is little doubt that recent interest in SCM is concentrated on the company's Coronastat line, principally the Model 55, and the potential for future earnings growth arising from this source. Under the circumstances, we believe SCM investors are almost entirely seekers of capital gains, and we would not anticipate that any cash dividend the company could reasonably pay would have an appreciable effect on the price of SCM stock. Consequently, we don't think the company should penalize its rate of internal earnings growth at this point by paying out a substantial part of its earnings in dividends.

Financial strength

We suggested above that financially strong companies can consider dividend policy apart from capital needs because they are able to raise capital externally on a reasonable basis. However, SCM's budgeted capital requirements, at least for the coming year, are very substantial indeed. Its 1966 budget indicates capitalization will be as follows:

	Millions of Dollars	*Percent*
Current bank loans*	14	15
Senior long-term debt	14	15
Conv. subordinated debt	7	8
Common equity	58	62
Total	93	100

* Included because they appear to represent permanently needed capital.

This compares with debt of about 20% of total capital for typical major industrial companies, whose earnings records are generally better than SCM's. We note also that the company's convertible debentures are rated double B by two rating agencies, and single B by the third, indicating that there is not a great deal of extra long-term borrowing capacity. We do not know if management is considering an equity financing. However, an offering of normal proportions would still leave SCM somewhat short on equity in terms of its growth expectations. Consequently, we believe that credit considerations suggest the minimization of cash dividends.

Statistical correlations

As we stated earlier, there are so many elements present in the market's appraisal of an industrial common stock that the effects of dividend policy are usually impossible to isolate. However, we did examine the office equipment industry, as well as a group of other companies which have some of the characteristics of SCM, to see if any significant correlations could be found between price-earnings and payout ratios. As we anticipated, the results did not show any clear relationship. Consequently, we are basing our dividend policy recommendations for SCM strictly on the general principles reviewed in this report.[6]

Recommendations

1. We believe that the establishment of a regular cash dividend would add to SCM's investment quality and would begin to lay the groundwork for eventual ownership of SCM stock by institutional investors with a dividend requirement or a dividend preference. We recommend that cash dividends be instituted in December coinciding with the time when the stock dividend is usually declared.
2. We recommend a $0.10 dividend—a $0.40 annual rate—as a starter. Our reasons for suggesting this low payout are: (1) our assumption that reinvestment of retained earnings offers a high potential return; (2) the fact that current interest in the stock is not dividend-oriented; and (3) SCM's need for capital.
3. We do not believe that stock dividends result in any real benefits to stockholders and recommend that SCM's stock dividend policy be dropped.

Comparable situations

[This section of the Report states that the record of listed stocks was studied to try to find situations comparable to SCM. Three companies were located that had eliminated cash dividends, switched to stock, and then switched back. A study of the data for these companies, the Irving Trust Report states, fails to show any significant change in market price as an immediate result of replacing stock dividends with cash. The Irving Trust Report states, however, that the experience of these companies "says nothing about the possible long-range benefits of such a transition."]

Dividend policy—long range

We believe that a long-range dividend policy for SCM can be designed on the basis of the principles reviewed in this report. There are several important factors we are not able to evaluate at the present time—the company's potential earning power and its capital structure goal—and we would be glad to review these points with SCM's management if this would be of interest. At the same time, we are satisfied that a low payout target is in order for the time being.

---

[6] Note: The full Irving Trust Report contained about 10 pages of supporting data and charts. This portion of the report is omitted from the case since the results, as anticipated, were inconclusive.

GENERAL PUBLIC UTILITIES CORPORATION (A)

^^

The dividend decision

In January, 1968, Mr. William Kuhns, president of General Public Utilities Corporation (GPU), was considering both the merit of a new dividend policy and the wisdom of inviting shareholder participation in deciding whether or not to adopt the policy. The dividend proposal which Mr. Kuhns was analyzing would eliminate three of the company's four quarterly cash dividends and substitute in their place stock dividends with a market value equal to the eliminated cash dividends. A large increase in the capital requirements of GPU prompted Mr. Kuhns to consider this policy in lieu of raising equity capital through rights offerings to GPU's stockholders.

Prior financing of capital needs

Over the period 1959 through 1967 GPU had issued common stock in 1960 and 1966. In each case, the shares were sold through rights offerings and the amount of new stock issued represented about 5% of the number of shares previously outstanding. Rights for over 50% of the shares in each instance were exercised by the individuals who initially received them.

Over the same nine-year period, the percentage of long-term debt in GPU's capital structure grew from 51.5% to 60.2% while preferred stock shrank from 9.9% to 5.4% (Exhibit 1). GPU had been able to provide the capital needed to support growth in customer electric power requirements mainly through a combination of internal cash throw-off and long-term debt additions. In 1967 the company began taking on significant amounts of short-term debt in addition to its traditional long-term borrowings. The Securities and Exchange Commission[1] gave the company authority to borrow up to $75 million by issuing commercial paper, and the company had sufficient bank lines of credit to give it a short-term borrowing capacity (including commercial paper) up to $150 million. So long as GPU wished to maintain a capital structure consisting of 60% debt, 5% preferred stock, and 35% common equity, the corporation had to limit long-term debt additions to

---

[1] The SEC held this authority under the Public Utility Holding Company Act of 1935.

170% of earnings retentions plus any new funds raised by the sale of common stock (i.e., 0.60/0.35 = 1.70).

According to Mr. George Schneider, financial vice president of GPU, a 60% long-term debt fraction was close to the limit that industry lenders and regulatory authorities would allow. Furthermore, certain states required that long-term debt be held below 60% of total capitalization if the securities of the company were to qualify as legal investments for savings banks and other regulated financial institutions. Although there was no formal regulation to establish this debt ceiling, few public utilities attempted to exceed it. A move in the direction of higher debt utilization could endanger a utility's bond rating (causing the interest rate to be higher on all its future debt issues) and/or invite additional regulation at the state and federal government levels.

Growing capital demands for the industry

Mr. Schneider outlined the reasons for a sudden surge in the capital-raising burden facing the electric utility industry.

> While the electric utilities as a group have been able to get by with occasional small stock issues in the past, in the immediate future and out as far as three to five years, we all face a dramatic acceleration in the needs for capital to finance our growth. This expansion in the need for capital has come about for six reasons.
>
> *First,* and perhaps most importantly, the rate of growth in electric power consumption is accelerating. Take "all electric"[2] homes as an example. These homes use almost five times as much electric power as comparable homes without this feature. Construction of "all electric" homes is increasing substantially.
>
> *Second,* the electric utility industry is becoming even more capital intensive than it has been in the past. The construction cost of a nuclear powered generating plant lies between $160 and $180 per kilowatt of installed capacity versus $135 per kilowatt for a fossil fired plant.
>
> *Third,* since the failure of the Northeast power grid at the end of 1965,[3] there has been a good deal of pressure for additional spending on redundant facilities to enhance system reliability.
>
> *Fourth,* the utilities face longer lead times in constructing power-generating facilities than we did 8 or 10 years ago. There used to be a four-year lead time on plant construction. Now it's six years. Since we make progress payments equal to 90% of the project's total price, a longer lead time substantially increases the size of our "plant under construction" account.
>
> *Fifth,* inflation has eroded the purchasing power of the dollar so that we're paying more for a unit of power-generating capacity than we were 10 years ago.
>
> *Finally,* expenditures for beautification such as wire-burying within cities add substantially to our needs for capital.

---

[2] "All electric" homes were built and sold with many electrical appliances, including oven, range, water heater, and furnace incorporated into the original home design.

[3] Early in the evening of November 9, 1965, a massive electric power failure threw most of the eastern seaboard of the United States and Canada into darkness. The blackout stretched from Toronto to Washington and lasted for more than 10 hours in some affected areas.

The future capital expenditures of GPU

Mr. Kuhns spoke specifically of the capital-raising burden in terms of its impact on GPU.

> Relating capital requirements more specifically to GPU, in the late 1950's and early 1960's, we expended an average of $80 million per year for new facilities. As late as 1964 we spent only $90 million. From 1968 through 1970, our capital spending will be in excess of $200 million annually, and at this time I cannot really foresee much of a letup after 1970.
>
> GPU's capital requirements made it clear to us that given our current dividend policy the company would have to raise additional equity capital through annual rights offerings to our shareholders for at least the next few years. Coincidentally, it appeared that the amount of equity financing required each year would approximate three quarters of the cash dividends which the company expected to pay out to its shareholders.

Exhibit 2 shows projections of GPU's sources and uses of funds through 1972. Since the elimination of three quarters of GPU's cash dividend would permit the company to meet its capital needs without resorting to additional annual equity financing (line 20 versus line 35 of Exhibit 2), the company began seriously to examine the feasibility of a dividend policy that would make this earnings retention possible.

Meeting the shareholders' needs for cash

The officers of GPU were sure that many of the company's shareholders preferred regular cash income. Any new GPU dividend plan would thus have to deal effectively with the shareholders' demands for regular cash payments. The company felt that this demand could be met if *stock* dividends equal in market value to the projected *cash* dividends were paid for the first three quarters of each year. By simply checking an IBM card, GPU shareholders would be able to specify anew each quarter whether they wished to sell their stock dividend for cash or receive certificates representing the number of GPU shares paid out as a dividend. Shareholders could round a fractional interest to a full share by either selling or buying the necessary fractional share. GPU was willing to absorb all transaction expenses (except brokerage commissions equal to about $33 per 100 shares) involved in selling dividend shares for cash.

A comparison—the old plan versus the new plan

When compared with a cash dividend payout ratio equal to 68% of earnings—coupled with an annual rights offering—the stock dividend alternative plus one quarterly cash dividend presented substantial tax savings to the investor (Exhibit 3).

A shareholder in the 20% federal income tax bracket[4] who normally

[4] As of 1967, the minimum marginal federal income tax rate for a married taxpayer was 14%. For taxable income between $4,000 and $8,000, the rate rose to 19%. For taxable income over $200,000, the marginal rate rose as high as 70%.

exercised his rights would receive $312 after taxes per 1,000 shares of GPU owned if the stock dividend plan were adopted, an increase of $234 over the $78 that would be received if the old cash dividend plan were continued. (See Basis A of Exhibit 3.)

The shareholder in the same tax bracket who normally *sold* his rights would receive $1,519 after taxes per 1,000 shares of GPU owned if the stock dividend plan were adopted, an increase of $117 over the $1,402 that would be received if the old cash dividend plan were continued.

Exhibit 4 shows that for shareholders in higher federal income tax brackets, the favorable impact of the stock dividend plan would be substantially greater. A shareholder in the 70% tax bracket would increase his after-tax cash receipts by more than $500 regardless of whether he chose to exercise or to sell his rights.

Comparative cost of administering the plan

The benefits of the stock dividend plan to the shareholders of GPU were fairly clear. In terms of the cost to the corporation, bank charges for each quarterly cash dividend payment were roughly $25,000. A single rights offering would cost the company about $450,000. A combination of four quarterly cash dividends plus one rights offering would thus cost the company $550,000. The stock dividends would cost roughly $175,000 each. The combination of three quarterly stock dividends and one cash dividend would thus cost GPU approximately $550,000. On balance, then, the cost to GPU of the two plans would be about the same provided that GPU anticipated a rights offering each year.

Some possible drawbacks in the stock dividend plan

GPU's dividend proposal was quite attractive from the standpoint of cash flow to any shareholder subject to income taxes. It was neutral from the standpoint of GPU's corporate administrative costs. Finally, the plan did have some drawbacks at both the shareholder and corporate levels. For example, GPU's officers were uncertain about the period of years during which heavy earnings retentions might be necessary. Comparatively speaking, quarterly stock dividends would be very expensive to administer unless the company faced an equally costly annual rights offering. Should GPU's capital requirements stabilize in the early 1970's, the company would rapidly increase the equity percentage in its overall capital structure under the stock dividend plan. Mr. Kuhns mentioned that another large utility had frozen the level of its per share cash dividend in 1952 to conserve cash for a large capital expenditure program. The utility in question had 35% equity in its capital structure in 1952. By 1962, the reduced cash payout coupled with stable capital expenditures had raised the equity percentage to 50% of total capital, and the frozen-dividend plan was finally abandoned. Mr. Kuhns did not want to make a fundamental change in GPU's dividend policy unless it could be justified by long-term benefits.

Other potential problem areas were evident in the new dividend policy proposal.

First, if a shareholder received cash in lieu of fractions of a share in a stock dividend, according to law these cash payments would be taxable to the recipient as ordinary income. A holder of 60 or less GPU shares would probably receive less than a single share in each quarterly stock dividend distribution. If this small holder wished to sell this fractional share, the cash received would have to be treated as ordinary income. The small GPU stockholder would thus gain no tax saving benefit from the stock dividend plan, and would in fact have to bear a small charge for selling the fractional share. This charge would have been avoided with a straight cash dividend. Since only about 4% of GPU's stock was held in lots of less than 60 shares (Exhibit 5), this drawback of the dividend plan did not appear to be a serious problem. However, some of the large holdings registered in the names of brokers might have been actually owned by a large number of small holders.

Second, since GPU would be establishing a convenient marketing mechanism for shareholders with the stock dividend plan, the company might have to maintain an effective registration statement continuously with the SEC on the theory that this was an indirect form of marketing shares of GPU. While this would not be a serious drawback (most mutual funds were in perpetual registration), it was inconvenient in that it would limit what GPU's management could report to the financial press regarding earnings projections or favorable company developments.

Finally, the most troublesome problem involving the proposed new dividend plan might arise with respect to shares held by estates and trusts. A conflict with regard to stock dividends could arise when the income beneficiary of a trust was not the same person as the beneficiary of trust principal (the remainderman). In such a situation, stock dividend shares were regarded as a distribution of principal in some states such as Massachusetts, while in other states such as New York and Pennsylvania they were treated as income. Where banks expected a conflict of interest between the income beneficiary and the remainderman, they might resolve the problem by selling their shares of GPU stock. GPU's officers were uncertain about how much selling pressure this problem might engender. The normal volume of GPU shares traded annually on the New York Stock Exchange totaled about 1.5 million shares. GPU's officers felt that if an extra million shares of selling pressure arose over a one-year period under normal circumstances the company's stock might have to decline 5% or more in order to attract the required number of new buyers.

If any such selling should develop, however, GPU's officers felt that the beneficial aspects of the new dividend plan might encourage new buyers to take up the extra available stock without any reduction in market price. GPU's managers examined the company's stockholder list to determine the number of shares held in trust accounts at Massachusetts banks, but they had no way of knowing how many of these shares were held in trusts where the income beneficiary and the remainderman were different persons (Exhibit 5). In addition they had no way of knowing the amount of buying interest which the new dividend plan might engender among existing GPU shareholders or investors as yet unknown to the company.

Checking shareholder reactions

Before making a decision on the new dividend plan, the officers of GPU felt that it might be useful on an informal basis to explore with some interested parties the acceptability of the new dividend proposal. GPU's officers were particularly concerned that some of the company's shares held by Massachusetts banks might have to be sold if the new dividend proposal was adopted. GPU's management was reluctant to make contact with Massachusetts bankers, however, since if the company were to do so, GPU's entire stockholder group would have to be simultaneously informed that the proposal was under consideration. A new ruling by the New York Stock Exchange Board of Governors[5] had made such disclosure necessary even though in the past companies had often sought out the opinions of major shareholders and others outside the management group—without such disclosure—before making financial policy changes.

If the shareholders were informed of the proposal, a logical extension of this action might be to ask the shareholders to vote on the matter. Since dividend policy had traditionally been determined at the level of the board of directors, Mr. Kuhns was somewhat wary of setting a new precedent by involving the shareholders in the dividend policy question.

Required decisions

In January, 1968, Mr. Kuhns thus faced the twin problems (1) of deciding whether the benefits of the proposed dividend plan were sufficiently attractive to merit an attempt to put them into practice, and (2) of deciding whether or not to involve the shareholder group in the making of this decision.

---

[5] Part of the text of the NYSE ruling follows:

"Negotiations leading to acquisitions and mergers, stock splits, the making of arrangements preparatory to an exchange or tender offer, changes in dividend rates or earnings, calls for redemption, new contracts, products or discoveries, are the type of developments where the risk of untimely and inadvertent disclosure of corporate plans is most likely to occur. Frequently, these matters require discussion and study by corporate officials before final decisions can be made. Accordingly, extreme care must be used in order to keep the information on a confidential basis.

. . . . .

"At some point it usually becomes necessary to involve persons other than top management of the company or companies to conduct preliminary studies or assist in other preparations for contemplated transactions, e.g., business appraisals, tentative financing arrangements, attitude of large outside holders, availability of major blocks of stock, engineering studies, market analyses and surveys, etc. Experience has shown that maintaining security at this point is virtually impossible. Accordingly, fairness requires that the company make an immediate public announcement as soon as confidential disclosures relating to such important matters are made to 'outsiders.'"

Exhibit 1

GENERAL PUBLIC UTILITIES CORPORATION (A)

INCOME AND BALANCE SHEET ITEMS FOR YEARS ENDED DECEMBER 31, 1959–67

(Dollar figures in millions except per share data)

INCOME ITEMS	*1959*	*1960*	*1961*	*1962*	*1963*	*1964*	*1965*	*1966*	*1967*
Revenues	$196.0	$204.8	$214.3	$ 227.2	$ 240.0	$ 253.2	$ 270.0	$ 289.3	$ 310.9
Net profit after taxes	33.1	35.1	36.5	40.7	41.6	44.1	46.4	48.7	51.9
BALANCE SHEET ITEMS									
Current assets	$ 55.1	$ 45.8	$ 47.1	$ 60.2	$ 59.8	$ 62.4	$ 60.4	$ 62.4	$ 75.4
Property, plant, and equipment	859.8	832.0	886.5	933.4	982.7	1,042.6	1,117.2	1,241.9	1,365.3
Other assets	21.0	53.0	52.9	82.0	77.3	72.3	66.5	60.6	68.9
Total assets	$935.9	$930.8	$986.5	$1,075.7	$1,119.8	$1,177.3	$1,244.1	$1,364.9	$1,509.6
Current liabilities	$ 55.3	$ 45.7	$ 51.1	$ 57.1	$ 75.0	$ 71.2	$ 52.6	$ 54.2	$ 50.6
Long-term debt	437.6	442.6	480.9	522.4	534.8	576.8	654.9	732.2	862.0
Preferred stock	84.2	84.2	84.2	84.2	84.2	83.7	79.7	77.5	77.5
Common equity	328.6	341.9	354.0	394.7	407.2	420.3	434.3	477.2	491.5
Other liabilities	30.2	16.4	16.3	17.3	18.6	25.3	22.6	23.8	28.0
Total liabilities	$935.9	$930.8	$986.5	$1,075.7	$1,119.8	$1,177.3	$1,244.1	$1,364.9	$1,509.6
Long-term debt/total capital	51.5%	50.9%	52.2%	52.2%	52.0%	53.4%	56.0%	56.8%	60.2%
Preferred stock/total capital	9.9	9.7	9.2	8.4	8.2	7.7	6.8	6.1	5.4
Common stock/total capital	38.6	39.4	38.6	39.4	39.8	38.9	37.2	37.1	34.4
	100.0%	100.0%	100.0%	100.0%	100.0%	100.0%	100.0%	100.0%	100.0%
Common shares outstanding (in millions)	22.6	23.7	23.8	23.8	23.8	23.8	23.8	23.9	24.8
PER SHARE ITEMS									
Earnings per share	$ 1.46	$ 1.48	$ 1.53	$ 1.71	$ 1.75	$ 1.85	$ 1.95	$ 2.04	$ 2.09
Dividends per share	$ 1.05	$ 1.09	$ 1.13	$ 1.15	$ 1.22	$ 1.30	$ 1.37	$ 1.42	$ 1.52
Average price per share	$24.20	$24.20	$30.30	$29.70	$33.30	$35.90	$37.20	$31.10	$29.70
Average price-earnings ratio	16.5	16.3	19.8	17.4	19.0	19.4	19.1	15.2	14.2
Average dividend yield	4.4%	4.5%	3.7%	3.7%	3.6%	3.6%	3.7%	4.6%	5.1%

Exhibit 2

GENERAL PUBLIC UTILITIES CORPORATION (A)
ESTIMATED FUNDS FLOW, 1967–72
(In millions)

		Actual	*Pro Forma*				
		1967	*1968*	*1969*	*1970*	*1971*	*1972*
1	Use of funds:						
2	Additions to plant including invest-						
3	ments in nuclear fuel	$176.5	$203.1	$250.9	$246.3	$235.0	$235.0
4	Working capital additions and						
5	other uses	13.6	4.0	4.0	4.0	4.0	4.0
6	Total funds applied	$190.1	$207.1	$254.9	$250.3	$239.0	$239.0
			New Dividend Plan				
11	Source of funds:						
12	Net income plus tax deferrals*	$ 55.3	$ 59.8	$ 64.6	$ 69.8	$ 75.5	$ 81.5
13	Less dividends (17%)†	37.6	10.2	11.0	11.9	12.9	13.8
14	Income retained	$ 17.7	$ 49.6	$ 53.6	$ 57.9	$ 62.6	$ 67.7
15	Depreciation	37.8	40.7	46.1	51.0	56.0	61.0
16	Total internal cash generation	$ 55.5	$ 90.3	$ 99.7	$108.9	$118.6	$128.7
17	Additions to short-term debt	27.8	24.4	55.3	34.0	4.2	(15.3)
18	Additions to long-term debt‡	106.8	85.3	92.3	99.1	107.2	116.0
19	Additions to preferred stock‡	—	7.1	7.6	8.3	9.0	9.6
20	Extra equity capital needed	—	—	—	—	—	—
21	Total funds available	$190.1	$207.1	$254.9	$250.3	$239.0	$239.0
			Old Dividend Plan				
26	Source of funds:						
27	Net income plus tax deferrals*	$ 55.3	$ 59.8	$ 64.6	$ 69.8	$ 75.5	$ 81.5
28	Less dividends (68%)†	37.6	40.0	44.0	47.5	51.3	55.5
29	Income retained	$ 17.7	$ 19.8	$ 20.6	$ 22.3	$ 24.2	$ 26.0
30	Depreciation	37.8	40.7	46.1	51.0	56.0	61.0
31	Total internal cash generation	$ 55.5	$ 60.5	$ 66.7	$ 73.3	$ 80.2	$ 87.0
32	Additions to short-term debt	27.8	24.4	55.3	34.0	4.2	(15.3)
33	Additions to long-term debt‡	106.8	85.3	92.3	99.1	107.2	116.0
34	Additions to preferred stock‡	—	7.1	7.6	8.3	9.0	9.6
35	Extra equity capital needed	—	29.8	33.0	35.6	38.4	41.7
36	Total funds available	$190.1	$207.1	$254.9	$250.3	$239.0	$239.0

* Assumes that net income plus tax deferrals would increase about 8% each year over the base year 1967.

† GPU's annual dividend payments had historically amounted to 68% of reported earnings and tax deferrals. Under the proposed stock dividend plan, one quarter of this amount (17%) of earnings and tax deferrals would be paid out in cash. An amount equivalent to 51% of earnings and tax deferrals would be declared in the form of stock dividends.

‡ Assuming a capital structure with 35% common equity, 5% preferred stock, and 60% debt, long-term debt additions equal to 0.60/0.35 = 1.70 times retained earnings could be made each year. Preferred stock additions equal to 0.05/0.35 = 0.143 times retained earnings could also be made annually.

Source: The company was unable to provide or substantiate data relating to income and dividend projections because of SEC regulations. GPU had a security in registration when the case was being prepared. Projections were thus made by the casewriter.

Exhibit 3

GENERAL PUBLIC UTILITIES CORPORATION (A)

Cash Effects of New Dividend Policy on Holder of 1,000 GPU Shares and on GPU as a Corporate Entity

I. Cash Effects of New Dividend Policy on Holder of 1,000 GPU Shares

	Shares	*Amount per Share*	*Cash Dividend*	*Stock Dividend*	*20% Income Tax*	*Net Receipts Stockholder*
Basis A—Shareholder Maintains Position by Exercising Rights or Accumulating Stock Dividends:						
Old dividend plan (use rights offering):						
Cash dividend received	1,000	$ 1.56	$1,560.00		$312.00	$1,248.00
Cash outlay to exercise rights to 50 shares	50	$23.40[a]				(1,170.00)
Total	1,050					$ 78.00
New stock dividend plan:						
Cash dividend received	1,000	$ 0.39	$ 390.00		$ 78.00	$ 312.00
Stock dividend accumulated	43⅓	$27.00		$1,170.00		
Total	1,043⅓					$ 312.00
Basis B—Shareholder Does Not Subscribe to Rights Offering or Sells Stock Dividend:						
Old dividend plan (use rights offering):						
Cash dividend received	1,000	$ 1.56	$1,560.00		$312.00	$1,248.00
Proceeds from sale of rights to 50 shares		$ 3.43[f]	171.50		17.15	154.35
Total	1,000		$1,731.50		$329.15	$1,402.35
New stock dividend plan:						
Cash dividend received	1,000	$ 0.39	$ 390.00		$ 78.00	$ 312.00
Proceeds from sale of stock dividend		$ 1.17[c,e]		$1,170.00	117.00	1,053.00
Proceeds from sale of additional shares	(6⅓)	$27.00[b,c,d,e]		171.50	17.15	154.35
Total	993⅔				$212.15	$1,519.35

Exhibit 3—Continued

II. Cash Effects of New Dividend Policy on GPU as a Corporate Entity
(In thousands)

	Shares	*Stock Dividend*	*(Disbursements)*
Old dividend plan (use rights offering):			
Cash dividend paid out	24,805 @ $ 1.56		$(38,696)
Cash received from exercise of rights	1,240 @ $23.40		29,016
Total	26,045		$ (9,680)
New stock dividend plan:			
Cash dividend paid out	24,805 @ $ 0.39		$ (9,680)
Stock dividend	1,075	$29,016	—
Total	25,880		$ (9,680)

[a] Assumes market value of common stock equals $27.00 and that one right is issued for each share of common stock held. One thousand rights entitle their owner to purchase 50 shares of GPU common stock at $23.40 per share. The 1,000 rights received by the GPU shareholder would thus have a total value equal to approximately 50 × ($27.00 − $23.40) = $180.00.

[b] Additional holdings are sold to maintain same equity position as under a rights offering wherein the rights are sold. In other words:

	Total Shares (In Thousands)	*Shareholder's Holdings*	*Shareholder's Equity*
Initial	24,805	1,000	0.00403%
Rights offering	26,045	1,050	0.00403
Sell rights	26,045	1,000	0.00384
Initial	24,805	1,000	0.00403
Stock dividend	25,880	1,043⅓	0.00403
Sell stock	25,880	1,000	0.00386
Sell additional shares	25,880	993⅔	0.00384

[c] Assumes stock has a cost basis for tax purposes of zero, the most conservative possible assumption.

[d] Under the stock dividend plan, the GPU shares retained by the shareholder would continue to have a zero tax basis. With cash dividends, the shareholder who exercised his rights would slowly build up a small tax basis for his stock. For this reason, the calculations assume that the shareholder does not sell his GPU holdings during his lifetime.

[e] All calculations assume that the GPU shareholder has owned his shares for at least six months and that capital gains are therefore taxed at reduced rates.

[f] The ex-rights price of the common stock should be [($27 × 20) + $23.40]/21 = $26.83. The proceeds from the sale of the rights would thus be 50 × ($26.83 − $23.40).

Exhibit 4

GENERAL PUBLIC UTILITIES CORPORATION (A)
INCREASED CASH IN HAND TO SHAREHOLDER UNDER STOCK DIVIDEND PLAN AS COMPARED WITH EXISTING DIVIDEND POLICY

Shareholder's Marginal Income Tax Bracket	*Extra Cash per 1,000 GPU Shares Owned*	
	*Basis A**	*Basis B†*
20%	$234	$117
30%	351	176
40%	468	234
50%	585	293
60%	702	410
70%	819	527

* Basis A—assumes that the shareholder would (1) subscribe to the rights offering under the old dividend plan or (2) accumulate his stock dividends under the new plan. Either action would leave his percentage equity interest in GPU intact.

† Basis B—assumes that the shareholder would (1) sell his rights under the old dividend plan or (2) sell his stock dividend and a small number of his common shares under the new plan. Either action would reduce slightly his percentage equity interest in GPU.

Exhibit 5

GENERAL PUBLIC UTILITIES CORPORATION (A)
COMMON SHAREHOLDERS OF GPU AT DECEMBER 31, 1967

I. DISTRIBUTION BY SIZE OF HOLDINGS

Size of Holdings	*Number of Holders*	*Percent*	*Number of Shares*	*Percent*
1 to 20 shares	17,089	22%	153,775	1%
21 to 60 shares	17,328	22	679,113	3
61 to 100 shares	11,152	14	949,203	4
101 to 300 shares	23,820	30	4,072,560	16
301 to 1,000 shares	7,469	10	3,680,096	15
1,001 shares and over	1,853	2	15,270,349	61
Total	78,711	100%	24,805,096	100%

II. INSTITUTIONAL HOLDERS

	Number of Shares (In Millions)
Bank trust departments:	
Pennsylvania	3.0
New York	2.9
Massachusetts	1.6
Other states	2.1
Mutual funds	1.5
Insurance companies	1.0
Pension funds	0.2
Total	12.3

Note: Some shares held by bank trust departments and insurance companies were beneficially owned by pension funds.

TEXAS NORTHERN ELECTRIC COMPANY

In early February, 1960, the board of directors of Texas Northern Electric Company (TENECO) met to discuss the following financial plan, which was prepared for the board by Stone & Webster Service Corporation. The latter was a consulting firm whose services TENECO customarily employed for advice on its planning.

* * * * *

To the Directors of

TEXAS NORTHERN ELECTRIC COMPANY

At the last directors' meeting you were informed of the rapidly growing demand for service in the territory served by the company. You also were advised of the necessity for raising substantial amounts of new capital to pay for major plant additions if the demands for service are to be satisfied. Since those preliminary discussions took place, in cooperation with company personnel we have made projections of loads and kilowatt-hour requirements and from them have prepared estimates of revenues, expenses, and construction requirements. These have been carefully reviewed and analyzed and represent our best judgment of what reasonably may be expected in the foreseeable future, assuming continuation of favorable economic levels. In accordance with your instructions, the results of our studies and our recommendations are presented herewith for your consideration.

The primary purpose of this report is to anticipate the effect of the expected growth on the company's earnings and to determine the extent of and the ability to finance cash requirements for the next few years. The following comments are therefore limited to a discussion of the financial aspects. The details of revenue, expense, and construction estimates and the assumptions and supporting data upon which the estimates are based have been omitted.

Construction Requirements

During the five-year period, cash required for construction is estimated to aggregate $20,536,000. Taken from the cash estimate, the amounts by years are as follows:

1960	$ 5,897,000
1961	4,568,000
1962	5,756,000
1963	2,767,000
1964	1,548,000
	$20,536,000

Construction costs shown include provision for new generating capacity and necessary additions to the transmission and distribution systems to serve the projected loads. The magnitude of this program in relation to the present plant is indicated by the fact that additions for 1960 through 1962 are equivalent to 62% of gross plant at the end of 1959 and for the five-year period are nearly 78%.

FIVE-YEAR FINANCING PROGRAM

In addition to the cash generated within the company through depreciation accruals and retained earnings, it is anticipated that $13,493,000 of cash will be needed from permanent financing and bank loans in the 1960–64 period. A proposed financing program to raise the required capital is summarized below:

Date	Security	(Dollar Figures in Thousands) 1960	1961	1962	1963	1964
6/60	50,000 shares common stock at $37 net	$1,850				
10/60	5⅜% first mortgage bonds	3,000				
10/61	15,000 shares 5¾% preferred stock		$1,500			
6/62	42,000 shares common stock at $41.50 net			$1,743		
10/62	5⅜% first mortgage bonds			4,000		
4/64	14,000 shares 5¾% preferred stock					$1,400
Bank loans—net change (decrease)			2,000	(1,300)	$1,100	(1,800)
Total proceeds		$4,850	$3,500	$4,443	$1,100	$(400)

Five-Year Totals

First mortgage bonds	$ 7,000
Preferred stock	2,900
Common stock	3,593
Bank loans (net)	0
Total proceeds	$13,493

RECOMMENDED FINANCING FOR THE YEAR 1960

Projected cash requirements for 1960 construction amount to $5,900,000. It is estimated that approximately $1,100,000 of this will be available from operations making it necessary to raise the balance of approximately $4,800,000 from outside sources.

During the past few years there has been a gradual improvement in the capital structure from that which existed at the time the company's stock was distributed to the public. Because of the need for additional common equity to balance out the overall financing, the company should take advantage of present favorable common stock markets.[1] We, therefore, recommend the sale of common stock as soon as possible to raise approximately $1,850,000 as the first step in the program for 1960, to be followed later this year by the sale of first mortgage bonds.

Since it appears appropriate to sell common stock in the immediate future, every attempt should be made to assure the attractiveness of the common stock from an investment standpoint. While it cannot be said with certainty what factors have the greatest effect on market values of utility common stocks, dividend policy

[1] Exhibit 1 charts Moody's common stock averages for 24 utilities for the period 1940–59. Footnote added.

undoubtedly plays a major part. For this reason we feel that consideration should be given now to increasing the quarterly dividend.

The present annual dividend of $1.40 per share established in early 1958 would represent a payment of 60% of estimated 1960 earnings of $2.33 per share on the 449,500 shares to be outstanding after a proposed sale of 50,000 shares in June of this year. On earnings of $2.44 per share based on average shares outstanding during the year, a dividend of $1.40 would be equivalent to 57% of earnings. We believe the dividend rate might be increased at this time to $1.70 per share or 73% of estimated 1960 earnings of $2.33 per share mentioned previously. This rate of payment is in line with the average payout ratio of other electric utility companies of its size. Assuming no adverse changes in the general price levels for utility securities, we would expect that if the proposed increase in dividends is made effective before the sale of new shares, it will improve considerably the price for the new stock. Accordingly, if our recommendation for the sale of common stock is acted upon favorably we think that the dividend rate should be increased at this meeting to a suggested quarterly rate of 42½ cents per share in order to have the company obtain the maximum benefit from the stock sale.

With respect to the amount of common stock to be sold, from an examination of the estimates of cash requirements for the years 1960, 1961, and 1962 it seems certain that some form of permanent financing will be needed in each of the three years. The estimates provide for part of this to be accomplished through the sales of common stock in 1960 and 1962. There appears to be little question as to the desirability of selling common stock this year, and the principal point for consideration should be the amount of stock to be sold. Utility stocks presently are in good demand, but the market for equity securities can disappear rapidly. For this reason we favor selling now enough shares of common stock to provide the equity needed for approximately the next two years. At an estimated net price to the company of $37 per share based on current market relationships[2] the sale of 50,000 shares of common stock would realize $1,850,000 in cash and provide sufficient common stock equity to maintain reasonable balance in the program for this year and next. Estimated earnings are sufficient to absorb the dilution caused by the increased number of shares and provide a modest further improvement over 1959 results. In consideration of the various factors it is our judgment that the sale of common stock in the amounts mentioned should be made and we so recommend.

With a sufficient amount of bondable property additions available, we believe the sale of $3,000,000 of first mortgage bonds is the logical step to raise the balance of 1960 capital requirements. We have projected such a sale for October 1. The 5⅜% rate of interest reflects the approximate level of rates for bonds of similar quality sold within the past 30 days.

Projected Financing for 1961 through 1964

The cash estimate shows that $3,500,000 of new money will be needed in 1961 and about $4,400,000 in 1962. At this point we need to sell preferred stock to restore proper balance to the capital structure. Consequently we have scheduled the sale of $1,500,000 preferred stock for October 1, 1961. The rate of 5¾% which has

[2] Calculated as follows:

$1.70 ÷ 0.044 = $38.50 − $1.50 = $37.00	(dividend ÷ yield − underwriter's commission)
$38.50 ÷ $2.33 = 16.5 price-earning ratio	(market price ÷ earnings per share expected in 1960)

been used in the estimates is an approximation based on today's situation. While the ratio of common equity temporarily will drop below the 32% level attained by the proposed sale of common stock in 1960, the change should not be sufficiently great to affect the bond rating. Aside from this, we believe it is desirable, where possible, to space common stock sales at less frequent intervals. The balance of 1961 requirements, estimated to be $2,000,000, should be obtainable through short-term bank credit.

In 1962 an additional common stock sale will be necessary if an improved common equity ratio is to be accomplished. Therefore permanent financing projected for that year consists of the sale of an estimated 42,000 shares of common stock on or about June 1, 1962, to net $1,743,000 and the sale on October 1 of $4,000,000 principal amount of first mortgage bonds. Assuming payment of common dividends in the range of 74% of available earnings, the annual rate could be $1.90 when the common stock is sold in 1962. Based on such a dividend and anticipating about the same yield basis as estimated for the 1960 sale, we have estimated a price of $41.50 per share net to the company.

Completion of the permanent financing program, insofar as it is possible to make recommendations for such future dates, contemplates the sale of an additional 14,000 shares ($1,400,000) of preferred stock on April 1, 1964, to retire bank loans assumed to be issued for temporary financing of 1963 construction and the balance carried over from 1962.

Capital Structure

The condensed table which follows shows the changes in capitalization ratios and related dollar figures over the period:

(In Thousands of Dollars)

	Actual	Estimated				
	1959	*1960*	*1961*	*1962*	*1963*	*1964*
Bonds (net of retirements)	$10,020	$12,960	$12,900	$16,840	$16,780	$16,720
Debentures (net of retirements)	2,825	2,750	2,675	2,600	2,525	2,450
Total long-term debt	$12,845	$15,710	$15,575	$19,440	$19,305	$19,170
Bank loans			2,000	700	1,800	
Total debt	$12,845	$15,710	$17,575	$20,140	$21,105	$19,170
Preferred stock (net of retirements)	2,750	2,750	4,168	4,085	3,957	5,229
Common equity	6,589	8,749	9,093	11,187	11,585	12,010
Total capitalization	$22,184	$27,209	$30,836	$35,412	$36,647	$36,409

(In Percent)

	Actual	Estimated				
	1959	*1960*	*1961*	*1962*	*1963*	*1964*
Bonds	45.2	47.6	41.8	47.5	45.8	45.9
Debentures	12.7	10.1	8.7	7.4	6.9	6.7
Total long-term debt	57.9	57.7	50.5	54.9	52.7	52.6
Bank loans			6.5	2.0	4.9	
Total debt	57.9	57.7	57.0	56.9	57.6	52.6
Preferred stock	12.4	10.1	13.5	11.5	10.8	14.4
Common equity	29.7	32.2	29.5	31.6	31.6	33.0
Total capitalization	100.0	100.0	100.0	100.0	100.0	100.0

The principal effect of the proposed financing schedule is a reduction in total long-term debt from 57.9% of the total capitalization at the beginning of the five-year period to 52.6% at the end of 1964. This reduction is brought about by increasing the proportion of preferred stock from 12.4% in 1959 to 14.4% estimated in 1964 and by an improvement in the common equity ratio from 29.7% for 1959 to 33.0% at the end of 1964, together with the operation of debenture sinking funds and the increase in total capitalization.

EARNINGS AND DIVIDENDS

The following tabulation summarizes estimated earnings and dividends and the percentages of earnings paid in the form of common dividends:

Year	*Earnings per Share*	*Annual Dividend Rate*	*Total Dividends as Percentage of Total Earnings*
1959 act.	$2.17	$1.40	64.5%
1960 est.	2.33	1.70	67.0
1961	2.46	1.70	69.0
1962	2.55	1.90	69.6
1963	2.71	1.90	70.1
1964	2.86	2.00	69.8

The earnings per share shown in the above tabulation are based on shares outstanding at the end of the year. Computed on average shares they would be $2.44 and $2.64 in 1960 and 1962, respectively. The annual dividend rate is the rate in effect at the year-end, and in 1960 and 1962 it reflects changes during the respective years. This explains the apparent discrepancies in those two years in the ratios of dividends paid to earnings available for common stock, which are computed on aggregate dollar dividends and earnings.

CONCLUSIONS AND RECOMMENDATIONS

It is our recommendation that the company proceed with the immediate sale of 50,000 shares of common stock. If work on this proposed sale is begun now, it should be possible to close on or about June 1. To improve the marketability of the stock and obtain the most advantageous price we also recommend increasing the dividend on the common stock from the present basis of $1.40 annually to $1.70 per annum by declaring a quarterly dividend of 42½ cents per share effective with the next dividend payable on May 1, 1960. Preliminary steps should also be taken looking to the sale of $3,000,000 of first mortgage bonds not later than the last quarter of this year.

The various financing steps suggested beyond these immediate proposals should be considered as tentative. It is felt that they represent a reasonable program for raising the amounts needed but because of changing market conditions and the possibility of revised operating requirements, they should be subject to review as each successive step is taken. Although changes are inevitable, the basic plan set forth should maintain the company's credit and permit a moderate increase in the earnings for the common shares.

Respectfully submitted,
STONE & WEBSTER SERVICE CORPORATION[3]

* * * * *

[3] A summary of data supporting the Stone & Webster report appears as Exhibit 2. Cumulative capital requirements assuming existing financial policies are shown in Exhibit 3.

The Texas Northern Electric Company began operations in Bordertown, Texas, during the early 1900's. The company engaged in the generation, purchase, and sale of electricity in an area of north-central Texas approximately 70 miles long and 30 miles wide centered around the city of Bordertown. For many years TENECO exhibited below-average growth, but by the early 1940's it was one of the country's more rapidly growing electric utilities. The population of the area served by the company increased by 20% from 1950 to 1960, until it currently numbered over 200,000 people. This annual rate of increase was about 4%, compared with 1.7% for the country as a whole.

Until 1955, all the company's outstanding common stock was held by three very wealthy individuals whose marginal tax rate on dividends was 87%. In 1955 the owners made a secondary stock offering to provide a market value for estate planning purposes and to create wider public interest in TENECO's affairs. The original stockholders had also wished to increase the diversity of their portfolios and were no longer willing to add further to their investments in TENECO. By 1960, these individuals had reduced their holdings to 40% of outstanding shares, and they contemplated no further sales of their stock. One block of common, constituting 20% of total shares, had been placed directly with a large nontaxable charitable foundation. Otherwise, the stock was owned by 2,700 individuals, most of whom owned 100 shares or less and lived in surrounding areas. In the future, management planned to sell any additional common stock offerings through a New York underwriter in order to attract wider interest in the company's securities, particularly among large eastern investors such as the pension trust funds. Management hoped that wider distribution would enhance the stock's market reputation and facilitate issuing bonds, debentures, and preferred stock on more favorable terms in the future.

Managements in the electric utility industry were usually able to plan their financial requirements with a high degree of accuracy for several years ahead. Previous five-year forecasts prepared by Stone & Webster had proved quite reliable because the stable rate of growth in TENECO's area provided a ready basis for forecasting kilowatt-hour demand and load requirements. In the past, facility needs beyond three years had occasionally been underestimated, but this did not prove serious as the first few years of the forecast were usually fairly accurate.

In the discussion that developed out of the 1960 Stone & Webster report for TENECO, the board focused its attention on three areas: (1) the recommendation to increase the common stock dividend; (2) a suggested change in debt policy; and (3) the sequence, amounts, and security types proposed by the report.

Prior to 1960, the company followed a policy of paying out approximately 60% of current earnings in dividends, although actual payment varied somewhat from year to year. In contrast, Stone & Webster recommended an increase in payout ratio to 70% of earnings in future years. This proposed change would place TENECO more in line with the industry average, which approximated 75% of earnings. In March, 1958, the board had increased the quarterly dividend rate from 30.0 cents to 35.0 cents per share. Stone & Webster proposed an immediate increase in the quarterly rate to 42.5 cents per share. It was hoped that the proposed change in payout would broaden the marketability of the stock and might drive up the common stock market price to a level where fewer shares would be required to support future capital requirements.

During the early postwar period when its debt was held privately, TENECO's debt capitalization was heavy compared with that of other, comparable companies. Beginning in 1955, management had attempted to bring capitalization ratios more in line with industry averages:

	1952	*1955*	*1958*	*Present Target Capitalization Ratio as per TENECO Policy*
Mortgage bonds	47%	49%	51%	46%
Debentures (general claims)	19	11	6	12
	66%	60%	57%	58%
Preferred stock	4%	6%	12%	12%
Common stock and surplus	30	34	31	30

First mortgage bond indentures contained a provision limiting total mortgage bonds to 60% of net utility property. This restriction did not affect TENECO's ability to issue debentures or borrow short-term funds.

In its 1960 report, Stone & Webster recommended that TENECO reduce the debt proportion to 52% of capitalization over the next five years. Ideal target capitalization ratios suggested by Stone & Webster were: long-term debt, 50%; preferred stock, 15%; and common stock, 35%. As a matter of long-standing practice, Stone & Webster had advocated these policies to its electric utility clients, and many utilities had debt ratios in line with this recommendation. Moreover, after passage of the Public Utility Holding Company Act of 1935, the Securities and Exchange Commission had actively encouraged electric and gas companies under its purview to reduce debt to 50% of capitalization.

Moody's Investors Service, widely used by utility analysts, had rated TENECO's public issues of mortgage bonds and debentures A and Baa respectively. Normally, the debentures[4] of a utility were rated one grade below its mortgage bonds. Although Moody's never divulged its bases for making bond evaluations, TENECO's small size and dependence on the prosperity of one area made it very unlikely that the company's mortgage debt would be rated above A by Moody's in the foreseeable future. However, TENECO could

[4] Recently, TENECO had paid approximately ⅛% more for its debentures than its bonds.

probably continue to earn A ratings on its mortgage bonds provided total debt did not exceed "prudent" levels, very generally regarded as about 57% of capitalization for companies of its size. The many financial and nonfinancial factors (attitudes of local regulatory authorities, marketability of the securities, etc.) considered by Moody's made a precise upper limit difficult to determine.

Generally speaking, for companies comparable to TENECO, the factors considered most important in Moody's bond ratings were as follows: earnings coverage of long-term debt charges; overall coverage; capitalization ratios; size of company (it was unusual for a company with total revenues under $10 million to have more than a Baa rating on its mortgage bonds); proportion of debt to net plant; and the distribution of revenues and customers by kind of service. (See Exhibits 4 and 5 for summaries of information relating to some of these factors on 20 companies comparable to TENECO). Other important factors included: territory served; degree of competition with public power; diversification of industrial customers; and overall evaluation of management. TENECO appeared favorably situated with regard to this latter group of factors.

In view of the magnitude of TENECO's estimated construction program (and, hence, future capital requirements), Stone & Webster recommended that the company aim at a 52% debt to capitalization policy for three primary reasons: The 52% ratio would be more in line with industry averages and might, as a consequence, have a favorable effect upon capital costs for preferred and common stock as well as debt. Such a ratio would better assure future A ratings on mortgage debt. (Since Moody's Investors Service revised ratings whenever circumstances seemed appropriate, a firm treading too near the A–Baa borderline might expose itself unduly to a lower bond rating in the event unforeseen adversity developed.) Finally, the new debt policy would allow greater flexibility in timing future capital issues.

Management was particularly anxious to preserve an A rating on TENECO's mortgage bonds. Once a Baa rating was placed on mortgage bonds, all the firm's securities would become more difficult to market (some institutional investors were restricted by law, others by policy, as to the quality of securities in their portfolios). As shown in Exhibit 6, Baa bonds sold at a higher yield than higher grade bonds. In addition, it was true that yields varied slightly within the A range, depending on market evaluation of quality. Bond ratings also affected preferred yields in a similar fashion, and lower ratings might adversely affect the market prices of a firm's common stock. Once a rating dropped to Baa, major improvement in corporate affairs was necessary to receive an improved rating; also, any reduction in bond rating was not easy to erase from the minds of potential investors.

Many insurance companies and pension trusts have staffs that independently appraise new bond issues. These ratings do not always agree with Moody's. It was generally believed that the debt restriction in the first mortgage bond indenture was likely to satisfy these institutional investors' safety requirements, provided TENECO's coverage of interest was not significantly out of line with the industry at the moment. These investors were actively seeking securities with higher yields and had found lower quality A or higher quality Baa bonds particularly attractive. As a result, yield differentials between lowest A and highest B were currently less than ⅛%, and occasionally Baa's carried lower yields than A's. (Bond marketability was a less important consideration for these investors.) In short, TENECO would not have immediate difficulty placing new debt issues, even those rated Baa, and the only disadvantage of current debt policy arose from the possibility of slightly higher interest costs.

It was accepted for purposes of analysis that the proposed changes in financial policies would not have any effect on future rate determinations by utility commissions. In short, TENECO management had the same incentives to minimize capital costs as any unregulated company.

Selected comments by the directors on debt policy are included as Exhibit 7.

Exhibit 1

TEXAS NORTHERN ELECTRIC COMPANY

MOODY'S COMMON STOCK AVERAGES
COVERING 24 UTILITIES

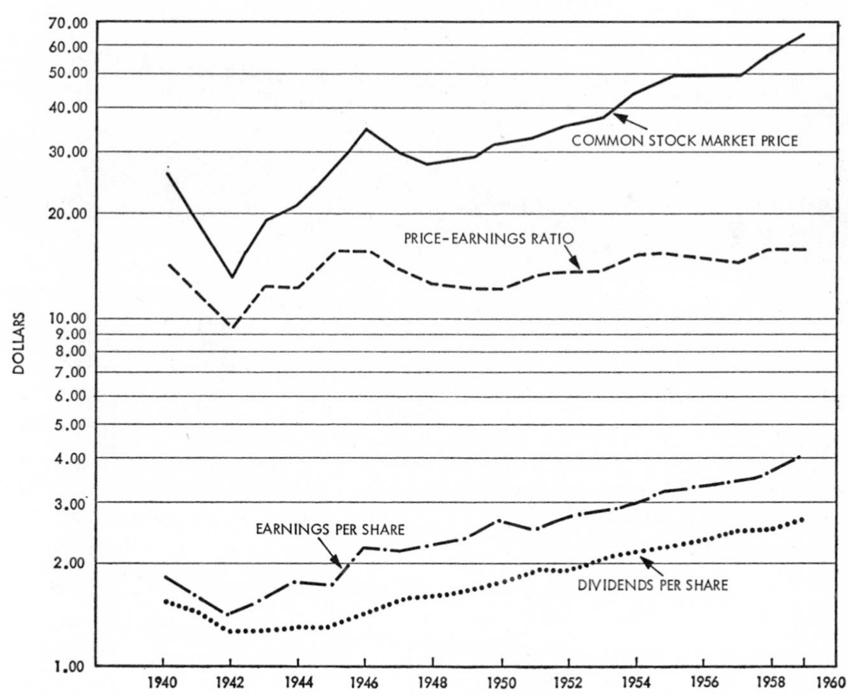

Exhibit 2

TEXAS NORTHERN ELECTRIC COMPANY

SUMMARY OF DATA SUPPORTING STONE & WEBSTER REPORT

(Dollar figures in thousands)

		Actual 1959	Estimated 1960	1961	1962	1963	1964
1	Operating revenues	$ 7,030	$ 7,682	$ 8,350	$ 9,530	$ 10,865	$ 11,864
2	Income before interest and taxes	2,249	2,707	2,932	3,414	3,777	4,111
3	Interest on present bonds	312	310	308	306	304	302
4	Interest on new bonds (@ 5⅜%)	...	41	162	216	377	377
5	Interest on debentures	97	95	92	89	87	85
6	Interest on short-term credit	21	37	58	93	58	35
7	Interest charged to construction*	(165)	(118)	(192)	(204)	(111)	(12)
8	Income before federal taxes	$ 1,984	$ 2,342	$ 2,504	$ 2,914	$ 3,062	$ 3,324
9	Federal taxes (@ 50%)	992	1,171	1,252	1,457	1,531	1,662
10	Net income	$ 992	$ 1,171	$ 1,252	$ 1,457	$ 1,531	$ 1,662
11	Preferred dividends on present stock	124	124	120	117	111	105
12	Preferred dividends on new stock (@ 5¾%)	...	...	24	87	88	149
13	Balance for common stock	$ 868	$ 1,047	$ 1,108	$ 1,253	$ 1,332	$ 1,408
14	Dividends on common stock	560	702	764	872	934	983
15	Balance to retained earnings	$ 308	$ 345	$ 344	$ 381	$ 398	$ 425
16	Shares outstanding (end of period)	399,500	449,500	449,500	491,500	491,500	491,500
17	Earnings per share (end of period)	$ 2.17	$ 2.33	$ 2.46	$ 2.55	$ 2.71	$ 2.86
18	Dividends per share (quarter made effective)	1.40	1.70(2)	1.70	1.90(2)	1.90	2.00
19	Fixed charges and preferred dividends, times earned†	3.23	3.14	2.93	2.77	2.46	2.35

* State regulatory commissions usually require that interest accrued during construction be capitalized.
† Coverage ratios computed as follows:

	1959	1960	1961	1962	1963	1964
Income before interest and taxes	$2,249	$2,707	$2,932	$3,414	$3,777	$4,111
Federal taxes (@ 50%)	992	1,171	1,252	1,457	1,531	1,662
Gross income	$1,257	$1,536	$1,680	$1,957	$2,246	$2,449
Interest charges (net of construction credit)	$ 265	$ 365	$ 428	$ 500	$ 715	$ 787
Preferred dividends	124	124	144	204	199	254
Total fixed charges and preferred dividends	$ 389	$ 489	$ 572	$ 704	$ 914	$1,041
Coverage ratios (gross income divided by total fixed charges and preferred dividends)	3.23	3.14	2.93	2.77	2.46	2.35

Exhibit 3

TEXAS NORTHERN ELECTRIC COMPANY

CUMULATIVE CAPITAL REQUIREMENTS
ASSUMING EXISTING FINANCIAL POLICIES
(Dollar figures in millions)

	1960		1961		1962		1964	
	Existing Policies	%	*Existing Policies*	%	*Existing Policies*	%	*Existing Policies*	%
Target year-end capitalizations:								
Bonds	$12.52	46	$14.18	46	$16.29	46	$16.75	46
Debentures	3.26	12	3.70	12	4.25	12	4.37	12
Preferred stock	3.26	12	3.70	12	4.25	12	4.37	12
Common equity	8.17	30	9.26	30	10.62	30	10.92	30
Total	$27.21	100	$30.84	100	$35.41	100	$36.41	100
Actual capital structure on December 31 (before consideration of new issues):								
Bonds (after sinking fund)	$ 9.96		$ 9.90		$ 9.84		$ 9.72	
Debentures (after sinking fund)	2.75		2.68		2.60		2.45	
Preferred stock	2.75		2.66		2.58		2.33	
Common equity (including additional retained earnings)*	7.01		7.45		7.95		9.05	
Total	$22.47		$22.69		$22.97		$23.55	
Cumulative additional capital requirements to meet target capitalization ratios:								
Bonds	$ 2.56		$ 4.28		$ 6.45		$ 7.03	
Debentures	0.51		1.02		1.65		1.92	
Preferred stock	0.51		1.04		1.67		2.04	
Common stock	1.16		1.81		2.67		1.87	
Total	$ 4.74		$ 8.15		$12.44		$12.86	
Maximum limit to total bonds under first mortgage bond indenture	$13.52		$15.61		$18.34		$18.98	

* Incremental dividends under 70% payout policy are:

1960	$ 74,000
1961	99,000
1962	120,000
1963	134,000
1964	138,000
Total	$565,000

Exhibit 4

TEXAS NORTHERN ELECTRIC COMPANY*

SELECTED INDUSTRY STATISTICS FOR COMPANIES WITH REVENUES LESS THAN $25 MILLION*

(Based on most recent data)

		Price-Earnings Ratio[1]	*Dividend Yield*[2]	*Growth Rate*[3]	*Payout Ratio*[4]	*Debt Ratio*	*Common Equity Ratio*	*1958 Times Interest Covered after Taxes*[5]	*1959 Times Fixed Charges + Preferred Dividends Covered*	*(Actual) or Estimated Moody's Bond Rating*	*Operating Revenue (Millions of Dollars)*
1	Public Service, New Mexico	23.3	2.8%	14.0%	66%	53.4%	33.5%	4.16	3.53	A	17.1
2	Central Louisiana Electric	21.5	4.0	3.6	86	57.1	31.2	3.12	2.73	(Baa)	19.2
3	Colorado Central Power	21.1	3.4	6.6	72	49.8	45.1	3.25	2.87	Baa	6.5
4	El Paso Electric	20.6	3.3	8.3	69	49.7	35.6	6.07	3.80	(Aa)	17.1
5	California Oregon Power	17.9	4.8	−3.4	85	57.2	33.4	2.84	2.15	(A)	23.7
6	Southwestern Electric	17.1	4.2	5.4	72	57.6	27.4	4.52	2.43	Baa	3.6
7	Upper Peninsular Power	16.6	5.6	−5.1	92	59.9	29.1	2.59	2.09	(Baa)	6.3
8	Missouri Utilities	16.6	4.9	−1.7	81	56.0	34.3	2.70	2.20	Baa	7.9
9	Southern Nevada Power	16.2	3.8	11.1	61	54.8	39.5	2.31	2.19	(Baa)	9.1
10	Arkansas-Missouri	16.1	4.6	4.2	75	58.2	30.2	2.86	2.29	Baa	12.3
11	Sierra Pacific Power	16.0	4.2	9.4	67	58.0	30.4	3.29	2.55	(Baa)	12.0
12	Southern Colorado Power	15.8	5.0	1.4	78	48.5	33.8	5.67	3.83	Baa	7.9
13	Green Mountain Power	15.3	5.7	2.6	88	57.9	35.6	3.18	2.68	Baa	6.7
14	Fitchburg Gas & Electric	15.2	5.4	0.4	82	43.9	48.2	4.02	3.16	Baa	5.4
15	Iowa Southern Utilities	14.1	4.8	5.7	67	57.3	38.1	2.81	2.55	(Baa)	16.5
16	Northwestern Public Service	13.9	5.2	1.3	72	56.0	30.3	2.91	2.22	(Baa)	11.5
17	Edison Sault Electric	13.4	4.7	5.1	63	57.9	31.9	2.93	2.48	Baa	2.7
18	Black Hills Power & Light	12.9	4.5†	4.5	59	54.6	36.3	3.24	2.43	Baa	6.8
19	Newport Electric	12.9	5.2	4.5	67	54.0	34.0	2.57	2.12	Baa	2.8
20	Bangor Hydro Electric	12.6	5.1	4.2	64	51.5	33.3	3.42	2.22	A	8.0
	Average of 20 companies	16.5	4.6	4.1	73	54.7‡	34.5	3.42	2.63		
21	Teneco	17.7	3.7	7.3	64	57.9	29.7	4.74	3.23	A	7.0

(1) Ratio market price 1/29/60 to most recent published earnings per share.
(2) Existing dividend rate divided by market price 1/29/60.
(3) The rate which will discount average 1958–59 eps to equal the average 1955–56 eps.
(4) Current dividend rate divided by most recent reported earnings per share.
(5) Earnings after taxes but before fixed charges divided by fixed charges.

* Common stock of all these companies was traded over-the-counter.
† Plus stock dividend.
‡ Average of 125 companies: 51.7% debt.
Sources: 1. Bear, Stearns & Co., *Monthly Comparison of Electric Utility Common Stocks.*
2. *Moody's Public Utility Manual.*

Exhibit 5

TEXAS NORTHERN ELECTRIC COMPANY

Graph Showing Relationship between Price-Earnings Ratio, Dividend Payout Rate, and Rate of Earnings Growth per Share

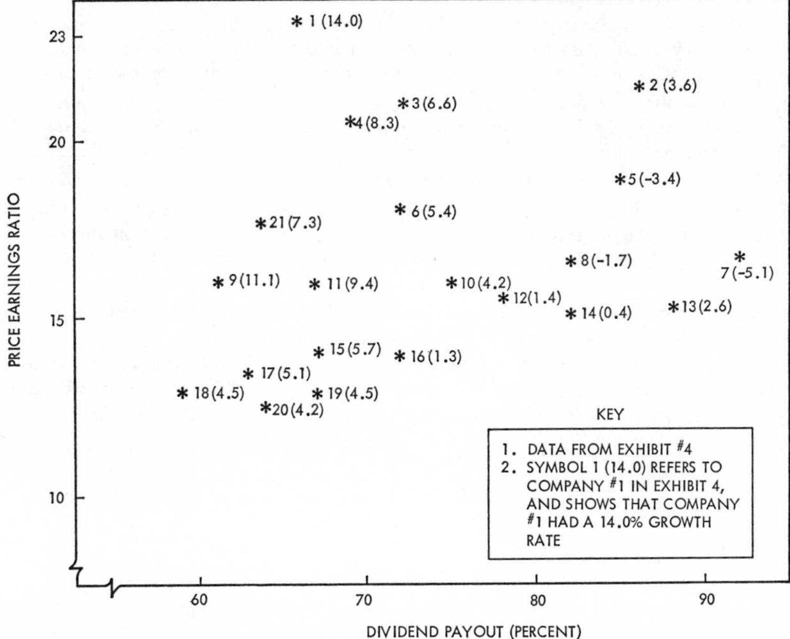

Exhibit 6

TEXAS NORTHERN ELECTRIC COMPANY

Moody's Public Utility Bond Yields by Ratings*

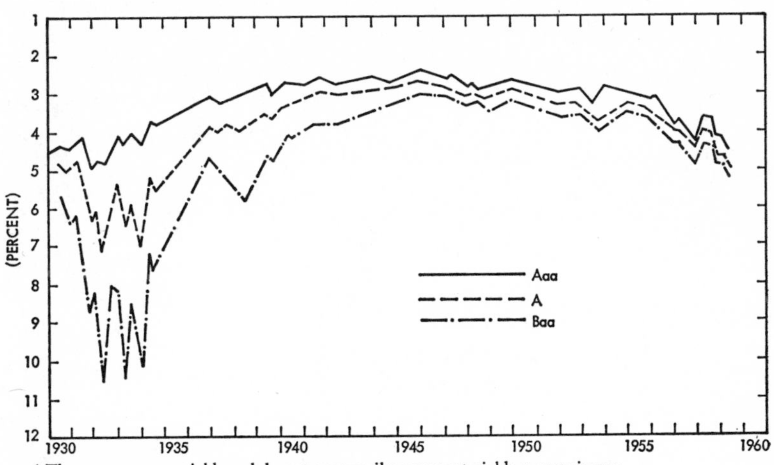

* These are average yields and do not necessarily represent yields on new issues.

Exhibit 7

TEXAS NORTHERN ELECTRIC COMPANY

Selected Comments by Directors on the Debt Policy Question

1. TENECO's president: "I've become convinced A bond ratings are extremely important in this industry and this factor should be our single most important consideration."
2. Manufacturing company president: "Current debt levels are much too risky for a company owned in part by small stockholders, and should be reduced. I would like to see TENECO move immediately to a 52% debt to total capitalization ratio."
3. Department store owner: "Companies in the department store industry often have comparably high debt to capitalization ratios (after capitalizing leases) despite less inherent profit stability."
4. A second manufacturing company president: "The financial plan requires too heavy dependence on short-term bank loans in view of money market uncertainties."
5. A retired manufacturer commented: "Reduction in debt proportions will increase new common equity requirements, add undesirable dilution, and unnecessarily limit appreciation opportunities in which our stockholders are most interested."
6. Commercial banker: "Too much emphasis has been placed upon bond ratings. We should instead continue present plans to minimize capital costs."

Although management personally valued the views of each board member, it was recognized that the board's inexperience in utility management occasionally created difficulties in areas where public utility problems were unique.

SPLASH SOAP CORPORATION

^^

In late December, 1958, Mr. William Cavanaugh, treasurer of Splash Soap Corporation, was considering how the company should finance a new plant in Chicago, Illinois. The expansion proposal introduced by Mr. Badin Farley, production vice president, called for the construction of a new plant to be completed late in 1960. After consulting several financing sources, Mr. Cavanaugh had obtained an offer of a mortgage loan from Morrissey Life Insurance Company and an offer from Dillon National Bank for a sale-and-leaseback arrangement. Splash Soap Corporation had used both methods of financing in the past. However, no decision had been reached until Mr. Cavanaugh could analyze the problem and present his recommendations at the next meeting of management to be held in January, 1959.

Splash Soap Corporation was a medium-sized company engaged in the manufacture and sale of powdered and liquid detergents and cleaning agents for commercial dishwashing and household use. In 1958 sales of commercial dishwashing and household products accounted for about 55% and 35% of total sales, respectively. The remaining 10% of sales came from different types of automatic dispensers of dry and liquid detergents. These dispensers were sold to customers for installation on dishwashing equipment to improve the efficiency of the company's detergents. (Exhibits 1–3 show recent financial data.)

In 1958, Splash Soap Corporation conducted manufacturing operations in three plants. The main plant and office building, located in Syracuse, New York, were leased from Morrissey Life Insurance Company under a sale-and-leaseback arrangement. Plants located in Chicago and Los Angeles were owned outright by the company. In addition, the company leased sales offices and space in public warehouses in various cities throughout the United States and Canada.

Mr. Cavanaugh had become acquainted with sale-and-leasebacks in December, 1952, when the company had sold its main plant and office building to Morrissey Life Insurance Company for $275,000 and leased it back for a period of 20 years with options to renew for an additional 15 years. Splash Soap Corporation had sold the facilities in Syracuse at a loss of $25,000 and had used the loss as an offset against excess profits taxes. In addition the company had been able to obtain rent deductions that were more favorable than depreciation allowances. For example, the Syracuse facilities had been constructed in the fall of 1947 at a cost of $280,000 for the building and $55,000 for land. The buildings were being depreciated over 40 years, at $7,000 a year. Under the terms of the sale-and-leaseback, rental payments for the first 20 years were $22,000 per annum.

Other terms of the sale-and-leaseback agreement had included the following:

1. Lease renewable for three periods of five years each at the following rental rates:
   a) $8,250 per year during the first five-year period.
   b) $6,875 per year during the next five-year period.
   c) $5,500 per year during the last five-year period.
2. Tenant shall pay all taxes and assessments.
3. Tenant shall maintain the improvements and every part thereof.
4. Tenant may construct and reconstruct accessory buildings.
5. Tenant to provide fire and extended coverage in amounts for not less than 80% of full insurable value.

In June, 1957, the management of Splash Soap Corporation had decided to open a plant on the West Coast. Mr. Cavanaugh had requested a sale-and-leaseback from Morrissey Life for a new plant scheduled for construction in Los Angeles. He had considered negotiating a temporary construction loan from Dillon National Bank to handle construction costs until the completed plant could be sold to Morrissey Life.

However, Mr. Harvey Zahm, vice president of Morrissey Life, had expressed a lack of interest in a sale-and-leaseback proposition at that time. He said that the insurance company had been out of the market for this investment medium since mid-1956. Because of factors peculiar to sale-and-leasebacks, the insurance company insisted on a yield at least one-half of 1% greater than other forms of investment media. This incremental interest rate was required by the insurance company to compensate for the risk assumed in making what was essentially a 100% loan on fixed assets. By assuming legal ownership, Morrissey Life would not have the position of a general creditor, which would be the case in a term loan. The general counsel of the insurance company had advised Mr. Zahm that in previous court cases, claims amounting only to the equivalent of one year's rental had been allowed in the case of straight bankruptcy, and three years in the case of reorganization.

A second reason for requiring a higher yield was the "nuisance" involved. In past sale-and-leaseback transactions, the insurance company had been asked to provide funds for improvements and renewal in the terms of the lease. As property owners, Morrissey Life felt a moral obligation to assist its tenants whenever possible. This had often involved the cost and nuisance of reconsidering and rewriting long leases and of committing additional funds at times when other investments seemed preferable.

In conjunction with this nuisance factor, Mr. Zahm had pointed out that the insurance company also viewed these periodic renewals and rewritings as postponements of its equity claims on the residual value of the leases. Morrissey Life considered real estate investment as one of two ways by which an insurance company could hedge against inflation; the other being common stocks. Since investments in common stocks were severely limited, insurers often hedged against rising prices by means of real estate ownership. As a result, the insurance company wanted to obtain residual value as soon as possible so that it could realize any capital appreciation that may have taken place.

Mr. Zahm had shown a chart to Mr. Cavanaugh that the insurance company used to compare yields from mortgage loans and yields from new issues of electric power utility bonds with "A" Moody ratings (Exhibit 4). He explained that the company considered a sale-and-leaseback to be comparable to a mortgage loan. Until August, 1956, mortgage loans had sold at a premium ranging between one half of 1% and 1% above new issues of "A" utility bonds. However, after August the yields had narrowed, and in June, 1957, "A" utility bonds and mortgage loans were both yielding about 5%. Mr. Zahm stated that the insurance company would not consider sale-and-leaseback at that time unless it could obtain a yield of 5½% to 6%.

Mr. Cavanaugh had considered the interest rate requested by Morrissey Life for a sale-and-leaseback too high. He subsequently had negotiated a 20-year term loan of $300,000 at 5% with Dillon National Bank for the construction of the Los Angeles plant. The provisions of the loan agreement had been as follows:

1. *Noncallable* prior to July 1, 1962.
2. *Indebtedness:* Additional term debt permitted if pro forma term debt would not exceed 33% of total capitalization.
3. *Consolidation and merger:* Not permitted without consent.
4. *Sales of assets:* Sale of all or substantially all assets prohibited.
5. *Minimum working capital:*
   a) Initially $800,000 to increase to $1,250,000 as of the date of issue of the additional debt.
   b) Current ratio not to be less than 2 to 1.
6. *Dividends and stock retirements:* Total amount of all dividends not to exceed $200,000 plus 75% of net income subsequent to June 30, 1957.
7. *Investments:* None permitted except:
   a) Direct obligations of the United States Government.
   b) Securities acquired to satisfy debts incurred in the ordinary course of business.

The present Chicago plant, a multistory building, had been built in 1946 at a cost of $140,000. Between 1946 and 1958 the number of products produced in the Chicago plant had increased from 2 to 18. Similarly, tonnage output had increased from 10,000 tons to 40,000 tons a year. Production operations had changed requiring more complex formulas and methods of mixing and packaging. Moreover, the loading and unloading facilities had become insufficient to handle the present volume of the plant.

Mr. Farley believed that the capacity of present mixing equipment, mixing pit, materials handling system, and packing equipment would be reached during 1959. The practical tonnage capacity of the plant for optimum operation was 40,000 tons. However, Mr. Farley thought that he could turn out close to 50,000 tons if hard pressed but cautioned that operations for incremental production above 40,000 tons would be less efficient. The marketing department estimated that sales in 1968 would be able to absorb somewhere between 60 and 70 thousand tons from the Chicago plant. Accordingly, Mr. Farley had convinced management that a new plant should be constructed in Chicago.

Mr. Farley proposed abandoning the present plant and constructing a completely new plant with capacity for annual production of 80,000 tons. The new plant would be located on a railroad siding and thus would decrease delivery expenses. It would be a one-story structure with air-conditioned offices. The new plant would permit a more straightforward layout and improved operating efficiencies. Mr. Farley considered the operating savings as nebulous and difficult to put on a monetary basis. He guessed that these savings would probably average $7,500 a year before taxes.

Because of the delays involved in purchasing the land, drawing up final blueprints, and obtaining bids from contractors, construction of the plant could not be started until August, 1959. Mr. Farley did not think the plant could be completed and equipped before January, 1961.

Mr. Farley estimated that the new plant would have about 28,000 square feet of floor space and would involve a total net investment of $450,000. He estimated the land would cost $50,000; buildings, $400,000; and equipment, $100,000. Mr. Farley then estimated that $100,000 net after capital gains taxes might be realized from the sale of the present plant. The new plant would be depreciated over 40 years on the basis of the declining balance method if it were owned outright, and the equipment would be depreciated over 10 years using the sum-of-the-years'-digits method. Exhibits 5 and 6 show the details of these depreciation schedules.

After the preliminary discussion in the December, 1958, meeting of management, the president of Splash Soap Corporation had requested Mr. Cavanaugh to prepare his recommendation for financing the new plant and to present it at the January meeting. Mr. Cavanaugh approached Mr. Zahm at Morrissey Life to see if the insurance company had renewed its interest in sale-and-leasebacks. Mr. Zahm replied that Morrissey Life was not entering into sale-and-leaseback transactions at the time because of uncertainties in the outlook for federal income taxes on life insurance companies. He said that Congress was in the process of revising life insurance tax laws and the 1958 tax rate had not been determined yet. Morrissey Life was not considering any sale-and-leasebacks until new legislation had been enacted.

In lieu of a sale-and-leaseback, Mr. Zahm offered Splash Soap Corporation a mortgage loan of $350,000 at 4½% with a takedown of $100,000 in August, 1959, and $250,000 in July, 1960. Splash Soap Corporation would begin annual payments of $32,600 in 1961, which would amortize the loan over 15 years. The amortization schedule would be as given in Exhibit 7.

Mr. Cavanaugh also called on Dillon National Bank to inquire about a sale-and-leaseback arrangement with a pension fund administered by the bank. Income received by these funds was not subject to federal income tax. Mr. Lyons, a trust officer of Dillon National Bank, expressed interest in the new building. He proposed a lease of 25 years with an annual rental of $31,572 payable monthly beginning in January, 1961. These payments would amortize the $450,000 net investment over the 25-year period at 5%. He also implied that the bank would be willing to include an option whereby Splash Soap Corporation could purchase the land and building at the end of 25 years. However, no specific repurchase price could be stated in the agreement because of rulings by the Bureau of Internal Revenue. The repurchase price would have to depend upon arm's-length market prices in 1985.

Under the sale-and-leaseback alternative Splash Soap Corporation would have to arrange a temporary construction loan until the building could be completed and sold to Dillon National Bank as trustee for the pension fund. Mr. Cavanaugh estimated that interest costs on the loan would be approximately $1,875 in 1959 and $10,125 in 1960. He also understood the bank would make a commitment and service charge in connection with the temporary construction loan, and a corresponding but smaller charge would probably be made by the insurance company under the mortgage arrangement. Not knowing the exact amounts, he estimated that the sale-and-leaseback would cost $1,500 more than the mortgage for commitment and service charges.

After reviewing these financing alternatives, Mr. Cavanaugh decided to compute the discounted cash flows under each alternative. He assumed a tax rate of 50% in all of his calculations. He did not include the repurchase cost of the land and building under the sale-and-leaseback because he was uncertain about what cost to use. He considered using the book value of $107,545 for the plant in 1985 after declining balance depreciation and the current value of the land of $50,000, but he had become concerned about inflation and wondered if this estimate was valid.

Before making a decision on the two financing alternatives, Mr. Cavanaugh discussed his computations with the controller, Mr. Patrick Stephanowsky. The latter did not agree with the use of book value of the new plant under the declining balance method of depreciation. He argued that this method of depreciation was merely a "gimmick" for tax purposes and was not related to the actual depreciation of the plant. Secondly, Mr. Stephanowsky questioned whether the two alternatives could be compared against each other at all since the sale-and-leaseback involved $100,000 more in net investment. He raised the point that perhaps Mr. Cavanaugh should adjust the cost of the sale-and-leaseback for the additional $100,000.

Mr. Cavanaugh decided to reanalyze his computations before deciding between the two financing alternatives.

Exhibit 1

SPLASH SOAP CORPORATION

COMPARATIVE BALANCE SHEETS AS OF DECEMBER 31

(Dollar figures in thousands)

		1957			*1958*	
ASSETS						
Current assets:						
Cash	$307			$342		
Accounts receivable	708			791		
Inventories	799			766		
Prepaid expenses	48			57		
Total current assets			$1,862			$1,956
Property, plant, and equipment:						
Land		$ 66			$ 66	
Building	$345			$540		
Less: Allowance for depreciation	39	306		62	478	
Machinery and equipment	$465			$465		
Less: Allowance for depreciation	255			323		
		210			142	
			582			686
Investments and other assets			66			66
Intangibles			99			92
Total assets			$2,609			$2,800
LIABILITIES						
Current liabilities:						
Accounts payable	$326			$315		
Dividends payable	27			29		
Federal and state taxes on income	232			214		
Current maturities for long-term debt	57			31		
Total current liabilities		$ 642			$ 589	
Long-term debt		216			344	
5% preferred stock		109			106	
Common stock and surplus:						
Common*	$400			$400		
Paid-in surplus	516			516		
Retained earnings	726			845		
		1,642			1,761	
Total liabilities			$2,609			$2,800

* The common stock had sold at an average price to earnings ratio of 8.0 for the three-year period ended December 31, 1955.

Exhibit 2

SPLASH SOAP CORPORATION

STATEMENT OF INCOME

(Dollar figures in thousands)

	1957		1958	
Net sales		$6,068		$6,545
Cost and expenses*				
Cost of sales	$2,622		$2,797	
Selling and advertising	2,334		2,607	
General and administrative	561		581	
Employees' retirement	47		47	
Other	35		39	
		5,599		6,071
Net income before taxes		$ 469		$ 474
Federal taxes on income		247		250
Net earnings		$ 222		$ 224

* Including provisions for depreciation and amortization of $91,286—1958; $76,265—1957.

Exhibit 3

SPLASH SOAP CORPORATION

SUMMARY DATA

(Dollar figures in thousands)

Year	*Net Sales*	*Earnings before Income Taxes*	*Federal Income Taxes*	*Net Earnings*	*Earnings Reinvested in the Business*	*Current Assets*	*Current Liabilities*	*Working Capital*
1949	$1,844	$ 76	$ 32	$ 44	$ 22	$ 338	$164	$ 174
1950	2,203	160	66	94	71	416	224	192
1951	2,697	158	72	86	61	572	320	252
1952	3,100	164	84	80	52	756	386	370
1953	3,490	150	65	85	58	817	441	376
1954	3,887	219	117	102	68	883	412	471
1955	4,527	351	189	162	119	1,320	604	716
1956	5,291	397	207	190	140	1,438	715	723
1957	6,068	469	247	222	142	1,862	642	1,220
1958	6,545	474	250	224	119	1,956	589	1,367

Exhibit 4

SPLASH SOAP CORPORATION

Comparative Yields, 1953–57

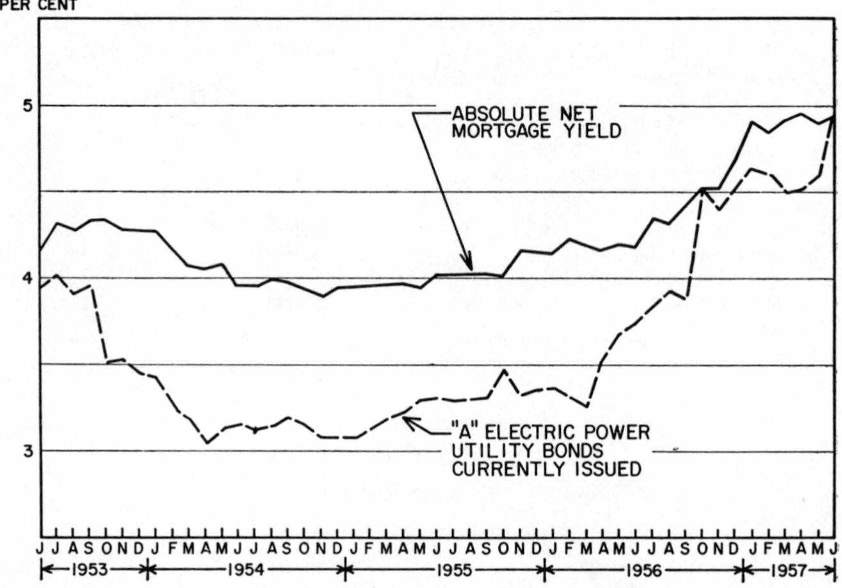

Exhibit 5

SPLASH SOAP CORPORATION

Depreciation Schedule for New Building

(Declining balance)

Year	*Opening Book Value*	*Depreciation—5% of Declining Balance*	*Closing Book Value*
1	$400,000	$20,000	$380,000
2	380,000	19,000	361,000
3	361,000	18,050	342,950
4	342,950	17,148	325,802
5	325,802	16,290	309,512
6	309,512	15,476	294,036
7	294,036	14,702	279,334
8	279,334	13,967	265,367
9	265,367	13,268	252,099
10	252,099	12,605	239,494
11	239,494	11,975	227,519
12	227,519	11,376	216,143
13	216,143	10,807	205,336
14	205,336	10,267	195,069
15	195,069	9,753	185,316
16	185,316	9,266	176,050
17	176,050	8,802	167,248
18	167,248	8,362	158,886
19	158,886	7,944	150,942
20	150,942	7,547	143,395
21	143,395	7,170	136,225
22–40*	136,225	7,170†	......

* Each year.

† The company expected to change to straight-line depreciation when the charge under the straight-line method became greater than the declining balance charge. For example in year 22, the straight-line charge would be $7,170 (book value of $136,225 divided by remaining life of 19 years) which is greater than $6,811 ($136,225 × declining balance rate of 5%).

Exhibit 6

SPLASH SOAP CORPORATION

Depreciation Schedule for Equipment

(Sum-of-the-years'-digits with useful life of 10 years on cost of $100,000)

Year	*Depreciation*
1	$18,182
2	16,364
3	14,545
4	12,727
5	10,909
6	9,091
7	7,273
8	5,455
9	3,636
10	1,818

Exhibit 7

SPLASH SOAP CORPORATION

AMORTIZATION SCHEDULE FOR 4½% MORTGAGE LOAN FROM MORRISSEY LIFE INSURANCE COMPANY

(Repayable in equal annual installments of $32,600 between 1961–75)

Year	*Principal at End of Year*	*Annual Payments*	
		Principal	*Interest*
1959	$100,000	.....	$ 1,875
1960	350,000	.....	10,125
1961	333,150	$16,850	15,750
1962	315,542	17,608	14,992
1963	297,141	18,401	14,199
1964	277,912	19,229	13,371
1965	257,818	20,094	12,506
1966	236,820	20,998	11,602
1967	214,877	21,943	10,657
1968	191,946	22,931	9,669
1969	167,984	23,962	8,638
1970	142,943	25,041	7,559
1971	116,775	26,168	6,432
1972	89,430	27,345	5,255
1973	60,854	28,576	4,024
1974	30,992	29,862	2,738
1975	.....	30,992	1,608

I.C.A. CORPORATION

On February 6, 1968, Mr. Simon Greenspan, president of I.C.A. Corporation, was considering whether his company should own outright or lease a new manufacturing facility. A new plant was needed by the company to meet the level of production required by a rapidly expanding backlog of orders. The directors of I.C.A. had recently approved in principle Mr. Greenspan's proposal to have a new manufacturing facility built to the company's specifications. Now Mr. Greenspan had to decide whether to (1) finance the new plant with a mortgage loan or (2) lease the plant from a group of private investors who would own and finance the property themselves.

Corporate history of I.C.A.

In October, 1958, Mr. Greenspan and two friends, who later became senior vice presidents, founded I.C.A. (then called Instruments Corporation of America) to conduct research and development for profit in technologically based industries. From its early days the company grew rapidly in terms of sales, profits, and assets, as evidenced by Exhibits 1 and 2. To sustain its early growth, the company raised capital in 1960 by offering to the public 50,000 shares of common stock. This security was not actively traded until 1965, when I.C.A. issued an additional 450,000 shares, this time to raise the cash necessary to finance an acquisition. The price behavior of the company's common stock after the 1965 offering is shown in Exhibit 3.

As the company grew, its profit-making activity, which was initially limited to contract research, soon expanded to include the manufacture of scientific instruments. I.C.A.'s entry into the field of instrument manufacture came about as a result of four highly profitable acquisitions between 1960 and 1966. By 1967 the company had diversified to the extent that its equipment was being used for precision measurement, integrated circuit production, and vacuum processing and joining of metals. Sales of laboratory apparatus and industrial equipment accounted for 77% of the company's revenue in 1967, while the revenues from contract research, a less profitable activity, declined to 23% of the combined corporate total.

In late 1967, I.C.A. markedly stepped up the pace of its merger activity. In November and December of that year I.C.A. and three privately owned companies signed merger agreements, which called for the issuance of a minimum of 330,000 and a maximum of 430,000 shares of I.C.A. common stock. The total number of shares ultimately issued would vary between these limits depending on the price of I.C.A.'s stock during a period of time immediately preceding the effective date of each particular merger. When consummated, the three mergers would substantially boost I.C.A.'s sales and profits.

Rapid growth causes shortage of facilities

By mid-1967 it was clear to Mr. Greenspan that I.C.A. was going to need an increase of 75% in its instrument manufacturing capability within the next two years simply to keep pace with internal growth opportunities. I.C.A. was already cramped for space in its two existing manufacturing facilities; a new plant would be needed to meet future production requirements. A plant of sufficient size would provide about 150,000 square feet of manufacturing floor space.

In August, 1967, Mr. Greenspan hired an architect to draft plans for a new plant and set out to locate a large plot of land for the new facility. Mr. Greenspan and the architect agreed on an ideal location for the plant and determined that the cost of suitable acreage would be $535,400. After the architect's plans had been drafted and approved, the treasurer of I.C.A. obtained construction bids from two building contractors. The lower bid was $2,464,600. The cost of the land and building together would amount to $3,000,000, and the treasurer calculated that the interest on interim loans used to finance construction would add an additional $185,400 to the project's total cost before the building could be occupied.

Financing via direct loan

In order to line up long-term financing for the proposed new plant, the treasurer had spoken at some length with the mortgage loan officers at the First National Bank. He found that I.C.A. could borrow the entire cost of construction by mortgaging both the proposed plant and one other plant, which the company owned outright. The bank offered an interest rate of 6%. No principal was to be payable on the loan of $3,185,400 in the first year. Thereafter the loan was to be amortized over a 30-year period in equal quarterly payments of $57,396 (equal to $229,584 annually), which included both principal and interest.

Financing via lease

Before hiring the architect, Mr. Greenspan had informally discussed the need for a new facility with some of the company's directors. During the course of one of these conversations he learned that a number of investment banking firms were offering a relatively new type of financial service. The partners of these firms or wealthy clients would put up the money needed to construct an office or factory tailored to the needs of a company such as I.C.A. On a property like the one under consideration, the investor group would put

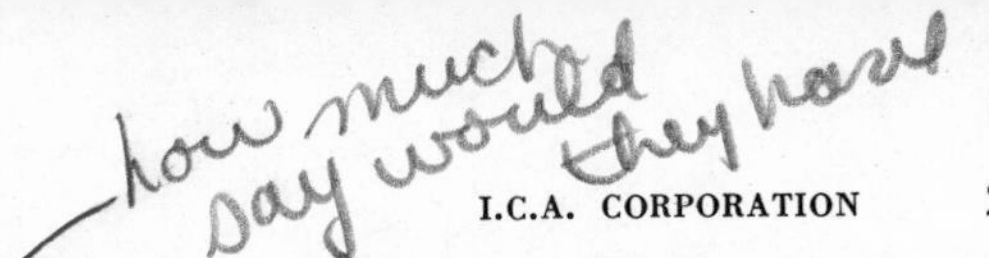

up a small fraction of the cost themselves and mortgage the property for the remaining amount. The company would then rent the property under a long-term noncancellable lease.

If I.C.A. financed by this method, it would pay a lease rate sufficient for the owners to recover the full cost of the building plus interest on their mortgage in 31 years, the initial term of the lease. At the end of the initial lease term the investor group would have recovered all of its original investment, and it would also own the building free and clear of any mortgage. I.C.A. could then renew the lease at a substantially reduced rate.

Mr. Greenspan decided to follow up the financing information he had received from the director, and shortly thereafter he asked the investment banking firm of Fare, Supple & Smarte, Inc. (FS&S), for a specific proposal under which I.C.A. could lease its new manufacturing facility. The representatives of FS&S appeared to be quite interested in submitting a lease proposal, and they offered to do a substantial part of the analysis necessary to enable the management of I.C.A. to make the lease versus ownership decision. Mr. Greenspan supplied them with the details of the financing package offered by the First National Bank, and the FS&S group returned three weeks later with their analysis and a proposal. Appendix A presents the FS&S analysis.

Exhibit 1

I.C.A. CORPORATION

CONSOLIDATED STATEMENT OF INCOME, 1962–67*

(In thousands)

	Years Ended September 30†					Nine Months Ended	
	1962	*1963*	*1964*	*1965*	*1966*	*July 3, 1966*	*June 30, 1967*
Net sales	$5,576	$7,308	$9,495	$9,973	$19,511	$14,301	$16,702
Cost of sales	4,751	6,172	7,906	8,049	14,523	10,533	12,203
Selling, general, administrative	391	498	793	979	2,373	1,804	2,100
Interest	33	42	57	117	375	282	305
Income before federal income tax	$ 401	$ 596	$ 739	$ 828	$ 2,240	$ 1,682	$ 2,094
Federal income tax	213	312	364	403	1,054	808	977
Net income	$ 188	$ 284	$ 375	$ 425	$ 1,186	$ 874	$ 1,117
Average number of shares outstanding	431	466	492	497	948‡	948	952
Income per common share§	$ 0.44	$ 0.61	$ 0.76	$ 0.85	$ 1.25	$ 0.92	$ 1.17

* This statement was prepared on the following basis:
On October 5, 1965, I.C.A. purchased all the outstanding stock of Instrumentation Company for approximately $10,300,000. The transaction was treated as a purchase, and accordingly the consolidated statement of income includes the operations of Instrumentation since the date of acquisition.

† Audited.

‡ Includes 450,000 shares issued in a public offering incident to the acquisition of the Instrumentation Company.

§ No dividends have been paid.

Exhibit 2

I.C.A. CORPORATION

CONSOLIDATED BALANCE SHEET AS OF JUNE 30, 1967

(Dollar figures in thousands)

ASSETS

Cash	$ 1,806
Accounts receivable	4,730
Inventories	5,356
Prepaid expenses	245
Total current assets	$12,137
Land and buildings	$ 2,772
Machinery and equipment	2,813
Less: Accumulated depreciation	(1,224)
Total property, plant, and equipment	$ 4,361
Excess of cost of investments in subsidiaries over net tangible assets acquired	6,269
Total assets	$22,767

LIABILITIES AND STOCKHOLDERS' EQUITY

Notes payable	$ 2,852
Accounts payable	1,126
Other accruals	2,038
Total current liabilities	$ 6,016
Long-term debt	4,239
Deferred taxes	106
Common stock: 1,500,000 shares authorized; 957,104 shares issued and outstanding	$ 545
Capital in excess of par value	7,948
Retained earnings	3,913
Total stockholders' equity	$12,406
Total liabilities and stockholders' equity	$22,767

Exhibit 3

I.C.A. CORPORATION

PRICE PERFORMANCE OF I.C.A. CORPORATION COMMON STOCK

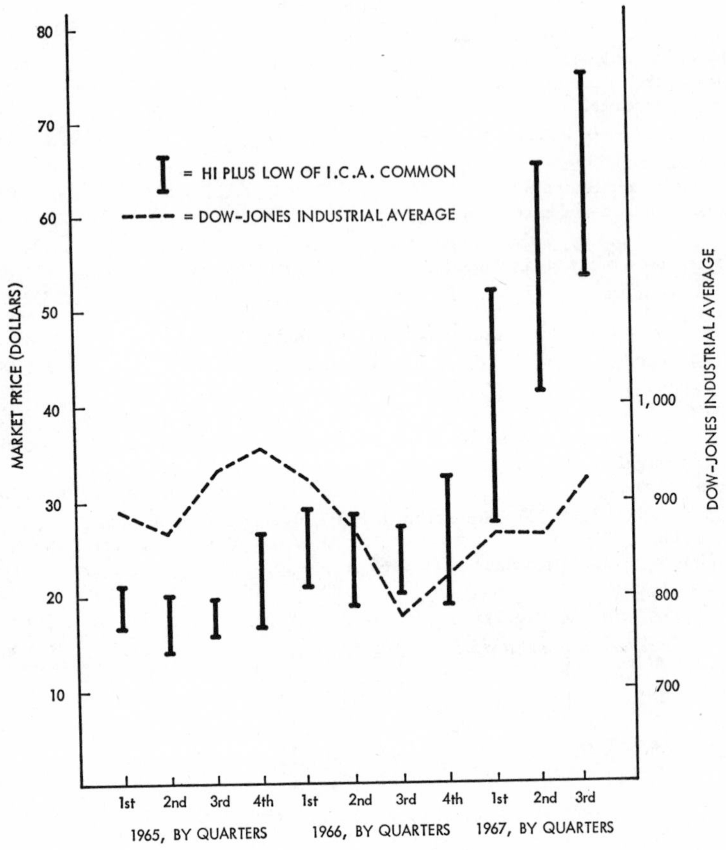

APPENDIX A

LEASE FINANCING PROPOSAL AND ANALYSIS PREPARED FOR I.C.A. CORPORATION BY THE FS&S INVESTOR GROUP

Proposal

FS&S Investor Group will build and lease to I.C.A. Corporation the proposed manufacturing facility, costing $3,185,400, under the following terms:

(1) I.C.A. Corporation will execute a noncancellable 31-year lease with FS&S Investor Group calling for quarterly rental payments of $54,159 (equal to $216,636 annually) except during the first year of the basic term.

During the first-year the quarterly rent will be $45,651 (equal to $182,604 annually).

(2) No rents will be payable by I.C.A. Corporation during construction.

(3) I.C.A. Corporation may, but is not required to, renew the lease at an annual rent equal to:

a) $53,067 from year 32 through year 46.

b) $37,798 from year 47 through year 52.

c) $26,535 from year 53 through year 62.

Analysis

The following discussion shows how the lease versus buy decision facing I.C.A. can be analyzed in terms of two important criteria. Part I of this report discusses the impact of the two possible decisions on I.C.A.'s earnings as reported to shareholders. Part II of the report discusses the impact of the two possible decisions on the net present value of I.C.A.'s cash outlays.

Part I. Effect of financing on corporate earnings as reported to shareholders

Exhibit A compares the effect of lease financing with that of ownership-debt financing on the annual income of I.C.A. over the 31-year basic term of the lease. Column 1 presents the years commencing when the plant construction is completed. Column 2 shows the expenses incurred under the leasing financing alternative. This expense amounts to $182,604 in the first year and $216,636 for each of the 30 years thereafter.

Columns 3, 4, and 5 of the exhibit show the cost of ownership-debt financing as it would be reflected in I.C.A.'s shareholder income statements. The interest expense on the mortgage loan is shown in column 3. This figure is naturally a declining amount since part of each mortgage payment reduces the principal outstanding on which the interest is computed. Straight-line depreciation calculated over a 45-year life is shown for each period in column 4. This building life and method of depreciation was chosen to reflect the most favorable way of reporting shareholder net income. If a shorter life or an accelerated method of depreciation were used, an already convincing argument in favor of the lease financing would become even more compelling. Column 5 sums the total cost of ownership-debt financing, i.e., the sum of columns 3 and 4.

Column 6 of Exhibit A shows for shareholder reporting the difference between the cost of ownership-debt financing (column 5) and the cost of lease financing (column 2). A positive figure indicates that lease financing will result in higher stated profits. For example, in the first year of plant occupancy, I.C.A.'s pretax profit would be higher by $67,485 if lease financing were chosen over ownership-debt financing. This differential would decline slowly until the 13th year, when I.C.A.'s profit would be higher if the building had been completed with ownership-debt financing. Since in a rapidly growing company current earnings are far more valuable than deferred earnings, we feel that if this analysis were made solely from the standpoint of reported earnings, I.C.A. should choose the lease financing over the ownership-debt financing alternative.

Part II. Effect of financing on net present value of cash outlays

Obviously I.C.A. will not want to make the lease versus buy decision based only on considering the implications for shareholder earnings. I.C.A. must also carefully weigh the impact of cash outflows arising under the two alternative choices.

In analyzing the lease versus buy decision according to net present value criteria, we need to choose a discount rate or opportunity cost of capital and apply that rate to the cash outflows associated with the ownership-debt financing and lease financing alternatives. Since we are dealing with the present value of a stream of cash *outflows* rather than *inflows,* in every case the alternative course of action with the *lower* net present value will be favored.

We in the FS&S Investor Group do not know what opportunity cost of capital I.C.A.'s management feels is appropriate for use in the company's investment decisions. Thus in our remaining calculations the present value of cash outlays will be computed with a number of possible discount factors ranging from 5% to 15%.

Exhibit B shows the actual cash outlays incurred in connection with ownership-debt financing and lease financing for the first quarter in each year of the initial lease term. Only the first quarter is shown for each year in order to limit the exhibit to a single page. To minimize the cash outflow under ownership-debt financing, depreciation in column 6 is calculated by double declining balance until the 22d year, at which point a switch to straight-line becomes advantageous.

Exhibit C, columns 2 and 3 respectively, show the net present value of all the cash outflows for 31 years associated with the ownership-debt financing and lease financing alternatives. The outflows discounted include all those shown in Exhibit B plus the intermediate quarterly flows that were omitted from Exhibit B in order to conserve space.

Column 4 of Exhibit C shows the net present value of the cash outflows associated with ownership-debt financing if no principal is repaid over the 31-year period. While in practice I.C.A. will have to repay principal, the impact of this cash outflow could be offset if I.C.A. were to borrow on a short-term basis amounts equivalent to the annual mortgage amortization. The total debt of I.C.A. would remain unchanged, but some long-term debt would shift into the short-term category. If this shift from long to short-term debt should prove bothersome, I.C.A. could increase its mortgage to the original amount after five or six years and use the cash made available from this transaction to repay short-term borrowings. Ownership-debt financing without debt amortization (column 4, Exhibit C) is clearly favored over the lease financing alternative presented in column 2 of Exhibit C. This comparison neglects, however, one major advantage of entering into a lease financing. The advantage is that lease financing does not use up as much of the borrowing capacity of a corporation as ownership-debt financing. (See attached excerpts from Alvin Zises' speech, "Equipment Leasing: Its Place in the Corporate Financial Design.") For example, assume that I.C.A. could borrow only about $3,000,000 within its present debt structure. If I.C.A. should enter into the lease financing, the company would still be able to borrow some additional funds. This would be true because lending institutions do not seem to weight the effects of lease financing as heavily as the effects of a direct loan. Columns 5 through 8 of Exhibit C take into account the value of additional borrowing power available to I.C.A. under the lease financing alternative. For instance, if I.C.A. should enter into the lease financing arrangement and could

1. Borrow an additional 25% of $3,185,400 @ 6% interest and
2. Invest that borrowing at an opportunity rate of 10%, then if we assume no debt amortization the lease financing alternative represents a net present value saving at $153,000. (Row 6, column 4, versus row 6, column 5, of Exhibit C.)

Residual values under two alternatives

To this point the analysis has assumed that I.C.A.'s "end position" 31 years after the plant construction is completed would be the same under the ownership-debt financing and lease financing alternatives. Since I.C.A. would *own* the facility under one alternative and merely have the option to renew the lease under the other alternative, the two "end positions" are not equivalent unless the plant has no value at the end of the initial lease term. Since this outcome is highly unlikely, additional adjustments are needed to make the end positions under the two alternatives equivalent.

At the end of 31 years, the market value of the land and building being considered by I.C.A. could be substantial. If this were the case, the rentals that could be charged on an "arm's length" lease might also be substantial. Assume that at the end of 31 years I.C.A.'s planned facility could be sold for exactly its original cost, $3,185,400. If I.C.A. owned the property, on its sale the company would realize a pretax gain of $1,959,856, an amount equal to the total depreciation taken on the property over the first 31 years of its life. Taxes of $489,964 would be due on the gain from the sale, leaving I.C.A. with a lump sum cash inflow of $2,695,436 at the end of 31 years (Table 1).

If I.C.A. leased the plant and the property retained its market value of $3,185,400 over 31 years of life, then the "arm's length" rental value would probably remain about equal to that amount paid by I.C.A. during the initial lease term. Since I.C.A. has the right to renew its plant lease at a large discount after 31 years, I.C.A. could exercise this option and sublease the plant to a third party, or continue to occupy the property itself at a "below market" cost. If the property were subleased, I.C.A. would receive a substan-

Table 1

Sale price	$3,185,400
Book value	1,225,544
Pretax gain	$1,959,856
Capital gain tax	489,964
After tax gain	$1,469,892
Add book value	1,225,544
Cash inflow	$2,695,436

tial cash inflow. If I.C.A. continued to occupy the property itself, however, the company could "impute" to this choice, for comparison purposes, a cash inflow equivalent to that which would have been received under a sublease. If a third party sublessee could be found who would be willing to pay $216,636 rent per year under a sublease, I.C.A. would realize an actual (or imputed) after-tax profit of $81,784 for 15 years, followed by a profit of $89,419 for 6 years, followed by $95,050 for 10 more years (Table 2).

Table 2

	Years 32–46	*Years 47–52*	*Years 53–62*
Lease revenue	$216,636	$216,636	$216,636
Lease cost	53,067	37,798	26,535
Pretax profit	$163,569	$178,838	$190,101
Income tax	81,785	89,419	95,051
Profit after tax	$ 81,784	$ 89,419	$ 95,050

If the lump cash inflow relating to the sale of I.C.A.'s plant 31 years in the future were discounted back to the present, the net present value of the cash outlays associated with ownership-debt financing, as shown in columns 2 and 4 of Exhibit C, would be reduced by $593,000 at the 5% opportunity rate (Exhibit D). If the after-tax cash flows from subleasing were similarly discounted at 5%, the net present value of the cash outlays associated with lease financing, as shown in columns 3 and 5–8 of Exhibit C, would be reduced by $293,000 (Exhibit D). By using Exhibit C and Exhibit D together, I.C.A.'s management can roughly test the impact of various assumed future plant values on the net present values of the ownership-debt financing and lease financing alternatives.

We, the FS&S investor group, feel that I.C.A. could not borrow much more than the $3,185,400 cost of the plant's construction on its present equity base. We also feel that if I.C.A. accepts the lease financing proposal, the company will still have borrowing power equal to at least 25% of $3,185,400. The value of this extra borrowing power is so substantial (as shown in Exhibit C) that if we ignore residual values the lease financing alternative is favored at every opportunity rate from 5% to 15%. At the upper end of this opportunity rate range, the lease financing alternative would still be favored under any reasonable assumption regarding plant residual values.

Since the analysis under criteria of (1) earnings and (2) present value of cash outflows both indicate that the lease financing is favored, we feel I.C.A. should accept our proposal.

Exhibit A

I.C.A. CORPORATION

COMPARISON OF THE LEASE FINANCING AND THE DIRECT LOAN AS TO THEIR EFFECT ON CORPORATE EARNINGS REPORTED TO STOCKHOLDERS

(1)	(2)	(3)	(4)	(5) = (3) + (4)	(6) = (5) − (2)
	Lease Plan	*Ownership-Debt Plan*			
Year	*Cost of Lease Financing*	*Interest Expense*	*Depreciation Expense*	*Total Cost of Direct Loan*	*Difference between Cost of Direct Loan and Lease Financing*
1	$182,604	$191,124	58,965	$250,089	$ 67,485
2	216,636	190,248	58,965	249,213	32,577
3	216,636	187,836	58,965	246,801	30,165
4	216,636	185,274	58,965	244,239	27,603
5	216,636	182,553	58,965	241,518	24,882
6	216,636	179,667	58,965	238,632	21,992
7	216,636	176,604	58,965	234,569	18,933
8	216,636	173,355	58,965	232,320	15,684
9	216,636	169,905	58,965	228,870	12,234
10	216,636	166,242	58,965	225,207	8,571
11	216,636	162,354	58,965	221,319	4,683
12	216,636	158,229	58,965	217,194	558
13	216,636	153,852	58,965	212,817	−3,819
14	216,636	149,205	58,965	208,170	−8,466
15	216,636	144,270	58,965	203,235	−13,401
16	216,636	139,035	58,965	198,000	−18,636
17	216,636	133,479	58,965	192,444	−24,192
18	216,636	127,584	58,965	186,549	−30,087
19	216,636	121,323	58,965	180,288	−36,348
20	216,636	114,681	58,965	173,646	−42,990
21	216,636	107,628	58,965	166,593	−50,043
22	216,636	99,846	58,965	159,111	−57,525
23	216,636	92,202	58,965	151,167	−65,469
24	216,636	83,772	58,965	142,737	−73,899
25	216,636	74,826	58,965	133,791	−82,845
26	216,636	65,228	58,965	124,293	−92,343
27	216,636	55,251	58,965	114,216	−102,420
28	216,636	44,553	58,965	103,518	−113,118
29	216,636	33,198	58,965	92,163	−124,473
30	216,636	21,147	58,965	60,112	−136,524
31	216,636	8,355	58,965	67,320	−149,316

Exhibit B

I.C.A. CORPORATION

COMPARISON OF AFTER-TAX CASH OUTFLOWS OF LEASE FINANCING AND DIRECT LOAN FINANCING

(1)	(2)	(3) = 0.5 x (2)	(4)	(5)	(6)	(7) = (4) − .5((5) + (6))	(8) = (7) − (3)
	Lease Plan		*Ownership-Debt Plan*				
Quarterly Rent Payment Number	*Lease Rentals*	*After-Tax Cash Outflow of Lease*	*Loan Payment*	*Loan Interest*	*Depreciation*	*After-Tax Cash Outflow of Loan*	*Amount by Which Cash Outflow with Direct Loan Exceeds Cash Outlay with Lease*
1	$45,651	$22,827	$47,781	$47,781	$29,481	$ 9,150	$−13,677
5	54,159	27,078	57,396	47,781	28,170	19,419	−7,659
9	54,159	27,078	57,396	47,190	26,919	20,340	−6,738
13	54,159	27,078	57,396	46,566	25,722	21,252	−5,826
17	54,159	27,078	57,396	45,900	24,579	22,155	−4,923
21	54,159	27,078	57,396	45,195	23,487	23,055	−4,023
25	54,159	27,078	57,396	44,445	22,443	23,952	−3,126
29	54,159	27,078	57,396	43,650	21,447	24,846	−2,232
33	54,159	27,078	57,396	42,807	20,493	25,746	−1,332
37	54,159	27,078	57,396	41,913	19,584	26,649	−429
41	54,159	27,078	57,396	40,962	18,711	27,558	480
45	54,159	27,078	57,396	39,954	17,880	28,479	1,401
49	54,159	27,078	57,396	38,883	17,085	29,412	2,331
53	54,159	27,078	57,396	37,749	16,326	30,360	3,279
57	54,159	27,078	57,396	36,543	15,600	31,326	4,245
61	54,159	27,078	57,396	35,262	14,907	32,310	5,232
65	54,159	27,078	57,396	33,903	14,244	33,321	6,243
69	54,159	27,078	57,396	32,463	13,611	34,359	7,281
73	54,159	27,078	57,396	30,933	13,005	35,427	8,349
77	54,159	27,078	57,396	29,310	12,429	36,528	9,450
81	54,159	27,078	57,396	27,585	11,877	37,665	10,587
85	54,159	27,078	57,396	25,755	11,349	38,844	11,766
89	54,159	27,078	57,396	23,814	10,845	40,068	12,987
93	54,159	27,078	57,396	21,753	10,599	41,220	14,142
97	54,159	27,078	57,396	19,566	10,599	42,315	15,234
101	54,159	27,078	57,396	17,244	10,599	43,476	16,395
105	54,159	27,078	57,396	14,781	10,599	44,706	17,028
109	54,159	27,078	57,396	12,165	10,599	46,014	18,936
113	54,159	27,078	57,396	9,390	10,599	47,403	20,222
117	54,159	27,078	57,396	6,444	10,599	48,876	21,795
121	54,159	27,078	.....	3,318	10,599	50,436	23,358

Exhibit C

I.C.A. CORPORATION

COMPARISON OF THE NET PRESENT VALUE OF CASH OUTFLOWS UNDER LEASE FINANCING VERSUS THE NET PRESENT VALUE OF CASH OUTFLOWS UNDER DEBT FINANCING

(Dollar figures in thousands)

(1)	(2)	(3)	(4)	(5)	(6)	(7)	(8)
After-Tax Discount Rate	*Present Value of Outflows Associated with 31-Year Loan Assuming Amortization*	*Present Value of Outflows Associated with 31-Year Lease*	*Present Value of Outflows Associated with 31-Year Loan with No Amortization*	*Present Value of Outflows Associated with 31-Year Lease Assuming Borrowing Power of I.C.A. Is Increased by:*			
				25%	*50%*	*75%*	*100%*
5%	$1,812	$1,686	$1,575	$1,434	$1,185	$ 936	$ 684
6	1,575	1,503	1,284	1,170	864	498	162
7	1,380	1,350	1,059	948	546	144	−258
8	1,218	1,221	885	768	312	−144	−597
9	1,080	1,110	747	615	117	−371	−879
10	996	1,017	639	486	−45	−579	−1,110
11	870	936	555	375	−183	−744	−1,302
12	789	864	486	282	−300	−882	−1,464
13	717	801	429	201	−399	−1,002	−1,602
14	657	747	384	129	−486	−1,104	−1,719
15	603	699	348	69	−561	−1,191	−1,824

Exhibit D

I.C.A. CORPORATION
PRESENT VALUE ADJUSTMENTS FOR PLANT'S RESIDUAL VALUE
(Dollar figures in thousands)

After-Tax Discount Rate	*Present Value of Lump Cash Inflow from Plant Sale—Ownership-Debt Financing*	*Present Value of Cash Inflows from Sublease of Plant—Lease Financing*
5%	$593	$293
6	443	194
7	331	130
8	248	88
9	186	60
10	140	41
11	106	28
12	80	20
13	60	14
14	46	10
15	35	7

APPENDIX B

EXCERPTS FROM "EQUIPMENT LEASING: ITS PLACE IN THE CORPORATE FINANCIAL DESIGN"[1]

by Alvin Zises

Attitude of investment community

Does the investment community recognize the junior nature of chattel leasing and its effect upon the equity and debt capital of a company if the lease is used prudently?

One of the largest banks in the United States in its credit analysis manual makes the following policy statement:

> Leases . . . are not necessarily similar to debt; nor are the properties assets since there is no ownership. These commitments are in the nature of contingent liabilities, similar to management contracts, purchase obligations, and the like . . . in bankruptcy or reorganization lease obligations and long-term debt are dissimilar. The lessor is limited to an award of damages which he must prove. . . .

Bennett R. Keenan of New England Merchants National Bank of Boston in his paper, "Financing a Leasing Corporation," circulated by the bank writes, "A lease is not debt . . . a lease has, to be sure, certain elements also found in debt . . . it lacks, however, one feature of debt, at least, that to a creditor should explode any notion that a lease is debt. In the event of bankruptcy of the debtor, debt is normally recognized in full as a claim; in bankruptcy of a lessee, this is not the case."

Frederick R. H. Witherby, Associate Counsel of New England Mutual Life Insurance Company, in "Personal Property Lease Financing," warns The

[1] Privately printed speech. Most footnotes omitted.

Association of Life Insurance Counsel that, "Since uncertainties in the enforceability of rental obligations militate against their ranking on the same level, in the hierarchy of priorities, as direct promises to pay . . . life insurance companies . . . [should be] . . . alert to the risks inherent in the enforceability of their position as creditors. . . ."

Ralph L. Gustin, Jr., Vice President of the John Hancock Mutual Life Insurance Company in his paper, "Financing by Contract and by Lease," stresses "the difference in the creditor position of the lender in [lease] financings from that of the lender in ordinary loan transactions . . ."

Gordon D. Brown, Vice President of The Bank of New York, stated:

> Going back through the history of finance, you will find that questions were asked about the conditional sales contract when the straight mortgage was a more common security form. Only a few years ago the term loan was not considered sensible for a business or a bank. The lease is filling a current need for supplemental financing and is probably in about the same status as consumer financing and the term loan were some 15–20 years ago.

Attitude of regulatory commissions

To learn the attitude of regulatory commissions, we asked a former chairman of the Securities and Exchange Commission what had been the attitude of the S.E.C. We were informed that where chattel leasing was used in amounts that were not material, the public had little interest in the transactions. We were referred to the S-X regulations.

To our best knowledge, whenever public service commissions regulating utility companies were requested to authorize approval of lease-back of equipment for utility companies, such agencies or their staffs after studying the economic effect have indicated such action as being in the interests of the company and the public. The commissions of Massachusetts, New Hampshire, Pennsylvania, Connecticut, New York, and California are among such regulatory bodies.

Statements of rating services

We wrote three security rating services to learn their attitude on fleet leasing. We quote excerpts from their replies:

Standard and Poor's Corporation wrote: "We would be inclined to agree that vehicle leasing would not ordinarily be a significant factor."

Fitch Investors Services wrote:

> . . . it is not our practice to regard this as an adverse factor where the amounts involved are not material to the assets of a utility or a sizeable industrial concern. It might even happen that we might regard such an arrangement as a favorable factor in the light of the advantages and freeing of capital for other purposes.

Moody's Investors Service stated:

> One analyst who has had close acquaintance with vehicle leasing programs was of the opinion that some such programs were indicative of astute management. We go along with this observation, particularly from the point of view of equity

owners, since we know of one situation where a company effected substantial savings per common share by changing over from ownership to leasing.

Harvard's survey of investment community's attitude

Probably the most extensive survey of the attitude of the investment community was conducted during 1959 for the *Harvard Business Review*. 512 of the largest financial institutions of the United States and Canada and the 1300 largest industrial and utility companies were solicited for information. Insurance company respondents represented 77% of total life insurance assets. Respondent banks represented 42% of total bank resources.[40]

Differences in negative covenants in debt agreements

In a study of negative covenants in formal debt agreements, it was disclosed that 50% of all such agreements placed no ceilings on the incurrence of additional lease commitments; such ceilings, if imposed, are far more prevalent in regard to realty than equipment leasing and applicable almost entirely to long-term noncancelable leases; such covenants are less restrictive and more flexible than limitations on debt. One conclusion of the study was:

> By far the most common restriction is one which establishes a fixed dollar or percentage limitation on annual lease payments. This . . . restriction, while serving to control the amount of lease financing, suggests that the lender considers a certain amount of such financing permissible in addition to the stated limits on long-term debt.[41]

Expanding the total financing pool

The final paragraph of the study which summarized the attitude of analysts and corporate officers, but only as to long-term and material leases, stated:

> 90% of the respondents to the analysts' survey and 65% of the respondents to our corporate survey state that the use of long-term, noncancelable leases makes it possible for a company to obtain a greater amount of credit than would be possible if debt financing were used. This may mean that they do not regard—or do not believe others regard—leasing as being exactly comparable with debt financing.[42]

It is an interesting commentary that lenders and investors hold to this doctrine in greater degree than do treasurers, controllers and financial vice presidents.

Because the lease offers to an investor a security position inferior to that of bonds or debentures, the other side of the coin enables the lessee to expand, through reasonable use of the lease, his total pool of financing.

. . . .

---

[40] R. F. Vancil and R. N. Anthony, "The Financial Community Looks at Leasing," *Harvard Business Review*, November–December, 1959, pp. 120 and 121.

[41] See (40) supra.

[42] See (40) supra.

Cost related to incremental debt

Each increase in the ratio of a company's senior debt likewise increases the comparative cost of incremental debt. The treasurer of a major oil company informed us that because his firm had not made sufficient use of junior financings like leasing, his company's ratio of senior debt securities was higher than that of comparable companies and consequently, he claimed, the interest rates on his company's incremental debt securities were also higher. His conclusion was that his company, by paying a higher rate on incremental debt, was paying the rate equivalent for junior financing but did not have its benefit in the capital structure. The prudent use of equipment leasing, according to institutional investors and financial analysts, will not be treated as a debt burden because of its junior nature.[54]

To a growing corporation the preservation of its capacity to borrow term debt at the lowest possible cost may be important if sizeable opportunities for future expansion present themselves. To the extent that a company uses the lease in prudent manner, it conserves such capacity.

. . . .

Comparison with total cost of alternatives

Before leasing or any form of financing should be acceptable, the total economic cost should be competitive with alternatives available to the company under the individual circumstances. To the extent that economical leasing extends the total pool of all capital and incurs a rate lower than that of earnings or of the required rate of return—and, more significantly, lower than the total cost of available alternatives—leasing is in the interest of the company, its shareholders, and customers.[65] Again, it is important to bear in mind that the interest rate on debt is not the total cost of alternatives.

---

[54] See (40) supra.

[65] Joel Dean, "Measuring the Productivity of Capital," *Harvard Business Review,* January, 1954.

NOTE: COMPUTER LEASING INDUSTRY

^^

The electronic data processing industry can be broken down into five major segments which include (1) main frame hardware[1] manufacturers, (2) peripheral equipment manufacturers, (3) supporting services (programming consultants, etc.), (4) computer utilities (sellers of computer time), and (5) computer leasing companies. This note will focus on the independent computer leasing industry. Since the policies of computer manufacturers play a key role in determining the operating environment of the computer leasing companies, introductory information will also be provided on the producers of main frame hardware.

BACKGROUND—COMPUTER HARDWARE MANUFACTURERS

Structure of industry

Only nine U.S. companies are significantly involved in the manufacture of main frame hardware. Most of these manufacturers decline to release the information necessary to determine market shares within the industry. For this reason, the statistics cited in the financial press relating to competitive positions are based on uncertain estimates. In spite of this uncertainty, it is clear that International Business Machines Corporation (IBM) is far and away the industry leader.

According to an article in *Forbes* magazine, IBM had, through 1965, installed 75% of the dollar value of computer equipment in use within the United States and 67% of the value of such equipment in use throughout the world.[2] Another trade source estimated the value of computers shipped by manufacturers during 1966 as shown in Exhibit 1.

Regarding IBM's share of the total computer market, the *Forbes* article went on to state:

IBM dominates the world computer business in a way no other giant industrial dominates any other major market. General Motors has about 52% of the U.S.

---

[1] "Main frame hardware" refers to the central processing units of a computer where numerical calculations are actually performed. This is distinct from input and output devices (peripheral equipment) such as card readers and tape drives.

[2] "International Business Machines," *Forbes*, September 15, 1966, p. 46.

Exhibit 1

COMPUTER LEASING INDUSTRY

ESTIMATED VALUE OF COMPUTERS SHIPPED BY MANUFACTURERS DURING 1966
(Dollar amounts in millions)

	Amount	*% of Total*
IBM	$2,500	68.3%
Honeywell	270	7.4
Control Data	200	5.5
Univac	195	5.3
General Electric	190	5.2
National Cash	95	2.6
Radio Corporation	95	2.6
Burroughs	60	1.6
Scientific Data	30	0.8
Others	25	0.7
Total	$3,660	100.0%

Source: "EDP Industry and Market Report," International Data Publishing Co.

auto business. . . . U.S. Steel has only about 25% of the domestic steel market, . . . [and] Standard Oil (N.J.) . . . [has] about 15% of the Free World crude production.[3]

Market growth

The estimated value of general-purpose computers shipped annually since 1955 and future demand projected through 1970 are shown in Exhibit 2. Between 1960 and 1965 industry shipments grew at a compounded rate of more than 25% annually. With deliveries of IBM's third-generation[4] "System/360" equipment beginning in earnest late in 1965, the 1965–66 annual rate of growth swelled to over 45%.

Computer manufacturers face financial problems similar to those of any industrial company experiencing rapid growth. Accounts receivable and in-process inventories of growing companies often jump sharply in response to rising sales levels. Plant and equipment expenditures may simultaneously increase if capacity must be expanded to bring production into a more reasonable balance with sales demand. In addition to the normal problems accompanying rapid growth, computer manufacturers face one additional financial problem that is *not* characteristic of most companies in fast-growing industries. That problem arises from the fact that computer users have traditionally leased rather than purchased more than 80% of the computer equipment they have accepted for installation.[5]

[3] *Ibid.*

[4] The "generation" of computer equipment is determined by the state of advancement in its electronic circuitry. First-generation equipment employed thousands of vacuum tubes in its circuitry. These relatively slow and inefficient machines were superseded in 1960 by second-generation equipment (such as IBM's 1401) employing transistors. The System/360 machines represent a third generation, which relies on integrated circuits (IC's) and hybrids of IC's and transistors.

[5] Barton M. Biggs, "Numbers Game," *Barron's*, July 24, 1967, p. 3.

Exhibit 2

COMPUTER LEASING INDUSTRY

ESTIMATED ANNUAL VALUE OF COMPUTER EQUIPMENT SHIPPED BY U.S. MANUFACTURERS

(In millions of dollars)

	General-Purpose Digital Computers	*Total**
1955	$ 75	$ 339
1960	720	2,225
1965	2,300	4,800
1966	3,660	6,535
1967	4,200–4,400	7,250– 7,640
1968	4,600–4,900	8,010– 8,660
1970	5,300–5,800	9,180–10,360

* Total includes general-purpose digital computers, special-purpose computers, independent peripheral equipment, software service bureau and consultants, and supplies and supporting services.

Source: "EDP Industry and Market Report," International Data Publishing Co.

Cash flow implications of leasing

The practice of leasing rather than selling a rapidly growing product line can place a terrific strain on a corporation's cash resources. A typical computer selling for $1,000,000 has a manufacturing cost of about $400,000. All other corporate operating expenses, such as engineering, selling, and administrative overhead, add another $300,000 to the machine's cost, leaving a pretax profit of $300,000 for the manufacturer if the machine is sold outright.[6,7] The same computer installed under a manufacturer's standard lease contract would produce annual revenues of about $238,000, but the expenses associated with earning this revenue would amount to $460,000 during the first year as shown in Exhibit 3.

Exhibit 3

COMPUTER LEASING INDUSTRY

FIRST-YEAR FINANCIAL STATEMENT RELATING TO THE LEASE OF A COMPUTER WITH A SALES PRICE EQUAL TO $1,000,000

Revenue		$ 238,000
Depreciation	$160,000	
Other costs	300,000	
Total costs		460,000
Pretax profit (loss)		$(222,000)
Income tax (credit)		(111,000)
After-tax profit (loss)		$(111,000)
Add: Depreciation		160,000
Cash inflow from lease		$ 49,000
Cash outflow to manufacture		400,000
Net cash outflow in first year		$ 351,000

[6] *Ibid.*

[7] Annual Report, 1967, Digital Equipment Corp.

If the computer's basic manufacturing cost of $400,000 is depreciated over four years using the sum-of-the-years'-digits method, the depreciation expense for the first year would be $160,000. This depreciation method is reported to be general industry practice for tax accounting.[8] The previously mentioned corporate operating expenses of $300,000 are not capitalized. Instead they are immediately charged off as an expense. This leads to a first year loss on the leased machine amounting to $222,000. If corporate income from other sources is available to offset the loss on this lease transaction, tax savings eliminate half of this loss, or $111,000. Adding depreciation, a noncash expense, to the after-tax loss gives $49,000 as the first year cash inflow from the leased computer. Since the manufacturer incurred an initial cash outflow of $400,000 to produce the machine, the lease transaction during the first year causes a net cash drain of $351,000. From this analysis it is easy to see why a large volume of computer shipments placed out on lease can be very damaging to a manufacturer from a cash standpoint.

Short-term leasing as a competitive weapon

Widespread leasing of equipment has long been a custom in the computer industry. Prior to 1956, this phenomenon could be explained by IBM's refusal to offer its data processing equipment for sale. As a result of a legal action in that year IBM must now "offer for sale all equipment which it offers for lease and must establish a sales price for such equipment which will have a commercially reasonable relationship to its lease charges for the same equipment."[9]

While the Consent Decree made the outright purchase of equipment possible, most users of IBM equipment still favor the one-year lease contract. A short-term lease frees the user from any risk of technological obsolescence and makes "trading-up" a simple matter if the user's data processing needs outgrow the capacity of the machine in question.

Almost through an accident of corporate history the popularity of one-year lease contracts has given IBM a strong competitive advantage within the computer industry. IBM enjoys the unique advantage of cash revenues in excess of a billion dollars annually from rentals of items such as punch card accounting equipment and typewriters placed in the field many years ago.[10] Other manufacturers without this cash flow have considerable difficulty meeting the huge cash drain that necessarily accompanies short-term leases. Cash shortages force manufacturers such as Honeywell to encourage outright sales or long-term leases (three to five years) against which they can immediately borrow almost the total value of future lease payments. Inability to offer one-year leases places a computer manufacturer such as Honeywell at a

---

[8] Biggs, *op. cit.*

[9] *United States* v. *International Business Machines Corporation,* 1956 Trade Cas. 71, 117 (S.D.N.Y. 1956).

[10] "Data Processing Equipment Leasing," Equity Research Associates, August 19, 1966.

competitive disadvantage since many lessees favor the one-year contract in order to avoid obsolescence risk and the necessity of showing a large future lease obligation in a footnote to their balance sheets.

Theoretically IBM assumes the risk of massive annual equipment returns since the company is protected only by one-year leases. In practice, however, a lessee rarely returns a piece of equipment in less than three to four years because of the considerable expense and time lost in converting existing programs to a new system. Lessees simply continue their contracts on a 90-day notification basis once they expire. Returned machines present only minor marketing problems. If the returned computer is new enough so that the model is still in production, IBM's large sales force will usually be able to place it with another lessee at the full rental rate enjoyed by a comparable piece of new equipment.

IBM cash shortage

Although the ability to offer a one-year lease contract represents a strong competitive weapon for IBM, customer acceptance of the System/360 line of computers was so great that in 1966 the company became a victim of its own success. The cash throw-off from operations, which amounted to $1,258,000,000 in 1966,[11] was no longer sufficient to sustain internally IBM's growth rate. Whereas in 1964 the corporation could boast of cash balances totaling nearly one billion dollars, the situation had changed markedly by 1966 and the company found it necessary to raise the money from external sources. Since IBM avoids debt of any consequence in proportion to equity, in 1966 its shareholders were called upon to supply the company with over $350,000,000 in new equity capital. It is clear that IBM's cash shortage in 1966 was unanticipated, since in 1964 the company had *prepaid* $160,000,000 of loans bearing 3½% interest to The Prudential Insurance Company. By 1966, however, in addition to raising the new equity capital already mentioned, the company had to establish new bank lines of credit equal to $160,000,000, this time at an interest rate of 5½%. In light of this fact, the Prudential prepayment decision ". . . stands as one IBM decision about which there is, in retrospect, no controversy—it was a mistake."[12]

The lease-sales ratio

System/360 was dramatically successful for IBM in terms of market acceptance, but the high percentage of shipments placed on a lease basis drained the corporation financially. Exhibit 4 presents estimates of IBM's cash requirements arising *solely* from shipments of System/360 equipment placed on lease.

In September, 1966, IBM moved to bring its lease-sales ratio down to a level consistent with the company's ability to finance its leases through

[11] Annual Report, IBM, 1966.

[12] T. A. Wise, "The Rocky Road to the Marketplace," *Fortune*, October, 1966, p. 206.

Exhibit 4

COMPUTER LEASING INDUSTRY

ESTIMATED IBM CASH FLOW ARISING SOLELY FROM SHIPMENTS OF SYSTEM/360 EQUIPMENT PLACED ON LEASE

($ Millions)

	1966	*1967*	*1968*	*1969*	*1970*
Total lease revenue	$518.3	$1,130.7	$1,800.3	$2,510.7	$3,272.5
Depreciation expense	348.4	673.0	933.2	1,108.2	1,198.3
Other costs	653.3	771.9	844.1	895.5	960.1
Pretax income	−483.4	−314.3	23.1	507.1	1,114.0
After-tax net	−241.7	−157.1	11.5	253.5	557.0
Total inflow from operation	106.7	515.9	944.7	1,361.7	1,755.3
Total equipment investment	871.1	1,029.2	1,125.4	1,194.0	1,280.2
Cash inflow-outflow	−764.4	−513.3	−180.7	167.7	475.1

	1966	*1967*	*1968*	*1969*	*1970*
Assumptions:					
1. Sales value of total industry computer shipments (billions) from Exhibit 2.	$3.66	$4.40	$4.90	$5.30	$5.80
2. IBM's share of above from Exhibit 1, plus casewriter's estimates.	0.70	0.68	0.66	0.64	0.62
3. IBM's lease-sales ratio from page 311, plus casewriter's estimates.	0.85	0.86	0.87	0.88	0.89

4. According to this exhibit, in 1966 IBM could expect to place out on lease System/360 computer equipment with a sales value of $2.18 billion. This figure can be derived by multiplying together three numbers: the sales value of industry shipments ($3.66 billion); IBM's share of total industry shipments (0.70); and IBM's lease-sales ratio (0.85).
Exhibit 3 shows the first-year cash flow relating to a leased computer with a sales price equal to $1,000,000. To arrive at IBM's 1966 cash flow arising from leasing equipment with a sales value of $2.18 billion, we simply multiply the figures in Exhibit 3 by 2,180.

Source: Publicly available estimates and casewriter's projections.

internal cash generation. IBM reduced the sales price of its computers by 3% and shortly thereafter raised its lease rental rates by 3%. The expectation of trade sources was that this new pricing schedule would stop and perhaps reverse the rising trend in IBM's lease-sales ratio. When the new pricing decision was announced, the value of shipments made on a lease basis was estimated to exceed the value of shipments sold outright by a very wide margin. If the new pricing schedule would reduce the lease to sales ratio significantly from its estimated level of 85%,[13] the immediate cash inflow would be substantial, and the downward pressure on corporate earnings implied by Exhibit 3 would be reduced. Since the heavy placements of leased systems were depressing earnings in 1966, this price change presumably helped the company maintain its historical uptrend in earnings per share.

INDEPENDENT COMPUTER LEASING INDUSTRY

Enter the financial entrepreneur

The cash squeeze at IBM, coupled with the fact that an entirely new generation of computers was being introduced, created a clear profit opportunity for financial entrepreneurs. IBM had widened substantially the spread between the revenues available to computer lessors and the cost of purchasing

[13] Biggs, *op. cit.*

computers to be placed on lease. Financial middlemen could purchase computers from IBM at standard prices and place them with lessees at rental rates ranging from 10% to 20% lower than those charged by IBM. If the machines were depreciated over 8 or 10 years in contrast to the manufacturer's practice of using 4 years, reported profits could be substantial even during the first year that the equipment was placed in service. Since the System/360 represented an entirely new computer generation when it was introduced in late 1965, the economic life of these machines was expected to extend well into the 1970's, limiting an early buyer's risk of premature technological obsolescence. Experience showed that second-generation equipment such as IBM's 1400 series was actively manufactured and marketed for as long as six years (1960–66), and the continued rental of existing equipment in this series was expected to remain profitable for a number of years to come.

Short-term versus long-term leases

While four or five publicly owned computer leasing companies were in existence prior to 1966 (Exhibit 5), the majority of the companies were created to take advantage of the profit opportunity afforded by IBM's pricing decision of September, 1966. With two exceptions the companies concentrate on writing leases of short duration, the average being about two years. Pricing policy among the companies is quite uniform, with the lessee usually paying the leasing company 90% of the standard manufacturer's rental rate on a two-year lease.

The rental rates charged by computer manufacturers allow them to recover the full sale price of their computers after about 47 months of continuous rental receipts. Since the independent computer leasing companies charge at most 90% of the manufacturer's rental rate, it takes the leasing companies at least 52 months to recover the full purchase price. With a purchase price payback of at least 52 months and an average lease term of 24 months, the computer leasing companies are obviously concerned with future marketability of returned machines. Concern with this problem leads most of the companies to restrict their computer purchases to models with proved market acceptance. Machines with large order backlogs or a large number of existing installations (such as IBM's System/360–30) are favored for purchase by the leasing companies. This is true because every user renting a System/360–30 from the manufacturer represents a potential future customer should the leasing company find itself with a returned machine of the same model. The concern with future marketability has led computer leasing companies to deal almost exclusively in IBM System/360 equipment.

Leasco Data Processing Equipment Corporation, the one company specializing in non-IBM equipment, writes only noncancellable full payout leases. In such a lease the entire purchase price plus interest is recovered during the initial lease term. Because Leasco carries essentially no obsolescence risk, its business is substantially different from that of the other computer leasing companies, which specialize in leases with much shorter terms. First, Leasco's

Exhibit 5

COMPUTER LEASING INDUSTRY

COMPARISON OF COMPUTER LEASING COMPANIES

Computer Leasing Companies	*Computer[1] Investment*	*Type of Computers*	*Type of Leases*	*Service*	*Marketing*	*Principals*
GC Computer Corp. (1966)	$73.1 MM gr. $51.1 MM net (12/31/66) 96 leases	IBM's ⅔—1400's 7000's ⅓— 360's	Length: Most 1–3 yrs. Range: 1 mo.–8 yrs. Rental: 90% of IBM's Costs recovery: 70–78 mos. (all costs)	No repair, maintenance, or programming.	Own marketing organization with five sales offices around the U.S.	Owned by Greyhound.
Randolph Computer Corp. (1965)	$35.9 MM gr. (2/10/67) 68 systems 31 lessees	IBM 360's Cost $225 M–$747 M	Length: 2–5 yrs. Rental: 90% of IBM's Cost recovery: 6 yrs. (*all* costs) 4–5 yrs. (machine cost) Options: Purchase options at 7½% per annum discount (purchase price always slightly above book value)	No repair or maintenance. In April, acquired United Data Processing, Inc., to add software capability.	The eight officers find most leasing opportunities. Work out of NY office.	Randolph (Pres.) from Boothe Leasing. Arbour (EVP) marketing man from IBM.
Levin-Townsend Computer Corp.	$20.5 MM gr. (3/10/67) 35 leases	IBM 360's	Length: Most 1 year Rental: About 90% of IBM	No maintenance or repair. Programming and systems consulting for a fee.	Own marketing force (about five men). Also representatives who find deals for commission. 67 employees.	Levin (Pres.) is former math professor and founded L-T as consulting firm in data processing.
Data Processing Financial & General Corp. (1961)	$18.2 MM gr. (11/30/66)	IBM's Cost $85 M–$2.3 MM	Length: 1 mo.–5 yrs. About 20% are monthly, about 40% are 1 yr. Rental: n.a. Options: A few leases have options at fair market value—exercisable any time.	No repair, maintenance, or programming.	Uses some brokers on commission basis. Has 10 full-time salesmen. (12/1967).	Harry Goodman (Pres.) data processing expert—formerly in IBM market forecasting.
Leasco Data Processing Equipment Corp. (1961)	$20–25 MM gr. (4/30/67 est.)	CDC and others	Length: 2–8 yrs. *full payout leases* Rentals: About 80% of manufacturers'. Options: a few have purchase option at fair market—end of lease. Most provide for renewal at lower rental.	No repair or maintenance. Plans to acquire Documentation, Inc., to provide software capability.	Has 37 salesmen among its 71 employees. Also trains manufacturer's salesmen in lease techniques. Manufacturer then sells lease package with machine. Has exclusive contract for CDC payout leases.	Steinberg Family controls. They are leasing, not computer experts. VP Sweetbaum is former accounting machine salesman.
Standard Computer Corp.	$8.2 MM gr. (2/28/67)	IBM's Cost $171 M–$3.9 MM	Length: 1 mo.–8 yrs. most 2 yrs. Cost recovery: 5–7 yrs. Options: None except in the case of an 8-yr. lease	No repair, maintenance, or programming.	Uses brokers and Lease Finance Co. (parent) to find deals.	Formed by: Auerbach (Tech. consulting firm which evaluates deals); Lease Finance Co. (management consultant which puts together deals); Blair & Co.; Pres. Affel is an engineer from Auerbach.

(1) Amounts shown are gross. "Net" amount is nearly as large in all cases. Most machines are less than 2 years old and are depreciated over an 8- to 10-year life.

sharply limited risk allows it to command a 4 to 1 debt to equity ratio, to be compared with about a 2 to 1 debt to equity ratio for its "short-term" counterparts. Second, Leasco has arranged its pricing policy to insulate the company from possible future increases in the cost of maintaining its computer equipment. Leasco accomplishes this by offering its lessees the standard 10% discount and adding to this amount a second deduction equal to the cost of the equipment manufacturer's full service maintenance contract at the time the lease is signed. The lessee must then assume the cost of a separate maintenance contract, which normally amounts to about 10% of the cost of renting the machine from its manufacturer. The companies specializing in short-term leases almost always assume the cost of maintenance contracts. While their higher rental charges offset this cost, the short-term leasing companies shoulder all the risk involved in future cost increases for the maintenance service.

Leasco enjoys the advantages of reduced risk and increased financial leverage, but these benefits do not come without cost. Leasco must give up a substantial part of the residual value in the equipment it leases in order to induce lessees to accept a longer term. "At the end of the initial lease term . . . , lessees may then renew the term at a negotiated rental rate which frequently ranges between 30% and 50% of the rental . . . originally charged."[14]

Importance of remarketing

Leasco's approach to computer leasing leaves the company practically immune from the problem of remarketing returned equipment. In contrast, the companies writing shorter leases face problems in two areas: (1) that of avoiding equipment inventories and (2) that of providing programming assistance to "second users."

1. It is of critical importance to these companies to keep all machines productively utilized since the average lease contract involves over $500,000 worth of computer equipment. Because the System/360 line of computers is so new, through 1967 no leasing company has yet had to remarket a returned machine in this series. Levin-Townsend Computer Corporation, a leasing company that occasionally purchases second generation equipment (at a considerable discount from its original purchase price), has had some experience with returns of this older equipment. Regarding the importance of rapidly remarketing equipment returns the company's president, Howard S. Levin, has said, "We hold sales contests with the salesman who places the computer keeping his job."[15] Presumably the comment was not made entirely with tongue in cheek. Leasing companies never purchase equipment for inventory: a lease agreement is always simultaneously executed. In fact, two simultaneous transactions generally occur in closing a deal. The leasing

[14] "Leasco—A Study for Institutional Investors," Goodbody and Co., February 1967.

[15] "Computer Leasing Stocks," *Fortune*, July, 1967, p. 171.

company signs a purchase agreement with the equipment manufacturer for a computer already chosen by company A. Company A simultaneously signs a contract with the leasing company to rent the machine for a period of from one to five years.

2. At present, it is IBM's policy to provide education, systems assistance, and other services to customers who are "first users" of its equipment but not necessarily to subsequent users. Through 1967 all System/360 lessees renting through leasing companies have been first users, but in future years as equipment is returned and remarketed, this will not continue to be the case. At some future time, therefore, computer leasing companies may be forced to furnish software support. Otherwise they might face a serious competitive disadvantage in the remarketing of equipment to second and later users.

Ease of growth

The growth rate of a manufacturing company is often constrained by the need for comparable expansion of such factors as capital resources, physical facilities, top-management talent, and a trained force of production employees. For the computer leasing business, available capital is the principal factor restricting growth. The "people" and "facilities" factors are far less critical. Indeed, Data Processing Financial & General Corporation was purchasing equipment at an annual rate of $50 million in September, 1967, with a staff of 10 people including the office secretaries.[16]

The computer leasing companies have purchased equipment at a spectacular rate since the end of 1965. Probably the only factor restraining even faster growth is the companies' limited cash resources. Yet even in the area of raising equity capital the companies have had few problems. Rapid price appreciation and growth in earnings per share have given the stocks in this industry a large market following. If we ignore the sharp general market setback between February and October, 1966, prices of the companies' common stocks have risen as dramatically as their equipment holdings, as shown in Exhibits 6 and 7. Almost everyone buying the securities of computer leasing companies has made money, a factor that greatly contributes to the ability of these corporations to keep coming to the market for additional financing.

Exhibit 7 shows the public financing pattern of three companies in the computer leasing industry. Each new security issue has been larger in absolute terms, and in many cases successive issues have grown larger and larger as a percentage of total computer equipment previously owned.

Accounting policies boost earnings

Corporate growth depends on the availability of funds and the availability of funds for computer leasing companies depends in large measure on a rising stock price. Price appreciation is the only return a common shareholder can

---

[16] *Preliminary Prospectus,* Data Processing Financial & General Corp., August 22, 1967.

Exhibit 6

LEVIN-TOWNSEND COMPUTER CORPORATION

STOCK PRICES AND VALUE OF EQUIPMENT OWNED

DECEMBER, 1965–SEPTEMBER, 1967

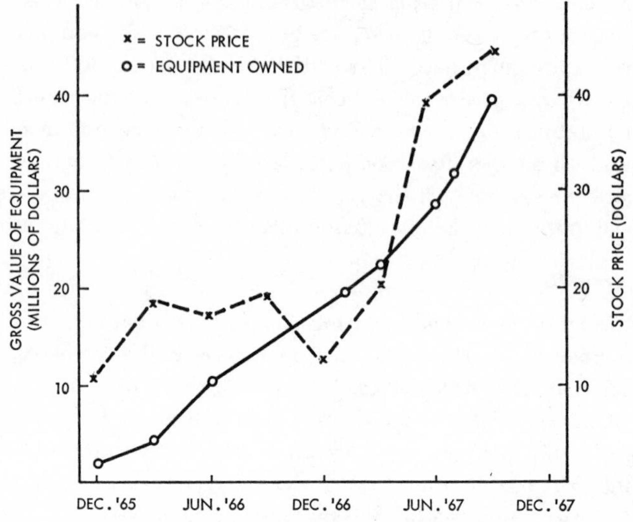

Exhibit 7

COMPUTER LEASING INDUSTRY

AMOUNTS AND PRICES OF PUBLIC SECURITY ISSUES OF SELECTED COMPANIES

Company	Date of Public Security Issue	*In Thousands of Dollars* Amount of Security Issue	Computer Equipment Owned	Elapsed Time Since Previous Security Issue	Common Stock Price $
Standard	April, 1966	2,500	6,000	....	5
Computer	March, 1967	4,000	12,143	11 mos.	15¾
Corporation	June, 1967	8,000	14,476	3 mos.	19½
Randolph	April, 1966	1,800	3,057	....	20
Computer	March, 1967	5,000	35,945	11 mos.	41¼
Corporation	July, 1967	10,000	44,913	4 mos.	46
Data Processing	December, 1965	3,300	6,000	....	11
Financial &	March, 1967	12,000	18,183	15 mos.	41⅛
General Corporation	September, 1967	50,000	38,941	6 mos.	73¼

expect for a number of years since loan covenants accepted by these companies severely restrict and generally prevent dividend payments.

Perhaps in an effort to provide the rising stock price necessary for growth in computer leasing, the companies in this industry have adopted accounting policies allowing them to report the highest possible current earnings. Thus, even though IBM depreciates a System/360–40 computer over 4 years using accelerated depreciation in its financial statements to its shareholders, most of the leasing companies depreciate the identical machine over 10 years using straight-line depreciation for shareholder reporting. To reduce their income tax liability, however, the companies use sum-of-the-years'-digits depreciation and an eight-year life for tax reporting. In a similar vein, leasing companies "flow through" the 7% investment tax credit as rapidly as possible rather than spreading the credit evenly over the life of the asset in question.

Automatic growth in reported earnings

Exhibit 8 shows pro forma financial statements relating to a typical short-term lease for a $1,000,000 computer system placed in service on January 1, 1966. The upper half of the page, lines 1–21, shows pro forma income statements as reported for purposes of calculating the annual federal income tax liability. The lower half of the page, lines 22–32, shows how the income statements would appear in a leasing company's shareholder reports.

Although the complexity of Exhibit 8 may at first appear overwhelming, detailed study of the numbers presented is unnecessary. Careful examination of a very few lines (those relating to depreciation expense and after-tax income) will provide most of the information needed for a thorough understanding of the importance of management accounting choices in the earnings reports of companies operating in this industry.

Lines 9 and 27 project the annual pretax profit for tax and shareholder reports, respectively. It is important to note that except for the depreciation charge, all the revenue and expense items used to calculate pretax profit in the tax and shareholder reports are exactly the same each year. Although tax loss carryforwards and the investment tax credit play a major role in determining after-tax income (lines 12 and 30), the striking numerical differences found in these two lines result entirely from the variation in depreciation charges.

While the importance of accounting policy in determining earnings is highlighted by Exhibit 8, two other key factors can be gleaned from the figures. First, net income for shareholder purposes (line 30) has a built-in increase of at least 15% per year during the first four years of the computer's life. This is caused by decreasing interest payments as the debt outstanding is reduced. Second, the first-year return on equity equals 10% ($32,799/$334,000). So long as equity for new equipment purchases is sold at a price exceeding 10 times current earnings, future earnings per share will be enhanced by simply buying and leasing additional equipment with the proceeds from new common stock issues. With leasing company equities selling at well above 20 times current earnings, the enhancement in earnings arising from simply selling additional stock to purchase and lease more computer equipment is dramatic.

The industry's future

While reported profits are currently moving even higher, a number of factors weigh heavily on the future prospects of the computer leasing indus-

Exhibit 8

COMPUTER LEASING INDUSTRY

Financial Statements Relating to a $1,000,000 Computer Placed under a Two-Year Lease Contract

Book versus Tax Accounting for a Typical Computer Leasing Company

		1966	1967	1968	1969	1970	1971	1972	1973	1974	1975	
1	IBM rental rate	256,000	256,000	256,000	256,000	256,000	256,000	256,000	256,000	256,000	256,000	
2	(1) Discount allowed	25,600	25,600	30,720	35,840	40,960	46,080	51,200	56,320	61,440	66,560	
3	Overtime premium	7,680	7,680	7,680	7,680	7,680	7,680	7,680	7,680	7,680	7,680	
4	Gross rentals	238,080	238,080	232,960	227,840	222,720	217,600	212,480	207,360	202,240	197,120	
5	Maintenance expense (10% of line 1)	25,600	25,600	25,600	25,600	25,600	25,600	25,600	25,600	25,600	25,600	
6	(2) Depreciation expense	188,889	165,278	141,667	118,056	94,444	70,833	47,222	23,611	.....	.....	
7	(3) Interest (9% of line 18)	59,940	48,354	35,726	22,375	8,238	.....	.....	.....	.....	.....	
8	Selling, general, and administrative	23,808	23,808	23,296	22,784	22,272	21,760	21,248	20,736	20,224	19,712	
9	Pretax profit (loss)	(60,157)	(24,960)	6,672	39,025	72,166	99,407	118,410	137,413	156,416	151,808	
10	Taxes (before investment credit)	.....	.....	.....	.....	16,373	49,703	59,204	68,706	78,208	75,904	
11	(4) Investment credit used	.....	.....	.....	.....	8,186	24,851	29,602	7,359	.....	.....	Leasing Company Tax Reports
12	Net profit	(60,157)	(24,960)	6,672	39,025	63,979	74,555	88,807	76,066	78,208	75,904	
13	Add depreciation	188,889	165,278	141,667	118,056	94,444	70,833	47,222	23,611	.....	.....	
14	Total cash inflow	128,732	140,318	148,338	157,081	158,424	145,388	136,030	99,677	78,208	75,904	
15	Debt repayment	128,732	140,318	148,338	157,081	91,531	.....	.....	.....	.....	.....	
16	Available for equity holders	.....	.....	.....	.....	66,893	145,388	136,030	99,677	78,208	75,904	
17	(5) After-tax cash flow from liquidation	.....	.....	.....	.....	.....	.....	.....	.....	.....	275,000	
18	Debt outstanding (start of yr.)	666,000	537,268	396,950	248,612	91,531	.....	.....	.....	.....	.....	
19	Equity invested (start of yr.)	334,000	334,000	334,000	334,000	334,000	267,107	121,719	(14,311)	(113,988)	(192,196)	
20	Remaining investment credit	70,000	70,000	70,000	70,000	61,813	36,962	7,359	.....	.....	.....	
21	Tax loss carry-forward	60,157	85,117	78,445	39,420	.....	.....	.....	.....	.....	.....	
22	Gross rentals	238,080	238,080	232,960	227,840	222,720	217,600	212,480	207,360	202,240	197,120	
23	(2) Depreciation	85,000	85,000	85,000	85,000	85,000	85,000	85,000	85,000	85,000	85,000	
24	Maintenance	25,600	25,600	25,600	25,600	25,600	25,600	25,600	25,600	25,600	25,600	
25	(3) Interest	59,940	48,354	35,726	22,375	8,238	.....	.....	.....	.....	.....	
26	Selling, general, and administrative	23,808	23,808	23,296	22,784	22,272	21,760	21,248	20,736	20,224	19,712	Leasing Company Shareholder Reports
27	Pretax profit	43,732	55,318	63.338	72,081	81,610	85,240	80,632	76,024	71,416	66,808	
28	Taxes (before investment credit)	21,866	27,659	31,669	36,040	40,805	42,620	40,316	38,012	35,708	33,404	
29	(4) Investment credit used	10,933	13,829	15,834	18,020	11,384	.....	.....	.....	.....	.....	
30	Net profit	32,799	41,488	47,503	54,061	52,189	42,620	40,316	38,012	35,708	33,404	
31	(5) After-tax cash flow from liquidation	.....	.....	.....	.....	.....	.....	.....	.....	.....	275,000	
32	Remaining investment credit	59,067	45,238	29,404	11,384	.....	.....	.....	.....	.....	.....	

Assumptions:

- (1) Discount: 10% of the IBM rate through 1967; increasing by 2 percentage points per year thereafter to 26% in 1975.
- (2) Depreciation: 8 yrs. sum of years' digits, 15% residual value for tax purposes; 10 yrs., straight line, 15% residual for shareholders.
- (3) Interest: 9% rate on outstanding balance which is reduced each year by the full cash flow.
- (4) Investment credit: 7% investment credit deducted from tax liability as fast as possible rather than evenly amortized over the life of asset.
- (5) Cash flow from liquidation: The computer is sold for 40% of original cost at the end of 1975; taxes paid at the corporate rate (0.50).

try. In the short run, the industry is threatened by the fact that it is dependent on the pricing strategy adopted by computer manufacturers. Should these manufacturers find their cash positions improving substantially in the next few years, they might wish to finance a higher proportion of computer shipments themselves. Higher computer sale prices relative to lease rental charges would tend to raise the manufacturers' lease to sales ratio. Higher computer maintenance fees would also tend to reduce the leasing companies' profit margins, thus slowing their growth and raising the manufacturers' lease to sales ratio.

Over the longer term, computer leasing companies are threatened by the obsolescence of their third-generation System/360 machines in less than the anticipated 10 years. Second-generation computers were manufactured and marketed for six full years from 1959 to 1965. Machines of this vintage dropped in used value from over 70% of the original purchase price to around 40% of the purchase price within a year after System/360 was introduced. With sales prices so sharply reduced, rental rates of the second generation machines were under considerable pressure. Whether this price pattern will be repeated with third-generation equipment remains a question for the future.

COMPULEASE CORPORATION (A)

Late in the evening of December 10, 1965, James A. Kralik, president of the newly formed Compulease Corporation, was in the process of deciding where his company should concentrate its lease-writing efforts.

Meeting with investment banker

Two hours previously Mr. Kralik had returned home after a successful meeting with the partner in charge of corporate finance at the investment banking firm of Bachman, Dillard and Hanover (BD&H). After a number of previous visits, Mr. Kralik felt that he had, at last, convinced the BD&H partner that an investment in a firm involved in computer leasing (see Note: Computer Leasing Industry, pp. 306–19) would offer a rewarding profit opportunity to a small syndicate of private investors. BD&H could quickly put together a financially sophisticated group of individuals willing to provide venture capital from among its partners and wealthy clients, and Compulease could represent a vehicle for the investor group to participate in the rapidly growing area of computer leasing.

While a specific financing proposal for Compulease was not made final during the meeting, the investment banker indicated that the BD&H group might be expected to put up $960,000 in return for a 78% interest in Compulease. Mr. Kralik and the other co-founders, John Bailey and Philip Jameson, would then receive a 22% interest in the company for $40,000 plus their efforts in organizing the new venture.

The investor group would be seeking capital gains. Their goal would also be to offer additional Compulease common stock to the public. The investment banker felt that a year of operating history would be sufficient to give Compulease the earnings base necessary to guarantee a successful public offering.

At the conclusion of the December 10 meeting the investment banker asked Mr. Kralik to meet with him again on December 22. The proposed meeting would be attended by a number of BD&H partners and the clients of BD&H who might be interested in participating in the Compulease financing. Prior to this meeting, BD&H would make sure that each member of the potential investor group was familiarized with the computer leasing industry. Instead of providing background information then, the main purpose of the December

22 meeting, aside from ascertaining investor interest, would be to discuss how Compulease ought to enter the field of computer leasing. The discussion would revolve around the pros and cons of writing long-term versus short-term computer leases. Mr. Kralik would be expected to present a convincing case for concentrating his company's efforts in one area or the other.

Mr. Kralik felt certain that the long-term versus short-term leasing decision he had to make in his proposal to the investors would be extremely important in the future development of his company. With this thought in mind, he set out to review the two types of leases.

The factors to be considered

Mr. Kralik knew that existing publicly owned firms specializing in the two types of leases differed markedly in at least four key areas: (1) the accounting principles adopted for reporting earnings to shareholders; (2) the amount of risk assumed in the course of normal business activity; (3) the potential return on investments in computer equipment; and (4) the type of technical expertise needed by management in order to assure long-run corporate success.

Reporting the earnings

Mr. Kralik was aware that for tax purposes, the accounting policies adopted by most computer leasing companies were the same, regardless of whether they specialized in long-term or short-term leases. In their tax accounts, both types of companies assumed a 15% salvage value and depreciated their machines over eight years by the sum-of-the-years'-digits method.

While their tax accounting conventions were similar, the accounting principles used by the two types of firms in reporting income to shareholders differed dramatically. Exhibits 1 and 2 show how a computer system costing $1,000,000 would appear for tax and shareholder reports under the two leasing strategies.

As shown in line 23 of Exhibit 2, companies specializing in short-term leases generally assumed a 15% salvage value and depreciated their equipment over *10* years using the *straight-line* method in the determination of earnings for shareholder reporting. For companies concentrating on long-term full payout leases, depreciation never entered shareholder financial statements at all. These companies recorded the total amount of future lease payments as an asset, effectively transforming a piece of equipment into an account receivable. Under this accounting convention, annual income was not determined by simply adding up the total monthly rental payments received during the year. Instead, as shown in line 20 of Exhibit 1, the total value of lease payments due during the six and one-half years that the lease remained in force was calculated, and from this amount the original cost of the machine (less a 10% estimated salvage value) was deducted. The remaining amount, called unearned income, was "earned" over the life of the lease. A sum-of-the-years'-digits technique, line 27 of Exhibit 1, was used to allocate "unearned income" in the annual profit and loss statements. The effect of this treatment was to throw the bulk of the income into the early years of the lease when the major cost item, interest expense, was highest.

In shareholder reports, both the long-term and short-term leases generated a profit in the first year. The initial profit in each case amounted to about 10% of the equity originally invested. ($19,800/$200,000 = 9.9% Exhibit 1; $32,799/$334,000 = 9.8% Exhibit 2.) Over the longer term a company writing short-term leases would report to shareholders (from this particular lease) steadily rising annual earnings for a period of four years, as shown in line 30 of Exhibit 2; whereas a company writing long-term leases would report steadily *declining* earnings over the entire period of the lease as shown in line 34 of Exhibit 1.

Risk

A wide gap separated the amount of risk that would be assumed by Compulease under the two leasing alternatives being considered by Mr. Kralik. If his decision took the company into the area of full payout leases, Mr. Kralik knew that the risk to Compulease from the standpoint of technological obsolescence would be greatly diminished. The only real threat from obsolescence would come in the options he would have to grant to lessees allowing them to "trade up" into larger computer systems (if they paid Compulease a small penalty fee) after three to four years of a six and one-half year lease. Mr. Kralik felt that computer manufacturers would probably retain their policy of allowing at least 40% of the original purchase price of four-year-old equipment on trade-ins for more expensive systems, so he was confident that losses could be avoided even if most options were exercised.

Companies writing short-term leases accepted almost all the risks of shortened machine life due to technological obsolescence. It was Mr. Kralik's opinion, however, that third-generation computers would not become technologically obsolete before 1974. A machine purchased in 1966 would thus have at minimum an eight-year life.

Borrowing capacity

Since the risk arising from technological obsolescence was small with full payout leases, the Manufacturers Chemical Bank of New York had given Mr. Kralik assurances that it would advance up to 80% of the cost of third-generation computer equipment placed under this type of lease. The effective interest rate on such a loan would be about 9%.

In contrast, the same bank would be willing to advance only two thirds of the cost of computer equipment placed on short-term leases, a figure Mr. Kralik understood to be practically standard for all companies writing similar leases in the industry.

Although commercial banks were willing to lend leasing companies a large fraction of the cost of acquiring computer systems, they also desired to have the loan on each system repaid as rapidly as possible. For this reason, leasing companies were generally required to amortize loan principal with the full after-tax cash flow resulting from lease payments (line 14 of Exhibit 1 and line 15 of Exhibit 2). For a computer system out on a short-term lease, the bank would be paid in 4 years and 7 months. For a system on a long-term lease, the banks were willing to wait 5½ years to recover their full loans.

Expertise required to compete successfully

Before committing Compulease to a particular leasing strategy, Mr. Kralik had to consider the differences in operating and technical expertise required for long-run corporate success under the two leasing alternatives. Exhibit 3 describes the management as it existed in December, 1965.

If Compulease concentrated on short-term leases, the ability to quickly remarket returned computer equipment to second users would be of key importance to the company's ultimate success. In that case, Compulease would require a staff of specialists to provide programming assistance to second users, and some systems experts to assist in installing used computers in situations where compatibility problems might reasonably be anticipated.

Most of the need for technical expertise in the computer field could be avoided if Mr. Kralik limited his company to full payout leases. The second-user problem would all but disappear with this strategy, and Compulease's problems would probably be more narrowly limited to those of a financial nature.

Returns

Mr. Kralik saw obvious advantages in terms of limited risk and greater debt leverage accruing to companies writing full payout leases, and this same fact had not escaped the notice of potential lessees. Indeed, the concessions demanded by potential lessees grew larger as the fixed term of a proposed computer lease grew longer. In order to get a 6½-year full payout lease, companies writing these leases were usually forced to forgo any overtime premium for machine usage over 176 hours per month, and to give the lessee an option allowing him to buy the machine at 40% of the original purchase price when the initial lease term expired. Leasing companies writing only short-term leases gave no such purchase options to their lessees, and if Mr. Kralik chose this strategy, he expected to be still collecting around 74% of the manufacturers' presently published standard rental rate some 10 years after the equipment was originally placed in service.

Those companies writing short-term leases accepted almost all the risk of shortened machine life due to technological obsolescence. In return they would enjoy any benefits that might result if (1) their machines could be profitably rented beyond the 10-year anticipated life, or (2) the computers could be sold at the end of 10 years for more than 40% of their original cost, or (3) the discount (below manufacturers' rental rates) needed to keep the machines in the field did not increase two percentage points per year, as assumed in Exhibit 2.

Working with the tax accounting reports in Exhibits 1 and 2, Mr. Kralik had done a discounted cash flow analysis of the return on equity after all debt had been repaid under the two leasing alternatives (Exhibit 4). The returns to investors in Compulease appeared to be comparable under both leasing strategies.

Mr. Kralik then decided to calculate how sensitive the return under the short-term leasing alternative might be to changes in anticipated life, resale value, and rental rates. Exhibit 5 shows the results of his analysis. Mr. Kralik based the study on his opinion that third-generation computers would not become technologically obsolete before 1974, giving a machine purchased in 1966 a minimum life of eight years. In a similar vein, he felt that lease discounts necessary to keep third-generation computers fully utilized would not increase faster than four percentage points per year before the machines became technologically obsolete. Once third-generation computers were finally superseded by fourth-generation computers, Mr. Kralik felt that he would still be able to sell his obsolete equipment for at least 40% of its original cost. The conclusion Mr. Kralik drew from Exhibit 5 was that under the most unfavorable circumstances, Compulease's return on equity would be about 10%. Under circumstances of long life, no deterioration in rental rates, and high resale values, the return might rise as high as 16%.

Exhibit 1

COMPULEASE CORPORATION (A)

FINANCIAL STATEMENTS RELATING TO A $1,000,000 COMPUTER ON A 6½-YEAR LEASE CONTRACT (FULL PAYOUT)

BOOK VERSUS TAX ACCOUNTING FOR COMPULEASE CORPORATION

		1966	*1967*	*1968*	*1969*	*1970*	*1971*	*Mid-1972*		
1	IBM rental rate	$ 256,000	$256,000	$256,000	$256,000	$256,000	$256,000	$128,000		Leasing Company Tax Reports (lines 2–17)
2	[1]Discount allowed	51,200	51,200	51,200	51,200	51,200	51,200	25,600		
3	Gross lease payments	204,800	204,800	204,800	204,800	204,800	204,800	102,400		
4	[2]Depreciation	189,000	165,000	142,000	118,000	94,500	70,500	23,700		
5	[3]Interest (9% of line 14)	72,000	64,300	52,500	39,800	25,800	10,600	0		
6	Selling, general and administrative	37,600	3,000	3,000	3,000	3,000	3,000	1,500		
7	Pretax profit (loss)	(93,800)	(27,500)	7,300	44,000	81,500	120,700	77,200		
8	Taxes (before investment credit)	0	0	0	0	5,700	60,300	38,600		
9	[4]Investment credit used	0	0	0	0	2,800	30,100	37,100		
10	Net profit	(93,800)	(27,500)	7,300	44,000	78,600	90,500	75,700		
11	Add depreciation	189,000	165,000	142,000	118,000	94,500	70,500	23,700		
12	Total cash inflow	95,200	137,500	149,300	162,000	173,100	161,000	99,400		
13	[5]Sale for residual value	0	0	0	0	0	0	298,700		
14	Debt outstanding (start of year)	800,000	704,800	567,300	418,000	256,000	82,900	0	0	
15	Equity invested (start of year)	200,000	200,000	200,000	200,000	200,000	200,000	121,900	(276,200)	
16	Remaining investment credit	70,000	70,000	70,000	70,000	67,200	37,100	0	0	
17	Tax loss carry-forward	93,800	121,300	114,000	70,000	0	0	0	0	
18	Gross rental payment	204,800								Leasing Company Shareholder Reports (lines 18–36)
19	Lease term 6½ years									
20	Total lease payments over term	1,331,200								
21	Cost of machine	1,000,000								
22	Less residual	100,000								
23	Net cost	900,000								
24	Unearned income available	431,200								
25	Less lease acquisition cost	37,600								
26	Remaining unearned income	393,600								
27	% taken of total above	.250	0.214	0.179	0.143	0.107	0.071	0.036		
28	Income	98,400	84,100	70,500	56,300	42,200	27,900	14,200		
29	Selling, general, and administrative	0	3,000	3,000	3,000	3,000	3,000	1,500		
30	Interest	72,000	64,300	52,500	39,800	25,800	10,600	0		
31	Pretax profit	26,400	16,800	15,000	13,500	13,400	14,300	12,700		
32	Taxes (before investment credit)	13,200	8,400	7,500	6,700	6,700	7,100	6,300		
33	Investment credit used	6,600	4,200	3,700	3,300	3,300	3,500	3,200		
34	After-tax profit	19,800	12,600	11,200	10,100	10,000	10,700	9,600		
35	Carry-forward investment credit	63,400	59,200	55,500	52,200	48,900	45,400	42,200		
36	Sale for residual value							292,200		

Assumptions:

[1] Discount: 20% of IBM rental rate.

[2] Depreciation: eight years sum-of-the-years' digits, 15% residual for tax purposes.

[3] Interest: 9% rate on outstanding balance, which is reduced each year by the full cash flow.

[4] Investment credit: 7% investment credit deducted from tax liability as fast as possible, rather than evenly amortized over the life of the asset.

[5] Cash flow from liquidation: the computer is sold for 40% of original cost at mid-1972; taxes paid at the corporate rate (0.5).

Exhibit 2

COMPULEASE CORPORATION (A)

Financial Statements Relating to a $1,000,000 Computer Placed under a Two-Year Lease Contract

Book versus Tax Accounting for Compulease Corporation

		1966	*1967*	*1968*	*1969*	*1970*	*1971*	*1972*	*1973*	*1974*	*1975*	
1	IBM rental rate	$256,000	$256,000	$256,000	$256,000	$256,000	$256,000	$256,000	$256,000	$256,000	$256,000	
2	(1)Discount allowed	25,600	25,600	30,720	35,840	40,960	46,080	51,200	56,320	61,440	66,560	
3	Overtime premium	7,680	7,680	7,680	7,680	7,680	7,680	7,680	7,680	7,680	7,680	
4	Gross rentals	238,080	238,080	232,960	227,840	222,720	217,600	212,480	207,360	202,240	197,120	
5	Maintenance expense (10% of line 1)	25,600	25,600	25,600	25,600	25,600	25,600	25,600	25,600	25,600	25,600	
6	(2)Depreciation expense	188,889	165,278	141,667	118,056	94,444	70,833	47,222	23,611	......	......	
7	(3)Interest (9% of line 18)	59,940	48,354	35,726	22,375	8,238	......	......	......	......	......	
8	Selling, general, and administrative	23,808	23,808	23,296	22,784	22,272	21,760	21,248	20,736	20,224	19,712	
9	Pretax profit (loss)	(60,157)	(24,960)	6,672	39,025	72,166	99,407	118,410	137,413	156,416	151,808	
10	Taxes (before investment credit)	......	......	......	......	16,373	49,703	59,204	68,706	78,208	75,904	
11	(4)Investment credit used	......	......	......	......	8,186	24,851	29,602	7,359	......	......	Leasing Company Tax Reports
12	Net profit	(60,157)	(24,960)	6,672	39,025	63,979	74,555	88,807	76,066	78,208	75,904	
13	Add depreciation	188,889	165,278	141,667	118,056	94,444	70,833	47,222	23,611	......	......	
14	Total cash inflow	128,732	140,318	148,338	157,081	158,424	145,388	136,030	99,677	78,208	75,904	
15	Debt repayment	128,732	140,318	148,338	157,081	91,531	......	......	......	......	......	
16	Available for equity holders	......	......	......	......	66,893	145,388	136,030	99,677	78,208	75,904	
17	(5)After tax cash flow from liquidation	......	......	......	......	......	......	......	......	......	275,000	
18	Debt outstanding (start of yr.)	666,000	537,268	396,950	248,612	91,531	......	......	......	......	......	
19	Equity invested (start of yr.)	334,000	334,000	334,000	334,000	334,000	267,107	121,719	(14,311)	(113,988)	(192,196)	
20	Remaining investment credit	70,000	70,000	70,000	70,000	61,813	36,962	7,359	......	......	......	
21	Tax loss carry-forward	60,157	85,117	78,445	39,420	......	......	......	......	......	......	
22	Gross rentals	238,080	238,080	232,960	227,840	222,720	217,600	212,480	207,360	202,240	197,120	
23	(2)Depreciation	85,000	85,000	85,000	85,000	85,000	85,000	85,000	85,000	85,000	85,000	
24	Maintenance	25,600	25,600	25,600	25,600	25,600	25,600	25,600	25,600	25,600	25,600	
25	(3)Interest	59,940	48,354	35,726	22,375	8,238	......	......	......	......	......	
26	Selling, general, and administrative	23,808	23,808	23,296	22,784	22,272	21,760	21,248	20,736	20,224	19,712	
27	Pretax profit	43,732	55,318	63,338	72,081	81,610	85,240	80,632	76,024	71,416	66,808	Leasing Company Shareholder Reports
28	Taxes (before investment credit)	21,866	27,659	31,669	36,040	40,805	42,620	40,316	38,012	35,708	33,404	
29	(4)Investment credit used	10,933	13,829	15,834	18,020	11,384	......	......	......	......	......	
30	Net profit	32,799	41,488	47,503	54,061	52,189	42,620	40,316	38,012	35,708	33,404	
31	(5)After-tax cash flow from liquidation	......	......	......	......	......	......	......	......	......	275,000	
32	Remaining investment credit	59,067	45,238	29,404	11,384	......	......	......	......	......	......	

Assumptions:

- (1) Discount: 10% of the IBM rate, through 1967; increasing by 2 percentage points per year thereafter to 26% in 1975.
- (2) Depreciation: 8 yrs. sum-of-the-years' digits, 15% residual value for tax purposes; 10 yrs, straight line, 15% residual for shareholders.
- (3) Interest: 9% rate on outstanding balance which is reduced each year by the full cash flow.
- (4) Investment Credit: 7% investment credit deducted from tax liability as fast as possible rather than evenly amortized over the life of asset.
- (5) Cash flow from liquidation: The computer is sold for 40% of original cost at the end of 1975; taxes paid at the corporate rate (50%).

Exhibit 3

COMPULEASE CORPORATION (A)

MANAGEMENT

Name	*Positions and Offices Held*
James A. Kralik	Chairman of the Board of Directors, and President
Philip R. Jameson	Executive Vice President and Director
John M. Bailey	Vice President of Marketing and Director
Sherman L. Gerard	Director

James A. Kralik was Vice President—Systems Analysis for The Data Control Corporation from 1963 to 1965. Prior to 1963 he was a consultant to various companies specializing in computer programming assistance.

Philip R. Jameson became treasurer of the Industrial Leasing Corporation in 1960 and still held that positio nin December, 1965.

John M. Bailey became a sales manager for the Digital Data Corporation in 1959 and still held that position in December, 1965.

Sherman L. Gerard was a partner in the investment banking firm of Bachman, Dillard and Hanover.

The company planned to hire two salesmen and one office secretary in the near future.

Exhibit 4

COMPULEASE CORPORATION (A)

CASH RETURN AFTER DEBT REPAYMENT ON $1,000,000 LEASE

	Short-Term Lease		*Full-Payout Lease*	
Year	*Outflow*	*Inflow*	*Outflow*	*Inflow*
1	$334,000	$ 0	$200,000	$ 0
2		0		0
3		0		0
4		0		0
5		66,893		0
6		145,388		78,100
7		136,029		398,100
8		99,676		
9		78,208		
10		350,904		
	Internal rate of return = 12.9%		Internal rate of return = 13.3%	

Exhibit 5

COMPULEASE CORPORATION (A)

SENSITIVITY ANALYSIS–DISCOUNTED CASH FLOW RATE OF RETURN ON EQUITY INVESTED IN COMPUTERS PLACED ON SHORT-TERM LEASES

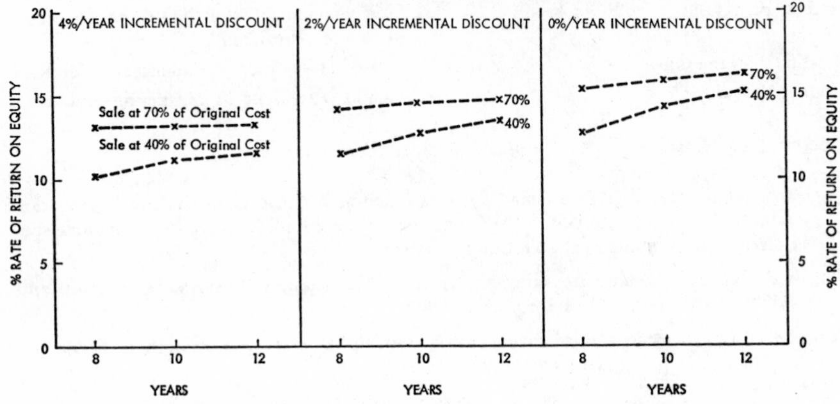

COMPULEASE CORPORATION (B)

^^

Late in December, 1967, Mr. James A. Kralik, president of Compulease Corporation, was considering whether his company should continue to purchase third-generation computer equipment.

Corporate history

Compulease Corporation had shown dramatic growth in the area of short-term leasing since its inception in 1965. The company had remained closely held during its first year. During this period the original investor group put together by BD&H had participated in three rounds of private financing. In the first round, which occurred in January, 1966, the BD&H group had purchased 77,777 shares of Compulease common stock at $12.34 for a total commitment of $960,000. The Compulease co-founders, James Kralik, Philip Jameson, and John Bailey, had received 22,223 shares for a total consideration of $40,000. In two later rounds of private financing during 1966, the BD&H group had purchased, for $10 a share, an additional 233,333 shares of the company's common stock. Since the Compulease co-founders had exhausted their personal resources in the first round of financing, they were not able to purchase additional shares in later financing.

As originally planned, Compulease went public early in January, 1967, by offering 317,144 shares at a price of $20 a share. By the end of 1967, the company's common stock price had risen to $46, giving handsome paper profits to the original investors in Compulease and the purchasers of shares in the initial public offering.

Compulease expected to report earnings per share of $1.63 for 1967, a figure up nearly 70% from the $0.97 earned in 1966. Based on the 1967 earnings estimate, the company's common stock was selling at over 28 times earnings, a conservative figure by industry standards, as Exhibit 1 indicates.

The company's return on equity

When his company had started purchasing third-generation computer equipment two years earlier, Mr. Kralik had been well aware that the useful life of these machines would *not* be determined by any physical deterioration. Since the obsolescence would be technological rather than physical, the remaining life of a third-generation computer purchased in 1965 would be the same as the remaining life of a similar machine purchased two years later, in December, 1967. The fact that similar equipment became obsolete at a specific *point* in time (shortly after the introduction of a new computer generation) rather than after an elapsed *period* of time made the continued purchase of third-generation machines a somewhat hazardous undertaking. This was true because those machines purchased earliest in the life cycle of the third generation were all but certain to earn the highest returns. Were Mr. Kralik to continue purchasing third-generation equipment for many more years, he could be certain of sustaining losses on those computers purchased too late in the product's life cycle to allow an economic return.

In his original 1965 projections (see Compulease Corporation [A]) Mr. Kralik estimated that the life cycle of third-generation computer equipment would extend through 1975. The passage of two years had not caused him to significantly revise these estimates. Thus, in calculating the return on equity invested in third-generation equipment purchased during 1968, he felt safe in assuming a remaining life of only eight years. Exhibit 2 shows that a two-year decline in life would cause the expected return on equity invested in third-generation equipment to drop from 12.9% to 11.7%.

Mr. Kralik was a little perturbed at the prospect of investing greater and greater sums of money at successively lower returns, and he wondered how the shareholders of Compulease would fare if the company continued its buying activity for at least another year. He was somewhat puzzled as to how he should go about evaluating the financial impact on shareholders of an additional year of purchasing third-generation equipment, but he decided to approach the problem from two different viewpoints, with an eye toward finally comparing the results of the two approaches.

First approach to shareholders' return on investment

Mr. Kralik's first attempt at estimating the impact of continuing computer purchases was based on valuing the cash flows generated through operations. Exhibit 3 shows Compulease's actual earnings reports through 1967 and estimated financial statements through 1975, assuming a halt in computer purchasing activity by the end of 1967. All future cash flows would be used first to retire outstanding debt, as was required in the company's agreement with its bank lenders. The cash flow remaining after debt amortization could then be returned to the shareholders, along with the cash realized from ultimately selling the computer equipment at the end of 1975.

At lines 25 and 26 of Exhibit 3, the company's cash flow is expressed on a per share basis to make possible a calculation of the rate of return to shareholders who bought the company's common stock at different prices.

According to Mr. Kralik's calculations (assuming all computer purchases were halted at the end of 1967), the original investors, who purchased their shares at an average cost of $10, would realize a rate of return equal to 17% on their investment if (1) they ignored all price gyrations in the stock market and held their shares through 1975, and (2) the company paid out its entire cash flow after debt amortization. Those investors who purchased their stock a year later at the initial public offering price of $20 a share would receive a return of only 8.8% under similar assumptions (line 28, Exhibit 3).

Mr. Kralik was a little unhappy about the return to the second group of investors. He wondered how a third group would fare under the same type of analysis if Compulease sold a new issue of common stock in 1968, thus allowing the company to continue purchasing third-generation computers for at least another year.

Mr. Kralik was advised by his investment banker that Compulease could easily raise enough equity through a common stock offering at $40 a share to enable the company to purchase some $40 million worth of third-generation computers in 1968. The sale of 306,000 shares of common stock would raise approximately $12,250,000. This amount, added to the earnings of $1,050,000 retained in 1967, would enlarge the company's equity base by $13,300,000. Compulease could borrow $26,700,000 (at a 2 to 1 debt-equity ratio) on this base, achieving a total potential cash infusion of nearly $40 million in 1968.

Exhibit 4 is Mr. Kralik's revision of the pro forma financial statements for Compulease Corporation for 1968–75, assuming a third round of external financing in 1968 and the purchase in that year of some $40 million worth of third-generation computer equipment. Mr. Kralik noted that under the continued buying assumption, the rate of return to the first two sets of investors rose from 17% to 21% and from 8.8% to 13.5% respectively (lines 27 and 28, Exhibits 3 and 4). Continued equipment purchases for at least another year would clearly be advantageous to these investors.

While the first two groups of investors profited substantially from a third year of purchasing activity, Mr. Kralik was startled to see that the last group of investors, who would purchase their shares at $40, could expect a return of only 4.4% (line 29, Exhibit 4) if they held their shares through 1975.

Second approach to shareholders' return on investment

Since no investor would knowingly place his capital at 4.4% in a situation as risky as computer leasing, Mr. Kralik felt that his valuation model based on discounting the cash flows from operations might be inappropriate. Investors were probably not looking to Compulease's future operating cash flows in making their stock purchase decisions. They were far more likely to count on getting their return through selling their shares in the open market at higher future prices. Their return might thus be entirely independent of Compulease's estimated future operating cash flows. The fact that the trading volume in Compulease's common stock was averaging 6% of the outstanding shares per week tended to give support to the idea that many investors were looking for profits from this security in the short run rather than through 1975. If investors were looking to a higher future stock price for their return on investment, Mr. Kralik felt they probably paid close attention to two factors contributing to future stock prices: (1) estimates of future earnings per share and (2) computer leasing industry price-earnings ratios.

Since Mr. Kralik was fairly confident of the earnings projections in Exhibits 3 and 4 (lines 38 and 39), he computed the price-earnings ratios necessary to keep the price of Compulease stock high enough to assure a 15% compound annual rate of return on his investment to an investor who purchased stock near the current price and held the stock over the next one to three years.

This analysis presented in Exhibit 5, indicated clearly that investors in Compulease would be far less vulnerable to a downward reevaluation of price-earnings ratios in the computer leasing industry if equipment purchases were continued another year. Indeed, Mr. Kralik feared that the high price-earnings ratios characteristic of this industry might be a direct result of investors' expectations that the high rate of earnings growth from 1966 to 1967 would be repeated in the future. If Compulease failed to purchase computers through 1968, the projected growth in its per share earnings in the period 1967–68 promised to drop from 52% to 15%. A decline of this magnitude in the growth rate might be the very factor to precipitate the drop that Mr. Kralik feared in the company's price-earnings ratio.

Comparing the models

From the analysis of both valuation models, Mr. Kralik saw strong arguments for continuing computer purchases through 1968 in spite of the increased hazards inherent in pursuing such a policy. On the other hand, he felt that similar arguments might lead him to continue equipment purchases right into the 1970's.

Looking to the future

Although the decision regarding a cutoff date for purchases of third-generation computer equipment was the most immediate corporate problem, Mr. Kralik recognized a second problem of equal significance looming in the future. When Compulease did finally stop purchasing third-generation computers, Mr. Kralik was counting on the lapse of a number of years before the company could begin buying fourth-generation machines. Similarly, because of debt repayment terms, it would be four years before the company could use any significant portion of its cash flow for reinvestment or return to the shareholders. During this "dead" period between the third and fourth generation, Compulease would have no growth in its existing business and no cash to get into a new business. Fortunately, reported earnings would still rise about 15% a year for three years after new purchases ceased (Exhibits 3 and 4, lines 38 and 39), but even so Mr. Kralik thought that investors would probably take an unfavorable view of any company that remained inactive for a long period of time and drastically reduced its price-earnings multiple.

Mr. Kralik currently felt boxed into a situation where to maintain the price of his company's stock, he might have to commit increasing sums of money in situations offering decreasing expected returns. To avoid this problem, he felt that Compulease would have to diversify into some new business area in the near future. He wondered whether this diversification move should be into the area of commercial finance or some area outside of finance within the computer industry. Exhibit 1 provides financial data on possible fields within the computer industry, and Exhibit 6 contains data on two commercial finance companies.

Exhibit 1

COMPULEASE CORPORATION (B)

FINANCIAL FACTS ON COMPANIES OPERATING IN THE DATA PROCESSING INDUSTRY

Company	*Sales (Thousands) Latest 12 Months*	*Principal Activity*	*Five-Year Earnings per Share* 1963	1964	1965	1966	1967E	*Recent Price*	*P-E Ratio ('67 Earns)*
Applied Data Research	$ 1,386	Software	$ 0.35D	$0.30	$ 0.21	$0.04	$0.30	17	57
ARIES Corp.	3,198	Software	0.09	0.25	0.13	0.50	0.50	23½	47
Automatic Data Proc.	8,900E	Svc. Bur.	0.03	0.09	0.19	0.50	c.80	43⅜	54
C-E-I-R	21,862	Svc. Bur.	(a—0.45D	0.65	0.79	0.13)	0.25	17⅜	69
			(b—1.20D	0.98	1.12	0.88)			
Calif. Computer Prod.	11,318	Hardware	0.18	0.58	0.55	0.67	c1.22	85¾	70
Computer Applications	24,542	Software	0.31	0.58	0.18	0.46	0.55	21¼	39
Computer Sciences	38,860	Software	0.12	0.07	(a—0.04D	0.17)	c.40	26⅛	65
					(b—0.07	0.66)			
Computer Usage	12,000E	Software	0.20	0.37	0.53	0.64	0.90	43½	48
Comp. & Software(f)	12,045	Svc. Bur.	0.09	0.19	0.33	0.44	0.75	33½	45
Data Proc. Fin. & Gen.	3,500	Leasing	0.02	0.04	0.17	0.60	1.50	71⅜	48
Data Products Corp.	12,500E	Hardware	0.40D	0.22	0.05D	0.04	c.21	14⅜	68
Decision Systems(g)	780	Software	0.35	0.41	0.03	0.79D	0.82D	2½	..
Digitek Corp.	825E	Software	0.03	0.07	0.15	0.28	1.35D	5¾	..
Elec. Comp. Prog. Inst.	2,406	Schools	0.13	0.18	0.34	0.54	0.85	42¼	50
Gerber Scientific Inst.	6,751	Hardware	0.24	0.14	0.56	0.62	0.95	39½	42
Informatics Inc.(h)	6,428	Software	0.14D	0.15	0.19	0.37	c.51	31¾	62
Leasco Data Proc.	3,250	Leasing	0.24	0.35	0.54	0.88	1.40	76⅞	55
Levin-Townsend Comp.	3,938	Leasing	0.01	0.27	0.32	0.41	c1.14	41⅝	37
Planning Research	16,021	Software	0.49	0.56	1.10	0.96	c1.29	47⅜	37
Programming & Syst.	1,283	Schools	0.01D	0.05D	0.11	0.12	c.30	16½	55
Randolph Computer	2,958	Leasing	n.a.	n.a.	0.12D	0.77	1.25	36⅞	30
Scientific Comp.(i)	2,000E	Svc. Bur.	0.42D	0.17D	0.12	(i)	0.25	6½	26
TBS Comp. Centers (j)	2,509	Svc. Bur.	0.15	0.35	0.37	0.43	c.33	11½	35
University Computing	9,000E	Svc. Bur.	0.04	0.21	0.40	0.93	2.00	113	57

D—Deficit. E—Estimated. n.a.—Not applicable.

a—Actual, from operations. b—As reported, after special credits and/or charges (later restated). c—Actual, as reported, for FY 1967. f—Formerly Telecomputing Corp.; now 61%—held by Whittaker Corp. g—Formerly Computronics, Inc. h—70%—held by Data Products Corp. i—23%—held by Control Data Corp.; changed to fiscal year basis in 1966; earnings for six months ended 6/30/66 reported as $0.09 per share. j—Formerly Tabulating & Business Services Inc.

Source: "THINKing Big," ***Barron's***, September 18, 1967.

Exhibit 2

COMPULEASE CORPORATION (B)

DISCOUNTED CASH FLOW RATE OF RETURN ON THE CORPORATION'S INVESTMENT IN THIRD-GENERATION COMPUTER EQUIPMENT

Life of Equipment (Years)	*Rate of Return*
4	Loss
5	7.0%
6	10.3
7	11.3
8	11.7
10	12.9

Source: Calculated from Exhibit 2, Compulease Corporation (A).

Exhibit 3

COMPULEASE CORPORATION (B)

Actual Financial Statements, 1966–67, and Pro Forma Statements, 1968–75 Assuming Purchasing Activity Ceases by the Close of 1967

		1966	1967	1968	1969	1970	1971	1972	1973	1974	1975	
1	Year	*1966*	*1967*	*1968*	*1969*	*1970*	*1971*	*1972*	*1973*	*1974*	*1975*	
2	Gross equipment purchases	10,000,000	20,000,000	0	0	0	0	0	0	0	0	
3	Gross equipment owned	10,000,000	30,000,000	30,000,000	30,000,000	30,000,000	30,000,000	30,000,000	30,000,000	30,000,000	30,000,000	
4	IBM rental rate	2,553,191	7,659,574	7,659,574	7,659,574	7,659,574	7,659,574	7,659,574	7,659,574	7,659,574	7,659,574	
5	Discount allowed	255,319	765,957	919,149	1,072,340	1,225,532	1,378,723	1,531,915	1,685,106	1,838,298	1,991,489	
6	Overtime premium	76,596	229,787	229,787	229,787	229,787	229,787	229,787	229,787	229,787	229,787	
7	Net rent received	2,374,468	7,123,404	6,970,213	6,817,021	6,663,830	6,510,638	6,357,447	6,204,255	6,051,064	5,897,872	
8	Maintenance expense	255,319	765,957	765,957	765,957	765,957	765,957	765,957	765,957	765,957	765,957	
9	Depreciation expense	1,888,889	5,430,555	4,722,222	4,013,889	3,305,555	2,597,222	1,888,889	1,180,556	472,222	0	
10	Interest expense	600,000	1,684,647	1,328,205	952,093	554,539	133,613	0	0	0	0	
11	General, selling, and administrative	237,447	712,340	697,021	681,702	666,383	651,064	635,745	620,426	605,106	589,787	
12	Pretax profit	−607,187	−1,470,096	−543,194	403,380	1,371,395	2,362,782	3,066,856	3,637,317	4,207,778	4,542,128	Tax Reports (lines 2–25)
13	Taxes	0	0	0	0	0	758,540	1,533,428	1,818,658	2,103,889	2,271,064	
14	After-tax profit	−607,187	−1,470,096	−543,194	403,380	1,371,395	1,983,511	2,300,142	2,727,987	2,148,576	2,271,064	
15	Depreciation expense	1,888,889	5,430,555	4,722,222	4,013,889	3,305,555	2,597,222	1,888,889	1,180,556	472,222	0	
16	Investment credit used	0	0	0	0	0	379,270	766,714	909,329	44,687	0	
17	Total cash inflow	1,281,702	3,960,460	4,179,028	4,417,269	4,676,951	4,580,734	4,189,031	3,908,543	2,620,798	2,271,064	
18	Liquidation inflow in 1976	8,250,000										
19	Debt outstanding	6,666,667	18,718,298	14,757,838	10,578,810	6,161,541	1,484,591	0	0	0	0	
20	Capital from investors	3,333,333	10,000,000	10,000,000	10,000,000	10,000,000	10,000,000	6,903,857	2,714,826	−1,193,717	−3,814,515	
21	Unused investment credit	700,000	2,100,000	2,100,000	2,100,000	2,100,000	1,720,730	954,016	44,687	0	0	
22	Tax loss carryover	607,187	2,077,283	2,620,476	2,217,096	845,701	0	0	0	0	0	
23	Shares sold in year	333,333	317,144	0	0	0	0	0	0	0	0	
24	Total shares outstanding	333,333	650,478	650,478	650,478	650,478	650,478	650,478	650,478	650,478	650,478	
25	Cash return per share	0	0	0	0	0	4.76	6.44	6.01	4.03	3.49	
26	Liquidation return per share in 1976	12.68										
27	ROR 1st investor	0.171										
28	ROR 2nd investor	0.088										
29	Net rent received	2,374,468	7,123,404	6,970,213	6,817,021	6,663,830	6,510,638	6,357,447	6,204,255	6,051,064	5,897,872	
30	Depreciation expense	850,000	2,550,000	2,550,000	2,550,000	2,550,000	2,550,000	2,550,000	2,550,000	2,550,000	2,550,000	
31	Maintenance expense	255,319	765,957	765,957	765,957	765,957	765,957	765,957	765,957	765,957	765,957	
32	Interest expense	600,000	1,684,647	1,328,205	952,093	554,539	133,613	0	0	0	0	
33	General, selling, and administrative	237,447	712,340	697,021	681,702	666,383	651,064	635,745	620,426	605,106	589,787	
34	Pretax profit	431,702	1,410,460	1,629,029	1,867,269	2,126,951	2,410,004	2,405,745	2,267,872	2,130,000	1,992,128	Shareholder Reports (lines 29–39)
35	Taxes	215,851	705,230	814,514	933,634	1,063,475	1,205,002	1,202,872	1,133,936	1,065,000	996,064	
36	Investment credit used	107,926	352,615	407,257	466,817	531,738	233,648	0	0	0	0	
37	After-tax profit	323,777	1,057,845	1,221,771	1,400,452	1,595,213	1,438,649	1,202,872	1,133,936	1,065,000	996,064	
38	Earnings per share	0.97	1.63	1.88	2.15	2.45	2.21	1.85	1.74	1.64	1.53	
39	Unused investment credit	592,074	1,639,460	1,232,202	765,385	233,648	0	0	0	0	0	

Assumptions: Investor No. 1 purchases @ $10 per share in January, 1966; Investor No. 2 purchases @ $20 per share in January, 1967.

Exhibit 4

COMPULEASE CORPORATION (B)

Actual Financial Statements, 1966–67, and Pro Forma Statements, 1968–75 Assuming Purchasing Activity Ceases by the Close of 1968

	1966	1967	1968	1969	1970	1971	1972	1973	1974	1975	
1 Year	*1966*	*1967*	*1968*	*1969*	*1970*	*1971*	*1972*	*1973*	*1974*	*1975*	
2 Gross equipment purchases	10,000,000	20,000,000	40,000,000	0	0	0	0	0	0	0	
3 Gross equipment owned	10,000,000	30,000,000	70,000,000	70,000,000	70,000,000	70,000,000	70,000,000	70,000,000	70,000,000	70,000,000	
4 IBM rental rate	2,553,191	7,659,574	17,872,340	17,872,340	17,872,340	17,872,340	17,872,340	17,872,340	17,872,340	17,872,340	
5 Discount allowed	255,319	765,957	2,144,681	2,502,128	2,859,574	3,217,021	3,574,468	3,931,915	4,289,362	4,646,808	
6 Overtime premium	76,596	229,787	536,170	536,170	536,170	536,170	536,170	536,170	536,170	536,170	
7 Net rent received	2,374,468	7,123,404	16,263,830	15,906,383	15,548,936	15,191,489	14,834,042	14,476,596	14,119,149	13,761,702	
8 Maintenance expense	255,319	765,957	1,787,234	1,787,234	1,787,234	1,787,234	1,787,234	1,787,234	1,787,234	1,787,234	
9 Depreciation expense	1,888,889	5,430,555	12,277,777	10,625,000	8,972,222	7,319,444	5,666,667	4,013,889	2,361,111	944,444	
10 Interest expense	600,000	1,684,647	3,728,205	2,907,225	2,041,309	1,126,414	158,132	0	0	0	
11 General, selling, and administrative	237,447	712,340	1,626,383	1,590,638	1,554,894	1,519,149	1,483,404	1,447,660	1,411,915	1,376,170	
12 Pretax profit	−607,187	−1,470,096	−3,155,770	−1,003,714	1,193,277	3,439,248	5,738,606	7,227,813	8,558,889	9,653,853	
13 Taxes	0	0	0	0	0	0	2,067,182	3,613,907	4,279,444	4,826,927	Tax Reports
14 After-tax profit	−607,187	−1,470,096	−3,155,770	−1,003,714	1,193,277	3,439,248	4,705,015	5,420,860	6,338,900	4,826,927	
15 Depreciation expense	1,888,889	5,430,555	12,277,777	10,625,000	8,972,222	7,319,444	5,666,667	4,013,889	2,361,111	944,444	
16 Investment credit used	0	0	0	0	0	0	1,033,591	1,806,953	2,059,456	0	
17 Total cash inflow	1,281,702	3,960,460	9,122,007	9,621,286	10,165,499	10,758,692	10,371,681	9,434,749	8,700,011	5,771,371	
18 Liquidation inflow in 1976	19,250,000										
19 Debt outstanding	6,666,667	18,718,298	41,424,505	32,302,498	22,681,212	12,515,713	1,757,021	0	0	0	
20 Capital from investors	3,333,333	10,000,000	23,333,333	23,333,333	23,333,333	23,333,333	23,333,333	14,718,673	5,283,925	−3,416,087	
21 Unused investment credit	700,000	2,100,000	4,900,000	4,900,000	4,900,000	4,900,000	3,866,409	2,059,456	0	0	
22 Tax loss carryover	607,187	2,077,283	5,233,053	6,236,767	5,043,490	1,604,242	0	0	0	0	
23 Shares sold in year	333,333	317,144	306,887	0	0	0	0	0	0	0	
24 Total shares outstanding	333,333	650,478	957,365	957,365	957,365	957,365	957,365	957,365	957,365	957,365	
25 Cash return per share	0	0	0	0	0	0	9.00	9.85	9.09	6.03	
26 Liquidation return per share in 1976	20.10										
27 ROR 1st investor	0.211										
28 ROR 2nd investor	0.135										
29 ROR 3rd investor	0.044										
30 Net rent received	2,374,468	7,123,404	16,263,830	15,906,383	15,548,936	15,191,489	14,834,042	14,476,596	14,119,149	13,761,702	
31 Depreciation expense	850,000	2,550,000	5,950,000	5,950,000	5,950,000	5,950,000	5,950,000	5,950,000	5,950,000	5,950,000	
32 Maintenance expense	255,319	765,957	1,787,234	1,787,234	1,787,234	1,787,234	1,787,234	1,787,234	1,787,234	1,787,234	
33 Interest expense	600,000	1,684,647	3,728,205	2,907,225	2,041,309	1,126,414	158,132	0	0	0	
34 General, selling, and administrative	237,447	712,340	1,626,383	1,590,638	1,554,894	1,519,149	1,483,404	1,447,660	1,411,915	1,376,170	
35 Pretax profit	431,702	1,410,460	3,172,007	3,671,286	4,215,499	4,808,692	5,455,272	5,291,702	4,970,000	4,648,298	Shareholder Reports
36 Taxes	215,851	705,230	1,586,004	1,835,643	2,107,750	2,404,346	2,727,636	2,645,851	2,485,000	2,324,149	
37 Investment credit used	107,926	352,615	793,002	917,821	1,053,875	1,202,173	472,588	0	0	0	
38 After-tax profit	323,777	1,057,845	2,379,005	2,753,464	3,161,624	3,606,519	3,200,225	2,645,851	2,485,000	2,324,149	
39 Earnings per share	0.97	1.63	2.48	2.88	3.30	3.77	3.34	2.76	2.60	2.43	
40 Unused investment credit	592,074	1,639,460	3,646,458	2,728,636	1,674,761	472,588	0	0	0	0	

Assumptions: Investor No. 1 purchases @ $10 per share in January, 1966; investor No. 2 purchases @ $20 per share in January, 1967; investor No. 3 purchases @ $40 per share in January, 1968.

Exhibit 5

COMPULEASE CORPORATION (B)

MARKET PRICES OF COMPULEASE CORPORATION COMMON STOCK NECESSARY TO SUSTAIN VARIOUS RATES OF RETURN TO INVESTORS

	Year	Projected Earnings per Share*	Market Price† Necessary for Compound Annual Rate of Return of— 5%	15%	25%	Price-Earnings Ratio Required for Compound Annual Rate of Return of— 5%	15%	25%
Assumes computer purchases cease after 1967	1968	$1.88	$42.00	$46.00	$50.00	22.3	24.5	26.6
	1969	2.15	44.20	53.00	62.50	20.6	24.7	29.0
	1970	2.45	46.40	61.00	78.30	18.9	24.9	32.0
Assumes computer purchases cease after 1968	1968	2.48	42.00	46.00	50.00	16.9	18.5	20.2
	1969	2.88	44.20	53.00	62.50	15.3	18.4	21.7
	1970	3.30	46.40	61.00	78.30	14.1	18.5	23.7

* Lines 38 and 39, Exhibits 3 and 4.
† Assumes initial purchase at $40 a share.

Exhibit 6

COMPULEASE CORPORATION (B)

FINANCIAL DATA—COMMERCIAL FINANCE COMPANIES

Year	*Earnings per share*	*Average P-E Ratio*	*Return on Equity**
Commercial Credit Corporation			
1966	$2.24	12.5	7.6%
1965	2.26	16.5	7.8
1964	3.07	13	11.2
1963	2.98	14.5	11.4
1962	2.97	15	11.9
C.I.T. Financial Corporation			
1966	2.74	10.5	12.5
1965	2.63	12.5	12.7
1964	2.54	14.5	12.7
1963	2.47	17.0	12.8
1962	2.43	16.5	13.0

* Defined as net profit/net worth.

ECONOMY SHIPPING COMPANY

I

In the spring of 1950 the controller of the Economy Shipping Company, located near Pittsburgh, was preparing a report for the executive committee regarding the feasibility of repairing one of the company's steam riverboats or of replacing the steamboat with a new diesel-powered boat.

The Economy Shipping Company was engaged mainly in the transportation of coal from the nearby mines to the steel mills, public utilities, and other industries in the Pittsburgh area. The company's several steamboats also on occasion carried cargoes to places as far away as New Orleans. All the boats owned by Economy were steam powered. All were at least 10 years old, and the majority were between 15 and 30 years old.

The steamboat the controller was concerned about, the *Cynthia,* was 23 years old and required immediate rehabilitation or replacement. It was estimated that the *Cynthia* had a useful life of another 20 years provided that adequate repairs and maintenance were made. Whereas the book value of the *Cynthia* was $39,500, it was believed that she would bring somewhat less than this amount, possibly around $25,000, if she was sold in 1950. The total of immediate rehabilitation costs for the *Cynthia* was estimated to be $115,000. It was estimated that these general rehabilitation expenditures would extend the useful life of the *Cynthia* for about 20 years.

New spare parts from another boat, which had been retired in 1948, were available for use in the rehabilitation of the *Cynthia.* If these parts were used on the *Cynthia,* an estimate of their fair value was $43,500, which was their book value. Use of these parts would in effect decrease the immediate rehabilitation costs from $115,000 to $71,500. It was believed that if these parts were sold on the market they would bring only around $30,000. They could not be used on any of the other Economy steamboats.

Currently, the *Cynthia* was operated by a 20-man crew. Annual operating costs for the 20-man crew would be approximately as follows:

Wages	$110,200
Vacation and sickness benefits	1,880
Social security payments	2,400
Life insurance	1,800
Commissary supplies	15,420
Repairs and maintenance	24,400
Fuel	34,500
Lubricants	550
Miscellaneous service and supplies	12,000
Total	$203,150

It was estimated that the cost of dismantling and scrapping the *Cynthia* at the end of her useful life after the overhaul would be offset by the value of the scrap and used parts taken off the boat.

II

An alternative to rehabilitating the steamboat was the purchase of a diesel-powered boat. The Quapelle Company, a local boat manufacturer, quoted the price of $325,000 for a diesel boat. An additional $75,000 for a basic parts inventory would be necessary to service a diesel boat, and such an inventory would be sufficient to service up to three diesel boats. If four or more diesels were purchased, however, it was estimated that additional spare parts inventory would be necessary.

The useful life of a diesel-powered boat was estimated to be 25 years; at the end of that time the boat would be scrapped or completely rehabilitated at a cost approximating that of a new boat. The possibility of diesel engine replacement during the 25-year life was not contemplated by the controller, since information from other companies having limited experience with diesel-powered riverboats did not indicate that such costs needed to be anticipated; but a general overhaul of the engines, costing at current prices $60,000, would be expected every 10 years.

One of the features the Quapelle Company pointed out was the 12% increase in average speed of diesel-powered boats over the steamboats. The controller discounted this feature, however. The short runs and lock-to-lock operations involved in local river shipping would prohibit the diesel boats from taking advantage of their greater speed, since there was little opportunity for passing and they would have to wait in turn at each lock for the slower steamboats. In 1950, out of about 40 boats only two diesel boats were operating on the river. The controller felt it would be many years, if at all, before diesel boats displaced the slower steamboats.

After consulting the Quapelle Company and other companies operating diesel-powered boats, the controller estimated that the annual operating costs of such a boat would total $156,640, broken down as follows:

Wages for a 13-man crew	$ 77,300
Vacation and sickness benefits	1,320
Social security payments	1,680
Life insurance	1,170
Commissary supplies	10,020
Repairs and maintenance*	21,700
Fuel	28,800
Extra stern repairs	2,000
Miscellaneous service and supplies	12,650
Total	$156,640

* Excluding possible major overhaul of diesel engines.

Although the Economy controller had not considered the matter, the user of this case may assume that at the end of the 20th year the diesel boat would have a realizable value of $32,500 and the inventory of parts of $37,500.

III

The controller was also concerned at this time with a city smoke ordinance, which had been signed in 1948 to take effect in 1952. To comply with the regulations of the ordinance, all hand-fired steamboats had to be converted to stoker firing. Several of the Economy steamboats were already stoker fired; the *Cynthia,* however, was hand fired. The additional cost of converting the *Cynthia* to stoker firing was estimated to be $40,000, provided it was done at the same time as the general rehabilitation. This $40,000 included the cost of stokers and extra hull conversion and was not included in the $115,000 rehabilitation figure. The controller also knew that if $115,000 were spent presently in rehabilitating the *Cynthia* and it was found later that no relief or only temporary relief for one or two years was to be granted under the smoke ordinance, the cost of converting to stoker firing would no longer be $40,000 but around $70,000. The higher cost would be due to rebuilding, which would not be necessary if the *Cynthia* was converted to stoker firing at the time of her general rehabilitation.

Conversion would reduce the crew from 20 to 18, with the following details:

Wages	$100,650
Vacation and sickness benefits	1,650
Social security payments	2,200
Life insurance	1,620
Commissary supplies	13,880
Repairs and maintenance*	24,400
Fuel*	34,500
Lubricants*	550
Miscellaneous service and supplies*	12,000
Total	$191,450

* These costs would remain the same, whether the crew was 20 or 18 men.

IV

All operating data the controller had collected pertaining to crew expenses were based on a 2-shift, 12-hour working day, which was standard on local riverboats. He had been informed, however, that the union representing crew members wanted a change to a three-shift, eight-hour day. If the union insisted on an eight-hour day, accommodations on board the steamers or the diesels would have to be enlarged. The controller was perturbed by this, because he knew the diesels could readily be converted to accommodate three crews whereas steamers could not. How strongly the union would insist on the change and when it would be put into effect, if ever, were questions for which the controller could get no satisfactory answers. He believed that the union might have a difficult time in getting acceptance of its demands for three eight-hour shifts on steamers, since because of space limitations it would be very difficult, if not impossible, to convert the steamers to hold a larger crew. The controller thought that the union might succeed in getting its demands accepted, however, in the case of diesel-powered boats. One of the diesel boats currently operating in the Pittsburgh area had accommodations for three crews, although it was still operating on a two-shift basis. The diesel boats that the Quapelle Company offered to build for Economy could be fitted to accommodate three crews at no additional cost.

V

Another factor the controller was considering at this time was alternative uses of funds. In the spring of 1950, Economy had sufficient funds to buy four diesel-powered boats; however, there were alternative uses for these funds. The other projects the management was considering at this time had an estimated return of at least 10% after taxes. The income tax rate at the time was 48%.

THE SUPER PROJECT

In March, 1967, Mr. Crosby Sanberg, manager, financial analysis at General Foods Corporation, told a casewriter, "What I learned about incremental analysis at the Business School doesn't always work." He was convinced that under some circumstances "sunk costs" were relevant to capital project evaluations. He was also concerned that financial and accounting systems did not provide an accurate estimate of "incremental costs and revenues" and that this was one of the most difficult problems in measuring the value of capital investment proposals. Mr. Sanberg used the Super project[1] as an example.

Super was a new instant dessert, based on a flavored, water soluble, agglomerated powder. Although a four-flavor line would be introduced, it was estimated that chocolate would account for 80% of total sales.

General Foods was organized along product lines in the United States. Foreign operations were under a separate division. Major U.S. product divisions included Post, Kool-Aid, Maxwell House, Jell-O, and Birds Eye. Financial data for General Foods are given in Exhibits 1, 2, and 3.

The capital investment project request for Super involved $200,000 as follows:

Building modifications	$ 80,000
Machinery and equipment	120,000
	$200,000

Part of the expenditure was required for modifying an existing building, where Jell-O was manufactured. Available capacity of a Jell-O agglomerator[2] would be used in the manufacture of Super, so that no cost for the key machine was included in the project. The $120,000 machinery and equipment item represented packaging machinery.

The market

The total dessert market was defined as including powdered desserts, ice creams, pie fillings, and cake mixes. According to a Nielsen survey, powdered

[1] The name and nature of this new product have been disguised to avoid the disclosure of confidential information.

[2] Agglomeration is a process by which the processed powder is passed through a steam bath and then dried. This "fluffs up" the powder particles and increases solubility.

desserts constituted a significant and growing segment of the market; their 1966 market share had increased over the preceding year. Results of the Nielsen survey follow:

DESSERT MARKET
AUGUST–SEPTEMBER, 1966, COMPARED WITH AUGUST–SEPTEMBER, 1965

	Market Share	% Change from August–September, 1965	
	August–September, 1966	Share	Volume
Jell-O	19.0%	+3.6	+40.0
Tasty	4.0	+4.0	(New)
Total powders	25.3	+7.6	+62.0
Pie fillings and cake mixes	32.0	−3.9	(No change)
Ice cream	42.7	−3.4	+ 5.0
Total market	100.0%		+13.0

On the basis of test market experience, General Foods expected Super to capture a 10% share of the total dessert market. Eighty percent of the expected volume of Super would come from a growth in total market share or growth in the total powdered segment, and 20% would come from erosion of Jell-O sales.

Production facilities

Test market volume was packaged on an existing line, inadequate to handle long-run requirements. Filling and packaging equipment to be purchased had a capacity of 1.9 million units on a two-shift, five-day workweek basis. This represented considerable excess capacity, since 1968 requirements were expected to reach 1.1 million units and the national potential was regarded as 1.6 million units. However, the extra capacity resulted from purchasing standard equipment, and a more economical alternative did not exist.

Capital budgeting procedure

Capital investment project proposals submitted under procedures covered in the General Foods Accounting and Financial Manual were identified as falling into one of the following classifications:

1. Safety and Convenience
2. Quality
3. Increase Profit
4. Other

These classifications served as a basis for establishing different procedures and criteria for accepting projects. For example, the Super project fell in the third classification, "increase profit." Criteria for evaluating projects are given in Exhibit 4. In discussing these criteria, Mr. Sanberg noted that the payback and return guidelines were not used as "cutoff" measures. Mr. Sanberg added: "Payback and return on investment are rarely the only measure of acceptability. Criteria vary significantly by type of project. A relatively high return might be required for a new product in a new business category. On the other hand, a much lower return might be acceptable for a new product entry which represented a continuing effort to maintain leadership in an existing business by, for example, filling out the product line."

Estimates of payback and return on funds employed were required for each profit-increasing project requiring a total of $50,000 or more of new capital funds and expense before taxes. The payback period was the length of time required for the project to repay the investment from the date the project became operational. In calculating the repayment period, only incremental income and expenses related to the project were used.

Return on funds employed (ROFE) was calculated by dividing 10-year average profit before taxes by the 10-year average funds employed. Funds employed included incremental net fixed assets plus or minus related working capital. Start-up costs and any profits or losses incurred prior to the time when the project became operational were included in the first profit and loss period in the financial evaluation calculation.

Capital budgeting atmosphere

A General Foods accounting executive commented on the atmosphere within which capital projects were reviewed, as follows: "Our problem is not one of capital rationing. Our problem is to find enough good solid projects to employ capital at an attractive return on investment. Of course, the rate of capital inputs must be balanced against a steady growth in earnings per share. The short-term impact of capital investments is usually an increase in the capital base without an immediate realization of profit potential. This is particularly true in the case of new products.

"The food industry should show a continuous growth. A cyclical industry can afford to let its profits vary. We want to expand faster than the gross national product. The key to our capital budgeting is to integrate the plans of our eight divisions into a balanced company plan which meets our overall growth objectives. Most new products show a loss in the first two or three years, but our divisions are big enough to introduce new products without showing a loss."

Documentation for the Super project

Exhibits 5 and 6 document the financial evaluation of the Super project. Exhibit 5 is the summary appropriation request prepared to justify the project to management and to secure management's authorization to expend funds on a capital project. Exhibit 6 presents the backup detail. Cost of the market test was included as "Other" expense in the first period because a new product had to pay for its test market expense, even though this might be a sunk cost at the time capital funds were requested. The "Adjustments" item represented erosion of the Jell-O market and was calculated by multiplying the volume of erosion times a variable profit contribution. In the preparation of Exhibit 6 costs of acquiring packaging machinery were included, but no cost was attributed to the 50% of the capacity of a Jell-O agglomerator to be used for the Super project because the General Foods Accounting and Financial Manual requested that capital projects be prepared on an incremental basis as follows:

"The incremental concept requires that project requests, profit projections, and funds-employed statements include only items of income and expense and investment in assets which will be realized, incurred, or made directly as a result of, or are attributed to, the new project."

Exchange of memos on the Super project

After receiving the paper work on the Super project, Mr. Sanberg studied the situation and wrote a memorandum arguing that the principle of the preceding quotation should not be applied to the Super project. His superior agreed with the memorandum and forwarded it to the corporate controller with the covering note contained in Appendix I. The controller's reply is given in Appendix II.

APPENDIX I

March 2, 1967

TO: J. C. Kresslin, Corporate Controller
FROM: J. E. Hooting, Director, Corporate Budgets and Analysis

Super Project

At the time we reviewed the Super project, I indicated to you that the return on investment looked significantly different if an allocation of the agglomerator and building, originally justified as a Jell-O project, were included in the Super investment. The pro rata allocation of these facilities, based on the share of capacity used, triples the initial gross investment in Super facilities from $200,000 to about $672,000.

I am forwarding a memorandum from Crosby Sanberg summarizing the results of three analyses evaluating the project on an:

I. Incremental basis
II. Facilities-used basis
III. Fully allocated facilities and costs basis

Crosby has calculated a 10-year average ROFE using these techniques.

Please read Crosby's memo before continuing with my note.

* * * * *

Crosby concludes that the fully allocated basis, or some variation of it, is necessary to understand the long-range potential of the project.

I agree. We launch a new project because of its potential to increase our sales and earning power for many years into the future. We must be mindful of short-term consequences, as indicated by an incremental analysis, but we must also have a long-range frame of reference if we are to really understand what we are committing ourselves to. This long-range frame of reference is best approximated by looking at fully allocated investment and "accounted" profits, which recognize fully allocated costs because, in fact, over the long run all costs are variable unless some major change occurs in the structure of the business.

Our current GF preoccupation with only the incremental costs and investment causes some real anomalies that confuse our decision making. Super is a good example. On an incremental basis the project looks particularly attractive because by using a share of the excess capacity built on the coat tails of the lucrative Jell-O project, the incremental investment in Super is low. If the excess Jell-O capacity did not exist, would the project be any less attractive? In the short term, perhaps yes because it would entail higher initial risk, but in the long term it is not a better project just because it fits a facility that is temporarily unused.

Looking at this point from a different angle, if the project exceeded our investment hurdle rate on a short-term basis but fell below it on a long-term basis (and Super comes close to doing this), should we reject the project? I say yes because over the long run as "fixed" costs become variable and as we have to commit new capital to support the business, the continuing ROFE will go under water.

In sum, we have to look at new project proposals from both the long-range and the short-term point of view. We plan to refine our techniques of using a fully allocated basis as a long-term point of reference and will hammer out a policy recommendation for your consideration. We would appreciate your comments.

February 17, 1967

TO: J. E. Hooting, Director, Corporate Budgets and Analysis
FROM: C. Sanberg, Manager, Financial Analysis

Super Project: A Case Example of Investment Evaluation Techniques

This will review the merits of alternative techniques of evaluating capital investment decisions using the Super project as an example. The purpose of the review is to provide an illustration of the problems and limitations inherent in using incremental ROFE and payback and thereby provide a rationale for adopting new techniques.

ALTERNATIVE TECHNIQUES

The alternative techniques to be reviewed are differentiated by the level of revenue and investment charged to the Super project in figuring a payback and ROFE, starting with incremental revenues and investment. Data related to the alternative techniques outlined below are summarized [at the end of this appendix].

Alternative I Incremental Basis

Method. The Super project as originally evaluated considered only incremental revenue and investment, which could be directly identified with the decision to produce Super. Incremental fixed capital ($200M) basically included packaging equipment.

Result. On this basis the project paid back in seven years with a ROFE of 63%.

Discussion. Although it is General Foods' current policy to evaluate capital projects on an incremental basis, this technique does not apply to the Super project. The reason is that Super extensively utilizes existing facilities, which are readily adaptable to known future alternative uses.

Super should be charged with the "opportunity loss" of agglomerating capacity and building space. Because of Super the opportunity is lost to use a portion of agglomerating capacity for Jell-O and other products that could potentially be agglomerated. In addition, the opportunity is lost to use the building space for existing or new product volume expansion. To the extent there is an opportunity loss of existing facilities, new facilities must be built to accommodate future expansion. In other words, because the business is expanding Super utilizes facilities that are adaptable to predictable alternative uses.

Alternative II Facilities-Used Basis

Method. Recognizing that Super will use half of an existing agglomerator and two thirds of an existing building, which were justified earlier in the Jell-O project, we added Super's pro rata share of these facilities ($453M) to the incremental capital. Overhead costs directly related to these existing facilities were also subtracted from incremental revenue on a shared basis.

Result. ROFE, 34%.

Discussion. Although the existing facilities utilized by Super are not incremental to this project, they are relevant to the evaluation of the project because potentially they can be put to alternative uses. Despite a high return on an incremental basis, if the ROFE on a project was unattractive after consideration of the shared use of existing facilities, the project would be questionable. Under these circumstances, we might look for a more profitable product for the facilities.

In summary, the facilities-used basis is a useful way of putting various projects on a common ground for purposes of *relative* evaluation. One product using existing capacity should not necesarily be judged to be more attractive than another practically identical product which necessitates an investment in additional facilities.

Alternative III Fully Allocated Basis

Method. Further recognizing that individual decisions to expand inevitably add to a higher overhead base, we increased the costs and investment base developed in Alternative II by a provision for overhead expenses and overhead capital. These increases were made in year 5 of the 10-year evaluation period, on the theory that at this point a number of decisions would result in more fixed costs and facilities. Overhead expenses included manufacturing costs, plus selling and general and administrative costs on a per unit basis equivalent to Jell-O. Overhead capital included a share of the distribution system assets ($40M).

Result. ROFE, 25%.

Discussion. Charging Super with an overhead burden recognizes that overhead costs in the long-run increase in proportion to the level of business activity, even though decisions to spend more overhead dollars are made separately from decisions to increase volume and provide the incremental facilities to support the higher volume level. To illustrate, the Division-F1968 Financial Plan budgets about a 75% increase in headquarters' overhead spending in F1968 over F1964. A contributing factor was the decision to increase the sales force by 50% to meet the demands of a growing and increasingly complex business. To further illustrate, about half the capital projects in the F1968 three-year Financial Plan are in the "nonpayback" category. This group of projects comprises largely "overhead facilities" (warehouses, utilities, etc.), which are not directly related to the manufacture of products but are necessary components of the total business. These facilities are made necessary by an increase in total business activity as a result of the cumulative effect of many decisions taken in the past.

The Super project is a significant decision which will most likely add to more overhead dollars as illustrated above. Super volume doubles the powdered dessert business category; it increases the Division businesses by 10%. Furthermore, Super requires a new production technology: agglomeration and packaging on a high-speed line.

CONCLUSIONS

1. The incremental basis for evaluating a project is an inadequate measure of a project's worth when existing facilities with a known future use will be utilized extensively.

2. A fully allocated basis of reviewing major new product proposals recognizes that overheads increase in proportion to the size and complexity of the business, and provides the best long-range projection of the financial consequences.

ALTERNATIVE EVALUATIONS OF SUPER PROJECT
(FIGURES BASED ON 10-YEAR AVERAGES;
IN THOUSANDS OF DOLLARS)

	I *Incremental Basis*	*II* *Facilities-Used Basis*	*III* *Fully Allocated Basis*
Investment:			
Working capital	267	267	267
Fixed capital:			
Gross	200	653	672
Net	113	358	367
Total net investment	380	625	634
*Profit before taxes**	239	211	157
ROFE	63%	34%	25%

Jell-O Project:

Building	$200 × ⅔ = $133
Agglomerator	640 × ½ = 320
	$453

* Note: Assumes 20% of Super volume will replace existing Jell-O business.

APPENDIX II

TO: Mr. J. E. Hooting, Director, Corporate Budgets and Analysis
FROM: Mr. J. C. Kresslin, Corporate Controller
SUBJECT: SUPER PROJECT

March 7, 1967

On March 2 you sent me a note describing Crosby Sanberg's and your thoughts about evaluating the Super project. In this memo you suggest that the project should be appraised on the basis of fully allocated facilities and production costs.

In order to continue the dialogue, I am raising a couple of questions below.

It seems to me that in a situation such as you describe for Super, the real question is a *management decision* as to whether to go ahead with the Super project or not go ahead. Or to put it another way, are we better off in the aggregate if we use half the agglomerator and two thirds of an existing building for Super, or are we not, on the basis of our current knowledge?

It might be assumed that, for example, half of the agglomerator is being used and half is not and that a minimum economical size agglomerator was necessary for Jell-O and, consequently, should be justified by the Jell-O project itself. If we find a way to utilize it sooner by producing Super on it, aren't we better off in the aggregate, and the different ROFE figure for the Super project by itself becomes somewhat irrelevant? A similar point of view might be applied to the portion of the building. Or if we charge the Super project with half an agglomerator and two thirds of an existing building, should we then go back and relieve the Jell-O projects of these costs in evaluating the management's original proposal?

To put it another way, since we are faced with making decisions at a certain time on the basis of what we then know, I see very little value in looking at the Super project all by itself. Better we should look at the total situation before and after to see how we fare.

As to allocated production costs, the point is not so clear. Undoubtedly, over the long haul, the selling prices will need to be determined on the basis of a satisfactory margin over fully allocated costs. Perhaps this should be an additional requirement in the course of evaluating capital projects, since we seem to have been surprised at the low margins for "Tasty" after allocating all costs to the product.

I look forward to discussing this subject with you and with Crosby at some length.

Exhibit 1

THE SUPER PROJECT

Consolidated Balance Sheet of General Foods Corporation
Fiscal Year Ended April 1, 1967
(Dollar figures in millions)

ASSETS	
Cash	$ 20
Marketable securities	89
Receivables	180
Inventories	261
Prepaid expenses	14
Total current assets	$564
Land, buildings, equipment (at cost, less depreciation)	332
Long-term receivables and sundry assets	7
Goodwill	26
Total assets	$929
LIABILITIES AND STOCKHOLDERS' EQUITY	
Notes payable	$ 22
Accounts payable	86
Accrued liabilities	73
Accrued income taxes	57
Total current liabilities	$238
Long-term notes	39
3⅜% debentures	22
Other noncurrent liabilities	10
Deferred investment tax credit	9
Stockholders' equity:	
Common stock issued	164
Retained earnings	449
Common stock held in treasury, at cost	(2)
Total stockholders' equity	$611
Total liabilities and stockholders' equity	$929
Common stock—shares outstanding at year-end	25,127,007

Exhibit 2
THE SUPER PROJECT
Common Stock Prices of General Foods Corporation 1958–67

Year	*Price Range*
1958	\$24 –\$ 39¾
1959	37⅛– 53⅞
1960	49⅛– 75½
1961	68⅝– 107¾
1962	57¾– 96
1963	77⅝– 90½
1964	78¼– 93¼
1965	77½– 89⅞
1966	62¾– 83
1967	65¼– 81¾

Exhibit 3

THE SUPER PROJECT

TEN-YEAR SUMMARY OF STATISTICAL DATA OF GENERAL FOODS CORPORATION, 1958–67
(All dollar amounts in millions, except assets per employee and figures on a share basis)

Fiscal years	*1958*	*1959*	*1960*	*1961*	*1962*	*1963*	*1964*	*1965*	*1966*	*1967*
EARNINGS										
Sales to customers (net)	$1,009	$1,053	$1,087	$1,160	$1,189	$1,216	$1,338	$1,478	$1,555	$1,652
Cost of sales	724	734	725	764	769	769	838	937	965	1,012
Marketing, administrative, and general expenses	181	205	236	261	267	274	322	362	406	449
Earnings before income taxes	$ 105	$ 115	$ 130	$ 138	$ 156	$ 170	$ 179	$ 177	$ 185	$ 193
Taxes on income	57	61	69	71	84	91	95	91	91	94
Net earnings	$ 48	$ 54	$ 61	$ 67	$ 72	$ 79	$ 84	$ 86	$ 94	$ 99
Dividends on common shares	24	28	32	35	40	45	50	50	53	55
Retained earnings—current year	24	26	29	32	32	34	34	36	41	44
Net earnings per common share	$ 1.99	$ 2.21	$ 2.48	$ 2.69	$ 2.90	$ 3.14	$ 3.33	$ 3.44	$ 3.73	$ 3.93
Dividends per common share	$ 1.00	$ 1.15	$ 1.30	$ 1.40	$ 1.60	$ 1.80	$ 2.00	$ 2.00	$ 2.10	$ 2.20
ASSETS, LIABILITIES, AND STOCKHOLDERS' EQUITY										
Inventories	$ 169	$ 149	$ 157	$ 189	$ 183	$ 205	$ 256	$ 214	$ 261	$ 261
Other current assets	144	180	200	171	204	206	180	230	266	303
Current liabilities	107	107	126	123	142	162	202	173	219	238
Working capital	$ 206	$ 222	$ 230	$ 237	$ 245	$ 249	$ 234	$ 271	$ 308	$ 326
Land, buildings, equipment, gross	$ 203	$ 221	$ 247	$ 289	$ 328	$ 375	$ 436	$ 477	$ 517	$ 569
Land, buildings, equipment, net	125	132	148	173	193	233	264	283	308	332
Long-term debt	49	44	40	37	35	34	23	37	54	61
Stockholders' equity	$ 287	$ 315	$ 347	$ 384	$ 419	$ 454	$ 490	$ 527	$ 569	$ 611
Stockholders' equity per common share	$11.78	$12.87	$14.07	$15.46	$16.80	$18.17	$19.53	$20.99	$22.64	$24.32
CAPITAL PROGRAM										
Capital additions	$ 28	$ 24	$ 35	$ 40	$ 42	$ 57	$ 70	$ 54	$ 65	$ 59
Depreciation	11	14	15	18	21	24	26	29	32	34
EMPLOYMENT DATA										
Wages, salaries, and benefits	$ 128	$ 138	$ 147	$ 162	$ 171	$ 180	$ 195	$ 204	$ 218	$ 237
Number of employees (in thousands)	21	22	22	25	28	28	30	30	30	32
Assets per employee (in thousands)	$ 21	$ 22	$ 23	$ 22	$ 22	$ 23	$ 24	$ 25	$ 29	$ 29

Per share figures calculated on shares outstanding at year-end and adjusted for 2 for 1 stock split in August, 1960.

Exhibit 4

THE SUPER PROJECT

Criteria for Evaluating Projects by General Foods Corporation

The basic criteria to be applied in evaluating projects within each of the classifications are set forth in the following schedule:

Purpose of Project	*Payback and ROFE Criteria*
a) SAFETY AND CONVENIENCE:	
1. Projects required for reasons of safety, sanitation, health, public convenience, or other overriding reason with no reasonable alternatives. Examples: sprinkler systems, elevators, fire escapes, smoke control, waste disposal, treatment of water pollution, etc.	Payback—return on funds projections not required but the request must clearly demonstrate the *immediate* need for the project and the lack or inadequacy of alternative solutions.
2. Additional nonproductive space requirements for which there are no financial criteria. Examples: office space, laboratories, service areas (kitchens, restrooms, etc.).	Requests for nonproductive facilities, such as warehouses, laboratories, and offices should indicate the advantages of owning rather than leasing, unless no possibility to lease exists. In those cases where the company owns a group of integrated facilities and wherein the introduction of rented or leased properties might complicate the long-range planning or development of the area, owning rather than leasing is recommended. If the project is designed to improve customer service (such as market centered warehouses) this factor is to be noted on the project request.
b) QUALITY: Projects designed primarily to improve quality.	If payback and ROFE cannot be computed, it must be clearly demonstrated that the improvement is identifiable and desirable.
c) INCREASE PROFIT:	
1. Projects that are justified primarily by reduced costs.	Projects with a payback period *up to 10 years* and a 10-year return *on* funds *as low as 20%* PBT are considered worthy of consideration, provided (1) the end product involved is believed to be a reasonably permanent part of our line or (2) the facilities involved are so flexible that they may be usable for successor products.
2. Projects that are designed primarily to increase production capacity for an existing product.	Projects for a proven product where the risk of mortality is small, such as coffee, Jell-O Gelatin, and cereals, should assure a payback in *no more than 10 years* and a 10-year PBT return on funds of *no less* than 20%.
3. Projects designed to provide facilities to manufacture and distribute a new product or product line.	Because of the greater risk involved such projects should show a high potential return *on* funds (not less than a 10-year PBT return of 40%). Payback period, however, might be as much as *10 years* because of losses incurred during the market development period.*
d) OTHER: This category includes projects which by definition are excluded from the three preceding categories. Examples: standby facilities intended to insure uninterrupted production, additional equipment not expected to improve profits or product quality and not required for reasons of safety and convenience, equipment to satisfy marketing requirements, etc.	While standards of return may be difficult to set, some calculation of financial benefits should be made where possible.

* These criteria apply to the United States and Canada only. Profit-increasing capital projects in other areas in categories c1 and c2 should offer at least a 10-year PBT return of 24% to compensate for the greater risk involved. Likewise, foreign operation projects in the c3 category should offer a 10-year PBT return of at least 48%.

Exhibit 5

THE SUPER PROJECT
CAPITAL PROJECT REQUEST FORM OF GENERAL FOODS CORPORATION

NY 1292-A 12-63
PTD. IN U.S.A.

December 23, 1966
Date

"Super" Facilities 66-42
Project Title & Number

New Request [X] Supplement [ ]

Expansion-New Product [X] A
Purpose [ ] R

Jell-O Division - St. Louis
Division & Location

PROJECT DESCRIPTION

To provide facilities for production of Super, chocolate dessert. This project included finishing a packing room in addition to filling and packaging equipment.

SUMMARY OF INVESTMENT	
NEW CAPITAL FUNDS REQUIRED	$ 200M
EXPENSE BEFORE TAXES	--
LESS: TRADE-IN OR SALVAGE, IF ANY	--
Total This Request	$ 200M
PREVIOUSLY APPROPRIATED	--
Total Project Cost	$ 200M

FINANCIAL JUSTIFICATION*	
ROFE (PBT BASIS) - 10 YR. AVERAGE	62.9 %
PAYBACK PERIOD April, F'68 (FROM) Feb. F'75 (TO)	6.83 YRS.
NOT REQUIRED -	[ ]
* BASED ON TOTAL PROJECT COST AND WORKING FUNDS OF	$ 510M

ESTIMATED EXPENDITURE RATE	
QUARTER ENDING Mar. F19 67	$ 160M
QUARTER ENDING June F19 68	40M
QUARTER ENDING F19	
QUARTER ENDING F19	
REMAINDER	

OTHER INFORMATION	
MAJOR [ ] SPECIFIC ORDINARY [ ] BLANKET [ ]	
INCLUDED IN ANNUAL PROGRAM YES [ ] NO [ ]	
PER CENT OF ENGINEERING COMPLETED	80 %
ESTIMATED START-UP COSTS	$ 15M
ESTIMATED START-UP DATE	April

LEVEL OF APPROVAL REQUIRED

[ ] BOARD [ ] CHAIRMAN [ ] EXEC. V.P. [ ] GEN. MGR.

SIGNATURES		DATE
DIRECTOR CORP. ENG.		
DIRECTOR B & A		
GENERAL MANAGER		
VICE PRESIDENT		
EXEC. VICE PRESIDENT		
PRESIDENT		
CHAIRMAN		

For Division Use - Signatures

NAME AND TITLE	DATE

Exhibit 5—Continued

INSTRUCTIONS FOR CAPITAL PROJECT REQUEST FORM NY 1292-A

The purpose of this form is to secure management's authorization to commit or expend funds on a capital project. Refer to Accounting and Financial Manual Statement No. 19 for information regarding projects to which this form applies.

NEW REQUEST—SUPPLEMENT: Check the appropriate box.

PURPOSE: Identify the primary purpose of the project in accordance with the classifications established in Accounting and Financial Statement No. 19, i.e., Sanitation, Health and Public Convenience, Non-Productive Space, Safety, Quality, Reduce Cost, Expansion—Existing Products, Expansion—New Products, Other (specify). Also indicate in the appropriate box whether the equipment represents an addition or a replacement.

PROJECT DESCRIPTION: Comments should be in sufficient detail to enable Corporate Management to appraise the benefits of the project. Where necessary, supplemental data should be attached to provide complete background for project evaluation.

SUMMARY OF INVESTMENT:

New Capital Funds Required: Show gross cost of assets to be acquired.

Expense before Taxes: Show incremental expense resulting from project.

Trade-in or Salvage: Show the amount expected to be realized on trade-in or sale of a replaced asset.

Previously Appropriated: When requesting a supplement to an approved project, show the amount previously appropriated even though authorization was given in a prior year.

FINANCIAL JUSTIFICATION:

ROFE: Show the return on funds employed (PBT basis) as calculated on Financial Evaluation Form NY 1292-C or 1292-F. The appropriate Financial Evaluation Form is to be attached to this form.

Not Required: Where financial benefits are not applicable or required or are not expected, check the box provided. The non-financial benefits should be explained in the comments.

In the space provided, show the sum of The Total Project Cost plus Total Working Funds (line 20, Form NY 1292-C or line 5, Form NY 1292-F) in either of the first three periods, whichever is higher.

ESTIMATED EXPENDITURE RATE: Expenditures are to be reported in accordance with accounting treatment of the asset and related expense portion of the project. Insert estimated quarterly expenditures beginning with the quarter in which the first expenditure will be made. The balance of authorized funds unspent after the fourth quarter should be reported in total.

OTHER INFORMATION: Check whether the project is a major, specific ordinary, or blanket, and whether or not the project was included in the Annual Program. Show estimated percentage of engineering completed; this is intended to give management an indication of the degree of reliability of the funds requested. Indicate the estimated start-up costs as shown on line 32 of Financial Evaluation Form NY 1292-C. Insert anticipated start-up date for the project; if start-up is to be staggered, explain in comments.

LEVEL OF APPROVAL REQUIRED: Check the appropriate box.

Exhibit 6

THE SUPER PROJECT
FINANCIAL EVALUATION FORM OF GENERAL FOODS CORPORATION
(Dollar figures in thousands)

NY 1292-C 10-64
PTD. IN U.S.A.

Division	Location	Project Title	Project No.	Date / Supplement No.
Jell-O	St. Louis	The Super Project	67-89	

PROJECT REQUEST DETAIL	1ST PER.	2ND PER.	___PER.	___PER.	___PER.
1. LAND	$				
2. BUILDINGS	80				
3. MACHINERY & EQUIPMENT	120				
4. ENGINEERING					
5. OTHER (EXPLAIN)					
6. EXPENSE PORTION (BEFORE TAX)					
7. SUB-TOTAL	$ 200				
8. LESS: SALVAGE VALUE (OLD ASSET)					
9. TOTAL PROJECT COST*	$ 200				
10. LESS: TAXES ON EXP. PORTION					
11. NET PROJECT COST	$ 200				

* Same as Project Request

RETURN ON NEW FUNDS EMPLOYED - 10-YR. AVG.	PAT (C ÷ A)	PBT (B ÷ A)
A - NEW FUNDS EMPLOYED (LINE 21)	$ 380	$ 380
B - PROFIT BEFORE TAXES (LINE 35)		$ 239
C - NET PROFIT (LINE 37)	$ 115	
D - CALCULATED RETURN	30.2 %	62.9 %

PAYBACK YEARS FROM OPERATIONAL DATE	
PART YEAR CALCULATION FOR FIRST PERIOD	- YRS.
NUMBER OF FULL YEARS TO PAY BACK	6.00 YRS.
PART YEAR CALCULATION FOR LAST PERIOD	0.83 YRS.
TOTAL YEARS TO PAY BACK	6.83 YRS.

	1ST PER. F 68	2ND PER. F 69	3RD PER. F 70	4TH PER. F 71	5TH PER. F 72	6TH PER. F 73	7TH PER. F 74	8TH PER. F 75	9TH PER. F 76	10TH PER. F 77	11TH PER.	10-YR. AVG.
FUNDS EMPLOYED												
12. NET PROJECT COST (LINE 11)	$ 200	200	200	200	200	200	200	200	200	200		
13. DEDUCT DEPRECIATION (CUM.)	19	37	54	70	85	98	110	121	131	140		
14. CAPITAL FUNDS EMPLOYED	$ 181	163	146	130	115	102	90	79	69	60		113
15. CASH	124	134	142	151	160	160	169	169	178	178		157
16. RECEIVABLES												
17. INVENTORIES	207	222	237	251	266	266	281	281	296	296		260
18. PREPAID & DEFERRED EXP.												
19. LESS CURRENT LIABILITIES	(2)	(82)	(108)	(138)	(185)	(184)	(195)	(195)	(207)	(207)		(150)
20. TOTAL WORKING FUNDS (15 THRU 19)	329	274	271	264	241	242	255	255	267	267		267
21. TOTAL NEW FUNDS EMPLOYED (14 + 20)	$ 510	437	417	394	356	344	345	334	336	327		380
PROFIT AND LOSS												
22. UNIT VOLUME (in thousands)	1100	1200	1300	1400	1500	1500	1600	1600	1700	1700		1460
23. GROSS SALES	$ 2200	2400	2600	2800	3000	3000	3200	3200	3400	3400		2920
24. DEDUCTIONS	88	96	104	112	120	120	128	128	136	136		117
25. NET SALES	2112	2304	2496	2688	2880	2880	3072	3072	3264	3264		2803
26. COST OF GOODS SOLD	1100	1200	1300	1400	1500	1500	1600	1600	1700	1700		1460
27. GROSS PROFIT	1012	1104	1196	1288	1380	1380	1472	1472	1564	1564		1343
GROSS PROFIT % NET SALES	%											
28. ADVERTISING EXPENSE												
29. SELLING EXPENSE	1100	1050	1000	900	700	700	730	730	750	750		841
30. GEN. AND ADMIN. COSTS												
31. RESEARCH EXPENSE												
32. START-UP COSTS	15											2
33. OTHER (EXPLAIN) Test Mkt.	360											36
34. ADJUSTMENTS (EXPLAIN) Erosion	180	200	210	220	230	230	240	240	250	250		225
35. PROFIT BEFORE TAXES	$ (643)	(146)	(14)	168	450	450	502	502	564	564		239
36. TAXES	(334)	(76)	(7)	87	234	234	261	261	293	293		125
36A. ADD: INVESTMENT CREDIT	(1)	(1)	(1)	(1)	(1)	(1)	(1)	(1)	-	-		(1)
37. NET PROFIT	(308)	(69)	(6)	82	217	217	242	242	271	271		115
38. CUMULATIVE NET PROFIT	$ (308)	(377)	(383)	(301)	(84)	133	375	617	888	1159		
39. NEW FUNDS TO REPAY (21 LESS 38)	$ 318	814	300	695	440	211	(30)	(283)	(552)	(832)		

Exhibit 6—Continued

INSTRUCTIONS FOR PREPARATION OF FORM NY 1292-C

FINANCIAL EVALUATION

This form is to be submitted to Corporate Budget and Analysis with each profit-increasing capital project request requiring $50,000 or more of capital funds and expense before taxes.

Note that the ten-year term has been divided into eleven periods. The first period is to end on the March 31st following the operational date of the project, and the P & L projection may thereby encompass any number of months from one to twelve, e.g., if the project becomes operational on November 1, 1964, the first period for P & L purposes would be 5 months (November 1, 1964 through March 31, 1965). The next nine periods would be fiscal years (F'66, F'67, etc.) and the eleventh period would be 7 months (April 1, 1974 through October 30, 1974). This has been done primarily to facilitate reporting of projected and actual P & L data by providing for fiscal years. See categorized instructions below for more specific details.

Project Request Detail: Lines 1 through 11 show the breakdown of the Net Project Cost to be used in the financial evaluation. *Line 8* is to show the amount expected to be realized on trade-in or sale of a replaced asset. *Line 9* should be the same as the "Total Project Cost" shown on Form NY 1292-A, Capital Project Request. Space has been provided for capital expenditures related to this project which are projected to take place subsequent to the first period. Indicate in such space the additional costs only; do not accumulate them.

Funds Employed:

Capital Funds Employed: *Line 12* will show the net project cost appearing on line 11 as a constant for the first ten periods except in any period in which additional expenditures are incurred; in that event show the accumulated amounts of line 11 in such period and in all future periods.

Deduct cumulative depreciation on *line 13*. Depreciation is to be computed on an incremental basis i.e., the net increase in depreciation over present depreciation on assets being replaced. In the first period depreciation will be computed at one half of the first year's annual rate; no depreciation is to be taken in the eleventh period. Depreciation rates are to be the same as those used for accounting purposes. *Exception:* When the depreciation rate used for accounting purposes differs materially from the rate for tax purposes, the higher rate should be used. A variation will be considered material when the first full year's depreciation on a book basis varies 20% or more from the first full year's depreciation on a tax basis.

The ten-year average of Capital Funds Employed shall be computed by adding line 14 in each of the first ten periods and dividing the total by ten.

Total Working Funds: Refer to Financial Policy No. 21 as a guide in computing new working fund requirements. Items which are not on a formula basis and which are normally computed on a five-quarter average shall be handled proportionately in the first period. For example, since the period involved may be less than 12 months, the average would be computed on the number of quarters involved. Generally, the balances should be approximately the same as they would be if the first period were a full year.

Cash, based on a formula which theorizes a two weeks' supply (2/52nds), should follow the same theory. If the first period is for three months, two-thirteenths (2/13ths) should be used; if it is for 5 months, two-twenty-firsts (2/21sts) should be used, and so forth. Current liabilities are to include one half of the tax expense as the tax liability. The ten-year averages of Working Funds shall be computed by adding each line across for the first ten periods and dividing each total by ten.

Profit and Loss Projection

P & L Categories (Lines 22 through 37): Reflect only the incremental amounts which will result from the proposed project; exclude all allocated charges. Include the P & L results expected in the individual periods comprising the first ten years of the life of the project. Refer to the second paragraph of these instructions regarding the fractional years' calculations during the first and eleventh periods.

Any loss or gain on the sale of a replaced asset (see line 8) shall be included in line 33.

As indicated in the caption Capital Funds Employed, no depreciation is to be taken in the eleventh period.

The ten-year averages of the P & L items shall be computed by adding each line across for the eleven periods (10 full years from the operational date) and dividing the total by ten.

Adjustments (Line 34): Show the adjustment necessary, on a before-tax basis, to indicate any adverse or favorable incremental effect the proposed project will have on any other products currently being produced by the corporation.

Investment Credit is to be included on Line 36-A. The Investment Credit will be spread over 8 years, or fractions thereof, as an addition to PAT.

Return on New Funds Employed: Ten-year average returns are to be calculated for PAT (projects requiring Board approval only) and PBT. The PAT return is calculated by dividing average PAT (line 37) by average new funds employed (line 21); the PBT return is derived by dividing average PBT (line 35) by average new funds employed (line 21).

Payback Years from Operational Date:

Part Year Calculatian for First Period: Divide number of months in the first period by twelve. If five months are involved, the calculation is 5/12 = .4 years.

Number of Full Years to Pay Back: Determined by the last period, excluding the first period, in which an amount is shown on line 39.

Part Year Calculation for Last Period: Divide amount still to be repaid at the end of the last full period (line 39) by net profit plus the *annual* depreciation in the following year when payback is completed.

Total Years to Pay Back: Sum of full and part years.

FRONTIER RUBBER COMPANY

At the December, 1958, meeting of the finance committee of Frontier Rubber Company, four capital expenditure proposals were brought up for review. The finance committee met quarterly to consider requests for the appropriation of funds for projects to be started within the next year. The committee previously had approved expenditures totaling $70 million for 1959, a figure that represented the highest appropriations since World War II. The committee had reviewed the projects currently under consideration earlier in the year but at that time had decided to allocate the available funds to projects promising a higher rate of return, considered to be more urgent, or appearing to be less risky. However, management expected 1959 profits to run higher than originally estimated, thereby providing an additional source of approximately $5 million. Therefore, the finance committee decided to rescreen requests that previously had been rejected to see whether any of these projects were sufficiently promising to merit approval.

Company background

Frontier Rubber Company was one of the major producers of rubber tires in the country. The company also produced a wide line of other rubber and nonrubber products. Rubber products included radiator hoses, floor mats, molded and extruded mechanical rubber goods, fan belts, latex thread, and cushion material for mattresses. During World War II the company had entered the chemicals and plastics field with the manufacture of vinyl, styrene, and other types of plastic resins; agricultural chemicals such as fungicides and nitricides; acids; textile resins and organic chemicals for use in petroleum, rubber, plastics, and other industries.

The company had been organized in 1911 as the result of a merger between two medium-sized rubber companies. In the period prior to World War II, growth had resulted from acquisitions of many smaller companies. In World War II, Frontier Rubber was a major supplier of military products for the government. After the war, sales increased from $443 million in 1946 to $907 million in 1957. Net income also increased from $26 million in 1949 to $60 million in 1957.

Capital expenditures for plant expansion and improvement since the end of World War II had been substantial. The company had undertaken two major programs prior to the current one. The first expansion program had been undertaken in the immediate postwar period as the company resumed production for civilian consumption. In 1949 the company had increased expenditures for the addition of facilities to handle new products in the plastics and chemicals fields and for improvements to existing plants. The current program had been started in 1955. The company had financed these expansion programs by the public sale of debentures and by retained earnings. On December 31, 1957, it had outstanding $151 million of long-term debt, which represented 28% of total capitalization (long-term debt plus common stock and surplus). Recent balance sheets are shown in Exhibit 1, and a 14-year summary of sales and earnings is shown in Exhibit 2.

Capital expenditure program

In 1947 the directors of Frontier Rubber had established long-range expansion goals with the hope of furnishing a basis for the budgeting of time, money, materials, and manpower in a purposeful manner. In conjunction with these long-range goals, the directors had approved a rolling five-year capital expenditure program. This program had been adopted to provide management with budgets beyond the yearly budget normally drawn up by the treasurer.

The objective of the capital expenditure programs was to increase earnings per share. The directors also wished in the implementation of the programs to stay within certain established financial policies. These involved maintaining a dividend payout ratio of approximately 65% and a long-term debt ratio of less than 35% of total capitalization. In December, 1958, Frontier's common stock price was 20 times the anticipated 1958 earnings per share.

In establishing capital expenditure policies, management set up minimum expected rates of return on investments, which had to be met before project proposals could be approved. These return criteria were disseminated throughout the organization to be used as a guide by division managers and their staffs. Division managers sponsored nearly all project proposals and, in turn, were held accountable for their forecasts and projections. Despite these minimum standards, more proposals were submitted than could be met by the funds available. As a result, all sizable proposals were given a critical appraisal throughout the review process. Typically, about one third of all projects submitted by the division managers were rejected during the screening process.

The minimum-return standards were based on the historical return on net assets of the company modified by comparisons with other companies in the rubber industry. For instance, during the five-year period, 1942–46, Frontier Rubber's average rate of return (net income after taxes divided by net assets) was 5.68%. Other large rubber companies, on the other hand, earned between 6.26% and 7.42% on net assets in that period. After reviewing this evidence, officers of Frontier Rubber had established the minimum acceptable rate of return for projects at 12% after taxes. Management hoped that a high cutoff rate of return would help to improve its earnings position more rapidly and raise its return on investment to levels comparable with competitors.

This minimum-return criterion was not applied uniformly to all projects because of the uncertainties involved in forecasting. The 12% rate was used for projects for improvement or replacement of existing facilities where expected earnings and expenditures could be forecast with reasonable accuracy over relatively long periods of time. Projects of this type generally involved laborsaving devices and other equipment purchases. Because of experience gained from equipment already in use, management had confidence in the estimates of division managers concerning these projects.

However, management expected higher rates of return from projects that appeared to be more uncertain. For instance, ventures into new products were expected to return at least 20% because of the greater risks that typically existed. New products could easily result in failure because demand did not match expectations or because of hidden costs that might not have been anticipated. Moreover, projects of this nature generally involved the expenditure of greater sums of money.

In another instance, management expected a minimum rate of return of 17% on projects for expansion of existing facilities. Although the company did not have to establish new markets, these projects were regarded as relatively risky because of the uncertainties involved in forecasting demands and costs.

In contrast to the emphasis placed on the rates of return for the above projects, the officers of Frontier Rubber considered return criteria less important for projects designed wholly to reduce costs. They believed that any savings in cost were beneficial to the company regardless of the rate of return. However, with a limited supply of funds for capital investment, management decided to restrict expenditures by some means. It therefore used the minimum acceptable rate of return of 12% for projects of cost reduction.

The method chosen for computing rates of return was based on the incremental investment required for the project and the 10-year average of expected earnings. Gross plant expenditures and funds required for working capital constituted the incremental investment. Expected earnings under "normal" future business conditions were computed after taxes and normal straight-line depreciation.[1] Division managers used detailed engineering and market surveys in their computations of expected earnings. Management did not require projections beyond 10 years because it did not think that accurate forecasts could be made beyond that period. Moreover, 10 years was a typical obsolescence period for many products in the rubber industry.

Frontier Rubber made an exception to its method of computing rates of return in the case of expenditures for replacement or improvement of facilities. In this instance, management believed that expected earnings should take

---

[1] The company used the declining balance method of depreciation for accounting purposes.

into consideration the income that would be lost if the existing facility under consideration were to cease operations. Moreover, it was believed that investment should include the net book value of the existing facility plus the new capital being requested. This procedure had been adopted to avoid sinking additional money into projects already yielding a low rate of return on existing book value.

Processing capital expenditure requests

The first step in the system of processing capital expenditure requests was separation of the proposed projects into three basic categories:

Class A—Projects amounting to $15,000 or more that covered new products, new plants, or new processes; or any project costing $100,000 or more.
Class B—Projects above $5,000 that did not fall into the Class A category.
Class C—Projects below $5,000.

In establishing these categories, management felt that closer surveillance should be given to all projects requiring large expenditures, and to new projects because of the inherent risks. As a result, Class A proposals went through a thorough system of review before they were approved. In Class B projects, the proposals did not go through so rigorous a review, but nevertheless, they were considered carefully before final approval was given. (See Exhibit 3 for a schematic diagram of the appropriations procedure for Class A and B projects.)

Class C projects, which included mainly maintenance expenditures, did not fall within the appropriations procedure but were allowed for and approved in total in the annual budget review. Division managers grouped requests for projects of less than $5,000 together and submitted them in a lump sum for budget approval. Officers of the company seldom questioned these requests but approved them on the basis of need. However, management felt that the system had a built-in control because each division manager was aware that he would decrease his chance for approval of Class A or B projects if he requested excessive amounts for Class C projects. Officers believed that in practice, division managers limited Class C expenditure to essential projects.

When the capital expenditure program had been established, the directors had appointed two committees, the budget committee and the finance committee, to review project proposals before they were submitted to the president and to the board of directors.

In the first step of the approval procedure, division managers submitted all proposed projects to the budget committee for inclusion in the five-year capital expenditure program. The committee was assigned the task of looking ahead, anticipating desirable expenditures opportunities, and testing the company's capacity to finance them. Each year at the May meeting, the committee revised the program and subsequently submitted it to the board of directors for approval. Unanticipated yet urgent requests were submitted to the directors as they were received. The budget committee included the president, the six division managers, the treasurer, the director of research and development, the personnel manager, and the assistant to the president. It reviewed projects as initially conceived—sometimes while still in advanced stages of research and often several years before they were ready for construction. Market information, process know-how, details on products, and estimated operating costs were used as a rough estimate to support each project proposal insofar as possible. Projects were evaluated on the basis of available resources, needs of the company, and expected rates of return on investment.

If the directors approved the projects in the five-year budget, the new projects were sent to the finance committee for more detailed analysis when the project was ready for construction. The division manager sponsoring the project prepared a detailed request for funds called an "appropriation request." This request embodied more detailed estimates of costs and earnings than the budget committee required. The time lag between approval by the budget committee and the appropriation of funds by the finance committee had varied from five months to five years. The finance committee consisted of the president, executive vice president, treasurer, director of research and development, the division manager sponsoring the project, and another division manager who was not concerned with the project.

The four projects under consideration in December, 1958, were at the finance committee awaiting the appropriation of funds. The projects were: (1) renovation of the molding process for rubber goods; (2) expansion of an existing acid plant; (3) construction of a laboratory for research into the commercial applications of atomic energy; and (4) construction of a new plastics plant on the West Coast. These projects had been approved by the budget committee at previous meetings and subsequently had been made a part of the company's five-year investment program. The appropriation requests had been submitted to the finance committee earlier in the year but had not been approved because funds had been limited and because other projects were expected to yield a higher rate of return, were less risky, or were more urgent. All of the projects that had been granted funds for 1959 were expected to yield at least 15% on the investment, or the equivalent.

Renovation of the molding process for rubber goods

In December, 1958, the factor of urgency became more imminent for one of the four projects listed above, renovation of the molding process for rubber goods at the Buffalo, New York, plant. Recurring mechanical failures had continued to plague the compression molding presses at Buffalo, one of the three plants of the company producing molded rubber goods. Mr. Jordan, the division manager for rubber goods, believed that the Buffalo plant would have to be shut down if renovation were not started within a few months. Work done at Buffalo could not be transferred to the other plants. A summary of Mr. Jordan's estimates appears as Exhibit 4.

Sales of molded rubber goods had declined during 1957 and 1958 because of the general economic recession. However, Mr. Jordan expressed his confidence that sales of nontire rubber products would continue to expand with the economy (i.e., about 4% per year) as it usually had in the past. Moreover, he pointed out that the plant had been earning between 14% in good years and 10% in poor years on net assets. In 1959, he expected the plant to earn about $230,000 after taxes and depreciation, provided repairs were undertaken immediately. On the basis of the December, 1958, net book value of the plant of $1.9 million, operations yielded a higher rate of return on net assets than the overall average for the company. In December, 1958, the appraised value of these assets was approximately $2.9 million, a sum that could possibly be realized in the event of liquidation of this facility. Mr. Jordan expected direct, nonrecurring costs of closing the plant to approximate $200,000, after taxes.

In the compression molding process, uncured compounded rubber was prepared to the correct weight, placed into the press cavity, and forced into the contour of the cavity by the pressure of the mold closing in the press. Cavities in the mold ran from one to hundreds, depending upon the size of the product being made. The plant had expanded gradually throughout the years so that many of the presses were small and inefficient. For example, in some cases rubber had to be inserted by hand into each of the cavities.

A minimum expenditure of $290,000 was now absolutely necessary to keep the presses in operation. Otherwise the plant would gradually have to be shut down. The repairs would be only a stop-gap measure, but Mr. Jordan estimated that probably no additional repairs would be required for another three years. The expenditure would be charged against current operations. The existing plant was being depreciated at a rate of $100,000 per year. The present molding presses were fully depreciated and had only nominal salvage value.

Mr. Jordan pointed out that the existing presses would eventually require a complete mechanical overhaul. If they were overhauled in conjunction with the repairs, the total cost (including repairs) would approximate $650,000. He estimated that through the elimination of inefficiencies $45,000 after taxes and straight-line depreciation could be saved each year after mechanical overhaul. When overhauled, the machines would have a new life for depreciation purposes of seven years. Mr. Jordan indicated that the cost for overhauling the presses would still approximate $650,000 at current market prices if the overhauling were done after the repairs had been made.

As a third possibility the company could replace the existing presses with new injection molding machines. These new presses utilized a power-driven plunger to force the unvulcanized rubber into a tightly closed mold. Forcing the rubber through small passages under high pressure increased the temperature of the injected compound sufficiently to reduce the curing time considerably. The machines would be automatic except for the removal of the product from the cavity. The new machines would cost a total of $2.4 million at current market prices but were not necessary to keep the plant in operation. They would have a life of 12 years for depreciation purposes.

As part of the request for appropriations, Mr. Jordan estimated that installation of the new equipment would result in average cost savings of about $230,000 per year, after taxes and straight-line depreciation. About 75% of these reduced operating costs would result from a reduction in the labor force since the new equipment would be almost fully automatic. The remaining cost savings would be realized from the use of less fuel. In his estimates Mr. Jordan included only those cost savings that he could definitely expect during the 10-year forecast. However, he believed that these savings would continue beyond the 10 years of the forecast. He expected the new machines to last for at least 20 years with only nominal interim repairs.

In addition to the labor and fuel savings, Mr. Jordan thought that approximately $500,000 after taxes could be saved by a reduction of indirect expenses during the first 10 years of their use. Since the new equipment would be more compact, he thought the machines, when installed, would free 20% of existing floor space for further expansion when this became desirable. Moreover, preventive maintenance and proper handling of the new equipment would cut repair bills, particularly in later years. This would also reduce time lost and would benefit the company by improving customer relations. With the repeated mechanical failures of the existing presses, the shipment of several orders had been held up. One of the company's more important customers had threatened to seek a new supplier if his orders were not delivered on schedule.

However, Mr. Jordan did not include these indirect savings in his return on investment computation because he could not be absolutely sure that they would be realized. He knew that he would be held accountable for the project when completed and would be expected to achieve the rate of return as forecasted. Until he had gained more experience with the new equipment, he did not want to assume the responsibility for the cost savings that were possible but either uncertain or intangible.

Acid plant expansion

The expansion of the sulfuric acid plant in Newark, New Jersey, had been planned as part of the original engineering work when the plant had been built in 1949. Demand at the time had not warranted building the entire plant, but it had been designed to allow an increase in capacity at a later date. Since the plant had been opened in 1949, the production of sulfuric acid in the United States had increased more than 50%, from 10.9 million short tons in 1947 to 16.5 million short tons in 1956. In December, 1957, Mr. Branner, the chemical division manager, had requested $2,225,000 for expansion of the plant. This request had included $1,200,000 for the plant, $800,000 for machinery and equipment, and $225,000 for working capital. However, funds had not been allocated because members of the finance committee had not been convinced that general business activity in 1958 would warrant expansion at that time.

Frontier Rubber had begun the production of industrial acids in 1949 as part of the company's diversification program. During 1957 Mr. Branner had felt that space limitations had placed pressure upon his plant personnel to fulfill the demands of his current customers. At one period, orders from new customers had been turned down. The economic recession in 1958 had left the plant operating at 80% of capacity. Mr. Branner had already noted an increase in the demand for acids by December, 1958, and expected them to be in short supply by mid-1959. The expansion program would double existing capacity.

With the recovery from the 1957–58 recession well under way by December, 1958, Mr. Branner was convinced that the industrial market would be able to absorb the output of the expanded plant within a few years' time. He therefore resubmitted his proposal. He further estimated that construction, machinery, and equipment costs would increase by approximately 5% and therefore requested an additional $100,000 for a total request of $2,325,000, summarized in Exhibit 5. Mr. Branner expected that earnings after taxes and straight-line depreciation would be approximately $200,000 a year for the first two years, when the plant would be operating at less than peak capacity. Thereafter, earnings would increase gradually to $600,000 per year in the fifth year as demand increased. The plant would be depreciated over 40 years, and the machinery and equipment would be depreciated over 10 years.

Mr. Branner decided to resubmit his proposal in conjunction with the company's policy of upgrading its acid products. Initially, the company had produced only heavy acids such as sulfuric, nitric, and hydrochloric acids. Recently, it had established a policy of converting the basic chemical products into higher grades of fine acids, which generally yielded higher profit margins, had stabler markets, and offered better returns on investment. For instance, the company now produced sulfuric acid to make ammonium sulphate for mixing into fertilizer. The company was also considering the manufacture of sulphonates for detergents. Expansion of the acid plant would be necessary if the company expected to continue its policy of upgrading its acid products yet wished to preserve the current basic acids market. Mr. Branner anticipated a strong growth pattern in the demand for end products such as detergents which, in turn, would increase the demand for fine acids. Consequently, additional heavy acids would be required for the manufacture of fine acids. His projections indicated that the present capacity would be entirely captive by 1965 (in contrast with being only 20% captive in 1958), suggesting further expansion would be necessary within a few years.

In discussing his proposal with the finance committee, Mr. Branner commented that product obsolescence was not a great problem. Sulfuric acid was used so widely that a decrease in one use was often offset by an increase in another. For instance, new and increased uses in rayon and film manufacture, and increased manufacture of sodium alkyl-sulfates as detergents, had offset the obsolescence of the salt-sulfuric acid process for manufacturing hydrochloric acid, petroleum refining by hydrogenation, and partial replacement in the fertilizer industry by nitric and phosphoric acids.

Mr. Branner felt confident that the expanded plant would be producing in the year 2000 with only moderate, interim equipment replacement. However, he pointed out the danger of the competition from other companies. In the past, a number of companies had been attracted to the chemical industry because of the high rate of return on investment and growth prospects. Because heavy acid plants required modest investment, an increasing number of companies were entering the field. Moreover, large users of sulfuric acid, such as fertilizer and explosive manufacturers, were acquiring smaller companies because they found it cheaper to make acid than to buy it. Consequently, occasional periods of overcapacity and cyclical fluctuations in plant usages had occurred. However, Mr. Branner pointed out that technical knowhow was an important factor, which tended to minimize the ease of entry into the sulfuric acid field.

An additional reason for resubmitting the proposal for expansion of the plant was Mr. Branner's argument that Frontier Rubber would be able to improve the return on investment of the entire sulfuric acid plant. The original plant costing $3.5 million (and returning profits of $400,000 on net assets of $3.0 million) had been built with excess floor space. Part of the basic structure had been designed to provide for further expansion. In addition some service facilities such as a power plant would not be required. Therefore, the plant expansion would provide a greater increase in capacity in proportion to the nominal investment expense, and the rate of return for the entire plant would be improved.

Construction of an atomic energy laboratory

The third project before the finance committee was a proposal by Mr. Wilbur, the director of research and development, for the construction of a new laboratory for research into atomic energy. He pointed out that the major rubber companies, as well as many companies in construction, mining, petroleum, chemicals, plastics, machine tools, electrical instruments, metals, and aircraft, were involved in some research of nuclear technology and its commercial counterparts. The function of the laboratory would be to explore the effects of radiation on chemical structures pertaining to the rubber industry and related products of Frontier Rubber.

Because of the hazards of radiation, a specially designed building would have to be constructed for the new research laboratory. After visiting other nuclear research laboratories and talking to architects and engineers, Mr. Wilbur had drawn up plans for a building, machinery, and equipment that would cost approximately $2.2 million. This amount included $200,000 for an air-conditioning system with an expected life of 10 years. He estimated that an additional $500,000 would be needed each year for manpower and other operating costs of the laboratory.

Mr. Wilbur recognized that the investment would have to be made with a look toward the long run. He admitted that he would be surprised if tangible benefits would result during the first five years because of immediate emphasis on basic research. He pointed out, however, that this form of basic research might eventually lead to extremely significant findings such as revolutionary new products or processes of major importance. Consequently, Mr. Wilbur believed the laboratory should be given high priority. He had become alarmed over the apathy shown by several officers of the company toward the project. These people, he felt, failed to recognize that all of the major competitors of Frontier Rubber were now actively engaged or about to begin research in atomic energy. The laboratory, he concluded, was necessary to keep up with competition and if postponed for another year would put the company behind its competitors. He thought research leadership was particularly important for establishing the company as a dynamic and aggressive organization.

Construction of a plastics plant

The fourth proposed project, summarized in Exhibit 6, was the construction of a plastics plant, which represented a completely new venture for Frontier Rubber. Recently the company had been offered an option to acquire the process rights to produce vinyl sheeting of a thinner gauge than currently on the market. This new sheeting would have the strength and quality of current plastics. The new finishing process would permit the production of more sheeting per pound of vinyl resin. The new process, combined with a nearby resin plant, would give Frontier a 15%–20% cost advantage over competing sheeting. Several companies were tooling up to produce this thinner gauge plastic in the East and Midwest but, at the moment, a market potential existed for entry into the West Coast area. In 1957, a number of relatively small vinyl chloride polymer plants had been built in various parts of the country, but the West Coast was still relatively free from competition in producing this material.

Rubber companies had played an important role in the plastics industry since the immediate post–World War II period when Goodrich began producing vinyl resin and film. By the time that Frontier Rubber had entered the vinyl resin industry, Firestone and Goodyear were producing both resin and film. Frontier had sold all of its resin to independent film and sheeting producers and manufacturers of end products such as vinyl garden hose, vinyl flooring, and vinyl-coated fabrics.

The vinyl industry had been highly competitive since 1952, and prices had been unstable. For instance, prices per pound of vinyl resin dropped from 38 cents to 31 cents in 1955 and to 27 cents in 1956. Imports of lower-priced foreign resin and pressure from vinyl film producers were largely responsible for the price cuts. On the other hand, vinyl film and sheeting manufacturers were able to maintain relatively stable price margins. Many vinyl resin producers began to produce their own vinyl film or sheeting in order to have a stable market for their vinyl resin without getting into the competitive pricing pressures from outside customers.

When the company policy of upgrading as many of the basic products as possible was formulated, management of Frontier began to look for an opportunity to manufacture its own vinyl film or sheeting. Several advantages of the new plastics plant had been pointed out by the division manager, Mr. Sterling. One important aspect would be the technical know-how gained with this product. If, at a later date, the company decided to upgrade its plastic products even further into production of consumer goods, this technical know-how would be an important factor. Secondly, the new plastic process would enable the company to begin building the sales force needed for further penetration into the fields of plastics and consumer goods.

A final important consideration with respect to the new process was the opportunity that it would give the company to avoid the competitive price struggle by establishing a captive market for its adjacent vinyl resin plant. Purchases of vinyl resin from the adjacent plant would probably absorb about 35% of its capacity. Moreover, the adjacent plant would realize a stable profit of $175,000. These profits were not included in the calculations on the rate of return by Mr. Sterling.

The project proposal for the manufacture of sheeting called for a special-purpose plant costing approximately $1.5 million and machinery and equipment of $800,000. Land adjacent to the existing plastics plant had been offered to the company for $200,000. (This land could also be used for construction of additional facilities in future years.) An additional $300,000 was requested for working capital. Although the plant would have limited value if the project did not work out as expected, it would have to be depreciated over 40 years. The machinery and equipment could be depreciated over 10 years. Management could foresee nothing that might replace vinyl products for the next three to four years. In fact trade publications estimated that production of vinyl resin for the entire industry would increase from 845 million pounds in 1957 to 1,200 million pounds by 1961. However, product obsolescence growing out of technical obsolescence in the plastic industry was quite high, with a typical product life expectancy of 8 to 10 years.

Mr. Sterling estimated earnings after taxes and straight-line deductions at $500,000 during the shakedown period of the first two years, $800,000 in years three through five, and $1 million thereafter. Some members of the finance committee had questioned these estimates when the project had been introduced earlier in the year. Mr. Sterling had based his projection on the expanding uses for vinyl sheeting such as vinyl-lined irrigation ditches and farm ponds, vinyl-covered greenhouses and home swimming pools. He assumed that a market already existed for these products and would result in production close to the capacity of the plant. Those who disagreed felt that the projection should be based on current production figures for the industry, which had shown a leveling off in the demand for vinyl sheeting. They had been doubtful that current demand would assure operations of more than 75% of operating capacity, or profits of $400,000 per year at this level.

Other members of the finance committee had believed that the sales potential was between full capacity and 75% of capacity. One committee member had suggested returning the proposal to Mr. Sterling for further study at the division level. With a nominal cost of approximately $25,000 for architectural and engineering fees, the capacity of the plant could be scaled down. He had estimated roughly that profit from the investment would be about 75% of Mr. Sterling's original estimate. He also had estimated that the cost of constructing the smaller plant would be about 90% of anticipated expenditures. After thorough discussion when the proposal had been introduced the first time, the members of the committee had agreed that all of the points of view concerning potential demand and earnings had some merit. Since they were generally agreed that the company would not know what the operating level would be until the plant was put on stream, Mr. Sterling had resubmitted his initial estimates.

In addition to questioning the potential market size for the vinyl sheeting, one committee member had questioned the availability of marketing personnel. The company had salesmen who were experienced in selling vinyl resin but did not have anyone skilled in selling film or sheeting. The two products, resin and sheeting, would be sold to different end-product markets. For instance, vinyl sheeting would be sold primarily to the upholstery field. Other uses would be for handbags, wallets, belts, and carrying cases. Vinyl resin, on the other hand, was sold to manufacturers of vinyl film and sheeting. Different selling techniques would have to be used for the two vinyl products because of the different end uses. The committee member who had raised the point questioned, first of all, whether the company could recruit enough good salesmen for the job and, secondly, whether the present vinyl resin salesmen would be able to train the new salesmen for the vinyl sheeting.

After reviewing the proposed projects the finance committee had to decide whether any or all of the projects should be allocated funds for construction in 1959.

Exhibit 1

FRONTIER RUBBER COMPANY

BALANCE SHEET, DECEMBER 31, 1956, AND 1957

(Dollar figures in millions)

ASSETS	1956		1957	
Current assets:				
Cash	$ 27.0		$ 23.6	
Marketable securities	63.6		32.3	
Accounts receivable	151.8		147.1	
Inventories	181.6		208.2	
Total current assets		$424.0		$411.2
Investments		26.9		32.7
Gross plant, machinery, and equipment	$286.6		$320.8	
Less: Reserve for depreciation	99.6		115.7	
Net fixed assets		187.0		205.1
Deferred charges		2.7		2.3
Total assets		$640.6		$651.3
LIABILITIES				
Current liabilities:				
Bank loan	$ 1.5		$ 5.3	
Accounts payable	39.4		35.7	
Accrued taxes	40.5		45.9	
Other accruals	22.7		23.3	
Total current liabilities		$104.1		$110.2
Long-term debt		159.7		151.3
Common and surplus		376.8		389.8
Total liabilities		$640.6		$651.3

Exhibit 2

FRONTIER RUBBER COMPANY

SUMMARY OF SALES AND EARNINGS

(Dollar figures in millions)

	Sales	*Income before Taxes*	*Income Tax*	*Net Income*
1944	$517	$ 32.7	$18.0	$14.7
1945	449	31.8	16.5	15.3
1946	443	65.3	33.7	31.6
1947	507	59.9	31.0	28.9
1948	523	60.7	31.6	29.1
1949	489	53.7	28.0	25.7
1950	680	90.2	46.4	43.8
1951	797	92.4	48.6	43.8
1952	780	85.7	45.3	40.4
1953	835	87.3	44.7	42.6
1954	781	100.2	51.9	48.3
1955	902	119.1	62.4	56.7
1956	891	112.6	58.5	54.1
1957	907	122.3	62.7	59.6

Exhibit 3

FRONTIER RUBBER COMPANY

Summary of Appropriation Request Procedure Review and Approval Requirements

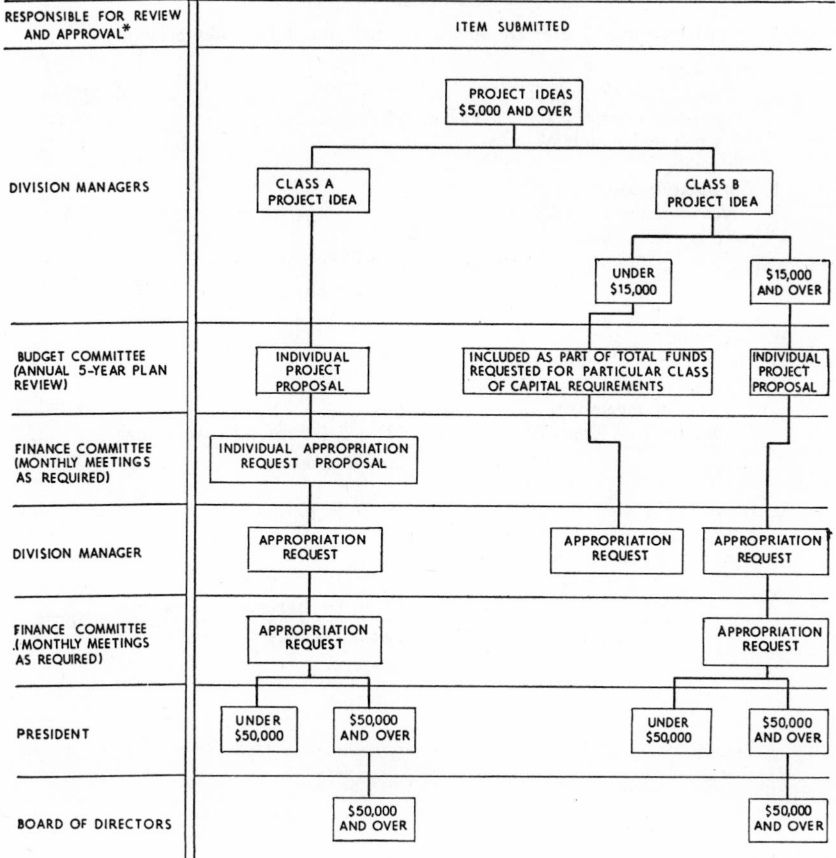

* Formal approval to spend funds comes only after approval is received from last authority noted on this diagram.

Exhibit 4

FRONTIER RUBBER COMPANY

SUMMARY OF EXPECTED RATES OF RETURN ON INVESTMENT AS CALCULATED BY THE COMPANY FOR RENOVATION OF THE MOLDING PROCESS FOR RUBBER GOODS

(All earnings figures are after taxes and straight-line depreciation)

Basic data:

Expected net earnings in 1958	$ 230,000
Net book value of plant (December, 1958)	1,900,000
Current return on book value	12.1%

I. Temporary repairs:
   Net investment—$290,000
   Return on investment—

$$\frac{\text{Income That Would Be Lost If Closed Down}}{\text{Net Book Value + Net Investment}} = 10.5\%$$

II. Overhaul:
   Net investment—$650,000
   Expected cost savings—$45,000
   Return on investment—

$$\frac{\text{Income That Would Be Lost If Closed Down + Expected Cost Savings}}{\text{Net Book Value + Net Investment}} = 10.8\%$$

III. Replacement with new machinery:
   Net investment—$2,400,000
   Expected cost savings—$230,000
   Return on investment—

$$\frac{\text{Income That Would Be Lost If Closed Down + Expected Cost Savings}}{\text{Net Book Value + Net Investment}} = 10.7\%$$

Exhibit 5

FRONTIER RUBBER COMPANY

SUMMARY OF EXPECTED RATE OF RETURN ON INVESTMENT AS CALCULATED BY THE COMPANY FOR EXPANSION OF THE ACID PLANT

(All earnings figures are after taxes and straight-line depreciation)

Net investment:	
Plant	$1,260,000
Machinery and equipment	840,000
Working capital	225,000
	$2,325,000

Expected earnings:

Year	*Earnings*
1	$ 200,000
2	200,000
3	330,000
4	460,000
5	600,000
6	600,000
7	600,000
8	600,000
9	600,000
10	600,000
	$4,790,000

Return on investment: $\frac{\text{Average Expected Earnings}}{\text{Net Investment}} = 20.6\%$

Exhibit 6

FRONTIER RUBBER COMPANY

SUMMARY OF EXPECTED RATES OF RETURN ON INVESTMENT AS CALCULATED BY THE COMPANY FOR CONSTRUCTION OF A PLASTICS PLANT

(All earnings figures are after taxes and straight-line depreciation)

Net investment:	
Plant	$1,500,000
Machinery and equipment	800,000
Land	200,000
Working capital	300,000
	$2,800,000

Expected earnings:

Year	*Per Year*
1–2	$ 500,000
3–5	800,000
6–10	1,000,000
Total expected earnings	$8,400,000

Return on investment: $\frac{\text{Average Expected Earnings}}{\text{Net Investment}} = 30.0\%$

MIDLAND-ROSS CORPORATION (A)

BACKGROUND INFORMATION

In 1966 the 13 divisions of the Midland-Ross Corporation had sales of over $340 million. No single division accounted for as much as 20% of the company's total sales, but the largest five divisions contributed 70% of total volume in that year. The product lines of the various divisions of Midland-Ross are shown in Exhibit 1. The most important products in terms of sales volume were (1) industrial furnaces and heat treating equipment; (2) parts used in the manufacture of railroad rolling stock and other foundry products; (3) rayon fiber for automobile tire cord and apparel fabrics; (4) auto, truck, and bus frames; and (5) power brake systems for autos, trucks, and buses.

Diversification through acquisition

Between 1957 and 1966 Midland-Ross had tripled total sales and nearly doubled per share earnings (Exhibit 2). During this period Midland-Ross had an active program of diversification by acquisition. These acquisitions were concluded at the average rate of one new company per year. The diversification program was intensified in response to a move toward unitized or "frameless" body construction started by Chrysler Corporation in 1959. The production of auto frames constituted 85% of the company's business in 1956. Thus, even though frameless construction never became popular in the 1960's, diversification lessened the company's vulnerability to technological change. The table below shows the company's acquisition history:

December, 1957:	Acquired J. O. Ross Engineering Corporation in exchange for 281,000 shares.
March, 1958:	Acquired Hartig Engine and Machine Company, Mountainside, New Jersey.
October, 1958:	Acquired Transportation Division of Consolidated Metal Products Corporation, Albany, New York, and moved operations to Owosso, Michigan, Division.
April, 1959:	Acquired Nelson Metal Products Company, Grand Rapids, Michigan.
November, 1959:	Acquired Surface Combustion Corporation, Toledo, Ohio, for $23 million cash.
May, 1961:	Merged Industrial Rayon Corporation by exchange of two common shares for each five Industrial Rayon shares.

January, 1962:	Acquired Wright Manufacturing Company, Phoenix, producer of air conditioning equipment.
March, 1962:	Acquired Fandaire Division, a producer of commercial air conditioning systems, from Yuba Consolidated Industries, Inc.
December 31, 1962:	Acquired the precision machine business of J. Leukart Machine Company, Columbus, Ohio.
April 1, 1963:	Purchased Steel City Electric Company from Martin Marietta Corporation.
April 22, 1965:	Merged National Castings Company, by exchange of 299,787 shares of $4.75 cumulative convertible preferred stock on basis of 45/100 share of preferred stock for each share of National Castings common stock. National Castings operated as two divisions.
Fall, 1965:	Acquired Grand Rapids Bright Metal Company.

Five of the acquisitions made during the period 1957 to 1966 were major acquisitions. Ross Engineering increased Midland-Ross sales in 1957 by $27 million. The Surface Combustion purchase in 1959 added about $38 million to annual sales. In 1961, Industrial Rayon boosted the company's growing sales volume by $50 million. The acquisition of Steel City Electric and National Castings in 1963 and 1965 added about $16 million and $73 million, respectively, to the Midland-Ross annual sales total.

Decentralized management

Midland-Ross operated with decentralized management responsibility. Each division had its own general manager (usually a vice president); and all sales, purchasing, personnel, advertising, and accounting functions were handled at the divisional level. The division manager was responsible for achieving certain sales and profit goals, which he had formulated and which were set forth in his division's annual budget and five-year plan. These two documents, the annual budget and the five-year plan, were submitted for review to the Midland-Ross executive office in Cleveland, Ohio, in November of each year. From this office, which occupied one and a half floors of a downtown building, the divisions were given legal, administrative, and financial assistance. The entire corporate staff at Midland-Ross numbered less than 90 people, at least 40 of whom would be classified as secretarial-clerical. Professional level personnel probably numbered about 25 in administrative, 15 in legal, and 10 in financial.

The division managers of Midland-Ross reported to one of two group vice presidents located at the executive office, or directly to the president, Mr. David E. Walbert. None of the division managers had their offices at the executive office, even though three of the largest divisions were located principally in Cleveland.

The business backgrounds of the division managers at Midland-Ross were varied, but the bulk of the experience of most of these men was in either an engineering or a sales capacity. As of a recent date, the 13 division managers had held their positions for the following lengths of time:

Number of Years in Position as Division Manager	*Number of Division Managers*
Since division became part of Midland-Ross	5
3 years	1
2 years	1
1 year	3
Less than 1 year	3
	13

FORMAL CAPITAL BUDGETING PROCEDURES

The formal capital budgeting procedures of Midland-Ross were outlined in a 49-page manual written for use at the divisional level and entitled "Expenditure Control Procedures." This document outlined (1) the classification scheme for types of funds requests, (2) the minimum levels of expenditure for which formal requests were required, (3) the maximum expenditure which could be authorized on the signature of corporate officers at various levels, (4) the format of the financial analysis required in a request for funds to carry out a project, and finally (5) the format of the report which followed the completion of the project and evaluated its success in terms of the original financial analysis outlined in (4).

Classification scheme for funds requests

The manual defined two basic classes of projects: profit improvement and necessity. Profit improvement projects included:

a) Cost reduction projects.
b) Capacity expansion projects in existing product lines.
c) New product line introductions.

Necessity projects included:

All projects where profit improvement was not the basic purpose of the project, such as those for service facilities, plant security, improved working conditions, employee relations and welfare, pollution and contamination prevention, extensive repairs and replacements, profit maintenance, and services of outside research and consultant agencies. Expense projects of an unusual or extraordinary character included in this class were those expenses which did not lend themselves to inclusion in the operating budget and could normally be expected to occur less than once per year.

Minimum amounts subject to formal request

Not all divisional requests for funds required formal and specific economic justification. Obviously, normal operating expenditures for items such as raw materials and wages were managed completely at the level of the divisions. Capital expenditures and certain nonrecurring operating expenditures were subject to formal requests and specific economic justification if they exceeded certain minimum amount levels specified below.

Project Appropriation Requests shall be issued as follows:

1. Capital:

Projects with a unit cost equal to or more than the unit cost in the following schedule shall be covered by a Project Appropriation Request; items with lesser unit costs shall be expensed.

Land improvements and buildings	$1,000
Machinery and equipment	500
Tools, patterns, dies, and jigs	250
Office furniture and office machines	100

2. Expense:

Expenses of an unusual or extraordinary character which do not lend themselves to inclusion in the operating budget and could normally be expected to occur less than once per year shall be covered by a Project Appropriation Request.

The minimum amount at which a Project Appropriation Request for expense is required is $10,000, the point at which the approval of a group vice president is required. Division managers may establish minimum limits for their respective divisions.

Approval limits of corporate officers

Officers at various management levels within Midland-Ross had the authority to approve a division's formal request for funds to carry out a project subject to the maximum limitations shown below.

Approvals:

Requests shall be processed from a lower approval level to a higher approval level in accordance with the chart below to secure the approving authorities' initials (and date approved) signifying approval. Lower approvals shall be completed in advance of submission to a higher level.

	Highest Approval Level Required
Expense projects:	
Minimum up to $10,000	Division manager
$10,000 up to $20,000	Group vice president
$20,000 up to $50,000	Corporate president
$50,000 and over	Board of directors
Capital projects:	
Minimum up to $5,000	Division manager
$ 5,000 up to $10,000	Group vice president
$10,000 up to $50,000	Corporate president
$50,000 and over	Board of directors

Expense and capital combinations:

Required approvals shall be the higher approved level required for either the capital or expense section in accordance with the above limits. For example, a project consisting of $8,000 expense and $8,000 capital would require the approval of a group vice president.

Project Appropriation Request

The formal financial analysis required in a request for funds was called a Project Appropriation Request (PAR). The format of a PAR is shown in

Exhibit 3. The key output factors in the analysis (which included the amount of the total appropriation, the discounted cash flow rate of return on the investment, and the payback period) are summarized on the opening page under "Financial Summary" for easy reference.

The PAR originated at the divisional level and circulated to the officers whose signatures were necessary to authorize the expenditure. If the project was large enough to require the approval of an officer higher than the division manager, then five other men in the corporate financial group also reviewed the proposal. This group included the controller, the tax manager, the director of financial planning, the treasurer, and the vice president of finance. These men did not review very small projects, however, since capital items under $5,000 never reached the corporate office. Division managers could authorize these small projects on their own signature.

Project Evaluation Report

On each PAR, the corporate controller had the option of indicating whether or not he desired a Project Evaluation Report (PER). When requested, the division manager submitted this report one year after the approved project was completed. The report indicated how well the project was performing in relation to its original cost, return on investment (ROI), and payback estimates.

The stream of PARs reaching the corporate office

During 1966, Midland-Ross approved 144 PARs calling for the expenditure of more than $46 million. Exhibits 4, 5, and 6 show a breakdown of these authorizations by (*a*) month of approval, (*b*) project size, and (*c*) the name of the division receiving the expenditure authorization.

A sample evaluation made in 1966 of some of the projects which the board of directors had approved in earlier years is reproduced as Exhibit 7.

THE INFORMAL ASPECTS OF CAPITAL BUDGETING

Pre-selling large projects

In discussing capital budgeting at Midland-Ross, Mr. David E. Walbert, president, stated that the largest projects, involving more than a million dollars, were almost always discussed informally between the president, the group vice president, and the division manager at least a year before a formal PAR was submitted. He said:

> Let's look at a project involving a facilities expansion. The need for a new plant addition in most of our business areas doesn't sneak up on you. It can be foreseen at least a couple of years in advance. An enormous amount of work is involved in submitting a detailed economic proposal for something like a new plant. Architects have to draft plans, proposed sites have to be outlined, and construction lead times need to be established. No division manager would submit

a complete request for a new facilities addition without first getting an informal green light that such a proposal could receive favorable attention. By the time a formal PAR is completed on a large plant addition, most of us are pretty well sold on the project.

Scrutinizing a PAR at the presidential level

In response to the question, "What are the most significant items that you look at when a new PAR lands on your desk?" Mr. Walbert responded as follows:

The size of the project is probably the first thing that I look at. Obviously, I won't spend much time on a $15,000 request for a new fork-lift truck from a division manager with an annual sales volume of $50 million.

I'd next look at the type of project we're dealing with to get a feel for the degree of certainty in the rate of return calculation. I feel a whole lot more comfortable with a *cost reduction* project promising a 20% return than I would with a *volume expansion* project which promises the same rate of return. Cost reduction is usually an engineering problem. You know exactly how much a new machine will cost and you can be fairly certain about how many man-hours will be saved. On a volume expansion you're betting on a marketing estimate and maybe the date for getting a plant on stream. These are fairly uncertain variables.

On a new product appropriation, things get even worse. Here you're betting on both price and volume estimates, and supporting data can get awfully thin. Over all I think our cost reduction projects have probably yielded higher returns and have been less risky than either plant expansion or new product proposals. They don't, of course, eat up anything like the amount of capital that the other two types of projects can require.

The third and perhaps most important item that I look for is the name of the division manager who sent the project up. We've got men at the top and at the bottom of the class just like any organization. If I get a project from a man who has been with the company for a few years, who has turned a division around, or shown that he has a better command of his business than anyone else in his industry, then I'll usually go with his judgment. If his business is going to pot, however, I may take a long hard look, challenge a lot of the assumptions, and ask for more justification.

Fourth, I look at the ROI figure. If the project is a large one, I have the finance people massage the numbers to see what happens to the ROI if some of the critical variables like volume, prices, and costs are varied. This is an area where knowing your division manager is enormously important. Some men, particularly those with a sales background, may be very optimistic on volume projections. In this kind of situation you feel more comfortable if you can knock the volume down 25% and still see a reasonable return.

Strategic capital investments

Mr. Walbert later commented on a question regarding the role of capital budgeting in overall corporate strategy.

In general we'll invest our capital in those business areas that promise the highest return. Usually you can't afford to establish a position in a market on just the hope that a return will materialize in the future. Du Pont can afford to invest $75 million in a new fiber like Qiana, but Midland-Ross can't. We can afford to invest a few million dollars in projects of this nature—and we have in areas like continuous casting, iron ore pelletizing, and polyester tire cord—but most of our projects have to promise a prompt return.

A group vice president looks at capital budgeting

Mr. Kenneth Selby, a group vice president of Midland-Ross, answered a number of questions about capital budgeting.

Ideas which may result in projects arise at all levels within the division, right down to the machine operator. Each plant manager has an "improvement book" in which employees are asked to suggest ideas which might reduce costs. The plant or division manager, of course, usually suggests the really large projects, although the ideas may have originated in plant engineering or sales.

Anywhere from a month to several years might elapse between conception of a new project idea and its approval. The smaller ones get through very rapidly. Larger projects with low returns sometimes bounce around for quite a while. I'd venture to say that 75% to 80% of all the projects needing approval at higher than the division manager level ultimately get through. For different divisions this percentage might vary considerably.

Most of the PARs that fail to get approval in my group don't get past me. I have a pretty good feel for what Dave [the president] will buy. If I know he won't accept a project, I usually send it back. For instance, one of my plant managers wants a new conference room, but I wouldn't consider submitting this for Dave's approval now, when business in our group is soft. We'll talk again about a new conference room when we've had a couple of fat years back to back. Very few of the projects that I approve are turned down by Dave, and I don't remember a single PAR that Dave has approved in the last three years that has been rejected at the board of directors level.

Mr. Selby then answered a question regarding the growth of various divisions.

It's a fact that some of the Midland-Ross divisions throw off more cash than they can reinvest at attractive returns. While other rapidly growing divisions gain the benefit of this cash generation, I don't feel that this creates any problems between divisions. For one thing, all of the corporation's cash collections flow into four lock-boxes located at banks throughout the country. The division managers get funds transferred to them only as they are needed for payrolls and payables. They never actually remit an annual check to corporate headquarters for the difference between their cash generation and their internal cash needs.

A realistic appraisal of the corporation's markets may indicate that it is difficult for a particular division to grow very much. Where this is true, the division manager can concentrate on accomplishing his mission at the lowest possible cost to yield the greatest profit. Sometimes this role can be frustrating.

In response to a question about the division manager's approval limits on capital expenditures, Mr. Selby commented: "I feel that the people running divisions with 30 and 40 and 50 million dollars in sales should be able to approve projects involving substantially more than $5,000."

Capital budgeting from the division level

Frank Linsalata had worked on a number of special assignments at both the corporate and the division levels at Midland-Ross. He commented on capital budgeting viewed from the division level:

Sometimes the numbers in a PAR strongly reflect a division manager's desire to get a project approved. If a project idea looks really great in terms of product line extension, market penetration, or a new business area, but the numbers just don't seem to justify it on the first ROI calculation, there's a strong inclination to play with the numbers. Sometimes the project is actually worked up backwards. You start with an ROI and see what volume, price, or cost change is needed to meet the ROI target. The division manager then sees if he can live with the resulting projections. If they're clearly out of line, the project is killed. If the division manager feels he might be able to meet the projection, however, and he wants the project badly enough, he'll usually go with the new set of numbers.

Somehow 15% has sort of gotten to be the magic number for ROIs on large projects at Midland-Ross, although it has never been mentioned as a cutoff rate and lower projects have been approved. Many of the division managers seem to hit near this number in any case. If their original estimates led to a lower project ROI, they may have followed the procedure I just outlined in order to raise it. If their original estimates led to a much higher ROI, however, they might lower the projections a little to give them a cushion as insurance. There is a fair amount of gamesmanship in capital budgeting.

Exhibit 1

MIDLAND-ROSS CORPORATION (A)

DIVISIONS OF MIDLAND-ROSS

Capitol Foundry

Cast alloy steel grinding balls; volume or job-lot production of gray, white, and nickel-chrome iron; chrome-molybdenum and austenitic-manganese steel castings.

IRC Fibers

Tyrex rayon tire yarns, cords, and fabrics; high tenacity rayon yarns, plied yarns, cords (adhesive-treated and untreated) for mechanical rubber goods; rayon textile yarns; rayon staple fiber; polyester tire yarn, cord, and fabric.

Janitrol Aero

Heat transfer equipment for aircraft and missiles; electronic cooling equipment; pneumatic, hydraulic, and cryogenic controls; high pressure couplings and duct supports; liquid heaters for ground support; aircraft and portable heaters; gas turbine combustion systems; gas turbine accessories; hot fuel priming units.

Janitrol

Heating and air conditioning equipment for residential, commercial, and industrial applications, including gas and oil-fired furnaces, unit heaters, gas conversion burners, gas and oil-fired boilers, central air conditioning systems, electric/gas year-round heat/cool packages, rooftop heating and cooling units, electric heat pumps, makeup air heaters.

Midland Frame

Passenger car, truck, and bus chassis frames; miscellaneous stampings and weldments.

National Castings

Couplers, draft gears, car trucks, cushioned underframes for railroad, mine, and industrial haulage systems; malleable, pearlitic malleable steel castings for metalworking industries.

Power Controls

Air-brake systems; vacuum power brake systems; power controls; electro-pneumatic door controls; air compressors; air actuating cylinders; emergency relay valves; zinc and aluminum die castings.

Ross Engineering

"Engineered Atmospheres" for processing, drying or curing pulp, paper, rubber, chemicals, food, textiles, wood and wood products, et al.; coil processing and metal decorating lines; textile dryers and curing machinery; air heaters; fume incinerators; web conditioners; dryer drainage systems; SUPERTHERM high temperature hot fluid heating systems.

Steel City

Switch, outlet, and floor boxes; conduit and cable fittings; hangers and supports; metal framing systems for conduit lighting and electrical equipment; slotted angle.

Surface Combustion

Industrial burners; heat-treat furnaces; heat-processing equipment for glass and ceramics; steel mill equipment; process and comfort air dehumidification and bacterial removal systems; continuous dryers; iron pelletizing and reducing equipment and plants; gas generators for metallurgical, food, and chemical applications.

Waldron-Hartig

Machinery for paper, film, foil, and textile coating, converting, laminating, embossing, and treating; metal coil coating and processing lines; plastics extruders, blow molding machinery, and film and sheeting lines; power transmission couplings.

Webster Engineering

Gas and oil burners for boilers in large buildings and industry; FANDAIRE air-cooled condensers, condensing units, and chillers.

Midland-Ross of Canada, Ltd.
Power Controls
Ross of Canada
Surface Combustion

Products similar to those of the Power Controls, Ross Engineering, and Surface Combustion Divisions in the United States.

MIDLAND-ROSS CORPORATION (A)

Ten-Year Summary of Financial Data

(Dollar figures in millions except for per share data)

	1957	1958	1959	1960	1961	1962	1963	1964	1965	1966
OPERATIONS										
Sales:										
Automotive and transportation	$ 76.4	$49.7	$56.8	$ 41.3	$ 57.8	$ 73.2	$ 80.9	$ 82.5	$ 94.2	$102.6
Capital goods	30.0	26.0	27.5	54.3	42.7	48.2	47.3	65.1	94.8	125.7
Building and construction	—	—	2.7	14.2	12.4	18.3	31.2	33.4	34.5	33.5
Railroad	—	—	—	—	—	—	—	—	39.6	42.7
Consumer goods	—	—	—	—	16.5	15.0	14.9	16.2	18.7	18.0
Aerospace and defense	0.9	0.7	1.8	8.3	8.3	11.6	15.7	13.9	14.3	21.6
Total	$107.3	$76.3	$88.7	$118.1	$137.6	$166.3	$190.1	$211.1	$296.1	$344.1
Net income	5.5	3.0	4.0	3.9	5.5	5.9	7.6	8.7	14.1	17.6
Depreciation and amortization of intangibles	1.4	1.5	1.7	2.3	4.3	4.6	5.2	5.1	6.9	7.4
Cash funds generated*	6.2	3.8	4.9	5.5	9.0	9.8	12.0	14.0	19.8	24.1
Federal income taxes	6.9	3.1	3.0	4.8	3.2	6.1	8.2	8.5	12.5	16.6
Profit margin	12.8%	10.0%	10.7%	9.6%	7.4%	9.1%	10.5%	9.8%	10.7%	11.4%
Depreciation rate	5.4	5.4	5.0	6.3	4.5	4.7	4.8	4.5	4.7	4.7
Earned on total capital	12.6	8.1	7.8	9.3	5.3	6.3	7.8	9.1	10.4	12.1
Earned on common equity	18.4	8.9	14.3	13.2	5.3	6.5	8.2	9.7	12.6	13.7
COMMON STOCK										
Net income per share†‡	$ 1.73	$ 0.82	$ 1.18	$ 1.16	$ 0.84	$ 0.97	$ 1.47	$ 1.82	$ 2.66	$ 3.33
Dividends per share†	0.94	0.79	0.75	0.75	0.75	0.75	0.75	0.85	0.95	1.22
Cash funds generated per share*†‡	2.29	1.38	1.78	2.01	1.60	1.85	2.57	2.96	4.15	4.90
Net tangible book value—per share†	8.95	9.02	8.06	8.60	15.86	17.00	17.64	18.63	20.70	22.52
Market price†	13–8	10–8	15–9	15–12	13–11	14–10	16–12	19–15	26–18	30–22
Dividend payout ratio	47%	65%	49%	47%	49%	45%	33%	31%	28%	31%
Average annual price-earnings ratio	6.5	12.1	10.3	11.5	15.1	11.3	10.5	10.3	8.2	7.9
Average annual dividend yield	8.4%	7.9%	6.2%	5.6%	5.8%	6.0%	4.9%	4.6%	4.4%	4.7%
Number of shareholders	5,975	5,800	5,875	6,075	13,125	12,165	11,750	12,725	12,750	15,150
FINANCIAL POSITION										
Working capital	$ 26.9	$22.5	$28.7	$ 29.0	$ 58.6	$ 47.4	$ 50.1	$ 49.3	$ 69.4	$ 70.2
Net property, plant, and equipment	15.6	16.0	23.1	22.5	42.4	43.8	44.6	49.3	66.6	72.4
Long-term debt	4.3	—	16.5	15.0	—	—	—	13.5	9.0	7.9
Preferred and common shareholders' equity	39.6	39.5	40.5	41.6	105.6	96.5	100.6	91.9	134.2	142.3
Additions to property, plant, and equipment	1.8	1.9	1.3	1.6	1.4	2.5	3.2	9.9	9.1	14.4
Number of employees	5,000	4,400	6,000	5,500	8,000	8,500	9,000	9,300	14,000	14,600

* Net income and provisions for depreciation, amortization of intangibles, and deferred income taxes, less preferred dividends.
† Adjusted for 2 for 1 splits in 1964 and 1966.
‡ Calculated on average number of shares outstanding during the year.
Figures have not been adjusted for years prior to mergers consummated in 1961 and 1965.

Exhibit 3

MIDLAND-ROSS CORPORATION (A)
PROJECT APPROPRIATION REQUEST

NUMBER-SUPPLEMENT

Division: Power Controls	Department	Location

Title: Disc Brake Manufacturing Facility

Profit Improvement	Necessity	Predicted Life	Underrun	Overrun	Starting Date	Completion Date
X		15 Years			July 1967	April 1969

1. DESCRIPTION AND JUSTIFICATION

The U.S. automotive industry is experiencing a trend to the use of disc braking systems for passenger cars and light trucks. Our market research indicates this type of braking system will be widespread within 5 years and the Power Controls Division can be a major supplier of these systems if we act now to provide the required manufacturing facilities.

2. FINANCIAL SUMMARY

	This Request	Previous Approved Requests	Total Project
Capital	4,875,000	———	4,875,000
Working Capital	1,950,000		1,950,000
Expense	975,000		975,000
Total	7,800,000		7,800,000
Less Salvage Value of Disposals			
Net			
Book Value of Disposals			
Project Budgeted Amount			7,800,000
Return on Investment (after Tax)			16%
Period to Amortize (after Tax)			3.6 Years

Approval and Distribution of Copies

Division	Date	No.	Corporate	Date	No.
Issued By			Group V.P.		
			Group V.P.		
			Controller		
			Tax Manager		
			Mgr. Fin. Planning		
			Treasurer		
			Financial V.P.		
Division Controller			President		
Division Manager			For the Board		

Accounting Distribution	Project Evaluation Report Required	Yes	No

Estimated Timing of Expenditures – By Quarter and Year

3/67	4/67	1/68	2/68	3/68	4/68	1/69	2/69
$ 75,000	$125,000	$1,125,000	$1,500,000	$1,500,000	$1,875,000	$ 900,000	$ 700,000

Exhibit 3—Continued

NUMBER-SUPPLEMENT

3. DETAIL COST

Item No.	Description	Material	Labor	Purchases	Total	Class *
	Capital					
	175,000 sq. ft. Bldg.				$1,750,000	
	Office Equipment			75,000	75,000	
	Machinery & Equipment			3,050,000	3,050,000	
	Total				4,875,000	
	Expense					
	Tooling				750,000	
	Rigging, etc.				225,000	
	Total				975,000	
	Grand Total					

* Class Codes: C–Capital and E–Expense

Exhibit 3—Continued

4. DETAIL OPERATING MARGIN CHANGES

Estimated Production Date	Calendar Year Income or (Loss) $000's														
	1969	1970	1971	1972	1973	1974	1975	1976	1977	1978	1979	1980	1981	1982	1983
Volume (unit sold 000's)	125	300	300	300	300	300	300	300	300	300	300	300	300	300	300
Sales @ $32.48/unit	4,060	9,744	9,744	9,744	9,744	9,744	9,744	9,744	9,744	9,744	9,744	9,744	9,744	9,744	9,744
Manufacturing Cost:															
Direct Material															
Direct Labor - Actual															
Manufacturing Expenses:															
Indirect Labor															
Maintenance Labor															
Fringe Benefits	3,035	6,768	6,901	7,006	7,107	7,162	7,184	7,190	7,198	7,199	7,380	7,563	7,399	7,397	7,090
Maintenance Material															
Tools															
Supplies															
Depreciation: (Building)	78	74	71	68	65	62	60	57	54	52	49	47	45	43	41
Depreciation: (Equipment)	521	434	362	301	251	209	174	174	174	174	174	174			
Total Mfg. Expense															
Permanent Tooling Amortization															
Total Manufacturing Cost															
Other Cost:															
Outbound Transportation															
G & A Expense:															
Warehousing															
Engineering															
Advertising															
Selling															
Administration															
Other Income & Deductions															
Startup	345														
Total Other Cost															
Total Cost	3,979	7,276	7,334	7,375	7,423	7,433	7,418	7,421	7,426	7,425	7,603	7,784	7,444	7,440	7,131
Operating Margin before Tax	81	2,468	2,410	2,369	2,321	2,311	2,326	2,323	2,318	2,319	2,141	1,960	2,300	2,304	2,613
Operating Margin after Tax	42	1,284	1,253	1,232	1,207	1,202	1,209	1,208	1,206	1,206	1,113	1,019	1,196	1,198	1,359
Depreciation	599	508	433	369	316	271	234	231	228	226	224	222	45	43	41
Permanent Tool Amortization															
Total Cash Return	641	1,792	1,686	1,601	1,523	1,473	1,443	1,439	1,434	1,432	1,337	1,241	1,241	1,241	1,400

Exhibit 3—Continued

NUMBER-SUPPLEMENT

5. PERIOD TO AMORTIZE ENTIRE PROJECT

A. PORTION CHARGEABLE TO CAPITAL	X	(100% - INVESTMENT CREDIT)	=	NET OUTLAY
$ 3,125,000 Eqpt.	X	(100% - 7 %)	=	$ 2,906,250
1,750,000 Bldg.	X	(100% - %)	=	1,750,000
	X	(100% - %)	=	
B. PORTION CHARGEABLE TO EXPENSE	X	(100% - FEDERAL INCOME TAX %)		
$ 975,000	X	(100% - 48 %)	=	507,000
C. TOTAL NET OUTLAY (A PLUS B)			=	$ 5,163,250
D. PERIOD TO AMORTIZE PROJECT - PAYOUT PERIOD (NUMBER OF YEARS FOR THE TOTAL CASH RETURN PER SECTION 4 TO EQUAL THE TOTAL NET OUTLAY OR TOTAL C)			=	3.6 YEARS

6. RETURN ON INVESTMENT - DISCOUNTED CASH FLOW METHOD

E. CAPITAL	$ 4,875,000
F. EXPENSE	975,000
G. WORKING CAPITAL CHANGES - RECEIVABLES, INVENTORIES, AND CONTRACTS	1,950,000
H. TOTAL INVESTMENT - SUM OF E. F. AND G	$ 7,800,000
I. RETURN ON INVESTMENT - AFTER TAX (CALCULATED PER SECTION 7, AND INTERPOLATED TO NEAREST PERCENT)	16 %

Exhibit 3—Continued

7. PRESENT VALUE OF CASH FLOWS

NUMBER-SUPPLEMENT

YEAR	YEAR OF OPER-ATION	DISBURSEMENTS	CASH RETURNS	15% TRIAL INTEREST RATE			16% TRIAL INTEREST RATE			% TRIAL INTEREST RATE		
				Factor	PRESENT WORTH Disbursements	PRESENT WORTH Cash Returns	Factor	PRESENT WORTH Disbursements	PRESENT WORTH Cash Returns	Factor	PRESENT WORTH Disbursements	PRESENT WORTH Cash Returns
1967	2 Prior	200					1.346	269				
1968	1 Prior	6,000	218				1.160	6,960	253			
← Beginning of Operations →												
1969	At 1	1,600	468	1.000		xxxxxxxxxxxx	1.000	1,132	xxxxxxxxxxxx	1.000		xxxxxxxxxxxx
1969	1		641		xxxxxxxxxxxx		.862	xxxxxxxxxxxx	553		xxxxxxxxxxxx	
	2		1,792				.743		1,331			
	3		1,686				.641		1,081			
	4		1,601				.552		884			
	5		1,523				.476		725			
	6		1,473				.410		604			
	7		1,443				.354		511			
	8		1,439				.305		439			
	9		1,434				.263		377			
	10		1,432				.227		325			
	11		1,337				.195		261			
	12		1,241				.168		208			
	13		1,241				.145		180			
	14		1,241				.125		155			
	15		1,400				.108		151			
	15	Return Work Cap.	1,950				.108		210			
	15	Residual Plant	885				.108		96			
	18											
	19											
	20											
	21											
	22											
	23											
	24											
	25											
	26											
	27											
	28											
	29											
	30											
TOTALS		7,800	24,445					8,361	8,344			
CASH RETURNS LESS DISBURSEMENTS		xxxxxxxxxxxx			xxxxxxxxxxxx			xxxxxxxxxxxx	(17)		xxxxxxxxxxxx	
DISBURSEMENTS / CASH RETURNS		xxxxxxxxxxxx			xxxxxxxxxxxx			xxxxxxxxxxxx	1.0		xxxxxxxxxxxxx	

Exhibit 4

MIDLAND-ROSS CORPORATION (A)
PARs Approved During 1966 by Month of Approval
(Dollar figures in thousands)

Month of 1966	*Capital Amount*	*Expense Amount*	*Number of Projects Approved*
January	$ 34	$ 17	2
February	3,150	700	13
March	6,000	650	20
April	2,100	530	14
May	370	40	11
June	2,350	60	23
July	25	—	4
August	1,450	690	11
September	2,680	140	14
October	200	38	12
November	1,500	51	8
December	23,400	50	12
	$43,259	$2,966	144

$46,225,000/144 = $321,000

Exhibit 5

MIDLAND-ROSS CORPORATION (A)
PARs Approved during 1966 by Size Groups

Size Class of Projects	*Number of Projects Approved in Size Class*	*Cumulative Number of Projects under Maximum Class Limit*
Less than $ 10,000	20	20
$ 10,000–$ 15,000	24	44
$ 15,001–$ 20,000	23	67
$ 20,001–$ 25,000	7	74
$ 25,001–$ 30,000	11	85
$ 30,001–$ 40,000	9	94
$ 40,001–$ 50,000	12	106
$ 50,001–$ 100,000	12	118
$ 100,001–$ 200,000	10	128
$ 200,001–$ 500,000	4	132
$ 500,001–$1,000,000	3	135
$1,000,001–$2,000,000	5	140
Over $2,000,000	4	144

Median project = $25,000

Exhibit 6

MIDLAND-ROSS CORPORATION (A)
PARs Approved during 1966 by Division Originating Requests

Division	*Total Value of Projects Approved (In Thousands)*	*Total Number of Projects Approved*
Surface Combustion	$ 1,000	6
Power Controls	9,500	13
National Castings	8,000	40
IRC Fibers	2,300	28
Ross Engineering	50	2
Waldron-Hartig	650	6
Steel City	600	10
Janitrol Aero	250	7
Janitrol Heating	75	4
Webster	100	2
Capitol Foundry	500	6
Frame	23,200	20
	$46,225	144

Exhibit 7

MIDLAND-ROSS CORPORATION (A)
SUMMARY OF SELECTED PROJECT EVALUATION REPORTS, AUGUST, 1966

Project Number	Description	Division	Date Approved	Project Amount		Rate of Return		Payback Period Years	
				Forecast	*Actual*	*Forecast*	*Actual*	*Forecast*	*Actual*
FA–157	Roll Forming Mill	Frame	1/65	$193 M	$193 M	37%	42%	2.5	2.3
FA–151	Univ. Paint Mach. Unloader	Frame	7/64	98	43	>30	>30	2.6	1.6
FA–147	Loading Equip. '65 Buick	Frame	7/64	80	79	29	29	3.1	3.3
D 53–63	Phenolic Molding Equip.	IRC	9/63	54	49	75	35	1.5	2.0
P 352–51	"V" Band Couplings Program	Jan. Aero	8/63	58	90	>30	Loss	0.7	Loss
P 328–29	New Gas Furnace Line	Jan.–Cols.	6/61	495	491	>50	43 est.	1.0	1.7 est.
P–532	Aluminum Die Cast Equip.	Power Cont.	5/64	86	86	>30	>30	2.2	2.0
P–547	(2) W–S #1 AC Chuckers	Power Cont.	7/64	66	66	>30	>30	2.0	1.4
64–129–C	(2) W–S Chuckers	Waldron-Hartig	12/64	116	114	12	Loss	5.5	Loss
62–MR–A2	Acquisition Yuba-Aimco	Webster	12/61	425	474	n.a	11 est.	n.a.	2.8 est.

MIDLAND-ROSS CORPORATION (B)

In mid-1966, top management of the Midland-Ross Corporation was considering a $30,500,000 capital budget proposal which would carry one of the company's divisions into the production of polyester fiber. Through its IRC division, the company was already heavily involved in the production of rayon fiber for tire cord, but this market was rapidly shrinking because of competitive inroads made by both nylon and polyester. An entry into polyester fiber, then, might allow Midland-Ross to preserve its market position in tire cord, and also move the company into the production of polyester fiber for other end uses.

BACKGROUND INFORMATION ON MIDLAND-ROSS CORPORATION

[Background information on the Midland-Ross Corporation, including its decentralized divisional organization, its growth and diversification through acquisitions, and a 10-year summary of its performance, has been given in the text and in Exhibit 2 of the (A) case, pp. 376–93.]

As noted in the (A) case, in the spring of 1961 the Midland-Ross Corporation merged with the Industrial Rayon Corporation (IRC) by exchanging two shares of Midland-Ross common stock for five shares of IRC common stock. The market value of the Midland-Ross stock involved in this transaction was $38.6 million. At the time of the merger IRC had working capital equal to $41.3 million (more than half of which was in cash and short-term marketable securities), no long-term debt, and property, plant, and equipment with book value equal to $23.9 million. From 1958 through 1960, IRC had average yearly sales of $53 million, and average pretax losses of $3.3 million. Almost all of IRC's sales consisted of rayon fiber, and more than 60% of these sales consisted of rayon tire cord used in the manufacture of automobile tires. At the time of the merger, IRC was the third largest U.S. producer of rayon and the future of this fiber was extremely uncertain.

BACKGROUND INFORMATION ON THE RAYON INDUSTRY

The U.S. rayon[1] industry was born when the American Viscose Corporation (AVC), then a wholly owned subsidiary of Courtaulds, Ltd., began pro-

[1] Rayon is a glossy fiber made by forcing a viscous solution of modified cellulose (wood pulp) through minute holes and drying the resulting filaments.

duction in 1910.[2] The industry grew very rapidly and was extremely profitable during its first 20 years of growth (see Table 1). Thanks to a patented process, AVC enjoyed a 100% share of the domestic rayon market until 1920. Once AVC's original patents expired, however, many other firms including Du Pont and Celanese entered the rayon market, reducing AVC's share to 73% by 1924; to 44% by 1931; and to 26% by 1949.

Table 1

AVERAGE ANNUAL INVESTMENT AND RATE OF RETURN FOR THE DOMESTIC RAYON INDUSTRY, 1915–40

Year	Total Average Annual Investment (In Millions)	Rate of Return %	Year	Total Average Annual Investment (In Millions)	Rate of Return %
1915	$ 7.8	26.3	1928	$208.9	24.5
1916	8.5	109.2	1929	241.5	18.1
1917	14.1	96.0	1930	260.0	5.0
1918	21.5	69.5	1931	247.5	3.4
1919	30.5	97.0	1932	235.9	1.5
1920	40.7	64.2	1933	251.7	12.2
1921	51.2	42.0	1934	260.4	6.9
1922	66.0	50.1	1935	265.8	6.7
1923	89.1	43.2	1936	277.3	11.5
1924	110.6	26.7	1937	292.1	12.1
1925	143.7	30.6	1938	309.2	2.5
1926	163.1	20.1	1939	305.6	N.A.
1927	170.6	25.8	1940	308.8	N.A.

Source of data: J. W. Markham, *Competition in the Rayon Industry* (Cambridge, Mass.: Harvard University Press, 1952), p. 227.

Spectacular early success in rayon

AVC's initial venture into the U.S. rayon market was enormously successful. "Starting with an initial investment by Courtaulds of only $930,000, the company has financed its rapid expansion completely out of earnings. In 24 years the company's aggregate net profits amounted to $354,000,000, or 38,000 percent of original investment. . . . The ratio of net profits to its sales . . . was 35 percent. *Fortune* has commented, 'American Viscose, modest, secretive, and unknown, is one of the industrial miracles of our times, a phenomenon comparable to Standard Oil, or the automobile empire of Henry Ford.' "[3]

Failure to respond to environmental change

Rayon began to falter in the early 1950's as other synthetics such as nylon and acrylic became popular. Style shifts also made cotton more attractive, forcing volume and production cutbacks in rayon. By the end of the 1950's many companies, including Du Pont, had left the rayon business entirely. In

[2] Jesse W. Markham, *Competition in the Rayon Industry* (Cambridge, Mass.: Harvard University Press, 1952), p. 16.

[3] *Ibid.*

1966, *Forbes* magazine was stating, "Today . . . [AVC] is a corporate shell in the process of liquidation. What is left of its business is now the subsidiary of another company. For the men who tied their careers and their investments to it, the company was a disappointment."[4]

While AVC was the most spectacular example of a rayon producer in trouble, the Industrial Rayon Corporation (the third largest U.S. producer of rayon) was also experiencing great difficulty in the late 1950's. The principal source of this difficulty could be directly traced to the declining use of rayon in automobile tire cord.

Use of rayon in tire cord slipping

Rayon had first been used in tire construction as a replacement for cotton cord in 1940. The use of rayon in tire manufacture reached an annual peak around 1955.[5] With the advent of nylon cord, rayon's market share in tire cord began to decline. Between 1955 and 1960, rayon's share of the total tire cord market dropped from 86% to 64% and the total poundage of rayon so used dropped 38% (see Table 2).

Table 2

CONSUMPTION OF TIRE CORD
(In millions)

	Rayon		Nylon		Cotton		Total
Year	*Pounds*	*Market Share*	*Pounds*	*Market Share*	*Pounds*	*Market Share*	*Pounds*
1947....	214.6	43%	n.a.	—	285.1	57%	499.7
1950....	297.0	64	n.a.	—	165.4	36	462.4
1955....	406.9	86	49.2	10%	16.7	4	472.8
1956....	343.0	83	58.6	14	10.6	3	412.2
1957....	318.5	77	83.2	20	10.3	3	412.0
1958....	253.0	71	97.9	27	7.1	2	358.0
1959....	287.1	70	120.3	29	3.9	1	411.2
1960....	251.3	64	138.1	35	3.1	1	392.5

Sources: 1947–55: U.S. Bureau of the Census, *Statistical Abstract of the United States–1967* (Washington, D.C.: U.S. Government Printing Office), p. 761; 1956–60: Industrial Rayon Corporation, Proxy Statement, March 28, 1961, p. 6.

Reducing IRC's dependence on tire cord

Over the period 1961–66, IRC, a division of Midland-Ross since 1961, performed profitably, though not satisfactorily in the latter years, as shown below:

	Sales Index of IRC Fibers Division	*Pretax Profit as a % of Sales*
1961....................	100	6%
1962....................	100	8
1963....................	112	10
1964....................	115	9
1965....................	118	7
1966....................	124	4

[4] "And Then There Was One," *Forbes*, January 15, 1966, p. 20.

[5] C. A. Litzler, "The Fluid Tire Cord Situation," *Modern Textiles Magazine*, September, 1966, p. 20.

The use of rayon in tire cord continued to decline during this period; and in an effort to reduce the division's dependence on this product, in 1964 Midland-Ross invested $8 million in a facility to produce high-wet modulus rayon staple fiber,[6] which was used principally in wearing apparel. At the time this project was proposed, the selling price of the fiber was between 44 and 45 cents a pound. IRC management felt that the price would decline to about 36 cents a pound within five years and stabilize there. At this reduced price level, the plant addition promised a five-year payback.

According to Mr. David E. Walbert, president of Midland-Ross:

> IRC had process problems during the first year after the facility opened. These problems cut heavily into the division's profits. We also had some problem in getting the textile manufacturers to switch to our fiber. The textile people won't switch to the fiber of a new manufacturer until it's been thoroughly tested and evaluated. This testing is a costly and time-consuming process.
>
> By the beginning of the second year after the plant was completed, the selling price of high-wet modulus rayon was down to 26 cents a pound.
>
> Man-made fiber manufacture is a continuous process production operation. You run the plants 24 hours a day, 7 days a week. The production costs are such that you have to run at close to capacity to make any profit. If you cut back production very far, you might as well shut down entirely. We had a choice. If you cut production, your unit costs skyrocket; if you keep producing, your inventories skyrocket. With us it was a question of whether we might be better off shutting the plant down completely until prices firmed. We finally decided to keep it running, and made staple fiber until it was coming out of our ears. Prices are firming now, but although we've had three price rises in the last 9 months, they are still not up to 36 cents a pound.

In 1966, IRC was still heavily dependent on rayon tire cord as the principal source of its business. During 1965, total industry production of rayon tire cord amounted to 210 million pounds. This production was "split very roughly equally by Industrial Rayon Division of Midland-Ross Corp.—25%; American Viscose Corp. Division of FMC—30%; Beaunit Mills—23%; and American Enka—23%."[7]

A threat to rayon tire cord's last remaining market

By 1966, the only real market remaining for rayon tire cord was the original equipment tire[8] market. Of the 210 million pounds of rayon tire cord used for all classes of tires in 1965, about 150 million pounds went into the 50 million passenger car tires required by the original equipment manufacturers (OEMs). The OEMs had purchased rayon cord tires almost exclusively through 1965, but nylon started to break into this market when the Chevrolet Division of General Motors Corporation indicated in 1966 that it would provide tires with nylon cord on 1968 models. "The use of . . . nylon for

---

[6] Staple fiber is "short length" fiber (approximately 1 to 1½ inches) such as is found in cotton balls.

[7] Litzler, *op. cit.*, p. 19.

[8] Original equipment tires are purchased from tire manufacturers and placed on new cars by automobile manufacturers.

Chevrolet production for this first year could mean a market of approximately 10,000,000 tires. . . ."[9]

If rayon cord were ultimately displaced from OEM passenger car tires, the rayon industry stood to lose approximately 150 million pounds of its market. As this last market started to switch, rayon producers would find it increasingly difficult to remain price competitive with nylon.

> The nylon producers may be in a position . . . to further reduce the price of their material. However, the rayon producers most probably will not be in a position to do the same because of the decrease . . . in usage of their materials.[10]
>
> Du Pont recently pointed to acetate yarn as an example of a fiber having passed the low point in raw material price and already having capitalized fully on the lower cost attainable through very large scale of production. . . . This may also be the case for rayon staple fiber.[11]

Polyester—the tire cord to displace nylon by 1970

While nylon was rapidly replacing rayon as the principal fiber in tire cord, a new fiber, polyester,[12] was becoming important. Five million pounds of this fiber were used in 1963 by tire manufacturers, 19 million pounds was the estimated use in 1966, and a Goodyear spokesman predicted that over 100 million pounds would be used in tire cord by 1970.[13]

Polyester was considered by some to be the "third generation" man-made fiber after rayon and nylon. The fiber had shown very rapid growth in recent years (Exhibit 1). After Du Pont's polyester patent expired in July, 1961, competition rapidly appeared, prices declined, and new markets opened up to the fiber. Much of polyester's success up to 1966 was due to the enthusiasm that greeted the introduction of stay-press fabric in wearing apparel. In 1956 the total production of polyester fiber for all uses was about 20 million pounds. By 1965 polyester output reached over 400 million pounds. Du Pont was the major producer of polyester fiber, accounting for well over one half of total U.S. production.

ALTERNATIVE COURSES OF ACTION IN THE FACE OF CHANGE

In mid-1966, the management of Midland-Ross was considering alternative courses of action with regard to the IRC division. The profits of this division

---

[9] Litzler, *op. cit.*, p. 22.

[10] *Ibid.*

[11] National Advisory Commission on Food and Fiber, *Cotton and Other Fiber Problems and Policies in the United States*, Technical Papers, Vol. 2 (Washington, D.C., 1967), p. 43.

[12] Polyester (polyethylene terephthalate) is a long chain polymer formed in the condensation reaction between ethylene glycol (permanent antifreeze) and dimethyl terephthalate. Du Pont's Dacron is the best known brand of polyester fiber.

[13] *Oil, Paint and Drug Reporter*, November 21, 1966, pp. 4 and 52.

were unsatisfactory when viewed in relation to the amount of capital required to support the division. With the market for IRC's major product line facing even greater near-term difficulty than it had in the past (due to the Chevrolet decision), the company had to (1) continue realizing progressively less satisfactory returns on the assets employed in the division, or (2) commit a substantial amount of new capital to production facilities for new fibers, or (3) get out of certain areas of the rayon business.

Leaving the market

The alternative of getting out of the rayon business entirely or in part presented a problem since the physical plant of IRC was on the books of the company at a net book value of about $20 million. If this were sold substantially below book value, Midland-Ross would have to absorb a substantial nonrecurring loss on the sale, which would probably reduce the company's 1966 earnings per share below the level achieved in 1965. Although this loss would be nonrecurring, Midland-Ross management felt that investors might confuse it with a downturn in earnings from normal operations. The company was in the middle of its fifth consecutive year of earnings progress in 1966. Its stock price had been moving up steadily since 1961 in response to these earnings gains, and management was reluctant to risk this share-price progress to investor misunderstanding.

Investing in new fibers—leapfrogging nylon

While selling the IRC division was not a particularly attractive alternative, investing in facilities for producing newer fibers also raised some difficult problems. First, since nylon seemed to have already neared a peak in tire cord use, an investment in a facility to produce this fiber would be practically obsolete by the time it was completed. On the other hand, polyester had not reached the point of acceptance in tire production to justify the construction of a large new plant just to serve this segment of the polyester market. New fiber plants had to be large to be economically competitive. As a representative example, Exhibit 2 shows the variation in production costs of rayon fiber as the size of the producing plant increases. Economies of scale are clearly evident here, as they are in most chemical production processes.[14] Similar production economies could be expected in polyester fiber production. For this reason, if Midland-Ross went into the production of polyester tire cord it would be necessary to produce polyester fiber for other uses as well. This would put the company into the textile fiber business against firms such as Du Pont. Except for the venture into high-wet modulus rayon staple fiber in 1964, the company had had little contact with textile mills, and had competed directly with the large apparel fiber manufacturers such as Du Pont only to a limited extent.

---

[14] S. C. Schuman, "How Plant Size Affects Unit Costs," *Chemical Engineering*, May, 1955, pp. 173–76.

THE POLYESTER PROPOSAL

In mid-1966, Midland-Ross was considering a proposal that would carry the corporation heavily into the production of polyester fiber for tire cord and apparel fabrics.

During the period 1966–71, the project would call for an investment of $30.5 million (Exhibit 3). About $20.2 million of this amount would be used to construct a new plant for the production of polyester fiber, $5.3 million would be used for plant additions to reduce the production costs of high-wet modulus rayon fiber and expand production capacity, and $5.0 million would be added to working capital in support of the increased level of sales.

Over a period of three years, the new facility would give IRC the capacity to produce up to 50 million pounds a year of polyester fiber and resin. Ten million pounds would go into tire cord, 30 million pounds would be marketed as staple fiber in competition with firms such as Du Pont, and 10 million pounds of resin chips would be sold to other polyester fabricators.

The economics of the venture

Exhibit 4 shows the profit and cash flow projections for the first five years of the project's life. The volume and price assumptions underlying these calculations are shown at the bottom of the exhibit. Although polyester staple fiber was selling for 84 cents a pound in mid-1966, the analysis assumes that this price will have declined to 70.5 cents a pound by 1969. Exhibit 5 shows the profit, cash flow, and ROI (return on investment) projections over the 15-year life of the facility assuming that the volume and price projections of 1971 continue through 1981. The second ROI calculation assumes that all polyester selling prices decline 10% in 1972 and remain at those levels for the final 10 years of the project's life.

The competitive environment in polyester

During the months that the Midland-Ross management was mulling over the new fiber project, the competitive situation in polyester was in considerable turmoil. In late March, 1966, Du Pont announced that it would build a new polyester facility capable of producing 200 million pounds a year by the end of 1968. The plant was to be twice the size of Du Pont's two other polyester plants and was to be called the Cape Fear plant. This facility, plus other announced additions at Du Pont's other polyester plants, would raise the company's capacity in polyester fiber from 240 million pounds a year in February, 1966 (versus 456 million pounds for the industry at that date), to over 600 million pounds a year by the end of 1968. Exhibit 6 shows the production capacity of the U.S. companies producing polyester resins at February, 1966, plus the announced capacity additions due to come on stream at least by the end of 1968. The exhibit also shows the 1965 total sales volume of these companies, the other fibers they manufactured, and their average return on total capital during the period 1961–65.

In April, 1966, an article in *Chemical Week* mentioned a number of other important competitive factors in the polyester situation:[15]

> Polyester sales in '65 increased 50% over '64 and '66 growth is projected for at least 35% to 500 million lbs. Demand got out of hand last year because a 14¢/lb. price decrease was coupled with an unexpectedly enthusiastic acceptance of polyester blends in durable-press apparel. . . .
>
> If all announced new capacity is built as scheduled, by the end of '68 U.S. production capability would be nearly 1.25 billion lbs./year. . . .
>
> With the Du Pont capacity disclosure, other polyester fiber producers theorize that marginal producers may scale down expansion plans and potential producers may think twice before entering the market. Intense competition in other fibers is in store as well.

The point of decision

It was in this environment that the management of Midland-Ross had to make its decision on the polyester fiber proposal.

[15] *Chemical Week,* April 2, 1966, p. 21.

Exhibit 1

MIDLAND-ROSS CORPORATION (B)
U.S. FIBER CONSUMPTION (IN MILLIONS OF POUNDS) AND PRICES
(IN DOLLARS PER POUND)

	Natural Fibers				*Man-Made Fibers*					
	Cotton		*Wool*		*Rayon*		*Nylon*		*Polyester*	
Year	*Pounds*	*Staple Price*	*Pounds*	*Staple Price*	*Pounds*	*Staple Price*	*Pounds*	*Staple Price*	*Pounds*	*Staple Price*
1910	n.a.	$	n.a.	$	*	$		$		$
1930	2,617		263		119	0.40				
1935	2,755		418		200	0.31				
1940	3,959		408		300	0.25	*			
1945	4,516	0.39	645		420	0.25	25			
1950	4,683	0.57	635	1.41	650	0.36	75	1.65	*	
1955	4,382	0.39	414	1.08	966	0.34	231	1.48	13	1.60
1956		0.33		1.08	870	0.32	246	1.30	20	1.35
1957		0.36		1.22	836	0.31	293	1.30	38	1.41
1958		0.33		0.90	750	0.31	293	1.20	44	1.41
1959		0.30		1.02	848	0.33	356	1.06	79	1.36
1960	4,191	0.31	411	1.07	716	0.28	376	0.92	110	1.36
1961		0.31		1.03	797	0.28	455	0.92	112	1.24
1962	4,188	0.30	429	1.09	884	0.28	551	0.92	162	1.14
1963	4,040	0.29	412	1.18	960	0.28	625	0.92	223	1.14
1964	4,244	0.29	357	1.28	975	0.28	754	0.92	274	0.98
1965	4,477	0.29	387	1.19	1,046	0.28	861	0.82	416	0.84
1966	4,633 est.		370 est.		1,026 est.		978 est.		545 est.	

Fibers compete for shares of the total fiber market principally on the basis of relative prices and relative quality characteristics. Relative prices appear to have been an important consideration in the substitution of rayon for cotton in certain uses. The noncellulose fibers offer serious price competition for apparel wool. However, price advantage has not accounted for the rapid increase in share of the fiber market gain by noncellulose fibers, although sharply reduced prices in recent years have undoubtedly expanded their use.

Synthetic fibers yield a greater amount of fabric from a pound of fiber than does cotton, thus reducing the price of synthetic fiber per unit of product output. The equivalent net weight pounds of cotton staple for each pound of man-made fiber is (*a*) rayon staple fiber, 1.10; and (*b*) nylon and polyester staple fiber, 1.37.

* Date of fiber introduction.

Sources: *Statistical Abstract of the United States—1967*, pp. 642, 760, 761. *Textile Organon:* December, 1966, p. 199; February, 1967, pp. 28, 29. *Modern Textiles Magazine*, December, 1965. National Advisory Commission on Food and Fiber, *Cotton and Other Fiber Problems and Policies in the United States*, Technical Papers, Vol. 2 (Washington, D.C., 1967), pp. 24, 33, 36, 39.

Exhibit 2

MIDLAND-ROSS CORPORATION (B)
VARIATION IN UNIT COST OF PRODUCTION WITH SIZE OF PLANT

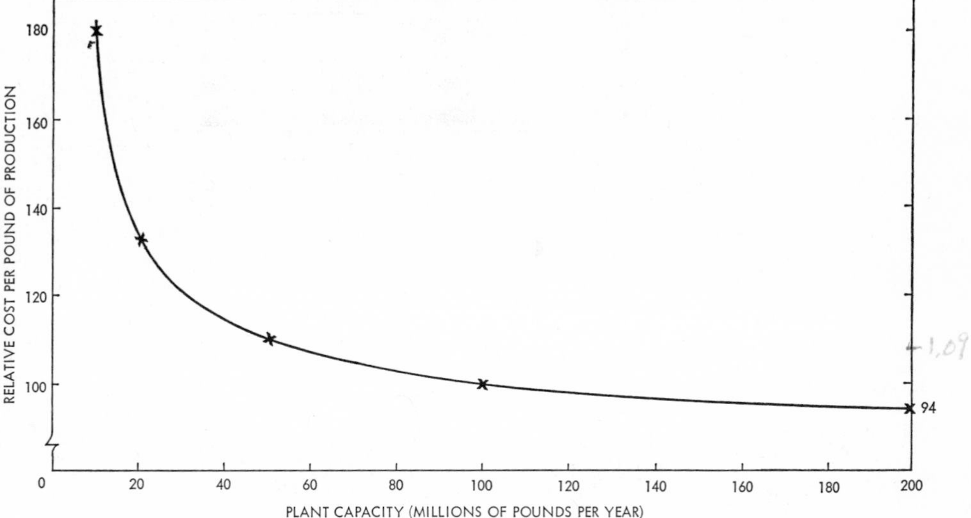

Based on a chart in Jesse W. Markham, *Competition in the Rayon Industry* (Cambridge, Mass.: Harvard University Press, 1952), p. 150.

Exhibit 3

MIDLAND-ROSS CORPORATION (B)
CAPITAL INVESTMENT IN POLYESTER
(In millions)

	IRC Division
Working capital	$ 6.5
Production facilities	20.3
Total existing investment	$26.8
Between 1/1/67 and 12/31/71, additional investments were to be made as follows:	
Polyester resin and fiber plant	$17.4
Polyester tire cord spinning facility	1.8
Other polyester facilities	1.0
Polyester plants	$20.2
Various rayon additions	5.3
Total plant additions	$25.5
Additional accounts receivable and inventories	5.0
Total additional investment	$30.5
Grand total	$57.3

The timing and size of the cash expenditure for the project would be as follows:

	1967	*1968*	*1969*	*1970*	*1971*	*Five-Year Totals*
Additions to plant	$16.9	$5.7	$0.9	$1.0	$1.0	$25.5
Additions to working capital	1.1	3.3	0.6	0	0	5.0
	$18.0	$9.0	$1.5	$1.0	$1.0	$30.5

Exhibit 4

MIDLAND-ROSS CORPORATION (B)
FIVE-YEAR SALES, PROFIT, CASH FLOW, AND PRICE FORECASTS OF PROJECT
(Dollar figures in millions)

	1967				1968			
	Total	*Poly-ester*	*Hi-Wet Modulus Rayon Staple*	*Rayon Tire Cord*	*Total*	*Poly-ester*	*Hi-Wet Modulus Rayon Staple*	*Rayon Tire Cord*
Net sales	$50.0	$ 6.4	$4.9	$38.7	$68.3	$21.5	$7.7	$39.1
Cost of sales:								
Normal	40.5							
Extraordinary start-up	0.5							
Depreciation	2.1	0.1		2.0	2.9	1.0		1.9
Total cost of sales	$43.1				$56.2			
Gross income	$ 6.9				$12.1			
Nonmanufacturing expense	4.0				6.3			
Income before interest and income taxes	$ 2.9	$(1.2)		$4.1	$ 5.8	$ 0.9		$4.9
Interest	0.0				0.0			
Income before taxes	$ 2.9				$ 5.8			
Income taxes @ approx. 50%:								
Current	1.4				2.5			
Deferred	—				0.4			
Total	$ 1.4				$ 2.9			
Less investment credit	0.2				$ 0.5			
Net provision	$ 1.2				$ 2.4			
Net income	$ 1.7				$ 3.4			
Depreciation and deferred taxes	2.1				3.3			
Cash flow	$ 3.8				$ 6.7			

	1967 *Product Sold (Millions of Lbs.)*	1967 *Price ($ per Lb.)*	1968 *Product Sold (Millions of Lbs.)*	1968 *Price ($ per Lb.)*
Rayon staple (hi-wet modulus)	16	$0.310	25	$0.310
Rayon tire cord	67	0.578	67.5	0.578
Polyester:				
Tire cord	7.5	0.850	10	0.809
Staple fiber	0.0	0.785	18.8	0.725
Resin (or polymer)	0.0	0.380	0.0	0.380
Total polyester	7.5	$0.850	28.8	$0.754

1969				1970				1971			
Total	*Polyester*	*Hi-Wet Modulus Rayon Staple*	*Rayon Tire Cord*	*Total*	*Polyester*	*Hi-Wet Modulus Rayon Staple*	*Rayon Tire Cord*	*Total*	*Polyester*	*Hi-Wet Modulus Rayon Staple*	*Rayon Tire Cord*
$79.8	$32.9	$7.7	$39.2	$79.7	$32.8	$7.7	$39.2	$79.5	$32.6	$7.7	$39.2
3.3	1.7		1.6	3.3	—		—	3.4	—		—
$57.8				$57.8				$57.8			
$22.0				$21.9				$21.7			
6.5				6.6				6.6			
$15.5	$10.5		$5.0	$15.3	$10.3		$5.0	$15.1	$10.1		$5.0
0.0				1.5				1.1			
$15.5				$13.8				$14.0			
6.9				5.7				6.2			
0.9				0.5				0.3			
$ 7.8				$ 6.2				$ 6.5			
0.7				0.1				0.1			
$ 7.1				$ 6.1				$ 6.4			
$ 8.4				$ 7.7				$ 7.6			
4.1				3.8				3.7			
$12.5				$11.5				$11.3			

1969		1970		1971	
Product Sold (Millions of Lbs.)	*Price ($ per Lb.)*	*Product Sold (Millions of Lbs.)*	*Price ($ per Lb.)*	*Product Sold (Millions of Lbs.)*	*Price ($ per Lb.)*
25	$0.310	25	$0.310	25	$0.310
67.8	0.578	67.8	0.578	67.8	0.578
10	0.795	10	0.795	10	0.795
30	0.705	30	0.705	30	0.705
10	0.380	10	0.372	10	0.350
50	$0.658	50	$0.656	50	$0.652

Exhibit 5

MIDLAND-ROSS CORPORATION (B)
CASH FLOWS FROM POLYESTER PROJECT, 1967–81
(In thousands)

Year	*Investment* *Existing*	*Investment* *New*	*Income after Tax*	*Cash Flow from Operations*
1967	$26,800	$18,029	$1,663	$ 3,788
1968		8,995	3,416	6,740
1969		1,480	8,397	12,543
1970		1,000	7,710	11,477
1971		1,000	7,597	11,286
1972			7,427	10,869
1973			7,659	10,611
1974			7,861	10,385
1975			8,034	10,184
1976			8,186	10,009
1977			8,317	9,853
1978			8,431	9,714
1979			8,529	9,590
1980			8,574	9,521
1981			8,574	{ 9,496 14,338←return of working capital and plant write-off

Discounted cash flow return on investment = 15.2%

DCF–ROI assuming 10% decline in selling prices of polyester, 1972–81 = 13.6%

Exhibit 6

MIDLAND-ROSS CORPORATION (B)

Current and Planned Capacity of Polyester Fiber Competitors

	Polyester Capacity Feb., 1966 (In Millions of Pounds)	*Announced Expansion by End of 1968 (In Millions of Pounds)*	*Number of Plants End of 1968*	*Other‡ Fibers Manufactured*	*Total Sales Volume of Company in 1965 (In Millions)*	*Average Return on Total Capital (1961–65)*
Allied Chemical	0	?	?	N	$1,121	10%
American Enka	0	?	?	N, R	193	11
American Viscose (Div. FMC)	0	?	?	A, R		
Beaunit Fibers (Div. Beaunit Corp.)	0	?	?	R		
Chemstrand (Div. Monsanto)	20	40	1	N	1,468	9
Du Pont	240	360	3	A, N	3,020	19
Fiber Industries*	95	155	2	A, N, R	862	8
Firestone Tire & Rubber	0	?	?	N	1,610	9
Goodyear Tire & Rubber	60	40	1		2,226	10
Hercules	0	30	1		532	13
IRC Fibers (Div. Midland-Ross)	0	?	?	R		
Phoenix Works, Inc. (Sub. Bates Mfg. Co.)	0	25	1			
Tennessee Eastman Co. (Div. Eastman Kodak)	50	100	2	A		
U.S. Rubber Company	0	?	?			
Vectra Co.† (Div. Nat. Plastic Products)	0	?	?	N		
	465	750	11			

* Owned 62.5% by Celanese Corp. of America.
† Jointly owned by Enjay Chemical Co. & J. P. Stevens & Co.
‡A = Acetate; N = Nylon; R = Rayon.

SUPER G CORPORATION[1]

On March 27, 1959, Mr. James Warfield, president of Super G, the fifth largest retail grocery chain in the United States (Exhibit 1), arrived at his office after a two-week vacation in Boca Raton, Florida. On his desk were proposals from his chief financial officer recommending the acquisition of two grocery firms, one located in Bakersfield, California, and the other located in Atlantic City, New Jersey. As of 1959, Super G had operations in neither city, but did operate stores in other areas in both states.

During his vacation, Mr. Warfield had spent a good deal of time thinking about a consulting study which had been undertaken in February and completed just prior to his departure to Florida. The consulting study examined both the profitability of Super G within the grocery chain industry and the profitability of individual Super G stores in different types of markets. After he had first read this report, Mr. Warfield made a mental note to review Super G's entire acquisition policy and new store construction program in light of the consulting report's conclusions and the trends that were clearly evident in the retail grocery business. The two acquisition proposals provided him with the impetus to make this review.

SUPER G CORPORATION—BACKGROUND AND ACQUISITION HISTORY

Early history

Super G was founded in Illinois in 1902. During the first decade of its existence, the firm expanded internally by opening new stores primarily in the Chicago area. In the early 1920's the firm shifted its approach to expansion and grew rapidly by acquisitions. By 1929 the firm was operating a chain of 1,600 stores and had total sales exceeding $90 million.

The depression was especially severe for Super G. The firm suffered three straight years of losses between 1936 and 1938, and sales declined from a $90 million peak just prior to the depression to $55.5 million in 1938.

---

[1] The data contained in the exhibits of this case are actual company and industry data taken from the public record. The material in the text of the case, in contrast, is derived from composite sources and should not be understood to apply to any specific company in real life.

Super G's fortunes changed considerably with the outbreak of World War II. When Mr. Warfield took over management control in 1947, Super G operated stores in eight states and had sales of over $200 million. Mr. Warfield continued the firm's progress; and 10 years later, in 1958, the firm was operating 932 stores in 18 states and had sales of $794 million (Exhibit 2).

Growth through acquisition

Between 1951 and 1958 Super G acquired 24 retail grocery firms, which operated a total of 485 stores (Exhibit 3). In their last full year of operation prior to acquisition, these firms had had sales in excess of $251 million (Exhibit 4).

During the year 1958 Mr. Warfield had, on several separate occasions, made the following comments concerning his long-run goals for the company:

> Although Super G now operates in only 18 states, we are looking forward to the 48.
>
> . . . . .
>
> Our future is pinpointed on the map. It is just a question of how far and how fast we can move—always, of course, living within our means for best operating results.
>
> . . . . .
>
> This is my aim. We plan to cover the United States like a book.

Earnings and book value tests

As a general rule, Super G paid about six times pretax (and 12 times after-tax) earnings for its acquisitions (Exhibit 5). This amount was usually somewhat in excess of the acquired firm's book value, although Super G occasionally acquired an unprofitable firm at a substantial discount from book value. As Super G's stock traditionally sold at about 14 times after-tax earnings, most acquisitions offered some earnings enhancement. Indeed, the prospect of dilution in earnings was often sufficient to rule out any proposed acquisition.

Per store volume test

Super G tried to acquire firms with sales volume per store averaging in excess of $750,000 a year. Mr. Warfield knew that customers were demanding larger and larger stores every year (Exhibit 6). This preference generally precluded the acquisition of most single store grocery firms, since these firms usually had dramatically lower per store sales volumes than the multistore chains (Exhibit 7). Larger stores generally meant a longer period of profitable operation at existing locations. Like almost all chains, Super G leased rather than owned its store sites. Consequently, the firm was flexible with regard to its store locations within an area. Nevertheless, moving operations from one location to another within a marketing area was expensive and moves were avoided whenever possible.

While Super G was very active in the merger area, it played a relatively passive role in selecting specific acquisition targets. Management generally did not take the initiative with respect to the acquisition of a particular firm until it received word that the firm might be for sale. If the store locations made sense from the standpoint of warehouse supply from an existing Super G facility, or if the acquisition candidate was large enough to have its own warehouse facility, further investigation was undertaken. This investigation generally took the form of ascertaining the earnings of the firm being reviewed and of discussing the price and terms with its owners.

A need to respond rapidly in acquisition negotiations

Super G acquired a very large number of stores each year. Indeed, half of the firm's growth between 1948 and 1958 could be directly traced to acquisitions (Exhibit 8). Since the firm accounted for by far the greatest number of grocery store acquisitions among the major chains (Exhibit 3), the need for rapid decision making meant that Super G could not afford to engage in laborious analysis of each acquisition. It had to utilize some rather simple tests, and the tests described earlier seemed to meet its needs.

Compensation problems lead to a study of profitability

Early in February, 1959, Mr. Warfield participated in a somewhat stormy meeting of the Super G Executive Bonus Committee.[2] At these meetings, which occurred annually, Mr. Warfield reviewed the earnings contribution of each of Super G's 11 geographic regions and assigned some fraction of Super G's total bonus pool (which amounted to slightly less than $1,000,000 in 1958) to each regional manager for distribution to himself and the individual store managers under his supervision.[3]

The fraction of the bonus pool assigned to each region was directly related[4] to that region's profit contribution. It was this feature of the bonus plan which had caused the difficulty in Mr. Warfield's February meeting. Some of the regional managers had argued quite forcefully, but without specific evidence, that both individual store and region profitability were closely related to the degree of market penetration that Super G enjoyed in different areas around the country. These regional managers claimed that

---

[2] The Bonus Committee met each year shortly after the taking of year-end inventories was completed and earnings figures were available for each of Super G's individual stores. Earnings figures for individual store units were generally ready by the end of January. By early February these data had been collected and totaled for the 11 regions into which Super G was organizationally divided.

[3] Each regional manager's share of the pool was fixed by Mr. Warfield. It usually ranged from 6% to 10% of the region's total allocation.

[4] The size of the bonus pool was zero until the corporation achieved a fixed return on capital. Once this level of return was exceeded, the bonus pool was credited with a fixed fraction of all profits above the minimum level and regions shared in the pool in proportion to their profit contribution in excess of the minimum return required on the capital they controlled.

where Super G was long established and represented the leading chain in a city, profitability was high. Where Super G was a newcomer to a city or was a relatively small participant in the city's total grocery sales, these managers claimed profitability was usually poor. An exceptionally good (or bad) store or regional manager, of course, had a significant and measurable impact on profitability, but this factor was often masked by the larger impact of the degree of market penetration.

As a result of these discussions and the obvious discontent of some of his most promising young managers, Mr. Warfield asked a consulting firm to analyze Super G's overall profitability. He was particularly interested in discovering those factors with the greatest degree of influence on profits, but he was also interested in some data on how Super G's profitability stacked up against the rest of the retail grocery industry. A short summary of the consulting report is presented below:

SUMMARY OF THE CONSULTING REPORT ON PROFITABILITY

Our investigation of the important factors influencing the profitability of Super G's stores has led us to the following conclusions:

1. The "contribution to corporate profit"[5] of an individual Super G store in any city seems to be directly related to the share of total grocery store sales made by all Super G stores in that city.

2. The relationship between store contribution to corporate profit and Super G's market share in any given city follows the pattern shown in Exhibit 9. The distribution of individual store performances about this average curve is relatively narrow. Only about 2 stores in 10 experienced a profitability rate that fell more than 1½ percentage points away from the graph.

3. The profitability-market share relationship demonstrated in Exhibit 9 holds consistently across cities of widely varying size (Exhibit 10).

4. The bulk of Super G's sales are concentrated in cities where Super G holds between 10% and 15% of the retail grocery market. Super G's weighted average market share for all cities in 1958 was 12.7% (Exhibit 11).

In looking at Super G's overall profitability in relation to its large retail grocery chain competitors, we find that Super G's recent performance is about average for the industry (Exhibit 12). While profit to net worth ratios for individual firms in the retail grocery industry are quite similar, one firm, Number 6, has consistently been a superior performer. It is interesting to note that this firm's weighted average market share in its cities of operation exceeds 20%, by far the highest rate in the industry.

---

[5] Store "contribution to corporate profit" is defined as sales minus cost of goods sold minus direct store expenses. Contribution to corporate profit does not include warehouse and corporate overhead expenses, which were fairly stable at about 2.0% of sales each year.

IMPLICATIONS OF THE PROFITABILITY STUDY AND INDUSTRY TRENDS

Although the consulting report was initially undertaken to solve a problem in the executive compensation area, Mr. Warfield thought he saw some implications extending beyond executive compensation. In terms of Super G's future acquisition opportunities and his expansion plans, Mr. Warfield wondered *if* and *how* the profitability study should influence his decision making. He was also concerned about how Super G should respond to two clear industry trends. First, the retail grocery business was rapidly consolidating, with fewer and fewer chains and store-association groups of various types controlling all the retail outlets (Exhibit 13). Second, individual city markets were experiencing a rapid increase in concentration among the top few firms (Exhibit 14).

Mr. Warfield felt that these trends might ultimately force some reevaluation of Super G's practice of moving into a new city marketing area with a small acquisition or two, and then building up this base with additional acquisitions and new store construction. Given these trends, and the results of the consulting report, Mr. Warfield wondered what he ought to do regarding the two acquisition proposals presented for his consideration (Exhibit 15).

Exhibit 1

SUPER G CORPORATION

SALES, OPERATING, AND MARKET SHARE DATA, TOP 20 RETAIL GROCERY CHAINS, 1958

Chain	*Sales (In Millions)*	*Number of Stores*	*Number of States*	*Percentage of U.S. Food Store Sales*
1	$ 4,736	4,082	37	9.7%
2	1,973	1,929	25	4.0
3	1,766	1,428	20	3.6
4	863	828	7	1.8
Super G	**794**	**932**	**18**	**1.6**
6	631	491	10	1.3
7	604	359	9	1.2
8	534	555	8	1.1
9	514	426	11	1.0
10	437	473	11	0.9
11	368	253	3	0.8
12	308	196	5	0.6
13	273	211	4	0.6
14	166	154	8	0.3
15	164	101	3	0.3
16	162	57	5	0.3
17	142	103	2	0.3
18	117	67	2	0.2
19	94	27	1	0.2
20	93	47	2	0.2
Total	$14,739	12,719		30.0%

Exhibit 2

SUPER G CORPORATION
FINANCIAL HISTORY, 1949–58
(Dollar figures in millions)

OPERATIONS	*1949*	*1950*	*1951*	*1952*	*1953*	*1954*	*1955*	*1956*	*1957*	*1958*
Sales	$274.3	$315.2	$361.3	$405.2	$462.3	$520.3	$575.6	$617.6	$681.1	$794.2
Profit before federal taxes	$ 7.4	$ 9.8	$ 7.2	$ 8.4	$ 10.0	$ 12.7	$ 15.2	$ 14.9	$ 16.8	$ 17.7
Federal taxes	2.8	4.6	3.6	4.7	5.2	6.2	8.0	7.9	8.7	8.9
Net profit	$ 4.6	$ 5.2	$ 3.6	$ 3.7	$ 4.8	$ 6.5	$ 7.2	$ 7.0	$ 8.1	$ 8.8
Profit to sales (ratio)	0.017	0.016	0.010	0.009	0.011	0.012	0.013	0.011	0.012	0.011
INVESTMENT										
Long-term debt	$ 5.1	$ 5.0	$ 4.6	$ 4.2	$ 16.2	$ 16.2	$ 30.7	$ 30.1	$ 42.5	$ 39.5
Equity	24.7	28.3	28.9	30.2	35.5	46.0	53.5	56.3	61.8	68.8
Total capital	$ 29.9	$ 33.3	$ 33.5	$ 34.4	$ 51.7	$ 62.1	$ 84.2	$ 86.4	$104.3	$108.3
Profit to equity (ratio)	0.19	0.18	0.12	0.12	0.14	0.14	0.13	0.12	0.13	0.13
Sales to capital (ratio)	9.17	9.47	10.79	11.78	8.94	8.38	6.84	7.15	6.53	7.33
Debt to equity (ratio)	0.21	0.18	0.16	0.14	0.46	0.35	0.57	0.53	0.69	0.57
Earnings per share (in dollars)	$2.89	$3.31	$2.14	$2.05	$2.65	$3.20	$3.41	$3.30	$3.76	$4.03
Average price-earnings ratio	—	—	—	—	—	11.2	14.2	13.5	11.5	14.6
Number of stores operating	655	634	624	765	688	711	744	761	883	932
Annual lease payments (in millions)	n.a.	n.a.	n.a.	n.a.	n.a.	n.a.	$ 7.2	$ 8.1	$ 10.7	$ 12.2

Exhibit 3

SUPER G CORPORATION

NUMBER OF STORES ACQUIRED BY THE LARGEST GROCERY CHAINS BY COMPANY AND YEAR, 1949–58

Chain	Number										1949–58 Stores Acquired	
	1949	*1950*	*1951*	*1952*	*1953*	*1954*	*1955*	*1956*	*1957*	*1958*	*Number*	*Percentage of Total*
Super G	—	—	**21**	**228**	**28**	**28**	**18**	**5**	**128**	**29**	**485**	**28.9%**
6	46	—	—	—	—	8	173	75	—	4	306	18.3
3	—	—	—	—	—	—	79	7	—	44	130	7.8
9	—	—	33	—	—	—	15	19	13	48	128	7.6
12	—	—	—	—	—	—	65	23	2	11	101	6.0
10	—	—	—	—	—	1	85	1	4	8	99	6.0
4	—	1	2	—	—	—	—	90	—	—	93	5.5
7	—	—	—	—	19	1	4	5	—	38	67	4.0
2	—	—	1	—	—	1	2	4	13	46	67	4.0
17	—	—	—	—	—	—	—	47	—	9	56	3.3
11	—	—	—	—	—	—	—	—	41	2	43	2.6
18	—	1	4	1	1	4	—	10	10	13	44	2.6
20	19	—	—	—	—	—	1	—	—	—	20	1.2
15	—	—	—	—	9	—	—	—	2	6	17	1.0
13	—	—	—	—	—	—	—	17	—	—	17	1.0
8	—	—	—	—	—	—	—	—	1	—	1	0.1
14	—	—	—	—	—	—	—	—	1	—	1	0.1
19	—	—	—	—	—	—	—	—	—	—	—	—
16	—	—	—	—	—	—	—	—	—	—	—	—
1	—	—	—	—	—	—	—	1	—	—	1	0.1
Total	65	2	61	229	57	43	442	304	215	258	1,676	100.0%
Total acquisitions of all grocery chains	68	5	69	273	73	79	551	482	357	584		

Exhibit 4

SUPER G CORPORATION
SALES VOLUME OF COMPANIES ACQUIRED BY SUPER G IN THE YEAR PRIOR TO THEIR ACQUISITION, 1951–58
(In millions)

Year	*Super G's Sales**	*Sales Volume of Acquired Companies in 12 Months Prior to Acquisition*
1951	$361.3	$ 8.4
1952	405.2	52.5
1953	462.3	30.5
1954	520.3	23.0
1955	575.6	18.6
1956	617.6	4.8
1957	681.1	77.2
1958	794.2	36.6
Total		$251.6†

* For years in which acquisitions were treated as a pooling of interests, no restatement of prior year's sales has been made in this exhibit.

† This total obviously underestimates the impact of acquisitions during 1951–58 on Super G's 1958 sales since it makes no allowance for internal growth in sales of the acquired stores subsequent to the date of acquisition.

Exhibit 5

SUPER G CORPORATION

Financial Data on Acquisitions by Super G, 1951–58

(Dollar figures in thousands)

Company	*Purchase Price*	*Book Value of Assets*	*Pretax Profit*	*Sales*	*Number of Stores Acquired*	*Weighted Average City Market Share*†	*Price/ Million Sales Volume*	*Price/ Book Value Ratio*	*Price/ Pretax Earnings Ratio*	*Average Sales per Store*	*Acquisition Date*
A	$ 964 C*			$ 8,362	21	4.9%	$115			$ 400	1951
B	1,068 C/S	$2,185	$ (40)	36,053	210		30	0.49	(26.7)	170	1952
C	440 C			2,927	6		150			490	..
D	725 C	496	115	6,737	6		108	1.46	6.3	1,120	..
E	297 C	257	29	6,825	6	18.7	44	1.15	10.3	1,140	..
F	5,079 C			30,467	28	11.0	167			1,090	1953
G	3,986 C	2,816	590	22,980	28	16.9	174	1.42	6.8	820	1954
H	101 C			802	1		126			800	1955
I	2,849 C			11,200	8	7.2	254			1,400	..
J	1,861 S	1,823		6,625	9		281	1.02		740	..
K	217 C			3,247	3		67			1,080	1956
L	69 C	67		908	1		76	1.02		900	..
M	117 C			633	1		185			630	..
N	7,578 C	4,770	1,228	42,499	27	21.0	179	1.59	6.2	1,570	1957
O	1,876 S	3,169	280	21,802	85	13.4	86	0.59	6.7	260	..
P	745 C			3,798	9		195			420	..
Q	625 S	354	100	9,099	7		69	1.77	6.3	1,300	..
R	714 S	513	178	6,053	7	10.6	118	1.39	4.0	870	1958
S	56 C			357	1		157			360	..
T	2,450 C	1,657	460	17,650	12		139	1.48	5.3	1,470	..
U	720 C			4,285	3		168			1,430	..
V	107 C			2,158	4		50			540	..
W	857 C	857	176	5,200	1		165	1.00	4.9	5,200	..
X	190 C	190		945	1		201	1.00		950	
Total				$251,612	485						

* C = Cash transaction.
S = Stock transaction.

† This concept is defined in Exhibit 11.

Exhibit 6

SUPER G CORPORATION
Shift in Consumer Preference Toward Large High-Volume Grocery Stores, 1948, 1954, 1958

	1948			
	Number of Stores in This Size Class	*% of Stores in This Size Class or Larger*	*Total Sales of Stores in This Size Class (In Millions)*	*% of Sales in This Size Class or Larger*
Store sales of:				
$1,000,000 and above	1,911	1%	$ 2,723	12%
500,000 to $999,999	5,360	3	3,680	28
300,000 to 499,999	6,197	5	2,391	38
299,999 or less	312,733	100	14,339	100
Total	326,201		$23,133	

	1954			
	Number of Stores in This Size Class	*% of Stores in This Size Class or Larger*	*Total Sales of Stores in This Size Class (In Millions)*	*% of Sales in This Size Class or Larger*
Store sales of:				
$1,000,000 and above	6,242	2%	$10,723	33%
500,000 to $999,999	7,507	5	5,294	49
300,000 to 499,999	7,711	8	2,978	58
299,999 or less	245,278	100	13,904	100
Total	266,738		$32,899	

	1958			
	Number of Stores in This Size Class	*% of Stores in This Size Class or Larger*	*Total Sales of Stores in This Size Class (In Millions)*	*% of Sales in This Size Class or Larger*
Store sales of:				
$5,000,000 and above	96	0%	$ 640	2%
2,000,000 to $4,999,999	2,888	1	7,777	20
1,000,000 to 1,999,999	7,348	4	10,340	46
500,000 to 999,999	9,092	8	6,445	61
300,000 to 499,999	8,369	11	3,227	69
299,999 or less	215,003	100	12,753	100
Total	242,796		$41,182	

Exhibit 7

SUPER G CORPORATION
CHAIN SIZE, STORE SIZE, AND VOLUME MIX OF RETAIL GROCERY FIRMS IN THE UNITED STATES, 1958

	Total Number of Firms in This Size Category	*Total Sales Volume of Firms in This Size Category (In Billions)*
Firms operating 101+ stores	16	$13.5
Firms operating 51 to 100 stores	21	1.7
Firms operating 26 to 50 stores	45	1.9
Firms operating 11 to 25 stores	92	1.4
Firms operating 6 to 10 stores	166	1.0
Firms operating 2 to 5 stores	1,950	2.8
Firms operating 1 store	219,142	18.9
Total	221,432	$41.2
Total number of stores	242,796	

	Number of Stores in This Size Class	*Total Sales of Stores in This Size Class (In Millions)*	*% of Sales in This Size Class or Larger*
Store sales of:		*Firms with 101+ Stores*	
$5,000,000 and above	12	$ 67	0%
2,000,000 to $4,999,999	1,599	4,170	31
1,000,000 to 1,999,999	4,156	5,939	75
500,000 to 999,999	3,382	2,485	94
300,000 to 499,999	1,321	534	98
299,999 or less	1,594	292	100
Total	12,064	$13,487	
		Single-Store Grocery Firms	
$5,000,000 and above	20	$ 150	1%
2,000,000 to $4,999,999	324	925	6
1,000,000 to 1,999,999	1,206	1,750	15
500,000 to 999,999	3,466	2,348	27
300,000 to 499,999	5,616	2,132	38
299,999 or less	208,510	11,672	100
Total	219,142	$18,977	

Exhibit 8

SUPER G CORPORATION

GROWTH AND ACQUISITION DATA FOR THE 20 LARGEST RETAIL GROCERY CHAINS, 1958*

(Dollar figures in millions)

Chain	(1) Sales in 1948	(2) Sales Volume Acquired 1948–58	(3) Sales Volume 1958	(4)† Growth in 10-Year Period	(5)‡ Growth in 10-Year Period from Acquisitions	(6)§ Growth in 10-Year Period Internally Generated
1	$ 2,837	$ 0	$ 5,095	80%	0%	80%
2	1,277	33	2,225	74	3	71
3	826	174	1,776	115	21	94
4	417	34	875	110	8	102
Super G	**270**	**252**	**794**	**194**	**94**	**100**
7	142	108	734	417	76	341
6	79	221	666	744	280	464
9	116	128	504	334	111	223
8	354	1	532	50	0	50
11	153	55	444	190	36	154
10	169	121	437	159	72	87
12	189	174	363	92	92	0
13	72	17	285	296	24	272
14	60	2	200	233	3	230
15	50	20	194	288	40	248
20	20	21	163	715	105	610
16	34	0	162	377	0	377
17	30	73	142	373	243	130
18	24	63	117	388	262	126
19	22	0	94	327	0	327
Total	$ 7,141	$1,497	$15,802			
Average				122%	21%	101%
GNP (in billions)	$ 258		$ 447	74%		
All grocery store sales (in millions)	$29,027		$46,105	59%		
Market share of 20 largest chains	24%		34%			

* The data in this exhibit are on a calendar year basis and the data in Exhibit 1 are on a fiscal year basis. In some cases acquisitions may be included in one exhibit but not in the other. These factors explain the apparent inconsistency between Exhibits 1 and 8.

† The value in column 4 is equal to ((3) − (1))/(1).

‡ The value in column 5 is equal to (2)/(1).

§ The value in column 6 is equal to (4) − (5).

Exhibit 9

SUPER G CORPORATION
COMPARISON OF MARKET SHARES AND STORE CONTRIBUTIONS TO CORPORATE PROFIT
1958

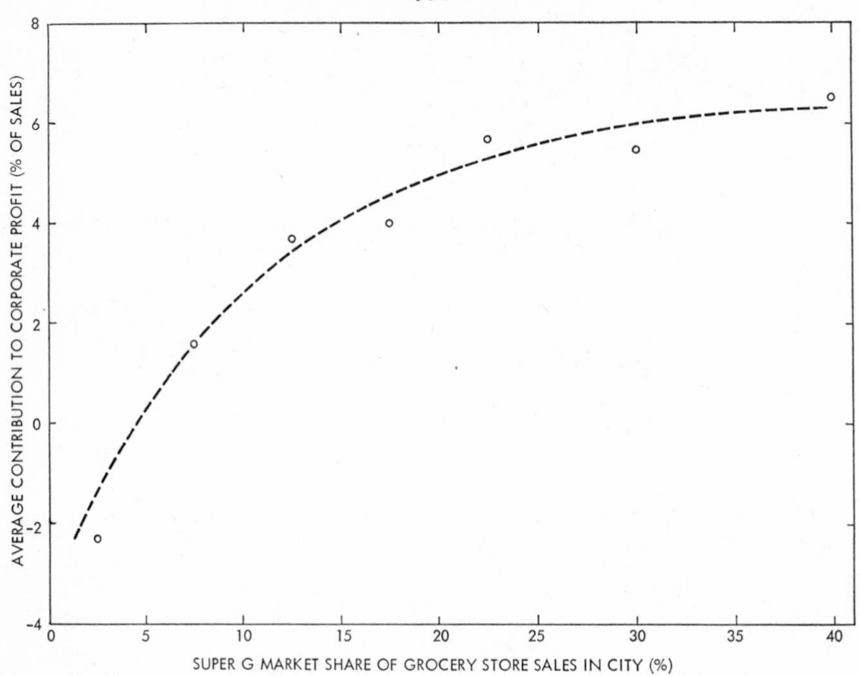

Exhibit 10

SUPER G CORPORATION

Comparison of Market Shares and Store Contributions to Corporate Profit by Groups of Cities—1958

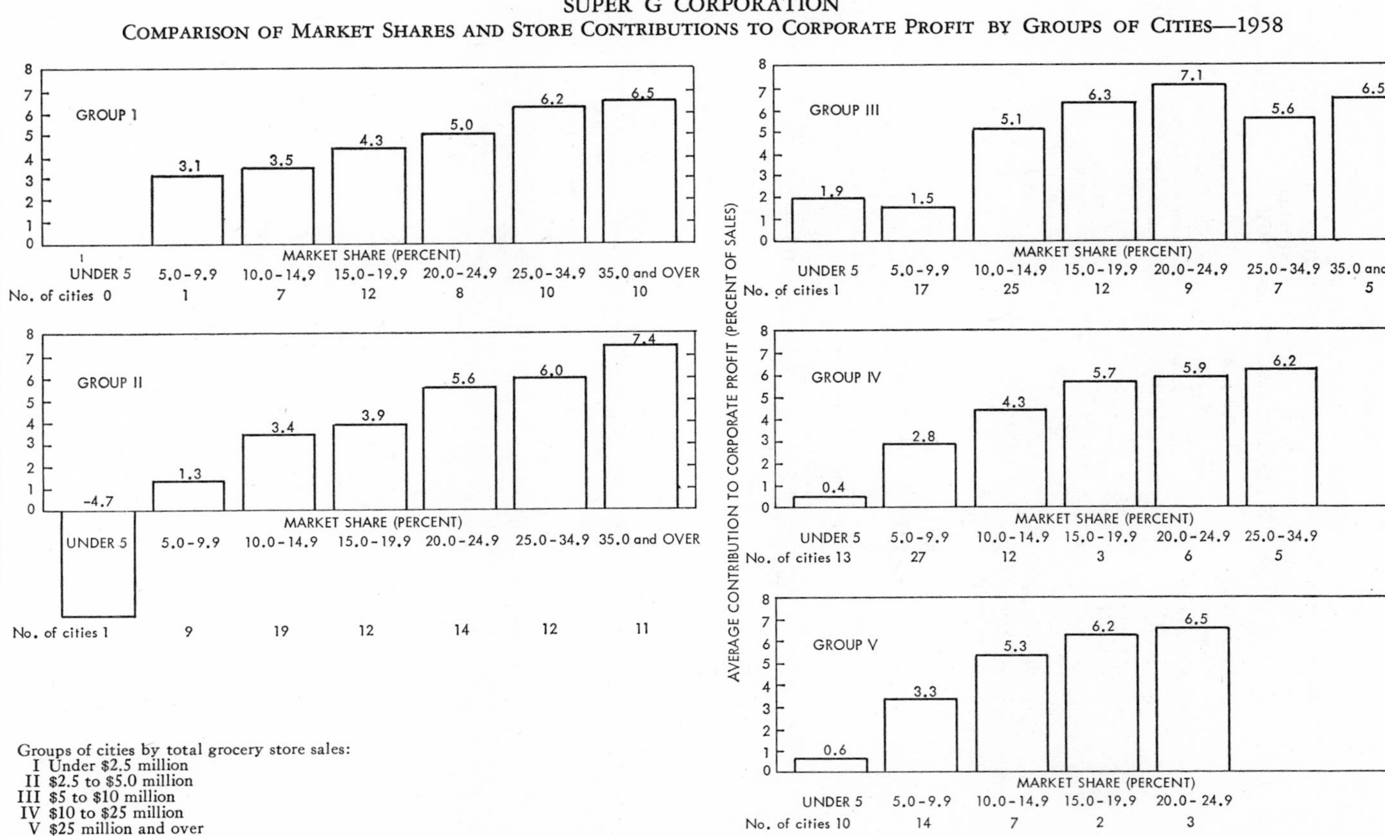

Groups of cities by total grocery store sales:
- I Under $2.5 million
- II $2.5 to $5.0 million
- III $5 to $10 million
- IV $10 to $25 million
- V $25 million and over

Exhibit 11

SUPER G CORPORATION

CUMULATIVE FRACTION OF SUPER G'S PROFITS CONTRIBUTED BY STORES OPERATING IN CITIES OF DIFFERENT SUPER G MARKET PENETRATION, 1958

Super G's Share of City Market (%)	*Percentage of Total Company Sales in Category*	*Percentage of Total Profit Contribution in Category*
35.0 and up	0.7	1.5
25.0 and up	7.7	15.1
20.0 and up	14.5	28.8
15.0 and up	24.6	42.9
10.0 and up	63.6	93.7
5.0 and up	89.7	108.4*
0.0 and up	100.0	100.0

Median† city market share = 12.0%
Mean‡ city market share = 12.7%

* Exhibit 10 includes data relating only to those Super G stores which had been in operation for two years or more in 1958. Exhibit 11 includes data for all stores, thus reflecting start-up losses on new store openings.

† One half of Super G's total sales were in cities where its market share was less than 12.0%, and one half of its total sales were in cities where its market share exceeded 12.0%.

‡ This figure was derived by summing (over all cities in which Super G operated) the product of Super G's market share in each city times the fraction of Super G's total sales made in that city.

Exhibit 12

SUPER G CORPORATION

Net Profit after Income Taxes as a Percentage of Net Worth for Leading Food Chains, 1948–58

(Data for fiscal years ending on or before June 30 are applicable to the prior year)

Chain and 1958 Sales Size	*1948*	*1949*	*1950*	*1951*	*1952*	*1953*	*1954*	*1955*	*1956*	*1957*	*1958*
Group 1: $500 million and over:											
1	16.4	13.6	12.5	9.9	10.2	10.1	10.1	10.5	11.6	13.2	12.8
2	12.0	15.0	12.6	6.5	5.3	10.1	8.1	7.6	13.0	14.4	14.6
3	15.8	16.6	14.8	13.5	12.2	12.0	13.2	12.0	13.1	14.4	13.6
4	13.3	13.4	12.9	8.8	8.4	11.4	10.0	11.0	11.3	11.3	11.3
7	20.1	22.7	17.6	13.7	14.8	17.1	18.9	19.0	17.2	18.4	18.4
Super G	**19.4**	**18.5**	**18.4**	**12.5**	**12.3**	**13.8**	**14.2**	**13.5**	**12.4**	**13.1**	**12.8**
6	23.8	25.9	18.6	19.4	20.4	20.5	22.8	23.7	24.0	23.6	23.2
11	18.0	17.2	16.3	13.0	11.1	9.9	11.5	12.6	13.9	14.2	14.4
8	14.4	15.5	12.7	12.0	13.9	13.2	14.3	13.5	11.8	12.1	12.2
9	15.7	16.6	14.9	11.2	10.2	12.4	13.6	12.5	14.2	13.7	11.4
Weighted average	15.5	15.1	13.4	10.2	9.9	11.3	11.4	11.5	13.0	14.0	13.8
Group 2: $150 to $500 million:											
10	17.3	17.7	17.2	14.5	13.0	14.2	16.6	16.9	15.9	16.0	11.9
12*	—	—	—	—	—	—	—	*	19.5	17.5	10.6
15	12.4	12.9	10.7	9.5	9.8	9.0	10.5	13.0	14.8	17.2	17.5
18	n.a.	2.1	5.8	5.6	3.8	5.2	8.1	8.4	8.7	8.1	7.2
14	12.5	15.8	14.3	9.7	9.5	8.5	9.0	10.8	14.2	14.5	13.4
17	8.9	10.0	14.0	9.0	12.0	11.8	12.8	14.0	15.0	16.3	15.9
20	14.4	16.3	15.0	13.6	14.6	16.1	10.4	9.9	11.5	9.8	10.8
19	n.a.	21.6	20.9	14.0	13.3	13.6	19.8	21.6	18.2	18.2	16.6
13	22.3	23.7	20.9	14.0	14.4	15.3	17.7	17.8	17.0	17.0	14.1
21	6.7	9.2	11.8	8.2	9.9	10.1	11.0	13.3	10.9	8.4	7.6
22	n.a.	28.1	25.8	15.5	12.6	16.2	20.4	18.4	18.3	15.4	13.8
16	24.0	22.2	16.5	12.0	9.5	9.4	12.6	9.7	9.4	10.3	10.3
Weighted average	15.1	15.6	14.9	11.5	10.9	11.0	12.7	13.1	14.1	14.1	12.3
Group 3: $50 to $150 million:											
23	13.6	8.6	10.2	9.3	9.5	10.3	11.9	11.0	10.5	12.9	10.4
24	23.9	21.1	21.5	14.8	11.7	13.4	18.9	25.7	23.9	23.1	18.1
25	n.a.	n.a.	n.a.	n.a.	6.1	8.7	12.1	16.4	10.4	14.8	15.1
26	n.a.	n.a.	n.a.	n.a.	n.a.	n.a.	n.a.	11.2	10.9	8.7	4.7
27	27.7	28.8	n.a.	n.a.	17.7	18.7	21.8	19.2	20.1	19.7	20.1
28	21.6	18.6	17.7	13.3	10.8	12.6	9.4	9.0	10.5	12.1	8.7
29	n.a.	n.a.	n.a.	n.a.	n.a.	n.a.	16.4	30.1	10.9	14.8	14.5
30	n.a.	n.a.	n.a.	11.8	11.5	13.3	12.7	14.5	12.4	13.0	13.0
Weighted average	19.4	19.6	17.6	13.0	11.7	12.9	16.3	16.4	14.2	14.9	12.9
Total weighted average	15.5	15.5	13.8	10.4	10.1	11.3	11.8	12.1	13.3	14.1	13.5

* Formed in 1956 by merger of several smaller chains.
Source: Company Annual Reports, *Moody's Industrial Manuals*, and other published sources.

Exhibit 13

SUPER G CORPORATION

PERCENTAGE DISTRIBUTION OF FOOD STORE SALES BY TYPE OF RETAILER, 1948, 1954, 1958

Type of Retailer	*Percentage of Food Store Sales* 1948	1954	1958
Top 20 chains	24.0%	30.1%	34.0%
Other chains	5.2	6.7	9.8
Cooperative members*	7.7	12.7	18.8
Voluntary members*	4.6	10.0	12.0
Unaffiliated independents	58.5	40.5	25.4
Total	100.0%	100.0%	100.0%

* In an effort to protect their markets, some wholesalers became partially integrated with their retail customers. Many independent retailers joined this trend because it promised the advantages of large scale buying and merchandising. Arrangements between wholesalers and independents have assumed two basic forms: the retailer-owned cooperative food wholesaler and the wholesaler-sponsored voluntary retail group. Groups of independents so affiliated with a particular wholesaler commonly are referred to as voluntary or cooperative groups or chains.

Exhibit 14

SUPER G CORPORATION

SEVENTEEN-CITY SAMPLE DESCRIBING THE MARKET STRUCTURE OF THE RETAIL GROCERY INDUSTRY IN 1958

	Total Sales (In Millions)	*Total Number of Firms*	*Total Number of Stores*	*Total Number of 1 Store Firms**	*Total Number of 2–3 Store Firms**	*Total Number of 4–10 Store Firms**	*Total Number of 11 or More Store Firms**	*Approximate Market Share of 4 Largest Firms in City:*		
								1954	*1958*	*Firms Also in Top 20 National Chains, 1958*
New York	$4,316	13,668	15,831	13,503	116	22	28	41%	37%	20%
Chicago	1,944	5,381	6,339	5,290	67	11	13	49	52	25
Akron	172	360	442	346	8	1	5	49	61	50
Albany	205	858	964	835	9	6	8	39	47	41
Alberquerque	71	147	189	138	3	2	4	50	60	60
Allentown	143	700	757	686	10	0	4	49	55	38
Anaheim	297	314	426	282	8	8	16	40	47	31
Atlanta	319	1,043	1,266	1,019	12	4	8	54	56	56
Atlantic City	*55*	*234*	*249*	*230*	*1*	*0*	*3*	*57*	*62*	*51*
Bakersfield	*96*	*285*	*316*	*265*	*13*	*2*	*5*	*31*	*31*	*19*
Baltimore	463	1,800	2,009	1,775	14	3	8	48	50	40
Beaumont	99	401	429	389	6	2	4	37	41	28
Binghamton	93	343	402	332	3	2	6	54	51	51
Birmingham	173	840	924	829	3	2	6	42	46	36
Boston	841	2,238	2,614	2,195	30	5	8	56	48	40
Bridgeport	121	404	440	389	7	1	7	n.a.	56	42
Buffalo	371	1,484	1,628	1,459	16	0	1	60	56	20
.										
.										
Average of 200 cities								45	49	

* Not all of these stores were necessarily located in the specific city market in question.

Exhibit 15

SUPER G CORPORATION
ACQUISITION POSSIBILITIES

Big Value Stores, Inc., Atlantic City, New Jersey

The following is a summary of the Big Value acquisition opportunity using 1958 figures. Big Value is a three-store chain that is the fourth largest factor in grocery sales in the Atlantic City area.

Sales	$6,050,000
Pretax income	130,000
Asking price	720,000
Book value	612,000
Pretax income after goodwill amortization*	130,000
After-tax income†	65,000

Number of Super G shares @ $59 for acquisition = 12,203
Earnings required to maintain 1959 EPS projection of $4.20 = $51,253

$$\text{Earnings contributed/earnings required} = \frac{65{,}000}{51{,}253} = 1.27$$

Total excess earnings contributed = $65,000 − $51,253 = $13,747

Pacific Giant, Inc., Bakersfield, California

The following is a summary of the Pacific Giant acquisition opportunity using 1958 figures. Pacific Giant is a six-store chain that is the fifth largest factor in grocery sales in the Bakersfield area.

Sales	$4,800,000
Pretax income	87,400
Asking price	656,000
Book value	560,000
Pretax income after goodwill amortization*	87,400
After-tax income†	43,700

Number of Super G shares @ $59 for acquisition = 11,119
Earnings required to maintain 1959 EPS projection of $4.20 = $46,700

$$\text{Earnings contributed/earnings required} = \frac{\$43{,}700}{\$46{,}700} = .94$$

Total excess earnings contributed = ($3,000)

* In a cash transaction, the price paid in excess of book value is assumed to be written off over a 20-year period and this expense is not tax deductible. In a stock transaction, there is no write-off as no goodwill account arises from the transaction.

† Assumes Super G's tax rate of 50%.

Note: Data on the market structure of the two cities are given in Exhibit 14.

GENERAL HOLDINGS CORPORATION

^^

One of the critical problems confronting management and the board of General Holdings Corporation in the early 1960's was the determination of a minimum acceptable rate of return on new capital investments. While this question had been under discussion within the company for several years, so far the people involved had been unable to agree even on what general concept of a minimum acceptable rate they should adopt. They were about evenly divided between using a single cutoff rate based on the company's overall weighted average cost of capital and a system of multiple cutoff rates said to reflect the risk–profit characteristics of the several businesses or economic sectors in which the company's subsidiaries operated. In late 1963, management was asked by the board to restudy the issue of single versus multiple cutoff rates and to recommend which approach the company should follow in the future.

General Holdings Corporation was formed in 1923 with the merger of several formerly independent firms operating in the oil refining, pipeline transportation, and industrial chemical fields. Over the following 40 years, the company integrated vertically into exploration and production of crude oil and marketing refined petroleum products, and horizontally into plastics, agricultural chemicals, and real estate development. The company was organized as a holding company with semiautonomous operating subsidiaries working in each of the above areas of activity. Its total assets exceeded $2 billion in 1963, and its capital expenditures averaged about $150 million a year in recent years.

Although management was unable to decide whether the company should use single or multiple cutoff rates, it had worked tentatively with a single corporationwide rate for about five years. The company's basic capital budgeting approach during this period had been to accept all proposed investments with a positive net present value when discounted at the company's estimated weighted average cost of capital. As cost of capital was defined and used in this process, the company, in effect, accepted projects down to the point where there would be no dilution in expected earnings per share of common stock.

The cost of capital discount rate used in the net present value discounting procedure was 10%, estimated as follows: First, an estimate was made of the expected proportions of future funds sources. Second, costs were assigned to each of these sources. Third, a weighted average cost of capital was calculated on the basis of these proportions and costs. Finally, this weighted average was adjusted upward to reflect the fact that no return at all was earned on a substantial proportion of the company's investments.

On the basis of the company's financing experience during the 1950's, company officials estimated that future capital investments would be financed about one third from debt and two thirds from depreciation and retained earnings combined. The company had not sold common stock for many years and had no plans to do so in the foreseeable future.

The primary consideration behind the costs assigned to the above funds sources was to avoid accepting projects with expected returns so low that the stockholders' expected earnings per share would be diluted. If the stockholders could reinvest their funds at a higher rate of return outside the company than management could inside, so the argument ran, the funds involved should be distributed to the stockholders rather than invested or reinvested internally. With this objective in mind, the company's future cost of debt was estimated at 2.5% after taxes, assuming a one third proportion of debt to total fund sources. Depreciation and retained earnings were thought to be exactly the same as common stock from the stockholders' point of view. In costing depreciation and retained earnings, therefore, the management started with the reciprocal of the company's probable long-term price–earnings ratio. This ratio was thought to be about 15 times. In addition, however, because this 15-times ratio was thought to reflect an assumed continuation of past growth in earnings per share, an adjustment was made, reducing the assumed price–earnings ratio to 10 times. The lower ratio was thought to reflect more accurately the long-term relationship between current market prices and expected earnings per share.

Combining these proportions and costs, the company's weighted average cost of capital came out at 7.5%.

Source	*Estimated Proportions of Future Funds Sources*	*Estimated Future Cost, after Taxes*
Debt	33%	2.5%
Depreciation and retained earnings	67	10.0
Weighted average cost		7.5%

This 7.5% assumed that at least 7.5% would be earned on the total capital employed by the company. In fact, however, total capital employed included not only successful projects but also unsuccessful projects and certain necessary investments that resulted in little, if any, return. About 25% of the company's investments typically fell into the second and third categories. Thus, to earn 7.5% on an overall basis it was necessary to earn at least 10%

after taxes on the 75% of the company's projects where an actual return was expected. This is the 10% discount rate that was used by the company in determining the net present value of proposed capital expenditures.

The idea of using the single 10% discount rate on a corporationwide basis had been strongly opposed from the beginning by several of the operating subsidiaries of General Holdings. These subsidiaries argued that the internal allocation of funds by the parent company among its principal operating subsidiaries should be based upon a system of multiple target rates of return reflecting the unique risk–profit characteristics of the industry or economic sector in which each subsidiary operated.

Those arguing in favor of multiple target rates of return usually began by pointing out that General Holdings Corporation was really just a holding company with a number of operating subsidiaries in several related and unrelated industries. Each of these operating affiliates faced numerous competitors and a unique risk–profit environment. Some of these competitors operated in only one industry or economic sector; others were parts of more complex groupings, such as General Holdings. However this might be, those arguing in favor of multiple cutoff rates did so on the grounds that given the underlying strategic decision to be in, say, pipelines or refining or plastics, the parent company had then to adopt minimum acceptable rates of return related to the competitive risk–profit characteristics inherent in each area.

To do otherwise was alleged to have two important undesirable outcomes. The first of these was that a high companywide rate, such as the company's present 10% discount rate, resulted in the company or its affiliates not going into some highly profitable ventures. Gas transmission pipelines were an often-cited example of this. Gas pipelines had been ruled out by General Holdings in the past because the regulated 6% return on invested capital was well below the company's 10% minimum. In spite of this low regulated return, however, gas transmission companies were typically highly leveraged because of the limited economic risk involved in their operation, and their common stocks often sold in the 30 times price–earnings range. Since this was double General Holdings' normal price–earnings ratio, it was argued that the company's stockholders would have benefited had the parent company allowed its pipeline affiliate to expand along with the gas transmission industry.

The second undesirable outcome of using a high single cutoff rate was that it was said to favor investment projects or alternatives with low initial funds commitments almost without regard to the subsequent operating cost streams that could be expected to follow. In part, this was simply reiterating the point that the company had been underinvesting in the low risk parts of its business or businesses. But more was involved. Where operating economies of scale were concerned, particularly in capital intensive areas, a higher than justified rate penalized high initial investment–low operating cost alternatives in favor of low initial investment–high operating cost alternatives or projects. In short, the company tended to underinvest initially at the expense of higher future operating costs, and deferred related investments whose importance was underrated as a result of using an inappropriately high discount rate in low risk situations.

The specific alternative proposed by the supporters of multiple cutoff rates in lieu of a single companywide rate involved determining several rates, based on the estimated cost of capital inherent in each of the economic sectors or industries in which the company's principal operating subsidiaries worked. Weighted average cost of capital cutoff rates reflecting their specific risk–profit environments would be determined for the company's production-exploration, pipeline transportation, refining, and marketing affiliates in the oil industry, as well as for its plastics, industrial chemicals, agricultural chemicals, and real estate subsidiaries operating outside the oil industry. For example, cutoff rates of 16%, 11%, 8%, and 6%, respectively, were proposed for the production-exploration, chemicals, real estate, and pipeline parts of the business. All the other rates proposed fell within this range. The suggestion was that these multiple cutoff rates determine the minimum acceptable rate of return on proposed capital investments in each of the main operating areas of the company.

It was proposed that the weighted average cost of capital in each operating sector be developed as follows. First, an estimate would be made of the usual debt and equity proportions of independently financed firms operating in each sector. Several such independents competed against each of the company's affiliates. Second, the costs of debt and equity given these proportions and sectors would be estimated in accordance with the concepts followed by the company in estimating its own costs of capital in the past. Third, these costs and proportions would be combined to determine the weighted average cost of capital, or minimum acceptable rate of return, for discounting purposes in each sector.

These multiple hurdle or discount rates had been calculated for several periods in the past, and invariably when their weighted average was weighted according to the company's relative investment in each sector, it exceeded the company's actual overall average cost of capital. This differential was attributed to the fact that the sector hurdle rates calculated as described above tended to overlook the risk diversification benefits of many investments undertaken by General Holdings. As compared with a nonintegrated enterprise operating in any given branch, a vertically and horizontally integrated firm such as General Holdings enjoyed some built-in asset diversification as well as important captive markets between certain of its vertically integrated parts. For example, the risks associated with a refinery investment by an integrated company like General Holdings were said to be much less than for an identical investment made by an independent. It was proposed that this diversification premium be allocated back and deducted from the multiple subsidiary discount rates in proportion to the relationship of the investment in each subsidiary to the company's total assets.

While it had been impossible to accurately appraise the overall impact of changing from a single rate to multiple target rates, it could be foreseen that both the company's asset structure and the probable size of its future capital expenditures would be affected. It was anticipated, for example, that up to one third of future capital expenditures might be shifted from one to another operating sector or affiliate with the adoption of multiple hurdle rates. In addition, the company's expected average annual capital budget could easily increase from $150 million to $175 million or more. An annual budget of this magnitude would force reconsideration of the company's traditional debt, common stock, and dividend policies.

As management and the board of General Holdings began their latest review of the controversy between using single or multiple minimum acceptable cutoff rates, the officers of the operating subsidiaries were asked to restate their positions. Those behind the present single target rate contended that the stockholders of General Holdings would expect the company to invest their funds in the highest return projects available. They suggested that without exception the affiliates backing multiple rates were those that were unable to compete effectively for new funds when measured against the corporate group's actual cost of capital. Against this, the multiple hurdle rate proponents pointed out again that if the parent company was serious about competing over the long run in industries with such disparate risk–profit characteristics as they faced, it was absolutely essential to relate internal target rates of return to these circumstances. They felt that division of the overall corporate investment pot should be based primarily on the company's long-term strategic plans. It was against this background that the final choice between single versus multiple cutoff rates had to be decided.

AMALGAMATED MANUFACTURING CORPORATION (A)

The Amalgamated Manufacturing Corporation was a large manufacturer of heavy industrial equipment with its main headquarters and production facilities located in the metropolitan Chicago area. The company had grown over a long period of years. Its principal sales volume was in a specialized line of industrial equipment, which accounted for more than half of its 1964 sales volume. Technological developments had limited sales of new equipment in this major line of the company's production in recent years, and it seemed unlikely that original equipment sales would expand beyond their 1965 volume. Although the demand for replacement parts would remain high for several years to come, it would eventually be limited by the cessation of growth and possible decline in the sale of new equipment.

The management of Amalgamated was thus confronted with the difficult task of maintaining a satisfactory rate of growth in the overall volume of the company's sales and earnings. Two main strategies were adopted. One was to intensify the company's research and development efforts in product lines that had previously accounted for a relatively small portion of Amalgamated's total volume but seemed to offer more promising opportunities for long-term growth than its main line of industrial equipment. The second was to inaugurate a vigorous search for companies Amalgamated might acquire in industries other than its main product line. The successful implementation of these strategies explains in part the growth of Amalgamated in recent years (Exhibit 1) and its sound financial position at the end of 1964 (Exhibit 2).

Amalgamated was particularly interested in acquiring small companies with promising products and management personnel but without established growth records. The management of Amalgamated hoped to be able to acquire several such companies each year, preferably before their earning capacity had been sufficiently well established to command a premium price. In this way it hoped over a period of years to build a broad base for expansion and diversification.

The management of Amalgamated was aware that the potential rate of growth of many small companies was limited by inadequate capital resources and distribution systems. It was convinced that Amalgamated's abundant capital resources and nationwide distribution system could greatly facilitate the growth of many such companies. Consequently, it hoped that Amalgamated would be able to acquire promising small companies on terms that would be mutually attractive because of the complementary character of the contributions that Amalgamated and any small companies it might acquire could make to the combined enterprise.

In following the strategy of expanding in part through acquisitions, the management of Amalgamated recognized that a variety of problems would be encountered. One was that such a policy would have to be in accord with the rather strict interpretation by the Supreme Court and the Justice Department of allowable mergers or acquisitions under the antitrust laws. Among other things, this would mean that most of the companies to be acquired by Amalgamated would have to be small in size. Even so, only a few companies could be acquired in any one year. Consequently, if these acquisitions were to have a significant impact on the growth rate of Amalgamated, it was important that wise decisions be made in selecting the companies to be purchased from the many potentially available for acquisition. The management of Amalgamated anticipated that for each company it should attempt to acquire, many companies might have to be screened.

(There are, of course, many facets to any decision concerning a potential acquisition. Among the most important is the caliber of the management of the company to be acquired, provided that the old management is expected to remain. Likewise, the quality of the company's product line, research capabilities, and patent position, if any, are prime considerations. Others are the degree to which the products of the two companies would mesh and the extent to which the value of the acquired company would be enhanced by an association with an established company. The acceptability of the acquisition under the antitrust laws would also have to be evaluated.)

Even after a prospective acquisition had passed the preliminary screening tests established by the management of Amalgamated, there still remained the difficult task of determining the maximum offering price that would be placed on the stock or assets of the company to be acquired. Until such an evaluation was made, serious negotiations with the potential sellers could not commence.

In order to apply consistent standards and to minimize the work load, the financial staff of Amalgamated had been requested by its top management to work out a standardized procedure to be used in evaluating potential acquisitions. The method used in evaluating the Norwood Screw Machinery Company, discussed below, is typical of that ordinarily used by Amalgamated.

The remainder of the case will describe very briefly the Norwood Screw Machinery Company and then discuss in more detail the method by which the financial staff arrived at a figure to recommend to management as a possible maximum purchase price. Not all the members of the management were convinced of the validity of the method of evaluation currently being used by Amalgamated. The final section of the case outlines briefly the doubts expressed by these members.

NORWOOD SCREW MACHINERY COMPANY

The Norwood Screw Machinery Company was a relatively small company with a diversified line of screw machinery products. It had a plant with approximately 75,000 square feet and employed about 75 persons. Its sales organization was rudimentary. In the opinion of both the Norwood and Amalgamated managements, this was one explanation for Norwood's relatively low volume of sales and profits.

Amalgamated had an interest in acquiring Norwood, if a satisfactory price could be agreed on, because Amalgamated was favorably impressed by the quality of Norwood's management and by its product lines. Norwood manufactured various standard screw machine products for which competition was severe and growth prospects were limited. It also had several proprietary products on which it earned a much higher rate of profit and from which it expected to achieve substantial growth. In addition, Norwood had several promising products scheduled to be put on the market in the near future. These items, several of which were revolutionary by industry standards, were expected to make a major contribution to Norwood's future growth. The management of Norwood also anticipated improvements in its production processes, which would increase its gross margin on sales above the relatively high level already prevailing.

Preliminary negotiations toward an acquisition of Norwood by Amalgamated were begun in mid-1965. The management of Amalgamated had considerable confidence in the quality of Norwood's management and shared its hopes that Norwood would be successful in developing new and improved products. Both managements believed that Norwood's products could be marketed much more successfully by the combined organization than by Norwood acting alone.

Amalgamated's information as to other aspects of Norwood's operations was much more scanty. Norwood had furnished Amalgamated with audited financial statements only for the year ending December 31, 1964 (Exhibits 3 and 4). The financial staff of Amalgamated was informed that the deficit in the retained earnings account (Exhibit 4) and the negligible charge against net income for income tax accruals (Exhibit 3) resulted from operating losses incurred in 1962 and 1963. These losses, however, were attributed to temporary conditions and were not regarded by the management of either company as indicative of Norwood's potential earning capacity. Preliminary unaudited statements for the first seven months of 1965 showed sales of approximately $550,000 and profits before taxes of about $100,000.

The management of Amalgamated recognized that a much more thorough examination would be necessary before a firm offer could be made to Norwood for the acquisition of its stock or assets. Among other things, much more detailed financial information would be needed for the years preceding 1964 and for the first part of 1965. Other aspects of Norwood's operations, such as the strength of its patent position, would also have to be subjected to detailed scrutiny by Amalgamated. In the meanwhile, however, preliminary negotiations were instituted. In connection with these negotiations, the financial staff of Amalgamated was requested by its top management to prepare an estimate of the maximum price at which Amalgamated might consider acquiring Norwood based on the limited information then available. Such an estimate might help to determine whether the probability that a deal could be worked out was high enough to justify the detailed examination of Norwood that would have to be undertaken before Amalgamated could make a firm offer.

AMALGAMATED'S METHOD OF EVALUATING ACQUISITIONS

Basic approach

As previously noted, Amalgamated's financial staff had worked out a fairly standardized method of evaluating potential acquisitions. This value was calculated by discounting at Amalgamated's cost of capital the future cash flow to be derived from the acquisition. The present worth of this future cash flow was the maximum price that Amalgamated would be willing to pay for an acquisition.

The future cash flow of a potential acquisition was obtained by forecasting the future profits, working capital, capital expenditures, depreciation, and other items affecting the cash flow to be derived from the acquisition. These forecasts were reviewed by the financial staff with other Amalgamated personnel who were familiar with the products and with the industry of the company under consideration.

Forecast of future cash flows

Typically three forecasts were considered in evaluating a company: an optimistic forecast (quite often the forecast submitted by the company to be purchased); a "most likely" forecast (the one that qualified Amalgamated personnel believed most likely to be realized); and, finally, a minimum forecast (reflecting the minimum growth reasonably to be expected from the potential acquisition). The cash flows resulting from each of these forecasts were then discounted at Amalgamated's cost of capital to arrive at a range of values for the company.

Although these three sets of forecasts were normally prepared, the management usually decided on the terms to be offered for a potential acquisition on the basis of the minimum forecast. This procedure was used because management had found that very frequently the *actual* growth rate of its acquisitions had not been as rapid as the minimum forecast.

As an illustration of the divergence often reflected in these forecasts, the president of Norwood estimated that the annual increase in sales would be about $400,000 a year for the next three years under *Norwood's* management, but the annual rate of growth could be as large as $2,000,000 if *Amalgamated* were to acquire Norwood. In contrast, on the assumption that Amalgamated acquired Norwood, the minumum forecast made by Amalgamated's staff for the same three years projected a growth in sales averaging about one third as large as that estimated by Norwood's management. This staff forecast, shown in Exhibit 5, assumes that Amalgamated would acquire Norwood at the beginning of 1966.

Amalgamated's normal procedure was to forecast for a five-year period the cash flows to be used in its evaluation. It then held constant the cash flow predicted for years 6 to 10. The staff preparing the forecasts recognized that this procedure introduced a conservative factor in its evaluation, but this element of conservatism was thought desirable as a means of counterbalancing the tendency cited above to overestimate the growth rate for the first five years. Finally, in year 10 a terminal value was placed on the company to be acquired. In effect, then, Amalgamated's procedure valued a potential acquisition as the sum of the present worth of the cash flow to be realized over the next 10 years plus the present worth of the terminal value at the end of the 10th year.

Assignment of terminal value

The decision to use a terminal value at the end of the 10th year was prompted by two factors. First, it was recognized that in the normal case Amalgamated would still own a company from which cash flows would be derived and which would, therefore, be of value to Amalgamated at the end of the 10-year period. Second, it seemed impractical to Amalgamated to attempt to forecast cash flows for longer than 10 years.

In the past Amalgamated had used several different approaches to set a terminal value on a potential acquisition at the end of the 10th year. These approaches included (1) the book value of the acquired company at this date; (2) its liquidating value at this date, that is, an estimate of the value of its assets but not as a going concern; and (3) a value based on an estimated sale of the acquired company at a specified multiple of earnings at the end of the 10th year.

However, Amalgamated's staff recognized that each of these procedures had serious limitations. Book value and liquidating value often would not reflect the worth of a company based on its present and potential earnings. The sale of a company at a specified multiple of 10-year earnings was regarded as a more adequate reflection of the value of the company in that year. The possible tax adjustments resulting from capital gains or losses arising from the sale, as well as the appropriate price-earnings multiplier for each company, were recognized as presenting additional complications for this method of determining a terminal value. Furthermore, Amalgamated's staff was concerned about a possible internal contradiction in this approach to the problem. It reasoned that to value the company in the 10th year at a specified price-earnings multiplier would be somewhat unrealistic: if the company's performance were satisfactory, Amalgamated probably would not be willing to sell; and if its performance were poor, Amalgamated probably would not be able to obtain the value indicated by the price-earnings multiplier.

At the time of the Norwood evaluation Amalgamated's staff was using a somewhat different approach. The terminal value of the company in year 10 was assumed to be the present worth of 20 years of additional cash flow. The annual rate of cash flow for years 11 through 30 was normally assumed to be equal to that for years 6 to 10, with the possible exception of adjustments for certain noncash expenses such as are shown in Exhibit 5. This procedure was believed to reflect more satisfactorily Amalgamated's intention in making an acquisition, that is, to realize a satisfactory cash flow over the long run.

Obviously, an assignment of a terminal value based on a discounting of the estimated cash flows (or earnings) from years 11 through 30 would not necessarily require Amalgamated to retain the company for 30 years in order for the acquisition to be profitable. For example, if Amalgamated could sell an acquisition at the end of the 10th year for the calculated terminal value, then, disregarding possible capital gains taxes, the investment would be just as profitable as if the assumed 20 years of additional earnings were realized in years 11–30. The Amalgamated procedure ignored years beyond year 30 because their contribution to the present worth of the terminal value with a discount rate as high as 10%, or thereabouts, would be negligible.

Working capital and capital expenditures

In determining the cash flows that would be caused by an acquisition, estimates also had to be made of changes in working capital requirements and of prospective capital outlays. If no better evidence was available, working capital requirements for a proposed acquisition were based on an historical analysis of relevant financial ratios of the company or industry for previous years. Expenditures on fixed assets were estimated at a level designed to maintain physical facilities in good working order and to handle the projected increases in sales volume.

Since sales volume was estimated to increase only for the first five years, as noted above, working capital requirements were generally considered to remain constant after year five. A typical assumption with respect to capital expenditures was that they would be equal to depreciation outlays after year five. The Norwood evaluation was made in this manner (Exhibit 5).

Treatment of debt

The financial staff of Amalgamated eliminated debt from the capital structure of potential acquisitions by assuming in its cash flow estimates that this debt would be paid off in full in year zero. As a corollary, interest charges associated with this debt were also eliminated from the estimates of cash outflows for subsequent years. The rationale for this treatment of debt and associated interest charges was that the future earnings of an acquisition should not be benefited by the use of leverage in the capital structure. This treatment was designed to permit all potential acquisitions to be evaluated on a comparable basis.

Estimate of cost of capital

Amalgamated's practice at the time of the Norwood acquisition was to discount its cash-flow estimates for future years at a rate of 10%. This figure was assumed to be an approximation of Amalgamated's cost of equity capital. As Exhibit 2 indicates, Amalgamated's capital structure consisted almost entirely of common equity. Management, however, was not committed to such a capital structure as a matter of company policy; it was, in fact, actively considering the possible benefits to be derived from a larger proportion of senior capital in its capital structure.

Application of procedure to Norwood

Exhibit 5 shows in detail how Amalgamated's procedure was applied in the evaluation of Norwood. The cash flow from Norwood was calculated first by estimating after-tax profits in years 1 to 10 and then adding back noncash expenses such as depreciation and amortization. From this sum the cash required for additions to working capital and new capital expenditures was subtracted. In addition, all long-term debt was assumed to be retired at the beginning of 1966 and was shown as an initial outlay. The resulting total represents the estimated cash contribution to be derived from Norwood over the 10-year period beginning January 1, 1966. The cash contribution of each year was then discounted at 10% to obtain an estimate of the present worth of contributions from operations over the next 10 years. The estimated terminal value of Norwood at the end of year 10 was then computed as the present worth of 20 additional years of earnings, that is, the earnings of years 11–30 discounted to year zero at 10%. The sum of the estimated present worth of the contribution from operations for the first 10 years and of the present worth of the terminal value assigned to Norwood represents Amalgamated's estimate of the purchase price that it would be justified in paying for all the outstanding stock of Norwood. This sum amounted to $4,465,000 for Norwood (Exhibit 5).

VIEWS OF OTHER MEMBERS OF AMALGAMATED'S MANAGEMENT

Although the evaluation procedure described in the preceding section was that currently used by Amalgamated, its merits were still under active debate within the company. Some members of management, for example, thought that in evaluating a potential acquisition more emphasis should be placed on the effect on Amalgamated's earnings per share. Mr. Simpson, a company director who was especially interested in Amalgamated's acquisition program, shared this view and contended vigorously that the $4,465,000 price for Norwood, as calculated in Exhibit 5, was far too high. He prepared the following illustrative data to support his position.

Hypothetical levels of profits after taxes to be derived from Norwood	$100,000	$200,000	$300,000	$400,000
Approximate earnings per share of Amalgamated without acquisition of Norwood	$5	$5	$5	$5
Number of shares of Amalgamated's stock that could be exchanged for all outstanding shares of Norwood without diluting Amalgamated's earnings per share	20,000	40,000	60,000	80,000
Approximate market value of Amalgamated's common stock at time of contemplated acquisition	$50	$50	$50	$50
Implicit value placed on Norwood by earnings-per-share criterion	$1,000,000	$2,000,000	$3,000,000	$4,000,000

Mr. Simpson pointed out that even if Norwood's profits after taxes were assumed to expand to $400,000, far in excess of its 1964 or probable 1965 level, the acquisition would result in a dilution of Amalgamated's earnings per share. In no circumstances, he contended, could Norwood's earnings expand sufficiently to overcome this dilution in earnings per share for at least several years. While Mr. Simpson did not deny that Norwood was a promising young company, he argued that no one could foresee the future well enough to predict with confidence that Norwood's profits after taxes would soon reach or exceed a level of $400,000 or $500,000, the minimum range needed to prevent a dilution in Amalgamated's earnings per share.

In this connection Mr. Simpson urged that his numerical illustration was highly conservative in that it assumed no growth in Amalgamated's future earnings per share. In fact, the $5 figure understated reported earnings in 1964 and even more so the projected earnings for 1965. A reasonable allowance for the growth in Amalgamated's earnings per share over the next several years, he pointed out, would require that Norwood's profits after taxes be substantially larger than the top figure of $400,000 shown in his numerical illustration to prevent a dilution in Amalgamated's earnings per share for an indefinite and possibly permanent period.

The proponents of the discounted cash flow method of evaluating acquisitions such as Norwood conceded to Mr. Simpson that it would be preferable for Amalgamated to acquire Norwood for cash rather than by an exchange of stock. But they pointed out to him that since Amalgamated was in a highly liquid position an outright purchase for cash was feasible. Thus Amalgamated's earnings per share would increase provided that the return on Amalgamated's investment in Norwood exceeded that available from money market securities.

Mr. Simpson responded that he recognized the validity of this argument if the Norwood acquisition were viewed in isolation. As a general principle, however, he stated that Norwood should be considered as one of a series of companies that Amalgamated hoped to acquire each year. Mr. Simpson pointed out that, although Amalgamated could probably acquire Norwood without resorting to outside financing, such financing would be required if

Amalgamated pressed its planned program of acquisitions vigorously. He concluded, therefore, that the Norwood acquisition should be required to pass the same earnings-per-share hurdle that he felt would have to be applied to subsequent acquisitions. In summary, then, Mr. Simpson continued to press his original contention, namely, that Norwood should be acquired only if the price were such that no dilution in earnings per share would result if the acquisition were made by an exchange of stock. The most he would concede was that a reasonable time should be allowed so that Norwood's profits would reflect the anticipated benefits from the combined operation before calculating the effect on Amalgamated's earnings per share of acquiring or not acquiring Norwood.

Other influential members of Amalgamated's management were concerned about the impact of the Norwood acquisition on Amalgamated's return on its book investment. They pointed out that Amalgamated was currently earning approximately 8% on the book value of its equity capital. If Norwood were to be acquired for $4,500,000, it would have to earn about $360,000 after taxes to match this rate of return. At best, they contended, several years would pass before earnings of this amount could be reasonably anticipated. Meanwhile the acquisition of Norwood would dilute Amalgamated's return on its book investment.

With these widely conflicting views regarding the appropriate means of evaluating potential acquisitions, all parties concerned were anxious to arrive at a consensus as to the best procedure as soon as possible. Without such a consensus, continuing differences of judgment were bound to occur. These differences would inevitably slow down the company's acquisition program. In addition, favorable opportunities might be rejected and poor ones accepted unless a consistent and defensible method of valuing potential acquisitions could be agreed upon as company policy.

Exhibit 1

AMALGAMATED MANUFACTURING CORPORATION (A)

SELECTED OPERATING DATA, 1960–64

Year	*Net Sales**	*Income after Taxes**	*Earnings per Common Share*	*Dividends per Common Share*	*Market Price of Common Stock*
1960	$157.8	$ 9.0	$3.87	$2.20	$33–57
1961	158.4	8.6	3.62	2.00	38–45
1962	167.0	8.2	3.41	2.00	38–54
1963	183.3	10.4	4.50	2.00	45–55
1964	200.6	11.8	5.11	2.00	45–55

* In millions of dollars.

Exhibit 2

AMALGAMATED MANUFACTURING CORPORATION (A)

Balance Sheet as of December 31, 1964

(In thousands of dollars)

ASSETS	
Current assets:	
Cash	$ 5,344
Marketable securities	8,752
Accounts and notes receivable	32,304
Inventories	48,674
Total current assets	$ 95,074
Net fixed assets	103,537
Patent rights and other intangibles	3,086
Other assets	2,304
Total assets	$204,001

LIABILITIES AND STOCKHOLDERS' EQUITY	
Current liabilities:	
Accounts and notes payable	$ 13,458
Income taxes payable	9,649
Accrued expenses and other liabilities	4,529
Total current liabilities	$ 27,636
Other liabilities (provision for pensions; various reserve accounts; and minority interest)	20,258
Mortgage notes and other noncurrent liabilities	2,927
Total liabilities	$ 50,821
Capital stock:	
Preferred stock	$ 8,478
Common stock	47,319
Retained earnings	97,383
Total stockholders' equity	$153,180
Total liabilities and stockholders' equity	$204,001

Exhibit 3

AMALGAMATED MANUFACTURING CORPORATION (A)

NORWOOD SCREW MACHINERY COMPANY

Income Statement for Year Ending December 31, 1964

(In thousands of dollars)

Net sales	$729.4
Deduct: Cost of goods sold	334.8
Gross profit on sales	$394.6
Deduct: Selling and administrative expenses	252.6
Net operating income	$142.0
Other income less other deductions	14.2
Net profit before income taxes	$156.2
Provision for income taxes	7.8
Net income	$148.4

Exhibit 4

AMALGAMATED MANUFACTURING CORPORATION (A)
NORWOOD SCREW MACHINERY COMPANY

BALANCE SHEET AS OF DECEMBER 31, 1964
(In thousands of dollars)

ASSETS	
Current assets:	
Cash	$ 109
Accounts receivable	130
Inventories	484
Prepaid expenses	37
Total current assets	$ 760
Net plant and equipment	456
Patents and other intangibles	230
Miscellaneous other assets (including large fire loss claim)	218
Total assets	$1,664

LIABILITIES AND STOCKHOLDERS' EQUITY	
Current liabilities:	
Accounts payable	$ 88
Advances from officers	84
Notes payable	116
Accrued expenses	19
Accrued taxes	26
Total current liabilities	$ 333
Debentures payable	273
Total liabilities	$ 606
Stockholders' equity:	
Common stock	$ 154
Paid-in capital	1,260
Retained earnings (deficit)	(356)
Total equity	$1,058
Total liabilities and equity	$1,664

Exhibit 5

AMALGAMATED MANUFACTURING CORPORATION (A)

Norwood Acquisition Study, Evaluation of Company

(In thousands of dollars)

	Initial Outlay	1966	1967	1968	1969	1970	1971	1972	1973	1974	1975	Total
I. OPERATING STATEMENT												
Net sales		$1,866	$2,500	$3,200	$3,800	$4,400	$4,400	$4,400	$4,400	$4,400	$4,400	$37,766
Cost of sales		840	1,050	1,280	1,444	1,672	1,672	1,672	1,672	1,672	1,672	14,646
Gross profit		$1,026	$1,450	$1,920	$2,356	$2,728	$2,728	$2,728	$2,728	$2,728	$2,728	$23,120
Deduct:												
Selling, general, and administrative		560	750	960	1,140	1,320	1,320	1,320	1,320	1,320	1,320	11,330
Research and development		94	126	160	190	220	220	220	220	220	220	1,890
Net profit before tax		$ 372	$ 574	$ 800	$1,026	$1,188	$1,188	$1,188	$1,188	$1,188	$1,188	$ 9,900
Tax at 50%		186	286	400	514	594	594	594	594	594	594	4,950
Net profit after tax		$ 186	$ 288	$ 400	$ 512	$ 594	$ 594	$ 594	$ 594	$ 594	$ 594	$ 4,950
Cash flow												
Add:												
Depreciation		88	96	96	96	120						496
Other noncash charges against income		28	28	28	28	28	28	28	28	28	20	272
Deduct:												
Increase in working capital		...	...	160	180	180						520
Capital expenditures		84	...	...	260	...						344
Long-term debt	$ 218*											218
Mortgages	22*											22
Cash contribution from 10 years' operations	$(240)	$ 218	$ 412	$ 364	$ 196	$ 562	$ 622	$ 622	$ 622	$ 622	$ 614	$ 4,614
Present worth contribution at 10%	(240)	198	340	273	134	349	351	319	290	264	237	2,515

II. TOTAL PRESENT WORTH VALUE OF COMPANY AT A 10% DISCOUNT FACTOR

Present worth contribution from operations	$2,515
Terminal value—present worth of 20 added years of earnings	1,950
Total present worth value of company	$4,465

* These outlays are assumed to be made on January 1, 1966.

AMALGAMATED MANUFACTURING CORPORATION (B)

As the case of Amalgamated Manufacturing Corporation (A) indicates (pp. 432–43), there was resistance within the Amalgamated top-management group to acquisitions that would dilute earnings per share even though such acquisitions could be justified by the use of Amalgamated's discounted-cash-flow method of evaluating acquisitions. Consequently, acquisitions that could be financed by cash rather than by an exchange of stock were favored by the management of Amalgamated. This preference was shared by the advocates of both the discounted-cash-flow method and the earnings-per-share method.

One reason for this preference was the low price-earnings multiple at which Amalgamated stock was selling. As Exhibit 1 of the (A) case (p. 440) shows, the average market price of Amalgamated stock was only about 10 times its earnings per share in 1964, and it had not greatly exceeded this figure during most of the 1960–64 period. In 1965 the market price of Amalgamated stock did not rise sufficiently to match the increase in earnings during the first half of 1965. Consequently, at the time of the Norwood negotiations the stock was selling at considerably less than 10 times current earnings per share.

The management of Amalgamated believed that for several years the stock market had valued its shares mainly in terms of the limited outlook for expansion in its main line of equipment rather than in terms of the growth that management believed would result from its aggressive research and development efforts in expanding product areas and from its acquisition program. Until the market placed more weight on these phases of Amalgamated's activities, management preferred to make acquisitions for cash rather than through an exchange of stock.

This preference posed a dilemma. If Amalgamated had to rely on internally generated cash, the pace of its acquisition program would be severely constrained. On the other hand, more acquisitions could be made if they were "paid for" by an exchange of stock, but the price of those acquired for stock would be likely to be excessive in the judgment of the management of Amalgamated.

As a means of resolving this dilemma and of accomplishing other company objectives, Amalgamated had developed a "buy-out" plan for financing acquisitions. Under this plan Amalgamated paid part of the purchase price when the purchase agreement was signed and agreed to make further payments conditional in amount on the future profits of the company being acquired.

From Amalgamated's viewpoint management thought that this method of purchase had several advantages. (1) It reduced Amalgamated's original investment and consequently the risk involved in a new acquisition. (2) It enabled the acquisition to pay for itself partially out of its future profits, thereby deferring and possibly reducing the cash drain on Amalgamated. (3) If the key executives of the company being acquired were also major stockholders, it provided them with a powerful incentive to remain with Amalgamated and to perform well since part of their payment depended on the profits generated by the acquired company. (4) It sometimes offered a tax advantage to selling stockholders, thereby enabling Amalgamated to negotiate more favorable terms for the acquisition than would otherwise have been possible. (5) Finally, it often served as a means of reconciling the divergent views of Amalgamated's management and the owners of the selling company concerning the profit potentialities of the selling company. If the future profits of the selling company proved to be relatively low, the total price that Amalgamated would be obligated to pay would be correspondingly reduced. On the other hand, if the normally optimistic profit estimates of the owners of the selling company proved to be correct, they would benefit by the profit sharing contingency in the buy-out plan. Moreover, in those instances in which the optimistic estimates of the sellers were correct Amalgamated could well afford to pay a premium price.

In reviewing the possible acquisition of the Norwood Screw Machinery Company the financial staff of Amalgamated had prepared a tentative buy-out proposal for the consideration of its top management. This plan was typical of others that had been employed by Amalgamated in previous acquisitions. The Norwood plan was based on the same profit projections and other financial data shown in Exhibit 5 of the (A) case (p. 443). This plan, as summarized in Exhibit 1, contained the following provisions:

1. On the closing of the purchase agreement (assumed to occur on December 31, 1965) Amalgamated would pay $2,000,000 to the stockholders of Norwood for all its outstanding stock. Amalgamated would also pay off Norwood's long-term debt of $240,000 as of this date.

2. The Norwood stockholders would be given 695,000 "certificates of participation" in the combined companies. Amalgamated would guarantee a payment of $3 for each certificate. The holders of the certificates would share in the profits of the Norwood division of Amalgamated over the next 10 years. The certificates could be redeemed at the option of the holders at the end of any year within the 10-year period. On redemption the certificate holder would receive his guaranteed $3 per certificate plus his share of the profits that had accrued at the time of redemption. All certificates had to be presented for redemption by the end of the 10th year.

This buy-out plan committed Amalgamated to a minimum payment of $4,325,000 for the acquisition of Norwood, nearly half of which would be deferred from 1 to 10 years. This guaranteed payment was significantly lower than the maximum cash outlay of $4,465,000—as estimated in Exhibit 5 of the (A) case—which Amalgamated could afford to make in an outright purchase of Norwood. The smaller guaranteed payment, however, was offset by the right of the former Norwood stockholders to share in part of the profits of the Norwood division under Amalgamated's ownership for the next 10 years.

3. For each of the 10 years after the acquisition, Amalgamated would subtract from the profits of the Norwood division 10% of its initial investment in Norwood, or $224,000. The remaining profits of each year would be split between Amalgamated and the holders of the certificates of participation, with 25% going to Amalgamated and 75% *accruing* to the certificate holders.

4. All the cash realized from the Norwood division would go to Amalgamated. Cash would be paid out to the holders of certificates of participation *only* when these certificates were turned in for redemption. When certificates were turned in for redemption, Amalgamated would be considered to be the holder of these certificates and would participate on a pro rata basis with the other certificate holders in the share of the profits accruing to the certificate holders. In effect, the 75% share of the annual profits in excess of $224,000 would be reduced in order to reflect the proportion of the certificates redeemed to date.

Outstanding certificates could be redeemed in any amount at the end of any year from 1 to 10. The timing of the redemption of the certificates would affect Amalgamated's profitability index. (The profitability index was defined by Amalgamated as the discount rate required to equate the present worth of all cash outlays with that of all cash inflows. The terminal value at the end of year 10, as described in the (A) case, was treated as a cash inflow. In other words, the profitability index was substantially equivalent to the estimated "internal rate of return" as this concept is commonly defined.)

* * * * *

Exhibit 1 illustrates the buy-out plan suggested by the Amalgamated staff for the Norwood acquisition. The data are taken from the preceding description and from the profit projections recorded in Exhibit 5 of the (A) case. Calculations are presented in Exhibit 1 for three possible patterns of redemption: (1) all certificates are assumed to be redeemed at the end of year 1; (2) the same assumption is made for year 5; and (3) for year 10. The profitability index for all combinations of redemptions of certificates in various years will be between those calculated for total redemption in years 1 and 10.

In computing the profitability indices shown in Exhibit 1 the cash outflows consist of the initial outlay of $2,240,000 at the beginning of the first year, and, as the case may be, the outlays required to redeem the outstanding certificates at the end of the 1st, 5th, or 10th years, respectively. The cash inflows are the same as those shown in the next to last line of the cash inflows recorded in Exhibit 5 of the (A) case. The terminal value is calculated as the present worth of an estimated level stream of annual cash inflows of $594,000 for years 11 through 30. Profits after taxes and cash flows are assumed to be equal for years 11 through 30: more explicitly, all noncash expenses except depreciation are assumed to have been exhausted by year 10; capital expenditures are assumed to be equal to depreciation; and net working capital is assumed to remain unchanged after year 10. Under the assumptions of Exhibit 1 the profitability indices range from 11.5% to 13.9% depending on the timing of the redemption of the certificates of participation.

* * * * *

The specific buy-out plan outlined for the Norwood acquisition was only one of several used by Amalgamated. In some cases, for example, the profits of the acquired company were split directly with the former shareholders without first allocating to Amalgamated all the profits up to 10% on its initial investment. However, the basic procedure and objective of Amalgamated remained the same—to set payment terms that would be consistent with the maximum purchase price as calculated in the (A) case and would give Amalgamated a satisfactory return (computed on a discounted-cash-flow basis) on its actual cash commitments.

Exhibit 1

AMALGAMATED MANUFACTURING CORPORATION (B)

NORWOOD ACQUISITION STUDY: BUY-OUT PLAN

(In thousands of dollars)

	Initial Outlay	1966	1967	1968	1969	1970	1971	1972	1973	1974	1975
I. BUY-OUT PLAN											
Original cash payment	$2,000										
Long-term debt repayment	240										
Net profit after taxes		$ 186	$ 288	$ 400	$ 512	$ 594	$ 594	$ 594	$ 594	$ 594	$ 594
Amalgamated's share at 10%		224	224	224	224	224	224	224	224	224	224
Balance available for accrual		0	26*	176	288	370	370	370	370	370	370
Amalgamated's share of profits (25%)		0	6	44	72	92	92	92	92	92	92
Accrue 75% to Norwood		0	20	132	216	278	278	278	278	278	278
Cumulative amount accrued to Norwood		$ 0	20	$ 152	$ 368	$ 646	$ 924	$1,202	$1,480	$1,758	$2,036
Add: Guaranteed amount ($3 a share)		2,085	2,085	2,085	2,085	2,085	2,085	2,085	2,085	2,085	2,085
Total delayed payment to Norwood		$2,085	$2,105	$2,237	$2,453	$2,731	$3,009	$3,287	$3,565	$3,843	$4,121
Profitability index to Amalgamated		11.5% (*If all certificates redeemed in 1966*)				12.5% (*If all certificates redeemed in 1970*)					13.9% (*If all certificates redeemed in 1975*)

II. CALCULATION OF PROFITABILITY INDEXES	Initial Outlay	1966	End of 1966	1967	1968	1969	1970	End of 1970	1971	1972	1973	1974	1975	End of 1975	Ter. Val. Yrs. 1976–95†	Profitability Index†
1. All certificates redeemed at end of 1966	−2,240	218	−2,085	412	364	196	562		622	622	622	622	614		594/yr.	11.5%
2. All certificates redeemed at end of 1970	−2,240	218		412	364	196	562	−2,731	622	622	622	622	614		594/yr.	12.5%
3. All certificates redeemed at end of 1975	−2,240	218		412	364	196	562		622	622	622	622	614	−4,121	594/yr.	13.9%

* Balance after adjustment for 1966 profit deficiency.

† The profitability index is the annual rate of discount at which the present worth of expected cash outlays is just equal to the present worth of expected cash inflows. Included in the cash inflows is an annuity of $594,000 annually received at the end of each year from 1976–95, inclusive.

THE CUNO ENGINEERING CORPORATION

^^

To provide for more orderly growth and improved evaluation of acquisition opportunities, Mr. Patterson, chairman and chief executive of the American Machine & Foundry Company, established a planning staff in 1958. By the spring of 1960 this group had produced several major special reports in addition to its more routine task of analysis of possible acquisitions. One of the areas to which the planning staff had directed its attention was water treatment. Early in 1960, Peter J. West of the AMF planning staff was again considering the desirability of acquiring The Cuno Engineering Corporation through an exchange of shares.

For some time, AMF's research and development laboratories had been exploring the area of dialytic treatment of salt and brackish water. In the process of dialytic treatment, the liquid to be conditioned was separated into compartments by ion-exchange membranes of alternate types, which would permit either negative or positive particles to pass. When current was applied to the solution, the particles in the solution flowed toward the proper electrodes and grouped themselves in alternate compartments as they were stopped by the ion-exchange membranes. As a result, the solution in half of the compartments was less saline than the original substance and the solution in the other compartments was more saline. AMF's research group was experimenting not only in water treatment but also in the use of the dialytic method in broader fields, such as the treatment of pickling liquors in the steel industry.

Members of the planning division recognized the long-range possibilities created by the increasing water shortage in many parts of the world. Many areas were served only by naturally brackish water, which required some treatment before it would be potable. Treatment of brackish water was one step, AMF executives believed, toward the treatment of sea water. Moreover, the possibility of using developments in the water desalinization area for still other purposes indicated to the planning staff that they should approach the problem in the general terms of liquid conditioning.

A liquid-conditioning system required a pump, a treatment section, and a polishing filter. The pump was a standard product, manufactured by many firms, and could easily be procured when AMF had developed a treatment system. The polishing filter would have to be improved beyond its current refinement, but these advances were probably well within the capabilities of engineers in the field. Successful entrance into the liquid-conditioning market also would require suitable marketing channels. AMF executives thought that they could acquire such a distribution system by purchase of a company already in the area, preferably closely related to the areas AMF had been exploring. However, the key problem in an entrance into the liquid-conditioning field was the necessity of overcoming the various technical difficulties, not the acquisition of the ancillary equipment lines or marketing channels. AMF executives were not concerned about competition because they felt that the company's research group could be expected to produce results at least as fast as the research laboratories of other major companies in the water treatment area. Partly as a by-product of recent findings developed from experiments involving more economical production of atomic energy, the AMF executives believed that AMF had gained a technological advantage, and they were anxious to push developments ahead rapidly.

Although in 1959 AMF had no immediate plans for acquiring any firms in the liquid-conditioning business, the planning staff had considered several companies as possible candidates for acquisition, and had made brief studies of their operation. Several firms had been approached informally, but no commitment had been made by the beginning of 1960.

One of the firms the planning group had investigated in the summer and fall of 1959 was The Cuno Engineering Corporation of Meriden, Connecticut. The reports prepared at that time pointed out the limited position that Cuno would offer in AMF's expansion into the water and liquid treatment field. As a result, Cuno was not formally approached by the AMF executives in 1959. Selected portions of the report concerning Cuno appear in Exhibit 1.

In February, 1960, Murray McConnel, president of Cuno, notified Morehead Patterson, chairman of AMF, that he and his associates were interested in selling their interest in Cuno and that a merger offer had been made to Cuno by another firm in the filter business. Mr. McConnel was interested in learning whether the AMF executives might want to merge AMF with Cuno and, if so, what terms would be satisfactory. Because Mr. Patterson and Walter Bedell Smith (AMF's vice chairman) had been members of Cuno's board of directors for some years and Mr. McConnel had been on AMF's board, the corporate officials were well aware of the potential conflicts of interest in the situation and agreed to conduct their negotiations on an arm's-length basis. Mr. Patterson requested the planning division to make a review of Cuno and prepare a recommendation for action, along with suggested purchase terms. Peter J. West, a recent graduate of the Harvard Business School and a member of AMF's planning staff, was assigned this task.

The Cuno Engineering Corporation

The Cuno Engineering Corporation had been founded in 1912. It was not the largest company in the filter industry, but it had a reputation for engineering excellence and market service in its segment of the market. By specializing in industrial filters rather than in the automotive filter market, the company had avoided the price competition involved in supplying original equipment to automobile manufacturers.

Cuno's products could be divided into three main classifications. The first included a broad line of industrial filters, which accounted for about 70% of net sales; the second, a line of home water filters, which accounted for about 10% of net sales; the third, a line of automobile cigarette lighters, which accounted for about 20% of net sales.

Industrial filters. The types of industrial filters manufactured by Cuno enabled it to produce and market equipment designed to filter any fluid—liquid or gas—that could be pumped. Such filtering was usually employed to remove foreign particles from a fluid used in a piece of equipment and so prevent damage to the working parts of the equipment, or to remove foreign particles from a consumer product such as paint, soap, or chocolate. In nearly all cases Cuno's filters were precision products engineered to do specific filtering tasks. They were produced in small quantities rather than in mass. The most important types of Cuno industrial filters were the following:

Auto-Klean. This precision filter contained equally spaced discs of metal and was capable of providing positive removal of all particles larger than 0.0035 inch. The filter was a permanent all-metal type that could be cleaned at any time, manually or automatically, without interrupting the flow of the fluid being filtered. The Auto-Klean filter was used in cleaning fluids, greases, lubricants, and coolants in machine tools, engines, compressors, and pumps.

Flo-Klean. This motor-driven filter was intended for use in filtering large volumes of liquids. The permanent, all-metal filtering element consisted of a stationary cylindrical cage; around the outer surface was wound a wire with the spacing between rows as close as 0.0025 inch. The filter had a continuous and automatic backwash cleaning mechanism. The Flo-Klean filter was used primarily for removing particles from water, coolants, cutting oil, and other like fluids, particularly in connection with large machines or groups of machines such as steel mills, grinding machines, and paper machines.

Micro-Klean. This filter of the replaceable cartridge type was capable of filtering micronic-size particles out of liquid or gas. The degree of filtration attainable ranged from 5 microns (0.0002) to 75 microns (0.003 inch). Important users of the filter included paint, varnish, and enamel manufacturers; jet engine producers, diesel engine manufacturers; and industries using air-operated instruments and tools.

Micro-Screen. This line of filters had elements of woven wire mesh, sometimes sintered. They were used for hydraulic and fuel systems on aircraft, missiles, and missile launching facilities, and in cleaning various process fluids.

Poro-Klean. This line had a filtering element of porous sintered metals produced from various powdered metals, notably stainless steel. The filters were particularly suited for handling fluids where extreme conditions of corrosion, temperature, and differential pressure could be encountered. Their unusual properties led to successful use in the rapidly expanding fields of atomic energy, aircraft and guided missiles, and the chemical process industries. These uses included fuel filtering on jet engines, filtering in hydraulic systems on aircraft and guided missiles, and filtering of various process fluids, including such chemicals as polymers for use in production of film and synthetic fibers.

Home water filters. The newest of Cuno's main product groups included a line of filters for the filtration of water in the home as it came from city and municipal water supplies, from wells, or from other private sources. The most important product in this group was the Aqua-Pure, which utilized a white cellulose replaceable cartridge contained in a durable plastic housing with a transparent sump. It removed particles of iron, rust, dirt, grit, sand, and algae from household water systems.

Automobile cigarette lighters. Cuno was one of the three largest manufacturers of automobile cigarette lighters in the United States. Its main customers for cigarette lighters were automobile manufacturers, which normally accounted for about 90% of Cuno's sales of lighters.

Financial background on Cuno

The filter business was a highly competitive one. In 1958 and 1959 a number of the larger companies in the industry had shown negligible profits or actual losses. Cuno, however, had an excellent financial record. Exhibit 2 gives 1957 and 1958 balance sheets, and Exhibit 3 gives income statements for 1955–58. Cuno's earnings had shown excellent growth except in 1958, when profits fell off because of the decline in the industrial segment of the economy and also because of unusual expenses incurred in the development of the Cuno line of home water filters. The company's sales in 1957 were 130% of 1955 sales, and 1957 net profits were 167% of 1955 profits. Final figures for 1959 sales and profits were expected to show gains over 1957.

In 1955 Cuno had reorganized its financial structure. To replace a two-class common stock capitalization, one class of common stock was created and a new preferred stock was issued.[1] The new preferred stock was offered to the public along with some of the new common stock. A total of 100,000 units was issued at $16.50 per unit of one preferred share and one common share. The net proceeds, $1.5 million, were used to help retire bank loans of about $2.2 million and to acquire the stock of the Connecticut Filter Corporation for $250,000.

Cuno had about 1,200 common stockholders in 1959, down from 1,367 at the end of 1956. Of the 287,260 shares of common stock outstanding at

[1] The new common stock had a par value of $1. The new preferred stock, which was entitled to annual cumulative dividends of $1, had a stated value of $14 a share and was callable in whole or in part at $17. Beginning on April 1, 1957, an annual sinking fund of 20% of net earnings, not exceeding $60,000 in any year, was to be used to retire preferred stock by purchase at not more than $17 or by call at $17. The consent of 50% of the preferred stock was required for the issue of debt of a maturity over one year for purposes other than to refund indebtedness or to retire all the preferred stock.

the end of 1959, Mr. McConnel, president of Cuno, and Mrs. McConnel held 36.1%, and the other directors and officers as a group held 29%. Directors and officers could also influence another 4%, held in trust or by their wives and children. The directors and officers as a group held about 6% of the preferred stock, either directly or as trustees. The Cuno stock was traded over the counter, but the market was thin.

Cuno had been aggressively managed. Its products distribution was well organized, production costs were falling as a percentage of sales, and about 1.5% of net sales was spent on its development department. The company's products were considered to be the most sophisticated in the industry, and its engineering capability was, according to customers, second to none. Mr. McConnel, who had been president since 1949, was becoming concerned about the company's continued existence after his retirement. In addition, Mr. and Mrs. McConnel had a substantial portion of their personal savings invested in Cuno stock and were interested in planning the disposition of their estate. Therefore in late 1959 Cuno's board of directors began to look for a prospective buyer.

Cuno-AMF relations

For several years, Morehead Patterson, board chairman of AMF, and Walter Bedell Smith, vice chairman, had served on the board of directors of Cuno, and Mr. McConnel had served as a director of AMF. The two groups of executives held each other in high regard, and it was natural that the interest of AMF's executives should be attracted to Cuno when they decided to enter the liquid-conditioning field. However, AMF had not made a formal offer to Cuno's management—in fact, had not yet made a decision regarding the desirability of acquiring Cuno—when word of the pending offer to Cuno was received. According to Mr. Patterson's information, the proposed acquisition was to be on the basis of a market-for-market exchange of stock, which at current prices (Exhibit 4 lists Cuno's stock prices) represented about $6 million for the common stock and about $1.4 million for the preferred. Because Cuno's management had a knowledge of AMF's manner of operation and knew AMF's management, it was anxious to know whether AMF would meet the alternative offer or on what terms AMF would be interested.

Mr. Patterson's position

Despite the relatively negative conclusions of AMF's 1959 reports on Cuno, Mr. Patterson argued that if AMF was going to enter the liquid-conditioning field and would eventually be interested in Cuno or a similar company, then AMF should buy Cuno at once. He believed that Cuno offered AMF several advantages which AMF would not have when going into a firm "cold turkey." AMF's management knew and respected the Cuno management. AMF's executives were reasonably familiar with Cuno's problems. Mr. McConnel was likewise familiar with AMF's practices and outlook. Moreover, if AMF delayed and Cuno was purchased by some other firm in the liquid-conditioning business, AMF might find it necessary at a later date to buy a much larger firm, some of whose divisions might not fit well into AMF's growth plans.

Mr. Patterson was also aware that AMF's stock was trading at a favorable price-earnings multiple in February, 1960. (Exhibit 5 gives prices of AMF common stock monthly from January, 1959, through February, 1960.) He did not know how long this condition would continue and believed that AMF should take immediate advantage of its favorable market evaluation to follow out its growth plan.

Mr. West's analysis

In approaching his analysis, Mr. West had the benefit of a substantial file on Cuno, which had been built up during the prior six months. One of the earliest memoranda, dated July 20, 1959, was written for a member of Mr. Patterson's staff. It read:

> If AMF plans to enter the chemical processing, water treating and fluid handling equipment field with a broad spectrum of products, then Cuno may be a desirable acquisition. If, on the other hand, AMF decides to operate primarily in the domestic water field, then we should not consider acquisition but perhaps we should consider only licensing Cuno's Aqua-Pure line. In any event, we would specify or use some Cuno filters in our industrial and domestic desalter applications.

After the decision had been made to take a broader view of the liquid treatment field, a more detailed analysis of Cuno was prepared. This document (Exhibit 1), written early in August, 1959, was far from enthusiastic, although it pointed out certain advantages that would result to AMF from the acquisition. After this report had been discussed for several weeks, the AMF executive office asked for a possible purchase price estimate. This estimate, prepared in October, 1959, before the 2 for 1 split of AMF stock in November 1959, appears as Exhibit 6.

The October, 1959, estimates had suggested a price substantially less than the price represented by the market-to-market offer of February, 1960. Mr. West therefore requested additional data on Cuno's 1959 sales and profits. The memorandum he was provided is reproduced as Exhibit 7.

Before he could make a meaningful recommendation, Mr. West decided he must make a four-phase analysis. First, he would study and perhaps revise the documents and reports he had been given in order to be sure that they provided the best calculations and projections of earnings. At the least they ought to be revised in light of Cuno's 1959 profits. Second, Mr. West was interested in the sort of alternatives to Cuno that might be offered by other sources. He therefore prepared information regarding some of the more profitable companies in the industry. Exhibit 8 presents sales, profit, and return figures for four firms in addition to Cuno. Third, he would consider how to acquire the preferred stock.[2] Since AMF had not previously been faced with the problem

[2] In January, 1960, the Cuno directors had voted to redeem 20,000 of the 87,605 preferred shares outstanding at the end of 1959. The sinking fund would retire a further 3,500 shares in April, 1960.

of buying preferred stock, no policies had been set regarding a desirable way of paying for it. Mr. West wondered whether any special treatment of the preferred stockholder was called for. Fourth, Mr. West thought that perhaps he ought to consider the advantages to AMF of acquiring a less successful, more stagnant company. Although he did not propose to do much detailed investigating, he thought he ought to answer to his own satisfaction the question of whether AMF might not profit most by buying a company in difficulty for a relatively depressed price and then rehabilitating it, rather than buying a firm like Cuno, which was doing well.

Exhibit 1

THE CUNO ENGINEERING CORPORATION

PRELIMINARY ANALYSIS OF THE CUNO ENGINEERING CORPORATION AS A PROPOSED ACQUISITION
EXCERPTS FROM REPORT PREPARED BY AMF PLANNING STAFF

Source: AMF Executive Office
Date Suggested: July, 1959 *Date of Analysis:* August 3, 1959

Location:

. . . . . .

Business:

. . . . . .

Price Asked:

It is understood that the principal Cuno stockholders desire a tax-free market-for-market exchange of common stock. Based on the study to date, from AMF's point of view the most desirable way of obtaining a tax-free reorganization would require retirement by Cuno of its 88,515 outstanding preferred shares. A total of $1,504,755 would be necessary for this purpose. The number of AMF common shares to obtain the Cuno common is 62,334.

Performance and Growth Aspects:

. . . . . .

Cuno's wide range of industrial filters indicates that they should be able to maintain a growth rate at least equal to the level of general industry. The recent emphasis on replacement type filters should give them an increasing volume of recurring business at probably attractive profit ratios. Continuation of their past aggressive product development program should encourage growth at a rate in excess of that for general industry. . . .

Discussion:

. . . . . .

A positive factor is that Cuno is in an industry with a volume in excess of $100 million per year and growing. There is every indication, moreover, that special engineered filter applications of particular interest to Cuno will continue to grow.

Cuno's reputation is highly respected in the segments of the filter industry where it operates. . . . Moreover, in analyzing Cuno's acquisition value, another positive factor is the very broad range of industries served. Therefore, it is not dependent on the vicissitudes of any one or even a few industries. This broad customer base will be even further expanded as Cuno establishes its line of Aqua-Pure home water filters.

The Cuno reputation has, in large part, been derived from its aggressive product development program. The exercise of sound applications engineering, research and development, and contract research with Johns Hopkins University have led to new product developments, such as the Micro-Klean cartridge, the Aqua-Pure domestic water filter, and the Poro-Klean porous stainless steel filter, as well as to unique and valuable applications of the above products. In 1958 Cuno spent $300,000 on engineering and R & D and $30,000 for R & D consulting. These expenses amounted to 5.5% of 1958 sales. It should be noted that Cuno's development work is directed toward improved methods of dealing with undissolved solids as opposed to chemical processes leading to the removal of dissolved impurities.

Exhibit 1—Continued

Cuno's pretax returns on total assets exceed the AMF criterion by a comfortable margin (Schedule III). . . .

A further positive factor is that Cuno's acquisition would give AMF Atomics another entry into the auxiliary equipment side of the nuclear power, propulsion, and research reactor fields. This fits in with AMF Atomics' objectives. In another area, it should be noted that our recently developed thin film, AMFab, has considerable potential as a filter material as do several of the other AMF films; therefore, the Cuno filter line might be married to our AMFab film with possible mutual benefit. Significantly, Cuno's lines of filter equipment have general application to the broad field of liquid conditioning, which is expected to experience above average growth in the future.

In the event that a "pooling of interests" type of merger may not be feasible, the consequences of a conventional acquisition approach must be considered. With a market-for-market common stock exchange and calling of the preferred stock, a total of $4,561,000 of goodwill would be created. By amortizing the goodwill created over 10 years, the yearly charge against future earnings would be $7.32 per AMF share exchanged (Schedule III). In all probability, this charge would result in a dilution of AMF's future stated earnings.

It should also be noted that Cuno's sales volume represents only a 3% to 6% share of the overall filter business, and thus would not make AMF a dominant company in the industry. This factor, however, is modified by the fact that Cuno maintains a strong position in certain specialized segments of that industry.

Finally, Cuno *would not* provide AMF with important technological know-how necessary to the solution of key problems relating to AMF's liquid-conditioning interest. The problems presented by dissolved minerals such as iron, calcium, magnesium, sulphur, and salt are considered to be the critical factors in liquid processing both domestically and industrially.

Furthermore, the presence of dissolved compounds is not only the immediate problem but also is expected to be the increasingly critical factor in the future. Cuno would bring to AMF an excellent pool of knowledge pertaining to the filtering of undissolved solids but relatively little know-how with respect to the removal of dissolved impurities. It should be mentioned, however, that in certain areas and applications there is a definite need for a liquid-conditioning filter, and in these applications Cuno might well provide the technology required. But in this case Cuno would provide the auxiliary or accessory equipment related to the field of liquid processing and not the technology critical to the solution of key liquid conditioning problems.

In summary, Cuno would offer the following opportunities and disadvantages.

POSITIVE

1. It is available.
2. Cuno is in a large, growing industry.
3. Cuno has an excellent reputation due to, among other things, its aggressive product development program.
4. Cuno serves a broad range of industries.
5. Cuno's profit performance exceeds AMF criteria.
6. Cuno could contribute to programs for AMF Atomics and GOVPG.

NEGATIVE

1. Cuno might be too small to qualify for a "pooling of interests" approach.* However, the size factor is only one of several considerations to be weighed before a definite conclusion can be made in this regard. The alternative is a high goodwill factor.
2. Cuno would not make AMF the dominant factor in filtering.
3. Cuno would not bring to AMF the key technology necessary to the solution of the critical liquid-conditioning problems expected in the future.

Recommendation:

Acquisition of Cuno Engineering Corporation by AMF is attractive only as a later adjunct to the prior establishment of a primary AMF proprietary position in: first, the water conditioning field; second, the water systems field.

[Schedules II, III, and IV below.]

Prepared by: Planning Division, American Machine & Foundry Company

* In an acquisition with pooling of interests, the balance sheet accounts of the two businesses are simply added for consolidated presentation. (Footnote supplied.)

Exhibit 1—Continued

SCHEDULE II—THE CUNO ENGINEERING CORPORATION, ANALYSIS OF BALANCE SHEET CHANGES
(000's omitted)

	At 6/30/59 Unaudited	*Loan to Retire Preferred at $17 Call Price*	*At 6/30/59 as Adjusted*	*Elimination of Preferred*	*Balance Sheet Assumed*
ASSETS					
Cash and governments	$ 916	$1,505	$2,421	$(1,505)	$ 916
Receivables	615		615		615
Inventories	1,316		1,316		1,316
Other	58		58		58
Total current assets	$2,905		$4,410		$2,905
Plant, property, and equipment (net)	801		801		801
Patents	32		32		32
Other (investment, Cuno Oil Filter Company)	110		110		110
Total assets	$3,848		$5,353		$3,848
LIABILITIES					
Notes payable	$ 125		$ 125		$ 125
Accruals	390		390		390
Income taxes	295		295		295
Total current liabilities	$ 810		$ 810		$ 810
Long-term debt (due 1960)	63		63		63
Long-term debt due AMF		1,505	1,505		1,505
Preferred stock ($14 stated value), 88,515 shares	1,239		1,239	$(1,239)	—
Common stock ($1 par), 280,502 shares	$ 281		$ 281		$ 281
Capital surplus	702		702	(266)	436
Earned surplus	753		753		753
Common stock net worth	$1,736		$1,736		$1,470
Total liabilities and equity	$3,848		$5,353		$3,848

Exhibit 1—Continued

SCHEDULE III—THE CUNO ENGINEERING CORPORATION, PRO FORMA HISTORICAL SALES, EARNINGS, RETURN RATIOS, ETC., BASED ON SUBSTITUTION OF LOAN AT 5% FOR PREFERRED STOCK ISSUE

($000's omitted except per share)

Period	Net Sales	Pretax Profits	% of Sales	Taxes	Net Profits	Total Assets Employed	% Pretax to T.A.E.	Net per Cuno‡ Share	Net per AMF Share Exchanged‖ Earned	Net per AMF Share Exchanged‖ Stated¶ 10-Yr.	Net per AMF Share Exchanged‖ Stated¶ 30-Yr.	AMF's Own Net/Share
6 mos. to:												
6/30/59	$ 3,430	$ 628*	18.3%	$ 327*	$ 301*	$ 3,848	32.6%†	$1.07	$ 4.82	$ 1.16	$3.60	$2.27
6/30/58	2,918	395*	13.5	205*	190*	3,870	20.4†	0.68	3.05	(0.61)	1.83	1.25
Year:												
1958	6,009	897*	14.9	466*	431*	3,769	23.8	1.54	6.91	(0.41)	4.47	2.96
1957	7,139	1,355*	19.0	705*	650*	3,971	34.1	2.32	10.43	3.11	7.99	3.17
1956	6,298	1,016*	16.1	528*	488*	3,560	28.5	1.74	7.83	0.51	5.39	2.39
1955	5,494	751	13.7	390	361	3,240	23.2	1.29	5.79	(1.53)	3.35	1.22
1954	4,123	462	11.2	168	185§	2,746	16.8	0.66	2.97	(4.35)	0.53	1.02
Avg. 1956–58	6,482	1,089	16.8	566	523	3,767	28.9	1.86	8.39	1.07	5.95	2.84
Data on AMF 1958	230,877	22,997	10.0	11,989	11,008	231,404	9.9	—	—	—	—	2.96

* Actual historical earnings plus preferred dividends, less $75,238 annual interest at 5% on [proposed] $1,504,755 loan to retire preferred stock, 88,515 shares at $17 call rate. [Preferred dividends: 1956, $98,350; 1957, $96,302; 1958, $93,563; 6 mos. to 6/30/59, $47,000.]

† Annualized.

‡ Based on 280,502 Cuno common shares outstanding, 6/30/59.

§ After deduction of investment loss of $109,000.

‖ Based on 62,334 AMF shares at $96.75 close, 8/3/59, to meet $21.50 market for Cuno common shares, or a total price of $6,030,793.

¶ After deductions for goodwill amortization. Total goodwill would be $4,561,000. This amounts to $7.32 per AMF share on a 10-year, and $2.44 on a 30-year, amortization basis.

** Based on 6 months to June 30 and 3,602,875 AMF shares outstanding.

Exhibit 1—Continued

SCHEDULE IV—THE CUNO ENGINEERING CORPORATION, OUTLOOK FOR SALES, EARNINGS, RETURN RATIOS FOR THE YEARS 1959 THROUGH 1964, BASED ON ACQUISITION BY AMF AND SUBSTITUTION OF LOAN ADVANCE AT 5% FOR PREFERRED STOCK ISSUE
($000's omitted except per share)
(Revised August 10, 1959)

								Net Earnings per AMF Share Exchanged‖			
									Stated¶		
Period	*Net Sales**	*Pretax Profits*	*Taxes†*	*Net Profits*	*Total Assets Employed‡*	*% Pretax to T.A.E.*	*Net Worth§*	*Earned*	*10-Yr.*	*30-Yr.*	*AMF's Own Outlook** per Share*
At acquisition	—	—	—	—	$3,848	—	$1,470	—	—	—	—
1959	$ 7,745	$1,554	$ 808	$ 746	4,136	37.6%	1,758	$11.97	$ 4.65	$ 9.53	$4.68
1960	8,708	1,723	896	827	4,882	35.3	2,504	13.27	5.95	10.83	5.88
1961	9,580	1,913	995	918	5,709	33.5	3,331	14.73	7.41	12.29	6.72
1962	10,610	2,135	1,110	1,025	6,627	32.2	4,249	16.44	9.12	14.00	7.25
1963	11,675	2,367	1,231	1,136	7,652	30.9	5,274	18.22	10.90	15.78	8.11
1964	12,810	2,590	1,347	1,243††	8,788	29.5	6,410	19.94	12.62	17.50	9.08

* Sales are based on Cuno's forecast without alteration. 1959 forecast appears slightly optimistic based on six months' performance.
† Taxes at 52%.
‡ Increased by amount of net profits.
§ At start of period.
‖ Based on 62,334 AMF shares at $96.75 close, 8/3/59, to meet $21.50 market for Cuno common shares, or a total price of $6,030,793.
¶ After deductions for goodwill amortization. Total goodwill would be $4,561,000. This amounts to $7.32 per AMF share on a 10-year amortization basis and $2.44 on a 30-year amortization basis.
** Per long-range forecast, 1959 through 1962, and on a straight-line percentage increase in 1963, 1964.
†† 1964 net profit calculated on the basis of 9.7% of net sales, which percentage was obtained from Cuno's profit forecasts for 1960–63.

Exhibit 2

THE CUNO ENGINEERING CORPORATION

BALANCE SHEETS OF THE CUNO ENGINEERING CORPORATION AND CONSOLIDATED SUBSIDIARIES AS OF DECEMBER 31, 1957, AND 1958*

(In thousands)

ASSETS	*1957*	*1958*
Cash	$ 816	$ 712
Accounts receivable, net	585	605
Inventories	1,603	1,432
Prepaid expenses and deposits	65	59
Total current assets	$3,069	$2,808
Investment in subsidiary, at cost	...	109
Plant, property, and equipment	$2,060	$2,118
Less: Depreciation and amortization	1,194	1,299
Net property	$ 866	$ 820
Patents and trademarks, less amortization	34	32
Deferred charges	3	...
Total assets	$3,971	$3,769
LIABILITIES AND STOCKHOLDERS' INVESTMENT		
Loans payable	$ 100	$ 125
Accounts payable	146	144
Accruals	260	222
Federal and state taxes	500	332
Total current liabilities	$1,006	$ 823
Loans payable	250	125
Preferred stock†	1,332	1,278
Common stock, $1 par‡	270	277
Capital surplus	569	662
Retained earnings	544	604
Total liabilities and stockholders' investment	$3,971	$3,769

* An unaudited balance sheet as of June 30, 1959, is contained in Schedule II of Exhibit 1

† $1 cumulative; no par; stated value $14; 95,121 shares outstanding in 1957, and 91,301 shares in 1958.

‡ 270,375 shares outstanding in 1957; 276,752 shares in 1958.

Note: Most of the figures in these exhibits have been rounded to the nearest whole number. Hence, totals do not always agree.

Source of data: Annual Reports of The Cuno Engineering Corporation.

Exhibit 3

THE CUNO ENGINEERING CORPORATION
CONSOLIDATED INCOME STATEMENT FOR YEARS
ENDED DECEMBER 31, 1955–58
(Dollar figures in thousands except for per share data)

	1955	*1956*	*1957*	*1958*
Net sales	$5,494	$6,298	$7,139	$6,009
Cost of sales	3,445	3,876	4,018	3,656
Selling, administrative, general expenses	1,242	1,460	1,842	1,546
Operating profit	$ 806	$ 962	$1,279	$ 807
Other income (deductions):				
Purchase discounts	11	13	.15	10
Discounts allowed	(35)	(43)	(45)	(44)
Royalties	2	4	1	2
Interest paid	(21)	(21)	(18)	(14)
Miscellaneous	(14)	(27)	1	17
Income before federal income taxes	$ 750	$ 887	$1,233	$ 777
Provision for federal income taxes	390	442	630	389
Net income	$ 361	$ 445	$ 602	$ 387
Dividends on preferred stock		98	96	94
Earnings applicable to common stock	$ 361	$ 347	$ 506	$ 294
Shares of common stock outstanding at end of period	250,000	262,500	270,375	276,752
Per share of common stock:				
Earnings	$1.44	$1.32	$1.87	$1.06
Cash dividends	...	...	0.12½	0.50
Stock dividends	...	5%	3%	2%

Source of data: Annual Reports of The Cuno Engineering Corporation.

Exhibit 4

THE CUNO ENGINEERING CORPORATION
BID AND ASKED PRICES OF COMMON AND PREFERRED STOCK*
OF THE CUNO ENGINEERING CORPORATION
JANUARY, 1958–FEBRUARY, 1960

	Common Stock		*Preferred Stock*	
	Bid	*Ask*	*Bid*	*Ask*
1958				
January	17	18⅝	15	16
February	15	16	14½	15½
March	16½	17¼	14¾	—
April	15¾	16½	15	16
May	14½	15½	15	16½
June	14	15	15	16½
July	13¾	14¼	15¾	16½
August	14	14¾	16	16¾
September	12½	13¼	15½	17
October	13¼	14⅞	16	17
November	14¾	15½	15¾	16¾
December	15½	16¼	15¾	16¾
1959				
January	16¼	17¼	16	16½
February	17	18	15¾	16¾
March	16½	17½	16	17
April	21¾	22½	16	16¾
May	20½	21¼	16	16¾
June	20¾	21½	16	16¾
July	20½	21¼	16	—
August	20¾	21¼	16	17
September	19½	20½	16	16¾
October	21	22	16¼	17¼
November	23	—	16¼	—
December	21	23	16¼	16¾
1960				
January	19½	21	16¼	17¼
February	20½	21½	16¼	—

* Prices as near as possible to closing day of month.
Source of data: *Bank and Quotation Record.*

Exhibit 5

THE CUNO ENGINEERING CORPORATION
COMMON STOCK PRICES OF AMERICAN MACHINE & FOUNDRY COMPANY
JANUARY, 1959–FEBRUARY, 1960
(Adjusted for 2 for 1 stock split in November, 1959)

	Low	*High*
1959		
January	26¾	29 7/16
February	27⅝	31¾
March	30⅝	36⅜
April	34½	44¾
May	38¾	44¾
June	37 5/16	47½
July	45¼	50
August	43¼	49 11/16
September	41⅝	45⅝
October	43⅜	50 15/16
November	46⅛	50
December	48⅛	52⅜
1960		
January	49½	59⅞
February	50	57

Source of data: *The Commercial and Financial Chronicle.*

Exhibit 6

THE CUNO ENGINEERING CORPORATION
ESTIMATE OF PURCHASE PRICE OF THE CUNO ENGINEERING CORPORATION

The Cuno Engineering Corporation—Acquisition Price Considerations

This study considers various approaches to the determination of a reasonable price for Cuno Engineering. The matter of a reasonable price cannot be divorced from a consideration of the peculiar advantages Cuno might contribute to attaining AMF's liquid-conditioning objectives. In my opinion, Cuno should not be considered as the keystone acquisition with which to launch AMF into this new field, since it will not bring with it any unique strengths in technology or market directly and significantly related to our objectives. Because of this view, I have arrived at a determination of price based on Cuno's inherent value as an investment independent of potential contributions which it might make to our efforts in the field of liquid conditioning.

Because of the very small percentage of Cuno's common stock in the hands of the public and because there is very limited trading in this stock (over the counter), the prices quoted are not considered to represent a true market evaluation of the company. In fact, it is doubtful that the major stockholders have an actual market for their stock. If Mr. McConnel, for example, were to put 10% to 20% of his common stock on the open market, it is probable that the price would be driven far below current quotations of 19½ bid, 21½ asked.

Cuno's projections of sales and earnings, as shown in Schedule IV of the Preliminary Analysis [Exhibit 1] dated August 3, 1959, and plotted in Schedule I attached, should not be used as a basis for an acquisition price because:

1. Actual sales and earnings for the first six months of 1959 [projected on an annual basis] are only 88.6% and 69.5% of Cuno's forecast.
2. A trend line projection of six-year historical earnings, as shown on Schedule I of this memorandum, indicates a much slower profit growth than estimated by Cuno.

It is further clear that AMF will, sooner or later, be forced to tie up, for an indeterminate period, at least $1 million to offset the cash drain that would be created by their retirement of $1,504,755 worth of preferred stock. This factor should be weighed heavily in the determination of a purchase price.

The following represent several approaches to establishment of a price:

Exhibit 6—Continued

1. Book value.
2. Capitalization of historical earnings.
3. Market price of Cuno common stock.
4. Present value of future earnings.
5. A 25% upgrading of expected AMF earnings on shares exchanged.

Book Value

As of 6/30/59, the common stock book value was $1,736,000; however, the premium of $266,000 for retirement of preferred reduces this to $1,470,000. The cash advance of $1 million would increase this to an effective price of $2,470,000.

The projected earnings for Cuno indicate that it would be unrealistic to assume that we could purchase Cuno for such a low price.

Capitalization of Historical Earnings

Current market prices of Fram and Purolator, both of which are considerably larger and more actively traded, are at an average of 10 times annualized 1959 earnings. On this basis, the earnings [as adjusted for an AMF purchase in Schedule III, Exhibit 1] of Cuno for 1956, 1957, 1958, and six months of 1959, which averaged $534,000, would establish a price of $5.34 million. The addition of 1954 and 1955 gives a 5½-year average of $446,000, or a price of $4.46 million.

If proper allowance is made for the expected cash advance of $1 million, the resultant price range of $3,460,000 to $4,340,000 is a more realistic evaluation than the book value.

Market Price of Cuno Common Stock

On the basis of the asked quotation of 21½ at September 25, 1959, the market price for the 280,504 common shares outstanding at June 30, 1959, would be $6.031 million.

As noted earlier, the artificial nature of the market for this common stock obviates this approach as a realistic price consideration.

Present Value of Future Earnings

Our projection of future net income and the present values of these earnings at 10%, 15%, and 20% discount rates are shown on Schedule II, attached. Further adjustment is made for an assumed residual value of the business after 10 years and subtraction of the AMF cash advance, which is expected to be at least $1 million. On this basis, the present value of future earnings, as adjusted, is:

At 10% discount......................	$5.462 million
At 15% discount......................	3.927
At 20% discount......................	2.885

This approach appears to contain more logic than any of the others mentioned because it makes due allowance for the element of risk inherent in entry into a new industry. It also evaluates Cuno as an investment for AMF and allows calculation of the purchase price at varying rates of return.

A 25% Upgrading of Expected AMF Earnings on Shares Exchanged

Schedule III, attached, shows the calculation of the number of AMF shares at the current price of $89 that would be exchanged for projected Cuno earnings to allow a 25% upgrade in expected AMF earnings per share. On this basis, it would appear that the maximum number of shares would be the 73,128 shown for 1964 earnings. At $89 this would amount to a price of $6.508 million. However, it is also clearly shown that the projected growth in AMF earnings far exceeds that for Cuno; therefore, at a constant $89 per share, the number of shares and the resultant price would continue to reduce each year.

In view of the disparity in growth rates of earnings projected for the two companies this approach to pricing provides a very unsatisfactory yardstick.

Recommendation

Any price up to approximately $4 million appears justified, provided a "pooling of interests" approach is assured.

Source: Prepared by the planning division in October, 1959.

Exhibit 6—Continued

SCHEDULE I—PROJECTED SALES AND PROFITS OF THE CUNO ENGINEERING CORPORATION

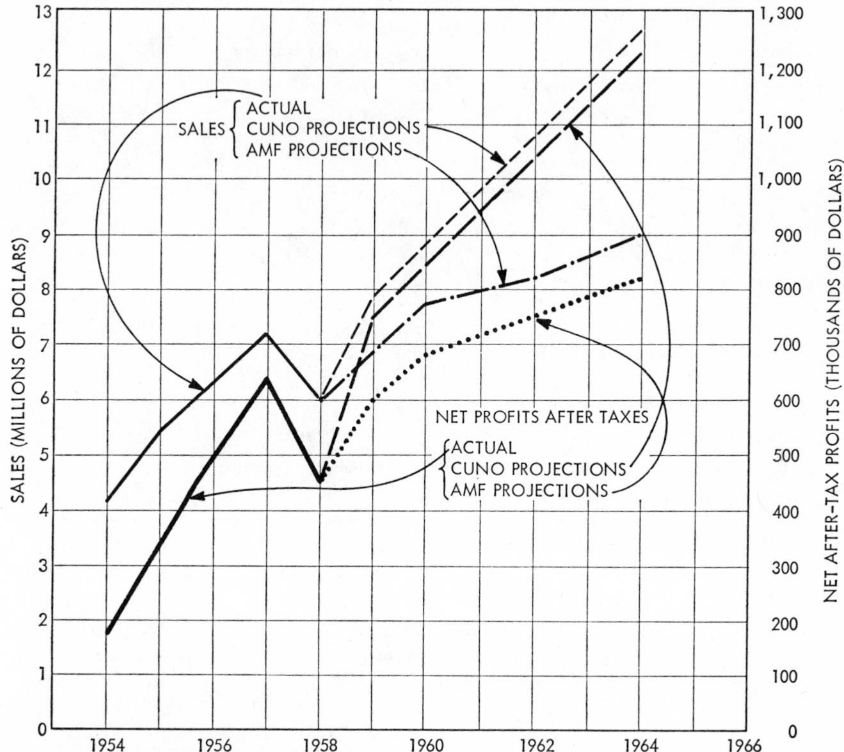

Source: See Exhibit 1, Schedules III and IV.

Exhibit 6—Continued

Schedule II—Present Value of Projected Cuno after Tax Earnings
(In thousands)

Year	Estimated Earnings (after Tax)	Present Value at Discount 10%	15%	20%
1960	$ 680	$ 618	$ 592	$ 566
1961	720	595	544	500
1962	750	563	494	434
1963	790	540	452	381
1964	830	515	413	334
1965	870*	491	376	291
1966	910*	467	342	254
1967	950*	444	311	221
1968	1,000*	424	284	194
1969	1,050*	405	259	170
Subtotal	$ 8,550	$5,062	$4,067	$3,345
Plus assumed residual value	$ 4,000	$1,400	$ 860	$ 540
Subtotal	$12,550	$6,462	$4,927	$3,885
Less AMF cash advance	$ 1,000	$1,000	$1,000	$1,000
Total	$11,550	$5,462	$3,927	$2,885

* Based on a conservative projection of the trend shown in Schedule I.

Schedule III—Calculation of AMF Shares Exchanged on Basis of 25% Upgrade of AMF Projected Earnings per Share

Year	Cuno Estimated Earnings after Tax		25% Upgrade on AMF Earnings per Share*		AMF Shares		Value at $89 per AMF Share
1959	$600	÷	5.85	=	102,564	=	$9,128,200
1960	680	÷	7.35	=	92,517	=	8,234,000
1961	720	÷	8.40	=	85,714	=	7,628,546
1962	750	÷	9.06	=	82,781	=	7,367,509
1963	790	÷	10.14	=	77,909	=	6,933,901
1964	830	÷	11.35	=	73,128	=	6,508,392

* See Schedule IV, Exhibit 1, for base figures.

Exhibit 7

THE CUNO ENGINEERING CORPORATION
REPORT ON 1959 EARNINGS OF THE CUNO ENGINEERING CORPORATION

February 15, 1960

In 1959 this company had net sales of $7.3 million and net income of $635,000. These results were slightly under the company's forecast, as shown following:

	Actual	*Forecast*	*% under Forecast*
Sales	7,260	7,745	6.3%
Net income	635	746	14.9%

Despite failure to meet its forecast, Cuno's sales reached a new high and the $1.1 million sales decline in 1958 was fully recovered. Similarly, the previous high in net income of $602,000 during 1957 was exceeded in 1959. It is interesting to note that Cuno's rather sharp dips in sales—16% —and in profits—36%—during 1958 were fully recovered in 1959. Cuno's vulnerability in previous recessions, such as 1949–50 and 1953–54, has not been studied.

Cuno's net worth at December 31, 1959, was $3.2 million and its market value is approximately double this, including preferred stock.

Because of the potential value of Cuno to AMF in the areas of (*a*) liquids filtering, i.e., home water use, (*b*) filtering materials, i.e., films; and (*c*) atomic energy filtering applications, this company should be kept firmly in mind as a possible follow-up to our more current acquisition plans in water conditioning.

Source: Prepared at American Machine & Foundry Company.

Exhibit 8

THE CUNO ENGINEERING CORPORATION
FIVE-YEAR COMPARISON OF THE CUNO ENGINEERING CORPORATION WITH FOUR OTHER COMPANIES IN THE INDUSTRY

	The Cuno Engineering Corporation	*American Machine & Metals, Inc.*
Net sales—index (1954 = 100):		
1954	100	100
1955	133	139
1956	153	161
1957	173	183
1958	146	177
Average, 1956–58	157	174
Pretax profits—index (1954 = 100):		
1954	100	100
1955	184	115
1956	217	157
1957	302	169
1958	190	132
Average, 1956–58	237	153

Pretax profits, return ratios on:	*Sales*	*Total Assets*	*Net Worth**	*Sales*	*Total Assets*	*Net Worth*
1954	9.9%	14.9%	23.5%	14.7%	24.6%	38.8%
1955	13.7	23.1	37.4	12.3	20.5	35.3
1956	14.1	24.7	38.0	14.3	25.2	42.7
1957	17.3	31.2	45.4	13.6	24.3	39.1
1958	12.9	20.6	27.4	10.9	16.9	28.6
Average, 1956–58	14.9	25.8	36.8	12.9	21.8	36.3

Ratios of market price to:†	*Book Value*		*Earnings‡*		*Book Value*		*Earnings*	
	High	*Low*	*High*	*Low*	*High*	*Low*	*High*	*Low*
1954	n.a.	n.a.	n.a.	n.a.	1.1×	0.7×	7.1×	4.2×
1955	n.a.	n.a.	n.a.	n.a.	1.5	1.0	8.3	5.5
1956	3.3×	1.4×	9.1×	3.8×	1.5	1.1	7.8	6.0
1957	4.0	2.3	11.0	6.4	1.7	1.2	9.2	6.4
1958	3.0	2.2	16.0	11.8	1.9	1.3	14.0	9.5
1958 net sales (in thousands of dollars)	$6,009				$43,613			

* Includes preferred stock: Cuno—all years; Duriron—1954.
† On shares outstanding each year-end.
‡ Common stock only.

Duriron Company, Inc.	*Fram Corporation*	*Purolator Products, Inc.*
100	100	100
119	112	117
155	108	143
172	114	161
140	129	150
156	117	152
100	100	100
101	141	154
172	93	82
191	93	101
101	165	100
155	117	94

Sales	*Total Assets*	*Net Worth*	*Sales*	*Total Assets*	*Net Worth*	*Sales*	*Total Assets*	*Net Worth*
13.3%	17.2%	26.7%*	8.5%	17.4%	31.5%	12.8%	24.6%	43.5%
11.2	14.2	28.5	10.6	21.8	38.1	16.8	31.5	52.5
14.7	21.2	40.5	7.3	14.1	21.7	7.4	13.3	22.8
14.8	22.4	34.4	6.9	13.5	21.2	8.0	15.8	26.7
9.6	11.8	17.6	10.8	17.6	33.4	8.6	15.4	25.6
13.2	18.4	29.8	8.5	15.4	25.8	8.0	14.9	25.3

Book Value		*Earnings‡*		*Book Value*		*Earnings*		*Book Value*		*Earnings*	
High	*Low*	*High*	*Low*	*High*	*Low*	*High*	*Low*	*High*	*Low*	*High*	*Low*
1.0×	0.7	6.7×	4.4×	n.a.	n.a.	n.a.	n.a.	1.9×	1.0×	9.4×	5.1×
1.1	0.9	8.1	6.6	n.a.	n.a.	n.a.	n.a.	3.0	1.6	10.9	5.9
1.4	0.9	7.2	4.6	1.3×	1.1×	12.2×	9.5×	2.3	1.7	25.4	19.0
1.5	1.0	8.8	6.2	1.3	0.8	13.1	7.7	1.6	1.0	13.0	7.7
1.2	0.9	13.6	10.7	1.7	0.8	9.7	4.9	2.1	1.1	15.2	8.1

$12,307	$30,285	$35,366

Exhibit 8—Continued

PRINCIPAL PRODUCTS

The Cuno Engineering Corporation

Industrial filters; automobile cigarette lighters.

American Machine & Metals, Inc.

Instruments to indicate, record, and control pressure, temperature, flow, level, or position for industrial processes and for other applications; pressure transducers for aircraft and missile systems; special-application fractional horsepower motors for industrial and commercial machinery, aircraft and automotive devices, and domestic appliances; filters and centrifugals for liquid-solid separation in process industries; materials testing equipment and related instrumentation; fans and blowers for industrial applications; commercial laundry machinery; springs, mechanical and electrical assemblies, fatigue testers, spring testers, and force indicators; manganese dioxide for dry cell batteries; manganese carbonate ores; zinc, lead, and silver concentrates.

Duriron Company, Inc.

Corrosion-resistant equipment and castings, such as pumps, valves, pipe, and fittings; fans, ejectors, steam jets, etc.

Fram Corporation

Lubricating oil filters, fluid separator filters, gasoline filters; crankcase ventilators and carburetor air filters; replacement cartridges.

Purolator Products, Inc.

Filters (and replaceable elements and cartridges) for filtration of such substances as oil, gasoline, air, water, paints, sugar, food products, toothpastes, drugs, beverages, chemicals, etc.

Source of data: *Moody's Industrial Manuals.*

ASSOCIATED TECHNOLOGY LABORATORIES, INC.

By late April, 1958, negotiations concerning the statutory merger of Magnus Controls, Inc., and Associated Technology Laboratories, Inc., (ATL) had reached their final stages. The primary problem remaining was to determine a basis on which shares of ATL common stock would be exchanged for those of Magnus Controls. Once the directors of each firm had agreed on this point, the proposed merger could be set before the stockholders of the two companies for their approval; and if two thirds of each organization's stockholders voted in favor of the move, the merger would be effected.

The price determination problem had been delayed until the end of the negotiations for several reasons. First, interest in the possibilities of a merger had been developed over more than a year's time, during which the stock market appraisal of each company's worth had been subject to considerable variation. Second, the management of each firm realized that there were significant difficulties involved in assessing the relative values of organizations as basically dissimilar as Magnus Controls and ATL. Finally, neither firm had at any time been fully committed to the merger from an operational standpoint; each had at its disposal alternative means of accomplishing the hoped-for objective of the merger. All of these considerations posed difficulties for the managements of the two firms in arriving at an exchange basis that they felt could be presented as reasonable to their respective shareholders.

Interest in the possibility of merger with Magnus Controls was a fairly recent development at ATL. Throughout most of its corporate history the company had received offers to merge or sell out on the average of twice per month, and invariably these offers had been discouraged. For more than a year, however, ATL had been engaged in contract negotiations with Magnus Controls aimed at the joint development and marketing of certain specialized industrial products. While no contract had ever actually been agreed upon, the management and various other employees of the two companies had developed a cordial relationship with each other. This factor, together with a number of other considerations noted below, had caused ATL management to reevaluate its position with respect to merger.

ATL was located in southern New England. The company was incorporated in 1945 to take over a laboratory that had been organized by Columbia University during World War II for work on electronic antisubmarine devices. The Columbia group was joined by personnel with similar skills from the Radiation Laboratory of Massachusetts Institute of Technology and the Radio Research Laboratory of Harvard University, both of which groups had similarly been established during the war for the development of electronic countermeasures. By April, 1958, the engineering staff had grown to about 400.

ATL was primarily occupied with the development of electronic systems ordered under government contracts or subcontracts, generally in the technical fields of radar moving target indicators, radar performance monitors, microwave components, and communications equipment. The company also produced analog and specialized digital computer devices for military applications, and electronic gauging and automatic control devices for industrial application. Historically these industrial products had accounted for less than 10% of annual sales volume, while approximately 90% of the company's sales had been to the government or to government agencies. In contrast, sales of the Magnus Controls organization were in almost the inverse ratio of industrial to government business.

A preponderant dependence on government business was not the ideal situation in which ATL management wished to be. For several years the company's top executives had advocated the development of products and a marketing force aimed at industrial customers. In part they were motivated by the potentially greater profitability of industrial sales; additionally, they viewed industrial sales as being inherently more stable than government work. For example, ATL's sales had leveled off in the 1954–56 period as a result of (*a*) the post-Korean decline in annual defense expenditures from $54 billion to $41 billion; (*b*) the completion of a $9 million government contract for a weapons control system; and (*c*) the shift in emphasis in defense spending from production to research and development work.

The possibilities for commercial products that were uncovered by ATL engineering and scientific personnel in the course of contract research and development work often stimulated the interest of company executives. Over a period of time a number of commercial products had actually been brought to the production stage by ATL's engineering staff. Since the firm specialized in electronics technology, most of these products were in the field of "automation controls," the process whereby industrial machining processes could be performed using an electronically programmed and controlled set of operations. A typical device which ATL had developed for this purpose, and which might ultimately be an important component of an automated process, was the Inchworm motor. The Inchworm permitted and controlled microscopic tool or workpiece movements under heavy loads in automated centerless grinder operations. As a single product the Inchworm had limited value, although as part of a fully automated system the device might often be invaluable.

The Inchworm had been developed not in response to a particular industrial customer's requirements but rather in the hope that once it had proved successful it could be marketed to a wide number of firms. Unfortunately, marketing efforts had developed into a greater problem than was originally anticipated. ATL's small industrial marketing staff discovered that unless the customer could be shown specific applications in his operations where the Inchworm could be utilized, he was generally not interested. Furthermore, even when an application was found, the customer normally resisted making major changes in his existing process.

The Inchworm experience served to point up several characteristics of industrial marketing that had not previously been fully appreciated by ATL management. In the first place they found that many potential industrial customers were skeptical of products emanating from small electronics firms. Purchasing agents and engineering personnel of many large firms were approached almost daily by salesmen who were totally unfamiliar to them, representing various electronics organizations and attempting to sell some new device or process. The customer personnel often did not have sufficient time to review all the new ideas and products presented to them and as a result they tended to rely on their established buying relationships to fulfill their needs.

In the second place, ATL's marketing personnel found that even when potential customers did express interest in the firm's product, they wanted to see a completely automated system rather than a single component part with limited applications. The cost of developing such a system was typically far greater than ATL could afford, or than the customer was willing to pay.

Finally, the ATL executives discovered that they had no really effective way of following the industrial markets sufficiently closely to be able to forecast future customer requirements. Knowing what the customer would want a year or more in advance of the actual need was critical to successful product development, but to be able to forecast these needs a firm had to maintain constant contact with the customer. Without adequate personnel ATL executives could not hope to achieve this sort of relationship; and unless they did they would not know which of the many available possibilities to pursue. This was viewed as a most critical problem.

A second major problem connected with dependence on government markets and of concern to ATL management was a disturbing trend evident in government purchasing procedures. Essentially, the trend was toward research and development contracts covering entire systems—in the case of communications, for example, "communications systems," which included not only the radio and electronic equipment involved but also antennae, power generators, and the like. Under this practice smaller firms were at a disadvantage in bidding for large contracts, since they were often unable to establish the degree of financial strength required by the contracting agent or officer. In such cases the small firms would be relegated to the position of subcontractor, which was even more risky than accepting government business at the prime contractor level.

The impact of this aspect of government purchasing policy had been driven home to ATL during early 1957, when an important project for which the firm had performed all preliminary research was contracted to a large airframe company for development. The amount involved in the development contract was approximately $20 million, and it promised to yield considerably greater profits than the preliminary research. In the eyes of the contracting officer, ATL—with peak annual sales up to that point of only $12.3 million—was not nearly strong enough financially to justify a contract of the size indicated. The fact that independent sources outside of ATL were willing to guarantee that the work would be adequately financed did not alter the contracting officer's stand. His position was that he would have to justify his decision to superiors on the basis of actual financial data and operating experience; the fact that bank credit or some other source of funds was available, if necessary, for the performance of the contract would not constitute the type of justification required.

In the period following the failure to get the $20 million contract and up to the time of negotiations with Magnus Controls, the trend toward fewer and larger contracts continued and ATL management encountered other instances where the company's relatively small size prohibited it from getting attractive prime contract business. By late 1957 ATL management was convinced that some method of increasing the organization's financial strength would have to be evolved if the company was to continue to operate effectively in the government market. Aside from joining with a larger organization two alternatives seemed feasible: a public sale of stock, or combination with a smaller firm. Both of these alternatives, however, had disadvantages.

A public sale of common stock in an amount sufficiently large to materially improve the company's financial position, according to ATL management's reasoning, might tend to restrict the freedom currently enjoyed by the company to pursue various basic research objectives. While not a particular threat to control, large numbers of public stockholders might obligate the firm to concentrate more on immediate profits than had historically been necessary, perhaps to the detriment of long-term growth and stability. As of early 1958, 35% of ATL stock was owned by employees, 55% by two large and highly regarded venture capital organizations, and only 10% by the public. The venture capital interests had consistently been willing to respect the judgment of management, although there had at times been minor disagreements. These organizations were primarily occupied with supplying capital for small, scientifically oriented firms to which other sources of funds were not available. Their influence was normally limited to financial affairs and was exerted only sparingly. By design, however, they attempted to keep their investments in young enterprises, and when a particular investment had "matured"—i.e., was no longer dependent on their support—they generally sought to withdraw from their position.

The large employee stockholdings and the small amount of publicly owned stock, combined with the traditionally agreeable attitude of the venture capital interests, had led to a high degree of flexibility for ATL in the past. Management believed that this situation might change if investment banking interests and new stockholder groups were to exercise influence in the future.

With respect to combining with smaller firms ATL management had initiated action on several occasions, but without success. Many smaller firms evidenced the same attitude toward ATL as ATL had historically shown toward larger firms interested in merger. By early 1958 ATL management conceded that while not impossible, it was unlikely that a smaller firm with the desired characteristics could be acquired, at least within the next few years. Moreover, a combination with a smaller firm would not really add the kind of financial strength that would be necessary. Consideration of the above factors by ATL coincided with the contract negotiations with Magnus Controls, and in early 1958 ATL management decided to reevaluate its position in relation to the larger organization.

ATL's original introduction to Magnus Controls had come in the fall of 1956 when Mr. Brown, an independent consultant, had inquired whether ATL management would be interested in discussing the possibility of merger with the larger firm. Magnus Controls, with central offices in the Midwest, was one of the largest manufacturers of electrical control devices in the United States. The firm produced a wide variety of switches and regulators for electrical motors and related equipment, ranging from refrigerator controls selling for less than one dollar apiece to electric machine tool control systems costing in excess of $500,000, for use in steel, paper, and textile mills. A detailed description of the firm's most important products in early 1958 was as follows:

> General purpose motor control and accessories for both A.C. and D.C. applications; machine tool control; mill and crane control; textile control; rubber mill control; marine and navy control; control centers; small motor switches for appliances and power tools; refrigeration control for refrigerators, freezers, and air conditioners; unit breakers for distribution of power and protection of electrical circuits; power relays and switches for commercial aircraft; and industrial safety switches.

Engineered electrical regulation systems included standard items of Magnus Controls equipment as components, as well as specially manufactured equipment. Such systems were designed for continuous process lines in steel mills, automotive plants, paper mills, aluminum mills, refineries, and rubber plants, as well as many other industries requiring synchronized operations.

The company operated eight manufacturing plants, of which five were located in the Midwest. Of the remaining three, which together accounted for only about 20% of Magnus Controls' productive capacity, one was located in New York City and two were on the West Coast. In addition to manufacturing facilities, the firm maintained 17 warehouses located in major market areas and 58 sales offices in principal cities throughout the United States. The latter were staffed by more than 300 sales engineers and had been instrumental in maintaining the company's position of strength in the industry.

ATL's initial response to Mr. Brown's inquiry was distinctly negative; nevertheless, a few weeks later ATL was again approached by a Magnus Controls representative, this time from Magnus Controls' product engineering department. He explained that Magnus Controls was very much interested in developing a line of "automation controls" to supplement and eventually supersede, in all likelihood, several of the company's existing product lines. To this end he suggested that the two concerns might collaborate in a joint research and development venture, and it was for this purpose that the two firms had been engaged in the contract negotiations mentioned above.

Specifically, the two firms would attempt to develop a continuous process system that would permit metal fabricators to use rolls of raw material in place of sheet metal. The system would probably incorporate a data accumulation center with such devices as Beta-Ray thickness gauges (on which ATL had done research work), photoelectric pinhole detectors, and other similar products. The heavy driving and regulation machinery would be developed by Magnus Controls and would be designed to use the electronic gear that ATL would develop. Work on the project had never commenced, owing to difficulties in determining the value of contributions made by each firm. The negotiations, however, ultimately led to the reconsideration of a potential merger.

The acceptance of merger as a possibility by ATL management had been a slow process. One very important favorable factor was the recognition that Magnus Controls was an "engineering" oriented organization rather than one primarily motivated by financial objectives. ATL personnel were consistently impressed by the relatively greater importance placed by Magnus Controls representatives on the technical aspects of the system as opposed to the cost considerations. In their opinion, this view contrasted with the attitudes evidenced by companies and financial organizations with whom they had previously had contact.

In addition, ATL personnel discovered that the more mechanical aspects of industrial product development deserved far greater consideration than had originally been assigned them. For this reason a skilled and experienced manufacturing staff was of great value.

Against this background actual merger negotiations were commenced with Magnus Controls in February, 1958. The chief responsibility for conducting negotiations on behalf of ATL was given to Mr. Henry Morse, treasurer of the firm. His counterpart for Magnus Controls was Mr. J. C. Walter, financial vice president.

Mr. Morse's position

In Mr. Morse's opinion the chief objective of Magnus Controls in negotiating the merger was to gain access to ATL's highly regarded electronics research staff. The use of electronic controls in industrial processes appeared to have a bright future; already many of Magnus Controls' competitors in the motor control field (among which were General Electric, Westinghouse,

Square D, Allen-Bradley, and some 30 others) had undertaken to apply electronics to their products. Magnus Controls, with an outstanding engineering staff but lacking an electronics research group, was certainly aware of this situation.

Mr. Morse recognized that if it wished, Magnus Controls could build up its own electronics research group. Such a move, however, would certainly involve a considerable amount of time—perhaps several years. Alternatively, there were a number of other small, research-oriented firms that Magnus Controls might seek to acquire or consolidate, although at present he was quite sure that none of these firms had been directly approached.

Mr. Morse and most others in ATL management, as well as Mr. Walter and his associates, were eager to conclude their negotiations as soon as possible. For this purpose a "final" meeting had been scheduled during the last week in April to determine a basis whereby the outstanding shares of ATL common stock, together with 20,833 shares reserved for conversion of ATL's 5¾% subordinated convertible notes due July 1, 1972 (see note 1 to Exhibit 3) and 21,025 shares reserved against the stock options outstanding, would be exchanged for stock in Magnus Controls. In preparation for this meeting Mr. Morse had set down the most important provisions to which the respective managements had tentatively agreed—contingent, of course, on an exchange price agreement:

1. ATL would operate as an autonomous division of Magnus Controls.
2. ATL would have one representative on Magnus Controls' Board of Directors, as soon as an opening occurred.
3. Merger would be effected by a tax-free exchange of stock.
4. No personnel changes would be involved in the merger. There would be, however, an exchange of personnel between Magnus Controls and the ATL division from time to time.

In addition to the provisions above, Mr. Morse wrote down a number of his own observations, based in part on his discussions with others in or connected with the ATL organization, which he wished to keep in mind during the price negotiation.

1. There should not be any difficulty with ——— and ——— (the 55% venture capital owners of ATL) if the price is in line with the market of the past few months. Those organizations have carried their investments in ATL at "market" value for their own reporting purposes. They might object if they were to end up with stock worth less than when last they reported to owners, which was on December 31, 1957. Otherwise, they would probably be happy with the move (and have so stated) since they feel that their money has had its maximum effect by now and they are eager to put it to work in a less mature investment situation. I doubt that they will object seriously to any reasonable price over 30, but this is a good arguing point. To the best of my knowledge they have not been in touch with Magnus and would not sell out without consulting us first.
2. Some of our [ATL] people have noted that the stock market has turned

up from last fall's lows. With the increasing interest in electronics companies they have mentioned that our stock "ought to hit $100 before very long." While I personally suspect that this is unlikely (based on our present earnings), we shall nevertheless have to keep these people happy.

3. Magnus Controls' sales organization would certainly be a great help to our existing industrial products as well as a guide to future developments.
4. We ought not to underestimate the value of their established manufacturing operations.
5. With Magnus Controls' backing we can probably win government prime contracts up to $40 or $50 million, versus our apparent limit of $6–8 million at present. This would increase our profitability enormously.

Pertinent data on earnings and balance sheets of the two companies appear in Exhibits 1–3. Exhibit 4 presents price ranges, earnings, and book values per common share.

Mr. Morse realized that both his observations and the provisions already agreed to were subject to change in the process of bargaining. He would, of course, discuss bargaining limits and strategy, as well as an initial bid and other relevant factors, with other ATL executives before the meeting with Mr. Walter; but in the end, he realized, he would be the one responsible for the success or failure of the negotiations from ATL's standpoint.

Exhibit 1

ASSOCIATED TECHNOLOGY LABORATORIES, INC.

SUMMARIES OF EARNINGS

(Dollar amounts in thousands, except for per share figures)

	Year Ended December 31										Two Months Ended			
											Feb. 28, 1957		Feb. 28, 1958	
Magnus Controls, Inc.	1953	%	1954	%	1955	%	1956	%	1957	%	(Unaudited)	%	(Unaudited)	%
Net sales	$62,482	100	$54,188	100	$61,575	100	$79,367	100	$74,870	100	$12,941	100	$11,632	100
Operating profit	12,060	19	8,431	16	12,103	20	15,380	19	13,234	18	2,518	19	1,729	15
Income before federal income tax	12,204	20	8,673	16	12,241	20	15,582	20	13,433	18	2,561	20	1,731	15
Provision for federal income tax	8,451	14	4,580	8	6,611	11	8,680	11	7,484	10	1,403	11	985	8
Net income	3,753	6	4,093	8	5,630	9	6,902	9	5,949	8	1,158	9	746	6
Earnings per common share*	2.84	...	3.10	...	4.26	...	5.23	...	4.51	...	0.88	...	0.57	...
Dividends per common share*	1.25	...	1.50	...	1.80	...	2.30	...	2.50	...	0.50	...	0.50	...
ATL, Inc.														
Net sales†	$ 6,563	100	$10,515	100	$ 9,178	100	$10,478	100	$12,272	100	$ 1,614	100	$ 1,659	100
Operating profit	388	6	884	8	731	8	655	6	844	7	109	7	112	7
Interest expense	122	2	97	1	34	...	31	...	120	1	9	1	33	2
Income before federal income tax	273	4	806	8	717	8	619	6	725	6	101	6	78	5
Provision for federal income tax	137	2	433	4	354	4	313	3	381	3	49	3	40	2
Net income	136	2	373	4	363	4	306	3	344	3	52	3	38	2
Special credit‡	...	...	39	...	...	...	...	...	98	1	...	...	...	...
Net income and special credit	136	2	412	4	363	4	306	3	442	4	52	3	38	2
Earnings per common share‡	0.72	...	1.92	...	1.84	...	1.55	...	1.73	...	0.26	...	0.19	...
Dividends per common share	...	...	...	...	...	...	...	...	...	...	...	...	...	...

* Adjusted for 2 for 1 stock split in 1956.

† Substantially all of the sales during the period were under U.S. government contracts or subcontracts, which are subject to termination.

‡ The special credits in 1954 and 1957 represent profit on sale of land (net of federal income tax of $13,833 in 1954 and $32,566 in 1957). The special credits are equivalent to $0.20 per share in 1954 and $0.49 in 1957. Net income and special credits for 1954 and 1957 amount to $2.12 and $2.22 per share, respectively.

Exhibit 2

ASSOCIATED TECHNOLOGY LABORATORIES, INC.

MAGNUS CONTROLS, INC., BALANCE SHEETS
DECEMBER 31, 1957 (AUDITED) AND FEBRUARY 28, 1958 (UNAUDITED)

(Dollar amounts in thousands)

ASSETS	December 31, 1957		February 28, 1958 (Unaudited)	
Cash and U.S. government securities		$ 2,939		$ 3,293
Accounts receivable (net of reserve)		7,472		7,469
Inventories:				
Raw materials and supplies	$ 1,785		$ 1,724	
Purchased parts	1,564		1,404	
Work in process	4,829		4,135	
Manufactured parts and finished apparatus	6,742		6,714	
Total inventories		$14,920		$13,977
Total current assets		$25,331		$24,739
Property, plant, and equipment (at cost):				
Land	$ 1,751		$ 1,751	
Buildings	11,751		11,755	
Machinery, equipment, tools, etc.	9,110		9,230	
Furniture, fixtures, etc.	2,279		2,341	
Construction in process	3,305		5,344	
	$28,196		$30,421	
Less: reserve for depreciation	7,813		8,097	
Property, plant and equipment (net)		$20,383		$22,324
Other assets		439		475
Total assets		$46,153		$47,538
LIABILITIES				
Accounts payable		$ 1,115		$ 1,080
Dividend payable				660
Accrued expenses		2,217		2,249
Accrued taxes		1,585		2,233
Total current liabilities		$ 4,917		$ 6,222
Reserve for deferred federal taxes on income*		2,861		2,854
Capital stock, surplus, and reserves:				
Common stock, par value $10.00 per share, authorized, 2,000,000 shares, issued and outstanding 1,319,996 shares	$13,200		$13,200	
Earned surplus	23,675		23,761	
Reserve for possible inventory losses and other contingencies	1,500		1,500	
Total capital stock, surplus, and reserves		$38,375		$38,461
Total liabilities and net worth		$46,153		$47,538

* Reserve for Deferred Federal Taxes on Income: This represents the balance of the temporary tax saving resulting from the company's election to claim depreciation for federal income taxes in excess of the normal provision included in operations on facilities covered by a necessity certificate. The reserve is now being used to offset federal income taxes on the normal depreciation not presently allowable.

Exhibit 3

ASSOCIATED TECHNOLOGY LABORATORIES, INC.

ATL, INC., BALANCE SHEETS
DECEMBER 31, 1957, AND FEBRUARY 28, 1958
(Dollar amounts in thousands)

ASSETS		*Dec. 31, 1957*		*Feb. 28, 1958 (Unaudited)*
Cash		$ 327		$ 278
Accounts receivable		2,632		2,289
Inventories (at the lower of cost or market):				
Finished goods	$ 286		$ 344	
Work in process (less progress payments received: 1957—$683,495; 1958—$972,384)	2,689		3,047	
Materials and supplies	146		141	
Total inventories		$ 3,121		$ 3,532
Total current assets		$ 6,080		$ 6,099
Investments and notes receivable		124		150
Property, plant, and equipment (at cost)	$ 2,233		$ 2,247	
Less: accumulated depreciation and amortization	939		968	
Property, plant, and equipment (net)		$ 1,294		$ 1,279
Prepaid expenses and deferred charges		71		71
Other assets		41		39
Total assets		$ 7,610		$ 7,638
LIABILITIES				
Notes payable to bank		$ 2,200		$ 2,500
Accounts payable		701		328
Accrued expenses		543		566
Accrued taxes		367		406
Total current liabilities		$ 3,811		$ 3,800
Long-term debt:				
5% mortgage note due 1959 to 1965	$ 300		$ 300	
5% mortgage note due May 14, 1960	50		50	
$5\frac{3}{4}$% subordinated convertible notes, due July 1, 1972*	1,000		1,000	
Total long-term debt		$ 1,350		$ 1,350
Stockholders' equity:				
Capital stock, par value $1 per share,† authorized—500,000 shares, issued and outstanding: 1957—199,605 shares; 1958—199,699 shares; at stated value	$ 893		$ 894	
Earned surplus	1,556		1,594	
Total stockholders' equity		$ 2,449		$ 2,488
Total liabilities and stockholders' equity		$ 7,610		$ 7,638

* Convertible at $48/share; 20,833 shares of capital stock are reserved for the purpose of conversion.
† Options are outstanding for 21,025 shares at prices from $18.50 to $43.00 per share; also, see note *.

Exhibit 4

ASSOCIATED TECHNOLOGY LABORATORIES, INC.

Common Stock Price Ranges, Earnings, and Book Value

I. COMMON STOCK PRICE RANGES*

	Magnus Controls, Inc.		*ATL, Inc.*			
			Bid		*Asked*	
	High	*Low*	*High*	*Low*	*High*	*Low*
1954†	32⅜	19½	18⅛	10	18⅝	10½
1955	43	28¼	36¼	17⅛	38⅛	23¾
1956:						
1st quarter	52	36½	44	29	46	30½
2nd quarter	55⅞	49⅛	51	38½	54	40
3rd quarter	61¼	53½	39½	37	41½	38½
4th quarter	65	53	37½	34	39½	36
1957:						
1st quarter	64¾	51½	37	29	39	31
2nd quarter	61¾	51½	52	34¼	54	36½
3rd quarter	63¼	45	51½	33	53½	36
4th quarter	46	38½	38	27	42	30
1958:						
1st quarter	46	40½	47	33	52	36

April 28, 1958, close: 45 April 30, 1958, bid: 43½–44

* The price ranges of the sales prices of Magnus Controls' common stock on the New York Stock Exchange and the bid and asked prices of ATL's capital stock in the over-the-counter market as reported by National Quotation Bureau, Inc., for the years 1954 and 1955 and the nine quarterly periods ended March 31, 1958.

† 1954 bid and asked prices for ATL capital stock are for the month of December only. Over-the-counter trading in ATL capital stock began in November 1954.

II. EARNINGS PER COMMON SHARE

	Magnus Controls, Inc.	*ATL, Inc.*
Year: 1953	$2.84	$0.72
1954	3.10	1.92
1955	4.26	1.84
1956	5.23	1.55
1957	4.51	1.73
Two months ended:		
February 28, 1958	0.57	0.19

Note: The foregoing tabulation has been prepared from information set forth in the summaries of earnings in Exhibit 1.

III. BOOK VALUES PER COMMON SHARE

	Magnus Controls, Inc.	*ATL, Inc.*
Book value, February 28, 1958	$29.14	$12.46

UNITED TERMINAL CORPORATION

In January, 1971, Jack Mason, vice president of San Francisco Capital Corporation, was reviewing the situation of United Terminal Corporation of Sunnyvale, California. United Terminal Corporation (UTC) was one of 49 companies in San Francisco Capital's portfolio of venture capital investments. (See Exhibit 1 for a summary of the portfolio.) Since San Francisco Capital's initial investment of $250,000 in UTC in December, 1969, UTC's sales and profit projections had not been met. In fact, UTC had posted a loss of over $1 million in its first nine months of operations. The company now needed an additional $600,000 to provide working capital to support the anticipated sales growth. The investment banker who had arranged the first-round financing was unprepared and unwilling, however, to help raise additional capital. Mr. Mason knew that he would have to take a leading role in structuring any second round of financing and in maintaining the interest and financial support of the other first-round investors in UTC.

THE COMPANY

UTC was a manufacturer of cathode ray tube[1] computer terminals for use principally in the newspaper industry. In the past, newspaper editors and reporters typed a story, corrected the story on the typed original, and then gave the corrected version to a typesetter operator who retyped the story on a typesetting machine. The UTC equipment eliminated the need to retype the story and saved time in transferring the news from the reporter to the "set type" form. With the UTC terminals, an editor or reporter typed a story, which was then displayed on the screen. The news copy could then be revised without retyping the entire article. The corrected copy was stored in the computer's memory bank until it was sent directly by wire to a typesetter machine, which set the story in type, ready to be printed. A single terminal sold for $13,000. UTC's more complete system sold for $130,000 to $200,000 and included a powerful memory capacity, several terminals, and a sophisticated minicomputer to coordinate the various terminals. (See Exhibit 2 for an illustration of the company's product.)

[1] A cathode ray tube (CRT) consists of an electron beam passing over a phosphor-coated glass surface. The most commonly known CRT is a television screen.

History of UTC

UTC began as a division of United Cable Co. of San Leandro, California. During the 1960's United Cable, a closely held manufacturer of electrical cable and hardware for electric power companies, had accumulated close to $1 million in excess working capital. The management decided to invest the excess working capital in the rapidly growing area of computer peripheral equipment. Lacking experience in the electronics field, the managers of United Cable sought a qualified person to develop the new division. In 1963, Charles Sill joined United Cable in that capacity.

Mr. Sill was well qualified for the job. He had graduated from the Massachusetts Institute of Technology with a B.A. in electrical engineering in 1955. After working with two large electric companies on government contracts, he formed Consulectric, Inc., in 1959 to do electronic consulting work for the government. In spite of Consulectric's growth to $5 million in revenue, several major investors became dissatisfied with Mr. Sill's handling of administrative and accounting details and finally were able to move for his replacement as president in 1963. Consulectric went bankrupt shortly thereafter. When Mr. Sill joined United Cable, he took with him many of the designs and ideas he had developed at Consulectric.

At United Cable Mr. Sill continued to work on his ideas for an improved cathode ray tube display terminal. After several important engineering accomplishments, some of which were later patented, he succeeded in producing a high-quality terminal with a display capacity significantly exceeding that of competitive equipment manufactured by such well-known names as Raytheon, RCA, General Electric, Bunker-Ramo, and IBM. This improved terminal was well received and within a short while several thousand requests for additional information and demonstrations were received. In terms of potential volume of business, the two most important inquiries came from American Telephone and Telegraph Company and Associated Press. Both leads were explored and subsequently resulted in some equipment installations.

By early 1969 it became apparent to the owners of United Cable that the management and financial commitment necessary to capitalize fully on the potential of their display equipment was beyond their capacity or interest. During the previous six years over $1 million had been spent on research and development in the electronics division to bring the terminal to market. The division had yet to show a profit. In addition to the division's losses, United Cable had experienced an overall decline in profitability which limited its ability to invest further in the division. The management of United Cable decided, therefore, to sell the designs, patents, inventory, current backlog, and all facilities of the electronics division as a package in order to recover the major part of its investment.

While United Cable management approached possible corporate customers about buying the electronics division, Mr. Sill began to assess his position in the proposed spin-off. The technical advances which had brought the CRT to its current stage had been the direct result of his technical leadership. A major part of the future value of the electronics division would depend on his innovative ability. Mr. Sill was uncomfortable with the thought that he—or at least his ideas—would be sold with the division. He mentioned the proposed sale of the division to Bill Hansen, whom he knew from joint work on various church committees. After discussing the situation, Mr. Hansen suggested that Mr. Sill should try to raise money from a venture capital source and buy the division himself.

The idea of again heading his own company appealed to Mr. Sill. He was eager to continue his research on cathode ray tube display terminals and to build a strong, healthy company on the basis of products of superior quality, partially to make up for the failure of Consulectric. He approached Ben Taylor, a partner in the San Francisco investment banking firm of Brown and Taylor, Inc., about venture capital financing. The firm was not very active in venture placements, but it had put together five deals previously and prided itself on never losing money for its investors. After reviewing the tentative structure for the proposed spin-off company and its financial needs, Mr. Taylor met with Mr. Sill to discuss the management of the proposed company. Mr. Sill admitted his dislike for housekeeping details of management. These details, he explained, took time that could be better spent designing new equipment. It was finally agreed that a man with a strong record of administrative competence should be sought to become president of the company. Clearly, an institutional investor would look critically at the management structure of the firm before investing money.

In June, 1969, Mr. Sill talked with Mr. Hansen and suggested that Mr. Hansen become president of the proposed company. Mr. Hansen had an excellent record of achievement with Mobil Oil Corporation. After graduating from Brigham Young University with a B.S. in marketing and a minor in accounting in 1952, he had joined Mobil Oil as a marketing representative in Los Angeles. He had progressed rapidly to Area Sales Manager; District Manager, Denver; Manager, Corporate National Sales, New York City; and in 1967, to Division General Manager for the Western States. He was respected as being a "straight shooter" and an excellent manager.

Mr. Hansen decided to accept the offer to become the president of the company, provided adequate financing could be arranged to buy the division from United Cable. The decision insured that he and his family would remain comfortably settled in northern California. He also respected Mr. Sill's technical competence and felt that Mr. Sill's ideas could be the basis for a very successful company.

Brown and Taylor was encouraged by the addition of Mr. Hansen to UTC's management team and was confident that it could raise the necessary money. A prospectus was drawn up in August, 1969, and a number of prospective investors were approached. Mr. Hansen had estimated that the company would need $2.3 million—$1.0 million to buy the division from United Cable and $1.3 million to provide working capital for at least the first 18 months of operation. The company was valued at $5.0 million and investors were offered 45% of the company for $2.25 million. The remainder of the ownership would be held by management and by Brown and Taylor in return for past and future services. Brown and Taylor began by approaching several insurance companies and small business investment companies (SBICs[2]). The prospective investors viewed the proposal with little interest. The most often cited reasons for investor reluctance were (1) Mr. Sill's previous association with Consulectric, (2) uncertainties about widespread acceptance of the product in the face of larger competitors, and (3) the high valuation of the company.

INITIAL INVESTMENT IN UTC

Jack Mason, vice president of San Francisco Bay National Bank's SBIC, agreed that the UTC deal was overpriced. He also believed that the venture had the potential for large profits. The market for UTC's systems seemed potentially enormous. Several personal checkings convinced Mr. Mason that Mr. Sill's technical ability in computer hardware and software was "near genius." While working with the electronics division, he had accomplished several engineering "firsts" which had substantially advanced the state of CRT technology. Mr. Sill and several of his customers felt that UTC's systems as applied to the newspaper field were 18 months ahead of any competitors. Mr. Mason believed that Mr. Sill had the capacity to maintain a technological superiority over such large manufacturers as IBM and Raytheon.

Mr. Mason called Mr. Taylor to inquire whether a more favorable price could be arranged. It was proposed that the company be valued at $3.8 million. The investors would receive 47% of the company for $1.8 million, with management and Brown and Taylor receiving the remaining 53%. Of the $1.8 million offering, $1.45 million was to be used primarily for working capital needs and for purchase of some capital equipment. The remaining $350,000 was allotted for the down payment to United Cable for the electronics division package. UTC would then owe United Cable an additional $650,000 to be secured by three noninterest-bearing notes of $100,000 due after the third year, $250,000 due after the fourth year, and $300,000 due after the fifth year, thus constituting the purchase price of $1 million. Exhibit 3 shows a pro forma balance sheet for the division as of August, 1969.

With the lower company valuation and with support from San Francisco

---

[2] Small business investment companies were authorized under the Small Business Investment Act of 1958. In order to encourage investors to invest in small companies the Act offers tax advantages to owners of SBICs and liberal borrowing terms to the SBICs. Prior to 1968 banks were allowed to establish wholly owned SBICs, and many banks took advantage of the SBIC opportunity. San Francisco Capital was a wholly owned subsidiary of the San Francisco Bay National Bank, which was one of the leading commercial banks in California with total assets in excess of $3.5 billion. Approximately 80% of San Francisco Capital's portfolio companies were also customers of the bank.

Capital, Brown and Taylor was able to obtain commitments for the rest of the issue. The deal was closed on December 5, 1969. Stock ownership of the company is listed in Exhibit 4.

In exchange for the $1.8 million financing, UTC issued 18,000 shares of 6¼% convertible preferred stock with $100 par value. Dividends would be payable after September 1, 1972 and each share of preferred stock was convertible into three common shares. The 18,000 preferred shares would thus convert into 54,000 common shares, which would represent 47.4% of the company's 114,000 common shares to be then outstanding. The preferred investors were allowed voting rights equal to their percentage of the common stock on a fully diluted basis. In order to protect the interests of the preferred shareholders, the shares held by Brown and Taylor could not be voted with management on close votes. In addition, the preferred investors were each allowed a seat on the board of directors.

UTC'S FIRST YEAR

The initial marketing efforts by UTC consisted of grading the hundreds of inquiries received and following up the most promising ones. Detailed discussions were held with a cable television group interested in providing a "newspaper of the air" and a British airline interested in engineering a cathode ray tube terminal reservation system. Mr. Sill and Mr. Hansen found the CATV and the airline discussions challenging but finally decided that financial and engineering limitations required concentration by the company on the already established newspaper and newswire market. Mr. Hansen felt that UTC's success depended on selecting one industry and serving it well.

The Associated Press newswire service represented a substantial opportunity for UTC. AP was counting on the UTC equipment to eliminate retyping in the editing process and to increase the speed of newswire transmission. This would reduce news backups, which plagued all the wire service companies, and would give AP an important competitive advantage over UPI. The Associated Press planned to install one memory unit with three or four display terminals in each of its 40 regional offices. This represented in excess of $4 million of sales. Although no contracts had been signed for any future deliveries, Mr. Hansen believed that Mr. Sill's excellent working relationship with the AP director of research and the excellent performance of the UTC system put UTC in an extremely strong position.

In April, 1970, UTC's competitive position was threatened unexpectedly by the development by Industrial Graphics Corporation of a text-editing terminal of superior quality. When the Industrial Graphics machine was shown at the American Newspaper Publishers Association Show in New Orleans in June, 1970, the machine appeared to be technically superior to UTC gear and it drew great interest. After recognizing that the performance of Industrial Graphics gear was better than that of UTC, Mr. Sill and Mr. Hansen decided that it would be necessary to entirely redesign the UTC terminal. Although the Industrial Graphics terminal was less flexible than the UTC system, it was easier to read and the equipment itself looked more professional. The redesign was necessary to change the terminal from a straight stroke generator system to a dot raster system of character delineation utilizing medium- and large-scale integrated circuits. This change had recently become economically feasible because the price of medium- and large-scale integrated circuits (upon which the dot raster system depends) had declined drastically. The dot raster system also generated more readable characters than the straight stroke.

After seeing the Industrial Graphics terminal Mr. Sill felt that all production of the UTC system should stop until a new terminal could be designed. "There's no use riding a dead horse," he commented. On the other hand, Mr. Hansen argued that the two systems then underway should be completed to meet customer commitments before redesign was begun. Mr. Sill was unhappy about finishing the systems and postponing redesign one and a half to two months. He felt the customers would be better off waiting six months for a better terminal. Mr. Hansen's argument—that developing a reputation for delivery of equipment on schedule would be more important in the long run than the extra 6–8 weeks of redesign time—finally prevailed and Mr. Sill reluctantly completed the two systems.

Once the two unfinished terminal systems were completed, all production and marketing efforts of the company were curtailed. The situation was desperate. Between December, 1969, and September, 1970, over $1 million had been lost on sales of only $121,000 and the company still did not have a superior product or a well-developed production process. (See Exhibits 5 and 6 for financial statements.) Mr. Sill and four other engineers went to work designing the new terminal. From September through December, 1970, no new systems were produced nor were any new sales commitments made. Basically, the company marked time while the engineers designed and redesigned the terminal. Finally in December Mr. Sill was satisfied that the company had produced a terminal superior to that of Industrial Graphics. In fact, he was confident that the UTC systems were now far superior because of their greater capacity, flexibility, speed, and lower cost. UTC's basic terminal would sell for $13,000 whereas the Industrial Graphics terminal sold for $16,000. In January, 1971, UTC had an order backlog of almost $400,000.

OUTLOOK FOR SECOND YEAR

Product

After the redesign was completed the UTC line consisted of three products: the 3400 Rotating Magnetic Storage Memory System, the smaller 3101 Disk Storage Memory System, and the 5200 Display Terminal which could be operated either as a stand-alone unit or in conjunction with either the

3400 or the 3101 data base. Basically the 3400 and 3101 systems served as memories for the large-scale storing of text, allowed text editing with the use of the 5200 CRT terminals, and accepted data from newswire service lines. They were also communications centers for originating and directing data to a variety of output devices.

A major selling point of the UTC equipment was its "systems" nature. The Industrial Graphics product consisted essentially of a terminal that had to be programmed to operate with a large central computer. In contrast, the 3400 and 3101 systems could be built up to meet customer specifications as an integrated system. For example, a small paper could start with a single 5200 terminal with its own data base to be used as a stand-alone copy editor, and then could gradually build up a system consisting of several 5200 terminals and a 3400 data base. Along with the equipment, UTC also provided all programming necessary to make it compatible with the customer's existing computer-controlled equipment.

UTC management believed that production of the redesigned terminals would be no problem. Approximately one third of UTC's production space would be used for making prototype integrated circuits. Once these circuits were checked out as having the characteristics needed in their particular application, production of additional printed circuits would be contracted out. Production of the various systems would consist mainly of assembling the 5200 terminal and the two data base systems to customer specifications. During the production assembly stages, each circuit would be thoroughly checked by a computer programmed to simulate the circuit's various functions. A failure to function properly would be immediately picked up by the simulation program and corrected. All of UTC's systems were built in modular configuration and each integrated circuit was a plug-in unit in itself. This made service easier and faster.

Market potential

The newspaper industry dwarfed Associated Press in terms of sales potential for UTC and offered a substantial base for long-term growth. In recent years, American newspapers had aggressively begun to modernize plant and automate office procedures. For example, a newsletter published in the fall of 1970 by Composition Information Services, Inc., stated that photocomposition processes had been adopted by 61% of all American newspapers in the last decade, creating a $35 to $40 million annual market for the several companies that manufactured photocomposition equipment. The management of UTC believed that automation of the flow of information was the next priority for the newspaper industry and that the market for the display terminals and memory devices was potentially greater than the market for photocomposition equipment. The size of the market for text editing terminals alone, for example, was projected in articles in 1970 in both *Electronic News* and *Editor & Publisher* to be $15 to $20 million annually; and sales of terminals for use in display and classified advertising would significantly increase the annual dollar volume of the terminal market as a whole. The magnitude of the industry's need for terminals was illustrated by the fact that a Midwest newspaper which was then evaluating the use of text editing terminals for editorial use would require 90 terminals to accommodate its editors; a West Coast newspaper would require 50 terminals for the classified advertising application alone.

The Associated Press was recommending UTC's equipment to subscribers in order to have a fully compatible and integrated system. From a competitive standpoint, a fully integrated system would "tie-up" subscribers and reduce the risk of losing them to UPI. In AP's roster of 1,200 subscribers, there were about 200 newspapers which could each use $1 million worth of equipment, another 300 each of which could use $500,000 worth, and yet another 400 each of which could use roughly $100,000 thus creating a potentially enormous market. (See Exhibit 7.)

There was the risk, however, that newspapers might be slow to adopt the equipment because of union problems. Photon, Inc., a manufacturer of automated typesetting equipment designed to eliminate several manual steps in the preparation of set type, had approached several newspapers that had had labor problems and had sold the equipment on the basis of reduced dependence on labor. The American Newspaper Guild and the typographical setters unions were incensed over the actions of Photon, and the word got out that any paper which did business with that company could expect labor troubles. As a result, Photon suffered considerable resistance on the part of large newspapers. In contrast, UTC designed its equipment to increase the productivity and speed of newspaper editors and typesetters, and by stressing these advantages—not the elimination of jobs—UTC had met a favorable response by most newspaper owners. Currently a jurisdictional dispute between the Associated Press and the Newspaper Guild concerning who would have control over UTC equipment was in court for settlement. AP was optimistic that the court would decide in its favor, thus allowing more freedom in future installation.

Competition

Competition came from other manufacturers of cathode ray tube display systems and from optical scanning producers. There were over 100 manufacturers of cathode ray tube terminals for various uses. To date, only Industrial Graphics and UTC had developed systems for the newspaper industry. Since there were many conventions peculiar to the newspaper uses, UTC management felt that it and Industrial Graphics were 18 months ahead of any other possible competitors. Mr. Sill recognized that other manufacturers could do what he had done from an engineering standpoint, but the money and time would be almost prohibitive. The only computer manufacturer with equipment capable of equaling the performance of the UTC system 3400 was IBM, and the IBM 360 would require significant modifications and sophisticated programming to meet the newspaper needs.

Somewhat indirect competition to UTC came from optical scanning manufacturers and from IBM. Optical scanning systems were used in book publishing to transfer printed material into machine language which could be fed into a typesetter. The systems eliminated the step of retyping once an original typed copy was available, but were very limited by the unavailability of editing features. The American Newspaper Publishers Association was supporting optical character recognition equipment as a significant innovation, but Mr. Sill felt that CRT systems would be much more important.

Management and staff

The company employed approximately 30 people, most of whom were in engineering, production, prototype printed circuit manufacturing, and drafting. The engineering staff included Mr. Sill and four other engineers. Recently the company had hired three computer programmers and was planning to add gradually to its technical staff as the company grew. The company was presently negotiating a sales and service agreement whereby a company in the graphic arts industry would distribute and service UTC's 5200 text-editing display terminal and 3101 memory system throughout the country. UTC intended to market directly its 3400 magnetic memory system and terminals to the Associated Press and other large systems users. AP men had been trained to maintain old equipment installations, although Mr. Sill had done special servicing by flying to several locations up to now.

Mr. Sill was looking forward to the time when Mr. Hansen and the marketing staff would know enough about the UTC system to be able to sell it effectively without his active assistance. He also hoped to give up some of the responsibility for production, programming, installation, and servicing and to concentrate on new product development.

Additional financing needs

Mr. Mason of San Francisco Capital still had confidence in Mr. Sill and Mr. Hansen and in their ability to make UTC profitable if given proper backing. He had spent a considerable amount of time at the company's plant during the past year and had participated in a number of the critical pricing and product-market decisions. He felt that Mr. Hansen had proved himself to be an able small business manager. Several things had changed since December, 1969, and most of the changes seemed for the better. The redesigned system was now technically better than the Industrial Graphics equipment. And the conservative sales and earnings forecasts, based largely on sales to the Associated Press, were encouraging. (See Exhibit 8 for projected statements.)

Mr. Mason could not detach himself totally, however, from the disastrous year that UTC had just completed. The company's product position and sales potential had appeared equally bright at the time of the initial financing in December, 1969. There certainly seemed to be justification for the concern among some of the other investors that UTC might be forced without warning into another major product redesign. The potential payoff from investing the additional $600,000 was large, but Mr. Mason wondered if it was sufficient to justify further investment in such a high-risk venture.

He was also considering what form the investment should take and the price at which the securities should be sold. Mr. Sill and Mr. Hansen wished to avoid the fixed financial charges of a debenture and were pressing for a common stock issue priced at $30 a share. They felt that the company was stronger than at the time of the initial financing when stock was sold, on a converted basis, for $33⅓ a share (the $100 preferred stock was convertible into three shares of common stock). A low issue price would result in substantial dilution of their ownership in UTC—a prospect which troubled each of them.

Mr. Mason did not believe that the other investors would accept a common stock issue for the second-round financing. For the majority of the venture capital industry, 1970 had been an extremely difficult period. Many portfolio companies had been forced into bankruptcy by the downturn in capital equipment purchasing and the slowdown in industrial sales and collections. As a result, many venture capitalists were working around the clock trying to keep their holdings in order. All had a few companies in trouble, and many had allocated personnel for direct management of such companies to keep them in business and under control while longer term solutions could be found. Most venture capitalists were still quite concerned about the state of the economy, the health of their portfolio companies, and the deterioration of their firms' stock prices. (See Exhibit 9.) In this mood of pessimism, venture capitalists seemed to want the greater security of a debt issue.

If it was decided to use a debt instrument, a decision would have to be made on the form of the debt. It seemed clear that a straight interest debenture could not provide adequate return, given the amount of risk, without imposing severe financial charges on the company. The choice was between a convertible debenture and a debenture with detachable warrants[3] to buy common stock at a price fixed at the time of closing the deal. Some of the investors favored debt with detachable warrants. This financing instrument would permit them to maintain the liquidity of their venture capital firms through annual receipt of principal repayments without forcing them to forgo the equity option. The investors would be able to get the "seed money" out of the investment while retaining the right to buy stock at a favorable price.

Mr. Mason appreciated the arguments for a warrant issue, but he felt that the alternative to a common stock issue should be a convertible debenture. He proposed issuance of $600,000 principal amount of a 7½% convertible, subordinated note due February 13, 1978, and convertible into 52,531 shares of the common stock of UTC. Interest would not accrue for 18 months from

[3] The debenture would provide for fixed interest and sinking fund payments and would not be convertible into common stock. However, investors would receive warrants that could be detached from the debenture and exercised independently of the debenture.

the date of the notes. The notes would be prepayable without penalty at UTC's option after five years or from the proceeds of a public offering of UTC's securities. Otherwise, the notes would not be callable.

The low conversion price reflected Mr. Mason's strong belief that all the initial investors in this syndicate should have the responsibility as well as the opportunity to increase their ownership of UTC. Therefore he felt that if one or more of the initial investors did not "step up" for their share of the second round, they should be willing to suffer substantial resultant dilution.

Mr. Mason was concerned, however, that the low conversion price would result in such severe ownership dilution for Mr. Sill and Mr. Hansen, who could not purchase any of the planned $600,000 issue, that their motivation would be adversely affected. Although UTC had not performed according to projections to date, he proposed that Mr. Sill and Mr. Hansen receive 10-year warrants to purchase an aggregate of 28,860 shares of common stock at a price of $11.42 a share. The exercise of the warrants would be subject to the attainment by UTC of certain performance standards. Specifically, 20% of the warrants could be exercised each year from 1971 through 1975 if the following pretax earnings levels were met or exceeded by the company:

	1971	*1972*	*1973*	*1974*	*1975*
Pretax earnings	0	$375,000	$650,000	$875,000	$1,100,000

At the board meeting in December, 1970, Mr. Hansen had said that he was anxious to have the additional financing soon. Therefore, Mr. Mason wanted to reach a decision within a week on whether to increase San Francisco Capital's investment in United Terminal by participating in the second-round financing and, if he decided to do so, on what terms he should recommend that the financing be structured.

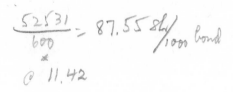

Exhibit 1

UNITED TERMINAL CORPORATION

Summary of the Portfolio of San Francisco Capital Corporation

Jack Mason and Ben Brooks, the two officers of San Francisco Capital, were responsible for making new investments and for monitoring the 49 companies already in the portfolio. San Francisco Capital had a total of $5.4 million invested in the 49 companies. The smallest investment was $2,000 in a wholesale distributor of electronic components. The largest investment was $345,000 in a manufacturer of industrial processing equipment using state-of-the-art high-energy electron and ion beams with pulsed power sources. Median investment size was $100,000.

The portfolio companies operated in the following areas: (1) Manufacture of data processing equipment; (2) manufacture of electronic transmitting and receiving equipment; (3) research and manufacturing in electronics; (4) manufacture of components for the electronics industry; (5) manufacture of microwave components; (6) cable television; (7) research and development of a computer system for block trading of securities; (8) manufacture of electronics equipment; (9) research in digital data communications; (10) production and design of automation devices; (11) manufacture of electronic connectors and connector modules; (12) wholesaling of electronic components; (13) manufacture of communications products for use in the loss-prevention market; (14) medical diagnostic services; (15) electronic assembly and manufacturing under contract or subcontract; (16) offshore lobster fishing; (17) maintenance of aviation, electronic, and heavy-duty equipment at U.S. government facilities; (18) AM radio stations; (19) manufacture of live magnetic tape cleaner for use in data processing centers; (20) manufacture of cookware, leisure and casual furniture, and giftware; (21) manufacture of a wide line of machinery for plastic packaging industry; (22) production of architectural precast concrete building wall panels; (23) design and manufacture of precision castings for wide industrial use; (24) design of automatic wave soldering systems for use in soldering printed circuits; (25) manufacture of electron volt parts which incorporate the concept of modular components to ion and electron beam technology with broad application for use in industrial, scientific, and educational laboratories; (26) operation of 17 self-service drive-in restaurants; (27) manufacture of rigid thermoplastic sheeting by the extrusion process; (28) development of a nonintervention heart assist device; (29) manufacture of a solid-state programmable digital controller; (30) development of an electro-optical mark reading system for direct conversion into computer language; (31) publication of mathematics textbooks; (32) production of wigs; (33) development of a steam engine for use in various on- and off-road motive power applications; (34) merchandising of men's and boys' clothing through leased departments in discount stores; (35) manufacture of plasma arc welding and cutting torches and systems; (36) research in thermionics; (37) manufacture of semiconductor components; (38) manufacture of information storage devices for the data processing industry; (39) distribution of gases, supplies and equipment for welding, industrial, and medical uses.

Exhibit 2

UNITED TERMINAL CORPORATION
ILLUSTRATION OF EDITING DISPLAY TERMINAL EDS/5200

Exhibit 3

UNITED TERMINAL CORPORATION
STATEMENT OF FINANCIAL POSITION AT AUGUST 1, 1969, PRO FORMA TO INCLUDE PROPOSED FINANCING
(Dollar figures in thousands)

ASSETS		LIABILITIES AND EQUITY	
Current assets:		*Current liabilities:*	
Cash	$1,337	n.a.	
Accounts receivable	20		
Inventory	154		
Work in process	377	*Long-term debt:*	
Value of leased equipment	96	Notes payable*	$ 650
Total current assets	$1,984		
		Owners' equity:	
		6¼% convertible preferred stock†	$1,800
Fixed assets:		Retained earnings	(350)
Capital equipment and tools	121	Common stock	5
		Total equity	$1,455
Total assets	$2,105	*Total liabilities and equity*	$2,105

Common stock outstanding: 54,696 shares

* Noninterest-bearing notes due to United Cable Co., subordinated to ordinary bank debt and without claim on assets. Retirement schedule: $100,000 after three years, $250,000 after four years, and $300,000 after five years.

† Convertible into 54,000 common shares. Dividend payments to commence after September 1, 1972.

Exhibit 4

UNITED TERMINAL CORPORATION
LIST OF STOCKHOLDERS AS OF JANUARY, 1971

	Cost	*Shares of Preferred Stock*	*Shares of Common Stock Assuming Conversion*	*% of Pro Forma Common Stock*
Preferred stockholders:				
California Life and Casualty	$ 500,000	5,000	15,000	13.2%
San Francisco Capital	250,000	2,500	7,500	6.6
Oakland Merchant Capital	250,000	2,500	7,500	6.6
San Francisco Bay National Bank Employees Trust Fund	250,000	2,500	7,500	6.6
Various Blacksmith Family Trusts	300,000	3,000	9,000	7.8
Two private investors	250,000	2,500	7,500	6.6
	$1,800,000	18,000	54,000	47.4%
Common stockholders:				
Bill Hansen	$ 0		23,940	21 %
Charles Sill	0		23,940	21
John Barron (production mgr.)	0		2,280	2
United Cable Co.	0		5,700	5
Brown and Taylor	0		4,140	3.6
			60,000	52.6%
Total			114,000	100.0%

Exhibit 5

UNITED TERMINAL CORPORATION
Balance Sheet at September 30, 1970
(In thousands)

ASSETS

Cash	$ 54
Short-term securities, at cost which approximates market	323
Accounts receivable, trade, less allowance of $1,150 for doubtful accounts	97
Inventories:	
Raw materials	$ 126
Discs, drums, and computers	166
Work in process	122
	$ 414
Prepaid expenses	7
Fixed assets:	
Used in operations, at cost	$ 221
Leased to others, at cost	60
	$ 281
Less accumulated depreciation	56
	$ 225
Deferred charges, patents, and other assets:	
Deferred interest expense	$ 172
Patents and other assets	33
	$ 205
	$1,325

LIABILITIES

Accounts payable, trade	$ 76
Accrued expenses	26
Long-term note payable	650
STOCKHOLDERS' EQUITY	
6¼% cumulative convertible preferred stock, $100 par value, authorized, issued and outstanding 18,000 shares	1,800
Common stock, $0.10 par value, authorized 150,000 shares, issued and outstanding 60,000 shares	6
Accumulated deficit	(1,233)
	$1,325

Exhibit 6

UNITED TERMINAL CORPORATION
STATEMENT OF OPERATIONS FROM INCEPTION (DECEMBER 5, 1969) TO SEPTEMBER 30, 1970
(In thousands except per share data)

Revenues:		
Sales		$ 121
Rental income		30
Interest income		56
		$ 207
Expenses:		
Engineering, production, and related costs:		
Research and development	$318	
Production costs	181	
Inventory losses	216	$ 715
Depreciation		70
Selling, general, and administrative expenses		183
Interest expense		35
Loss before extraordinary item		$ 796
Extraordinary item:		
Reduction of values assigned to assets acquired from United Cable Co. (Note A)		304
Net loss		$1,100
Losses per common share:		
Loss before extraordinary item		$ 13.19
Extraordinary item		5.03
Net loss		$ 18.22

Note A: As of September 30, 1970, United Terminal reduced the amounts at which certain assets acquired from United Cable Co. were originally stated to amounts which in its opinion are representative of the minimum value of such assets in the company's future business activities. Such reduction appears as an extraordinary item in the statement of operations.

Exhibit 7

UNITED TERMINAL CORPORATION
Market Potential Analysis
(Dollar figures in thousands)

Circulation	*Number of Papers*	*Product Line* 3400 *High*	3400 *Low*	3101 *High*	3101 *Low*	5200 *High*	5200 *Low*
500,000–over	11						
Single paper requirements		$ 1,400	$ 700			$ 4,000	$ 1,300
Group dollar total		15,400	7,700			39,000	13,000
250,000–500,000	28						
Single paper requirements		700	350			2,000	650
Group dollar total		19,600	9,800			56,000	18,000
100,000–250,000	91						
Single paper requirements		350	175			1,000	325
Group dollar total		32,000	16,000			91,000	27,000
50,000–100,000	119						
Single paper requirements		140	70			160	100
Group dollar total		17,000	8,000			19,000	12,000
25,000–50,000	249						
Single paper requirements				$ 39	$ 13	104	52
Group dollar total				9,700	3,200	25,700	12,800
10,000–25,000	472						
Single paper requirements				13	—	52	13
Group dollar total				6,100	—	24,500	6,100
00,000–10,000	468						
Single paper requirements						13	—
Group dollar total						6,000	—
Total		$84,000	$41,500	$15,800	$3,200	$261,200	$88,900

Note: The value of each product was extended for a sample paper in the group and brought to a total for the group. A wide range exists between the high and the low assumptions. However, using the low for all products, a very large market exists within the newspaper industry. This approach is for newspapers only and looks at the total market size if the newspapers ordered all of their equipment needs. The market potential analysis excludes commercial printing and all foreign newspapers, commercial printers, and newswire services, domestic and foreign.

Exhibit 8

UNITED TERMINAL CORPORATION

PROJECTED INCOME AND CASH FLOW STATEMENTS FOR 1971, TOGETHER WITH ANNUAL FORECAST FOR 1972

(In thousands)

	Projected Monthly Income Statements, 1971													1972
	Jan.	*Feb.*	*Mar.*	*Apr.*	*May*	*June*	*July*	*Aug.*	*Sept.*	*Oct.*	*Nov.*	*Dec.*	*Totals*	*Forecast*
Sales and lease income	$ 5	$ 35	$ 100	$175	$200	$230	$250	$270	$300	$320	$350	$380	$2,615	$4,950
Cost of sales	—	$ 14	$ 43	$ 75	$ 86	$ 99	$101	$116	$129	$138	$150	$163	$1,114	$2,138
Depreciation	$ 6	6	$ 6	6	6	6	6	6	6	6	6	6	72	145
Salaries	20	20	30	35	35	45	45	50	55	55	60	65	515	1,150
Outside services	5	7	1	—	—	1	—	—	1	—	—	4	19	34
Total cost of sales	$ 31	$ 47	$ 80	$116	$127	$151	$152	$172	$191	$199	$216	$238	$1,720	$3,467
Gross margin	$(26)	$(12)	$ 20	$ 59	$ 73	$ 79	$ 98	$ 98	$109	$121	$134	$142	$ 895	$1,483
Operating expenses	18	18	20	22	23	25	25	25	25	27	30	30	288	475
Operating income	$(44)	$(30)	$ 0	$ 37	$ 50	$ 54	$ 73	$ 73	$ 84	$ 94	$104	$112	$ 607	$1,008
Other charges*	1	—	1	1	1	1	2	3	3	3	3	4	23	78
Net income before research and development	$(45)	$(30)	$ (1)	$ 36	$ 49	$ 53	$ 71	$ 70	$ 81	$ 91	$101	$108	$ 584	$ 930
Research and development	20	20	20	20	20	25	35	35	30	30	30	30	315	475
Net income before taxes	$(65)	$(50)	$ (21)	$ 16	$ 29	$ 28	$ 36	$ 35	$ 51	$ 61	$ 71	$ 78	$ 269	$ 455

* Includes interest.

Projected Monthly Cash Flows, 1971

	Jan.	*Feb.*	*Mar.*	*Apr.*	*May*	*June*	*July*	*Aug.*	*Sept.*	*Oct.*	*Nov.*	*Dec.*	*Totals*
Raw material and component purchases	—	$132	$ 86	$ 98	$100	$116	$129	$137	$150	$163	$160	$160	$1,431
Monthly cash expenses	$63	65	72	78	79	87	106	111	112	113	120	130	1,136
Collections	—	—	—	35	100	175	200	230	250	270	300	320	1,880
Monthly cash need	$63	$197	$158	$141	$ 79	$ 28	$ 35	$ 18	$ 12	$ 6	$(20)	$(30)	$ 687
Cumulative cash need	63	260	418	559	638	666	701	719	731	737	717	687	

1971 Working Capital Requirements

Requirements		*Sources*	
1. Peak cash need (October)	$737	January cash position	$100
2. Manufacturing equipment	50	New financing	600
3. Retained leases	100	Accounts receivable financing	287
4. Short-term demonstration models	100	Total	$987
Total	$987		

Exhibit 9

UNITED TERMINAL CORPORATION
STOCK PRICES OF SBICS AND VENTURE CAPITAL COMPANIES

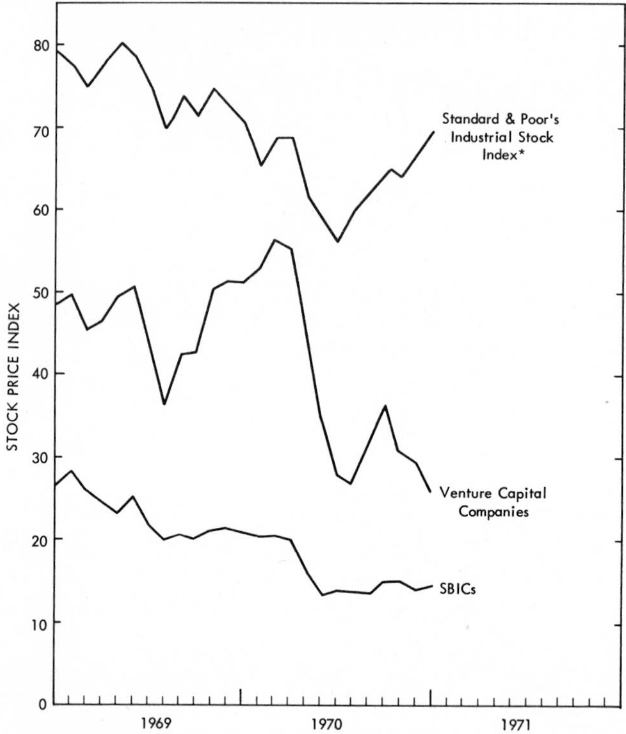

* Scaled to 1941–43 = 7.
Source: *SBIC/Venture Capital*, published by S. M. Rubel & Company, various monthly issues.

THE FORMATION AND GROWTH OF POLAROID CORPORATION

^^

This case was written (in April, 1971) with a variety of teaching purposes in mind. (1) The first portion provides an exciting story of the formation and early problems of a new company, which is relevant for today's problems even though it is set in the 1930's. The essential problems of new enterprises have not changed greatly over this span of time. (2) The case also summarizes the dramatic growth of Polaroid under a single management from a totally new enterprise to a major company with sales of over one-half billion dollars (including unconsolidated foreign subsidiaries), all from internally developed products over the short period of a quarter of a century. (3) Finally, the case concludes with a summary of the basic management philosophy of the Polaroid management and provides the background for a fruitful discussion of the fundamental confrontation of Eastman Kodak and Polaroid as of 1970–71.

Formative years of Polaroid

The early history of Polaroid as of many new enterprises is essentially a biography of one man, in this case Edwin H. Land. Land started his scientific experiments while still in grammar school. At that time he was primarily interested in television, but the importance for that purpose of work on polarizers soon became clear. Land continued his experiments throughout his preparatory schooling and at Harvard College. His first important patent was applied for in 1929, when he was about 20 years of age. He left college in his senior year to devote his entire time to experimentation with polarized light. In 1932 Land and G. W. Wheelwright, a laboratory assistant at Harvard, set up the Land-Wheelwright Laboratories, Inc., in Wellesley, Massachusetts. Shortly thereafter, the laboratory was moved to a basement on Dartmouth Street, Boston.

During these early stages the enterprise was financed largely by moderate advances from the families of Land and Wheelwright. Great economy was practiced; the young inventors worked in dingy surroundings and spent as little as possible.

Their early interest was in the development, manufacture, and sale of light-polarizing materials and of accessories necessary for their utilization. Polarized light had long been a subject of scientific research and experimentation, but its commercial applications prior to Polaroid had been effectively limited by the absence of any plentiful, low-cost material for polarizing light. Land's initial breakthrough was the invention of a commercially practicable light polarizer. His invention made possible the production, at relatively low cost, of a continuous cellulosic sheeting, capable of polarizing or arranging light vibrations as light passes through the sheeting.

The first applications selected for development required small amounts of material. On November 30, 1934, Eastman Kodak Company signed a contract calling for the manufacture by Polaroid of photographic light filters called Polascreens.[1] Revenue from the resulting sales to Eastman was instrumental in financing subsequent research.

A second important contract, signed on November 5, 1935, called for the manufacture of Polaroid Day Glasses by the American Optical Company. These glasses, the first Polaroid product intended for popular use, were introduced by the American Optical Company in December, 1936. Meanwhile, Polaroid sheeting was being sold in the form of small discs for demonstration purposes in school and college laboratories. Public announcement of the invention in January, 1936, attracted widespread interest. By July, 1936, larger quarters were needed to house the growing organization.

The rapid strides in product development made by the newly formed enterprise are well illustrated by the following quotation from *Fortune* magazine:

> . . . Polaroid, while expensive in comparison with glass, involves no big investment. It has now been on the market only three years [as of 1938]. But already people are wearing it in sunglasses, researching with it in microscopes, telescopes, and other optical instruments, reading by it in lamps, using it in advertising color displays, taking pictures with it in cameras, and looking through it in binoculars. Children play with it in educational toys. It has—experimentally—produced colored movies *in three dimensions*. And every automobile driver in America may soon be clamoring for it because it is capable of eliminating headlight glare completely and forever. . . .[2]

Initial acquisition of outside capital

By 1937 Polaroid was in need of outside capital. A staff of some 50 individuals had been acquired. As the preceding summary statement indicates, numerous applications of light polarization had been developed to the stage where investment prospects appeared promising. Contracts had been signed with Eastman Kodak and American Optical. Beginning in early 1937, negotiations for outside financing were carried on, first through an intermediary, and later directly with Schroder Rockefeller & Co., Inc., and Kuhn, Loeb & Co.

---

[1] In retrospect it is interesting to note that Eastman was Polaroid's first commercial customer of any significance. In contrast, during the 1950's and 1960's Polaroid became one of Eastman's largest customers. As of early 1971 Polaroid constituted a serious competitive threat to Eastman.

[2] "In the Light of Polaroid," *Fortune*, September, 1938, p. 74.

of New York. After early negotiations had failed to materialize, an agreement was finally reached in a contract dated August 10, 1937.

Under this contract the Land-Wheelwright interests agreed to organize the present Polaroid Corporation with authorized capital stock of:

> 7,500 shares of 5% cumulative, Class A stock with a par value of $100 a share,
> 2,500 shares of $5 cumulative, Class B stock with a par value of $5 a share, and
> 100,000 shares of common stock with a par value of $1 a share.

The Lands and Wheelwright also agreed to transfer to the new corporation all patents and patent applications owned by Land and all other interests of the Lands and Wheelwright in the development. This contribution was valued at $132,627, the total cost of the development to August, 1937. Moreover, Land agreed to enter into an employment contract with the new company for a period of 10 years.

Outside capital amounting to $750,000 was supplied through Kuhn, Loeb & Co. and Schroder Rockefeller & Co., Inc. Half of this amount was to be paid immediately; the remainder was to be paid at any time prior to December 31, 1939, at the call of the company, and was so paid.

The ownership and control of the new corporation was governed by a series of complicated agreements, the gist of which can be described as follows:

1. The Lands and Wheelwright, predominantly the Lands, received the entire issue of 2,500 shares of Class B stock and, in effect, a little over 60% of the common stock.
2. An additional 16.7% of the common stock was initially turned over to the Lands and Wheelwright, but these shares were immediately sold by them at a nominal price of $1 a share to compensate other individuals who had participated in the financing negotiations.
3. The Kuhn-Loeb and Schroder-Rockefeller interests received the entire issue of 7,500 shares of Class A stock, which had first preference as to dividends and assets, and 22,500 shares, or 22.5% of the common stock. In effect, a block of one share of Class A stock and three shares of common stock was sold for $100, the par value of the Class A stock.
4. By mutual agreement 71,500 shares of common stock were deposited in a Voting Trust. The Voting Trust Agreement gave Land unlimited voting power over the stock deposited in the Trust and hence over the company until the expiration of the Trust in September, 1947. Nominally, there were three voting trustees, but Land was given the power to remove the other trustees at his discretion, and no action would be taken by the Voting Trust without Land's approval.[3]

The terms of this financing and the care taken to preserve absolute control in the hands of Land clearly reflected (1) the high regard of the investment bankers for the potential of the company, and (2) the fact that

[3] Certain minor options that were later exercised to the extent of 7,000 shares of common stock are omitted from this summary as are other details. This statement attempts to report in simple terms the essence of a very complicated set of transactions.

the investment bankers attributed this potential largely to the contributions that Land as a person would make to the newly formed company. Land attached a strong premium to the maintenance of his control of the enterprise, and his financial backers were glad to leave the control in his hands.

The 1937 financing was regarded as a private placement when the transaction was undertaken, and it was so treated. Later, however, at the request of the Securities and Exchange Commission the three securities issued in this transaction were registered with the SEC.

Expansion through World War II

Sales and profits. As shown in Exhibit 1, the sales of the new company increased rapidly during the prewar years from $142,000 in 1937 to about $750,000 in 1939 and 1940. No profits were accumulated in this period; substantial sums were invested in research and development, and, in addition, the normal problems of forming a new organization and of placing a variety of new products on the market were encountered. In fact, a net deficit of $134,000 was reported for the years 1937–40, inclusive. No preferred dividends were paid during these years and substantial arrearages were accumulated. Nevertheless, the company was still in a comfortable financial position as of December 31, 1940, as Exhibit 2 shows. Current assets amounted to $245,000 as against current liabilities of $66,000. Most of the remaining assets consisted of expenditures for patents and patent applications and of deferred experimental and development costs, both of which were capitalized during these early years. Total equity amounted to $757,000, but the equity represented by preferred stock came to $762,500. The net deficits incurred in 1937–40 had completely eroded the common equity leaving a book deficit of about $5,000.

The war years brought a sharp change. Sales expanded from $720,000 in 1940 to $13,155,000 in 1944 and to $16,752,000 in 1945. Net income after taxes, however, grew much more slowly, as shown in Exhibit 1, primarily because of the severe excess profits taxes in effect throughout the war years. Despite the skyrocketing sales volume during the war years the financial condition of the company became much more precarious. As of December 31, 1944, for example, current assets amounted to $3,779,000 and current liabilities to $2,723,000, as Exhibit 3 shows, leaving a net working capital of $1,056,000 and reducing the current ratio from the comfortable level of 3.7 as of December 30, 1940, to 1.4 as of December 31, 1944. Most of the remaining assets consisted of capitalized patents and developmental costs. Despite these capitalizations, some of which never generated subsequent revenues, the book value of the common stock amounted to only $631,000 as of December 31, 1944. Dividends on the preferred stock were paid for the first time beginning in 1942, but arrearages on preferred dividends of over $240,000 remained outstanding at the end of 1944.

Products and processes, 1937–45. The research and product development of Polaroid during these early years is difficult to summarize in succinct form. Any brief statement undoubtedly does injustice to the facts. The one statement that can be made with confidence is that Polaroid under the guidance of Land moved forward on a wide variety of fronts, many of which never came to the stage of producing commercial revenues.

The discussion of the company's product development during this stage of its history can best be broken down into the years prior to World War II and then into the war years. Three lines of research and product development appear to have characterized the years prior to World War II. All were concerned with applications of Land's basic interest and critical breakthroughs in the field of polarized light.

1. The first and most lasting commercial application consisted of applications of the Land polarizing process to the field of optical goods, primarily Polaroid sun glasses. The 1939 annual report stated that more than a million pairs of Polaroid glasses were sold to the public in this year. Sun glasses were the bread-and-butter source of commercial revenue for Polaroid during its crucial early years of 1937–39.
2. The major hope of the Polaroid management for the attainment of a sizable volume of sales and significant profits during its early years was in the application of the Polaroid process to the field of automobile headlights. Reference to this application was made in each annual report from 1938 through the early postwar years. Though no figures are available, a major fraction of the company's limited resources throughout the prewar years was undoubtedly devoted to the difficult problem of adapting the Polaroid process to this important application. Not only did it appear to be a major source of potential sales and profits, but, equally important, it was regarded by Land and other members of the Polaroid management as a crucial advance in automotive safety. The emotional energy expended on this development and the frustrations encountered by the Polaroid management as a result of the negative or uninterested response of the automotive industry and of related regulatory agencies would be difficult to overstate. Anyone who has attended the annual stockholders meetings of the Polaroid Corporation as late as the 1950's and 1960's can attest to this fact. Yet, so far as the author of this case knows, Polaroid never received one dime of revenue from this effort—its principal hope of becoming a substantial company in its early years and an endeavor that absorbed a major portion of its limited capital during the 1930's and again in the immediate postwar years.
3. A third important line of publicly announced research and product development during the 1937–39 period was the application of the Polaroid process to photography, specifically to the production of three-dimensional pictures. Unlike the automotive application, this line of development produced significant revenues during the war years, and, in a brief flurry, the production of three-dimensional movies stimulated the sale of Polaroid viewers after the war. While Polaroid has maintained interest in this application, it does not currently constitute a sizable source of revenue.

Undoubtedly Polaroid was engaged in other areas of research and exploratory product development during the 1937–39 period, but the management naturally regarded much of its research and development activity as highly confidential, and no public record of its other endeavors is available.

As has already been stated, Polaroid's sales volume expanded enormously from 1940 through 1945 as its efforts were directed almost entirely to military business. Substantial quantities of Vectographic materials and field processing equipment were produced for making three-dimensional aerial views of terrain. Much of the company's wartime activity remained veiled by the cloak of wartime censorship, but the 1943 Annual Report lists some of its products of this period as follows:

Goggles for a variety of services:

Variable-Density Goggles, for aircraft and antiaircraft gunners to use in reducing glare from the sky and sun; Dark-Adaptor Goggles, for preconditioning the eyes for night vision; All-Purpose Goggles, for general use by all branches of the Service, as protection against glare, wind and dust; Aviation Goggles, for Army and Navy flying personnel; and Fog-Free Goggles, for eye protection under conditions which cause lens-fog in ordinary goggles.

Polarizing Filters and *Nonpolarizing Colored Filters*, for use in gunsights, range finders, periscopes, binoculars, and other military instruments.

Precision Plastic Optical Parts, for telescopes, fire control and signaling devices, and other instruments.

Blind Flying Training Equipment, for blacking out aircraft used in training pilots to fly at night.

Position Angle Finders, for finding the elevation of aircraft above the horizon.

Antiaircraft *Machine Gun Trainers*, for teaching gunners how to use tracer-bullet observation in the control of antiaircraft gunfire.

Polaroid's research and development even during this period ranged far beyond its initial concentration on the field of polarized light. Perhaps the best illustration of Polaroid's sponsorship of basic scientific and industrial research in quite a diverse field is its 1944 announcement of its total synthesis of quinine, a classic problem in organic chemistry. This development was undertaken on Polaroid's own initiative and successfully completed "not with a view to manufacturing the product, but as one of Polaroid's war contributions in case other anti-malarial controls should prove inadequate"[4] —this despite the fact that the government and a large chemical company believed that the project would at best require too much time to be completed for use during the war and might be completely insoluble.

Polaroid's problems as of V-J Day

Polaroid was faced with a potential financial crisis at the end of World War II. Its volume of business had expanded more than 20 times from 1940 to 1945. But its financial resources had not grown commensurately because of the severe impact of the excess profits tax on companies such as Polaroid that had no history of prewar earnings. The process of cutting back to peacetime levels of production was almost certain to involve large losses no matter how efficiently it was conducted.

---

[4] Annual Report to Stockholders, 1944.

The future also contained much uncertainty as to Polaroid's postwar financial needs. The management grouped the company's financial needs into four categories: (1) current working capital, (2) financing of research and development expenditures that might not yield a monetary return for some years, (3) financing of the acquisition of much needed new facilities to replace the inefficient wartime setup, and (4) the maintenance of a "financial cushion" to give the company flexibility of operation and protection against unforeseen contingencies.

Reliable estimates could not be made of the amounts of capital that would be needed for any of these categories. Working capital needs, for example, would depend on sales; and the postwar sales pattern was extremely difficult to predict as of mid-1945. For the near term, the management believed that sales of the company's prewar products with adaptations and improvements would amount to at least $2 million in the first postwar year and, barring unforeseen difficulties, should reach a volume of $5 million within two or three years. Sales of $2 million undoubtedly would involve a sizable operating deficit. Beyond this point the most significant factor in determining the future expansion of sales would be the introduction of radically new products.

Some of these products, such as the company's system for eliminating headlight glare and the use of Polaroid products in the manufacture of three-dimensional movies, had already been announced. Sufficient experience had been accumulated, however, to raise doubts about the successful commercial introduction of either of these products in the near future, since each depended on the cooperation of a large established industry.

Other potential products were closely guarded secrets. No significant time or resources were devoted during the war period to the company's later developments in the field of instant photography. This potential product was in the mind of the Polaroid management at the time, however, partly because it met the joint requirements of having a large potential market and of being sold directly to consumers without dependence on the collaboration of a large established industry such as the automobile manufacturers.

Once these new products were taken into consideration, the management believed that any attempt to estimate the company's sales potential 5 to 10 years ahead was like picking a number from a hat; $50 million or $100 million seemed about as reasonable as $5 million or $10 million.

The extent to which heavy outlays on research and development would be required before they would yield a monetary return was also difficult to estimate. The company's system of eliminating headlight glare and the potential use of the Polaroid process in making three-dimensional movies were in advanced stages of development, but the possibility of marketing these products depended on the whims of other industries and, in the case of automobile headlights, of regulatory authorities. Polaroid's tentative plans in the field of instant photography did not suffer from this impediment, but the Polaroid camera was just a gleam in the eye of Land in 1945 and might never come to fruition. At best it would require years of intensive and costly research and development with no certainty of success at the end of the road.

As of 1945 Polaroid was also badly in need of an efficient plant for its postwar activities. Throughout the war and prewar periods Polaroid had never purchased any real estate, preferring to conserve its limited capital for other purposes. During the war, as the company's volume expanded, one small piece of property after another was leased wherever vacant space could be located. The management believed that as much as $750,000 might be needed to acquire efficient manufacturing and laboratory space adequate for the company's immediate postwar needs. These expenditures would have to be multiplied severalfold in the relatively near future, however, if the company's postwar expansion was rapid.

To summarize, the company's financial requirements as of mid-1945 were highly indeterminate. It was, however, clear that the company could not enter the postwar readjustment period in sound financial condition with its existing limited resources. Indeed, it was entirely possible that a large additional influx of new capital would be needed to enable the company to survive the adjustment to peacetime operations.

Second round of external financing in 1945

Faced with all these pressures for additional funds and with the high risk confronting the company in the immediate postwar future, the Polaroid management decided to go to the market for new equity funds. This decision was difficult because of the importance attached by Land to maintaining control of the company and because of the management's optimistic appraisal of the company's future potential. As of mid-1945, for example, the Land family ownership in the company's common stock had declined to 33.6% and the Voting Trust that gave Land absolute voting control was due to expire in 1947.

The feasibility of raising external equity capital, fortunately, was enhanced by a very favorable market for the company's stock. By August, 1945, the price of the company's common stock on the over-the-counter market had risen to over $30 a share whereas it had traded at as little as $3 a share in 1942 and under $7 a share in 1944 (see Exhibit 4).[5] The peak level of earnings per share prior to 1945 was $0.92 in 1944 (Exhibit 1) so that the August, 1945, price for the common stock represented a price-earnings multiple of over 30, this for a company that had no proved peacetime product representing any sizable sales volume and no significant record of profitable peacetime operations.

As an aside, it is worthwhile noting the extreme volatility of the market for

[5] It should be stressed that the prices quoted in Exhibit 4 for the entire 1938–50 period reflect the three for one stock split undertaken immediately prior to the 1945 financing. No other stock splits or dividends were made during this 12-year period. To put the data of Exhibit 4 into perspective, one share of Polaroid stock as of 1950, if held until 1971, would represent 72 current shares after accounting for all stock splits and stock dividends from 1950 through 1970. One share as of the original outside financing in 1937 now represents 216 shares.

Polaroid stock in the 1938–45 period, or for that matter for the entire 1938–50 period, as compared with the general level of the stock market. The occasions when an untested firm has access to the equity market on attractive terms are limited, as the extreme fluctuations in the price of Polaroid stock during its early years so clearly indicate. Fortunately for Polaroid the market for the company's stock was strong when the need for outside financing became imperative.

As a prelude to the 1945 financing, a plan of recapitalization was undertaken in September, 1945. The essential elements of this recapitalization were as follows:

1. Dividend arrearages of $150,000 on the Class A stock and of $100,000 on the Class B stock were eliminated by issuing additional shares of these two classes of stock.[6]
2. Three shares of new common stock were exchanged for each outstanding share. The basic purpose of this move was to bring the price of the stock into a better trading range.
3. The number of shares of authorized common stock was increased to accommodate this exchange and to provide additional authorized stock for outside financing.

Shortly thereafter the company raised $2,096,140 in exchange for 80,875 shares of new common stock. These funds were raised through an underwritten rights offering in which each stockholder was entitled to subscribe to one new share of stock at $28 for each four shares that he owned. The underwriters received a maximum commission of $2.50 a share so that the net proceeds to the company were $25.50 a share.[7] With the proceeds of this new financing, Polaroid's financial position was greatly strengthened. Its net working capital increased from $1,056,000 at the end of 1944 to $3,618,000 at the end of 1945. Similarly, the book value of its common stock increased from $631,000 at the end of 1944 to $3,131,000 at the end of 1945. These additional financial resources proved to be of critical importance during the difficult period of transition to peacetime production.

Postwar conversion period: 1946–48

The postwar conversion period proved to be long and costly for Polaroid. Deficits before taking account of tax refunds from loss carry-backs amounted to $4,388,000 during the years 1946–48, inclusive (Exhibit 1). Tax refunds

[6] The names of these two preferred issues of stock, their par values, and the number of shares issued were also changed, in addition to the adjustment for dividend arrearages, but except for this adjustment the essential relationships remained unchanged.

[7] Actually, the proceeds to the company were slightly larger than this and the underwriters' commissions were slightly smaller since the amount of the underwriter's commission was reduced by $1.50 for each share subscribed for by the stockholders upon the exercise of their warrants. The actual net proceeds to the company were $25.92 ($2,096,140 divided by 80,875 shares), indicating that most of the shares were sold to the public rather than to existing stockholders. This was to be expected because of the heavy financial commitments to the company of the largest existing stockholders, especially Land.

on account of deficits incurred in 1946 and 1947 absorbed $2,233,000 of these deficits leaving losses chargeable to net worth of $2,155,000, more than the total amount of new equity raised in 1945. As a consequence, the company's net working capital fell from $3,618,000 at the end of 1945 to $1,136,000 at the end of 1948 and the book value of its common equity declined from $3,131,000 at the end of 1945 to only $849,000 at the end of 1948. No dividends had ever been paid on the common stock and dividend arrearages of $78,125 were accumulated on the two classes of preferred stock during the 1946–48 period.

A number of factors contributed to the company's large deficits during these years. Sales of prewar products and their adaptations proved disappointing. Indeed, as Exhibit 1 shows, sales fell to $1.5 million in 1947 and 1948, less than 10% of their 1945 level. The organization had grown sufficiently large during the war so that profitable operation at this level of sales was difficult or impossible. Moreover, in addition to the normal costs of operation, large-scale research and development efforts on peacetime products were resumed as soon as the company's war effort was completed.

One major line of developmental effort involving large expenditures was the Polaroid headlight system, but to this date these expenditures have been fruitless. The Polaroid management was never able to persuade the automotive industry and regulatory agencies to authorize the adoption of this system. Lengthy statements in the 1946 and 1947 Annual Reports vividly portray the frustration felt by the Polaroid management because of its inability to obtain the cooperation needed for this major breakthrough. Likewise, despite substantial research outlays the management's hopes for major commercial applications of three-dimensional moving pictures failed to materialize in the immediate postwar years.

In effect, the failure of these two major lines of research and developmental work to produce commercial revenues meant that the management had to bet the future of the company on its efforts in the field of instant photography. Initial research and experimentation on this revolutionary product was begun on a very small scale during the war. Intensive research in the field of instant photography, however, did not begin until the war had ended. Even so, by February 21, 1947, sufficient progress had been made so that Land felt free to make a public announcement of the company's progress in this field. The 1946 Annual Report stated in part: ". . . our major research project in the field of *photography* was announced by your President . . . on February 21, 1947, when he described a way to produce finished positive prints directly from the camera within one minute after the exposure is made."

Work on this project proceeded with increasing intensity during 1947 and 1948. The Land camera and photographic process were described in detail in the company's 1947 Annual Report. On November 26, 1948, little more than three years after research and development on this project was begun on a significant scale, the Polaroid Land camera was publicly marketed in limited quantities in Boston.

This date marked the end of the postwar transition for Polaroid and the beginning of its sensational growth over the next 20 years. Polaroid had won the race to complete the development and commercial introduction of a product that could be sold in volume directly to the consumer before its financial resources had been exhausted. The margin of victory was narrow as the previously reported financial data indicate. The cost of failure or even of extended delay would have been great. The price of Polaroid common stock declined sharply during 1947 and early 1948 (Exhibit 4), despite the company's favorable progress in the photographic field. If the company had run out of financial resources before the Land camera had been marketed, the cost of new capital would have been prohibitively high if, indeed, it would have been available on any terms.

Twenty years of rapid growth: 1949–70

Polaroid entered into an entirely new phase of its history with the introduction of the Land camera at the end of 1948. A steady stream of new photographic products and processes emerged from the Polaroid laboratories throughout this entire 20-year period, and with few exceptions each succeeding product proved to be more successful than its predecessor. The main lines of this product development will be briefly sketched. Against this background the company's sales and profit experience will be interpreted. A few brief comments will be made on the company's marketing strategy. Finally, Polaroid's financial policies during the 1950's and 1960's will be summarized.

Product development. The Polaroid photographic process introduced in late 1948 constituted a remarkable scientific achievement, but both the camera and the film were very imperfect. The camera was large, bulky, and inconvenient to handle. The sepia film was of uneven quality and durability. Except for the novelty of having a picture in a minute, the initial Polaroid camera and film were far inferior to competitive products. It was by no means clear in 1949 whether Polaroid's photographic process represented the foundation of a new industry or merely an intriguing scientific gadget of ephemeral significance. The stock market apparently was inclined to the latter view. Despite sharp increases in sales and earnings, Polaroid's stock dropped steadily in price during most of 1949 and sold throughout almost all of 1950 at less than one third of its previous high reached in the deficit year of 1946 (Exhibit 4). Polaroid's stock price, in fact, remained sluggish until 1953.

During the 1950's, however, innovations were introduced at a rapid pace. As early as the summer of 1950 a major forward step was taken when black-and-white film with an ASA rating of 100 replaced the inferior sepia film. Steady progress was then made in developing black-and-white images of greater sharpness and brilliance and in attaining higher and higher film speeds. By 1955 the transition was made to panchromatic film with ASA speeds of 200 and 400. Other types of films such as X-ray packets for one-step radiography and transparency films for projection were developed during these years. Finally, in 1959 a major step forward was taken with the marketing of 3000-speed film which made it possible to take indoor pictures without flashbulbs.

Two additional important advances were made in 1960. First, the time to produce a finished print was reduced from 60 seconds to 10 seconds. Second, a film for professional use was developed from which a positive print and a negative could be produced simultaneously for use in making multiple prints and enlargements.

With these developments the black-and-white film had reached a high degree of sophistication. The only major advance yet to be announced for the black-and-white film was the later development of a "dry process," eliminating the troublesome coating heretofore necessary to preserve black-and-white prints.

Simultaneously with this progress in the development of film, and largely dependent on it, came a steady improvement in the company's cameras during the 1950's. The original Model 95 was introduced at the relatively high suggested list price of $89.75 in November, 1948. Various accessories that added to sales volume were developed shortly thereafter, including close-up lens kits, meters and carrying cases, new flash guns, and a kit for adapting the standard camera for identification photography. Late in 1952 the Pathfinder Model 110, designed for professional and commercial users, was introduced to list at $249.50.

Polaroid made its first tentative move toward a lower priced camera in 1954 with its smaller Highlander model. This model, however, was not priced low enough to challenge Eastman in the low-price field. Various other models and numerous special adaptations for technical and specialized uses were introduced almost annually. The next really major development for the amateur market, however, was the Model 900 and Model 850 Electric Eye cameras introduced in 1960 to accompany the 3000-speed, 10-second film marketed at this time.

This series of developments in both black-and-white film and cameras can be said to mark the culmination of the first stage of Polaroid's expansion in the photographic field. These dramatic technical achievements were accompanied by equally impressive advances in the company's sales, earnings, and stock price. From 1951 to 1959, sales increased at an average annual rate of 33%, earnings per share at an average annual rate of 48%, and the company's stock price at the still faster rate of over 70% (Exhibits 5, 6, and 7).

Beginning in 1960, however, for the first time since 1949 Polaroid began to encounter difficulty in expanding its sales and profits, despite the important innovations introduced in 1960 and 1961. The $100 million sales level appeared to present a barrier difficult to cross. After several years of stagnant sales and earnings skepticism began to develop concerning the future growth of the company. Consequently, at the low point of the 1962 stock market decline, the price of Polaroid stock fell to less than one third of its 1960 high.

The skeptics, however, failed to reckon with the progress being made in the company's research and development laboratories. Simultaneously with the advances in black-and-white film, work had been underway for a long period on color film. As early as December 12, 1957, Polaroid announced that research in the field of color had advanced in its laboratories to the point where full color prints were being made directly in Polaroid Land cameras. At the same time, however, the management cautioned that experience with other basic new color processes in the photographic industry indicated it could not predict when its color film would be ready for marketing. Reference was made at this time to a contract with Eastman Kodak Company providing for Kodak to develop methods which, if successful, would enable Polaroid to look to Kodak as a supplier of the negative materials needed for the color film.

Despite the advances previously reported in other areas, the 1958 and 1959 Annual Reports stated that the major research and development energies of the company were being devoted to the development of color prints. At the annual stockholders meeting of April, 1960, Dr. Land publicly demonstrated for the first time full color pictures made in a standard model of the Polaroid Land camera, using laboratory film. Finally, on January 28, 1963, Polacolor picture-in-a-minute color film was released for sale to the public in limited quantities in Florida. This announcement signaled the beginning of another phase of rapid growth for Polaroid.

Shortly on the heels of the introduction of the color film, major new advances were announced in Polaroid's line of cameras. In August, 1963, the Automatic 100 Color Pack camera was introduced. It weighed only 2½ pounds, about half that of the previous awkward roll-type cameras, but took the same size 3¼ × 4¼ pictures. The film pack to be used in this camera had many advantages over the previous roll-type film, most notably that the picture was developed outside the camera so that the user could take one picture right after another.

In 1964 a lower priced version of the Color Pack camera was introduced. Then in 1965, Polaroid for the first time introduced a truly low-priced camera, the Swinger, that competed directly with Eastman's dominance in the mass consumer market. The Swinger was offered for sale at a suggested list price of $19.95. Even though this camera took only small-sized black-and-white pictures, it was an immediate success and was on allocation to dealers throughout 1965 and 1966. The number of cameras sold in 1965 was four times the 1964 total and exceeded the total number of cameras sold in the first 10 years of Polaroid's history. The resulting stimulus to film sales is obvious.

In 1967 a new series of the company's full line of automatic pack cameras was introduced extending them to a somewhat lower priced range. No dramatic advances, however, were involved in this new 200 series. In 1968 the Big Swinger, taking larger pictures, 3¼ × 4¼, and utilizing pack film, in contrast to roll-type film utilized by the original Swinger, was marketed at a suggested list price of $24.95. The Big Swinger largely eliminated the market for the original Swinger.

Finally, in 1969 the Colorpack II Land camera was introduced. This camera, listed for $29.95, took color pictures as well as black-and-white, was equipped with an electric eye mechanism, and had a new flash cube attachment. A new 300 series of the company's basic automatic pack cameras was also introduced in 1969, ranging in suggested list price from $59.95 to $199.95. The 1969 Annual Report describes the Colorpack II camera as quickly becoming the most successful camera in the company's history. It was sold on allocation in 1969. It stimulated the sale of film and greatly increased the sales of color film in relation to black-and-white film. The Big Swinger and the Colorpack II cameras, in succession, largely made obsolete their lower priced and less sophisticated predecessors. Many of the older models still in stock had to be unloaded at marked-down prices through such outlets as discount houses and department stores.

New products introduced since 1969 have represented an extension and perfection of the company's existing product line. An improved 400 line of the company's basic series of automatic cameras was announced to the public in April, 1971. The company planned to introduce in May, 1971, its Big Shot color portrait camera with a suggested list price of $19.95. Polaroid described this camera as "one of the most unusual cameras ever put on the market." The major attention of the company for the last several years, however, has been on the perfection and eventual marketing of a totally new series of products which it expects will be more revolutionary than the initial developments in the 1948–60 period and, again, in the 1963–69 period.

In terms of sales, earnings per share, and market price, 1963–70 largely duplicated the 1949–62 period except that the time span was telescoped.

Beginning in 1963 explosive sales growth was resumed with commensurate increases in earnings per share and in the company's stock price. This growth was especially rapid from 1964 through 1967 when the full impact of the color film, the automatic and improved pack cameras, and the company's entry into the low-price mass market was felt. During this three-year period Polaroid's average annual sales increased at a rate of 40%, earnings per share increased at a rate of 46%, and the market price of the company's stock increased at a rate of about 75% (Exhibits 5, 6, and 7). Beginning in 1968 and 1969, however, the rate of domestic sales growth declined despite the highly successful introduction of the Colorpack II camera in 1969. In 1970, for the first time in 20 years, domestic sales of photographic products failed to register an increase over sales of the previous year.[8]

Earnings per share from domestic activities were affected even more sharply than sales. Earnings per share were essentially constant from 1967 to 1971; they were depressed by the slower rate of sales growth, and, in addition, they had to absorb the heavy research and developmental expenses on

[8] The small decline in overall company sales in 1954 as compared with 1953 is accounted for by the sudden but temporary burst of activity in three-dimensional movies in late 1952 and 1953. This episode has been omitted from the case because of its short-lived effect on company sales. It is still possible, however, that a sophisticated version of the company's work in the three-dimensional movie field may become important at some future date.

the revolutionary new products to which the company's major efforts have been devoted for the last several years. As in the 1960–62 period, the slowdown in sales and earnings growth affected investor sentiment. Polaroid's common stock plummeted from a late 1969 high of $145 a share to a low of $51 a share at the bottom of the market in mid-1970. Then, however, the stock price recovered to around $90 a share as of early April, 1971.

Investor sentiment naturally reflected a wide divergence of opinion in April, 1971. Three years of relatively constant earnings per share naturally raised questions in the minds of analysts appraising a stock currently selling at a price-earnings multiple of over 45. The feasibility of engendering another burst of sales and earnings growth from a sales base of $500 million, as contrasted with $6–9 million in 1950–51, or even $100 million in 1960–62, posed new and difficult problems for the Polaroid management. Likewise, the fact that any resumption of sales and earnings growth comparable to the past almost certainly would involve, to some degree, a head-on confrontation with Eastman Kodak, raised new dimensions to the problem that were not previously present. On top of all this, the Polaroid management was naturally extraordinarily secretive and uncommunicative about the immediate future, a fact totally understandable in view of the competitive situation but nevertheless extremely frustrating to investment analysts.

As against these factors which pessimists could cite, the analogy of the 1970–71 period of consolidation to the similar periods of 1946–48 and 1960–62 had to be weighed. Skeptics doubted the potential of Polaroid during each of these periods of consolidation and temporary interruptions of sales and earnings growth. They lived to regret their doubts. Moreover, there was no doubt as to the expectations of the Polaroid management. One only needs to cite the company's investments in fixed assets to demonstrate this point. The company's net fixed assets expanded from $37.5 million at the end of 1965, to $80.0 million at the end of 1967, to $172.4 million (of which $63 million represented construction in progress) at the end of 1970.

Before leaving this portion of the story, a word should be said about Polaroid's unconsolidated foreign subsidiaries. After an initial period of difficulty in gaining acceptance in the overseas market, Polaroid's overseas sales and earnings expanded rapidly after 1965 despite the slowdown in the recent rate of domestic growth. Sales of foreign unconsolidated subsidiaries expanded from $24 million in 1965 to $89 million in 1970, and earnings per share increased from a deficit of $0.02 in 1966 to $0.34 in 1970 (Exhibit 8). These figures were still small in relation to the company's overall results, but they were beginning to assume significant size.

We turn now to products still under development in 1971. These comments will be brief because little was known about them as of April, 1971. Speculation, supported in part by specific statements and demonstrations by the Polaroid management, centered on four main lines of new products.

1. A radically new Polaroid camera. This camera was described as entirely different in concept and design from the current family of Polaroid Land cameras. It was reported to be extraordinarily light and compact and to be

capable of producing pictures of unprecedented brilliance and depth of color. Polaroid planned to manufacture this camera itself whereas it had traditionally subcontracted the manufacture of its cameras. The plant for this purpose was already constructed.

2. A unique instant color film incorporating a new color negative. For the first time Polaroid planned to manufacture its own negative. Heretofore Polaroid had always purchased its negative from Eastman. The Polaroid Annual Report for 1970 stated that it already had the capacity to produce significant amounts of commercial quality negative in its Waltham plant and that its major new plant for film production was nearing completion in New Bedford.
3. A third major line of new development was in the field of color transparencies that could be instantly developed and instantly projected for group viewing. As early as March, 1969, Dr. Land reported in the 1968 Annual Report that "our belief is that the new fields of application opened by our transparency materials will lead to a significant expansion of the whole photographic industry."
4. Finally, there was considerable speculation that Polaroid might introduce an instant version of color film to be used for amateur movies. In the 1969 annual stockholders meeting, Dr. Land took colored 16-mm. motion pictures with a conventional movie camera, processed the film on the spot, and projected it minutes later to the assembled stockholders.

Several of these developments raised the possibility that Polaroid's new materials might be usable in both Polaroid Land cameras and ordinary still and movie cameras. Therein lay part of the threat that Polaroid currently posed for Eastman. Eastman, in turn, was reported to be working on its own version of instant photography. Reports to this effect emanated from Eastman, and the possibility of this development was briefly alluded to by Dr. Land in the 1969 Polaroid Annual Report. Thus, the potential of a direct confrontation between the two companies existed in 1971 with an outcome that was currently unpredictable.

Marketing. Polaroid's marketing policy will not be discussed in detail in this case.[9] It should, however, be noted that Polaroid's current marketing effort is heavily consumer oriented. This orientation is no accident. As the early portions of this case point out, Polaroid's future as a small company in the 1940's was gravely threatened because it could not persuade the automobile manufacturers to adopt its headlight system or the motion picture industry to produce three-dimensional movies.

This inability to market its products through established industries convinced the management of the critical importance of developing a product that could be sold in large volume directly to consumers. The search for such a product was one factor that stimulated the management's initial interest in instant photography. In a marketing sense the success of the Polaroid Land

[9] An excellent case devoted primarily to Polaroid's marketing policy can be ordered separately from the Harvard Business School. This case is entitled Polaroid France (S.A.): Marketing in a Multinational Company (9–513–119, M 340R [1969]).

camera has depended from the outset on its direct appeal to the consumer. As *Fortune* magazine has put the matter: "Land's revolution was at first derided by all the experts . . . [including] virtually every camera dealer in the country, every 'advanced' amateur photographer, and nearly everyone on Wall Street."[10] Fortunately for Polaroid, however, it was the verdict of the ordinary consumer rather than that of "the expert" that mattered. And this verdict was favorable. Thus, in its early critical days the Polaroid Land camera provided the link that was missing in its other major product lines—direct access to the consumer without reliance on other parties. Polaroid has carefully nurtured this relationship ever since.

Financial policy. Polaroid followed a consistent financial policy throughout its 1949–70 period of rapid growth. The main components of this financial policy can be summarized as follows:

1. Polaroid relied almost exclusively on retained earnings to finance its 1949–70 growth. During this 22-year period its net earnings after taxes amounted to $408 million, of which $356 million, or 87%, were retained in the business to finance the company's growth.
2. It follows from the preceding statement that only a small proportion of the company's earnings was paid out as dividends. Dividends on the preferred stock resulting from the 1937 and 1945 financing were paid at an annual rate of $62,500 until the preferred stock was retired in 1963. The first dividend on the common stock was paid in 1952. Since then common stock dividends have been paid in every year. For the entire 1949–70 period common stock dividends amounted to slightly less than 13% of the earnings available to common stock, and in most individual years the annual ratio of dividends to available earnings did not deviate widely from this figure.
3. At no time during the postwar period did Polaroid rely on debt financing *in any form*, short term or long term. The *only* liabilities that appeared on its balance sheets throughout the postwar period were standard current liabilities, principally a provision for taxes and routine payables.
4. On two occasions since 1945 outside equity financing was undertaken in the form of newly issued common stock. In 1958, as plans were being made for the introduction of color film, the company raised $11,877,000 through a rights issue to existing shareholders. In 1969, in preparation for the major expansion program currently in process, the company raised $98,721,000 of new common equity, again by means of a rights offering to existing shareholders. As of March 5, 1969, stockholders were offered the right to subscribe for 1,057,800 shares of common stock at the rate of one share for each 30 shares held. The net effect of this financing was to increase the book value of the shareholders' equity by over 35% while increasing the number of shares of common stock outstanding by only slightly over 3%.
5. A study of the company's balance sheets after the 1958 and 1969 financing points to the conclusion that both these rounds of financing were essentially precautionary in character. The funds raised in 1958 and 1969 appear in the company's subsequent financial statements in the form of additions to

[10] Francis Bello, "The Magic That Made Polaroid," *Fortune*, April, 1959, p. 125.

the marketable securities held by Polaroid rather than as funds immediately needed for operating purposes.

6. Over the years the combined effect of the above policies has been to increase steadily the strength of the company's financial position. The cumulative impact of these policies is clearly reflected in the company's balance sheet as of December 31, 1970 (Exhibit 9). Just to highlight a few of the main points, this balance sheet shows that at the end of 1970:
   a) Polaroid had cash and marketable securities of over $201 million as compared with total liabilities (all current) of $47 million.
   b) The company's ratio of current assets to current liabilities amounted to 7.4 times. There were no other liabilities.
   c) All research and development expenses and all outlays for patents and trademarks had been charged against income and are shown on the balance sheet at the nominal figure of one dollar.
   d) The company's net worth of $475 million, all in the form of common equity, exceeded the company's total liabilities of $47 million by a ratio of more than 10 to 1.
   e) Even so, the book value of the common stock at December 31, 1970, amounted to only $14.45 a share as compared with a current market price of approximately $90 a share as of late April, 1971.

The Polaroid philosophy

No comprehensive case on the Polaroid Corporation would be complete without an attempt to summarize the basic philosophy of Polaroid as Dr. Land has often stated it over the years. We do so in this case by selecting representative excerpts from Dr. Land's letters to shareholders of recent years.

In the 1965 Annual Report Dr. Land stated:

As you know, the policy of our company since its inception has been to do basic scientific research in the wide variety of areas that excite our intellectual interest. Then from time to time we pick a field of applied research in a domain so important that its value is indisputable and so difficult that we gain the benefits of the pioneer. In the intensive development of these difficult domains we draw upon all the experience we have accumulated in our basic research.

In the 1967 Annual Report Dr. Land commented in a similar vein:

Thus we pursue our policy of not doing what others can do, and of not displacing what others are doing well, but rather of trying to discern a domain which we can enter through basic research and which, having entered, we can then seek to expand with the view of making the whole field larger than it has ever been before.

* * * * *

In this discussion, we have seen the phased relationship between evolution and revolution in laboratory, factory, and market. Yet, while one speaks of a product evolving in the laboratory, it would perhaps be as accurate to say that it is the people and their insights which are evolving. . . . The satisfaction one feels in seeing the whole history of ideas utilized is matched by the sense of pleasure in seeing that the new generation has taken over with the same excitement and drive which we were experiencing when we were initiating this field. The interplay between evolution and revolution gives the young the responsibilities of the old and the old the excitement of the young. It keeps in the big company an intimacy and freshness almost indistinguishable from the personally rewarding conditions in a small company.

In these troubled times, how can we keep our minds on the satisfaction in our life here at Polaroid while the nation as a whole is deeply involved not merely in military difficulties abroad but also in social difficulties at home? Our conviction has been for a whole generation that without a growing industrial base what one accomplishes outside of industry is frequently only a temporary remedy, that the health of society is determined within industry where jobs must be made. Industries that are not evolving from new science to new products do not make jobs—rather with increasing efficiency they eliminate jobs. If we are to make more jobs then we must make new industries.

Fortunately, our company has been one which has been dedicated throughout its life to making only things which others cannot make. We proceed from basic science through applied science to highly desirable products, so that new opportunities are produced year by year. . . . Thus, particularly in these troubled times, we turn to our tasks at Polaroid with conviction and enthusiasm about our potential social as well as technical contribution to American society.

As the final excerpt in this case we reproduce in full the letter to Polaroid shareholders written by Dr. Land in the 1970 Annual Report and dated March 18, 1971. This letter has been read with much interest and with varying interpretations by those in search of a clue concerning the future course of affairs at Polaroid.

We are happy to report that the equipment we have designed and built for coating multi-layer color negative performs very well, so that we now have our own facility in Waltham with competence to produce significant amounts of commercial quality negative. Of course, our major capacity will derive from our new plant nearing completion in New Bedford. The first units of assembly equipment for our new kind of film are installed and operative in Waltham. New dyes for the new films are in quantity production in our own chemical plant, as are some remarkable new reagents that we will not be free to describe until the product appears on the market. The basic equipment for the transparency film is operating. Our extraordinary new camera is coming along very well indeed; the tooling for many parts is proceeding.

In this period of high technological drama at Polaroid, it occurs to me that we sometimes forget to tell our shareholders that the continuum between sensing a significant human need in our field and delivering the final product involves not only the chain of inventions in the laboratory, but also the creation of wholly new manufacturing equipment. The factory experience becomes a continuation of the research experience and the period during which these two experiences are joined to make an operative process is one of the best parts of the industrial adventure. These undertakings—research through manufacturing-development into actual manufacture—cannot be fractionated.

Yet the people involved in each component of the activity are necessarily diverse in kind of mind, temperament, value system and motivational structure. Contrary to popular opinion, scientists differ from each other at least as much as, if not more than, non-scientists, and while each subculture of the technological world seems to be built around a common denominator of personality, even within the subcultures there is an intensification of small differences analogous perhaps to genetic accentuation from inbreeding. Certainly we can never know whether it is the field of science that generates a certain kind of person appropriate for that field, or whether it is the aggregation of people of that certain kind that determines the nature of a field of science. Physical chemists differ from organic chemists as Frenchmen from Englishmen, and similarly mechanical engineers differ from electronic engineers and design engineers from production engineers. Then there is the most extreme dichotomy of all—the men who organize ideas and the men who organize men.

I take you as shareholders into this discussion of the subcultures of technology to make clear that a really new field cannot be brought into being by an orderly sequence in time; (*a*) an idea, (*b*) an early research program, (*c*) a pilot development period, (*d*) a program of manufacturing-development, (*e*) manufacturing. In a world changing as rapidly as ours, the old rule of nine years from test tube to tank car would be disastrous. The science would change, the scientists would change, the markets would change. More significantly, the simultaneous interaction between the large variety of technological subcultures would, by definition, be non-existent.

Clearly then, massive, modern programs require nearly complete overlap in time of all phases of the activity from research through development, through manufacturing-development, through manufacturing. Consequently, each of the technological subcultures associated with these overlapping phases, while retaining its own identity and effectiveness, must be interacting constructively with all the others. At the same time, within each subculture, each member, while retaining his own identity and effectiveness, must be interacting constructively with all others in his group.

When this vast, elaborate human process is working well, the people involved keep growing and changing, the ideas keep growing and changing, the processes keep growing and changing and so, too, does the pilot equipment. When this human process is working well, there is a sense of inevitable convergence of all this diversification of personality and action towards one goal.

As the whole group approaches its goal, as we at Polaroid are approaching ours, it sloughs off extraneous concepts and premises which had been carried along in the event of intellectual emergency. The principal insights are now crystallized and with this simplification there is a sudden sense of unity. Where there were thousands of notions in the minds of hundreds of people there is now at last a unified statement of common insight expressed in the smooth running factory process.

The picture I have given of corporate activity makes clear that one cannot answer the questions of how far along a product is in its development by saying it is out of research or into pilot or into manufacturing-development or anywhere in the old-fashioned sequence. A significant new product in contemporary corporate life emerges on all these fronts at once and then quite suddenly is complete.

Exhibit 1

POLAROID CORPORATION
SELECTED HISTORICAL FINANCIAL DATA
(In thousands except per share data)

Year	Sales	Net Earnings before Taxes*	Income and Excess Profits Taxes*	Net Earnings after Taxes*	Preferred Dividends	Earnings Available to Common Stock	Number of Shares of Common Stock	Earnings per Share†	Market Price per Share†
1937	$ 142	$ 9	$ 2	$ 7	$—	$ 7	—	$ —	$ —
1938	195	(73)	0	(73)	—	(73)	321	(0.27)	—
1939	761	35	7	28	—	28	321	0.09	23–12
1940	720	(96)	0	(96)	—	(96)	321	(0.30)	14–7
1941	1,032	153	27	126	—	126	321	0.39	7–4
1942	4,119	429	281	98	9	89	321	0.27	5–3
1943	10,739	760	558	152	9	143	321	0.44	13–7
1944	13,155	1,640	1,274	344	50	294	321	0.92	14–7
1945	16,752	1,735	1,286	449	44	405	404	1.00	42–13
1946	4,366	(1,433)	(1,098)	(336)	63	(399)	404	(0.98)	51–28
1947	1,504	(2,089)	(1,135)	(954)	47	(1,003)	404	(2.51)	47–18
1948	1,481	(866)	(1)	(865)	—	(865)	404	(2.29)	21–14
1949	6,678	770	49	721	68	653	404	1.63	31–17
1950	6,390	794	68	726	68	658	404	1.64	18–14

* In some years net earnings before taxes, the provision for income and excess profits taxes, and net earnings after taxes appear inconsistent because of minor accounting adjustments.

† The number of shares of common stock outstanding and the per share data shown in this exhibit have been adjusted to reflect the 3 for 1 split of the common stock undertaken as part of the 1945 recapitalization plan. To put the data of this exhibit into perspective it should be emphasized that one share of common stock as shown here would represent 72 shares of the 1970 common stock after adjustment for all stock dividends and stock splits from 1950 through 1970.

Sources: Annual Reports of Polaroid Corporation and *Bank and Quotation Record.*

Exhibit 2

POLAROID CORPORATION
STATEMENT OF FINANCIAL CONDITION
DECEMBER 31, 1940
(In thousands)

ASSETS	
Cash	$ 117
Receivables	48
Inventories	80
Total current assets	$ 245
Plant and equipment	$ 215
Less: Reserve for depreciation	64
Net plant and equipment	$ 151
Patents and trademarks	156
Deferred experimental and development costs	262
Deferred expenses and other assets	9
Total assets	$ 823
LIABILITIES AND NET WORTH	
Payables and accruals	$ 58
Federal and state income taxes	8
Total liabilities	$ 66
Preferred stock:	
5% cumulative Class A	750
$5.00 cumulative Class B	12
Common stock	107
Additional paid-in capital	32
Retained earnings	(144)
Total liabilities and net worth	$ 823

Source: Polaroid Corporation, Annual Report for 1940.

Exhibit 3

POLAROID CORPORATION
STATEMENT OF FINANCIAL CONDITION
DECEMBER 31, 1944
(In thousands)

ASSETS	
Cash	$ 569
Marketable securities	100
Receivables	2,106
Inventories	862
Advances to subcontractors	142
Total current assets	$3,779
Plant and equipment	544
Less: Reserve for depreciation	316
Net plant and equipment	$ 228
Patents and trademarks	129
Postwar refund on excess profits taxes	128
Deferred expenses and other assets	52
Total assets	$4,316

LIABILITIES AND NET WORTH	
Payables and accruals	$1,065
Federal and state income taxes	1,658
Total liabilities	$2,723
Reserve for contingencies	200
Preferred stock:	
5% cumulative Class A	750
$5.00 cumulative Class B	12
Common stock	107
Additional paid-in capital	32
Retained earnings	492
Total liabilities and net worth	$4,316

Source: Polaroid Corporation, Annual Report for 1944.

Exhibit 4

POLAROID CORPORATION
PRICES OF POLAROID COMMON STOCK AND DOW JONES INDEX OF 30 INDUSTRIAL STOCKS, 1938–50

Sources: *Bank and Quotation Record* and *Survey of Current Business.*

Exhibit 5

POLAROID CORPORATION
POLAROID CORPORATION AND ITS DOMESTIC SUBSIDIARIES
SELECTED HISTORICAL FINANCIAL DATA
(Dollar figures in millions except per share data)

Year	*Sales*	*Net Earnings after Taxes*	*Earnings per Share**	*Dividends per Share**	*Market Price per Share**	*Price-Earnings Ratio**	*Dividend Yield**
1951	$ 9.2	$ 0.51	$0.015	$ 0	$0.34–0.20	18	0
1952	13.4	0.60	0.018	0.0035	0.39–0.26	18	0.011
1953	26.0	1.41	0.046	0.0069	0.69–0.37	11	0.013
1954	23.3	1.15	0.037	0.0104	1.07–0.68	24	0.012
1955	26.1	2.43	0.080	0.0104	1.71–0.89	16	0.008
1956	34.1	3.6	0.12	0.0156	3–2	21	0.006
1957	47.5	5.4	0.18	0.0180	7–3	27	0.004
1958	64.8	7.3	0.23	0.0250	13–5	42	0.003
1959	88.5	10.7	0.35	0.0250	23–12	50	0.001
1960	98.3	8.8	0.29	0.0250	33–20	90	0.001
1961	100.1	8.0	0.26	0.0250	30–22	90	0.001
1962	102.6	9.9	0.32	0.0250	26–10	57	0.001
1963	122.3	11.1	0.35	0.0250	26–15	59	0.001
1964	138.1	18.1	0.58	0.0312	23–16	34	0.002
1965	202.2	28.9	0.92	0.0625	65–22	47	0.001
1966	316.5	47.6	1.51	0.125	87–54	47	0.001
1967	374.3	57.4	1.81	0.23	127–77	56	0.002
1968	402.0	58.9	1.86	0.32	134–87	59	0.003
1969	465.6	63.1	1.94	0.32	145–103	64	0.002
1970	444.3	61.1	1.86	0.32	131–51	45	0.003

* All per share figures adjusted for all stock splits and stock dividends, 1951–70. Price-earnings ratio based on average of high and low prices for year divided by earnings per share for current year. Market prices per share rounded to nearest dollar.

Sources: Annual Reports of Polaroid Corporation and *Moody's Industrial Manuals.*

Exhibit 6

POLAROID CORPORATION
EARNINGS PER SHARE, 1951–70*
COMPARISON OF POLAROID WITH EASTMAN KODAK

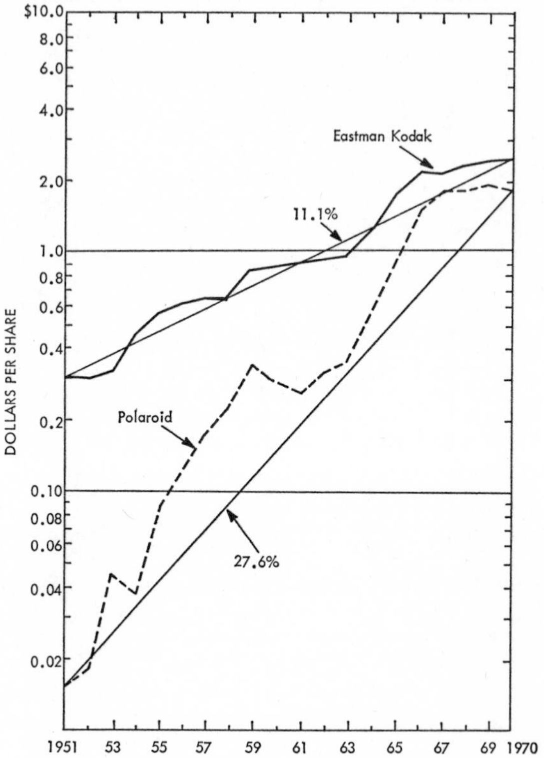

* All data are adjusted for stock splits and major stock dividends, 1951–70. No adjustment for fractional stock dividends and rights issues.

Exhibit 7

POLAROID CORPORATION

AVERAGE MARKET PRICE PER SHARE, 1951–70*

COMPARISON OF POLAROID WITH EASTMAN KODAK

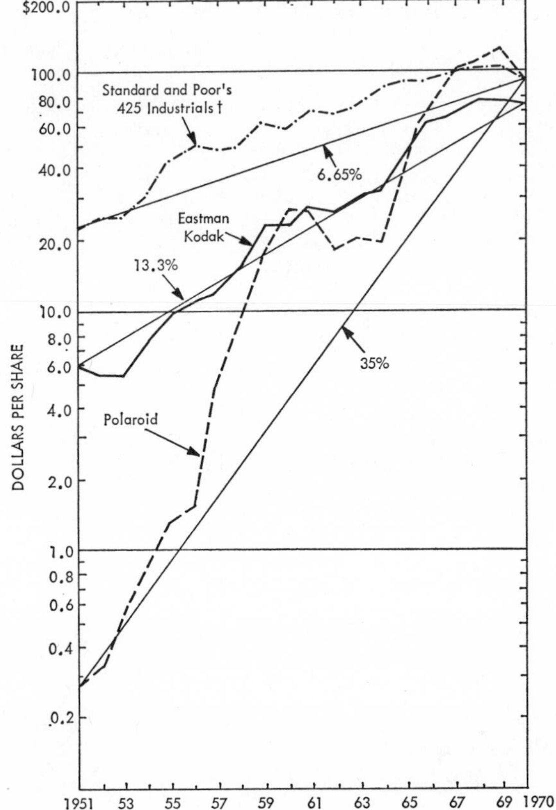

* Data show the average of the high and low market prices of the year. All data for years prior to 1970 are adjusted for stock splits and major stock dividends but not for fractional stock dividends and rights issues.

† 1941–43 = 10.

Exhibit 8

POLAROID CORPORATION
POLAROID CORPORATION: UNCONSOLIDATED SUBSIDIARIES OUTSIDE THE UNITED STATES
SELECTED HISTORICAL FINANCIAL DATA
(In millions except per share data)

Year	*Sales*	*Net Earnings after Tax*	*Earnings per Share*
1961	$ 4.7	$ 0.2	$ 0.01
1962	5.6	0.4	0.01
1963	9.2	0.5	0.01
1964	12.1	0.6	0.02
1965	24.3	0.6	0.02
1966	46.1	(0.6)	(0.02)
1967	52.1	1.1	0.03
1968	52.9	3.5	0.11
1969	70.5	8.5	0.26
1970	88.8	11.0	0.34

Source: Polaroid Corporation, Annual Report for 1970.

Exhibit 9

POLAROID CORPORATION
POLAROID CORPORATION AND ITS DOMESTIC SUBSIDIARIES
STATEMENT OF FINANCIAL CONDITION
DECEMBER 31, 1970
(In thousands)

ASSETS	
Cash	$ 6,118
Marketable securities	195,363
Receivables	103,987
Inventories	39,899
Prepaid expenses	2,781
Total current assets	$348,148
Land	$ 2,742
Buildings	69,064
Machinery and equipment	112,360
Construction in progress	63,192
	$247,358
Less: Accumulated depreciation	74,909
Net property, plant, and equipment	$172,449
Investments in and advances to unconsolidated foreign subsidiaries, at cost	1,163
Patents and trademarks (at nominal value of $1)	—
Total assets	$521,760
LIABILITIES AND NET WORTH	
Payables and accruals	$ 31,291
Federal and state income taxes	15,824
Total liabilities	$ 47,115
Common stock, $1 par value	32,832
Additional paid-in capital	119,843
Retained earnings	321,970
Total liabilities and net worth	$521,760

Source: Polaroid Corporation, Annual Report for 1970.

THE LAND DEVELOPERS—1968

^^

There are numerous companies involved in the land development business. This note discusses the historical development of one segment of the industry —a segment characterized by companies with large marketing organizations that make the total economic picture of these companies unlike that of any other real estate company. The primary business of these developers is the acquisition of large tracts of raw, unimproved land for subsequent resale as subdivided lots. Each tract is usually designed as a recreational or retirement community containing numerous amenities such as golf courses, lakes, riding stables, marinas, and many other attractions. But it is the marketing arm that, in fact, creates the value of these "national land sales" companies, not the real estate on the balance sheet. (A point borne out by the fact that the cost of the raw land is typically less than 10% of the selling price!) These land developers are akin to such marketing organizations as Avon Products, Inc., the Encyclopaedia Britannica, and Combined Insurance Company of America. They actively seek their customers through massive marketing efforts, which include entertaining the customer and offering him low cost inspection trips to the property and installment terms often extending to seven to eight years.

The customers of land sales companies

For some Americans, purchase of a lot in Florida or near the ski slopes of Mt. Snow will result in their construction of a vacation—or retirement—home. However, for many customers of the national land sales companies, a large part of their purchase motivation is investment. Certainly, during the 1960's, land often earned exceptionally attractive returns—a point that salesmen of the land sales companies and industry experts are quick to point out.

"We're living in a society with a rising real income and a rising dollar income, which creates the capacity to buy more automobiles, more television sets, more everything—except land," observes Allan D. Kotin, director of research for California-based Property Research Corporation. "We can increase production of goods to meet almost any demand within reason, but we can't produce more land. So, in the long run, the increase in the value of land not only keeps up with inflation, it actually outstrips it. . . . What land provides even more than long-term growth is insurance against any real possibility of long-term decline; except for excessively speculative ventures or short-run possibilities, land is a kind of loss-proof investment."[1]

New day dawning?[2]

All this may have a familiar ring to investors who went wild over Florida land once or twice before. The most sensational boom was that memorable bubble of the twenties. In those days, as a mangrove patch was being transformed into the fabulous pink-and-white fairyland called Miami Beach—and Henry Flagler was crisscrossing the barren countryside with railroads, and then resorts—Florida caught the nation's fancy. Everyone wanted to buy a piece of paradise. After a while, it seemed as though everyone had. "It was one of those periods of mass insanity that are strewn throughout history," says Carl Bertoch [executive director in 1966 of the Florida Installment Land Sales Board—an agency set up to police the industry]. "Appropriately enough, it was a perfect prelude to the even greater madness that ended a few years later with the '29 crash."

In the mid-fifties, the Florida real estate game again became a national pastime. Only $10 down and $10 a month would buy a chunk—however remote—of the country's fastest growing state. Shivering Midwesterners and Down Easterners, by the hundreds of thousands, took the plunge. Prices boomed. Developers became millionaires. But abuses began to cloud the picture, and by 1962 the public was up in arms. So were state legislatures. New laws went on the books and new agencies went into action. One of the most effective, Mr. Bertoch's Florida Installment Land Sales Board, set about reviewing industry promotion, saw to it that purchasers got a detailed property report, and followed up by requiring developers to make good on their promises of roads, sewers, and the like.

Before the cleanup campaign began, however, something else happened that hit the Florida land market like a hurricane. The something was called Fidel Castro. Cuban threats to lob missiles a mere 90 miles into Sunshine State back yards—no matter how cold it got up North—really put a chill on business. "Selling land was next to impossible," recalls one developer. Accordingly, fringe operations pulled up stakes and fled the scene. Of an estimated 1,200 to 1,600 firms selling Florida land on installment plans in the early sixties, less than 200 are registered today [1966].

The Florida land developers

The shake-out left the industry greatly strengthened. The surviving firms, indeed, began putting their resources to use in new fields, hoping to gain stability through diversification. Canaveral International took a turn at resorting on the high seas. "Every study we made suggested that this would be the greatest thing since the repeal of prohibition," recalls Dan Dubbin, Canaveral's president, "but it just didn't work." Another venture, however,

---

[1] Quoted in "Land Rush," *Forbes,* November 1, 1967, p. 56.

[2] The sections "New Day Dawning?" through "Promised Land" are taken from the article, "Sand in Their Shoes," *Barron's,* June 13, 1966, pp. 3, 8, and 14.

came off much better. Operating three converted LSDs, Canaveral now [in 1966] grosses about $500,000 annually providing logistical support for Cape Kennedy's downrange tracking stations.

Others have found the luxury hotel-motel business anything but a last resort. Arvida grossed $4.4 million last year from the operations of its Boca Raton Hotel and Club. General Development runs the posh St. Lucie Country Club. Deltona opened a new motor inn last year [in 1965], then hired a veteran hotel executive to head up a department with responsibility for all of its growing resort activities.

Gulf American, most diversified of them all, has holdings ranging from a life insurance firm to an airline, and owns a string of hotels, motels, and commercial buildings as well. Hoping to diversify further, it has picked up a 46% interest in Fenestra, a steel products manufacturer that did $36 million worth of business last year.

Mainly, of course, the developers have poured their talents and capital into creating Florida's new, permanent communities. This seems to be a business with all but unlimited potential. "In most parts of the country," says Deltona's Frank Mackle, "a man who has an income of $250 a month either has to live with relatives or in substandard housing. At Deltona, that same $250 will buy a $7,900 home that can be mortgaged out with ease. We've got a beautiful climate here, great fishing, and all the rest. But that's the icing on the cake. What we're really selling is value." Located midway between Orlando and Daytona Beach, the town of Deltona was 15,000 acres of wooded countryside just 3½ years ago [in 1962]. Today [1966] it has schools, churches, shopping centers, and a population of 2,000.

A few miles to the west is Rainbow Lakes Estates, an American Realty project boasting 300 homes with over 1,000 residents. American Realty gets $995 for a quarter-acre lot, $2,495 for a full acre. The price includes roads and utility connections which already are in, three years ahead of schedule, according to Secretary Howard Friedman. South, toward Sarasota, is Bird Key, Arvida's tropical island, complete with yacht club, winding waterways, rambling homes and 511 homesites (ranging from $9,000 to $33,000 each). . . .

Just below Bird Key on the West Coast lies Port Charlotte, biggest of General Development's communities. Further south is Cape Coral, the 52,530-acre pride-and-joy of Gulf American. Boasting everything from yacht club and golf course to apartment buildings, single-family homes and a well-developed downtown shopping area, the eight-year-old community is home to some 5,000 residents. Best of all, hardly a soul among these thousands of new Sunshine Staters—from Deltona to Cape Coral—can be found who isn't happy with his lot.

Merchandising efforts

All the Florida developers, of course, are dependent on keeping 'em happy and—even more important to corporate growth—keeping 'em coming. To that end, the industry's merchandising efforts have acquired a new look. For one thing, they are being pointed increasingly abroad, aimed at both foreign nations and U.S. servicemen who have sold their stateside homes and who will be retiring after 20 years of duty. Deltona, as an example, has grossed over $10 million this way during the three years it has been active overseas.

Back home, the old mail-order pitch has given way to a new way of selling —the "gala" party. Though these social affairs vary from one company to the next, the technique follows a basic pattern. Invitations go out to a preselected group of couples in a given market, anywhere in the country. The group is wined and dined, shown a film extolling the wonders of Florida, then asked to sign up. Despite its cost—the tab for a cocktail party runs to $3 per person, a dinner to $4—the party, one developer says, is "the most efficient way to get our story across to the greatest number of people."

So it would seem. Some developers report the sale of either a home or a homesite to as many as one of every five couples feted. Down payments from the dinner guests are bigger, too. In place of the outmoded $10 down, Deltona says it averages $135; Gulf American [which hosts 12,000 parties annually], about $250. "When someone has put that kind of money into something," notes one satisfied host, "he thinks twice about letting it go down the drain."

Promised land?

To clinch a sale, most developers offer a money-back guarantee if, within six months, the purchaser finds his lot to be anything other than the promised land. They also make it amazingly easy for the buyer to get his all-important look at it. In what amounts to a fairly typical program, Gulf American provides round trip, New York to Florida transportation, including three days of food and lodging, for only $59.95.

As anyone in the industry is quick to acknowledge, this combination[3] clearly adds up to "hard sell." (One doesn't refer to "salesmen." In this business, there are only "land counselors" and "real estate consultants.") In some audiences, developers' men are planted to help stir up excitement. Closings are accomplished with scientific precision and dispatch. But hard sell or soft, techniques really are not so different from those of other fields: encyclopedias, insurance, mutual funds, even charitable fund-raising, to cite a few.

In any event, the satisfied customer—and, one day, that happy homeowner

---

[3] [Casewriter's comment:] Having land projects located away from their markets offers several additional merchandising advantages. First, the typical customer located in New York and buying land in Florida or the Southwest does not know whether the real estate market in these areas is going up or down. Therefore, regardless of the real estate market in Florida or the Southwest, the bulk, if not all, of the companies' sales will not be affected since they are probably quite a distance from the project. Second, and more important, the developers' prices cannot be compared with other prices as a home buyer would do if buying a house in his locality. Since this is the case, the land developers can peg their prices. The industry has found that raising prices by 5% to 15% per year is a very effective sales tool when presenting past price appreciation to the prospective customer. The most common complaint to the Florida Land Sales Board is that salesmen misrepresent the investment potential of Florida land.

—would seem to offer proof that today's methods are not heading the industry into the kind of trouble it's been in before. Says Harry Schloss, Gulf American's treasurer: "Something like 80% of our sales are made to people who have seen what they are buying or who see it within six months. In most of the latter cases, they wind up buying more." Charles Kellstadt, retired board chairman of Sears, Roebuck & Company, and now the big man at General Development, adds a forceful footnote: "If I catch any of our salesmen exaggerating, pretty soon he's got himself a new boss. We don't have to exaggerate."

Sizzling sales

A glance at the sales figures for Florida land companies (Exhibit 1) convincingly demonstrates that the cry to "come on down" has been heard by investors and retirees throughout the United States. By 1967 Crescent Corporation, the largest of the Florida land companies, had sold land to over 150,000 customers. Sales of most companies had more than doubled since the shake-out in 1963–64, and sharp increases were forecast for 1968. As *Fortune* reported in late 1968,

> Real estate is not just hot these days. It is sizzling. There is in general an intense, new corporate involvement in real estate. A number of corporate giants have jumped into the field: Chrysler, Westinghouse, I.T.T., Gulf & Western, and the Norfolk & Western Railway, to name some of the most recent. They are creating brand-new communities, building homes and apartment houses, and backing a wide range of other projects, from office buildings and industrial parks to shopping centers and plush resorts. In most instances they are not directly involved in brick-and-mortar construction. Indeed, a majority of them are concentrating on land development, i.e., planning the use of large tracts of land and increasing its value by grading it, building streets, putting in utility lines, adding amenities such as greenbelts and golf courses, and then selling the land at a profit to others who do the actual building.[4]

Exhibit 1

THE LAND DEVELOPERS—1968

SALES GROWTH OF SELECTED FLORIDA LAND DEVELOPERS, 1962–68

(In millions)

	1962	*1963*	*1964*	*1965*	*1966*	*1967*	*Est. 1968*
Arvida Corporation	$ 8	$ 7	$ 5	$ 13	$ 9	$ 12	$15
Canaveral International Corporation	5	3	2	3	4	5	6
General Development Corporation	54	29	30	33	42	54	81
AMREP Corporation	13	8	6	8	12	18	33
Deltona Corporation	2	11	18	16	21	45	56
Crescent Corporation	74	70	91	107	144	131	*

* No forecast available.
Sources: *Moody's Bank & Finance Manuals; Moody's Industrial Manuals.*

[4] "Look Who's Rushing into Real Estate," *Fortune*, October, 1968, p. 160.

Record earnings

Sales were not all that were sizzling for the Florida land companies. Earnings expanded sharply in the years following the depressed industry conditions of 1963, as shown in Exhibit 2. General Development swung from loss operations in 1963 to earnings per share of $0.81 in 1967. AMREP's net jumped from $0.24 per share in 1963 to $1.24 in 1967, and industry sources anticipated a further rise to $2 in 1968. Even Canaveral International, although suffering from cutbacks at the Canaveral space center, showed improved earnings. With continued annual sales increases of 15–20% anticipated, the Florida land companies seemed poised in 1968 for rapidly rising reported earnings.

Exhibit 2

THE LAND DEVELOPERS—1968

EARNINGS PER SHARE OF SELECTED FLORIDA LAND DEVELOPERS, 1962–68

	1962	*1963*	*1964*	*1965*	*1966*	*1967*	*Est. 1968*
Arvida Corporation	*	*	$0.04	$0.09	$0.17	$0.18	$0.40
Canaveral International Corporation	$1.00	$0.17	*	*	0.79	0.53	0.20
General Development Corporation	*	*	0.19	0.27	0.51	0.81	1.00
AMREP Corporation	0.99	0.24	0.23	0.48	0.91	1.24	2.00
Deltona Corporation	0.03	0.33	0.48	0.60	0.67	0.85	1.25
Crescent Corporation	1.17	0.71	1.13	1.42	2.30	1.74	†

* = Deficit.
† = No forecast available.
Sources: *Moody's Bank & Finance Manuals; Moody's Industrial Manuals.*

Financial accounting

The sources of the improved profit margins were not entirely clear, however. Some industry observers pointed to product price increases, more effective selling practices, and increased operating efficiency, but the accounting practices of the industry created some uncertainty.

Like other installment plan enterprises, whether General Motors Acceptance Corporation or Investors Diversified Services, Inc., the land development companies record as sales the full price of a homesite as soon as the cash deposit and the first one or two monthly payments have been received. Crescent Corporation is fairly typical of the national land sales companies in its accounting.

For accounting purposes the Company [Crescent] records a transaction as a sale when it has been paid an amount equivalent to two monthly installments or 2½% of the sales price, whichever first occurs. All actual and estimated direct costs related to the sale are charged against income at that time. These costs consist of (1) cost of land, (2) estimated cost of required improvements and (3) sales commissions. Income is also charged with amounts deemed to be sufficient to provide for contract cancellations.[5] Selling and administrative expenses, real estate taxes and purchase money mortgage interest are charged to income as incurred. Sales commissions are charged to income in the full amount payable when the sale is recorded, although in the event of cancellation all or a part of the commission may also be cancelled.[6]

A basic accounting question, which was raised by the Securities and Exchange Commission in its 1962 Release[7] on certain real estate transactions (land developers were *not* cited specifically), is the appropriateness of the recognition of all of the estimated profit at the time of sale. The SEC was concerned not only with property sales that were mere fictions designed to create the illusion of profits or value as a basis for the sale of securities but also with bona fide transactions in which the degree of uncertainty as to the ultimate realization of profit was so great that business prudence, as well as generally accepted accounting principles, would preclude the recognition of gain at the time of sale. The SEC stated that the following circumstances raise a question as to the propriety of current recognition of profit:

a) Evidence of financial weakness of the purchaser.
b) Substantial uncertainty as to the amount of costs and expenses to be incurred.
c) Substantial uncertainty as to the amount of proceeds to be realized because of the form of consideration or the method of settlement; e.g., nonrecourse notes.
d) Retention of effective control of the property by the seller.
e) Limitations and restrictions on the purchaser's profits and on the development or disposition of the property.
f) Simultaneous sale and repurchase by the same or affiliated interests.
g) Concurrent loans to purchasers.
h) Small or no down payment.
i) Simultaneous sale-and-leaseback of property.

Some of the criteria would seem to fit the land sales companies inasmuch as they sell to people on terms involving small down payments, long payment periods, and no recourse in the event of default on payment. Often, the land

[5] Approximately 20–30% of sales are canceled in the same fiscal year in which the sale is recorded, and all entries pertaining to such sales are reversed. In addition, a substantial portion of land sales are canceled during a fiscal year subsequent to the year of the sale. For example, Crescent Corporation experienced cancellations of land sales of prior years totaling $116 million during the 1964 through 1968 period. These cancellations compare with net land sales of $501 million during the same period. If a contract is canceled during a fiscal year subsequent to the year of sale, the allowance for contract cancellation is reduced by the amount by which the remaining unpaid balance of the contract receivable exceeds (1) cost of land and (2) estimated cost of required improvements. Correspondingly, liabilities for estimated costs, required improvements, and unearned sales commissions are reduced, and the land is restored to inventory at cost. (Footnote added.)

[6] Proxy Statement, Crescent Corporation, January 15, 1969, p. B-7.

[7] "Accounting for Real Estate Transactions Where Circumstances Indicate That Profits Were Not Earned at the Time the Transactions Were Recorded," *SEC Accounting Series, Release No. 95,* December 28, 1962.

companies make no credit check on the purchasers and contract cancellation rates are high. Finally, the seller may retain title to the property for 5–7 years after the point of sale. However, the SEC never challenged the recognition of income by land companies at the time of sale.[8]

The land sales industry claimed support for immediate income recognition from the 1966 Omnibus Opinion of the Accounting Principles Board. The Opinion reaffirmed the recommendation of *Accounting Research Bulletin No. 43* that "Profit is deemed to be realized when a sale in the ordinary course of business is effected, unless the circumstances are such that the collection of the sales price is not reasonably assured." The Board recognized that there are exceptional cases "where receivables are collected over an extended period of time and, because of the terms of the transactions or other conditions, there is no reasonable basis for estimating the degree of collectibility. When such circumstances exist and as long as they exist, either the installment method or the cost recovery method of accounting may be used. (Under the cost recovery method, equal amounts of revenue and expense are recognized as collections are made until all costs have been recovered, postponing any recognition of profit until that time.) In the absence of such circumstances, however, the installment method of recognizing revenue is *not* acceptable."[9]

The accounting profession apparently felt that the land companies were not "exceptional cases." Their financial statements, prepared on the basis of immediate income recognition, were certified by such major national accounting firms as Lybrand, Ross Bros. & Montgomery, and Peat, Marwick, Mitchell & Co. as being consistent with generally accepted accounting principles.

For the land sales industry, allowance of immediate income recognition was central to the high earnings reported during the 1964–68 period of rapid sales growth. Exhibits 6 and 7[10] provide insight into the sharp disparities in the level and pattern of earnings that would be reported under various methods of income recognition by a rapidly growing company selling on long installment terms. Exhibit 3 compares the net incomes developed in these two exhibits. Recognition of income at the time of sale results in net earnings of $36 million by the 20th year after the formation of the company. In contrast,

---

[8] In fact, the Commission rejected a petition in 1968 by one land company to shift its accounting from immediate income recognition to a partial installment basis. (On the installment basis income is recognized over the installment payment period rather than entirely at the point of sale—see Exhibit 7.) The SEC rejection was based on the grounds that recognition on an installment basis would deviate from the accepted industry practices, and also that retroactive restatement of income on an installment basis would have the effect of "recycling" earnings which had been reported in prior years.

[9] *Omnibus Opinion*, 1966, p. 149.

[10] Exhibits 6 and 7 assume that general and administrative expenses and other selling expenses vary directly with sales. No effect is shown representing the differential effect (reduction) on fixed costs (as a percentage of sales) resulting from higher sales volume. Recognition of these areas of scale economy would raise the net income and the return on investment in both exhibits.

Exhibit 3

THE LAND DEVELOPERS—1968
COMPARISON OF INCOME RECOGNITION AT TIME OF SALE
AND BY INSTALLMENT METHOD

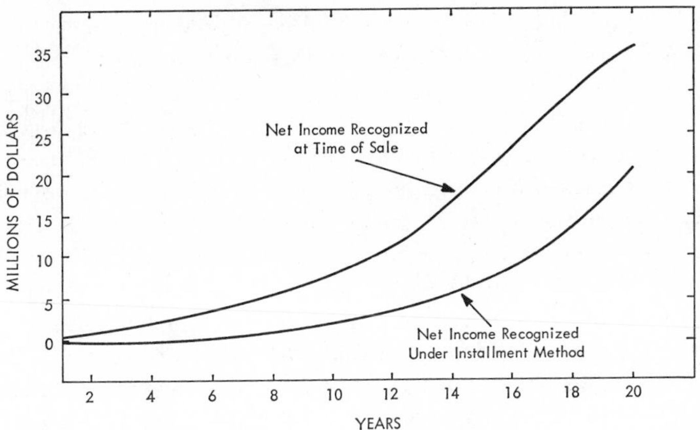

earnings would be only $21 million in the 20th year if income is recognized under the installment method.

Investor Interest

In 1968 investors seemed unconcerned, for the most part, with the philosophical arguments on income recognition. Six years had passed since the stock prices of land sales companies had collapsed in 1960–63. The price of General Development stock, for instance, had dropped from a high of $30 in 1958. Wall Street was showing a renewed and lively interest in the land companies, spurred by the rapid earnings gains and the belief that the industry had moved into stronger hands since the debacle of the early 1960's; and the stocks were selling on the basis of reported earnings.

By September, 1968, many land sales stocks had doubled and even quadrupled from their 1967 price levels (Exhibit 4) and were selling at price-earnings ratios of 20–30 times earnings.

Exhibit 4

THE LAND DEVELOPERS—1968
MARKET PRICES (MIDPOINT) OF COMMON STOCK OF SELECTED FLORIDA
LAND DEVELOPERS, 1962–SEPTEMBER, 1968

	1962	*1963*	*1964*	*1965*	*1966*	*1967*	*Sept., 1968*
Arvida Corporation	$ 8	$5	$5	$7	$ 7	$ 7	$16
Canaveral International Corporation	8	6	5	2	4	9	10
General Development Corporation	9	6	5	4	6	10	21
AMREP Corporation	5	4	2	3	3	8	31
Deltona Corporation	8	6	5	6	6	8	38
Crescent Corporation	10	6	5	9	10	10	23

Sources: *Moody's Bank & Finance Manuals; Moody's Industrial Manuals.*

The companies were also gaining greater acceptance from financial institutions. In the past, some of the land developers had been forced to borrow money at 15–20% from third-rate finance concerns. By the mid-1960's less restrictive bank lines were becoming available. The industry had matured and the golf pros that a decade earlier had been hired to promote the sale of undeveloped sites had been replaced by professional businessmen.

Negative cash flows

For rapidly growing land companies selling on 10–12 year terms, favorable investor attitudes and access to funds were essential. There is often a great disparity between the reported earnings and the cash generation from earnings. For example, reported earnings of the assumed company characterized in Exhibit 6 increased rapidly from $618,000 in its first year of operation to $30 million by the 18th year (under the generally accepted industry practice of income recognition at the time of sale). As indicated in Exhibits 5 and 8, however, the company generated a cash deficit in every year through year 18, by which time the cumulative deficit exceeded $57 million. If tax payments were based on reported earnings rather than on the installment tax option,[11] the cash deficit would approach $240 million.

The response by the land sales companies to the financing needs was influenced strongly by the corporate marketing strategy. The land sales industry is segregated into at least two distinct groups of companies. In one group are the community builders—firms that typically sell to a carefully preselected list of prospects. The basic appeal is to buy a vacation or retirement site and to build on it within a very few years. Sale usually involves a substantial down payment (perhaps 20%) and relatively short terms (4–6 years) and the purchaser's credit worthiness is checked prior to the signing of a contract. The market is narrowed by the terms of sale and credit check, but the resultant high quality of the contract receivables facilitates bank financing of the company's growth. Financing is also facilitated by the marketing requirement that the land either be fully developed prior to sale or that development be completed well before the purchaser wishes to build.

In sharp contrast to the community builders are the land companies that mass merchandise raw land, appealing in large measure to the investment potential. In time, the land will be developed and houses will be built, but the initial purchase is frequently motivated by hopes of high returns and by hard-sell "land counselors." The market encompasses that broad segment of the American households that earns annual incomes of $7,000–$12,000. The down payments are low (4–6%) and the installment contracts often stretch over 10–15 years to keep the monthly payments at manageable levels.[12] And

[11] Under the installment option a company is taxed as sales are collected and not when the sale is recorded. The cost of goods sold is allocated over the period of the installment contract. Other costs are considered expenses of the period.

[12] Monthly payments on a $4,000 receivable written at a 6% interest cost are $77 on a five-year contract. The same $4,000 receivable requires a monthly payment of only $40 if written on an 11-year repayment period.

the investment orientation of the buyer allows the companies to defer development of the land for 5–7 years to alleviate any financial pressures. Title to the land does not pass to the buyer for 6–7 years.

The financing needs of the mass merchandisers of land are large, however, during periods of rapid sales growth. Deferment of land development expenditures is an important source of funds, although such a policy runs the risk, especially in inflationary periods, of forcing the company into massive

Exhibit 5

THE LAND DEVELOPERS—1968

COMPARISON OF NET INCOME AND CUMULATIVE CASH FLOW

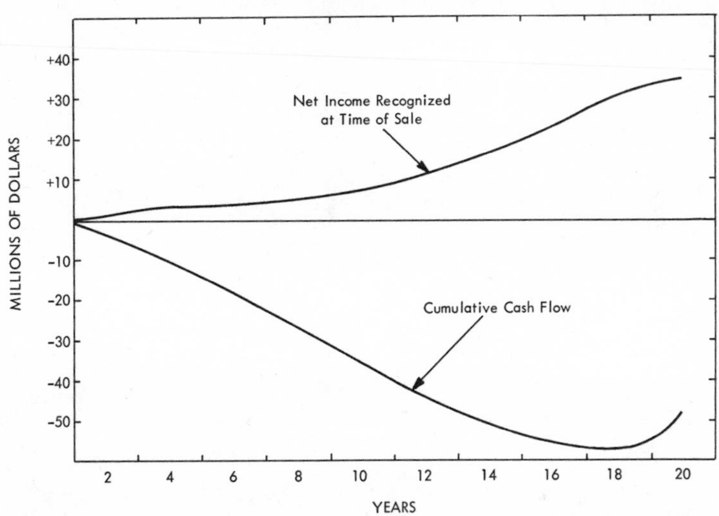

required development outlays to bring the program back on schedule. Deferment of development work may be seen by lenders as jeopardizing the company's ability to deliver a finished site on time to the customer and may reduce lenders' willingness to lend against receivables, which are based upon a contract that is valid only if all development work is completed within a stipulated period (6–7 years).

Banks and insurance companies are troubled by the characteristics of the contract receivables against which they lend, for reasons in addition to the development requirement. The receivables result in part from hard-sell techniques, are created typically without a credit check, and are subject to high default rates (primarily in the first year they are on the books) without any recourse to the buyer, who simply forfeits any payments made. Lenders, however, have gained experience with the receivables of land companies and while they certainly are unwilling to loan against receivables at 70%–80% of their book value, they have extended credit lines of 20%–33% of the value of receivables. Exhibit 8 indicates the relationship between the borrowing needs and the level of receivables at various points in time.

The mass merchandisers have also secured long-term funds from foundations, insurance companies, and the general public, although equity sweeteners (convertible issues or warrants) have frequently been necessary; and have usually acquired land on installment terms. Exhibit 9 provides some insight into the sources of finance used by five land sales companies in 1967.

Exhibit 6

THE LAND DEVELOPERS—1968
Reported Earnings under Income Recognition at Time of Sale
(Dollar figures in millions)

	Years since Formation of Company											
	1	2	3	*4*	*5*	*6*	7	*8*	*9*	*10*	*15*	*20*
Sales	$3	$5	$8	$10	$12	$14.4	$17.3	$20.8	$25	$30	$72	$112
Raw land cost[a]	0.12	0.20	0.32	0.40	0.48	0.58	0.69	0.83	1.0	1.2	2.88	4.48
Est. development cost[b]	0.48	0.80	1.28	1.60	1.92	2.30	2.77	3.33	4.0	4.8	11.52	17.92
Selling expense[c]	1.05	1.75	2.80	3.50	4.20	5.04	6.06	7.28	8.75	10.5	25.2	39.2
Gen. and admin. expense[d]	0.21	0.35	0.56	0.70	0.84	1.01	1.21	1.46	1.75	2.10	5.04	7.84
Interest expense[e]	0	0.152	0.384	0.730	1.112	1.51	1.921	2.342	2.768	3.191	5.019	5.541
Interest income[f]	0.095	0.348	0.741	1.272	1.888	2.592	3.397	4.326	5.399	6.638	16.864	34.262
Pretax profits	$1.235	$2.096	$3.397	$ 4.342	$ 5.336	$ 6.552	$ 8.046	$ 9.884	$12.131	$14.847	$39.205	$ 71.281
Taxes[g]	0.617	1.048	1.699	2.171	2.668	3.276	4.023	4.942	6.066	7.423	19.602	35.640
Net income	$0.618	$1.048	$1.698	$ 2.171	$ 2.668	$ 3.276	$ 4.023	$ 4.942	$ 6.065	$ 7.424	$19.603	$ 35.641
Percent earned on—												
Equity[h]	38%				29%					21%	19%	14%
Capital[i]	20				16					15	16	14

Notes:
[a] Raw land cost = 4% of sales.
[b] Development cost = 16% of sales.
[c] Selling expense = 35% of sales.
[d] General and administrative costs = 7% of sales.
[e] Interest expense = 10% of cumulative cash deficit at the beginning of the year.
[f] Interest income = 7% of contract receivables outstanding.
[g] Taxes = 50% of pretax profits.
[h] Year-end book equity, assuming no payment of dividends.
[i] Assumes that the cash deficit indicated in Exhibit 3 is met by borrowings. Capital = equity plus all borrowings.

Exhibit 7

THE LAND DEVELOPERS—1968

Reported Earnings under Installment Method of Income Recognition*

(Dollars figures in millions)

	Years since Formation of Company											
	1	2	3	*4*	*5*	*6*	*7*	*8*	*9*	*10*	*15*	*20*
Sales (repayment of principal)	$ 0.2412	$ 0.5844	$ 1.1467	$ 1.8338	$ 2.6843	$ 3.7399	$5.0461	$6.6581	$8.638	$11.0582	$30.647	$64.648
Allocated costs	0.0905	0.2192	0.43	0.6877	1.0066	1.4025	1.8923	2.4968	3.2393	4.1468	11.4926	24.243
Period costs	0.735	1.377	2.344	3.180	4.052	5.04	6.161	7.442	8.893	10.541	22.659	32.981
Interest income	0.095	0.3476	0.7413	1.2722	1.8877	2.5921	3.3969	4.326	5.399	6.6379	16.864	34.262
Pretax earnings (loss)	$(0.489)	$(0.664)	$(0.886)	$(0.762)	$(0.487)	$(0.111)	$0.390	$1.045	$1.905	$ 3.008	$13.359	$41.686
Taxes	0.244	0.332	0.443	0.381	0.244	0.055	0.195	0.522	0.953	1.504	6.679	20.843
Net income (loss)	$(0.245)	$(0.332)	$(0.443)	$(0.381)	$(0.243)	$(0.056)	$0.195	$0.523	$0.952	$ 1.504	$ 6.68	$20.843

* Under the installment method of income recognition, reported sales equal the collection in that period of principal owed on the contracts receivable. Allocated costs in a period are determined by multiplying the estimated cost of goods sold as a percent of sales (for the entire transaction) times the collection of principal during that period. For example, it was assumed in Exhibit 6 and in this exhibit that land cost = 4% of sales, development cost = 16% of sales, and salesmen's commissions = 17.5% of sales. The cost of goods sold as a percent of sales = 37.5% (salesmen's commissions were included because of their size and the distortions that would result from their treatment as a period cost). The allocated costs in period 1, therefore, were calculated by multiplying 37.5% times $.2412. Period costs = interest expense, general and administrative expense, and all selling expenses other than salesmen's commissions. Interest income on contracts receivable was included in income in the period in which it was collected. The operating patterns assumed in Exhibit 7 were identical with those upon which Exhibit 6 was based; the only difference was in accounting.

Exhibit 8

THE LAND DEVELOPERS—1968
CASH FLOW ANALYSIS
(Dollar figures in millions)

Year since Formation of Company	*Collections*	*Land Development*	*Selling Expense*	*G & A Expense*	*Interest*	*Tax Payments*[a]	*Cash Flow*	*Cumulative Cash Flow*	*Contracts Receivable*
1	$ 0.336	$ 0.60	$ 1.05	$0.210	$ 0	$ 0	$ (1.524)		$ 2.8
2	0.932	1.00	1.75	0.35	0.152	0	(2.320)	$ (3.844)	7.2
3	1.888	1.60	2.80	0.56	0.384	0	(3.456)	(7.300)	14
4	3.106	2.00	3.5	0.70	0.730	0	(3.824)	(11.124)	22
5	4.572	2.40	4.2	0.84	1.1124	0	(3.9804)	(15.1044)	32
6	6.332	2.88	5.04	1.01	1.5104	0	(4.1084)	(19.2128)	42
7	8.443	3.46	6.06	1.21	1.9213	0	(4.2083)	(23.4211)	54
8	10.984	4.16	7.28	1.46	2.3421	0	(4.2581)	(27.6792)	69
9	14.037	5.00	8.75	1.75	2.7679	0	(4.2309)	(31.9101)	85
10	17.696	6.00	10.5	2.10	3.1910	0	(4.095)	(36.005)	104
11	22.102	7.20	12.6	2.52	3.6005	0	(3.8185)	(39.8235)	126
12	27.186	8.64	15.1	3.02	3.9824	0	(3.5564)	(43.3799)	152
13	33.089	10.40	18.2	3.64	4.338	0	(3.489)	(46.8689)	182
14	39.808	12.40	21.7	4.34	4.6869	0	(3.3189)	(50.1878)	219
15	47.511	14.40	25.2	5.04	5.0188	0	(2.1478)	(52.336)	260
16	56.205	16.40	28.7	5.74	5.2336	1.3626	(1.2312)	(53.567)	306
17	65.86	18.40	32.2	6.44	5.3567	6.093	(2.6297)	(56.197)	355
18	76.44	20.40	35.7	7.14	5.6197	8.381	(0.8007)	(56.998)	408
19	87.85	22.40	39.2	7.84	5.6998	11.117	1.5932	(55.405)	462
20	98.91	22.40	39.2	7.84	5.5405	15.936	7.9935	(47.412)	510
21	109.396	22.40	39.2	7.84	4.7412	20.833	14.382	(33.030)	550
22	119.20	22.40	39.2	7.84	3.303	25.763	20.694	(12.336)	582
23	128.184	22.40	39.2	7.84	1.234	30.664	26.846	14.51	608
24	136.174	22.40	39.2	7.84	0	34.731	32.003	(b)	628
25	142.998	22.40	39.2	7.84	0	37.688	35.870		641
26	148.579	22.40	39.2	7.84	0	40.1149	39.024		650
27	152.92	22.40	39.2	7.84	0	42.0126	41.467		656
28	156.02	22.40	39.2	7.84	0	43.3808	43.199		658
29	157.88	22.40	39.2	7.84	0	44.2198	44.22		658
30	158.50	22.40	39.2	7.84	0	44.53	44.53		658
31	145.95	0	0	6.0	0	59.793	80.157		555
32	132.05	0	0	5.5	0	54.111	72.439		459
33	118.15	0	0	5.0	0	48.429	64.721		370
34	104.25	0	0	4.5	0	42.748	52.002		289
35	90.35	0	0	4.0	0	37.066	49.284		217
36	76.45	0	0	3.2	0	31.534	41.716		154
37	62.55	0	0	2.6	0	25.902	34.048		101
38	48.65	0	0	2.0	0	20.27	26.38		58
39	34.75	0	0	1.6	0	14.539	18.611		26
40	20.85	0	0	1.3	0	8.757	10.793		7
41	6.95	0	0	1.0	0	2.975	2.975		0

[a] The company operated at a tax loss over the first 10 years and tax-loss carry-forwards offset taxable income in years 11 through 15. (Expiration of tax-loss carry-forwards can be a problem.)
[b] Assumed that the positive cash flows are paid out to stockholders after year 22.
Note: The present value of the cash flows shown above equals zero at an assumed interest rate of 16%.

Exhibit 9

THE LAND DEVELOPERS—1968

COMPOSITE BALANCE SHEET OF FIVE LAND SALES COMPANIES—1967

ASSETS		LIABILITIES AND NET WORTH	
Cash	3%	Accounts payable	6%
Receivables	67	Notes and loans payable	14
Inventory (land, etc.)	21	Liability for development	8
Fixed assets	7	Deferred taxes	18
Other	2	Other	2
	100%	Subordinated debentures	4
		Mortgages payable	13
		Equity	35
			100%

UNIVERSAL FINANCE COMPANY (A)

Universal Finance Company, a finance company based in Columbus, Ohio, was no stranger to acquisitions. Its 35-year history had been marked by above average expansion of sales as the company absorbed small, regional finance companies. In just the nine years ended 1968, Universal had made over 16 acquisitions, which had helped to increase the company's assets, net income, and employees over fourfold and had catapulted it into insurance, computer leasing, and the manufacturing of steel products and truck trailers. But never before in its history had the management of Universal been faced with such a monumental decision as the proposed acquisition in 1968 of Crescent Corporation—the Florida land sales company whose fortunes had faltered recently under a series of charges by the Florida Land Sales Board. For Ben Moore, the 41-year-old president of Universal, the growth and profitability prospects of the land sales business provided an exciting contrast to the maturing finance industry. This single acquisition would more than double Universal's earnings and promised some hope for greater investor interest in the company's stock. Mr. Moore's conviction had been somewhat lessened, however, by a strong report in opposition to the acquisition and he felt that an immediate review of the proposed acquisition was necessary prior to a final recommendation in three days to the board of directors at its October, 1968, meeting.

History of Universal Finance Company

Universal Finance Company was formed in 1933, after F. R. Moore took over the Columbus Thrift Company. In those days the "finance industry" had a strong small-business flavor; most of its members were operating on a local basis. Credit cards were virtually unheard of, and credit unions were less significant as competitors than they later became. Most commercial banks had not yet begun to compete aggressively in personal loans and sales finance, the two staples of the finance industry. In addition to having these fields mostly to themselves, finance companies were freer than they are now to pass money costs on to their customers; almost none of the present regulation of sales finance charges were then in effect. Many finance companies thrived in this environment, and very few felt any inclination to change.

F. R. Moore was nevertheless astute enough to see that the small companies would not have protected local markets forever. Big nationwide companies would have one crucial advantage over small ones: the cost of their raw material, money, would be lower because they would be better credit risks. Mr. Moore decided that he was faced with two choices: either sell out to another larger finance company or make Universal itself grow. Rapid growth obviously meant dilution of the Moore family's controlling interest in Universal (it was 59% at one point), for the company's cash was tied up in its operations, and acquisitions would necessarily involve stock. Mr. Moore nevertheless decided that Universal would grow by acquisition. Ben Moore, son of F. R. Moore, and the president of Universal in 1968, is certain that his father had already settled on this course before World War II (and there were in fact some small acquisitions then), but it was not formalized until a directors meeting in Colorado Springs in 1958. According to the minutes, F. R. Moore explained that "due to the competitive factors of the larger companies with low money costs and larger capital funds, it became more difficult for small companies to survive and that this, in turn, might cause the smaller companies to consider the sale of their assets to the larger companies. . . ." Mr. Moore then continued to discuss the future conduct of the corporation and stated that "the corporation should take the following steps: (1) continue to build by acquisitions. . . ."[1]

Universal wasted little time in following the game plan. Eleven companies or parts of companies were acquired during the five years ended December, 1964. The acquisitions provided Universal with 145 additional finance offices, often in states not previously served. (The total number of Universal offices increased during the period from 208 to 395.) The acquisitions also allowed the company to build its borrowing base by issuance of common and preferred stock at favorable prices. By 1964 Universal had reached a size at which it clearly was a member of that elite club of finance companies that could borrow at low cost from a broad range of investors. The commercial paper was rated prime[2] and lines from some 350 banks totaled $223 million. Borrowings were at the prime rate. Universal had gained the size and geographic diversification necessary to compete successfully.

UNIVERSAL FINANCE COMPANY
(In millions)

	1959	*1964*
Receivables, net of reserve	$139.00	$431.00
Total assets	161.00	495.00
Net income	2.62	4.89

[1] The first two paragraphs of the section on the history of Universal Finance Company are based on an article published in *Fortune*. The names of the companies and of management are disguised.

[2] Prime is the top rating accorded an issuer's commercial paper by the National Credit Office of Dun & Bradstreet, the national rating service.

A matter of control[3]

Universal's rapid expansion was not without difficulties, however. The company ventured into insurance with the acquisition in 1945 of the Puritan Insurance Company of Springfield, a small fire-and-casualty company. In 1953, Universal put the company into credit life insurance; and in the mid-1950's it expanded still further, into fire-and-casualty reinsurance—i.e., insuring contracts already written by other underwriters. But in this case Universal went too far too fast and let its internal controls get out of hand. Automobile casualty claims ran far ahead of expectations, and hurricanes and other bad-weather problems were also compounding the difficulties (and hurting casualty companies generally); Universal's venture was soon in big trouble. In 1963 the reinsurance operation was discontinued, and the casualty business was cut back sharply as cumulative underwriting losses exceeded $12 million.

The company's alarming experiences in some of its insurance operations fortified a conviction that Ben Moore had been developing for some time—that Universal had grown to a point at which it sorely needed some stronger central controls. One of his first acts as president in 1964 was to set up a "control group," under a vice president, which continuously audited Universal's varied operations and reported findings directly to him. Mr. Moore now consults with the head of the group every working day.

Acquisition of Frontier Finance Company

Universal's beefed-up internal controls allowed it to take a growing interest in troubled finance companies whose receivables looked as though they might be bought at bargain prices. Such considerations were evident in Universal's move on Frontier Finance Company.

The woes of Frontier were rooted in overexpansion. Its difficulties dated back to 1959 when it entered shell-house financing in a big way. By 1962 shell housing accounted for $60 million, or 51%, of Frontier's total receivables. Financing the purchase of a shell and letting the buyer put his own "sweat equity" into it looked like a promising avenue of growth. But as things turned out, many shells never were completed, and only a handful of shell-house builders managed to survive.

Frontier itself still seemed to be in good enough shape in the early 1960's. By granting extensions on shell-house loans and refinancing accounts on extended terms, Frontier was able to look healthier than it really was. But its difficulties finally came out into the open after it brought in a new auditor, Ross & Sayles, in the summer of 1965. The firm appears to have taken a tougher line than its predecessor and after the first Ross & Sayles audit, a

---

[3] The sections "A Matter of Control" through "An Inside Track for Universal" are based on an article published in *Fortune*. The names of the companies and of management are disguised.

special charge of $2,500,000 was made, mostly to provide for an additional allowance for losses on shell-housing paper.

Even before the new audit was made public, one of Frontier's biggest bank creditors, the National Bank of Chicago, decided to take a closer look at the company. It found that Frontier had lost some other lines of credit during the preceding six months; it also found out about the $2,500,000 special charge. National Bank of Chicago decided not to renew its own line of credit to Frontier. This meant that the company would not be able to pay off other short-term loans coming due; furthermore, the $2,500,000 special charge had reduced Frontier's capital below the level specified in its loan agreements—and these things meant that the company was in technical default on all of its $118 million of loans. Frontier was not immediately thrown into bankruptcy because most of its creditors felt there would be more to salvage through a merger or sale of assets; bankruptcy proceedings, furthermore, would be costly and time consuming. But it turned out that not even Ross & Sayles had fully realized the extent of Frontier's troubles; in the spring another special provision of $11,100,000 had to be made for anticipated losses, and an additional charge of $6 million was made to reflect changes in Frontier's accounting practices. Frontier ended with a deficit of $16,400,000 in the fiscal year ended March 31, 1966 (in contrast to a profit of $963,000 for the previous fiscal year).

An inside track for Universal

Meanwhile, Universal had sent a team of specialists to Chicago to evaluate Frontier's receivables. Another team was dispatched to Florida to check out the company's loan offices there. Universal negotiated a contract to help collect Frontier's receivables as they came due and seemed to have the inside track when it came to buying any pieces of the company. But as things turned out, buying *anything* from Frontier was difficult, because the company had seven different classes of stockholders and a variety of creditors as well, all of whom had to approve the terms of the merger.

Universal wanted a merger with Frontier. The specific attractions were some $60 million of net sales-finance receivables, most of them in mobile (not shell) housing; some $13 million of net personal-loan receivables; and about $40 million in cash. The acquisition would, of course, enable Universal to expand its sales-finance and personal-loan business in several areas of the United States in which Frontier had strong positions, notably Michigan and Florida. But far more important to Mr. Moore was an unparalleled opportunity he saw in the deal to raise capital at a low cost—no mean trick in 1966—and to increase his company's borrowing power. He proposed to pay for the Frontier package with a package of his own consisting mostly of debt securities: Universal would give Frontier's stockholders and creditors about $20 million of its own preferred stock and subordinated debt and $80 million of newly issued senior notes paying only 4% to 5%. When the merger became effective, Universal also paid Frontier's creditors about $15 million in cash.

Diversified operations

The financial community gained considerable respect from the Frontier acquisition for Universal's ability to work profitably in troubled waters. Some lenders grew increasingly wary, however, as the company began to move outside the finance industry. Such diversification moves were not new to finance companies. Beneficial Finance Company, the second largest small-loan company in the United States, realized almost one third of its net income in 1965 from its retailing subsidiary, Western Auto Supply Company (acquired in 1961), and was negotiating the acquisition of Spiegel Inc., the nationwide mail-order merchandiser. And Household Finance Corporation had acquired Coast-to-Coast Stores Inc., a chain of 976 franchised retail stores, in 1961 and Badger Paint & Hardware Stores Inc., in 1963. Precedents aside, however, lenders were anxious over Universal's rapid expansion through acquisition of ailing companies.

Universal's first excursion beyond the confines of the finance (and insurance) industry was its 1965 acquisition of National Trailer Industries, a manufacturer of trailers, whose primary competitor was Fruehauf Corporation. National Trailer was losing money in large amounts, was plagued by stockholder suits, and had directors who had been indicted for illegal stock promotion (they were ultimately acquitted) when acquired by Universal.

Universal had been financing National Trailer since 1961 and was acutely aware of the nature of the problems undermining National's operation. Institution of a vigorous and experienced management and cost-cutting measures seemed to improve the situation. National Trailer swung from a loss of $1.7 million in 1965 to profits of $2.9 million and $2.4 million in 1966 and 1967, respectively.

The National Trailer acquisition was followed by the acquisition in 1967 of Aetna Steel Products Corporation of Pottsville, Pennsylvania, a manufacturer of movable steel office partitions and steel shelving. Kahr Bearing Corporation, a California producer of bearings used in the aircraft industry, joined Universal's manufacturing operations in March, 1967. And Trump, Ltd., of Canada was acquired in December, 1967, to expand Universal's utilities construction and maintenance equipment product line. With the acquisition of Dean Phipps Stores in April, 1968, Universal entered into the retail merchandising business with 72 stores in Pennsylvania, New Jersey, and New York. (Exhibit 1 lists Universal's acquisitions since 1960.) At the same time as its entry into retailing, Universal announced that it was making a major commitment to the computer leasing industry. For several years management had observed the rapid growth in the use of computers and their integration into virtually every type of business. Pricing policies of IBM seemed to provide Universal with an excellent and profitable opportunity to finance the use of computers by other companies.

Availability of Crescent Corporation

But the most exciting move was Universal's possible entry into the national land sales business through the acquisition of Crescent Corporation, the largest of the Florida land companies. (For background information on the industry, see the note entitled "The Land Developers—1968.") The possibility that Leonard and Sam Julius, founders and majority stockholders of Crescent, might want to sell out was first rumored in early 1968. The company was in serious political straits with the Florida Land Sales Board and the repercussions were being felt in its sales and financing efforts. The company had long been under the watchful eye of the Land Sales Board. Almost one half of the customer complaints filed with the Board in 1964–66 had been registered against Crescent,[4] but this was in part the natural outgrowth of an aggressive mass marketing strategy. And when Claude Kirk campaigned for and won the Florida governorship on a platform of cleaning up the land business, Crescent faced turbulent times.

In June, 1967, the Florida Land Sales Board charged Crescent with flagrant misrepresentation in sales of land, of selling lots bearing specific numbers and then switching the lot numbers to other land, and of concealing key information from the regulatory agency. The situation deteriorated even further when Governor Kirk ordered an investigation aimed at criminal prosecution of a purported "representative" of Crescent who allegedly tried to blackmail the Governor's staff into suppressing the Board's investigation.

Crescent moved to avoid the spotlight of public hearings. It pleaded guilty to the five counts lodged by the Board and was suspended from all land sales in November, 1967, for 30 days. The suspension had barely ended, however, when the Board announced a new investigation of the company's selling practices, questioned its ability to make millions of dollars worth of improvements promised for existing developments, and denied Crescent's petition to register and open for sale eight new areas in various Florida developments. Leonard Julius reacted with a vitriolic attack on the members of the Board. "We thought they wanted a pound of flesh," exclaimed Mr. Julius. "They didn't want the pound of flesh, they wanted our blood."

The breakdown of relations with the Land Sales Board was publicized by such national media as *The Wall Street Journal.* The adverse publicity severely hurt Crescent's operations. Management feared that sales in the fiscal year ended August, 1968, would not exceed $100 million and that a small operating loss might be reported. A substantial portion of the company's salaries was fixed over short time periods and sharp reductions in sales would inevitably result in substantial declines in earnings.[5] The publicity might also lead to an increase in contract cancellations.

But of greatest significance was the impact on Crescent's ability to raise funds. Crescent had fallen far behind in its development program. This, coupled with the Land Sales Board investigation, led lenders to refuse to

---

[4] Crescent accounted for approximately one quarter of total Florida land sales.

[5] Crescent had about 3,500 full-time employees: administrative and clerical (900), sales department (1,000; of which 500 were salesmen and the rest were sales support), construction (800), operations of company-owned motels and restaurants (500), and airlines operations (300).

extend additional credit; and the sale of stock seemed excessively expensive in view of the 38% plunge in the price of the company's stock between June, 1967, and March, 1968 (a period in which market prices of stocks of other Florida land developers increased by 30%–40%). The shortage of funds almost ensured continued reluctance by the Land Sales Board to register Crescent land for sale,[6] and the company was faced with the prospect of exhausting its land inventory. Sale of the company seemed to be the most acceptable alternative open to the Julius brothers.

Appeal of Crescent to Universal

The possibility of acquiring Crescent appealed to Ben Moore. The finance industry appeared to be approaching maturity with growing competition from commercial banks, captive finance companies, and credit cards. Profit margins were being squeezed in the vise of rising cost of funds and state statutory ceilings on loan rates. Operating profit margins and the return earned on equity in the industry had fallen by almost one third during the period 1959–67 and further declines were expected. Earnings per share had increased despite the deteriorating profit margins, but this was accomplished by increasing the use of debt and preferred stock. By 1967, earnings coverage of the interest on borrowings in the industry had fallen to 2.05 from 2.79 in 1959, and opportunities to substitute debt for equity seemed limited (the decline was the result of higher interest rates as well as increased financial leverage).

FINANCE COMPANIES INDEX*

	1959	*1967*
Operating profit margin†	33%	22%
Return on equity	14%	11%
Earnings per share‡	100	163
Times interest earned§	2.79	2.05

* The index includes Beneficial Finance Company, C.I.T. Financial Corporation, Family Finance Corporation, Walter E. Heller & Company, Household Finance Corporation, James Talcott, Inc., and Liberty Loan Corporation.

† Operating profit margin = profit (after operating expenses, interest, and provision for loan losses) as percentage of total revenues. The calculations are limited to the finance operations and exclude nonfinance activities.

‡ 1959 earnings per share are set at a base of 100.

§ Calculated on a pretax basis.

The deterioration of industry fundamentals and investor fascination with growth stocks contributed to a downgrading of the price-earnings ratios on

FINANCE COMPANIES INDEX (1959-100)

	1959	*1962*	*1967*
Earnings per share	100	118	163
Price-earnings ratio	100	147	89
Market price	100	171	140

[6] Land must be registered with the Land Sales Board prior to its being offered for sale.

finance company stocks. After selling as high as 16–20 times earnings in 1962, the stocks declined to price-earnings ratios of only 10–12 times in 1967.

Universal was swept by the same trends as the other major finance companies. Operating margins narrowed; and while earnings per share rose at a more rapid rate than for the industry sample, the company's price-earnings ratio plunged steadily from 16 times in 1962 to only 8 times in 1967 (10 times fully diluted earnings per share after conversion of all convertible securities). Despite a 76% increase in earnings per share, the common stock was lower in price in 1967 than in 1962. (Exhibit 2 shows the operating results of Universal during the period 1962–67.)

The disenchantment of investors over the industry and the major revaluation of the equities also placed Universal in some jeopardy of unwanted courtship by a free-wheeling conglomerate. Gulf & Western Industries, Inc., had acquired Associates Investment Company (with year-end 1967 assets of $1.6 billion) earlier in 1968, and the rise in price of finance company stocks in 1968 reflected investor belief that more take-overs by conglomerates were in the wind. A major commitment to the land development industry seemed a promising solution to these pressures. Profits reported by the land companies were high and rising rapidly, and the stocks were commanding price-earnings ratios of 20–30 times (up substantially from the earnings multiples of 6–12 times that had prevailed in 1965–67).

The land development business seemed very similar to the finance business, and Mr. Moore felt that the results of acquiring Crescent might be more than additive. The principal assets of Crescent were some $258 million of contracts receivable, which required both collection and financing. (Exhibit 3 provides a balance sheet of Crescent and an aging schedule of the receivables.) Universal had excellent contacts with lenders throughout the capital markets, and management felt that the borrowing needs of a rapidly expanding land development subsidiary could be financed either directly or through Universal's finance subsidiary. (Exhibit 4 shows a consolidated balance sheet of Universal.)

What interested Mr. Moore was *not* merely the $258 million of receivables already on the books, however, but Crescent's sales force and marketing program. Crescent's nationwide sales force[7] was as strong as any in the industry and was supported by mass mailings, heavy national advertising, and easy sales terms (low down payment and low monthly payments). The aggressive sales program had propelled sales from only $7 million in 1958 to $144 million by 1966; net income had shot from $400,000 to $22 million. (See Exhibit 5 for the operating record of Crescent.) By 1968, over 175,000

[7] The approximately 125 independent brokers who sold land for Crescent received commissions at rates ranging from 15% to 18½% of their net sales. In addition, approximately 150 salesmen who showed land to potential purchasers at the subdivisions received commissions ranging from 1% to 5% of their net sales depending on the amount of down payment received. Also, approximately 50 persons were engaged as telephone salesmen (accounting for 10% of land sales) and received commissions of 7½% to 9%.

Americans had bought acreage in one of the Crescent developments. (See Exhibit 6 for information on Crescent's acreage.)

A project team headed by Alan Strassman, the Universal vice president responsible for all acquisitions, swung into action. Twenty-five of the company's employees and eight outside consulting firms spent four months studying the full range of Crescent's operations. In the most comprehensive acquisition analysis ever undertaken by Universal, the assets, control systems, organization, morale, and personnel of each of Crescent's divisions were analyzed and evaluated; and the magnitude of any post-acquisition changes was determined. Major deficiencies were found in some critical areas, but Mr. Moore felt that Universal was almost uniquely experienced in dealing with problems of control and organization.

What seemed critical to any serious consideration of the acquisition of Crescent were (1) sound relations with the Florida regulatory authorities, (2) careful consideration of the real meaning of Crescent's balance sheet and its future profit potential, and (3) assurance that the Juliuses would not gain any material control of Universal.

Mr. Moore was assured by authorities in Florida that the Land Sales Board would view with favor the acquisition of Crescent by Universal and that while tighter controls over salesmen's activities were mandatory, required changes in the basic marketing program would be small. It seemed likely that the combination of Universal's financial capacity and control systems and Crescent's sales force might drive sales to $150–$180 million in 1969 and earnings to $22–$25 million. Sales might increase by roughly $30 million per year thereafter, with a correspondingly rapid rise in earnings. (A forecast of sales and earnings for Crescent under Universal ownership is provided in Exhibit 7.)

Attention was then focused on the practice of Crescent (and the land sales industry generally) of full recognition of income after 2½% of the total sales price, or two monthly payments, had been received from the customer. After discussions with several accounting firms, Mr. Strassman considered a modified installment method for recognizing income. The accounting change, which would necessitate restatement of the results of prior years, would reduce estimated 1969 earnings (reported) by roughly 25%–30% from $22–$25 million to $15–$18 million. The management of Universal felt, however, that the accounting change would provide a sounder measure of the profitability of operations.

The SEC rejected the proposal on the grounds that the proposed accounting method would differ materially from the practices of the industry and would create a possibly misleading picture of stability in the operations of the company. Generally speaking, the SEC has chosen, as a matter of operating policy, to support and rely on the accounting profession to take the leadership, through the work of the Accounting Principles Board, in the development of accounting principles in the private sector. Its policy in this respect is complemented by its insistence on unqualified opinions of independent accountants as to the conformity with "generally accepted accounting principles" on financial statements required to be filed with the SEC or over which it otherwise exercises jurisdiction. Universal retained, therefore, the industrywide practice of recognizing income at the time of sale. (Exhibit 7 was generated on this basis.)

Proposed acquisition price

Negotiations between Universal and the Juliuses started in the spring of 1968. Announcement of agreement in principle on the merger was made on July 17, 1968. Under the terms of the agreement, each share of Crescent common stock would be entitled, at the election of the holder, to 0.416 of a share of Universal common stock or 0.188 of a share of Universal voting preference stock $1.06 Convertible Series. The $1.06 Convertible Series would have a stated value of $75, would be entitled to cumulative dividends of $1.06 per annum, would be callable at any time after five years from the date of merger at $100 plus accrued dividends, and would be convertible at any time after three years from such date into 2.53 shares of Universal common stock. It was anticipated that there would not be an active secondary market for the $1.06 Convertible Series. The implications for Crescent stockholders of accepting the offer are outlined in Exhibit 8.

Exhibit 8 is complicated and confusing. It is an exact reproduction of the information provided in the offering prospectus to stockholders of Crescent as a basis for their decision on the merger offer. The exhibit is complicated by (*a*) uncertainty as to the securities which Crescent shareholders would elect to receive in exchange for their stock and (*b*) the basis for calculating earnings per share (basically, the extent to which convertible securities would be, in fact, converted). It is very apparent that stockholders of Crescent were confronted with considerable uncertainty as to the claim on earnings (reported, partially diluted, and fully diluted) that they would have as the result of exchanging their shares either for Universal common stock or for Universal voting preference stock. The uncertainty stemmed from uncertainty as to (*a*) future operations and profitability of the merged companies; (*b*) the election by other Crescent stockholders to receive common stock or voting preference stock of Universal; (*c*) the basis on which Universal and investors would calculate earnings per share (e.g., the basis of common stock outstanding versus common stock and common stock equivalents outstanding); and (*d*) the rate at which convertible securities, in fact, would be converted in the future.

The Juliuses, owners of approximately 53% of the shares of Crescent, agreed to vote not less than 5,000,000 shares of Crescent common stock in favor of the merger[8] and to convert their Crescent shares into not less than

---

[8] This agreement ensured that the necessary majority of the outstanding shares (there were 9,791,490 shares of Crescent common stock outstanding) of Crescent would be voted in favor of the merger and, therefore, that *all* of the common stock of Crescent would be acquired by Universal. Stockholders of Crescent who dissented from the proposed merger

826,000 shares of the $1.06 Convertible Series.[9] All other Crescent stockholders would have the right to elect either form of exchange. The exchange of stock would be tax-free to stockholders of Crescent.

Financing diversification

The moves by Universal into manufacturing, retailing, land sales, and computer leasing (as well as planned expansion into mortgage banking and savings and loan operations) were viewed by management as strategically sound.

> The initial steps that were taken for diversification in the late 1950's by your company and many of its competitors were sound. We must continue to broaden our concept of today's and tomorrow's marketplace. The skills and services we are now assembling go well beyond the old definitions of the finance industry, but are related to them.
>
> For example, a finance company's ability to raise substantial amounts of capital helps to satisfy the requirements of computer leasing. Our expertise in distribution and consumer credit contributes to success in the retail merchandising field. The type of individual we serve in many of our operations is similar to the savings and loan customer and to the mortgage banking customer. Likewise, the sources of funds are basically the same in all our operations.
>
> Ben Moore, *Chairman and President*
> 1968 Message to Stockholders

However, the traditional suppliers of funds to Universal were made increasingly concerned by the company's diversification moves. The lenders' anxiety seemed to stem from (*a*) their unfamiliarity with mobile home financing and computer leasing, (*b*) their distaste for finance companies that lend to their own nonfinance subsidiaries, and (*c*) the heavy use of borrowed funds by finance companies generally, and Universal in particular. The solvency of the company could be threatened by a relatively small shrinkage in the value of its assets. All of Universal's diversified activities were commingled with the company's finance operation and some lenders were uncertain as to the possible profile of the company in the years to come and the quality of the advances by Universal Finance to its nonfinance subsidiaries. The advances had increased sharply, relative to gross receivables,[10] and the fact that they were not arm's-length transactions was troubling.

---

would be given the right to cash payment for their shares in an amount established by negotiations with Universal or by court appraisal.

[9] The agreement by the Juliuses to accept not less than 826,000 shares of the $1.06 Convertible Series was important in assuring that they would not secure any material control of Universal. Each share had one tenth of the voting power of a share of common stock, and the Juliuses agreed that at such time as the voting power of their stockholdings in Universal should exceed 8% of the total number of votes represented by the shares of the corporation, they would place the shares representing such excess in a voting trust. The trustee would be required to vote the shares held in the voting trust in the same proportion as the votes of the remaining shares of Universal voting on a proposition.

[10] Gross receivables = total receivables before deduction of balances withheld pending collection, allowance for losses, and unearned finance charges.

	Year-end			June,
	1965	*1966*	*1967*	*1968*
Gross receivables (in millions).......	$575	$622	$679	$681
Advances to subsidiaries (in millions)..................	12	21	38	48

During 1968 a complete reorganization of the company was made in response to these concerns and the finance operation was established as a subsidiary separate from all other corporate activities. (See Exhibit 9 for the new organizational structure of Universal.) Institutional lenders to the Universal Finance division also imposed a restriction that advances to the other affiliates (formerly subsidiaries of Universal Finance) could not exceed 20% of the gross receivables of the Universal Finance division (10% after 1972).

The restriction did not appear to be very burdensome, however. Universal's decision to lease computers on very conservative terms (five-year contracts with no assumed residual value), in comparison with its competitors' terms, limited the sales potential and resultant borrowing needs of this operation. And the appetite for cash of a rapidly expanding land sales operation might be held to very manageable proportions by (1) increasing all land prices by 10 to 20%, and then giving the increase back to the customer as an incentive to prepay his account and (2) development of a deferred sales commission program.[11] It was estimated that the land sales operation would need $30 million in 1969, of which $18 million would be required for repayment of existent indebtedness. An additional $30 million would be needed in 1970, of which $17 million would be for refunding.

Acquire Crescent?

Mr. Moore felt that a price of $214 million[12] for all the outstanding stock of Crescent was reasonable. Although this was considerably greater than Crescent's book value, the proposed price was less than 10 times the estimated earnings for 1969—a low earnings multiple when compared with the price-earnings ratios of 15–30 times for other land companies in 1968. (Crescent's stock had sold historically at a low earnings multiple relative to the stocks of other land developers. This resulted, in part, from the controversy surrounding the company's selling and development practices.)

---

[11] Commissions were generally fully earned when an equivalent of five months' payments were received (this often was the case at the time of the down payment). A lengthening of the period over which commissions were paid would alleviate both the cash flow problem and the problem of the salesman with short-range plans who promised anything to make a sale knowing that the problems would develop after he had collected his commission and left the company.

[12] The price of $214 million was based on an exchange of 826,000 shares of Universal voting preference stock (valued at $75 a share) and 2,539,220 shares of Universal common stock (October, 1968, market price of $60 a share) for all the outstanding stock and convertible securities of Crescent. For financial reporting purposes, it was planned to value the package of securities using the market price for Universal common stock ($30 a share) that prevailed in the spring of 1968, prior to negotiations with Crescent.

The acquisition would make Universal a major force in the rapidly growing land development business and, if the estimated earnings of $22–$25 million were realized by Crescent, would increase earnings per share of Universal substantially.

	Estimated 1969 Earnings per Share—Universal	
	Based on Common Shares Outstanding	*Based on Common Stock Outstanding and Common Stock Equivalents*
Universal without Crescent.............	$3.20	$2.80
Universal with Crescent*...............	5.60	4.05

* Assumes that the Juliuses exchange 4.4 million shares of Crescent common stock for shares of the $1.06 convertible preference series and that all remaining shares of Crescent common stock (and the convertible debentures) are exchanged for shares of common stock of Universal.

It seemed clear from the performance of Universal's common stock that the apparent benefits from the acquisition had not gone unnoticed by the investing public. Trading volume in the stock increased from an average of roughly 50,000 shares a month during the period January, 1967, through April, 1968, to 250,000 shares in May, 1968, and averaged approximately 170,000 shares a month through October. The price more than doubled during the March through October period, acting considerably more like the stocks of real estate companies than like those of finance companies. (During the March–October, 1968, period, the price index of five finance companies' stocks increased by 35%, while the price of Standard & Poor's 425 Industrials rose by less than 25%.) By October, Universal's stock had reached $62 and was selling at an earnings multiple of 23 times 1967 earnings per share.

Mr. Moore was concerned, however, because of an unfavorable reaction to the acquisition by a prominent Wall Street investment house, which felt that the proposed price was excessive in view of the uncertainties surrounding Crescent's operations. The report stressed that "a repetition of the disastrous 1968 results of Crescent would reduce Universal's earnings per share severely. Furthermore, a significant portion of the acquisition benefits seems to result from the use of convertible securities. While the probability of a rush to convert the securities seems remote, the possibility that the company, along with the rest of the corporate world, might have to report solely on a fully converted basis certainly isn't."

Mr. Moore felt that a thorough review of the proposed acquisition was necessary. It was essential that any doubts on its merits be resolved prior to submission of the acquisition terms to Universal directors for consideration at their meeting three days later.

Exhibit 1

UNIVERSAL FINANCE COMPANY (A)

RECENT ACQUISITIONS BY UNIVERSAL FINANCE COMPANY

June, 1960:	Acquired Consumer Finance Corporation of America, Denver, Colo., with 28 offices in 7 states.
February, 1961:	Acquired S. W. Coe & Co., Springfield, Ill., with 33 offices in 4 states.
August, 1961:	Acquired Securities Credit Corporation, Denver, Colo., with 14 offices in 2 states.
December, 1961:	Acquired Doty Discount Corporation, Detroit, Mich., with 17 offices in 2 states. (Also acquired an affiliate of Doty, which was involved in the mobile home finance business in 4 states.)
July, 1962:	Acquired the retail and wholesale mobile home and miscellaneous commercial and mortgage receivables from Crusader Finance Company, Dallas, Tex.
October, 1962:	Acquired Equitable Finance Corporation, Ltd., Toronto, with 5 offices in the Toronto metropolitan area.
November, 1962:	Acquired I.C.C. Loan Company, Chester, Pa., with 6 offices in the Chester-Philadelphia area.
April, 1963:	Acquired all of the receivables and business of Mobile Home Finance Company, the credit subsidiary of Detroiter Mobile Homes, Inc.
December, 1964:	Acquired Aid Investment & Discount, Inc., with 42 offices in 5 states.
October, 1965:	Acquired National Trailer Industries, Inc.
Summer, 1966:	Acquired $44 million of receivables and 105 offices of Atlantic Acceptance Corporation.
February, 1967:	Acquired Frontier Finance Company.
March, 1967:	Acquired Aetna Steel Products Corporation, of Pottsville, Pa.
March, 1967:	Acquired Kahr Bearing Corporation, of Burbank, Calif.
September, 1967:	Acquired First Finance Corporation, Chelmsford, Mass.
September, 1967:	Acquired Continental Commercial Corporation.
December, 1967:	Acquired Trump, Ltd., of Oliver, British Columbia.
March, 1968:	Acquired New Hampshire Finance Company.
April, 1968:	Acquired Dean Phipps Stores.
September, 1968:	Acquired $64 million of mortgage receivables and the long-term debt of Modern Homes Construction Company.

Pending Acquisitions as of October, 1968:

- Equitable Savings & Loan Association.
- Miller Trailers, Inc., of Bradenton, Fla.—a manufacturer of commercial trailers.
- Home and Auto Division of Eckmar Corporation—this transaction would add 58 stores.
- Commonwealth, Inc., headquartered in Portland, Oreg.—a mortgage banking company in the business of originating and servicing residential and commercial mortgages.
- Deseret Farms, a large tract (265,000 acres) of land in Central Florida (conditional upon the acquisition of Crescent).

Exhibit 2

UNIVERSAL FINANCE COMPANY (A)
OPERATING RESULTS OF UNIVERSAL FINANCE COMPANY
FOR YEARS ENDED DECEMBER 31, 1962–67
(In millions except per share data)

	*1962**	*1963**	*1964*	*1965*	*1966*	*1967*
Finance charges, interest earned	$42.00	$52.00	$57.00	$65.00	$75.00	$82.00
Operating expenses	22.00	24.00	27.00	31.00	34.00	41.00
Provision for losses	4.00	5.00	5.00	7.00	10.00	10.00
Cost of borrowings	12.00	16.00	19.00	22.00	28.00	29.00
Income of finance group before taxes	$ 4.00	$ 7.00	$ 4.87	$ 4.50	$ 2.77	$ 2.65
Provision for taxes on income			1.57	1.27	1.32	1.00
Net income of finance group			$ 3.29	$ 3.23	$ 1.45	$ 1.65
Equity in net income of:						
Casualty insurance subsidiaries			(1.09)	(1.05)	0.12	1.87
Life insurance subsidiaries			2.70	3.45	3.18	2.70
Manufacturing subsidiaries			0	0.24	1.27	1.25
Banking subsidiaries			0	(0.06)	0.04	0.03
Income before extraordinary items			$ 4.89	$ 5.82	$ 6.05	$ 7.49
Extraordinary items			0	0	1.10	1.72
Net income	$ 3.93	$ 4.44	$ 4.89	$ 5.82	$ 7.15	$ 9.21
Per share of common stock:						
Earnings before extraordinary items	$ 1.40	$ 1.53	$ 1.63	$ 1.91	$ 1.73	$ 2.00
Earnings after extraordinary items	1.40	1.53	1.63	1.91	2.21	2.65
Dividends	1.00	1.00	1.025	1.125	1.20	1.30
Market price	17–27	17–22	18–22	20–22	17–24	20–35
Price-earnings ratio†	15.7	12.7	12.3	11.0	9.3	10.4

* Financial statements for 1962 and 1963 were not available in the same format as for the years 1964 through 1967.

† Based on earnings after extraordinary items and on midpoint of the market range.

Exhibit 3

UNIVERSAL FINANCE COMPANY (A)
BALANCE SHEET OF CRESCENT CORPORATION AS OF AUGUST 31, 1968
(In millions)

ASSETS		
Cash and equivalent		$ 4
Contracts receivable*	$258	
Less: Allowance for cancellations†	31	227
Other receivables, net		3
Land and other inventories		48
Investment in unconsolidated subsidiary		2
Fixed assets		52
Other		4
Total assets		$340
LIABILITIES AND STOCKHOLDERS' EQUITY		
Notes payable		$ 2
Accounts payable		5
Accrued liabilities		5
Mortgages payable		66
Estimated cost of development of land sold‡		64
7% subordinated convertible notes		1
6½% convertible subordinated debentures		7
Other		8
		$158
Deferred federal income taxes		86
		$244
Common stockholders' equity		96
Total liabilities and stockholders' equity		$340

NOTES TO BALANCE SHEET

* An analysis of contracts receivable at August 31, 1968, is set forth below:

	Millions
Current and paid to date	$231
Past due 1 to 30 days	21
Past due 31 to 60 days	5
Past due 61 days and over	1
	$258

† The following tabulation reflects land sales cancellation statistics for the periods shown:

	Millions of Dollars			
Year Ended	*Net Land Sales*	*Contracts Receivable Balance at Year-end*	*Cancellations of Land Sales of Prior Years*	*Allowance for Cancellations at Year-end*
8/31/64	$ 85	$161	$14	$19
8/31/65	98	202	17	23
8/31/66	130	261	20	30
8/31/67	114	281	28	32
8/31/68	74	258	37	31

Note: The cancellations are of sales made in prior years (usually the year immediately preceding) and do not include sales canceled in the same year as initially recorded. Such cancellations totaled $22 million for the year ended 8/31/68; for 1967, $21 million; for 1966, $35 million; for 1965, $28 million.

‡ It is believed that inadequate provision has been made for future development costs and that the liability for the estimated cost of development of land sold is understated by $18 million.

Exhibit 4

UNIVERSAL FINANCE COMPANY (A)
Consolidated Balance Sheet of Universal Finance Company and Subsidiaries as of December 31, 1967
(In millions)

ASSETS		
Cash and equivalent		$ 47
Receivables (including installments due after one year of $283 million)	$679	
Less: Balances withheld pending collection of receivables	37	
Allowance for losses	14	
Unearned finance charges	54	
Net receivables		573
Other		4
Total current assets		$624
Investment in nonfinance subsidiaries		42
Fixed assets		1
Other		4
Total assets		$671

LIABILITIES AND NET WORTH	
Notes payable:	
Banks	$101
Other	170
Accounts payable and accruals	11
Current requirements—long-term debt	21
Other	8
Total current liabilities	$312
Senior debt	180
Subordinated debt	86
Convertible preferred stock	11
Preferred stock	34
Common stock	48
Total liabilities and net worth	$671

Exhibit 5

UNIVERSAL FINANCE COMPANY (A)

OPERATING RECORD OF CRESCENT CORPORATION FOR FISCAL YEARS ENDED AUGUST 31, 1958–68

(Dollar figures in millions)

	1958	*1959*	*1960*	*1961*	*1962*	*1963*	*1964*	*1965*	*1966*	*1967*	*1968*
Sales*	$6.60	$14.16	$26.56	$39.72	$73.60	$69.70	$94.40	$111.20	$143.90	$131.40	$95.70
Cost of sales	3.08	5.24	8.50	12.70	23.40	24.00	32.00	39.00	42.00	34.00	37.00
Selling expense	0.70	2.49	4.56	7.38	17.00	20.00	25.00	31.00	39.00	43.00	34.00
Provision for contract cancellations	1.38	2.15	3.93	5.23	8.87	10.80	13.00	15.00	20.00	21.00	26.00
General and administrative	0.56	1.23	2.89	2.86	3.79	4.10	4.80	5.70	6.30	7.80	7.70
Interest and other expenses	0.05	0.17	0.43	0.52	1.39	3.10	5.30	5.20	6.90	8.60	9.10
Interest income	0.02	0.20	0.90	1.69	3.64	5.80	7.70	9.80	13.00	15.00	16.00
Profits before taxes	$0.85	$ 3.08	$ 7.15	$12.72	$22.80	$14.00	$22.60	$ 25.20	$ 42.10	$ 32.30	$(2.80)
Deferred taxes	0.45	1.63	3.89	6.57	12.00	7.48	12.00	11.80	20.00	15.50	1.20
Profits after taxes	$0.40	$ 1.45	$ 3.26	$ 6.15	$10.80	$ 6.52	$10.60	$ 13.40	$ 22.10	$ 16.80	$(1.60)
Per share data:											
Earnings	$0.06	$ 0.20	$ 0.42	$ 0.74	$ 1.18	$ 0.71	$ 1.14	$ 1.43	$ 2.31	$ 1.75	$(0.17)
Dividends	0	0	0	0	0	0	0	0	0	0	0
Market price†	—	—	—	—	$4–16	$4–7	$4–6	$5–12	$7–13	$7–13	$8–23
Price-earnings ratio‡	—	—	—	—	8.5	7.7	4.4	5.9	4.3	5.7	
Book value	—	—	$ 0.82	$ 1.51	$ 2.68	$ 3.38	$ 4.49	$ 5.90	$ 8.24	$ 9.97	
Percent of sales:											
Cost of sales	47.0%	37.0%	32.0%	32.0%	31.0%	34.0%	34.0%	35.0%	29.0%	26.0%	39.0%
Selling expense	11.0	18.0	17.0	18.0	23.0	29.0	27.0	28.0	27.0	33.0	35.0
Provision for contract cancellations	21.0	15.0	15.0	13.0	12.0	15.0	14.0	14.0	14.0	16.0	27.0
General and administrative	8.5	8.7	10.9	7.1	5.1	5.8	5.1	5.1	4.4	5.9	8.0
Interest and other expenses	0.8	1.2	1.6	1.3	1.9	4.4	5.6	4.7	4.8	6.6	9.5§
Interest income	0.3	1.4	3.4	4.2	4.9	8.3	8.2	8.8	9.0	11.4	16.7
Pretax earnings	12.0	21.5	26.9	32.8	31.9	20.1	22.5	22.0	29.8	23.9	(1.8)

* Revenues and expenses include products other than land.
† Calendar year.
‡ Based on midpoint of market range.
§ Includes sales discounts, which increased sharply in 1968.

Exhibit 6

UNIVERSAL FINANCE COMPANY (A)
LAND INVENTORY OF CRESCENT CORPORATION AT AUGUST 31, 1968

Location	*Total Acreage*	*Acres Sold*	*Development Costs* — *Total* (In Millions)	*Development Costs* — *Spent to Date* (In Millions)	*Families in Residence*
FLORIDA*					
Cape Coral	55,500	37,100	$86	$25	3,800
Golden Gate	2,500	1,400 }	$30	$11	295
Golden Gate Estates	105,000	95,200 }			
Golden Gate Acres	3,800	3,000	Sold as unimproved land		
Remuda Ranch Grants	68,300	25,900	Sold as unimproved land		
River Ranch Acres	50,100	31,700	Sold as unimproved land		
Miscellaneous	70,540	0	No present plans for development		
ARIZONA					
Rio Rico	55,000	0			
Miscellaneous	10,600	0			
NEW MEXICO	51,000	0			
UTAH	5,700	0			
MARYLAND	700	0			
BRITISH HONDURAS	95,100	0			

* At August 31, 1968, approximately $93 million of contracts receivable had been assigned under bonding agreements between Crescent and two Florida counties, providing for completion of development on dates approximately coinciding with full collection of applicable installment sales contracts.

Exhibit 7

UNIVERSAL FINANCE COMPANY (A)
FORECASTS OF SALES AND EARNINGS OF CRESCENT CORPORATION AND OF THE IMPACT OF ITS ACQUISITION ON PER SHARE EARNINGS OF UNIVERSAL FINANCE COMPANY

Year	*Crescent** — *Sales* (In Millions)	*Crescent** — *Net Income*† (In Millions)	*Universal Excluding Crescent* — *Net Income* (In Millions)	*Universal Excluding Crescent* — *E.P.S.*‡	*Universal Including Crescent* — *Net Income* (In Millions)	*Universal Including Crescent* — *E.P.S.*§
1963	$ 69.7	$ 6.57				
1964	94.4	10.60				
1965	111.2	13.44				
1966	143.9	22.08				
1967	131.4	16.81				
1968	95.7	(1.65)				
1969	187.0	25.21	$13.0	$2.80	$37.66	$4.05
1970	213.5	30.07	16.2	3.47	46.27	4.98
1971	230.5	33.85	19.3	4.14	53.15	5.72
1972	258.5	39.58	22.3	4.79	61.88	6.67
1973	283.5	44.21	25.8	5.53	70.01	7.53

* Assumes that the acquisition is treated as a purchase for reporting purposes and that the excess of the cost of the Universal stock over its adjusted cash value will be regarded as permanent goodwill, not subject to amortization.

† The forecasts for 1969–73 assume acquisition of Crescent by Universal.

‡ Earnings per share are on a fully diluted basis, based on 4,658,000 shares and share equivalents.

§ Earnings per share are on a fully diluted basis, based on 9,287,000 shares and share equivalents, of which 4,629,000 shares are assumed to be issued for all outstanding shares and convertible securities of Crescent.

Exhibit 8

UNIVERSAL FINANCE COMPANY (A)

IMPACT OF EXCHANGE OFFER ON STOCKHOLDERS OF CRESCENT CORPORATION

	Applicable to One Share of	
	Universal Common	*Crescent Common*
Historical data:		
Cash dividends	$1.50	0
Earnings reported:		
Before issuance of shares reserved for conversion of convertible securities:		
1967 twelve-month period	2.65	1.75
1968 twelve-month period	2.85	(0.17)
Assuming conversion of all outstanding convertible securities:		
1967 twelve-month period	2.05	1.59
1968 twelve-month period	2.39	(0.15)
Pro forma Universal and Crescent assuming issuance in exchange for Crescent (including shares presently reserved for convertible debt):		
A. 2,033,000 shares of Universal Voting Preference Stock $1.06 Convertible Series:		
Cash dividends:		
Before conversion of $1.06 Convertible Series	1.50	0.20
After conversion of $1.06 Convertible Series	1.50	0.71
Earnings:		
Before conversion (treating the $1.06 Convertible Series as a nonresidual security):		
1967 twelve-month period	7.54	0.20[a]
1968 twelve-month period	1.10	0.20[a]
Assuming conversion of $1.06 Convertible Series:		
1967 twelve-month period	2.84	1.35
1968 twelve month period	0.68	.32
Assuming conversion of all convertible securities:		
1967 twelve-month period	2.52	1.20
1968 twelve-month period	0.68	0.32
B. 826,000 shares of Universal Voting Preference Stock $1.06 Convertible Series and 2,539,220 shares of Universal Common Stock:[b]		
Cash dividends:		
$1.06 Convertible Series	—	0.20
Common stock	1.50	0.62
After conversion of $1.06 Convertible Series	1.50	0.71
Earnings:		
Before conversion of $1.06 Convertible Series (treating the $1.06 Convertible Series as a nonresidual security):		
1967 twelve-month period	4.18	1.74
1968 twelve-month period	0.92	0.38
Assuming conversion of $1.06 Convertible Series:		
1967 twelve-month period	3.10	1.37
1968 twelve-month period	0.78	0.35
Assuming conversion of all convertible securities:		
1967 twelve-month period	2.72	1.20
1968 twelve-month period	0.77	0.34

[a] Amount shown is dividend on Voting Preference Stock $1.06 Convertible Series.

[b] The principal stockholders of Crescent have agreed to exchange 4,383,617 Crescent common shares for 826,000 shares of Universal Voting Preference Stock $1.06 Convertible Series. If no other Crescent stockholders elect to exchange their shares for Voting Preference Stock, 2,539,220 shares of Universal Common Stock would be issued in exchange for the remaining Crescent shares.

Exhibit 8—Continued

MARKET INFORMATION

	0.416 Share Universal Common		1 Share Crescent Common	
	High	*Low*	*High*	*Low*
1967:				
First quarter	$10.14	$ 8.16	$12.00	$ 6.83
Second quarter	11.54	9.41	13.75	9.00
Third quarter	13.83	10.45	9.83	7.75
Fourth quarter	14.56	11.02	9.38	6.63
1968:				
First quarter	14.56	11.65	10.13	7.63
Second quarter	17.89	12.27	17.50	8.00
Third quarter	25.90	16.85	23.75	14.63

Exhibit 9

UNIVERSAL FINANCE COMPANY (A)
ORGANIZATIONAL STRUCTURE OF UNIVERSAL FINANCE COMPANY AFTER REORGANIZATION EFFECTIVE JULY 1, 1968, AND INCLUDING PROPOSED ACQUISITION OF CRESCENT

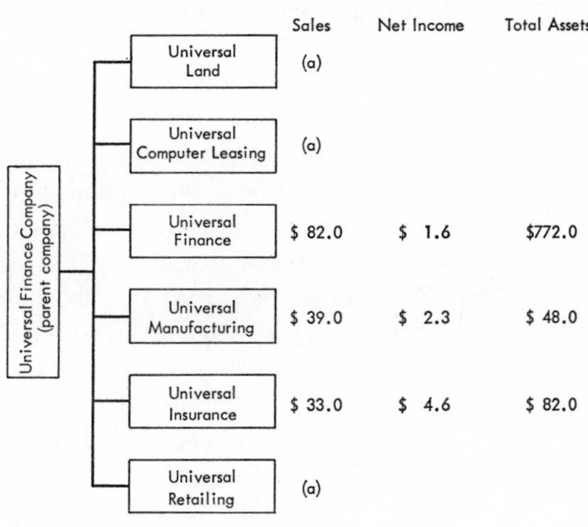

a) Not a part of Universal in 1967.

UNIVERSAL FINANCE COMPANY (B)

Ben Moore, president of Universal Finance Company, was convinced that the acquisition of Crescent Corporation made sense in terms of both its "fit" and its favorable impact on Universal's growth prospects and valuation. He was also certain that the Julius brothers, founders and majority stockholders of Crescent Corporation, must have no control of the future operations of the combined companies. Their reputations in financial circles and with the Florida regulatory authorities were extremely bad. (See Universal Finance Company (A).) The future financing programs and operations would be jeopardized by any continued association of the Juliuses with the merged companies.

It was easy to keep the Juliuses out of the management, but minimizing their voting power was more difficult. If allowed to exchange their shares of Crescent stock for common stock in Universal, the Julius brothers would control over 25% of the outstanding stock of the combined companies. They would be the largest stockholders by a wide margin and could exercise considerable control over the company's future operations. This was unacceptable to Mr. Moore, to sources of financing, and to the Florida Land Sales Board.

Mr. Moore decided to offer two types of securities to the shareholders of Crescent. Under the terms of the proposed merger, each share of Crescent common stock would be entitled, at the election of the holder thereof, to 0.416 of a share of Universal common stock or 0.188 of a share of Universal's voting preference stock $1.06 Convertible Series. The $1.06 Convertible Series would have a stated value of $75, would be entitled to cumulative dividends of $1.06 per annum, would be convertible after three years into 2.53 shares of common stock, and would have one tenth of a vote per share.

The Juliuses, who owned or controlled beneficially approximately 53% of the 10 million shares of Crescent common stock outstanding, agreed to convert not less than 4.4 million shares into the $1.06 Convertible Series. Furthermore, at such a time as the voting power of their stockholdings in Universal exceeded 8% of the total number of votes represented by the shares of Universal, they would place the shares representing such excess into a voting trust. The trustee would be required to vote the shares held in the voting trust in the same proportion as the votes of the remaining shares of Universal voting on a proposition.

The form of the transaction satisfied the Julius brothers' demand that the exchange be tax-free.[1] The terms of the $1.06 convertible preference series also compensated the Juliuses for the loss of dividend income resulting from their acceptance of the $1.06 preference stock instead of the common stock. The economics of accepting each of the two exchange offers and holding the securities for three years is shown below.[2] The high personal tax rates of the Juliuses made the preference issue especially attractive to them:

	Exchange One Share of Crescent Common Stock for Either (1) or (2)	
	(1) 0.188 Shares of Universal $1.06 Preference Stock	*(2) 0.416 Shares of Universal Common Stock*
Dividends		
Year 1	$ 0.20	$ 0.62
Year 2	0.20	0.62*
Year 3	0.20	0.62*
	$ 0.60	$ 1.86
Shares of common stock	0.476†	0.416
Price of common stock‡	$30.00	$30.00
Value of common stock holdings	$14.28	$12.48
Value of dividends + common	$14.88	$14.34

* Assumes no increase in the common dividend rate.
† Assumes conversion of the preference stock into common stock at the end of the third year.
‡ Price of the common stock of Universal at the time negotiations commenced.

The use of convertible preference stock, combined with the restriction on the voting rights of the Julius brothers, insured that they would exercise no control over the operations of the combined companies. The convertible preference also would result in higher reported earnings per share than if the transaction were effected solely for the common stock, as shown in the following figures:

ESTIMATED 1969 EARNINGS PER SHARE—UNIVERSAL*

Based on Common Shares Outstanding†	*Based on Common Stock Outstanding and Common Stock Equivalents*
$5.60	$4.05

* See Exhibit 7 of Universal Finance Company (A).
† Treats the $1.06 preference as a nonresidual security.

The significance of the impact of the $1.06 preference on earnings per share seemed small, however. It was clear in the fall of 1968 that new accounting rules proposed by the Accounting Principles Board soon would require Universal to report on a fully diluted basis. Furthermore, investors were in-

[1] Under the Internal Revenue Code, the acquiring corporation must offer voting stock for the stock of the acquired corporation to qualify the transaction as a tax-free Type B acquisition. A capital gains tax would be levied at the time of the transaction if (*a*) the $1.06 convertible preference series did not have voting rights or (*b*) the shares of Crescent were acquired for cash or in exchange for a debenture of Universal.

[2] The $1.06 preference stock could be converted into common stock after three years.

creasingly wary of potential earnings per share dilution from convertible securities, and stocks seemed to trade on a fully diluted basis.

The plan to curtail sharply the control of the Juliuses might involve a cost. It might be necessary to account for the acquisition as a purchase since two of the three primary criteria for its treatment as a pooling of interests were not met. Specifically, the elimination of the Juliuses from the management of the combined companies violated the test of management continuity, and the restriction of voting rights would not satisfy the requirement of ownership continuity.

Substantial accounting differences would result from handling the acquisition of Crescent as a pooling of interests, rather than a purchase. Under pooling-of-interest accounting, the assets and liabilities of the two firms would be combined at their book values and operating results of prior years would have to be restated to reflect the combined operations. In contrast, under purchase accounting, Universal would not be required to restate the results of prior years; but the assets of Crescent would be brought onto the books of Universal at the market price for which Crescent was acquired. The market value of Universal's securities to be exchanged for Crescent's securities exceeded the book value of Crescent by some $66 million.[3] Discussion with the SEC led to an agreement to amortize the $66 million of goodwill at an annual rate of $2.3 million. The $2.3 million charge would not be deductible for tax purposes.

Mr. Moore was very uncertain whether Universal's auditors and the SEC would agree to accounting for the acquisition of Crescent as a pooling of interests. In fact, it was not clear to him that he should even attempt to persuade them to permit a pooling. The required restatement of operating results of prior years under pooling-of-interest accounting seemed as painful as a $2.3 million annual charge against earnings over the next 29 years as shown below:

REPORTED EARNINGS PER SHARE—UNIVERSAL

	1964	*1965*	*1966*	*1967*	*1968 Est.*
Purchase accounting	$1.63	$1.91	$2.21	$2.65	$2.85
Pooling-of-interest accounting	1.44	1.94	3.06	2.52	0.68

[3] The securities of Universal Finance Company were valued as of early spring 1968 when the negotiations commenced.

ROGERS, WILDE & COMPANY (Abridged)

On the morning of November 14, 1960, Messrs. Robert Woodruff and Sheldon Wylie of the large New York investment banking house of Rogers, Wilde & Company were attempting to hammer out a pricing recommendation to be made to the president of the Pennsylvania Electronics Company (PENELCO) that afternoon. Mr. Wylie, partner in charge of Syndication, had the final responsibility for deciding at what price the firm would be willing to underwrite. Mr. Woodruff was also concerned since his buying department had initiated and developed the contact and carried on the negotiations with PENELCO throughout the preparation of the new issue. They both realized that contingent upon their success in arriving at a price acceptable to both the company and Rogers, Wilde, the Securities and Exchange Commission would clear PENELCO's Registration Statement the following day, thus permitting the public offering to be made on the over-the-counter market on Wednesday, November 16.

HISTORY OF PENELCO

PENELCO was founded in 1923 in Pittsburgh, Pennsylvania, by Gustav Trumbilee, a Swedish-born engineer who had developed a new vacuum tube which met with immediate success in the burgeoning radio receiver industry. Sales of the vacuum tube grew rapidly in spite of the economic depression of the 1930's. Profits had reached $260,000 on sales of $2.5 million by 1934, when the company was incorporated as the Pennsylvania Electronics Company. In the years leading up to World War II, PENELCO sustained modest, continuing growth and undertook substantial research activities in an effort to broaden its line of radio parts. By 1940 sales totaled $7 million with profits of $565,000.

With the commencement of World War II, PENELCO, along with others in the electronics industry, turned its efforts to the development and production of a variety of military communications equipment. During the war, production facilities and employees increased threefold, and of the company's sales of $26.5 million in 1944, over 90% were the direct result of research and development conducted by the company's own engineers and technicians. In 1944 Gustav Trumbilee died and was succeeded as head of PENELCO by his son, Ralph, a graduate of the Massachusetts Institute of Technology and the Wharton School of Finance and Commerce at the University of Pennsylvania.

Postwar developments

It was obvious to PENELCO's management that postwar demand for radio tubes would utilize only a fraction of the company's war-expanded facilities and that at this level of sales it would not be possible to support the research team which PENELCO had assembled during the war years. There appeared to be two courses of action open to PENELCO. Either the company could permanently contract its operations to a size commensurate with the demand for radio tubes, or it could attempt to hold together its production and research facilities by diversifying into other, related areas. Ralph Trumbilee chose to follow the latter course. The company thereupon embarked on the development and manufacture of a variety of electronic components for other manufacturers of end products. These efforts proved unprofitable, however, and between 1945 and 1948 sales fell by almost 60%—to $11 million—and the company suffered repeated losses, which had grown to an annual rate of $1.3 million by December, 1948.

When the United States moved to rearm in 1948, PENELCO began to compete aggressively for defense contracts. By 1951, sales had rebounded to $19 million (mainly as the result of several large research and development contracts awarded to PENELCO by the Navy) and the company recorded a profit of almost $875,000 for that year. Then, too, sales of TV components began to increase as the sales of TV receivers boomed. By the end of 1959, sales had reached an annual rate of $44 million with profits of $600,000.

Although the company had continued to manufacture items for the radio and television receiver industry in recent years, the bulk of its efforts had been directed toward the development and manufacture of components for electronic communication equipment, aircraft, guided missiles, and computers. PENELCO's product line in this area could be divided into four categories:

1. Microwave equipment—signal generators, power meters, devices for waveguard and coaxial systems. These were used in research, production and maintenance of microwave communications, radar, air navigation, and guided missile control.
2. Electronic counters and frequency measurement equipment, which were used in nuclear research and industrial automation.
3. Oscillators and vacuum tube voltmeters—essential components used in all areas of electronics.
4. Oscilloscopes—another basic tool. PENELCO entered this field in 1955 and believed it promised substantial volume in the future.

Although a number of competitors produced one or more of its lines, in 1960 PENELCO was one of the largest producers of its types of electronic components in the United States and 40% of its gross sales comprised components not being manufactured by any other company. In fact, the PENELCO name had become almost generically associated with certain types of oscillators and vacuum tube voltmeters, the development of which PENELCO had pioneered. The company's annual expenditure for research and development had approximated 6% of sales in recent years, and in 1960 there were 120 engineers and technicians employed in the research division.

The company's backlog of orders as of June 30, 1960, aggregated $7.5 million as compared with $8.9 million for the same date a year earlier. The percentages of total sales under government prime contracts and subcontracts during the past five years had respectively remained at approximately 6% and 64%. Almost all of these contracts were subject to renegotiation. In addition, a considerable part of the remainder of the company's sales could be directly attributed to the defense program.

The company's products were distributed throughout the United States, in Canada, and in a number of foreign countries. In 1959 sales were made to more than 5,500 customers through 42 factory representatives and field sales engineering offices as well as 510 distributors. Although the company's 25 largest customers accounted for 40% of sales, no single customer accounted for more than 10% of total sales in 1959. Foreign sales amounted to approximately 4% of total sales in 1959, and to approximately 5% in the six months' period ended June 30, 1960. The company had begun negotiations to establish a manufacturing subsidiary in Luxembourg to serve the Common Market and other European countries. Its U.S. manufacturing facilities were located in Pennsylvania, California, and Missouri.

Capitalization

In 1960 the capital stock of PENELCO—5,250 shares of voting common stock with a par value of $10 per share—was held in four equal lots by the surviving children of Gustav Trumbilee. Ralph, 45—the only heir who was presently active in the business—and his younger sister, Mrs. Maralyn Trumbilee Baker, 37, were retaining their full quarter interest in PENELCO. Ralph's older brother, Dr. Edward Trumbilee, 49, and his older sister, Miss Anne Trumbilee, 51, had determined to dispose of approximately 27% of their holdings (354 shares each).

Aside from the original capital of the company, all subsequent funds to finance PENELCO's growth had been raised through short-term and long-term borrowing and through the issuance in 1949 of $2 million of 6% cumulative preferred stock, which had been retired in 1955. In 1960 the company had notes outstanding with the Rocky Mountains Life Insurance Company totaling $4.2 million, at an interest rate of 5½% and repayable in installments extending to 1974. The covenants of the loans required that:

1. Working capital must be maintained at a minimum of $5.7 million.
2. Dividends on common stock were to be limited to 50% of aggregate earnings since the date of the initial loan agreement (January 1, 1957).

It had been the policy of the PENELCO board of directors to declare a modest yearly dividend for the benefit of those shareholders in the Trumbilee family who depended either completely or in part on these dividends for their livelihood. PENELCO's management intended, however, to end the cash dividend payments entirely now that Edward and Anne Trumbilee were diversifying their portfolios, presumably into securities some of which would have income-producing features. The board believed that without the cash drain of dividend payments in the future, the company could expect to finance all of its future expansion from internally generated funds and from the present level of long-term debt financing.

Exhibit 1 presents the comparative income statements of PENELCO for the years ended December 31, 1955–59, and for the six months ended June 30, 1960. Exhibit 2 presents PENELCO's balance sheet for June 30, 1960.

BACKGROUND OF ROGERS, WILDE'S ASSOCIATION WITH PENELCO

Mr. Woodruff had first learned of the company's plans to float a secondary issue at a dinner dance given in December, 1958, in Pittsburgh in honor of the eldest daughter of PENELCO's president, Ralph Trumbilee. Mr. Trumbilee and Mr. Woodruff had been casually acquainted for some time, and as they chatted together during a lull in the evening, Mr. Trumbilee mentioned his family's interest in marketing a portion of its holdings of PENELCO stock.

"You see," he explained, "My brother Ed and sister Anne have been chafing for quite a while at having all their eggs in one basket, so to speak. At one time I had thought of trying to buy some of their PENELCO stock from them but I just couldn't raise that much cash. Now, I'm beginning to feel that it wouldn't be such a bad idea to put some of the stock on the open market, as long as control isn't threatened. It would help to put a value on our holdings for estate tax purposes, and should we want to sell some more of our stock in the future, there'd be a ready market for it.

"They've asked me to handle the details for them and, quite frankly, I feel like a babe in the woods on these matters. I want to do right by them—get them the best deal I can—but I just don't know where to start!"

Mr. Woodruff expressed considerable interest in helping Mr. Trumbilee in this matter and they agreed to get together to discuss the matter further after the Christmas holidays.

When they met in early January at PENELCO's Pittsburgh headquarters Mr. Woodruff collected a variety of information and impressions from PENELCO's management, legal counsel, and public accountants. An examination of financial data showed a downturn in earnings for 1958, but the company executives felt that this was attributable largely to the recession of that year. By the end of March Mr. Woodruff and his associates at Rogers, Wilde felt sufficiently familiar with PENELCO's operations and were encouraged enough by Mr. Trumbilee's optimism over 1959 earnings prospects to prepare a confidential memorandum containing a financing proposal for the consideration of PENELCO's board of directors (see Appendix). The memorandum recommended that in view of the current favorable reception for issues of this kind, the company move quickly to permit the public offering to be made as soon as possible.

Not long thereafter, however, Mr. Woodruff received PENELCO's unaudited income statement for the first quarter of 1959. Not only had the upturn in profits predicted by Mr. Trumbilee failed to materialize, but earnings were actually considerably below those of the same period in 1958. PENELCO attributed the disappointing profits to a slower-than-anticipated recovery from the recent recession and to an unforeseen delay of a congressional appropriation for a defense contract on which the company had been counting heavily. The company's executives also disclosed that a strike in connection with the expiration of a contract with one of its unions in June of that year might be unavoidable and that considerable expense would be incurred when the company moved some of its manufacturing operations from Pittsburgh to a new plant being built in St. Louis. In view of these developments, Mr. Woodruff advised PENELCO to postpone consideration of a public issue for an indefinite period.

PREPARATIONS FOR A PUBLIC ISSUE

Recalling a recommendation he had made in his recent financing memorandum, Mr. Woodruff urged PENELCO to undertake a thorough housecleaning during the current fiscal year, writing off all anticipated extraordinary expenses so as to allow the following year's operations to reflect a hoped-for upturn in earnings.

The company thereupon undertook a drive to reduce costs and overhead, although the savings effected were not expected to be reflected in increased earnings until the following year. In June, 1959, one of the AFL–CIO industrial unions struck the company's Pittsburgh plants for nine weeks, until arbitration finally settled the issues in conflict.

In November of that year the company finished construction of a microwave plant in St. Louis and during November and December completed the transfer of 160 employees, their families, and a considerable amount of heavy machinery to the new plant location.

When Mr. Woodruff received the unaudited year-end operating statement from PENELCO's treasurer in January, 1960, he noted that the figures were every bit as depressed as he had anticipated (see Exhibit 1). Shortly after this he recommended to Mr. Trumbilee that PENELCO engage a firm of nationally known auditors to assist the company's regular public accountants in handling the intricacies associated with the preparation for a new public issue. In proposing this move to Mr. Trumbilee in a telephone conversation on January 16, Mr. Woodruff explained that potential investors felt more ready to accept the word of an accounting firm with a national reputation than the certification of an unfamiliar, local firm, no matter what the quality of its work. When Mr. Trumbilee expressed concern at the considerable extra expense involved in such a move, Mr. Woodruff assured him that it would be more than offset by the better reception which the stock would receive when it was placed on the market. In the end, Mr. Trumbilee agreed to call in De Tocqueville, Hobbes, & Company, a nationally known public accounting firm which had performed similar services for several other Rogers, Wilde clients in the past.

Decision to go ahead

In early April Mr. Woodruff received unaudited earnings figures for the first quarter of 1960 and he was sufficiently encouraged by their upward trend to recommend resumption of active preparation for a public issue of PENELCO's stock. During April and May, representatives of the PENELCO management and their legal counsel, Bodine & Tutt, met with representatives from Rogers, Wilde and their legal counsel, Van Roden & Tindell, to discuss the financing proposal that should be made to PENELCO's board, to begin preparation of the Registration Statement, and to draw up the Agreement among Underwriters.

Mr. Woodruff had also discussed with PENELCO's management the relative comparability to its various competitors. After much reflection, Mr. Trumbilee had presented the investment banker with a list of other companies, in order of their relative similarity: (1) Amphenol-Borg, (2) AMP, (3) Burndy, and (4) Thomas & Betts. The financial data that had been assembled on these and other related companies was now on Mr. Woodruff's desk (Exhibit 3).

In June, 1960, PENELCO's board met and adopted substantially the same plan of refinancing proposed by Mr. Woodruff in his memorandum of a year earlier (Appendix). At the time of the board's action, Mr. Woodruff reminded Mr. Trumbilee that the stretch-out in the filing period for the Registration Statement made it even more likely that it would be necessary to make another adjustment in the company's capital structure in order to take account of subsequent changes in market conditions.

During the summer months Mr. Woodruff had numerous telephone talks with Mr. Trumbilee. Almost invariably the latter at some point in the conversation would bring up the subject of price. Mr. Woodruff had on all occasions sought to avoid making a price estimation that might be construed by Mr. Trumbilee to be a moral or verbal commitment on the part of Rogers, Wilde. Mr. Woodruff remembered one such conversation in which he had attempted to explain the intricacies of the pricing decision and the impossibility of making any sort of firm price estimate until just before the stock was to be offered to the public. It had started when Mr. Trumbilee had asked, "Bob, what do you suppose we'd get for the stock if it were offered tomorrow? I mean, the market looks pretty good, doesn't it?"

MR. WOODRUFF: Yes, Ralph, the over-the-counter market is still pretty strong. But remember two things. First, we won't be ready to go to the market for some time yet. A lot can happen between now and then to change the whole picture. Second, it doesn't matter that you and I know that PENELCO is basically a very strong company with excellent long-term prospects. Its earnings record in the past couple of years just hasn't been good—and that's one of the biggest things that potential investors will be looking at!

MR. TRUMBILEE: Okay, okay, but just take a guess. Say we were going to issue 125,000 shares tomorrow. What would we get?

MR. WOODRUFF: Ralph, I wouldn't LET you issue that small a block! As I stated in that memo I wrote last year, the very *minimum* number of shares that you'll have to issue in order to have an adequate floating supply is between 150,000 and 200,000, and frankly I'd feel a hell of a lot better about 200,000.

MR. TRUMBILEE: That means a further stock split, huh? You know, some of the lower priced new issues are selling awfully well these days. Because it's important to us for a number of reasons that the after market be strong, maybe we should think about pricing the shares at around $4 or $5 each. At a price in this range we could increase the size of the issue considerably without giving away a larger block of the equity.

MR. WOODRUFF: Well, it's true that the dollar price range is extremely important, but I can tell you right now that Rogers, Wilde wouldn't want PENELCO to be associated with a low-priced "doggie" issue such as that! No, I think that what we want to do is price it in the dollar range of 12 and 20—which is more in keeping with PENELCO's prestige—and still ensure that there will be a sufficient floating supply to make an active after market in the stock.

MR. TRUMBILEE: Have you given any more thought to what price-earnings ratio to use in our case?

MR. WOODRUFF: Frankly, no. We're waiting for De Tocqueville's preliminary earnings figures for the first half of 1960 (Exhibit 1). As I have said before, PENELCO is in a glamorous industry but hasn't had the explosive record of sales and earnings increases which has characterized the real electronics market leaders, such as Litton and Texas Instruments.

If a company has a good growth record it can get an excellent price in a rising market and even in a falling market you can still do pretty well. If it has "up and down" growth—but can satisfactorily explain the dips—then it can usually get a good price in a rising market but may run into trouble in a falling market. Once we determine how PENELCO fits into the overall market picture, we'll get a price-earnings multiple. Generally, it should be slightly below the multiple that would apply to a company that is already publicly held and has withstood the test of the open market.

At a luncheon meeting held in Pittsburgh in late August, Mr. Sheldon Wylie, the Rogers, Wilde partner in charge of Syndication, was introduced by Mr. Woodruff to Mr. Trumbilee and other members of PENELCO's management. Mr. Wylie explained to the group that now that the proposed stock offering was progressing towards a definite public issue date, he was entering the picture to give advice on further refinements in the pricing decision and to marshal the efforts of a group of underwriters to sell the issue when the public offering was actually made.

Gross spread

During the meeting Mr. Trumbilee queried both Mr. Woodruff and Mr. Wylie more closely on the breakdown of the gross spread. He reminded the investment bankers that Mr. Woodruff's memo had estimated that the spread would fall somewhere between 6½% and 7½% of the dollar value of the issue, and he wondered how this would be broken down into expenses and profits. Wasn't it possible that because of the good reception by the market for this type of security, the expenses of placing the issue could be reduced?

Mr. Wylie explained that the three main components of the gross spread were (1) the selling concession, (2) the management fee, and (3) the underwriting profit. The selling concession tended to vary with the anticipated difficulty in placing the issue. The management fee, in Mr. Woodruff's experience, had tended to equal 15% of the gross spread; and the underwriting profit was whatever was left over after these two items had been covered. Mr. Woodruff hastened to point out, however, that out of this remainder had to be deducted legal fees, advertising expenses, and applicable taxes, which were prorated to each underwriter in proportion to the size of its participation in the issue.

Mr. Woodruff added that at this point it was too early to tell how much of an incentive would be needed to induce the security salesmen to put forth their best efforts to place the stock with investors. He anticipated, however, that the gross spread would still fall within the 6½% to 7½% range.

On September 23, the stockholders of PENELCO authorized a 50% stock dividend to become effective as soon as state regulatory authorities could give their approval. The stock dividend was accomplished by issuing an additional 525,000 shares of $1 par value common stock and decreasing retained earnings by an equivalent amount. Mr. Woodruff had recommended this move in order to put the offering into what he believed was the most acceptable dollar price range and to provide a sufficient number of shares for the first offering (210,000) to maintain an active secondary market in the securities.

Formation of syndicate

Mr. Wylie had no trouble in recruiting an underwriting syndicate, since PENELCO was a well-known and respected name in an industry that had been surrounded with an aura of glamour by the investing public in recent years. Rather, his job had been to pick and choose among the many firms who wanted to be included. For a few days following the filing of the Registration Statement on September 26 and the immediate newspaper reports thereof, Mr. Wylie had bided his time, waiting to see which firms had sufficient interest to approach Rogers, Wilde for a participation in the offering on their own initiative. Then, on the following Friday, he made a tentative list of underwriters for the syndicate and obtained Mr. Trumbilee's approval. This list included some of the firms that had approached Rogers, Wilde specifically about the PENELCO issue and others that had not approached Rogers, Wilde but that Mr. Wylie felt certain would want to be included.

The difficult task of working out the details of the agreements between PENELCO and the underwriters, the Agreement among Underwriters, and the processing of the issue through the Securities and Exchange Commission proceeded normally. On November 11, with SEC clearance all but assured within four or five days, Mr. Wylie began stepping up the selling pressure on the other members of the syndicate. Although federal statute permitted the solicitation of "indications of interest" in the period between the filing of the Registration Statement and its final clearance by the SEC, no firm orders for the securities could be solicited by anyone connected with the syndicate. It was important to the successful placement of the issue, however, that enough bona fide "indications of interest" be accumulated to ensure the quick sale of all of the securities once the public offering was actually made.

Mr. Wylie was almost constantly on the telephone in these last few days, attempting to ascertain the extent of the "indications of interest" which each underwriter had secured to date. His job had not been made easier by the fact that security salesmen were by nature overoptimistic and tended to give glowing forecasts of sales, which often bore little or no relation to fact. Mr. Wylie had been forced to press them until he had obtained what he thought was a fairly realistic appraisal of the securities that would actually be sold. Then, with these estimates in front of him, he had juggled the shares among the underwriters and selling group members in an effort to satisfy excess demand in some firms and to move uncommitted securities assigned to others. He was somewhat disturbed to find that several of the syndicate's leading underwriters were now asking to be dropped from the selling group[1] altogether, leaving them only their participation in the syndicate itself to sell.

Coming to a pricing decision

On Monday morning, November 14, both Mr. Woodruff and Mr. Wylie felt that a final pricing decision should be reached that day since SEC clearance of the Registration Statement could be obtained on Tuesday afternoon if the final price amendment had been filed with the SEC on Tuesday morning. On Monday a three-way telephone hookup was arranged between Messrs. Trumbilee, Woodruff, and Wylie, during which the following conversation took place:

MR. WYLIE: The enthusiasm for this issue has really cooled down during the past week or so, Ralph [Trumbilee]. I've really had to beat the bushes trying to get the stuff placed.

MR. TRUMBILEE: What do the other underwriters say about the price, Shel [Wylie]?

MR. WYLIE: Well, you see, we don't solicit pricing suggestions from anyone else since we feel that it is primarily the concern of the issuing company and the managing firm of the syndicate. The other underwriters can assume that if Rogers, Wilde is taking a major position, then it'll recommend a price at which it can

[1] A "selling group" was composed of selected dealers who received a smaller concession than did the members of the syndicate and were not subject to the same liability that bound the underwriters. The group was usually composed of any members of the National Association of Securities Dealers who had requested inclusion. Occasionally, however, the manager used the group as a way to include a relative's firm or a small regional broker who had done business with the managing firm in the past but whom the manager did not, for one reason or another, want to include in the underwriting group itself. Sometimes the selling group included members of the underwriting group who wanted a larger number of shares than the manager was willing to give them as members of the syndicate.

place its shares. And if Rogers, Wilde can place its shares, so can the other syndicate members. Of course, we're glad to listen to any pricing ideas the other syndicate members want to offer. I've gotten a lot of this type of advice in the past few days and it's all tended to follow the same theme: don't try to price this one too full in the present uncertain market.

MR. TRUMBILEE: I understand the problems you guys are facing but look at my side of it for a minute. I've promised my brother and sister that I'd get the very best deal I could for them. I chose to put myself in your hands with the confidence that you'd get the very best price possible in the current market. What I'm afraid of is that once the stock hits the market it'll rise to a premium considerably above the offering price and then my family'll be on my neck! Remember, every 50 cents of variation in the price means a $100,000 difference in the proceeds to them!

Mr. Woodruff expressed appreciation for Mr. Trumbilee's position and promised to call him back later in the day with a final pricing recommendation. In the meantime, he explained, both he and Mr. Wylie wanted to review the available data once more before coming to a price recommendation.

As additional aids in the pricing decision, the two men had additional

Exhibit 1

ROGERS, WILDE & COMPANY
COMPARATIVE INCOME STATEMENTS OF PENELCO FOR
YEARS ENDED DECEMBER 31, 1955–59, AND SIX MONTHS ENDED JUNE 30, 1960
(In millions except per share data)

	1955	*1956*	*1957*	*1958*	*1959*	*Six Months Ended June 30, 1960 (Unaudited)*
Gross sales, less returns and allowances	$20.3	$26.1	$36.6	$34.7	$44.0	$24.0
Cost of goods sold	14.1	18.1	25.7	24.0	33.9	16.2
Net sales	$ 6.2	$ 8.0	$10.9	$10.7	$10.1	$ 7.8
Selling and administrative expenses	4.2	5.2	6.7	7.2	8.7	5.7
Income before federal income tax	$ 2.0	$ 2.7	4.1	$ 3.4	$ 1.3	$ 2.0
Provision for federal income tax	1.0	1.4	2.1	1.7	0.7	1.1
Net income for the period	$ 1.0	$ 1.3	$ 2.0	$ 1.7	$ 0.6	$ 1.0
Retained earnings, beginning of period	3.1	4.1	5.3	7.2	8.8	9.3
Cash dividends paid:						
Preferred stock	(0.03)	—	—	—	—	—
Common stock	(0.03)	(0.04)	(0.11)	(0.11)	(0.11)	(0.05)
Amount transferred to common stock account attributable to stock split and change in par value						1.0
Retained earnings at end of period	$ 4.1	$ 5.3	$ 7.2	$ 8.8	$ 9.3	$ 9.2
Earnings and dividends per share applicable to common stock, calculated on 1,575,000 common shares to give effect to stock dividend voted September 23, 1960:						
Earnings per share	$ 0.63	$ 0.83	$ 1.27	$ 1.08	$ 0.38	$ 0.63
Dividends per share	0.03	0.03	0.07	0.07	0.07	0.03

current data on the condition of the stock market (Exhibit 4), information as to the market behavior of recent over-the-counter equity issues (Exhibit 5), and quotations for companies in the same general industry plus overall stock market indexes (Exhibits 6 and 7).

Exhibit 2

ROGERS, WILDE & COMPANY
PENELCO BALANCE SHEET AS OF JUNE 30, 1960
(In thousands)

Current assets:		
Cash		$ 653
Marketable securities		368
Receivables, net		4,921
Inventories		11,584
Prepaid expenses		265
Total current assets		$17,791
Property and equipment:		
Buildings	$3,052	
Machinery and equipment	5,528	
Leasehold improvements	310	
	$8,890	
Less: Accumulated depreciation and amortization	4,288	
	$4,601	
Land	640	
Construction in progress	212	
Property and equipment, net		5,453
Total assets		$23,244
Current liabilities:		
Unsecured bank loans and current installments on long-term notes		$ 909
Accounts payable		1,925
Accrued expenses		1,723
Federal income tax		2,824
Total current liabilities		$ 7,381
Unsecured notes, 5½%, excluding current installments		4,202
Stockholders' equity:		
Common stock, $1 par value; authorized 2,100,000 shares; issued and outstanding 1,575,000 shares (giving effect to stock dividend subsequently voted on Sept. 23, 1960)	$1,575	
Contributed capital	1,442	
Retained earnings	8,644	
Total stockholders' equity		11,661
Total liabilities and stockholders' equity		$23,244

Note: The company reported income for tax purposes computed with inventories determined by a standard cost formula and until June, 1960, maintained its books on the same basis. With minor adjustments the Treasury Department accepted this formula in its examination of the company's tax returns to and including 1955, the most recent year examined. In Exhibits 1 and 2 inventories for each period have been priced at actual average cost, not in excess of market (and the books adjusted accordingly), with the result that net income before provision for taxes shown in the statements differs from that determined under the standard cost formula. The accrual for estimated taxes is based on income shown in the statement; a significant portion of such accrual will not be payable as long as the use of the standard cost formula is continued for tax purposes.

Exhibit 3

ROGERS, WILDE & COMPANY
FINANCIAL DATA FOR COMPANIES COMPARABLE TO PENELCO

	PENELCO		*AMP, Inc.*		*Amphenol-Borg*		*Burndy Corp.*	
Fiscal year to:	12/31		12/31		12/31		12/31	
Market price (11/11/60)			58½		41½		20	
Indicated cash dividend			$ 0.50		$ 1.40		$ 0.60	
Yield			0.85%		3.4%		3.0%	
Price × 1960 est. EPS			23.10(*e*)		13.2		20.0	
× 1959 EPS			24.80(*e*)		15.0		23.8	
× 1958 EPS			43.70(*e*)		18.8		32.8	
× 1955–59 average EPS			36.70(*e*)		14.1		21.1	
× 1950–59 average EPS			62.10(*e*)		14.4		—	
6 mos.—1960 vs. 1959 EPS	$0.63		$1.21	$1.11	$1.36–$1.17		$0.66–$0.42	
1960 est. EPS	1.33		2.45(*e*)(*g*)		2.85(*i*)		1.00(*g*)	
Earns. (E) Divids. (D)	(*E*)	(*D*)	(*E*)	(*D*)	(*E*)	(*D*)	(*E*)	(*D*)
for common shares: 1959	$0.38	$0.07	$2.28	$0.60	$2.50	$1.40	$0.84	$0.60
1958	1.08	0.07	1.29	0.50	2.00	1.29	0.61	0.60
1957	1.27	0.07	1.66	0.50	3.03	—	1.22	0.30
1956	0.83	0.03	1.66	0.23	2.64	—	1.43	nil
1955	0.63	0.03	0.83	0.11	3.20	—	0.60	nil
1954	0.55	—	0.46	0.04	2.31	—	0.32	nil
1953	0.31	—	0.23	0.02	2.40	—	0.69	nil
1952	0.43	—	0.27	0.02	3.01	—	0.84	n.a.
1951	0.56	—	0.23	0.01	2.29	—	n.a.	n.a.
1950	0.13	—	0.31	nil	2.80	—	n.a.	n.a.
Avg. EPS 1955–59	$0.84		$1.54	$2.67	$2.67		$0.95	
Avg. EPS 1950–59	0.62		0.91	2.62	2.62		—	

Exchange on which traded	*PENELCO*	*AMP, Inc.* O.C.	*Amphenol-Borg* N.Y.S.	*Burndy Corp.* N.Y.S.
Sales (millions):				
6 mos. 1960 and 1959	$24.0	$24.9–20.4	$31.4–28.1	$18.4–13.3
1959	44.0	43.2	56.5	29.8
1958	34.7	31.4	46.3	21.1
1957	36.6	36.1	54.1(*a*)	23.8
1956	26.1	32.3	47.0	21.4
1955	20.3	21.7	43.4	15.0
1954	16.7	16.0	43.3	14.2
1953	18.9	15.3	55.2	15.4
1952	21.7	11.6	52.1	14.9
1951	19.3	10.2	37.2	n.a.
1950	13.0	5.5	23.4	n.a.
Capitalization (millions) date	12/31/59	12/31/59	6/30/60	12/31/59
Debt	$ 4.2	$ 1.0	$ 0.7	$ 2.8
Preferred	—	—	—	—
Common and surplus	11.6	15.9	34.0	11.7
Total	$15.8	$16.9	$34.7	$14.5
Number of shares outstanding	1,575,000	2,617,496	1,176,074	1,138,637
Net current assets/share	$ 6.61	$ 4.40	$15.45	$ 3.70
Book value per share	7.42	7.83	28.87	9.86
Market as % of book value	—	747%	144%	203%

a) Pro forma combined statements of Amphenol and Borg prior to 1958.
b) Twenty-five weeks to June 25, 1960, and June 21, 1959.
c) Eleven months to June 30.
e) Excluding nonconsolidated foreign earnings of $0.40 est. in 1960; $0.22 in 1959; and $0.10 in 1958. Price-earnings ratio for 1960 and 1959 including foreign earnings would be 20.2 and 23.0 respectively.

Exhibit 3—Continued

P. R. Mallory	*Sprague Electric*	*Erie Resistor*	*International Resistance*	*Avnet Electronics*	*Thomas & Betts Co.*
12/31	12/31	12/31	12/31	6/30	12/31
39	43	8¾	27⅜	16⅜	26¼
$ 1.40	$ 1.30	nil	$ 0.50	nil	$ 0.80
3.6%	3.0%	—	1.8%	—	3.0%
12.8	14.5	—	17.5	22.8(*f*)	—
12.2	16.7	24.6	19.7	30.0	14.5
18.6	30.9	15.1	68.7	85.0	25.5
16.2	21.9	9.0	40.3	109.0	18.1
16.6	18.6	9.3	43.8	—	24.8
$1.32–$1.30	$1.51–$1.47	$0.20–$0.20(*h*)	$0.75–$0.68(*g*)	$0.52–$0.43	$0.95–$0.88
2.75	3.00(*g*)		1.45(*i*)	0.67(*f*)	

(*E*)	(*D*)	(*E*)	(*D*)	(*E*)	(*D*)	(*E*)	(*D*)	(*E*)	(*D*)	(*E*)	(*D*)
$2.87	$1.40	$2.61	$1.20	$0.35	$0.10	$1.23	$0.35	$ 0.51	—	$1.72	$0.60
1.89	1.40	1.41	1.20	0.57	0.15	0.37	0.20	0.18	—	0.98	0.65
2.06	1.40	1.78	1.20	0.68	0.40	0.35	0.20	0.05	—	1.45	0.59
1.99	1.40	1.75	1.20	1.59	0.40	0.59	0.20	(0.01)(*c*)	—	1.67	0.49
2.05	1.35	2.43	1.20	1.60	0.80	0.59	0.20	(0.04)	—	1.09	0.32
0.81	1.32	2.68	1.10	0.44	0.40	0.45	0.30	(0.05)	—	0.72	0.24
2.49	1.13	2.50	1.07	1.01	0.40	0.53	0.30	—	—	0.32	0.21
2.08	0.67	2.79	0.93	0.81	0.40	0.44	0.30	—	—	0.55	0.26
2.13	0.80	2.42	0.89	0.66	0.37½	0.71	0.40	—	—	0.62	0.11
2.82	0.63	3.04	0.60	1.60	0.10	1.01	0.30	—	—	0.72	0.13
$2.17		$1.99		$0.96		$0.63		$ 0.14		$1.38	
2.12		2.34		0.93		0.58		—		1.01	

P. R. Mallory *N.Y.S.*	*Sprague Electric* *O.C.*	*Erie Resistor* *O.C.*	*International Resistance* *N.Y.S.*	*Avnet Electronics* *N.Y.S.*	*Thomas & Betts Co.* *O.C.*
$43.7–42.5	$32.3–27.4	—	$10.3–9.4(*h*)	$9.3–6.4(*f*)	$11.6–10.6
86.5	56.4	$24.5	19.8	6.4	21.6
68.3	43.2	21.2	13.7	3.5	17.1
77.6	46.2	24.7	15.4	2.0	17.8
68.4	44.7	23.3	16.8	1.0(*c*)	18.3
63.9	44.6	22.6	15.7	0.7	14.8
54.6	42.6	14.9	13.2	0.4	12.4
70.9	46.8	17.1	12.8	—	13.0
53.4	43.4	14.5	11.8	—	12.7
45.4	38.3	14.2	13.0	—	13.0
39.8	28.6	13.7	11.1	—	9.2
12/31/59	12/31/59	12/27/59	6/26/60	3/31/60	12/31/59
$10.2	$ 1.1	$ 1.5	—	$0.2	$ 1.2
3.7	—	1.3	—	—	1.4
30.4	29.8	8.9	$ 8.0	2.5	10.4
$44.3	$30.9	$11.7	$ 8.0	$2.7	$13.0
1,441,009	1,340,289	768,083	1,382,998	1,513,200	1,480,153
$ 2.63	$11.65	$ 3.52	$ 3.68	$1.19	$ 4.32
21.15	21.94	11.39	5.65	1.67	7.62
184%	196%	77%	484%	980%	344%

f) Figures for fiscal year to 6/30/60.
g) Estimate by R. W. & Co. Research Dept.
h) Twenty-four weeks to June 12, 1960, and June 14, 1959.
i) Company estimate.

Exhibit 4

ROGERS, WILDE & COMPANY
Current Information on Condition of Stock Market

New York Times, November 14, 1960:

"Except for selected specialty issues among industrial stocks, over-the-counter shares generally went their own way last week. Most issues failed to take a clue from the post-election rally on the New York Stock Exchange.

"There was no general forward movement among the over-the-counter stocks. . . .

"The National Quotation Bureau's price average of thirty-five over-the-counter stocks closed Friday at 99.21, up 1.58 points, and the high for the week. The week's low of 98.13 was established on Wednesday." [On September 26, 1960, the *New York Times* reported that the index's high (109.39) for the year was reached on January 6 and the low (100.77) on March 11.]

* * * * *

"New issues moved ahead smartly."

New York Times, November 15, 1960:

"Investor attention turned reluctantly yesterday from the envisioned bright mornings of 1961 and 1962 to the setting sun of 1960. There were discouraging developments for steels and motors and some of the oils and the market took them into account.

"Wall Street analysts seemed gradually to be coming to agreement on a wary appraisal of the market's future. Between now and the end of the year most brokers expect tax-selling but nothing like a general sell-off. There is, they believe, too much excitement in the economic air. Investors do not sell easily when tomorrow or the day after can bring new developments and new hope. There might even be a general but small bulge in prices, it was said.

"After mid-January, however, analysts would not be surprised to see a shakedown of 10 per cent or so, followed rather promptly by a recovery taking the market into the kind of trading range it enjoyed between 1946 and 1949. This could mean a channel allowing a swing of about 15 to 20 per cent."

Exhibit 5

ROGERS, WILDE & COMPANY
A LIST OF RECENT OVER-THE-COUNTER EQUITY ISSUES

	Offering Price	*Current Bid (11/11/60)*	*Current Asked (11/11/60)*
Allied Maintenance Corp.	$ 15½	$ 21¼	$ 23
American Optical Co. 4.40s—1980	100	105½	107¼
Associated Sales Analysts, Inc.	3½	3⅝	4⅜
Cenco Instruments Corp. 4½s—1980	102	113½	115½
Del Electronics Corp.	4	8¼	9½
Electro-Science Investors, Inc.	11	12¼	13⅞
Electronics International Capital Ltd.	10	8⅜	9⅛
Florida Hillsboro, Inc.—units	500	n.a	n.a.
Fotochrome Inc.	11	14	15⅛
Green Shoe Manufacturing Co.	20	21	22½
Gulf Resources	8	7⅞	8¾
Interstate Vending Co.	14⅞	16⅜	17⅝
Jahncke Service, Inc.	11	10¾	11½
Klondex Inc.	2	6	6¾
Mid-States Business Capital Corp.	11	10¾	*
NAFI Corp. 5¼s—1980	102½	94½	97
Nissen Trampoline Co.	9	12¼	13⅜
Nixon-Baldwin Chemicals Inc.—units	500	495	525
Scantlin Electronics, Inc.	12	16⅞	18⅛
Scott, Foresman & Co.	27½	25⅛	25⅞
Stephan Company	4	5	...
Technical Materiel Corp.	27	24¾	26
Techno Fund, Inc.	12½	12⅛	10⅞
Variable Annuity Life Insurance Co.	12	8½	9½
Vogue Instrument Corp.	3	4⅛	4⅝
Welded Tube Co. of America	6	5¼	5⅞
Melpar, Inc.	14	14¾	16

* Syndicate bid.
Source of data: *New York Times*, November 14, 1960.

Exhibit 6

ROGERS, WILDE & COMPANY
Market Quotations for Common Stock of Texas Instruments Incorporated and Litton Industries, Inc.

	Texas Instruments Incorporated	*Litton Industries, Inc.*
September 1–15, 1960	\$187 –\$214⅛	\$79 –\$86⅜
September 16–30, 1960	176¾– 185¼	70½– 79¼
October 1–15, 1960	172 – 182¾	73½– 78½
October 17	167¼	79
18	167	76¾
19	168½	77⅛
20	162	77½
21	161	75½
24	150¼	73
25	151¼	70⅞
26	158	71
27	165¼	73⅛
28	160¼	75¼
31	161	72½
November 1	165¼	72⅛
2	167¼	73½
3	167⅜	74
4	167¾	74⅝
7	171⅛	74⅞
8	176	76
9	176	76
10	178¼	76⅛
11	187¾	81⅛
14	185	80⅜

Exhibit 7

ROGERS, WILDE & COMPANY
Weekly and Daily Averages for Dow Jones Industrials

		The Year's High	*The Year's Low*
September 8	611.42	677.66	602.31
15	602.69	677.66	602.31
22	592.15	677.66	602.31
29	570.59	677.66	592.15
October 6	583.69	677.66	570.59
13	591.41	677.66	570.59
20	582.69	677.66	570.59
27	580.95	677.66	570.59
November 3	590.82	677.66	570.59
10	612.01	677.66	570.59
November 4	596.41		
7	599.14		
9	591.08		
10	605.62		
11	608.69		

APPENDIX

ROGERS, WILDE & COMPANY
Confidential Memorandum

PENNSYLVANIA ELECTRONICS COMPANY
SUMMARY OF FINANCING RECOMMENDATIONS

The stock of Pennsylvania Electronics Company is owned in equal parts by four brothers and sisters—the two sons and two daughters of the late Mr. Gustav Trumbilee, who founded the company in 1923. We have been asked to summarize our recommendations and opinions with respect to the public sale of common stock by the present shareholders and/or by the company.

There are a number of advantages in establishing a public market for the stock of a privately owned company, including the following:

1. An established public market should greatly facilitate the estate planning of the controlling stockholders, possibly eliminating a distress sale of stock at an inopportune time and avoiding arbitrary valuation placed on the shares for estate tax purposes.
2. When stock is publicly held, the stockholders constitute a "ready-made" market should the company wish to raise additional equity money in the future.
3. An established market for common stock provides management with much greater flexibility in planning the financing of new capital requirements. It places the company in a position to consider Debentures, Subordinated Debentures and/or Preferred Stock convertible into common stock. We have found that such convertible securities are particularly desirable for growing companies.
4. The acquisition of additional companies sometimes can be effectively consummated only through the issuance of stock. An active market can be of great assistance in such negotiations.
5. A public market affords a company's employees an opportunity to purchase stock thereby giving them an added interest in the company. If desirable, added incentive can be given key employees through stock options.

Pennsylvania Electronics Company is a name of long standing and excellent reputation in its field but because of the closely held nature of its stock, the company is not well known in the investment market. We believe that it is of utmost importance that the initial public offering of a company's stock be successful and that sufficient shares be distributed to provide an active market. We would plan in connection with any public offering of shares of your company to conduct an educational campaign to assure a successful offering on the best possible terms and to achieve broad distribution. This would also prove beneficial in creating a continued interest in the shares both with dealers whom we would expect to maintain a trading market and with investors. We

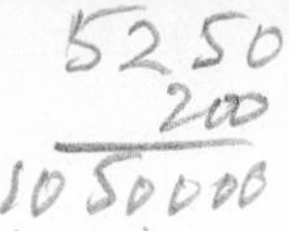

would plan ourselves to take a trading position in the stock and maintain an active market as soon after the public offering as SEC regulations permit. Such sponsorship of investment dealers is important if an issue is to sell at a fair value in relation to other securities in the market.

Recommended recapitalization

Present capitalization consists of 5,250 shares of common stock, par value $10 per share, all of which is issued and outstanding. We suggest that the company be recapitalized to split the common stock on a 200 for 1 basis and reduce the par value per share from $10 to $1. There appears to be sufficient capital surplus available for this purpose. The recapitalization would result in 1,000,000 shares of $1 par value common stock, all of which would be outstanding. We further suggest that as a part of the recapitalization an additional 1,000,000 $1 par shares be authorized for future issuance as needed.

The ratio of the stock split should be reviewed at the time action is to be taken and adjusted, if necessary, so as to give the split shares a value within a range that would be considered most attractive for an initial public offering. We generally consider a price in the range of 15 to 25 as most attractive for obtaining the broadest distribution and best investor interest. Most investors prefer to buy so-called "round lots" of 100 or a few hundred shares rather than to make an equivalent dollar investment in less than 100 shares of a high-priced stock. Moreover, in order to obtain broad distribution in an offering of this type, we endeavor to restrict the number of shares which any individual may purchase. It is more effective to do this in lots of a few hundred shares than in amounts of less than 100 shares.

Also, many investors believe a stock at a price in this range offers better potentialities of appreciation than a stock at a higher level. Illogical as this may seem, it is a real factor in the minds of a large percentage of security buyers.

Pricing the stock

We would be glad to discuss our ideas as to the price at which the shares of your company might be sold. In general it would be our objective to agree with you on a public offering price which would provide the maximum amount of proceeds and at the same time insure the successful distribution of the stock. It is of the utmost importance that the initial offering of stock be properly priced so that the entire issue can be distributed within a relatively short period at the initial offering price, and be traded at a slight premium in the secondary market. With proper pricing of its initial offering, the company will acquire a group of satisfied stockholders and will reap the benefit of their good will, especially in connection with subsequent financing programs.

Size of issue

To establish a reliable market the original distribution should be broad and the issue should be of sufficient size to insure a trading supply of stock thereafter. Under these conditions, the necessary dealer and investor interest can be secured and maintained. Based upon experience we believe that not less than 150,000 shares of stock should be distributed and we would prefer to see not less than 200,000 shares. The initial distribution might consist entirely of shares presently outstanding; or if the company can profitably employ additional funds, the offering might consist of new shares or include both outstanding and new shares.

Time of offering

The market is now favorable for the sale of equity securities, and we would recommend that should you decide to sell stock you proceed immediately with preparations for the offering. The preparation of the registration statement will require approximately three weeks to a month. To this must be added the 20-day registration period, during which the registration statement would be on file with the SEC.

Underwriting

We would be pleased to manage an underwriting of a public offering of your stock. We would envision a strong geographically distributed underwriting group, and it would be our desire to underwrite a substantial portion of the total offering ourselves as we feel confident our sales organization could do an excellent distributing job. The underwriting group would be discussed with you prior to formation.

As far as underwriting fees are concerned, enough compensation should be paid to stimulate the interest of dealers; their active interest will result in a higher price and wider distribution. Our present estimate is that the underwriting commission should be between 6½% and 7½% of the public offering price. During the course of the registration work and our educational campaign, we would be in a position to evaluate the buildup in investor interest and refine the commission accordingly. However, to repeat, enough compensation should be paid to stimulate the interest of underwriters and dealers and to get the best job done.

Expenses of registration

The principal costs of the registration would be legal fees, accounting fees, and printing fees. We would estimate that the total expenses of registration in your case, assuming an offering involving about $3,000,000, would approximate $40,000 to $50,000. For many years the SEC was insistent that all such expenses be paid by the actual seller of the stock notwithstanding, in the case of a secondary sale by a stockholder, the benefits accruing to the company and the other stockholders in terms of improved marketability for the stock. More recently the SEC has shown a tendency to modify its position, and should one or more of your shareholders decide to sell a portion of their holdings we are confident that a substantial part of the expenses, other than transfer taxes, could be paid by the company without objection by the Commission. In any event, we are confident that we can be of help in holding the expenses of registration to a minimum.

General

We would suggest that prior to any offering of your stock you have competent counsel review your charter and bylaws with a view to recommending changes and additions. It is always worthwhile to "clean house" before acquiring outside stockholders. We would be glad to have our counsel, Messrs. Van Roden and Tindell, help in this connection should you wish. This review could run concurrently with the preparation of a registration statement and should cover such things as pre-emptive rights, cumulative voting, etc.

We would suggest that in connection with a public offering, you appoint a transfer agent and a registrar in New York. We believe that this would improve the market for your shares and would help in maintaining nationwide distribution.

As to dividends, we believe that in the case of a company such as yours, they are of secondary importance under present market conditions.

Rogers, Wilde & Company
March 10, 1959

RAW/rj

BECTON, DICKINSON AND COMPANY

In mid-June, 1968, Douglas Brash and Harry Mosle of F. Eberstadt & Co. (FE & Co.), a New York investment banking firm, were involved in setting the final terms for a $25,000,000 issue of convertible subordinated debentures of Becton, Dickinson and Company (B-D). Most of the detailed features of the issue had been worked out with B-D over the preceding three months in preparation for the offering, which was planned for June 18. A general understanding had been reached with the company on the coupon rate for the debentures, the conversion premium above the current price of the common stock, and the underwriters' spread; but the final terms were to be set only at the last minute and would be based upon market conditions just before the offering date. A meeting between the top management of FE & Co. and B-D had been called for the afternoon of June 17, after the close of the market; and Douglas Brash was expected to recommend the final terms of the issue at that time.

Ben Harter, B-D's vice president for finance, had called on Ferdinand Eberstadt early in March, 1968, for advice and assistance in raising between $15 and $20 million later in the year. He said that on the basis of the company's current projections, B-D would need at least $15 million and perhaps as much as $25 million for new capital within the next two years. The bulk of the funds would be used to finance expansion of domestic manufacturing and distribution facilities, and the remainder would be needed for additional working capital, principally to carry increased inventories and accounts receivable. He asked for Mr. Eberstadt's views on the various ways in which B-D might raise these funds. Mr. Eberstadt said immediately that B-D should consider as one alternative the possibility of a convertible subordinated debenture, and indicated that his firm would come up with a specific recommendation as soon as a detailed analysis could be made. He indicated that because the firm was so familiar with B-D and its needs, he believed that a concrete proposal could be developed promptly.

Mr. Harter said that he had been in touch recently with the insurance company that held its 5⅛% promissory notes due in 1982. These notes had been placed privately in 1962 with the assistance of the Eberstadt firm. He told Mr. Eberstadt that the insurance company had indicated that it would lend B-D $20 million for 20 years, nonrefundable for the first 10 years, with interest at 7%. He said that in addition to the possibility of straight long-term debt, the company had been considering as alternatives another common stock issue, or arranging a revolving-term loan credit agreement with commercial banks.

F. Eberstadt & Co. had arranged six earlier financings for B-D. The first of these had been a private placement of $7 million of notes in 1958. Since that date it had placed privately another $9 million issue of notes and had handled four common stock issues for the company. The stock issues were all public offerings. Three were combined offerings of the company and certain selling stockholders; the fourth was entirely a registered secondary offering. The selling stockholders were members of the Dickinson and Becton families as well as other substantial holders who had acquired B-D stock through acquisition of their companies by B-D. The most recent issue had been a common stock offering of more than 500,000 shares just a year before; hence the financial affairs of B-D were well known to the firm. (See Exhibit 1.)

THE COMPANY

Becton, Dickinson and Company was incorporated under the laws of New Jersey in 1906 to succeed to a partnership established in 1897. The company and its subsidiaries are engaged principally in the manufacture and sale of a broad line of medical, surgical, laboratory, and diagnostic products used by doctors, hospitals, laboratories, pharmaceutical companies, medical schools, dentists, and veterinarians. The company also manufactures and sells gloves and mittens for industry, farm, home, and recreational uses and electronic and electromechanical products and engineered subassemblies primarily for industrial customers. It also engages in custom contract packaging and the leasing of packaging machinery. In its fiscal year ended September 30, 1967, approximately 75% of its sales were attributable to health care products.

The original business of the company was the manufacture and sale of clinical thermometers. Over the years B-D had diversified its activities and added many product lines, primarily in the medical, surgical, and laboratory areas, both through its own development activities and through acquisitions. It had become one of the leading companies in the expanding health care field. B-D's broad product line provided valuable diversification to lessen the possible impact of any adverse technological or competitive development relating to any one product. Moreover, this diversification across wide areas of medical activity meant that B-D would be exposed to most of the new product opportunities that were likely to develop. Therefore, the company, which had strong research and product development capabilities, could be expected to continue to participate significantly in the expanding health care field.

The company manufactures and sells several thousand individual items within its various product lines. Approximately 92% of its sales are currently derived from items of its own manufacture; the remaining products are made for it by others, generally to its specifications. The company's products include both reusable and disposable items. In recent years there had been substantial growth in the demand for disposable items, and currently they accounted for about 70% of the company's sales of medical, surgical, and laboratory products.

The company has, throughout its history, laid great emphasis on quality control and on biological safety. Particular care is exercised in the control of disposable medical devices, especially in the areas of sterility, toxicity, and pyrogenicity, to ensure that its products are not harmful, when used as indicated, in the care of human beings. B-D's standards for quality and safety have assumed even greater significance with the increased sales of sterile products and products for human implant.

Research and development

The company is actively engaged in the development of new products and in devising new and improved methods of manufacturing existing products. It carries on its research and development activities both at the corporate level and in each of the seven operating divisions.

The corporate research and development group is concerned primarily with areas of investigation not related to the company's existing products. It attempts to satisfy the needs of the medical profession for new and improved instrumentation through research and development. In addition, the corporate research and development group coordinates research and development activities among the various operating units of the company. It is B-D's general policy to delegate as far as possible research and development work relating to the products of an operating facility to that facility. This includes both immediate and advanced product development, as well as extension of product lines and improvement of existing products.

The company owns numerous domestic and foreign patents and is licensed under patents owned by others. It does not believe that any of its patents or licenses give it a substantial competitive advantage with respect to any of the activities in which it is engaged, or that its patents or licenses are of material importance to the overall success of its business. The company relies primarily on the development and manufacturing ability of its technical and engineering staffs rather than upon patents.

Competition

The company is faced with substantial competition in all areas in which it is active, in most cases from companies which provide competition for only a part of B-D's product lines. Some of the company's competitors have greater financial resources and sales than those of B-D. In recent years there has been a tendency on the part of some firms engaged in the distribution of medical products to become manufacturers as well. In addition, the company is faced with competition from products manufactured abroad, particularly reusable hypodermic syringes and needles, clinical thermometers and disposable needles. The rapid progress of medical technology means that new methods or techniques can render B-D's current products in some fields obsolete and, therefore, the company stresses its research and development programs and the orderly introduction of new products.

Property

The executive offices of the company are located in East Rutherford, New Jersey. Principal domestic manufacturing units, some with research and significant warehousing facilities, are located in California, Connecticut, Illinois, Indiana, Louisiana, Maryland, Massachusetts, Michigan, Nebraska, New Jersey, New Mexico, New York, and Ohio. Sales offices and distribution points are also located in other sections of the United States.

The company owns approximately 1,800,000 square feet and leases approximately 800,000 square feet of floor space at its various locations in the United States. Its manufacturing equipment consists in large part of specialized machinery for the precision grinding, processing, shaping, sewing, forming, marking and sealing of glass, rubber, fabric, plastic, and metal. In many instances this machinery has been specially designed by its technical staff and manufactured in its machine shops. Of particular importance to the company because of the nature of its products are various types of sterilization and testing equipment. B-D owns all of its machinery and equipment except for certain items, not of significance, which are furnished by customers in connection with contract business or leased from others.

Major plant facilities are currently being used at or near full capacity. The company has a continuing program for expansion of its plant facilities. The capital expenditures of the company and its consolidated subsidiaries, net of retirements, for property, plant, and equipment for the five fiscal years ended September 30, 1967, were approximately as follows:

1963	$ 5,273,000
1964	6,126,000
1965	8,247,000
1966	8,504,000
1967	10,910,000

Financial data

A statement of consolidated income of B-D for five fiscal years ended September 30, 1963, to 1967 and for the six-month periods ended March 31, 1967, and 1968 is set forth in Exhibit 2. Consolidated balance sheets on September 30, 1967, and March 31, 1968, appear in Exhibit 3.

The common stock of B-D has been listed on the New York Stock Exchange since September 25, 1963. The holders of the stock have noncumulative voting rights and do not have preemptive rights. The range of sale prices of the common stock, from 1964 to June 17, 1968, adjusted for a 1 for 1 stock distribution in November, 1966, is as follows:

	High	*Low*
1964	19¾	13⅝
1965	32	17⅞
1966	40⅜	26⅝
1967	63	39½
1968 (through June 17)	71⅞	55¼

SELECTING THE SECURITY

A second meeting with B-D officials took place on March 15 to discuss the form of financing that was to be recommended by the Eberstadt firm. The recommendation was that B-D finance its needs by a public offering of convertible subordinated debentures. The approximate terms suggested for such an issue were a 4½% coupon, convertible at about 15% above the stock price at the time of issue, and a gross spread no higher than 1½%, all terms being subject to market conditions.

In the discussion that followed, three alternatives to the convertible debenture were also discussed—a long-term straight debt issue, a revolving-term loan with banks, and a common stock offering. In regard to the possibility of a common stock offering, concern was expressed about the potential dilution involved in such an issue. B-D was now considering an issue of $25 million. An equity issue to raise this amount would involve a substantial number of shares, and the announcement of such a large offering would almost certainly cause the market price of B-D's stock to decline. Depending on the extent of the market reaction, an offering of as many as 500,000 shares might be required. Despite the fact that the resulting capital structure after such an issue of common stock would provide advantageous flexibility for future financings, the potential adverse effect on the company's stock price was believed to be too substantial. A rights offering to minimize the effects of dilution had also been considered, but the idea had been discarded. A substantial amount of the outstanding stock of the company was still in the hands of the Becton and Dickinson families and their interests, and such holders could not be expected to subscribe for additional stock. They had been reducing their holdings through the earlier secondary offerings in order to diversify their investments. Consequently, a rights offering was not considered a realistic alternative.

As indicated earlier, B-D was also reluctant to assume the relatively high cost involved in a long-term, straight debt placement such as had been suggested by the insurance company holding its 1962 debt issue. B-D did express an interest in bank debt, however, with perhaps a five-year term. The Eberstadt representatives, however, thought it unwise to consider relatively short-term bank financing of long-term capital requirements, especially during a period of current and prospective rapid growth of the company.

In regard to a long-term straight debt issue, the Eberstadt people were also concerned about the lack of flexibility inherent in the tight repayment schedule as well as the high interest rate that would be required, whether the debt was offered publicly or placed privately. The repayment provisions were considered to be especially important, because of B-D's desire to retain a maximum amount of earnings for reinvestment in the company rather than for debt repayment. On a long-term straight debt issue the sinking fund would probably commence no later than the beginning of the sixth year and thereafter the entire amount would have to be repaid in approximately equal installments. The FE & Co. representatives also pointed out that long-term straight debt would require call protection for at least 5 and perhaps as many as 10 years, which would reduce B-D's freedom to refinance in the event that interest rates declined. Finally, they expressed concern over B-D's flexibility for future financings if it issued straight debt now. Its debt ratio and interest coverage now were excellent, but both would be reduced with an additional issue of $25 million of senior debt. This would have an adverse impact on whatever rating the bond services would put on B-D's debt securities in the future, and thus make future debt financings more expensive.

The Eberstadt people saw the subordinated convertible debenture as the most attractive alternative at the time. The primary advantage lay in the reduced burden of the security. In the first place the coupon rate would be lower, say 4½% as compared with over 6½% for a public offering of straight debt. In addition, the indenture would be much less restrictive. Furthermore, the sinking fund would require no repayments at all for 10 years and then the repayment of only half of the issue prior to the final maturity date. At the same time there could be an optional sinking fund for repayments at no premium, which could add additional flexibility to the company's financial planning. Moreover, there might be no need for any repayments because if B-D continued to prosper and grow, its stock price might be expected to rise above the conversion price, leading either to voluntary conversions or to forced conversion in the event the company called the debentures. In either case there would be no required repayments at all for the first 10 years and, to the extent that the conversions took place, required repayments could be further delayed.

In addition, such an issue would be considered as quasi equity and would expand the company's senior borrowing base. And there would be an even clearer case of increased flexibility in future financing after conversion took place. Finally, because of the great interest and enthusiasm for B-D stock as evidenced by its price-earnings ratio above 50, a good conversion premium would be possible, which in turn would minimize dilution. On all these grounds the Eberstadt people believed that a convertible subordinated debenture would best meet B-D's needs at the present time.

As to the tentative terms suggested, these were based on the Eberstadt firm's judgment as to what would be salable in the then current securities market after analyzing the terms of recent convertible issues as of March 12, 1968. Exhibit 4 includes data assembled at that time on eight such issues of industrial corporations which were at least somewhat comparable in size and quality to the proposed B-D issue. Only two of the issuers, Will Ross and Baxter Laboratories, were in the same general industry group as B-D, and both of these companies had high price-earnings ratios and strong growth rates comparable to B-D. On the basis of these figures and the then market conditions, the Eberstadt firm was confident it could sell B-D convertibles at a 4½% coupon, 15% conversion premium, and 1½% spread.

No decision was reached at the March 15 meeting, but on March 20, B-D's executive vice president, John Simmons, called Douglas Brash to say that B-D's finance committee had decided to proceed expeditiously to raise $25 million through the sale of subordinated convertible debentures. He said that the company would have to hold a special meeting of shareholders to approve the issuance of the recommended securities, but he did not envisage any problem on that score. Mr. Simmons asked the Eberstadt firm to proceed to work out the schedule for the financing and to develop with counsel the detailed covenants for the debentures.

INDENTURE PROVISIONS

On the basis of its experience in designing securities and of a detailed review of the provisions of a number of indentures relating to recent convertible issues by companies of comparable quality, the Eberstadt firm recommended and B-D accepted the following important indenture provisions:

The debentures are to be limited to the principal amount of $25 million being offered hereby, and are to be unsecured obligations of the company. They are to be issuable as definitive registered debentures without coupons in denominations of $1,000, and any multiple of $1,000. Interest will be payable semiannually on June 1 and December 1 of each year (commencing December 1, 1968) to holders of record on the preceding May 15 or November 15, and the debentures will mature on June 1, 1988.

Redemption

The debentures are to be subject to redemption prior to maturity, at the option of the company, as a whole at any time, or from time to time in part, during the respective 12-month period ending May 31 in each of the years set forth in the tabulation below, upon payment of the applicable percentage of the principal amount set forth under the heading "Redemption Price," together with interest accrued to the date fixed for redemption.

Year Ending May 31	*Redemption Price*	*Year Ending May 31*	*Redemption Price*
1969	100% plus coupon rate	1979	
1970		1980	
1971		1981	
1972	Scaled down in equal	1982	
1973	intervals to 100% in	1983	
1974	1986	1984	
1975		1985	
1976		1986	100.00
1977		1987	100.00
1978		1988	100.00

At least 30 days' notice of redemption shall be given by mail to the registered holders of the debentures being redeemed. If less than all of the debentures are to redeemed, the trustee will select those to be redeemed in any manner it deems fair and appropriate.

The debentures will be redeemable on similar notice through the operation of a sinking fund (optional and mandatory) described below at the principal amount thereof (no premium), together with accrued interest to the redemption date.

Sinking fund

The indenture will require the company to retire $1,250,000 principal amount of debentures on June 1 in each of the years 1978 to and including 1987, subject to credits for debentures converted prior to such June 1 or redeemed or canceled otherwise than through the operation of the sinking fund. In addition, the company may at its option provide cash for the retirement, on June 1 in each of the years 1973 to 1987, both inclusive, of debentures up to a maximum principal amount equal to, but not to exceed, $1,250,000. Such optional right of redemption will be noncumulative and without payment of premium.

Conversion

Any debenture or any portion of the principal amount thereof which is $1,000 or a multiple of $1,000 will be convertible, at its principal amount, into common stock of the company, at any time or from time to time at the option of the holder, on or before June 1, 1988, at the conversion price. The conversion price is to be subject to adjustment in the case of dividends in common stock and in certain other cases, including the issuance or sale of common stock at less than the conversion price then in effect. The conversion price will also be subject to adjustment upon any subdivision or combination of the outstanding shares of common stock, or reclassification of other securities into common stock. No adjustment in the conversion price is to be made with respect to (*a*) the shares issued upon conversion of the debentures offered hereby; (*b*) issuance of shares of common stock or securities convertible into shares of common stock in exchange for the assets, or at least 80% of the voting shares, of a going business, or in connection with a merger of another company into B-D; and (*c*) all shares issued to employees (including officers) under stock options granted under any plan (now or hereafter existing) for the benefit of such employees in connection with their employment. No adjustment in the conversion price will be made until the adjustment formula set forth in the indenture requires a total adjustment per share of 50 cents or more.

Subordination provisions

Upon any distribution of assets of B-D or upon any dissolution, winding up, liquidation, or reorganization of the company, payment of the principal of and premium and interest on the debentures will be subordinated to the prior payment in full of all senior indebtedness. No payment may be made on the debentures while payment of principal of, or interest on, any senior indebtedness is in default or while there is any other default on senior indebtedness which permits its acceleration.

Senior indebtedness includes the principal of and premium, if any, and interest on (*a*) indebtedness (other than the debentures) of or guaranteed by the company for money borrowed; (*b*) indebtedness of the company evidenced by notes or debentures (other than these debentures) issued under the provisions of an indenture or similar instrument between the company and a financial institution; (*c*) any such indebtedness of another person, firm, or corporation incurred, assumed or guaranteed by the company in connection with the acquisition by B-D of any businesses, properties, or other assets; or (*d*) indebtedness of the company under any deferrals, renewals or extensions of any such foregoing indebtedness, or under any debentures, notes or other evidences of indebtedness issued in exchange for such foregoing indebtedness —unless, in each case, by the terms of the instrument by which the company incurred, assumed or guaranteed such indebtedness, it is expressly provided that such indebtedness is not superior in right of payment to the debentures. (As of March 31, 1968, the principal amount of senior indebtedness was approximately $18,300,000.)

Dividend restrictions

The indenture will provide that no dividend or other distribution (except in stock of the company) may be declared on any stock of the company unless after giving effect thereto, the aggregate amount expended for such purposes since September 30, 1967, does not exceed the sum of (*a*) the consolidated net income of the company earned subsequent to September 30, 1967; (*b*) the aggregate net proceeds of sales after June 1, 1968, of any capital stock of the company; (*c*) the aggregate net cash proceeds of the sales after June 1, 1968, of any indebtedness (including the debentures) of the company thereafter converted into stock; and (*d*) $7,500,000. (If this provision had been in effect on March 31, 1968, approximately $12,250,000 would have been available for cash dividends.)

FINAL TERMS FOR THE ISSUE

It had been estimated that it would require about three months to take all the necessary steps to prepare and file the registration statement, to prepare and mail the proxy statement to obtain the approval of B-D's stockholders, and to have the registration statement become effective. B-D made the first public announcement of the issue on April 8 at the time it filled its preliminary proxy material with the SEC. A second announcement was made when the registration statement was filed on May 14, 1968. After the latter date the Eberstadt firm proceeded to form an underwriting syndicate for the forthcoming issue and, as the red herring prospectuses became available, to ascertain the extent of dealer and investor interest in the debentures.

Interest in the securities was strong and immediate. Invitations to participate in the underwriting went to the investment banking firms which had handled so successfully the previous issues of B-D's common stock under the Eberstadt management. Not only were such invitations readily accepted, but the underwriters generally sought larger participations. In addition, requests for participations came in increasing numbers during the registration period from all across the country as did requests by dealers for selling allotments. A final list of 95 underwriters was submitted to and approved by B-D just after the stockholders had approved on May 21 the issuance of the debentures.

There was no question of the strength of the appetite for the debentures among investors and dealers alike, and the interest seemed to increase as the offering date approached. In addition, the market stayed strong for B-D stock with no significant adverse reaction immediately after the announcement of the issue or later. B-D's stock price strengthened in April and May, and there was no significant weakening as the offering date approached. (See Exhibit 5.)

This was the general situation on Monday, June 17, as Douglas Brash met with Mr. Eberstadt and other top partners of the firm after the close of the market to settle on the final terms of the issue to be negotiated with B-D. To assist them Mr. Mosle had assembled the data appearing in Exhibit 6. He also indicated that the price of B-D's stock at the close of the market was $64⅝. The final terms of the issue to be negotiated later that afternoon with the top officials of B-D included (*a*) the coupon rate of the debentures, (*b*) the conversion premium above the current market price or the conversion price itself, and (*c*) the contemplated gross spread.

Exhibit 1

BECTON, DICKINSON AND COMPANY
CHRONOLOGICAL LIST OF FINANCINGS FOR BECTON, DICKINSON AND COMPANY MANAGED BY F. EBERSTADT & CO. THROUGH MARCH, 1968

January 22, 1958:	Private placement of: $ 500,000 4½% promissory notes due 1963 $4,500,000 5½% promissory notes due 1978 $2,000,000 6% subordinated notes due 1983
April 23, 1962:	Registered public offering of 480,000 shares of common stock at $25 ($9⅜):* 200,000 shares for company 280,000 shares for selling stockholders Aggregate prices to public = $12,000,000
December 18, 1962:	Private placement of: $9,000,000 5⅛% promissory notes due 1982
May 4, 1965:	Registered public offering of 250,000 shares of common stock at $40⅛ ($20¹⁄₁₆)* for selling stockholders: Aggregate price to public = $10,031,250
April 5, 1966:	Registered public offering of 368,250 shares of common stock at $56.75 ($28⅜):* 125,000 shares for company 243,250 shares for selling stockholders Aggregate price to public = $20,898,188 (Joint with White, Weld & Co., Incorporated)
March 22, 1967:	Registered public offering of 526,769 shares of common stock at $49.50: 283,200 shares for company 243,569 shares for selling stockholders Aggregate price to public = $26,075,066

* Stock Prices in ( ) represent adjusted prices to take account of a 4 for 3 stock split in 1963 and a 100% stock dividend in 1966.

Exhibit 2

BECTON, DICKINSON AND COMPANY
STATEMENT OF CONSOLIDATED INCOME
(In thousands, except for per share data)

	Year Ended September 30					Six Months Ended March 31	
	1963	*1964*	*1965*	*1966*	*1967*	*1967 (Unaudited)*	*1968 (Unaudited)*
Revenues:							
Net sales	$88,207	$100,908	$116,001	$140,750	$157,019	$76,507	$85,254
Company's share of undistributed income (net) of unconsolidated subsidiaries	878	1,018	731	845	1,311	439	1,082
Interest and other	695	654	711	836	1,130	375	863
	$89,781	$102,580	$117,443	$142,431	$159,460	$77,321	$87,199
Costs and expenses:							
Cost of products sold	$55,287	$ 62,175	$ 69,632	$ 82,349	$ 91,349	$44,803	$50,067
Selling, general and administrative, and research and development expenses	24,449	27,697	32,292	39,324	45,040	21,917	25,207
Interest on long-term notes	539	690	850	936	1,003	498	516
Other	147	146	89	109	181	71	88
	$80,422	$ 90,709	$102,864	$122,718	$137,573	$67,289	$75,878
Income before federal income taxes	$ 9,358	$ 11,872	$ 14,579	$ 19,713	$ 21,888	$10,032	$11,321
Federal income taxes	4,155	5,203	6,612	9,208	9,799	4,731	4,994
Net income	$ 5,203	$ 6,669	$ 7,967	$ 10,505	$ 12,089	$ 5,301	$ 6,327
Net income per share*	$0.55	$0.71	$0.84	$1.05	$1.17	$0.52	$0.60
Dividends per share†	$0.11¼	$0.15	$0.20	$0.20	$0.30	$0.15	$0.15

* Based on the number of shares outstanding at the end of each period (except for the year ended September 30, 1967, and the six months ended March 31, 1967, and 1968 which are based on the average number of shares outstanding for the period) after giving retroactive effect to shares issued in poolings of interests, a 4 for 3 stock split in December, 1963, and a 1 for 1 stock distribution in November, 1966.

† Adjusted to reflect the 4 for 3 stock split in December, 1963, and the 1 for 1 stock distribution in November, 1966.

Figures may not add because of rounding.

Exhibit 3

BECTON, DICKINSON AND COMPANY
CONSOLIDATED BALANCE SHEET
(In thousands)

	September 30, 1967	*March 31, 1968 (Unaudited)*
ASSETS		
Current assets:		
Cash	$ 2,307	$ 3,209
Short-term investments at cost (approximate market)	18,453	10,038
Trade receivables—less allowances of $453,750 ($477,944 at March 31, 1968)	21,359	22,514
Inventories, generally at the lower of cost (first-in, first-out) or market:		
Raw materials and supplies	$ 9,996	$ 10,530
Work in process	9,751	11,774
Finished products	15,925	16,495
	$ 35,672	$ 38,800
Prepaid expenses	1,798	1,839
Total current assets	$ 79,590	$ 76,399
Investments and other assets:		
Investments in unconsolidated subsidiaries, including advances of $3,311,444 ($3,170,606 at March 31, 1968)	13,851	14,677
Other	1,052	1,101
Property, plant, and equipment—on the basis of cost:		
Land	$ 3,035	$ 3,583
Buildings	21,147	23,671
Machinery, equipment, and fixtures	35,044	38,287
Leasehold improvements	861	864
	$ 60,086	$ 66,405
Less: Allowances for depreciation and amortization	21,247	23,165
	$ 38,839	$ 43,241
Intangible assets (patents, trade-marks, goodwill, etc.)	1,138	1,317
Total assets	$ 134,470	$ 136,735
LIABILITIES AND SHAREHOLDERS' EQUITY		
Current liabilities:		
Trade payables	$ 4,956	$ 4,115
Salaries, wages, and related items	3,328	4,006
Federal income taxes	8,056	5,194
Other	3,246	4,173
Current portion of long-term notes payable—Note A	1,822	1,821
Total current liabilities	$ 21,408	$ 19,309
Long-term notes payable—Note A	17,404	16,230
Shareholders' equity:		
Common stock—par value $1—authorized 12,000,000 shares (15,000,000 at March 31, 1968); issued 10,749,136 shares (10,783,033 at March 31, 1968) including 90,524 shares in treasury (83,301 at March 31, 1968) and 111,112 shares held by a wholly owned subsidiary	$ 18,221	$ 18,255
Capital in excess of par value	25,025	25,778
Retained earnings	53,435	58,174
	$ 96,681	$ 102,207
Less treasury stock—at cost	1,023	1,011
Total shareholders' equity	$ 95,658	101,196
Total liabilities and shareholders' equity	$ 134,470	$ 136,735

Exhibit 3—Continued

NOTE A—LONG-TERM NOTES PAYABLE

	September 30, 1967	March 31, 1968 (Unaudited)
Notes payable to an insurance company and a pension trust:		
5½% promissory notes, due December 31, 1978	$ 3,600,000	$ 3,300,000
6% subordinated notes, due December 31, 1983	1,700,000	1,600,000
5⅛% promissory notes, due December 31, 1982	9,000,000	8,500,000
Notes (5%) payable to banks as trustees and agents, due in quarterly installments through October 1, 1985	1,893,209	1,860,953
6½% term loan (7½% at March 31, 1968) payable to bank December 31, 1969, to 1971	1,163,750	1,163,750
Sundry notes (5% to 6½%), with varied repayments through 1981	1,869,011	1,625,610
	$19,225,970	$18,050,313
Less portion included in current liabilities	1,822,339	1,820,626
	$17,403,631	$16,229,687

Notes payable to an insurance company and a pension trust are subject to fixed sinking fund payments of $900,000 annually. The company has optional prepayment privileges under certain conditions. These notes provide, among other things, that the company and its consolidated subsidiaries will limit: (1) indebtedness for borrowed money; (2) investments in companies other than restricted subsidiaries, as defined; (3) annual rentals under long-term leases, as defined. Such limitations vary with conditions related generally to the growth of the company. The company has agreed to maintain specified amounts of consolidated net current assets, as defined. At September 30, 1967, and March 31, 1968, there was an excess of approximately $36,000,000 and $37,000,000, respectively, over the then required amounts of consolidated net current assets. In addition, declaration or payment of cash dividends and the acquisition or retirement of the company's capital stock are limited to an amount equivalent to consolidated net income, as defined, subsequent to September 30, 1961. At September 30, 1967, and March 31, 1968, retained earnings of approximately $31,000,000 and $35,000,000, respectively, were unrestricted under such limitation.

The aggregate annual maturities (including sinking fund payments) of long-term notes payable during the fiscal years ending September 30, 1968 to 1972, are as follows: 1968, $1,824,320; 1969, $1,300,478; 1970, $1,431,278; 1971, $1,626,347; 1972, $1,309,874.

Exhibit 4

BECTON, DICKINSON AND COMPANY
DATA ON SELECTED RECENT ISSUES OF SUBORDINATED CONVERTIBLE DEBENTURES AS COMPILED MARCH 12, 1968

Rating	*Offering Date*	*Company*	*Size of Offering (000)*	*Coupon Rate*	*Conversion Price*	*Market Price at Offering*	*Conversion Premium*
NR	9/06/67	Monogram Ind.	$25,000	4%	$45	41½(2)	8.4%
BB	9/06/67	Will Ross	12,000	4¼	74½	60	24.2
BB	9/14/67	Parker Hannifin	20,000	4	76	65½	16.0
B	11/21/67	Sanders Assoc.	35,000	5	67	60¾	10.3
BB	12/01/67	General Instrument	50,000	5	67	63	6.3
BB	12/05/67	Fischer & Porter	6,000	5½	32⅓	29	11.5
BB	1/17/68	Walt Disney Prod.	40,000	4½	65	56⅞	14.3
BBB	3/05/68	Baxter Labs.	25,000	4½	42	35	20.0
		Becton, Dickinson	25,000				

(1) At the time of the offering, giving effect to the offering.
(2) Adjusted for 3 for 1 split.

	Current Prices				
	Com. Price	*Com. Div.*	*Com. Yield*	*Deb. Price*	*Deb. Yield*
Monogram Ind. 4s	47	nil	already called		
Will Ross 4¼s	73½	$0.50	0.68%	$111	3.83%
Parker Hannifin 4s	45½	1.20	2.64	84¾	4.72
Sanders Assoc. 5s	47⅛	0.30	0.64	102½	4.88
General Instrument 5s	47⅛	1.08	2.29	92	5.43
Fischer & Porter 5½s	21	0.98	4.67	92	5.98
Walt Disney Prod. 4½s	48⅜	0.30	0.62	98¼	4.58
Baxter Labs. 4½s	36¾	0.16	0.44	105	4.29
Becton, Dickinson	59⅞	0.30	0.50	—	—

Exhibit 4—Continued

EPS 1967	1966	1965	1964	1963	P/E Ratio (1)		LTD as % Total Cap. (1)	Book Value per $1,000 LTD (1)	Market Value per $1,000 LTD (1)
$0.96	$0.52	$0.27	$0.19	$0.09	43.2X	Lehman, Blyth	63.5	$ 575	$ 3,333
1.53E	1.42	1.24	1.07	0.93	39.2X	White, Weld	43.2	1,315	7,966
3.41	3.06	2.23	1.65	1.43	19.2X	Kidder	41.8	1,394	5,165
1.23	0.67	0.70	0.73	0.72	49.4X	Lehman	46.0	1,175	7,727
2.00E	2.27	1.38	0.82	0.46	31.5X	Loeb Rhoades	46.3	1,158	3,857
1.81	1.63	1.54	1.03	0.75	19.9X	Drexel	44.7	1,209	1,907
2.52	3.17	3.04	1.98	1.91	22.6X	Kidder, Lehman	36.1	1,767	5,505
0.70	0.53	0.37	0.27	0.26	50.0X	M.L.P., F.& S.	49.8	1,007	8,736
1.17	1.05	0.84	0.71	0.55			32.8	2,242	15,080

Assume $25 MM Offering

Gross Spread	*When Callable*	
1.50%	At any time	Usually with 30 days' notice
1.25	At any time	Plus various sinking fund provisions
1.25	At any time	At various premiums
1.25	At any time	In whole or in part
1.25	At any time	
2.75	At any time	
1.25	At any time	
1.25	At any time	
—		Unless in default

Exhibit 5

BECTON, DICKINSON AND COMPANY
Common Stock Prices and Volume of Trading
March 11 to June 17, 1968

	Closing Price	Volume
March 11	59⅞	3,800
12	58⅞	5,500
13	59⅝	2,600
14	57¼	5,000
15	57¼	7,000
March 18	57¾	14,900
19	57⅞	1,500
20	56⅞	3,100
21	56⅞	2,100
22	56¾	3,900
March 29	59⅞	6,100
April 15	64	7,600
30	64¾	1,300
May 13	69¼	4,300
14	67⅞	3,800
15	67½	1,900
16	67	1,000
17	66⅜	3,300
May 20	65¾	1,300
21	67¼	2,500
22	66⅛	2,400
23	66½	2,100
24	65⅞	8,800
May 27	66½	1,200
28	66¼	12,700
29	66¼	5,400
30	Holiday	
31	68½	2,600
June 3	67	3,800
4	66⅝	3,200
5	66¾	4,300
6	67⅜	3,000
7	67⅞	3,400
June 10	67⅜	1,200
11	66½	3,700
12	Market closed	
13	65¾	4,400
14	66⅛	8,800
June 17	64⅝	5,300

Exhibit 6

BECTON, DICKINSON AND COMPANY
Convertible Subordinated Debentures Pricing Comparison
(as compiled June 14, 1968)

Rating S & P	Rating Moody	Company	Coupon and Maturity	Size of Issue (Millions)	Date of Issue	Conversion Price	Current Market Price of Stock (1)	Current Market Price of Bond
					1967			
BB	Ba	Will Ross	4¼s '87	12.0	9/6	74.50	90	120
BB	Ba	Parker Hannifin	4s '92	20.0	9/14	76.00	57⅛	90¼
B	Ba	Sanders Associates	5s '92	35.0	11/21	67.00	58¼	111¼
BB	Ba	Fischer & Porter	5½s '87	6.0	12/5	32 33	25	105
BB	Ba	General Instrument	5s '92	50.0	12/01	67.00	53¼	104
					1968			
BB	Ba	Walt Disney	4½s '93	40.0	1/17	65.00	68¼	127
BBB	Ba	Baxter Labs.	4½s '88	25.0	3/5	42.00	51½	134
BBB	Baa	White Motor	5¼s '93	25.0	3/12	54.50	54⅛	112
B	Ba	Sundstrand	5s '93	30.0	4/4	71.00	89¼	132
B	B	Indian Head	5½s '93	25.0	4/10	38.50	37¼	109
BB	B	Lucky Stores	5s '93	28.0	4/23	45.00	45⅝	115
BBB	Baa	Burroughs	3¾s '93	75.0	5/16	253.50	213⅞	102
BB	Ba	Ogden Corp.	5s '93	50.0	6/4	50.00	48¾	108¾
B	Ba	Am. Hoist & Derrick	5½s '93	18.0	6/5	21.50	18½	99¾
BBB	Baa	Becton, Dickinson	— '88	25.0	—	—	65¾	—

(1) Closing prices June 13, 1968.
(2) *Conversion Value*—Current common market price × number of shares into which convertible.

Exhibit 6—Continued

Conversion Value (2) per $1000 Bond	*Conversion Premium*	*Current Bond Yield*	*Current Conversion Yield (3)*	*Common Stock Price Range 1967–68*	*Gross Spread*	*Yield*	*Conversion Premium*	*Managing Underwriter*
120.78		3.54	0.56	90–36½	1.25%	4.25%	24.2%	White, Weld
75.18	20.0	4.71	1.75	67¼–38¾	1.25	4.00	16.0	Kidder Peabody
86.97	27.9	4.49	0.40	77¼–26⅝	1.25	5.00	10.3	Lehman—Kidder Peabody
77.33	35.8	5.24	—	37⅛–16⅛	2.75	5.50	11.5	Drexel
79.50	30.8	4.81	—	86–40⅛	1.25	5.00	6.3	Loeb Rhoades
104.97	21.0	3.54	0.36	68½–37½	1.25	4.50	14.3	Kidder Peabody—Lehman
122.62	9.3	3.36	0.28	54⅞–19⅜	1.25	4.50	20.0	MLPFS—White, Weld
99.32	12.8	4.69	3.28	57½–36⅞	0.875(4)	5.25	13.5	Blyth
125.66	5.0	3.79	0.85	90¾–29½	1.25	5.00	16.2	Hornblower—White, Weld
96.74	12.7	5.05	1.43	46–18⅝	1.875	5.50	11.6	White Weld—Blair
101.38	13.4	4.35	2.32	47⅛–16¼	1.75	5.00	13.2	MLPFS—Lehman—Goldman Sachs
84.27	21.0	3.68	0.38	220⅜–80⅞	1.125	3.75	20.5	Kidder Peabody
97.50	11.5	4.60	1.47	52–15¼	1.75	5.00	8.0	Allen—Wertheim
86.04	15.9	5.51	3.26	24⅜–10½	1.50	5.50	10.2	Lehman
—	—	—	—	71⅞–39½	—	—	—	F. Eberstadt & Co.

(3) *Conversion Yield*—Common dividend × number of shares into which convertible as % of bond price.
(4) This issue was combined in a package with an issue of $22 million in common stock.

MIDWESTERN TRANSMISSION COMPANY (A)

In late February, 1964, Mr. John Truscott, senior partner of Morehead, Dormer & Co., was considering the recommendation he should make to Midwestern Transmission Co. (MTC) concerning how that company should best meet immediate needs for capital. As Mr. Frank Michaels, president of MTC, had explained during a mid-December trip to New York City, the company needed approximately \$2.6 million new equity capital to complete the financing of its 1964 expansion program. Mr. Michaels had been concerned about the recent softness in the market price of the company's common stock. He emphasized, however, that he did not want to see the momentum of the company interrupted by the meanderings of the stock market, and expressed his belief that Mr. Truscott could raise the \$2.6 million without "giving the company away" or otherwise impairing the market potential of the company's shares. Mr. Truscott had played a major role in the large, complex, and successful initial financing of MTC and hoped that resourcefulness and imagination might point to an effective resolution of the current financing problem.

Currently, MTC's capital structure was as follows:

		Million
6%	First mortgage pipeline bonds	\$40.0
6%	Convertible promissory note*	3.0
5¼%	Promissory notes	6.0
6½%	Subordinated debentures	20.5
	Common stock (1,838,700 shares)	14.0
		\$83.5

* Convertible into common stock at \$10.

Mr. Truscott was well aware of a widespread opinion among major investors that MTC was "leveraged to the hilt," particularly as compared with other companies with pipeline interests (see Exhibit 1). For this reason alone, Mr. Truscott and Mr. Michaels realized that additional debt financing would not be feasible at this point. Moreover, the covenants of the outstanding senior debt issue, as well as of the \$6 million bank term loan closed on February 14, required the prior consent of these creditors to any further issues of funded debt or execution of sale-leaseback agreements. Northern Mutual Life Insurance Co., the senior debtholder, had given such consent in the past, but in conjunction with the bankers had insisted that the next MTC move be to strengthen its equity base.

Mr. Truscott first had considered two conventional methods of raising equity funds, a straight common issue and one of convertible preferred stock. As he reviewed MTC's unique history, however, he thought that an entirely new approach—that of selling warrants to buy common stock—might have some very attractive possibilities. Mr. Truscott believed that in order to protect MTC's current stockholders a rights offering would be appropriate, regardless of the security selected. Before his scheduled meeting with Mr. Michaels at the end of the week, he expected to reach a conclusion as to which of these alternatives would best meet MTC's needs.

ORIGINS

In 1957 officers of the Prairie Railroad Co., looking for diversification opportunities, conceived the idea of building a pipeline for the transportation of liquefied petroleum gas (LPG). The original plan was to build a line from West Texas to Albany, New York, in partnership with an eastern railroad, using as much of their combined rights-of-way as possible. After a year and a half of study the idea was dropped because of lack of shipper support, reductions in railroad tank car charges, and the threat of imports along the East Coast.

In early 1959, Mr. Michaels, chairman of the executive committee of Prairie, found that a number of shippers were interested in moving LPG to central Kansas and the upper Middle West. Despite the facts that Prairie's rights-of-way were not in ideal places and that only a large pipeline would be economically feasible, Mr. Michaels went ahead with preliminary engineering and design, setting the route and securing letters of intent.[1] A feasibility study based on 13 letters of intent was completed in November, projecting volume sufficient for profitable operation. On December 1, 1959, Mr. Michaels made the decision to go ahead. He promised the skeptical LP gas industry that the system would be in operation within a year. As he explained later, "The reason for the haste was simple. It appeared to me that if we did not get the system built in 1960, by 1961 the industry might have found some way to do it themselves and push us out of the picture."

The pipeline was in full operation on December 8, 1960.

In addition to his position with Prairie, Mr. Michaels had been for seven years vice president of the Park Avenue Fund, and had known Mr. Truscott in this capacity. In early December, 1959, he called on Mr. Truscott and told his story. On the basis of the feasibility study, the letters of intent from the shippers and their confidence in Mr. Michaels' ability, Morehead, Dormer & Co. agreed to go ahead with the financing.

[1] Letters of intent simply expressed the shippers' expectations that they would use the proposed pipeline when the pipeline was constructed and operating at planned rate schedules. Unlike take-or-pay and throughput contracts, letters of intent in no way legally bound the signer to use the proposed facilities.

INITIAL FINANCING

The original capitalization of MTC was $600,000, distributed as follows: Morehead, Dormer & Co. and Prairie Management Co. (wholly owned subsidiary of Prairie) each put up $60,000 original capital for 39,500 shares of common stock; and Prairie Management Co. took a note for $480,000, converted automatically into 316,000 shares of common upon a successful public offering, in exchange for $215,000 cash and rights to various preliminary reports, surveys, material orders, etc.

The group projected the cost of the pipeline at $70 million, Mr. Michaels having agreed to add a $3 million contingency reserve to his original $67 million estimate. The bankers suggested that they attempt to raise $42 million of senior money and the rest through a junior debt-equity package.

After discussions with signers of the letters of intent, Northern Mutual in mid-January agreed to purchase a $42 million issue of 6% first mortgage pipeline bonds and a $3 million 6% convertible promissory note. Northern Mutual paid $42 million cash for the $45 million debt package. The $42 million mortgage bonds were repayable in 25 semiannual installments from May 1, 1963, to May 1, 1975, in amounts increasing gradually from $1.1 to a $2.2 million final payment. The $3 million note, due May 1, 1975, was convertible into 300,000 shares of common stock.

On March 30, 1960, a syndicate managed by Morehead, Dormer & Co. made a public offering of $20.5 million 6½% subordinated debentures and 1,435,000 shares of common stock packaged into 410,000 units. Each unit, consisting of $50 principal amount of debentures and 3½ shares of stock, was priced at $73.50. Of the total proceeds of the successful offering, $30.1 million, MTC netted $28.6 million. On the basis of debenture and common stock market performance after the two started trading separately, the total financing was accounted for as follows:

ASSET ENTRIES		LIABILITY ENTRIES	
	Northern Mutual Financing		
Cash	$42,000,000	First mortgage bonds	$42,000,000
Bond discount	3,000,000	Convertible note	3,000,000
	Public Offering		
Cash	28,600,000		
Bond discount	3,400,000	Subordinated debentures	20,500,000
Bond expense	1,500,000	Common stock	13,000,000
	$78,500,000		$78,500,000

The terms of the $20.5 million subordinated debenture issue contained two provisions calculated to add flexibility to MTC's short and medium-term finances: (1) those semiannual interest payments due up to March 1, 1964 would be deferred if not covered by "Earnings Available for Interest," which was defined as net income plus noncash charges less the sinking fund payments required under the mortgage bond agreement; (2) sinking fund payments were $500,000 annually from 1970 to 1975 contingent on earnings coverage and $2.5 million mandatory payments from 1976 to the final maturity, March, 1980.

OPERATIONS

MTC's pipeline currently extended from sources in Texas, New Mexico, and Oklahoma to nine states in the Midwest. Since it began operations in December, 1960, MTC had serviced an increasing share of the growing propane market in its nine-state area:

	1958	*1959*	*1960*	*1961*	*1962*	*1963*
Sales of propane*.......	72,800	88,700	97,800	98,800	109,400	n.a.
Delivered by MTC*.....	—	—	—	27,040	44,900	55,290

* In annual average barrels per day.

The principal use of propane in 1964 was for home and commercial heating, but the demand for cooking and major appliance operation also was significant. Because use for domestic and commercial heating accounted for 85% of total propane use, demand was highly seasonal in nature. The company had built large underground storage facilities in both its source and market areas, in order to increase use of the pipeline during the summer months and to increase deliverability of the system during peak cold weather periods. Present peak deliverability was estimated to be 135,000 barrels per day, with about 20% originating from the market area storage capacity.

COMPETITION

The company's most immediate competition as a supplier of propane came from shippers by railroad tank cars. At its delivery terminals MTC's rates were often 30% to 50% below the railroads' rates. Mr. Michaels believed MTC offered greater dependability of supply than the railroads as well as lower costs of handling and expediting the product. Nevertheless, the railroads remained important suppliers of propane because many shipper-producers owned fleets of tank cars and planned to use them until they were ready to be scrapped. Of course, railroad tank cars as well as trucks were used for short hauls from MTC delivery terminals.

Natural gas, fuel oil, and coal were also used as fuel in the market area. As a rule, only natural gas was competitive with propane on a price basis, and was generally less expensive than propane at locations served by natural gas mains. Electricity was competitive for uses other than space and central heating.

Since the summer of 1963, Northern Natural Gas Co. had moved LP gas by pipeline into MTC's market area, with terminals located in four states. Mr. Michaels felt that Northern's entry and possibly further expansion would have some but by no means an important adverse effect on MTC's revenues.

Only one of the several other pipelines in and around MTC's market area currently was equipped to carry LPG. Owned by a large integrated oil company, this pipeline carried the company's products to terminals on the southeastern fringe of MTC's area and was not considered a major competitor. Mr. Michaels believed that shippers owning the other pipelines would continue to use MTC rather than make the alterations and additions necessary to handle LPG in their own lines. Since apparently such alterations had been uneconomic in the late 1950's when railroad tank cars were the only alternative, Mr. Michaels thought they would make even less sense currently under MTC's reduced rate schedules.

FUNDS FLOWS AND EXPANSION

As had been projected in the original feasibility study, MTC showed \$3.2 million in losses prior to the last quarter of 1961, when it was able to report a nominal profit (see Exhibit 2). On a cash basis, these losses were offset by \$3.1 million of depreciation and amortization of deferred charges. Additionally, MTC began operations with substantial cash reserves, as evidenced in its balance sheet of December 31, 1960 (see Exhibit 3), resulting from the fact that the pipeline system was built for \$63.1 million, more than \$5 million below budget, and, as Mr. Michaels pointed out with pride, with a higher throughput capacity than originally planned.

Mr. Michaels immediately began using these surplus funds to improve the system and to further increase its capacity. MTC's yearly expansion programs included two lateral pipelines increasing the company's effective market area, additions to pumping power and underground storage capacity, and a diversifying move into oil and gas properties.

In September, 1963, MTC acquired for \$4.4 million various oil- and gas-producing properties, including natural gas liquids under 234,000 acres in the West Panhandle field in Texas, various interests in oil and gas properties in eight states, and a partially constructed gasoline plant, producing LPG in an unfractionated stream. MTC completed construction of the gasoline plant by November at a cost of \$1.3 million. The properties were purchased subject to "reserved interests" totaling \$19.6 million. These "reserved interests" were obligations not of MTC but of the properties themselves, and were to be retired (including approximately 5¾% interest on the outstanding balance) entirely from revenues derived from the properties, after deductions of (1) MTC's operating expenses and (2) \$25,000 per month for 60 months, to reimburse the company for gasoline plant construction costs. MTC would receive no material cash flows from production properties until the reserved interests were retired, which the company estimated should take 9 to 11 years, subject to significant changes in prices or allowed levels of production.

The underground storage facilities cost \$2.6 million and with Northern Mutual's permission were financed by a sale-leaseback arrangement. The other programs, which cost \$16.7 million, were financed by MTC's original cash resources, net cash flows in 1962 and 1963 of \$4.5 and \$3.4 million, and a 1963 short-term bank loan of $3.5 million. The bank loan was arranged to allow the cash purchase of the production properties with the explicit understanding that the loan would be repaid soon out of the proceeds of long-term financing. As the 1964 expansion program began to take shape, Mr. Michaels realized that the company would have to make another trip to the market.

After registering sizable increases in 1962 and 1963 (see Exhibit 2), MTC's earnings turned sharply downward in January, 1964. Contributing to the lower results for January were unusually warm weather and the delivery by MTC of propane produced by new government-sponsored helium plants in southwestern Kansas, resulting in shorter deliveries and lower average revenue per barrel. Also, in late 1963 the company had exhausted its tax loss carry-forward and was for the first time required to bear the normal tax burden.

The unseasonable weather was widely predicted to continue through March. Thus company projections of 12 months' earnings to March 31, 1964, showed that despite a 10% increase in barrels delivered, pretax income would drop to $0.83 per share from $1.01 for the previous 12 months. Mr. Michaels was confident that the downturn would be reversed in short order. His long-term expansion plans covered a broad spectrum of projects, including additions to present pipelines, storage, and production operations; petrochemical plants in MTC's market area; pipelines for nonpetroleum products; and, as Mr. Michaels put it, "anything that will make money for the stockholder."

THE 1964 FINANCING

Common stock

Mr. Truscott's review of the materials he had assembled on MTC reinforced his impressions that (1) new equity money for MTC was called for from every point of view and (2) the timing of an equity financing was unfortunate. His preliminary analysis suggested that an announcement of an imminent offering of common stock, in conjunction with MTC's disappointing and fully taxed current earnings, would result in a decline in the market price of the common from its present level of $17 to $15. As a result, the new issue would be priced at around $13½, and MTC would net about $12½ after all issue costs. A price of $13½ would represent a 50% premium over the 1960 imputed offering price of about $9, and a much greater premium over the founders' investment of $1.52 per share. Yet such a price would be below the lowest bid price for MTC stock since shortly after the 1960 offering, and less than half the 1961 high of $27¼ (see Exhibit 4).

MTC's price-earnings ratio of 16 was similar to ratios of the pipeline companies listed in Exhibit 1, which ranged from 15 to 18. However, certain factors limited the comparability of MTC with the other pipeline companies. First, MTC's 1963 earnings were not taxed. Second, the other companies were paying dividends ranging upward of 60% of earnings, while it was MTC's current policy to pay no dividends. Third, the other companies were typically much larger and had a longer growth record. Fourth, the other companies were regulated public utilities, which contributed to a stability of earnings and cash flows that MTC could not yet demonstrate. Thus a precise assessment of the value of MTC's unique operation was difficult; however, Mr. Truscott believed that since MTC's future looked no less promising than originally projected, and since the company's 1965 and 1966 pretax earnings were estimated by Mr. Michaels to reach several times their 1963 level, MTC's common stock was at present underpriced.

Apart from the near-term impact on the market price, a major disadvantage of a common offering was that the 210,000 shares which would have to be issued in order that MTC net \$2.6 million (at \$12½ per share) would result in immediate earnings dilution of approximately 10%.

On the other hand, Mr. Truscott's discussions with his associates had suggested several potential advantages of a common offering:

1. The market for MTC common would be broadened, which would have a beneficial effect on the marketability and perhaps the price of future common offerings, partially offsetting the depressing effects of the current offering.

2. A common offering would add solidity to the company's current financial structure and flexibility in meeting future needs. It was apparent that Mr. Michaels' aggressive plans would require future trips to the market. Using common now would leave more doors open for his next trip.

3. Common, as opposed to preferred, would reduce leverage and thus risk, rather than accentuate it; and it would not require dividends.

4. Common, as opposed to warrants, would be viewed as a conventional and appropriate source for MTC's needs by all parties concerned.

Convertible preferred stock

A successful issue of preferred stock would require a cash dividend, and in MTC's circumstances a sizable one. MTC had no immediate plans for paying a cash dividend on its common, and planned to use all cash generated by operations for expansion. If the company prospered, conversion could be forced through call within a short period, and the sale of convertible preferred stock could be viewed as a deferred sale of common above the market, and consequently as causing less long-term dilution of earnings. Until conversion, assuming a minimum dividend rate of 6%, preferred dividend requirements would be \$156,000, or on a pretax basis \$290,000, or 13% of MTC's 1963 pretax earnings of \$2.2 million. Thus immediate reduction of EPS would exceed the 10% dilution projected under a common offering. Moreover, a convertible preferred issue would add an element of complexity to the company's capital structure and while outstanding might make more difficult the sale of further equity issues.

Warrants

Mr. Truscott was also considering another method of selling common stock above the market, a direct sale of warrants. To his knowledge no company had ever used warrants as a direct source of equity funds. Nonetheless, he thought the possibility worth a full analysis. For purposes of review, he turned to a file containing material he had collected on warrants.

Like an option, a warrant entitled its holder to exchange it for common stock of a company at a fixed price and in a given ratio for either a specified time period or in perpetuity. Warrants had no value other than as an option to buy common stock; they carried no voting or dividend rights (but typically were protected by antidilution provisions) and in themselves had no claim on either assets or earnings. The warrants issued by a number of firms were traded freely in the over-the-counter market. The movement in the market value of the warrants was closely tied to that of the related common stock, but the warrants' price movements were often much greater than the fluctuations of the stock because of leverage, which could be substantial. For example, Company A had warrants outstanding which entitled the holder to purchase one share of common for $20. Since the market price of "A" common was $25, the warrant price would in theory have been $5. A prospective investor might have reflected that if "A" common should go to $30, the warrant would presumably sell for $10; thus he might have chosen the warrant for one of two reasons. First, he could get the same "play" on 20% of the cash outlay, in effect a 20% margin with the advantage that he would pay no interest on the $20 differential. Second, for an equal investment he could purchase five times as much play—on both the upside and the downside!

In fact, because of the speculative appeal, perhaps to a limited segment of the market, of "more bang for the buck," warrants with a significant remaining life had consistently sold at a premium.[2] A contributing factor may have been their scarcity value; of some 150 warrant issues currently outstanding, less than half were actively traded, and most issues were quite small relative to the associated common stock outstanding. Warrants had been created for several purposes: (1) as a "sweetener," they had sometimes been attached to a debt issue; (2) they had occasionally arisen from a merger, as a device to make the deal more attractive to the owners of the acquired company; (3) they had been used at the time of a company's organization or afterwards as a means of noncash payment to underwriters and others for services rendered.

Although he knew that warrants had commanded a premium in the marketplace, Mr. Truscott had not followed particular warrant issues closely and had wanted additional information to determine the features which would be most appropriate for an MTC warrant issue and the approximate size of the premium MTC warrants could command.

At Mr. Truscott's request, one of his assistants had prepared a report on the current warrant market. This report indicated that many aspects of the

---

[2] That is, above the level at which the buyer would be indifferent between (*a*) buying the common and (*b*) buying the warrant and "exercising" it, or exchanging the warrant plus a specified amount of cash for a new share of common. Using the example of Company A above, with an "exercise price" of $20 and the common selling at $25, the warrant might sell for $8, in which case the premium would be $3.

market behavior of warrants generally remained obscure or ambiguous. However, it seemed clear that, *ceteris paribus*, a larger premium was likely when the warrant was:

1. Of significant life;
2. Issued by a company with dynamic growth records and prospects as compared with those of companies with "flatter" earnings records and less exciting outlooks;
3. Highly leveraged.

Roughing out possible terms for a warrant issue by MTC, Mr. Truscott first determined that 8 to 10 years would be an appropriate term for the warrants. With respect to the degree of leverage to be built into the warrants, Mr. Truscott tentatively concluded that a warrant price about equal to the exercise price should have adequate investor appeal. A higher price would, of course, reduce the number of warrants that would have to be issued in order to raise the desired $2.6 million, but might well dissipate the speculative attractiveness of the warrants.

Mr. Truscott also had reached the tentative conclusion to add a unique feature—a provision that warrants remaining unexercised at expiry date would not become valueless but would instead be converted automatically into one-half share of common stock.

With these tentative provisions in mind, Mr. Truscott called a number of potential investors for their reaction to such an issue. Many reacted with enthusiasm, and Mr. Truscott concluded that with MTC common selling at $17, warrants to purchase one share at $9 could be priced at $9 to stockholders. In effect, stock would be sold for $18 per share. The enthusiasm of potential investors for the proposal, however, raised the possibility that existing shareholders holding MTC common for capital gains might well find the warrants a more attractive speculative vehicle than the stock itself. If many were to sell the common in order to exercise their warrant rights or purchase warrants after a market was established, the price of MTC common would be driven down. From his knowledge of the potential market for MTC shares, Mr. Truscott believed that Morehead, Dormer & Co. could find enough buyers to keep the price from falling below $15.50. If the warrants sold up to $10 after the offering (as would be the case in a successful offering), the resulting premium would be 3½ points per share (19–15½) or 23% of the price of the common, which did not appear to be out of line with the current warrant market.

In discussions of a potential warrant offering with his associates, several possible advantages to MTC were put forward:

1. MTC could in effect sell common above the market at $18, as opposed to $13½ if common were offered directly.
2. The proceeds of the warrant offering would be credited directly to capital as would be the proceeds of the alternative offerings; however, a warrant offering would postpone *reported* dilution of earnings per share until they

were exercised. Presumably, they would not be exercised until near their expiry date in eight years. This would be attributable to the premium. As long as the warrants sold at a premium, warrantholders desiring to acquire the stock would find it cheaper to sell the warrant and buy the desired shares directly in the market. Although warrants would be entitled to neither dividends nor votes, there would appear to be some justification for taking them into account when reporting earnings per share; but to date reporting services had sidestepped the issue by ignoring them.

3. Because it appeared that warrants would have an especial appeal for certain types of investors, it was estimated that investment bankers could sell a warrant issue much more readily and at less expense than a straight issue of stock. Mr. Truscott believed that the underwriting charge would be approximately $0.30 per warrant, as opposed to as much as 10% if common were issued.
4. Eight years hence, assuming the warrants would be exercised at that time, MTC would receive an additional $2.6 million with no financing charge.

Several observations were expressed regarding possible disadvantages to MTC:

1. Approximately 300,000 warrants would have to be issued in order for MTC to net $2.6 million. This would mean an ultimate increase in outstanding shares of 300,000 (conceivably 150,000 if MTC common were selling below $18 in 1982 and thus the warrants were not exercised) resulting in per share earnings dilution of 14%. Since MTC did not expect to pay dividends for many years, a warrantholder who exercised his warrants in 1972 would acquire a pro rata share in all undistributed earnings of the company to that date as well as in future earnings.
2. No company had made a direct warrants offering before. Moreover, many warrants had been issued to add appeal to an otherwise unattractive security issue. Few of the "blue-chip" companies had warrants outstanding. At the minimum, they would add a relatively unfamiliar element to MTC's capital structure, and might tend to limit the company's flexibility and the marketability of its future equity issues.
3. To the extent that a warrant issue would encourage a speculative image for MTC's stock, the stock would tend to be held by active traders rather than long-term investors; the resulting amplified price swings might further restrict the breadth of the investor market for MTC common, and might make it especially difficult for MTC to raise equity funds in depressed market periods.

Exhibit 1

MIDWESTERN TRANSMISSION COMPANY (A)
CAPITALIZATION OF PIPELINE COMPANIES

Company	*Total Capitalization (in Millions of Dollars)*	*Term Debt*	*Preferred*	*Common*
Buckeye Pipe Line Co.	$ 69.3	45%	—	55%
El Paso Natural Gas Company	1,208.4	70	10%	20
Mississippi River Fuel Corporation	138.9	61	—	39
Northern Natural Gas Company	531.0	54	9	37
Panhandle Eastern Pipe Line Company	295.6	57	9	34
Southern Natural Gas Company	249.9	53	—	47
Tennessee Gas Transmission Company	1,836.8	59	13	28
MTC	83.5	83	—	17

Exhibit 2

MIDWESTERN TRANSMISSION COMPANY (A)
INCOME STATEMENTS, YEARS ENDED DECEMBER 31
(In thousands except per share data)

	1960	*1961*	*1962*	*1963*
Revenues	$ 556	$ 7,120	$11,988	$14,748
Expenses:				
Operating	265	1,633	1,893	2,789
General and administrative	187	928	928	1,095
Depreciation and depletion	315	2,225	2,351	2,889
State and local taxes	19	435	612	717
Interest	336	3,819	4,042	4,396
Amortization	54	648	654	648
Pretax income	$(620)	$(2,568)	$ 1,508	$ 2,214
Income taxes	—	—	—	245
Net income	(620)	(2,568)	1,508	1,969
Earnings per share	$(0.34)	$ (1.40)	$ 0.82	$ 1.07

Exhibit 3

MIDWESTERN TRANSMISSION COMPANY (A)
BALANCE SHEETS, DECEMBER 31
(In thousands)

	1960	*1961*	*1962*	*1963*
ASSETS				
Cash	$ 1,899	$ 699	$ 548	$ 672
U.S. securities	4,100	3,274	1,702	—
Receivables	544	1,274	1,869	2,499
Inventory	—	235	383	466
Total current assets	$ 6,543	$ 5,452	$ 4,502	$ 3,637
Special deposits, etc.	4,172	259	53	—
Marketable securities	—	—	1,019	1,426
Fixed assets	62,221	64,025	66,254	71,518
Deferred charges	8,602	7,990	7,362	6,697
Total assets	$81,538	$77,726	$79,190	$83,278
LIABILITIES				
Notes payable	—	—	—	$ 3,500
Accounts payable	$ 2,977	$ 489	$ 263	573
Current term debt	—	—	2,213	2,347
Accrued interest	—	894	894	897
Other	44	292	409	699
Total current liabilities	$ 3,021	$ 1,675	$ 3,779	$ 8,016
Construction advances	—	100	158	128
First mortgage bonds	42,000	42,000	39,787	37,440
Promissory note	3,000	3,000	3,000	3,000
Subordinated debentures	20,500	20,500	20,500	20,500
Deferred taxes	—	—	—	228
Common stock	13,637	13,639	13,646	13,677
Retained earnings	(620)	(3,188)	(1,680)	289
Total liabilities	$81,538	$77,726	$79,190	$83,278

Exhibit 4

MIDWESTERN TRANSMISSION COMPANY (A)
Bid Price of MTC Common Stock*

	1960	*1961*	*1962*	*1963*	*1964*
January		24¾	22	19¼	16
February		23¼	22	20	
March	9¼	22¾	20	18¾	
April	8⅞	20⅛	21	17½	
May	10½	21	16	18¼	
June	12¾	19¾	15¾	19⅞	
July	11¾	20	16¾	18¾	
August	14⅛	21½	17½	18⅞	
September	14½	22¼	15¾	16⅞	
October	16	22¼	14½	16¼	
November	19½	21½	16½	16¼	
December	20½	20	17½	17½	
Bid price range for year:					
High	21¾	27¼	24½	20¼	17½
Low	8¾	18¾	13¾	15¾	16

* On last day of month.
Source: *Bank and Quotation Record.*

AMERICAN WOOLEN COMPANY

^^

In June, 1946, the preferred and common stockholders of the American Woolen Company were asked to approve a plan of recapitalization proposed by the directors of the company. Since the plan involved basic changes in the company's articles of incorporation, the approval of stockholders owning two thirds of each class of stock, preferred and common, was required.

The recapitalization plan sought to eliminate dividend arrearages on the 350,000 shares of 7% cumulative, noncallable, preferred stock outstanding. Elimination of the arrearages, which on June 3, 1946, amounted to $20,475,000 or $58.50 a share, would make legally possible the resumption of dividend payments on the 400,000 shares of common stock of the company. The common stockholders had received no dividends for 22 years, the last payment having been made in July, 1924.

After many years of low profits or operating deficits, the company had made substantial profits during the war years. Earnings and preferred dividend payments are shown in Exhibit 1.

In the annual report to stockholders dated February 20, 1946, the president of American Woolen had discussed the problem of the arrearages in the light of recent profitable operations of the company. He said:

> During the ten years ended December 31, 1945 the company paid dividends totaling $70.00 per share on the Preferred stock, an average of $7.00 per year, which was just enough to keep the Preferred dividends current without reduction of the unpaid accumulations which were $58.75 on December 31, 1935 and the same amount on December 31, 1945. While some of the years during this ten-year period were years of loss or less than average earnings, the war years were profitable and the whole period should be regarded as one of more than average prosperity with average earnings at least equal and probably in excess of what may be expected during the reconversion period and thereafter. A net reduction of the accumulations on the Preferred stock during the next few years is not impossible and may even be regarded as probable, but it is highly improbable that earnings will permit the payment of the entire accumulations, which must happen before dividends can be paid on the Common stock.
>
> For this and other reasons, and with the benefit of suggestions from many interested stockholders, both Preferred and Common, the Officers and Directors, during the past year and particularly during recent months, have given a great

deal of thought and consideration to the question of recapitalization for the purpose of eliminating the accumulated unpaid dividends on the Preferred stock which amounted, as previously stated, to $58.75 per share on December 31, 1945, or a total of $20,562,500.00. If the many legal technicalities and other difficulties can be satisfactorily overcome, a detailed plan will be submitted to the stockholders for approval at a special meeting to be called for that purpose. The Management is hopeful that the problem will be solved, but no definite assurance can be given at this time.

On March 26, 1946, at the annual meeting of stockholders a tentative plan of recapitalization was disclosed. At the same meeting, according to newspaper reports,[1] President Moses Pendleton said he expected that distribution of at least 75% of earnings would be made in 1946 with the larger part of the payment in the second half of the year.

Despite many uncertainties operations in the early months of 1946 continued at a high and very profitable rate.

At a special meeting on April 30, the board of directors voted to recommend a revised plan of recapitalization to the stockholders.

A letter describing the proposed plan and calling a stockholders meeting for July 3 to vote on the proposal was mailed on June 3. A major portion of the letter follows:

To the Stockholders of
AMERICAN WOOLEN COMPANY:

Accompanying this letter is a Notice of Meeting and Proxy Statement, together with a Proxy, relating to a Special Meeting of Stockholders to be held July 3, 1946. The purpose of the meeting is to consider and take action upon a Plan of Recapitalization of your Company.

It has long been apparent that a revision of the capital structure of the Company is desirable. As you have been advised in the Annual Reports, this subject has been given almost constant study for the past several years. During this period dozens of plans submitted by stockholders, banking houses and independent financial experts have been reviewed and a great deal of time and effort has gone into the preparation of the Plan now submitted to you. It is presented with the unanimous approval of your Directors as being fair and equitable and in the interest of both Preferred and Common stockholders. Please give it careful consideration and mail in your proxy promptly.

Historical Review

The predecessor American Woolen Company was organized in 1899 and the terms of the present 7% noncallable Preferred stock and the Common stock were created at that time. The history of the company since then falls naturally into three periods. Until shortly after the First World War the company maintained a relatively stable earning power. During the next period, up to the outbreak of the recent War, profit margins declined sharply as a result of price competition induced by the substantial over-capacity that had been built up in

[1] *The Commercial and Financial Chronicle,* April 1, 1946.

the industry, the development of competing fabrics and the increasing competition from woolen imports produced by cheap foreign labor. The present period, beginning with the outbreak of the last World War, saw an abnormal demand for woolen fabrics and the practical elimination of imports so that the Company has been able to operate steadily at a high rate of production.

. . . .

The mills are now working at a high rate of capacity and earnings are currently running at a very favorable rate. It is impossible to predict how long these conditions will continue. The Wool Textile Industry in the United States has much too great a productive capacity in relation to the normal demand. English and European mills are making every effort to resume volume production. Once the present world shortage of woolens is satisfied, we must look forward to a return of the highly competitive conditions existing prior to the war. The problem of meeting foreign competition under the lower tariffs established in 1939 will be intensified by high labor costs.

The Present Situation

For many years the Company has been seriously burdened by the excessive amount of non-callable Preferred stock carrying a fixed dividend rate of 7%. Dividend accumulations on this stock now amount to $20,475,000 and one of the most serious problems confronting the company is the elimination of these dividend accumulations and the correction of the present inflexible capital structure.

The Company now has outstanding 350,000 shares of 7% non-callable Preferred stock of $100 par value and 400,000 shares of Common stock without par value. Dividend accumulations on the Preferred stock amount to $58.50 per share, or an aggregate of $20,475,000. The annual dividend requirement on the Preferred stock of $2,450,000 is currently being earned by a wide margin but from the organization of the predecessor company in 1899 through 1942 average earnings were less than the annual dividend requirement on the Preferred stock now outstanding. Even including the high earnings of the past three years, such dividend requirements would have been covered by only a slight margin.

In the opinion of your Directors, the present inflexible and topheavy capital structure will prove a serious burden unless corrected.

Exchange of Stock

The Plan contemplates the creation of a new class of $4 Cumulative Convertible Prior Preference stock to be offered in exchange for the present 7% cumulative Preferred stock on the basis of 1½ shares of the new Prior Preference stock, plus $8.50 in cash, for each share of the present Preferred stock with its right to accrued dividends. The new Prior Preference stock will be without par value, will be preferred over any unexchanged 7% Preferred stock and the Common stock as to dividends to the extent of $4 per share per year and as to assets to the extent of $105 per share in voluntary and $100 per share in involuntary liquidation, in each case plus accrued dividends; will be callable at any time on or after September 15, 1951, at $105 per share plus accrued dividends and will be convertible at any time into 2 shares of Common stock. For a more complete statement of the provisions of the new Prior Preference stock, reference is made to the Proxy Statement.

Advantages of the New Capital Structure

To the extent exchanges are made pursuant to the Plan, the dividend accumulations on the present Preferred stock will be eliminated without any substantial cash drain upon the Company, and, since it is intended to pay promptly accrued dividends on any unexchanged Preferred stock, the way will immediately be opened for dividends upon the Common stock. At the same time regular preferred dividend requirements will be reduced and provison made for the eventual reduction of senior capital either by redemption, or through conversion of the new Prior Preference stock into Common stock.

The Plan in Relation to the Preferred Stockholders

The holders of the present 7% cumulative Preferred stock now have a first claim upon the earnings of the company to the extent of $7 per share annually, plus accrued dividends of $58.50 per share. Furthermore, their present stock is non-callable. Under the Plan they will be offered the right to exchange each share of present Preferred stock with its right to accrued dividends, for 1½ shares of $4 Prior Preference stock plus $8.50 in cash. Each share of such stock will be convertible into 2 shares of Common stock and may be redeemed after five years at $105 per share plus accrued dividends. The new Prior Preference stock received in exchange for each share of present Preferred will have an aggregate dividend preference of $6 annually.

While the Preferred stockholders who make the exchange will forego any right to receive payment of the accrued dividends on their present stock, and will accept a reduction of $1 per share in the aggregate dividend rate, they will receive new stock having a liquidation and redemption value, plus cash, equal to or greater than the par value plus accrued dividends of their present stock. Furthermore, each share of the new Prior Preference stock will be convertible into 2 shares of Common stock or a total of 3 shares for the 1½ shares of new Prior Preference stock for which the present Preferred stock may be exchanged. Thus, holders of Preferred stock who make the exchange will place themselves in a position to participate in the future earnings of the company as Common stockholders by converting the new Prior Preference stock into Common stock.

Upon consummation of the Plan it is intended to pay promptly the dividend accumulation on any unexchanged Preferred stock.

A vote in favor of the plan does not in any way commit a Preferred stockholder to make the exchange. It is intended that, following approval of the Plan and completion of registration, the exchange offer will be made to holders of Preferred stock for a limited period, but acceptance or rejection of the offer will be entirely optional with the stockholder.

The Plan in Relation to Common Stockholders

The Common stockholders now own the entire equity of the company subject to the preferences of the Preferred stock, including the dividend accumulations thereon. However, these preferences are so large that no dividends have been paid on the Common stock since 1924 and no dividends can be paid under the present capital structure until the present dividend accumulations of $20,-475,000 have been eliminated. Currently the regular dividend upon the Preferred stock is being earned by a wide margin but the average annual earnings of the company and its predecessor since 1899 have been only slightly in excess of the present annual dividend requirement upon the Preferred stock.

It is impossible to determine how much of the Preferred stock may be exchanged pursuant to the Plan but, to the extent that exchanges are made, the dividend accumulations on such stock will be eliminated and the annual dividend requirement will be reduced by $1 for each share exchanged. To the extent that any new Prior Preference stock may subsequently be converted into Common stock, the amount of Common stock outstanding will be increased at the rate of 2 shares for each share of Prior Preference stock so converted, but this would be accompanied by a proportionate decrease of senior capital now coming ahead of the Common stock.

Upon consummation of the Plan the Company intends to pay promptly the accrued dividends on the unexchanged Preferred stock and to initiate dividends on the Common stock. The rate and continuity of Common stock dividends will obviously depend on the trend of earnings but, if the Plan is consummated, the Directors expect to pay dividends on the Common stock of at least $5 a share in 1946.

. . . .

Conclusion

After a careful study, the Directors believe that the proposed Plan is in the interests of holders of both classes of stock and recommend that all stockholders vote in favor of the Plan.

Adoption of the Plan will require the affirmative vote of two-thirds of each class of stock outstanding. It is important, therefore, that every stockholder make sure that his stock is represented at the meeting by filling in, signing and returning the enclosed Proxy promptly.

(*Signed*) M. Pendleton
President

June 3, 1946

The stockholders convened as scheduled on July 3, with results as described in *The Commercial and Financial Chronicle* of July 15th:

The special meeting of stockholders called to act upon a plan of recapitalization was adjourned on July 3 for two weeks to July 17. Additional time is sought for further stockholder responses to the proposed plan.

Over 60% of the common stock and over 75% of the preferred already have registered approval, it was said.

Moses Pendleton, President, stated the plan would automatically go into effect when holders of 80% of preferred have deposited their stock and registered their approval of the plan. He also said that the company is operating at capacity. Terming earnings highly satisfactory, he said that unaudited profits for the first five months of the year were at a somewhat better annual rate than reported for the first quarter.

Unfilled orders on June 1 were $62,000,000, or almost equivalent to the wartime volume of a year ago.

Exhibit 1

AMERICAN WOOLEN COMPANY

Year	*Sales in Thousands*	*Net Income after Taxes in Thousands*	*Preferred Dividends Paid per Share*	*Preferred Dividends in Arrears per Share*		*Preferred Stock Prices on NYSE*		*Common Stock Prices on NYSE*	
						High	*Low*	*High*	*Low*
1927.....	*	$ 600	$ 1.75	$ 5.25		$ 86½	$ 46⅞	$33⅜	$16½
1928.....	*	1,262d	....	12.25		65¾	39	32⅜	14
1929.....	*	4,228d	....	19.25		58¾	15½	27⅞	5⅞
1930.....	*	4,898d	....	26.25		44⅞	15⅝	20¼	5½
1931.....	*	2,837d	....	33.25		40	15¼	11⅞	2⅝
1932.....	*	7,270d	....	40.25		39⅞	15½	10	1⅝
1933.....	*	7,053	....	47.25		67½	22⅝	17	3½
1934.....	$ 48,711	5,465d	2.50	51.75		83¾	36	17⅛	7
1935.....	70,317	2,741	....	58.75		68¾	35½	10¾	4⅞
1936.....	71,023	1,930	4.00	61.75		70¾	52¾	11½	7⅝
1937.....	75,062	1,855d	3.00	65.75		79	25¼	14⅜	3½
1938.....	42,038	4,912d	....	72.75		45	23⅝	7⅜	3¾
1939.....	64,936	2,312	....	79.75		28⅜	64¾	15¼	3⅝
1940.....	76,560	3,154	7.00	79.75		61⅜	25½	12	6
1941.....	145,749	6,944†	12.00	74.75		81¼	51	8⅝	3½
1942.....	196,031	4,824†	8.00	73.75		76⅜	51¾	5⅜	3½
1943.....	197,505	5,475†	8.00	72.75		79½	55¼	8⅝	3¾
1944.....	183,009	5,295†	12.00	67.75		107	67½	9½	6⅛
1945.....	162,680	8,301†	16.00	58.75		140	100⅛	31⅞	9
1/1/46–3/31/46 (unaudited)		3,937†	....	....	1946 J	150	128	57¾	29½
					F	147½	134	51	40
					M	150	138¾	49⅝	41¼
					A	154⅞	142	60⅛	45⅜
					M	168	150	67½	51¼
					J	182½	165	70¾	60¾

* The company did not disclose sales figures prior to 1934.

† Figures through 1945 are from annual reports. During the war the figures reported for income were influenced greatly by amounts set aside for possible renegotiation and reserves. In 1946 in a registration statement filed with the SEC in connection with the recapitalization, net income was restated as follows:

1941..................	9,175
1942..................	7,039
1943..................	10,810
1944..................	7,556
1945..................	6,075

Exhibit 2

AMERICAN WOOLEN COMPANY

Balance Sheet, December 31, 1945

(Thousands of dollars)

ASSETS		LIABILITIES	
Cash	$ 23,926	Accounts payable—trade	$ 828
U.S. government securities at cost	5,100	Accrued liabilities	3,202
Accounts receivable—net	11,594	Reserve for federal income taxes	19,361
Inventories	37,701	Reserve for renegotiation refunds	700
Other current assets	1,636	Other current liabilities	777
Total current assets	$ 79,957	*Total current liabilities*	$ 24,868
Investment in subsidiary	9	$3\frac{1}{2}$% mortgage on real estate	940
Fixed assets—net	22,861	Special reserve for war contingencies	9,000
Other assets	1,510	7% preferred stock—350,000 shares outstanding*	35,000
		Common stock—400,000 shares—no-par at $5 stated value	2,000
		Capital surplus	21,290
		Earned surplus since January 1, 1941	11,239
	$104,337		$104,337

* Preferred arrearages to date are $20,562,500 or $58.75 per share.

EASTERN GAS AND FUEL ASSOCIATES

On July 26, 1962, the management of Eastern Gas and Fuel Associates was reviewing its policy with respect to the company's investment, to the extent of 967,236 shares, in the common stock of the Norfolk and Western Railway Company (Norfolk). Although Eastern annually received substantial income in the form of dividends from Norfolk, and although only 15% of such income was subject to federal taxation,[1] a number of Eastern's officers had raised questions concerning the advisability of continued retention of Norfolk common stock in light of potential alternative uses of the funds committed, including in particular their use to reacquire outstanding capital stock of Eastern. Also raised were further questions regarding Eastern's obligations to its various stockholder groups.

At the time of review, the book value of Eastern's shareholdings in Norfolk stood at $23 million—the cost of acquisition (see Exhibit 1 for balance sheet data); the market value was $87 million, or approximately $90 per Norfolk share. Dividends received from Norfolk during 1962 through July 26 had totaled $1.9 million ($2 per Norfolk share); further dividends of $2.9 million ($3 per Norfolk share) were expected before the close of the calendar year. (See Exhibits 2a and 2b for income data.)

History and business

Eastern Gas and Fuel Associates was organized in 1929. At the time of formation, it acquired (1) a majority of the common and preferred stocks of Massachusetts Gas Companies, which owned the Boston Consolidated Gas Company (later the Boston Gas Company) and, through other subsidiaries, operated bituminous coal mines, company stores, colliers and tugboats, a coke plant and a blast furnace; and (2) all of the common stock of two coke plant companies.

Over the years, a variety of acquisitions, consolidations, and dissolutions was effected; additionally, many investments were undertaken or liquidated, and many operations and activities initiated or terminated. By 1962, Eastern Gas and Fuel Associates and its commercial subsidiaries were engaged in the production, preparation, and sale of bituminous coal; the operation of a

---

[1] Under Section 243 of the Internal Revenue Code of 1954, corporations were generally entitled to deduct from their income 85% of the amount received as dividends.

number of small department stores, principally in communities adjacent to its coal mines; the conversion of coal into coke, gas, and other coke-oven products, and the distribution and sale of such products; the operation of inland waterway towboats and barges; the operation of bulk cargo ships in coastal and worldwide trade, and of a fleet of tugboats in Boston Harbor; and the carrying on of other allied operations. (See Exhibit 3 for a breakdown of revenues by type of activity for the 10-year period 1952–61.) Eastern's major wholly owned subsidiaries included (1) the Boston Gas Company, a public utility, which distributed gas in the Boston metropolitan area; (2) Midland Enterprises Inc., which, in conjunction with its wholly owned subsidiary, the Ohio River Company, owned and operated a fleet of barges and towboats; and (3) the Virginian Corporation, which held title to the 967,236 shares of common stock constituting (on a consolidated basis) Eastern's investment in Norfolk. Also included among the list of companies affiliated with Eastern was the Algonquin Gas Transmission Company, a natural gas pipeline company servicing the New England area. Eastern owned 37% of Algonquin's outstanding common stock.

Coal operations

Eastern was the fifth largest commercial bituminous coal producer in the United States. Its mines, located in West Virginia and Pennsylvania, yielded nearly 10 million tons of coal annually, most of which was of a premium grade suitable for metallurgical purposes. Domestically, and apart from Eastern's own coke plants which consumed the major portion of the company's annual output of metallurgical coal, steel companies formed the principal market for Eastern's premium grade coal. Electric utilities were the main customers for its lower grade steam coal. Over 25% of Eastern's coal revenues was accounted for by foreign markets.

Although Eastern had for many years been continuously engaged in efforts to reduce operating costs, both through the termination of marginal mining activities and through the introduction of highly mechanized mining and processing equipment, the profitability of Eastern's coal operations in any given year depended to a large extent on the volume of demand. During the four-year period beginning with the recession of 1958, and as a result of depressed conditions in the steel industry, of increasing competition for both coal and coke from other fuels and energy sources, and of the closing down in 1960 of Eastern's largest coke plant, located in Everett, Massachusetts, demand declined to levels that made mining operations unprofitable from 1959 on (see Exhibit 2*b*).

Store operations

Principally as an adjunct to its coal mining activities, Eastern operated a number of small department stores. Most of these were located in towns adjacent to Eastern's mining properties and catered to the needs of the mining community. Although some 20-odd stores were in operation in 1962, almost an equal number had been closed over the years, in part because of depressed conditions in the particular communities they served and the resulting decline in sales. Except during periods of great demand for coal (e.g., 1957) those stores that had continued to function returned only modest profits.

Coke plant operations

Eastern operated two coke plants, one in Philadelphia, Pennsylvania, and the other in New Haven, Connecticut. (A third plant in Everett, Massachusetts, discontinued activities in 1960, as previously noted, and was later demolished to make room for other facilities.) The principal customers for the coke produced at these plants were steel producers, both domestic and foreign, and demand was thus related to conditions in the steel industry. Coke-oven gas, the main by-product of Eastern's production of coke, was sold principally to utilities, especially gas companies. Because of the increasing use of natural gas in the Northeast occasioned by extension into the region of natural gas pipelines, demand for Eastern's coke-oven gas had shown a generally declining trend, and operations had been unprofitable for a number of years.

Inland waterway operations

On August 22, 1961, in exchange for 494,500 shares of Eastern common, Eastern Gas and Fuel Associates acquired Midland Enterprises Inc. and its wholly owned subsidiary, the Ohio River Company. Midland Enterprises Inc. and its subsidiary owned and operated one of the major barge lines on the inland waterways. The major portion of tonnage carried was steam coal hauled under long-term contracts with utilities located along or near the Ohio and Illinois Rivers. During periods of heavy activity in the steel industry, substantial amounts of metallurgical coal were also hauled, with benefit to both operating efficiency and profits.

Other marine operations

Through its Mystic Steamship Division, Eastern operated a fleet of eight Liberty ships for the transportation, primarily along the eastern seaboard, of coal and other bulk commodities. Through a Liberian subsidiary, Eastern also operated two ocean-going bulk cargo ships for worldwide trade. As of July 26, 1962, and excluding a new 23,000-ton vessel scheduled for subsequent delivery to the Liberian subsidiary, the combined net weight of Eastern's two fleets amounted to 151,000 deadweight tons. The profitability of these fleets depended to a great extent on the domestic and export market demand for coal as well as the presence or absence of a general surplus of bulk cargo vessels.

In addition to the activities noted above, Eastern also operated nine tugboats for docking vessels and general service in Boston Harbor and nearby waters.

Boston Gas Company

The Boston Gas Company supplied gas for cooking and heating in a region encompassing the city of Boston and 31 adjoining communities. Although Boston and 27 of these communities had been included within the company's service area as early as 1953, and although the total population of Boston and its environs had shown little change since then, the company had experienced a substantial growth in sales during the same period (see Exhibit 3).

In the main, this growth was attributable to three interrelated factors. The first was the extension of natural gas pipelines into the New England area, which enabled the Boston Gas Company to shift from the distribution of manufactured gas to the distribution of mixtures containing a higher and higher natural gas content. By 1960, manufactured gas was used only during periods of peak load. This resulted in reduced costs for gas as well as substantial distribution economies. Since the B.T.U. content of natural gas is almost double that of manufactured gas, system capacity was significantly increased without the necessity for major capital expenditure programs.

The second was the initiation and continuation of an aggressive promotional campaign by the Boston Gas Company to secure additional customers and thus to secure the advantages of additional volume. An integral part of this campaign was a reduced rate schedule designed to induce further use of gas for space and water heating and cooking.

The third was the increasing acceptance of gas by the industrial, commercial, and residential population in the area served by the Boston Gas Company. For example, it was estimated by the company that gas central heating was installed in 80% of all homes built in 1961 within reach of its lines.

In part because of its status as a utility and the nature of its operations, and in part because of the increased volume of sales, the Boston Gas Company was both the largest of the operating divisions or subsidiaries of Eastern Gas and Fuel Associates and the most stable contributor to profits.

Algonquin Gas Transmission Company

The Algonquin Gas Transmission Company (Algonquin) was formed by Eastern Gas and Fuel Associates in conjunction with the New England Gas and Electric Association and the Providence Gas Company. It operated a pipeline system that distributed gas purchased from the Texas Eastern Transmission Corporation—a stockholder in Algonquin since shortly after the latter's inception—to utilities in the New England area, as well as to a number of customers in New Jersey and New York located near its pipeline route.

Eastern's investment in Algonquin was slightly over $5 million, represented by 51,711 shares of $100 par common stock. Dividends received from Algonquin during the year 1961 amounted to $440,000. Eastern's equity in Algonquin's undistributed earnings for the year 1961 amounted to $800,000.

Norfolk and Western

The Norfolk and Western Railway Company operated some 2,747 miles of road and 5,738 miles of track, and, with over $1 billion in assets, was one of the major railroads in the United States. (See Exhibit 4 for balance sheet data.) Its main lines extended westward from tidewater ports and docks in Virginia through the West Virginia bituminous coal fields to Columbus and Cincinnati, Ohio, and from Walton to Bristol, Virginia. Important branch or feeder lines extended into Maryland, Kentucky, and North Carolina.

Norfolk was one of the nation's important coal-hauling railroads, with 71% of its freight revenues in 1961 coming from coal and coke traffic and 29% from other traffic. Of its total bituminous coal tonnage in 1961 of 61.0 million (of which Eastern accounted for over 10%), 25% was shipped to companies in the steel industry and 18% to electric utilities. Export tonnage accounted for an additional 26%.

Because of its location and because of the large bulk of its freight traffic and the consequent requirement for relatively small amounts of labor, the Norfolk and Western Railway system ranked high relative to other major railroads with respect to many traditional measures of railroad operating efficiency and competitive strength. For example, its operating ratio (operating expenses/operating revenues) for 1961 was one of the lowest in the nation. (See Exhibit 5 for income data.) A related measure, the transportation ratio (transportation expenses/operating revenues), was lower for Norfolk in 1961 than for any other major railroad—26.3% versus 31.0% for the second ranking Bangor and Aroostook system. Similarly, Norfolk led all other major railroads in percentage of tonnage originated and in revenue freight density (ton-miles per miles of road). Moreover, although Norfolk's operating revenues in 1961 were only modestly (21%) above the system's 1947–49 average—computed to include operations of the Virginian Railway Company, merged with Norfolk and Western in 1959—its performance in this respect compared favorably with Class I[2] railroads as a whole, whose operating revenues increased only 2% during the same period. (Norfolk's operating revenues and related data for the 10-year period 1952–61 are presented in Exhibit 6.)

Effective control of the Norfolk and Western Railway Company rested with Pennsylvania Railroad Company, which directly or through its wholly owned subsidiary, the Pennsylvania Company, owned 2,397,284 shares of Norfolk common, which was 32.5% of the amount outstanding. Eastern's investment, which consisted of 967,236 shares and which enabled it to place two of its own directors on Norfolk's board, represented 13.1% of the amount outstanding.

Management's review of Eastern's Norfolk and Western holdings

The review by management of its policy with respect to Eastern's investment in Norfolk and Western was prompted by a number of factors. Among these was increasing pessimism on the part of most of Eastern's officers regarding prospects for further significant price advancement by Norfolk common stock. Several of the younger officers in particular considered such prospects quite limited relative to opportunities for profitable employment of the funds involved for expanding Eastern's gas and barge operations and for revitalizing its coal business. Contributing to this skepticism was the feeling that Norfolk's earnings in recent years were overstated because of the latter's use of "pass-through" tax accounting and the consequent failure to reduce reported net income by an allowance for deferred taxes. One executive who shared this sentiment summed up his objections to the status quo as follows:

[2] All railroads with annual operating revenues of $3,000,000 or over are considered "Class I" railroads.

"I have yet to meet anyone who advocates our investing additional funds in Norfolk common. As far as I'm concerned, if the stock doesn't warrant additional investment, our original commitment should be liquidated, at least to the extent that there are suitable alternative uses for the funds released." Together with most of his fellow officers, however, this individual was hesitant to have Eastern undertake any disposition of the Norfolk holdings, which would subject it to a large tax liability or which would, as in the case of a distribution in kind to stockholders, subject the majority of Eastern's stockholders to income tax liability at ordinary rates.

An additional factor prompting review was the growing desire on the part of some of Eastern's executives to utilize the company's Norfolk holdings to reduce the number of shares of Eastern common stock outstanding. It was the contention of these executives that this would have the same general effect on a per share basis as selling the Norfolk holdings and employing the proceeds to expand Eastern's other operations.

The proposed means for achieving the reduction was an exchange, with consenting shareholders of Eastern, of Norfolk common shares for shares of Eastern. Tenders were to be actively solicited by Eastern, and a precise exchange ratio stipulated.

To help insure the success of the exchange offer were it to be undertaken, Eastern's principal stockholder group, which formerly controlled Midland Enterprises Inc., and currently owned between 10% and 15% of Eastern's outstanding common shares, was prepared to tender some of its own holdings. If such tenders were not needed, however, it was the intention of this group to retain its shares and interest in Eastern.

In contrast to a direct sale of the Norfolk holdings, which would result in a taxable gain to Eastern, the proposed exchange could be consummated without Eastern's incurring gain or loss for tax purposes. As for exchanging shareholders, it was believed that under most circumstances they could limit their tax liability to capital gain rates by careful adherence to guidelines specified in the tax code.

As explained by one high-ranking executive, the increased leverage that would result from the proposed exchange was the principal merit and justification of the proposal. He said:

> One of the things I concluded upon joining Eastern early in 1962 after my previous association with Midland Enterprises was that it would be very difficult to raise the per-share earnings of the merged company with over three million shares of common outstanding. Any reduction in the equity base would directly enhance our ability to boost these earnings. In addition, in my view, the greater potential for both upside and downside movement in earnings per share would increase the challenge to management.
>
> Of course, this emphasis on the structure of the liability and net worth side of the balance sheet differs from what I suppose could be called the traditional management viewpoint, which emphasizes assets and their utilization and control while tending to regard the amount of equity as a static quantity subject only

to increase. The net worth or right-hand side of the balance sheet is also important, however, and frequently involves matters of greater subtlety and significance than asset management.

As anyone who has reviewed our financial statements would know, we could achieve an immediate increase in earnings per share if we liquidated our coal and coke operations, which have shown losses for the past three years. This would produce a tax loss and free up a large quantity of funds now committed to inventories and receivables. But almost 4,000 jobs are at stake and we feel obligated to the employees associated with these activities. About the only employee involved in connection with our Norfolk and Western investment is the man who walks down to the bank every three months and deposits our dividend check. It should also be borne in mind that it is difficult for Eastern's managers to prove their worth unless the results of their efforts can be readily reflected in the financial statements; the more we divest ourselves of enterprises that require active management on our part, the more of an investment company we become and the less opportunity and incentive there are for the successful pursuit of the management art.

Alternative proposals for utilization of the Norfolk holdings

In addition to the proposed exchange of stock, alternative means for utilizing the Norfolk holdings without the incurrence of tax liability by Eastern had been investigated by Eastern's management. Foremost among these was the use of the Norfolk shares to acquire other operating concerns through the process of statutory merger or consolidation. In part because stockholders of firms so acquired would be subject to capital gains tax, and in part because Eastern could qualify for tax-free treatment only if it surrendered large blocks of its own stock along with its Norfolk holdings, such use had ultimately been deemed inadvisable, and by July 26, 1962, the Norfolk-for-Eastern exchange was the only proposal under active consideration.

The proposed exchange in the context of management's responsibilities to individual stockholder groups

Among the questions encountered by Eastern's management in evaluating different proposals regarding the specific nature and scope of any Norfolk-for-Eastern exchange offer were:

1. If state legal requirements could be satisfied, and if otherwise deemed preferable, should the offer be limited to a selected group of common stockholders (e.g., holders of large blocks of stock such as mutual funds and other institutional investors)? Or should it be extended as a matter of equity to all common stockholders? and
2. More generally, with respect to the determination both of the advisability of an exchange offer and of its terms, what standards should govern management's concern for the different stockholder groups, i.e., what were management's responsibilities towards individual shareholder groups?

As regards the first question, although Eastern's management had at one time given preliminary consideration to limiting any exchange offer to some of the company's larger shareholders, the issue became moot upon a review by

Eastern's legal department of the company's listing agreement with the New York Stock Exchange. The terms of this agreement prohibited selection, other than by lot, of particular stockholders for offers of redemption. (A manual of the New York Stock Exchange offers the following summary statement of the Exchange's position: "This Exchange believes it is important that all stockholders of a company be given an opportunity to participate on equal terms in any offer made which may affect the rights or benefits of such stockholders.")

As to management's responsibilities towards individual shareholder groups, a top executive of Eastern offered the following comments:

> Any decision regarding a matter such as an exchange offer should be approached in two stages. Initially you have to disassociate the company from its stockholders and address yourself to the question "What is best for the company?" Once this is resolved you proceed to the problem of how to achieve the stipulated goal in a way that is equitable to each of the stockholder groups concerned.
>
> In the present case, our aim is to increase earnings per share. We feel that we can facilitate this by reducing our equity base through an exchange of stock with some of our shareholders. Were we to proceed to undertake such an exchange, one element of our task would be to settle on some exchange formula which would be fair to both those who would stay with the company and those who would tender their stock. It is especially important that the formula be fair to the latter group if the principal members of management—as I believe would prove to be true in the present case—were to decide to retain their investment in the company. For if things went poorly, and management encountered criticism from those who had stayed, the response would always be available that management had themselves elected to be in the same boat. But if things went well, there would be no counter to the criticism from those who had surrendered their stock except that they had been given full information and had been treated fairly at the time they submitted their tenders.
>
> As matters stand now, we are thinking in terms of offering one share of Norfolk and Western common in exchange for two shares of Eastern common. [See Exhibit 7 for per-share price, earnings and dividend data.] We would offer a total of roughly 225,000 shares of Norfolk and, depending on the outcome, possibly the remainder of our holdings at some later date.

The executive added that if the initial exchange venture was undertaken and was successful, the preferred shareholders of Eastern would probably be included in plans for any subsequent exchange transaction. "Actually, we gave serious consideration to including them in our proposed first offering," he said. "However, in view of the differing effects of a reduction in preferred as contrasted with a reduction in common, and in view of our uncertainty as to the outcome of even a common-for-common offer, we finally decided to keep things as simple as possible on our first try."

On the basis of July 25th's closing prices and the one-for-two exchange ratio, tendering shareholders would receive $90 of market value (the price of one Norfolk share) in exchange for $82 (the price of two Eastern shares). If dividends were maintained at current rates, they would receive annual dividends of $5 as opposed to $3.20 (2 × $1.60). On the basis of the results of the six months ending June 30, 1962, and projections for the rest of the year, they would be giving up approximately $4.70 in earnings (i.e., approximately $2.35 per share) and receiving between $8 and $9.

Viewed from a different perspective, Eastern's remaining stockholders would be gaining approximately $4.70 in earnings for every two shares surrendered, and losing $4.61 (i.e., $5 [1 – (0.15) (0.52)]).

Exhibit 1

EASTERN GAS AND FUEL ASSOCIATES

CONSOLIDATED BALANCE SHEETS AS OF DECEMBER 31, 1958–61

(In millions of dollars)

ASSETS	*1958*	*1959*	*1960*	*1961**
Current assets:				
Cash and marketable securities	$ 9.3	$ 7.8	$ 7.9	$ 12.0
Accounts receivable, net	19.3	22.2	21.0	20.1
Inventories	25.6	21.9	17.9	17.4
Prepaid expenses	0.7	0.9	0.9	0.7
Total current assets	$ 54.9	$ 52.8	$ 47.7	$ 50.2
Investments and other assets:				
Common stock of Norfolk and Western Railway Company, at cost	$ ...	$ 23.6†	$ 22.9†	$ 22.9†
Common stock of the Virginian Railway Company, at cost‡	23.5	...	...	...
Common stock of Algonquin Gas Transmission Company, at cost	5.2	5.2	5.2	5.2
Miscellaneous securities, notes and accounts	3.1	3.2	3.0	3.0
Total investments and other assets	$ 31.8	$ 32.0	$ 31.1	$ 31.1
Property, plant, and equipment:				
Commercial and coal mining properties	$152.4	$150.0	$126.3	$170.5
Less depreciation, depletion, and other allowances	85.4	87.8	69.3	81.7
	$ 67.0	$ 62.2	$ 57.0	$ 88.8
Utility properties	$ 69.9	$ 71.3	$ 73.9	$ 77.0
Less depreciation	18.3	18.5	19.3	20.1
	$ 51.6	$ 52.8	$ 54.6	$ 56.9
Total property, plant, and equipment	$118.6	$115.0	$111.6	$145.7
Deferred charges	5.6	5.3	7.0	7.3
Total assets	$210.9	$205.1	$197.4	$234.3
LIABILITIES AND NET WORTH				
Current liabilities:				
Notes payable to banks	$ 5.2	$ 4.0	$ 3.0	$ 4.0
Long-term debt due within one year	3.7	3.0	2.9	6.0
Other	12.3	13.9	12.6	16.7
Total current liabilities	$ 21.2	$ 20.9	$ 18.5	$ 26.7
Long-term debt (except portion due within one year)	68.7	66.6	63.1	76.9
Reserves and other liabilities	4.8	7.6	4.9	11.8
Stockholders equity:				
Preferred stock—4½% cumulative	$ 24.6	$ 24.6	$ 24.6	$ 24.6
Common stock	28.0	28.0	28.2	33.3
Capital surplus	39.4	39.4	39.4	40.0
Retained earnings	24.2	18.0	18.7	21.0
Total stockholders' equity	$116.2	$110.0	$110.9	$118.9
Total liabilities and net worth	$210.9	$205.1	$197.4	$234.3

* Includes Midland Enterprises Inc., with which Eastern merged during 1961.

† In 1959, 1960, and 1961, Eastern's investment in Norfolk common consisted of 994,348 shares, 967,236 shares, and 967,236 shares, respectively.

‡ The Virginian Railway Company was merged into the Norfolk and Western Railway Company on December 1, 1959. As a result of the merger, Eastern received, in exchange for its investment in the Virginian Railway Company (roughly 50% of the outstanding shares), 994,348 shares of Norfolk and Western common stock.

Exhibit 2a

EASTERN GAS AND FUEL ASSOCIATES

CONSOLIDATED INCOME STATEMENTS, 1958–61 AND SIX MONTHS ENDING JUNE 30, 1962
(In millions of dollars)

	1958	*1959*	*1960*	*1961**	*1962*†*
Net sales and operating revenues	$161.5	$157.5	$139.1	$147.0	$81.5
Costs of sales and expenses of operation:					
Depreciation and depletion:					
Commercial and coal mining	$ 6.8	$ 6.8	$ 5.2	$ 7.7	
Utility	1.3	1.4	1.4	1.3	
Other costs and expenses	148.7	145.3	128.2	129.0	
Total costs and expenses	$156.8	$153.5	$134.8	$138.0	$72.5
Operating profit	$ 4.7	$ 4.0	$ 4.3	$ 9.0	$ 9.0
Other income and (deductions):					
Dividends from railroad investment	$ 3.6	$ 3.6	$ 4.9	$ 4.8	$ 1.9
Interest on long-term debt	(2.8)	(3.0)	(2.9)	(3.8)	(1.9)
Miscellaneous, net	0.3	0.4	0.5	0.8	(0.3)
	$ 1.1	$ 1.0	$ 2.5	$ 1.8	$(0.3)
Income before federal income taxes	$ 5.8	$ 5.0	$ 6.8	$ 10.8	$ 8.7
Provision for federal income taxes	...	...	0.3	2.5	3.5
Net income	$ 5.8	$ 5.0	$ 6.5	$ 8.3	$ 5.2
Preferred dividends	1.1	1.1	1.1	1.1	0.6
Earnings applicable to common	$ 4.7	$ 3.9	$ 5.4	$ 7.2	$ 4.6

* Income statements for the year 1961 and the six months ending June 30, 1962, include operating data for Midland Enterprises Inc. for those respective periods.
† Six months ending June 30, 1962.

Exhibit 2b

EASTERN GAS AND FUEL ASSOCIATES

STATEMENT OF EARNINGS, 1958–61 AND SIX MONTHS ENDING JUNE 30, 1962
(In millions of dollars)

	1958	*1959*	*1960*	*1961*	*1962‡*
Pretax earnings:					
Coal	$ 1.4	$(0.2)	$(0.5)	$(0.6)	$0.0
Coke plant*	(2.2)	(2.0)	(1.1)	(0.8)	0.0
Public utility	4.1	4.8	5.1	5.6	5.5
Marine†	1.1	0.7	0.3	4.1	2.4
Stores	0.2	0.2	0.1	0.1	0.0
Railroad dividends	3.6	3.6	4.9	4.8	1.9
	$ 8.2	$ 7.1	$ 8.8	$13.2	$9.8
Less general expenses	2.4	2.1	2.0	2.4	1.1
Income before federal income taxes	$ 5.8	$ 5.0	$ 6.8	$10.8	$8.7

* Up until 1960, Eastern operated a blast furnace at Everett, Mass. Operating results for this activity, including results of inventory liquidation in 1960, are combined with coke plant data.
† Includes pretax earnings by Midland Enterprises Inc. of $3.5 million for 1961 and $2.4 million for the six months ending June 30, 1962.
‡ Six months ending June 30, 1962.

Exhibit 3

EASTERN GAS AND FUEL ASSOCIATES

STATEMENT OF SALES AND REVENUES, 1952–61

(In millions of dollars)

	Sales and Revenues						
Year	*Coal*	*Coke Plants*	*Public Utility*	*Marine*	*Stores*	*Pig Iron*	*Total*
1952	$75.2	$41.6	$25.9	$9.0	$9.5	$7.4	$168.6
1953	60.4	34.4	25.5	8.6	7.2	7.1	143.3
1954	52.4	27.2	27.2	6.5	5.3	6.0	124.6
1955	67.6	33.6	27.1	9.2	5.5	8.1	151.1
1956	89.8	35.6	30.0	10.6	5.8	5.1	176.9
1957	103.7	30.6	30.9	10.3	6.9	6.9	189.3
1958	76.9	21.4	34.3	7.3	5.6	5.9	151.4*
1959	66.4	24.3	36.4	6.0	5.3	8.5	146.9*
1960	62.7	20.7	38.8	7.3	5.1	2.5	137.1*
1961	58.8	18.6	40.6	24.5†	4.5	..	147.0

* Total sales and revenues for the years 1958, 1959, and 1960 differ from the totals shown in Exhibit 2*a* for the same years by $10.1 million, $10.6 million, and $2.0 million, respectively. The higher figures in Exhibit 2*a* reflect primarily the consolidation of operating data for a Philadelphia subsidiary, sold in 1960, which had been engaged in the distribution and storage of fuel oils and other liquids.

† Includes revenues of Midland Enterprises Inc. for the entire year 1961. During the period 1952 through 1960, revenues for Midland totaled (in millions of dollars) 6.0, 7.0, 6.4, 9.5, 12.2, 14.6, 14.0, 17.8, and 16.1 respectively.

Exhibit 4

EASTERN GAS AND FUEL ASSOCIATES

CONSOLIDATED BALANCE SHEETS FOR NORFOLK AND WESTERN RAILWAY COMPANY AS OF DECEMBER 31, 1958–61

(In millions of dollars)

ASSETS	*1958*	*1959**	*1960**	*1961**
Current assets:				
Cash and cash investments	$ 47.9	$ 77.4	$ 77.9	$ 87.3
Other current assets	35.8	44.3	33.8	35.7
Total current assets	$ 83.7	$121.7	$111.7	$ 123.0
Investments in affiliated companies	10.6	17.1	26.4	25.2
Properties:				
Road	$448.1	$584.6	$573.7	$ 565.7
Less depreciation and other allowances	55.1	75.6	67.7	64.6
	$393.0	$509.0	$506.0	$ 501.1
Equipment	$367.8	$484.4	$485.6	$ 500.3
Less depreciation and other allowances	155.0	184.3	175.4	186.3
	$212.8	$300.1	$310.2	$ 314.0
Miscellaneous, net	16.2	24.8	29.4	30.0
Total properties	$622.0	$833.9	$845.6	$ 845.1
Other assets, net	9.9	6.1	5.5	11.7
Total assets	$726.2	$978.8	$989.2	$1,005.0
LIABILITIES AND NET WORTH				
Current and accrued liabilities	$ 28.5	$ 40.2	$ 35.3	$ 43.2
Miscellaneous liabilities and reserves	10.5	9.6	10.7	11.5
Equipment obligations and funded debt	91.6	217.3	208.4	198.9
Stockholders' equity:				
Preferred stock	$ 22.7	$ 27.3	$ 26.5	$ 25.6
Common stock	140.7	183.7	183.9	184.3
Capital surplus	0.6	0.2	0.7	1.7
Retained earnings	431.6	500.5	523.7	539.8
Total stockholders' equity	$595.6	$711.7	$734.8	$ 751.4
Total liabilities and net worth	$726.2	$978.8	$989.2	$1,005.0

* Includes data for the Virginian Railway Company.

Exhibit 5

EASTERN GAS AND FUEL ASSOCIATES

CONSOLIDATED INCOME STATEMENTS FOR NORFOLK AND WESTERN RAILWAY COMPANY, 1958–61, AND SIX MONTHS ENDING JUNE 30, 1962*

(In millions of dollars)

	1958	*1959*	*1960*	*1961*	*1962†*
Operating revenues	$203.9	$205.0	$241.3	$243.7	$130.0
Operating expenses:					
Maintenance of way and structure:					
Maintenance	$ 20.5	$ 18.4	$ 21.4	$ 19.2	$ 9.9
Depreciation	3.9	4.1	4.7	4.6	2.2
Maintenance of equipment:					
Maintenance	23.7	20.4	21.2	20.1	10.2
Depreciation	12.5	13.8	17.5	18.2	9.5
Traffic	4.3	4.4	4.9	4.8	2.5
Transportation	60.2	56.2	64.4	64.0	33.2
Miscellaneous and general	8.3	10.1	10.0	9.8	4.0
Total operating expenses	$133.4	$127.4	$144.1	$140.7	$ 71.5
Net railway operating revenues	$ 70.5	$ 77.6	$ 97.2	$103.0	$ 58.5
Operating ratio	65.6%	62.2%	59.7%	57.7%	55.0%
Federal income taxes‡	$ 18.5	$ 22.4	$ 25.2	$ 29.6	$ 22.6
Other taxes	16.0	16.6	21.4	20.5	10.6
Total taxes	$ 34.5	$ 39.0	$ 46.6	$ 50.1	$ 33.2
Railway operating income	$ 36.0	$ 38.6	$ 50.6	$ 52.9	$ 25.3
Interest charges, net	(2.9)	(4.4)	(8.4)	(8.0)	(3.9)
Other income and deductions, net	10.4	17.4	19.0	15.4	6.8
Net income	$ 43.5	$ 51.6	$ 61.2	$ 60.3	$ 28.2
Preferred dividends	0.9	1.0	1.2	1.1	0.5
Earnings applicable to common	$ 42.6	$ 50.6	$ 60.0	$ 59.2	$ 27.7

* Includes operating data for the Virginian Railway Company from December 1, 1959, on.
† Six months ending June 30, 1962.
‡ Does not include taxes deferred because of accelerated amortization or depreciation. Such taxes amounted to $10.1 million, $10.2 million, $10.8 million, $10.1 million, and $1.7 million, respectively, for the four years 1958–61 and for the six months ending June 30, 1962.

Exhibit 6

EASTERN GAS AND FUEL ASSOCIATES

NORFOLK AND WESTERN RAILWAY COMPANY

SELECTED FINANCIAL DATA*

Year	*Operating Revenues†*	*Operating Ratio*	*Net Income†*
1952	$239.7	69.3%	$36.1
1953	227.5	71.3	33.5
1954	207.0	71.7	32.6
1955	253.1	64.4	49.2
1956	296.2	64.8	56.8
1957	315.8	63.8	61.6
1958	233.7	62.7	55.1
1959	247.0	61.1	60.7
1960	241.3	59.7	61.2
1961	243.7	57.7	60.3
1962‡	130.0	55.0	28.2

* All figures include operating data for the Virginian Railway Company.
† In millions of dollars.
† Six months ending June 30, 1962.

Exhibit 7

EASTERN GAS AND FUEL ASSOCIATES

SELECTED FINANCIAL DATA*

	Norfolk and Western Common				Eastern Gas and Fuel Common			
Year	Earnings per Share[ac]	Dividends per Share	Price Range	No. of Shares Outstanding†	Earnings per Share[a]	Dividends per Share	Price Range	No. of Shares Outstanding†
1952	$5.05	$3.50	$46⅝– 52¼	5,630	$2.10	$1.00	$12⅜–15⅝	2,580
1953	4.83	3.50	39¾– 53⅛	5,630	1.19	1.00	9 –13½	2,580
1954	4.52	3.50	39⅝– 51⅞	5,630	0.67	0.85	7⅛–10¾	2,580
1955	6.70	3.75	48¼– 61⅞	5,630	1.56	0.70	9⅞–16	2,590
1956	7.39	3.75	60⅛– 73¾	5,630	3.61	1.40	15⅜–37⅞	2,670
1957	7.75	4.00	51½– 70¾	5,630	4.41	1.60	23⅛–42½	2,790
1958	7.57	4.00	53¾– 92	5,630	1.67	1.60	22⅛–30¾	2,800
1959	6.88	4.70	84¼–108	7,350	1.38	1.60	25⅝–34¼	2,800
1960	8.15	5.00	90⅛–106¼	7,360	1.93	1.60	24½–30¾	2,810
1961	8.04	5.00	97¼–117	7,370	2.17[b]	1.60	29½–54½	3,330
1962‡	3.76	2.00	85¾–109⅞	7,380	1.38[b]	0.80	31¾–55⅜	3,350

* Per share and price data in dollars.
† To the nearest 10 thousand shares. Based on shares outstanding at end of period.
‡ Six months ending June 30, 1962.
[a] Based on the number of shares outstanding at end of period.
[b] Includes operations of Midland Enterprises Inc.
[c] Includes operations of the Virginian Railway Company from December 1, 1959, on.

ELECTRICIRCUIT, INC.

In late May, 1964, Mr. Vito Rappasadi, treasurer of Electricircuit, Inc., was considering the company's future investment and financing program. Anticipated normal growth, introduction of a new product line, and modification of the company's present inventory control system together would require substantial external financing. The opportunities for such financing were severely restricted, however, by the company's financial condition.

Company background information

Electricircuit, Inc., had been founded on Long Island and incorporated in New York in 1954 by four young electrical engineers. At the outset, stock in the company had been wholly owned by this group of four. Later, stock options had been granted to three particularly desirable managers as an inducement to join the company. These options had been exercised, and in 1964 the entire equity was owned by the seven men, in approximately equal blocks. The seven also held all of the top-management positions and constituted the board of directors.

In the period from formation through 1963 Electricircuit had enjoyed considerable success. The product line had been expanded from one original product to include several lines of proprietary items sold as components for digital systems. In the form of packaged circuits (modules), these products performed decision control, storage, and ancillary functions as components of digital systems. They were primarily produced for off-the-shelf sale to customers who used them in systems of their own design and manufacture. Company profit came principally from the sale of these proprietary products.

As the company had expanded, it had also begun the manufacture-to-order of a variety of special-purpose systems, which applied digital techniques to computing, information handling, control tasks, and data processing. The systems were used in space equipment, navigation and positioning systems, signal processing, data converters, and a variety of other end uses associated directly or indirectly with government expenditures for military and nonmilitary purposes. This business accounted for roughly one fourth of Electricircuit's billings. The company profited from the inclusion of its products in these systems, but little, if any, additional profit had been gained from the provision of engineering services.

Electricircuit's proprietary products were subject to a high rate of obsolescence in an extremely competitive market. Although protected by patents, these items were always exposed to the competition of alternatively engineered products performing the same function. Typically the company's new products had achieved about three fourths of their highest sales level in the year in which they were introduced. Peak volumes had been reached and maintained in the second and third years, but these years normally had been followed by steep decay and virtual worthlessness by the sixth or seventh year. This six- to seven-year cycle had been cut short by competitive developments for about 10% of the new products that the company had introduced during the past 10 years, and on those occasions Electricircuit had been forced to absorb substantial inventory write-offs.

Thus, the danger of being leapfrogged technically was a very real one. It had been met by unstinting expenditures on research and development to improve existing product lines and add new ones. Company officials had been successful in recruiting and holding a strong research group, and this group, supported by ample budgetary allocations, had created enviable market respect for the quality of the company's products. The seven owner-managers were determined to maintain that reputation.

Over the years continuing expansion had led to a number of changes in Electricircuit's internal organization. Sales outlets had been established in southern California, and late in 1962 a plant had been constructed there for the design and production of systems for the West Coast space industry. Earlier, production of proprietary products had been shifted from Long Island to a wholly owned subsidiary in North Carolina, largely because of the availability in that area of a low-wage labor force. Production operations at the subsidiary consisted almost entirely of hand assembly and wiring of modules and allied components. Other managerial offices remained at the original site on Long Island.

In the period after 1960, rapidly widening product acceptance had almost trebled the company's sales (Exhibit 1), and its investment in current assets had expanded accordingly (Exhibit 2). Short-term loans, secured by the pledge of receivables, had been obtained from Electricircuit's Long Island bank to support this growing requirement. With isolated exceptions, the bank had been willing to lend 85% of the face amount of the receivables, and this banking arrangement had proved generally satisfactory until early 1964. At that time an officer of the bank had made it clear that Electricircuit had reached the limit of the credit line that the bank was willing to extend in the absence of some improvement in the company's capital structure. New equity or junior debt financing would qualify Electricircuit for a larger loan, if the company so desired and the requisite security was available, but the loan limit would continue to be set in terms of the ratio of bank debt to junior claims (equity plus subordinated debt, if any) that existed at the end of 1963. This assumed no deterioration in earnings or financial condition.

As 1964 had worn on and sales had continued to increase, the company had been forced to cut its cash balance sharply to meet its growing financing needs. Positive earnings had been realized in approximately the same proportion to sales as in 1963, but the retention of these earnings had failed to alter the bank's stand on additional financing. When approached in April, the loan officer had been reluctant to extend additional credit on the basis of unaudited interim statements, but more importantly, he had pointed out that the growth of equity had produced only a modest change in the company's debt/equity ratio. Moreover, about one half of the earnings had been invested in highly specialized equipment, and to that extent the bank had not benefited either from replenishment of the company's deposit balance or, as a creditor, from the increased protection that investment in more liquid assets might have provided.

Growth prospects

In late May, Mr. Rappasadi prepared the following forecast of Electricircuit's year-end current asset position, to help in assessing the company's immediate financing problems.

Cash		$ 135,000
Receivables		2,720,000
Inventory:		
Raw materials	$436,000	
Work in process	529,000	
Finished goods	311,000	1,276,000
		$4,131,000

The forecast assumed a year-end sales rate of $13.6 million and a corresponding cost of goods sold figure of $8.1 million. Actual sales for the year were estimated at $12.0 million. These estimates had been employed with some confidence in projecting working capital requirements, since sales in recent months and impressions of customers' production plans for the rest of the year pointed unmistakably toward continued growth. Receivables had been estimated at 20% of sales, and raw materials and work in process at a four-week rate of usage. Finished goods, on the other hand, had been projected at little more than a two-week supply.

During preceding months finished goods inventory had been deliberately reduced in relation to sales as other cash requirements had mounted. Mr. Rappasadi believed that continued curtailment of investment in finished goods inventory was likely to be costly, but lacking other immediate sources of funds, he also felt that the stock of finished goods would have to be held to the projected level if the company was to avoid an acute cash emergency. As it was, cash had been projected at merely its current level.

Beyond 1964, the marketing manager had estimated that sales of the company's current products would reach $16 million in 1965. Without major product innovation, he thought that sales could probably be maintained at that level in 1966, but if past patterns prevailed, he expected that the following year would see a decline, which might amount to as much as $4 million or $5 million. The exact forecast for 1965 was based primarily on the marketing group's knowledge of government appropriations for ongoing defense and space programs. It could be upset by project cancellations, but that was considered highly unlikely for the projects concerned. On the other hand, the plateau and descent pattern of the more distant estimates emphasized the importance of maintaining Electricircuit's technical preeminence.

Investment possibilities

Mr. Rappasadi saw two possible opportunities for investment that might improve the projected sales pattern and its profit consequences in the future. One involved the introduction of a major new product line and the other, a revision of the company's finished goods inventory control system.

The new product line, which had been under development for the past two years, performed comfortably to military specifications and was believed to possess technical qualities that would give it significant competitive advantages. All of the items making up the line were in a late stage of development, and the line was currently scheduled for introduction at the turn of the year. Market reception was difficult to estimate with any degree of precision, but the marketing manager was confident that the line would contribute sales of at least $2.0 million in 1965 and a further increment of at least $0.5 million in 1966. The line would be priced to give the same coverage of costs as was provided by the company's other proprietary products.

To put the line into production in the North Carolina plant would require about $100,000 for specialized equipment. That plant had been built to accommodate more growth than had yet been realized, and therefore no additional outlays were anticipated for production facilities. However, the marketing manager had estimated that a budget allocation of $35,000 would be needed to introduce and promote the line if it was to achieve its full potential.

The second investment possibility—that of increasing stocks of finished goods—grew out of widespread feeling that economizing in that direction had already been pushed far beyond justifiable limits. Expediting had become commonplace in juggling production schedules, with costly consequences, and orders had been lost to competitors with disturbing frequency when customers had been notified of long but necessary delivery delays. Mr. Rappasadi, therefore, had ordered a review of the company's entire inventory control system.

The area of concern, as a result of that study, had been narrowed to the finished goods segment of total inventory. Some improvements seemed possible in balancing raw material stocks, but it was not thought that this would lead to any appreciable change in the relationship of total raw material inventory to production volume. Lead time required by the purchasing department and limited interchangeability of parts among product lines combined to fix the required total at roughly a four-week supply level. Work in process inventory seemed similarly intractable. Allocation of shop labor, timing of lot starts, schedules, and so on, were already being decided on grounds of optimum production arrangements, as the production manager saw them. Technical changes, necessitating work stoppages, often had to be introduced during the in-process stage, and therefore the production manager, and the engineering group as well, attached considerable value to the flexibility allowed by a four-week production period.

By contrast with its approval of current raw material and in-process control practices, the report recommended complete revamping of the system being used to determine finished goods inventory levels. The current system, in brief, was based on specific item-by-item sales forecasts for the coming quarter. Given those forecasts, goods were scheduled into production in quantities that would raise the level of existing stocks to the anticipated sales requirement. Recently, as noted above, financial circumstances had made it necessary to cut stocks below the target levels that would have been set in more normal circumstances, but the report's condemnation of the system was independent of that experience.

Its basic criticism centered on the system's dependence on quarterly sales forecasts and the invariable inaccuracy of such estimates. Replacement demand could be predicted with tolerable margins of error, but the same was not true of new orders. They were typically received at erratic intervals. Moreover, they constituted a large part of the total demand for most products.

To cope with the problem the report urged adoption of a system of buffer stocks, which would be set with more careful regard to the costs, returns, and risks associated with inventory maintenance. To that end data had been compiled on five possible inventory-sales levels representing substantially different inventory policies (Exhibit 3). In each case the lost-sales estimate had been derived from computer simulations (using appropriate reorder points and reorder quantities) of the demand experience of major product lines.

Since Electricircuit was currently operating with lower finished goods stocks than those contemplated by any one of the five policies, Mr. Rappasadi was particularly impressed by the magnitude of the lost-sales figures. On the other hand, he was also impressed by the inventory investment required to cut those losses by appreciable amounts. Any significant change in inventory policy would therefore tend to enlarge the financing problems that already lay ahead.

Financing alternatives

As noted earlier, those problems had come to a head at the beginning of 1964, when Electricircuit's bank had refused to increase its line of credit in the absence of some prior strengthening of the company's capital structure. That development had not been completely unanticipated. In 1963 Mr. Rappasadi had begun to explore the possible issuance of subordinated long-term debt with several investment bankers and representatives of lending institutions. The discussions had all been unsuccessful, however, and as a result Electricircuit had been forced to finance the acquisition of a new headquarters building and its West Coast plant with sale-and-leaseback financing. The two buildings together had been constructed at a cost of $950,000 and had been leased by Electricircuit for a 10-year period at a combined annual rental of $280,000. The leases contained 10-year renewal options at the same annual rentals, but no repurchase option. Mr. Rappasadi, at the time, had estimated that the two plants probably would be worth half their original cost at the end of 10 years and little or nothing at the end of 20 years. Both deals had been arranged with a private group of wealthy New York investors.

The same group had also indicated its willingness to lend the company an additional $500,000 to $1,000,000 at any time at an annual interest rate of 18%. While the loan would be subordinated to bank debt and would permit an increase of the type of secured financing that the bank was currently providing, it would not be without its own restrictive covenants:

1. Cash dividend payments and company purchase of its own stock would be prohibited.
2. No additional debt would be allowed other than bank borrowing and other short-term liabilities arising in the normal course of business, or long-term debt specifically subordinated to this loan.
3. Current assets would have to exceed the sum of current liabilities and all long-term debt by at least $800,000.
4. Default on any provision would automatically accelerate the due date of principal and accrued interest to the date of default.

Interest payments would be payable semiannually, but the principal would not become due for five years. Prepayment in full would become permissible at the end of three years at a penalty of 10% and at the end of four years at 6%, but only with funds from operations.

Concern about weakening of control and earnings dilution made a public sale of common stock seem highly questionable to some of the company's owner-managers. They felt that earnings would continue to improve and cited the company's recent growth record as evidence of the possible cost of bringing in outside shareholders at an inopportune point in the company's development. On the other hand, Mr. Rappasadi had found that underwriters repeatedly expressed the opinion that Electricircuit's only hope for adequate long-term financing was additional common stock. That meant a public offering since none of the current stockholders had additional funds to invest.

Increasingly tight financial straits during 1964 had pressed Mr. Rappasadi to pursue the subject. Expressions of interest had been obtained from several underwriters, but only one, Bayles and Bayles, had expressed willingness to underwrite a stock issue. After many conversations, company visits, and a preliminary study of Electricircuit's financial records, the senior partner of Bayles and Bayles had indicated to Mr. Rappasadi that an issue of common stock to net the company up to $1,000,000 would probably be feasible in early autumn. Offering price to the public would be about $10.50 a share. The brevity of Electricircuit's history of good earnings would be a drawback, but Mr. Bayles explained that he counted on the company's unusual growth record to make that price attainable. The net proceeds to Electricircuit, however, would be closer to $8. The spread between the two prices would cover the underwriter's compensation and risk and all costs of preparing the issue. In addition, the company would agree to sell warrants to Bayles and Bayles for $10,000 to purchase 10,000 shares of stock. The warrants would be exercisable after one year at a price of $13.50 a share.

If the terms of a deal were finally agreed on, Bayles and Bayles would attempt to assemble a syndicate for which it would act as lead underwriter. The syndicate would be organized to provide wide geographic dispersion and insure a distribution of shares that would pose no threat to existing management. For a period of a year or so after the sale Bayles and Bayles would make an informal market for Electricircuit's stock in limited quantities. Although the firm was not an active over-the-counter dealer, it sometimes made an "after market" in issues it had originated, largely for the benefit of customers who might be forced to dispose of their stock in emergency circumstances.

Mr. Rappasadi found it difficult to evaluate the terms of this offer. Inquiries addressed to acquaintances in the financial community uncovered some opinion that the company should hold out for a higher price. These sources cited a number of recent growth issues that had sold in the 30 times price-earnings range. In addition, they noted that the economy showed strong signs of extending its longest postwar boom and that the stock market was currently at a record high.

Although Mr. Rappasadi realized that of all the firms approached Bayles and Bayles had been the only one to express any interest in underwriting a new issue, he decided to review the opinions above with Mr. Bayles. While Mr. Bayles agreed that both the economy and the stock market were unusually strong, he interpreted these developments as cause for apprehension concerning the new-issues market. He was uncertain about how long these favorable conditions could continue, and foresaw a possible break in the market at any time. In a sharply falling market an unseasoned over-the-counter stock such as Electricircuit's was apt to fare much worse than average. In pricing Electricircuit's proposed issue, the underwriter therefore had tried to allow both for some immediate capital appreciation and for the fact that it would be selling the issue to its customers at or near the top of a particularly strong market. Bayles and Bayles was particularly mindful of the second fact because of its agreement to maintain an informal market for Electricircuit common stock. As for the price of so-called comparable issues, the firm disagreed with the critics. The issues referred to were generally smaller, often had a small cash dividend to provide downside price support, and had been sold two or three months earlier in quite different market conditions. For all of these reasons, Bayles and Bayles declined to reconsider the offering price.

An alternative to external equity financing was continued reliance on the plowback of earnings with no payment of dividends. Mr. Rappasadi thought that the outlook for expansion and the profitability of contemplated funds commitments probably threw doubt on the wisdom of that policy, but he was uncertain about the amount and type, or types, of outside financing to recommend to his fellow shareholders.

Exhibit 1

ELECTRICIRCUIT, INC.

INCOME STATEMENTS FOR YEARS ENDED DECEMBER 31, 1961–63
(Dollar figures in thousands)

	1961	*1962*	*1963*
Net sales	$3,616	$5,544	$10,637
Cost of goods sold*	2,368	3,758	6,325
Gross profit	$1,248	$1,786	$ 4,312
Research and development expense	422	529	1,097
Selling, general, and administrative expense†	782	1,105	2,376
Interest expense	30	40	93
Income from operations	$ 13	$ 112	$ 746
Other income	2	7	20
Other deductions	(7)	(9)	(92)
Income before tax	$ 8	$ 110	$ 675
Federal income tax	3	45	329
Net income	$ 5	$ 65	$ 346

* Included in cost of goods sold:			
Depreciation, amortization, and maintenance	$31	$ 52	$117
Rental charges	40	80	210
State and local taxes (excluding payroll)	1	1	4
Total	$72	$133	$331
† Included in selling, general, and administrative expense:			
Depreciation, amortization, and maintenance	$11	$ 18	$ 40
Rental charges	19	39	101
State and local taxes (excluding payroll)	10	17	66
Total	$40	$ 74	$207

Exhibit 2

ELECTRICIRCUIT, INC.

BALANCE SHEETS AS OF DECEMBER 31, 1961–63
(Dollar figures in thousands)

ASSETS	1961		1962		1963	
Cash		$ 279		$ 303		$ 347
Accounts receivable		693		1,260		2,255
Inventories:						
Raw materials	$128		$337		$372	
Work in process	187		373		537	
Finished goods	244		311		407	
Total inventory		559		1,022		1,317
Prepaid expenses		8		13		24
Total current assets		$1,539		$2,598		$3,943
Gross fixed assets	$212		$298		$537	
Less: Accumulated depreciation	72		120		155	
Net fixed assets		140		178		382
Total assets		$1,679		$2,776		$4,325
LIABILITIES						
Notes payable*		$ 541		$1,072		$1,804
Trade accounts payable		159		401		484
Accrued expenses		129		246		240
Provision for taxes		9		56		383
Other		20		102		160
Total current liabilities		$ 858		$1,876		$3,072
Common stock, stated value 50 cents		$ 318		$ 328		$ 360
Paid-in surplus		486		489		464
Retained earnings		17		83		429
Total stockholders' equity		$ 821		$ 900		$1,253
Total liabilities and capital		$1,679		$2,776		$4,325
Number of shares outstanding		636,086		655,122		719,746

* Secured by the pledge of all receivables.

Exhibit 3

ELECTRICIRCUIT, INC.

SELECTED FINANCIAL DATA ON POSSIBLE INVENTORY POLICIES
(Dollar figures in thousands)

Alternative	*Ratio of Inventory to Cost of Goods Sold**	*Total Investment in Finished Goods Inventory**	*Annual Sales Loss because of Stockouts*	*Annual Combined Setup, Warehouse, Handling, and Insurance Costs†*
A	4.9% (18 days' sales)	$ 381	$495	$21
B	6.5 (24 days' sales)	505	301	25
C	8.9 (32 days' sales)	692	150	30
D	11.8 (42 days' sales)	917	56	35
E	14.2 (51 days' sales)	1,103	17	37

* Based on forecast annual cost of sales rate of $8.1 million. Inventory valued at direct cost.
† Interest expense and/or other financing costs are not included.

Exhibit 4

ELECTRICIRCUIT, INC.

BALANCE SHEET, AS OF APRIL 30, 1964, UNAUDITED
(Dollar figures in thousands)

ASSETS		
Cash		$ 135
Accounts receivable		2,510
Inventories:		
Raw materials	$410	
Work in process	506	
Finished goods	310	1,226
Prepaid expenses		30
Total current assets		$3,901
Gross fixed assets	$612	
Less: Accumulated depreciation	168	
Net fixed assets		444
Total assets		$4,345
LIABILITIES		
Notes payable*		$1,795
Trade accounts payable		530
Accrued expenses		246
Provision for taxes†		245
Other		143
Total current liabilities		$2,959
Common stock, stated value 50 cents		$ 360
Paid-in surplus		464
Retained earnings		562
Total stockholders' equity		$1,386
Total liabilities and capital		$4,345
Number of shares outstanding		719,746

* Secured by the pledge of receivables.

† Tax liabilities as of April 30 reflect a large, first-quarter adjusting payment. At year-end, "Provision for taxes" normally equals the federal corporate income tax for the year just ended, plus approximately $75,000 state and local tax accruals.

WINCO DISTRIBUTION COMPANY

In early June, 1965, the directors of Winco Distribution Company were faced with two major financial decisions that would have a long-run impact on the future of the firm. The first was the possible acquisition of Taylor Markets, Inc. The second was a major overhaul of the long-term capital structure of the company.

The first part of this case will present in summary form background information about Winco Distribution Company, stressing its growth and financing in the years immediately preceding 1965. Thereafter the information relevant to the acquisition of Taylor Markets and to alternative methods of reconstructing Winco's long-term capital structure will be summarized.

Growth of Winco Distribution Company

Winco was founded in 1907 to sell supplies to cotton plantations in the vicinity of Memphis, Tennessee. Through the years it expanded and underwent several changes in the nature of its business. By the end of World War II it had evolved into a grocery wholesaler with headquarters in Memphis servicing grocery stores in 10 states; it also owned and operated a chain of 18 retail food stores in Nashville, Tennessee.

Winco grew steadily from 1945 until 1965. The number of affiliated stores increased from 300 in 1945 to 1,350 in 1965 (Exhibit 1). This growth was also reflected in its operating statements and balance sheets for recent years (Exhibits 2 and 3). By 1965 the company's distribution system had expanded from the original single warehouse to a network of eight distribution points and three marine terminals from which it supplied ships calling in port.

In 1965 Winco was by far the larger of the two independent wholesale grocers in Memphis. It provided a wide range of ancillary services for affiliated retail stores. Stores could operate under their own names with standard brands or under a wide variety of advertising groups sponsored by Winco. Winco's staff was available to help plan all aspects of store operations from advertising to insurance and renovations. Financial support was also available to its retail associates. This support was given in the form of direct loans to 180 stores; of guarantees by Winco of liabilities of affiliates or suppliers; and of leases for prime store space signed by Winco and then sublet at cost to its retail affiliates. Management believed that these arrangements were basically quite secure and that they did not expose Winco to major financial risks.

Despite heavy competition from national chains such as A&P, Kroger, and National Tea, Winco's management believed that the sales volume of its own stores and its affiliates was equal to or larger than that of any chain or similar wholesale group in its area of operation. Independent studies by brokerage houses confirmed the ability of Winco and several large grocery wholesalers in other parts of the country to compete effectively with the national chains.

Background information on acquisitions prior to 1965

Part of the rapid expansion of Winco during the 1961–65 period was accounted for by acquisitions rather than by internal growth.

Certain assets of the Henstock Company, a wholesale grocery business operating in southeastern Texas and southwestern Louisiana, were acquired in July, 1962, for $700,000 in cash and common stock of Winco valued at $1.4 million (108,655 shares with a market price at the time of acquisition of about $13). Henstock's after-tax earnings were about $175,000 in the most recent year before acquisition. The book value of the assets acquired, after the deduction of certain liabilities assumed, was $1.7 million. The financial statements for Winco shown in Exhibits 2 and 3 have not been adjusted for the years prior to fiscal year 1963 to show the operations of the combined companies because the transaction was a purchase of assets rather than a merger.

In May, 1964, Winco acquired the principal operating assets of the Warrilow Corporation, a closely held wholesale grocery business and retail store chain operating in Nashville, Tennessee, and nearby areas. Winco paid the owners of Warrilow slightly over $12 million. Payment was made in three parts: (1) $4.8 million in cash; (2) $5 million of 6% cumulative preferred stock (described in more detail in the next section); and (3) the assumption by Winco of $2.4 million of the liabilities of Warrilow. The price paid was estimated by Winco's management at approximately 13 times Warrilow's earnings after taxes. The assets purchased had been carried on Warrilow's books at about $2 million less than the net price Winco paid for them. Most of this amount was assigned to individual asset accounts on Winco's books on the basis of an independent professional appraisal of the acquired assets. The remainder was carried as goodwill.

Financing in connection with the Warrilow acquisition

As previously indicated, Winco issued $5 million of 6% cumulative preferred stock to the owners of the Warrilow Corporation as partial payment for this acquisition. The terms of the preferred stock provided for the retirement of the entire issue in May, 1968, although Winco was given the right to call at par part or all of the issue for retirement prior to that date. If the preferred stock were not retired by May, 1968, the preferred stockholders would be entitled to elect a majority of the board of directors. Furthermore, the holders of the preferred stock could require redemption of their shares on 30 days' notice if the paid-in surplus and retained earnings of Winco should fall below $5.5 million.

The management of Winco did not expect to be able to generate funds from its own working capital position to cover all the $4.8 million cash payment and the $2.4 million in increased liabilities assumed in the Warrilow Corporation purchase. It did anticipate, however, that a smaller amount of current assets would be required to operate the combined businesses than the sum of their current assets before the acquisition. Inventory duplications could be eliminated, and other efficiencies were expected to reduce somewhat the need for working capital. Because the Winco management was uncertain about the exact amount of funds required to finance the expanded scale of operations, it decided to seek interim financing rather than longer term debt.

The cash required for the Warrilow acquisition was therefore raised mainly through an intermediate-term loan negotiated in June, 1964, with banks in Memphis and Nashville. The banks gave Winco a revolving line of credit at 5¼% in addition to the balance outstanding on a 5¼% loan previously made to Winco in 1963. The new loan was granted with the understanding that it would be paid off or replaced by longer term debt when a more precise estimate of the company's financial requirements could be made. On June 27, 1964, the end of Winco's 1964 fiscal year, $5 million of the new line of credit had been drawn down. By the end of fiscal year 1965, Winco was only borrowing $1.9 million under this arrangement.

Future plans

Except for the possible acquisition of Taylor Markets, Inc., which will be discussed below, the management of Winco knew of no future possible acquisitions of retail or wholesale grocery firms. Moreover, in the foreseeable future the management did not expect to commit funds to integrate operations backward into processing, packaging, and manufacturing. No major additions were planned for Winco's physical plant; funds generated from depreciation charges would be sufficient to cover construction of whatever new fixed assets might be required. Growth was expected to come primarily from an increased volume of business in existing market areas. The region served by Winco was attracting industry at a significant rate; standards of living were rising and population was increasing. Moreover, as previously noted, the management of Winco was confident of its ability to compete effectively with the national chains. It anticipated a probable growth rate of sales of about 13% for the foreseeable future and set the likely boundaries on the range of this growth rate as 10% and 16%. The existing physical plant, with relatively minor additions, was more than adequate to accommodate this rate of growth for some years to come.

Taylor Markets, Inc.

The management of Winco knew of only one prospect for expansion by acquisition in the foreseeable future. It had recently learned that the owners of Taylor Markets, an aggressive retail chain of 10 stores in Memphis, were willing to sell their chain to Winco if suitable terms could be negotiated. The Taylor chain had grown from a single store opened in 1947 to its current size. An independent market survey conducted early in 1964 indicated that Taylor had 18% of the Memphis food store business.

Winco had maintained a long and close relationship with Taylor Markets, which had been a member of Winco's voluntary plan since the first Taylor store was opened. The Taylor management had been very impressive, generating sufficient profits to open new stores with a minimum of financial assistance from Winco. Taylor Markets paid approximately $261,000 annually for the properties it leased. Many of these properties had been subleased from Winco and thus were already contingent liabilities of Winco.

The only severe difficulty Taylor Markets had encountered was caused by a labor dispute growing out of an acquisition the chain had made in 1961. As a consequence the company had shown losses for several years, but the issue had been completely resolved by 1965. The management of Winco regarded Taylor Markets' earnings of $220,000 in fiscal year 1965 as reasonably reflecting its true earning power. This figure was also considered a reasonable estimate of Taylor Markets' earning capacity on its existing stores over the next several years. (Recent earning statements of Taylor Markets are shown in Exhibit 4. Its estimated balance sheet for June 26, 1965, is given in Exhibit 5).

The owners of Taylor Markets wished to continue operating the business after its sale. For tax reasons they preferred to sell by means of an exchange of stock rather than for cash. A sale for cash would involve immediate heavy capital gains taxes whereas an exchange of stock would qualify as a taxfree transaction.

A merger with Taylor Markets might be considered as containing seeds of conflict with the independent retail affiliates of Winco. The Winco management, however, had found no ill will generated from its acquisition of the Warrilow stores in Nashville. All retailers, including wholly owned stores, were given the same terms and treatment. Management had concluded that under these circumstances there was little difference between supplying, on the one hand, a wholly owned store and its independent competitor and, on the other hand, two independent retailers who were competing with each other.

Long-term financing

Winco's long-term debt structure as of June 26, 1965, can be summarized as follows:

Current maturities on long-term debt	$ 300,000
Balloon maturity due in 1968 on 5¼% note of 1963	2,000,000
Amount outstanding on revolving 5¼% loan in connection with Warrilow acquisition	1,900,000
Other long-term debt (about half of which was scheduled to mature during or prior to 1968)	1,400,000
	$5,600,000

In addition to the long-term debt owed by Winco, Taylor Markets had \$650,000 outstanding in short-term notes payable. If Taylor was acquired, \$650,000 would be required to pay off these notes.[1]

In reviewing its debt position the management of Winco had definitely decided to refinance \$5.0 million of its existing debt (\$5.65 million if Taylor was acquired). An insurance company had expressed a willingness to share a loan of this size with Winco's banks. The interest rate on the outstanding balance would be between 5% and 5¼%. The principal of the loan would be amortized at an even rate over a 20-year period. If the loan was for \$5.0 million, the banks would loan \$1.25 million and the insurance company \$3.75 million. The loan would be paid off at the rate of \$250,000 a year, with the full amount going to the banks for the first five years and the remainder to the insurance company for the last 15 years. The covenants on the new loan would be less restrictive than those on the company's existing indebtedness.

Refinancing the \$5 million of preferred stock along with the outstanding debt was also under consideration. The lending institutions had indicated that they would be willing to increase the size of the new 20-year loan to a maximum of \$7.5 to \$8.0 million on the same terms except for a proportionate increase in the annual payments needed to retire the principal of the loan in 20 years. An \$8.0 million loan, however, was the maximum amount that they would grant at this time.

In addition to these needs for long-term or equity funds, Winco required seasonal financing each year. Peak needs occurred during the fall months and had amounted to about \$1 million in recent years. These funds were borrowed through Winco's Memphis bank, where a 90-day line of credit of \$3.5 million was maintained for seasonal financing. No change was expected in this arrangement for seasonal financing.

In its consideration of the restructuring of its long-run financing, Winco's management was considering two other sources of funds to refinance part or all of its needs above the amount that it expected to borrow on a 20-year basis.

Possible issue of common stock

The first was a public issue of common stock. Winco stock, which was traded over the counter, had recently reached an all time high of \$28⅞ a share, bid. (Exhibit 6 shows the range of Winco stock prices to June 10, 1965.) The bid price had only declined to about \$28 during the recent softening of the stock market in the second quarter of 1965. During the same period the Dow-Jones average of 30 industrial stocks had declined from 920 to 875.

The company's investment banker had indicated that a new issue of up to \$5 million of common stock could probably be sold at a price of about \$25 a

[1] Winco also had contingent liabilities and lease obligations for its affiliates and suppliers amounting to \$900,000, and it leased property in its own name involving annual rental payments of \$850,000. Neither of these items was shown on its balance sheet.

share to the public provided that the price of Winco common stock did not decline any further. The management of Winco did not want to price the stock so high as to "crowd the market" for fear that the stock might perform unfavorably thereafter. Fees and expenses were estimated at about 7% of the gross receipts of a $5 million issue and, because of the fixed costs involved, at a somewhat higher percentage of a smaller issue.

Winco common stock had first been made available to the public in July, 1961. At that time the company had sold 115,500 shares to raise funds to retire debt and for general purposes; members of the founder's family had sold 201,000 shares of their personal holdings at the same time. In order to minimize the cash drain from dividends during the first years of public ownership, the family had converted some of the shares they retained into a Class A common stock. The Class A stock was identical with the regular common stock except that it did not participate in dividends. It was convertible share for share into regular common stock according to a fixed schedule. After converting the remaining 109,638 shares of Class A stock on July 1, 1965, the founder's family would own about 437,000 shares of common stock. Other officers and directors owned about 90,000 regular common shares.

Management considered the public stock issue in 1961 a success. It was priced at $12 a share and subsequently rose to a high of $18½ before the stock market decline in April, 1962. At that time the price fell back to about $12.

By 1965 Winco had 1,373 registered stockholders located in 37 states. Some of the stock was held in "street names," the ultimate owner having left the stock in the name of his bank or brokerage house. Some mutual and pension funds had taken positions in the stock. Nevertheless, the number of round lots (100-share lots) held by the public was still small.

An investment banking firm with a special interest in the leading wholesale grocers had noted the limited marketability, the relatively small capitalization, and the lack of listing of these stocks as drawbacks. It expected, though, that these problems would diminish in intensity during the next several years for the larger wholesale grocers such as Winco. Exhibit 7 includes some financial statistics for several large wholesale grocers.

Possible issue of convertible debentures

The management of Winco had also discussed the possibility of issuing a subordinated convertible debenture to the public. Its investment banker had indicated that a company like Winco could raise roughly $5 million by issuing a 15-year or 20-year subordinated convertible debenture bearing interest at a rate of between 4% and 4½%. This rate was lower than Winco could obtain on a straight debt issue because of the potential value of the convertible feature to the lender. The conversion price would be set about 20% above the market price of the common stock at the time the debenture was sold, or at about $34 a share on the basis of the $28 market price. In other words, each $1,000 bond would be convertible into 29.41 shares of common stock. Fees and expenses would be 3½% to 4% of gross funds raised. The banks and insurance company that had offered to lend up to $8 million on a 20-year amortization basis had indicated that they would not object to an issue of convertible debentures provided that these debentures were subordinated to the 20-year loan.

It was normally expected that the price of the common stock of a growing company would rise sufficiently within a few years to make a conversion privilege attractive, thereby enabling the company to force conversion by calling the debenture issue for redemption. Consequently, it was not customary to require a sinking fund for the first few years of a convertible debenture's life. If Winco should issue a 20-year convertible debenture, for example, the repayments on principal would be scheduled to begin after five years and to be sufficient to retire the debt over the remaining 15 years, assuming that it had not been converted in the meantime.

Timing of issue of common stock or convertible debentures

Although an issue of stock or debt could be canceled at the last minute if the market proved extremely unfavorable, a public issue had to be planned several months in advance so that the necessary registration information could be compiled and filed with appropriate authorities. The nature of the information would differ depending on whether management had decided tentatively to issue stock or debt. A decision to shift from one type of issue to the other after planning was well under way would require a substantial revision of the preparatory paper work. The date of issue would be delayed, and an additional investment in management time and in legal and accounting fees would be necessary. For this reason, if a public issue of Winco securities was selected, management was anxious to choose a form of security that would not have to be changed because of moderate changes in stock market conditions during the next several months.

* * * * *

With the preceding facts in mind, the management of Winco had to decide (1) what action to take with respect to the merger with Taylor Markets; (2) whether to raise more than the $5 million it had already decided to secure by an issue of bonds; and (3) if so, the amount and the source of these additional funds. Management had prepared the forecasts shown in Exhibit 8 as background information for these decisions.

Exhibit 1

WINCO DISTRIBUTION COMPANY

NUMBER OF CLIENT STORES

	Fiscal Year				
	1961	*1962*	*1963*	*1964*	*1965*
Number of stores, beginning of year	747	767	774	797	1,197
Number of stores added	53	64	41	418*	161*
Number of stores dropped	33	57	18	18	8
Number of stores at year-end	767	774	797	1,197	1,350

* Of the 418 stores added in fiscal year 1964 and the 161 stores added in 1965, 376 and 128 respectively were formerly served by the Warrilow Corporation and became affiliated stores of Winco as a result of the acquisition of Warrilow or by affiliation with Winco after the acquisition.

Exhibit 2

WINCO DISTRIBUTION COMPANY

INCOME STATEMENTS FOR THE FISCAL YEARS 1961–65

(Dollar figures in millions)

Fiscal year ended	*June 24, 1961*		*June 30, 1962*		*June 29, 1963*		*June 27, 1964*		*(Preliminary) June 26, 1965*	
Net sales and service fees*	$ 74.4	100.0%	$ 86.3	100.0%	$121.4	100.0%	$138.7	100.0%	$211.8	100.0%
Cost of sales less discounts	69.5	93.4	80.6	93.4	112.6	92.8	128.1	92.3	192.0	90.7
Gross profit on sales and service fees	$ 4.9	6.6%	$ 5.7	6.6%	$ 8.8	7.2%	$ 10.6	7.7%	$ 19.8	9.3%
Operating expenses:										
Warehouse and delivery	$ 1.7		$ 1.9		$ 2.8		$ 3.1		$ 4.9	
Selling, general, and administrative	1.9		2.3		3.9		5.2		10.6	
Total operating expenses	$ 3.6	4.8	$ 4.2	4.9	$ 6.7	5.5	$ 8.3	6.0	$ 15.5	7.3
Income from operations	$ 1.3	1.8%	$ 1.5	1.7%	$ 2.1	1.7%	$ 2.3	1.7%	$ 4.3	2.0%
Add: Other income (expenses) net	0.1		0.1		0.1		0.1		(0.2)‡	
Less: Interest	0.1		0.1		0.2		0.2		0.4	
Income before taxes	$ 1.3	1.8%	$ 1.5	1.7%	$ 2.0	1.6%	$ 2.2	1.6%	$ 3.7	1.8%
Provision for income taxes	0.7	1.0	0.8	0.9	1.0	0.8	1.1	0.8	1.8	0.9
Net income after tax	$ 0.6	0.8%	$ 0.7	0.8%	$ 1.0	0.8%	$ 1.1	0.8%	$ 1.9	0.9%
Preferred dividends	...		...		...		...		$ 0.3	
Net income applicable to common shares	$ 0.6		$ 0.7		$ 1.0		$ 1.1		$ 1.6	
Number of shares of common stock outstanding at end of each period†	704,411		819,911		928,566		932,901		938,393	
Net income per share†	$ 0.85		$ 0.86		$ 1.07		$ 1.21		$ 1.66	
Dividends per share paid on common shares only	$ 0.04		$ 0.26		$ 0.34		$ 0.41		$ 0.50	
Depreciation (millions)	n.a.		n.a.		$ 0.4		$ 0.5		$ 0.9	

* In fiscal year 1964 includes $10.3 million in sales and a negligible amount in net profits from Warrilow for the period May 4, 1964–June 27, 1964. For the full fiscal year 1965, Warrilow contributed sales of $70.0 million and income from operations of $1.5 million.

† Includes both classes of common stock.

‡ Includes $0.3 million loss on abandonment of equipment in the Warrilow operation.

Exhibit 3

WINCO DISTRIBUTION COMPANY

BALANCE SHEETS AS OF END OF FISCAL YEARS 1961–65

(Dollar figures in millions)

ASSETS	*June 24, 1961**	*June 30, 1962*	*June 29, 1963*	*June 27, 1964*	*(Preliminary) June 26, 1965*
Current assets:					
Cash	$1.0	$ 1.6	$ 2.4	$ 4.2	$ 2.5
Receivables (net)	1.8	3.3	4.7	8.5	10.2
Inventories of merchandise and supplies	4.3	4.5	7.0	12.7	13.0
Total current assets	$7.1	$ 9.4	$14.1	$25.4	$25.7
Investments, advances to affiliates, and other assets	$1.2	$ 0.5	$ 1.8	$ 1.7	$ 1.8
Property and equipment:					
Property and equipment	$2.2	$ 2.5	$ 3.5	$ 7.0	$ 6.9
Less: Accumulated depreciation	0.7	1.0	1.3	2.1	2.4
Net property and equipment	$1.5	$ 1.5	$ 2.2	$ 4.9	$ 4.5
Goodwill, deferred charges, and other assets	...	...	0.1	0.8	0.8
Total assets	$9.8	$11.4	$18.2	$32.8	$32.8
LIABILITIES					
Current liabilities:					
Notes payable, bank	$1.5	$ 0.5	$ ...	$ 0.1	$ 0.4
Current maturities, long-term debt	0.1	0.1	0.3	0.3	0.3
Trade accounts payable and other accruals	2.2	2.8	4.7	8.6	10.0
Income taxes payable	0.6	0.6	0.8	0.9	1.4
Total current liabilities	$4.4	$ 4.0	$ 5.8	$ 9.9	$12.1
Long-term debt	$0.9	$ 0.8	$ 4.1	$ 8.8	$ 5.3
Stockholders' equity:					
4% preferred stock, noncumulative	$0.4	$ 0.4	$ ...	$ ...	$ ...
6% preferred stock, cumulative, due 1968	...	...	...	5.0	5.0
Common stock, $1 par value†	0.4	0.5	0.6	0.7	0.8
Common stock Class A, $1 par value†	0.3	0.3	0.3	0.2	0.1
Paid-in surplus	0.5	1.8	3.1	3.1	3.2
Retained earnings	2.9	3.6	4.3	5.1	6.3
Total stockholders' equity	$4.5	$ 6.6	$ 8.3	$14.1	$15.4
Total liabilities and stockholders' equity	$9.8	$11.4	$18.2	$32.8	$32.8

* The statement as of June 24, 1961, has not been restated to allow for certain subsidiaries consolidated in 1962 and subsequent years. The assets of these subsidiaries totalled about $350,000.

† Total number of shares outstanding in each period shown in Exhibit 2.

Exhibit 4

TAYLOR MARKETS, INC.

INCOME STATEMENTS

(Dollar figures in thousands)

Fiscal year ended	*June 29, 1963*		*June 27, 1964*		*(Preliminary) June 26, 1965*	
Net sales	$16,463	100.0%	$18,504	100.0%	$18,162	100.0%
Cost of sales	13,270	80.6	14,833	80.2	14,379	79.2
Gross profit on sales	$ 3,193	19.4%	$ 3,671	19.8%	$ 3,783	20.8%
Operating expenses:						
Direct store expenses	$ 2,041	12.4%	$ 2,203	11.9%	$ 2,176	12.0%
Selling, general, and administrative	1,112	6.8	1,238	6.7	1,100	6.0
Total operating expenses	$ 3,153	19.2%	$ 3,441	18.6%	$ 3,276	18.0%
Income from operations	$ 40	0.2%	$ 230	1.2%	$ 507	2.8%
Other income	19	0.1	46	0.3	3	...
	$ 59	0.3%	$ 276	1.5%	$ 510	2.8%
Other expenses:						
Interest	$ 70		$ 71		$ 66	
Other	15		2		5	
Total other expenses	$ 85	0.5%	$ 73	0.4%	$ 71	0.4%
Net income (loss) before taxes	$ (26)	(0.2%)	$ 203	1.1%	$ 439	2.4%
Provision for state and federal income taxes	...	...	95	0.5	219	1.2
Net income (loss)	$ (26)	(0.2%)	$ 108	0.6%	$ 220	1.2%

Exhibit 5

TAYLOR MARKETS, INC.

PRELIMINARY BALANCE SHEET AS OF JUNE 26, 1965

(Dollar figures in thousands)

ASSETS		
Current assets:		
Cash		$ 884
Accounts receivable		10
Inventory		600
Prepaid expenses		116
Total current assets		$1,610
Cash value of life insurance		16
Total property and equipment	$1,659	
Less: Depreciation	808	
Net property and equipment		851
Deferred charges		1
Total assets		$2,478
LIABILITIES		
Current liabilities:		
Note payable		$ 650
Current maturities, long-term debt		125
Accounts payable and miscellaneous accruals		501
Accrued state and federal taxes		219
Total current liabilities		$1,495
Long-term debt:		
4% note payable		$ 42
5% note payable		130
		$ 172
Stockholders' equity:		
Common stock, $100 par, 536 shares outstanding		$ 54
Paid-in surplus		71
Retained earnings		686
Total stockholders' equity		$ 811
Total liabilities		$2,478

Exhibit 6

WINCO DISTRIBUTION COMPANY

Market Price of Common Stock*

Calendar Years	*High*	*Low*
1962:		
First quarter	$18½	$16½
Second	15¾	12¼
Third	14¼	12½
Fourth	13½	13
1963:		
First	14	13⅜
Second	17⅝	14¾
Third	17⅛	17
Fourth	17⅜	16⅜
1964:		
First	17	16½
Second	21⅝	19
Third	21½	21⅜
Fourth	24	21½
1965:		
First	25	24
Second (to June 10)	28⅞	24

* Bid price in over-the-counter market.

Exhibit 7

WINCO DISTRIBUTION COMPANY

Financial Statistics, Four Grocery Wholesalers

	Winco Distribution Company	*Fleming Company*	*Scot Lad Foods*	*Super Value Stores*
Most recent fiscal year ended	*June, 1964*	*Dec., 1964*	*June, 1964*	*Dec., 1964*
Most recent fiscal year:				
Sales (millions)	$139	$313	$183	$466
Profit after taxes (millions)	$ 1.1	$ 2.6	$ 1.4	$ 3.2
Gross margin (%)	7.7%	6.6%	11.8%	6.2%
Common dividends as a percentage of profit after taxes	25.5%*	47.5%	21%	43.8%
Stock price, fiscal 1964 range	16⅜–21⅝	22¼–28½	19⅝–27¼	27⅛–35½
Price-earnings ratio (based on average price for fiscal year 1964)	15.7	18.5	12.3	18.3
Yield (fiscal 1964 figures)	2.2%	2.6%	1.7%	2.4%
Quoted bid price, June 11, 1965	$ 28¼	$ 29¾	$ 24¾	$ 33½
Capitalization:				
Long-term debt	38.3%	25.6%	38.5%	22.3%
Preferred stock	21.8	3.4	...	8.6
Common stock and surplus	39.9	71.0	61.5	69.1
	100.0%	100.0%	100.0%	100.0%
Five-year compound growth rate:				
Sales	15.0%	11.6%	21%	17.2%
Profits after taxes	13.3	12.6	28	15.5
Earnings per share	8.4	8.8	18	9.8

* Based on dividends actually paid on the common stock. If dividends at the same rate had been paid on both the regular common and the Class A common stock, dividends would have been 34.8% of profit after taxes.

Exhibit 8

WINCO DISTRIBUTION COMPANY

PRO FORMA PROJECTIONS, FISCAL YEARS 1966 THROUGH 1968*

(Dollar figures in millions)

	Actual	*Projected, 1966–68*		
	1965	*1966*	*1967*	*1968*
1. *Sales and Earnings:*				
Sales—13% annual growth	$211.8	$239.3	$270.4	$305.6
Earnings before interest and taxes	4.1	4.4	4.9	5.6
2. *Projected balance sheet data*†				
Current assets and advances to affiliates:				
Cash	$ 2.5	$ 3.6	$ 4.0	$ 4.6
Receivables (net)	10.2	11.0	12.4	13.9
Inventories	13.0	14.6	16.4	18.5
Advances to affiliates	1.8	1.9	2.0	2.1
Total	$ 27.5	$ 31.1	$ 34.8	$ 39.1
Current liabilities:				
Accounts payable	$ 10.0	$ 10.8	$ 12.2	$ 13.7
Income taxes payable	1.4	1.5	1.7	2.0
Other	0.7	0.7	0.7	0.7
Total	$ 12.1	$ 13.0	$ 14.6	$ 16.4
Net working capital and advances to affiliates	$ 15.4	$ 18.1	$ 20.2	$ 22.7
Incremental funds required for NWC and advances to affiliates	...	2.7	2.1	2.5
Cumulative increase in funds required for NWC and advances to affiliates	...	2.7	4.8	7.3
3. *Minimum financial charges following the proposed $5 million refinancing*‡:				
Interest on the $5 million of long-term debt	...	$ 0.25	$ 0.24	$ 0.22
Interest on other remaining long-term debt	...	0.04	0.03	0.03
Debt repayment—$5 million of long-term debt	...	0.25	0.25	0.25
Debt repayment—other remaining long-term debt	...	0.09	0.09	0.09

* Note: The projections in this exhibit do *not* include any adjustments to reflect the possible acquisition of Taylor Markets currently under consideration by the management of Winco.

† The balance sheet data in this section include only current assets and current liabilities with the single exception that "advances to affiliates" is classified here with current assets. As stated in the text, expenditures on fixed assets were expected to be about equal to depreciation expenses.

‡ These charges are computed on the assumption that $5 million of new long-term debt is borrowed at an interest rate of 5% with repayments of principal of $250,000 per annum. If more than $5 million of long-term debt were borrowed, then charges related to long-term borrowings would have to be increased proportionately.

HOLIDAY GREETINGS, INC.

On Tuesday, July 21, 1970, Karl Augspach, president of Holiday Greetings, Inc., met with David Kingston, a friend and financial consultant. They had been discussing the future of Holiday in relation to the research Mr. Kingston had been doing on the firm. Mr. Augspach commented:

> Money is tight and, quite frankly, the cost of financing growth is now so high that I wish we could sit still for a year. But we really can't do that.
>
> If we should start refusing orders from new customers, we would demoralize our salesmen since part of their compensation is based on the volume of orders they generate. Similarly, if we can't respond to increased order sizes from existing customers, these customers might take all of their business to some other company that can meet their needs. Were we to come looking for their business later, they wouldn't let us in the door. You know the record and you saw our growth for last year. We're projecting 20% increases in sales and even larger increases in earnings for next year [see Exhibits 1 and 2 for the company's income statements, projections, and balance sheets]. The momentum we're generating is based mainly on larger orders from existing customers—in fact, already we've seen the size of some orders increase anywhere from 5% to 500% over last year. However, we are keenly aware that growth from this source can't go on forever. Ultimately we will have to expand our customer base and our production operations, not just the size of our orders. If you can come up with some suggestions concerning the financing of our expansion, we can talk about them on Saturday morning; right now I've got to go upstairs to see about the cutting of that new line of round cards, and then look at the Christmas 1971 designs.

With this dismissal from Mr. Augspach, Mr. Kingston left to consider the information that he had collected to date. He knew that he would have to develop some precise recommendations by the end of the week.

INDUSTRY BACKGROUND DATA

In 1968, the greeting card industry consisted of about 215 companies; the "Big Five" (see Exhibits 3 and 4) dominated the scene with an overwhelming market share. Of these five, two were publicly owned (American Greetings and Rust Craft), two were private (Hallmark and Norcross), and one (Gibson) had been purchased by a financial corporation (CIT) in 1964.

The rest of the industry was made up predominantly of small firms, many of which were privately owned and family controlled; 60% of them employed fewer than 20 people and most manufactured seasonal card lines (such as Christmas cards, Valentines, etc.). Growth, however, was most prominent in the larger firms, which had larger, more diversified product lines (as many as 1,200 different cards for Christmas) and more efficient national distribution channels. Smaller companies were often crippled by the expense of setting up a large sales system, of producing a full line and constantly reviewing it, and of designing and preparing new cards. As a result, from 1954 to 1963 the total number of firms in the industry had declined 12%, and from 1963 to 1967 the decline was 15%. Most of this decline occurred within companies of less than 50 employees.[1]

In order to compete successfully, all firms had to deal effectively with high fixed costs. Companies ran large inventory costs because of the necessity of keeping stock for reorders. In addition, many retailers could return unsold or soiled cards to the manufacturer, who would have to bear the expense. Production was costly since long lead times prevented rerunning successful designs.

Because of these high fixed costs and the overall competitiveness of the industry, distribution costs were very important to overall firm profitability. Most large companies used their own sales force to sell directly to various kinds of outlets (see Exhibits 5 and 6); few dealt with supermarkets and little was known about effective marketing strategy in this area. Often, companies would try to increase sales by expanding the distribution network although the policy at Hallmark was to maintain the number of outlets while increasing card turnover. Some firms also marketed different lines for different kinds of stores (such as college versus general drugstores) in order to widen distribution, but the trend appeared to be moving away from this expensive strategy. Sales trends within the industry were quite distinctive; they were often characterized (especially in the case of smaller companies) by seasonal peaks, as most of the actual sales occurred in a short period of time even though cards were in production all year. As an example, for the industry as a whole 37% of dollar sales (and 50% of the total piece volume) occurred at Christmas, with Valentine's Day (7% of sales), Mother's Day (5%), and Father's Day (2%) being other examples where the selling season was short but the revenues were large. Within the industry, companies had been placing

---

[1] Most of these small firms disappeared through failure or merger with other small greeting card firms. The U.S. Department of Justice generally challenged a merger between two firms operating in a highly concentrated industry if these firms' market shares exceeded those shown below:

Acquiring Firm	*Acquired Firm*
4%	4% or more
10%	2% or more
15% or more	1% or more

Source: U.S. Department of Justice, *Merger Guidelines*, "Enforcement Policy" [for Section 7, Clayton Act], May 30, 1968, p. 13.

an increasing emphasis on variety offering and a rapid replacement of slow sellers to encourage more impulse buying of everyday cards. This had been successful to the extent that in 1954 25% of card volume was represented by everyday sales, and in 1969 this figure was 40%.

Within the industry, trends included a conscious move away from relying solely on greeting card sales. To provide more year-round revenue, firms had been diversifying into different kinds of cards (such as Friendship, Black holidays) as well as related products. Hallmark, for example, also marketed glassware, jewelry, candles, silverware, and giftbooks in its national "Hall Galleries"; American Greetings diversified into gift wrap (16% of sales) and stationery goods (such as playing cards, giftbooks and college study guides—2% of sales). Rust Craft produced art prints, stationery, announcements (wedding, birth, etc.) and owned and operated several TV stations. However, greeting cards still represented 75% of this company's sales in 1968. In a further attempt to even out revenue, the four "giants" had also started licensees and subsidiaries all over the world.

HOLIDAY GREETINGS, INC.

In 1956, four years after coming to the United States, Karl Augspach founded Augspach's Greeting Card Co. in New York City with $1,500. A citizen of Holland, born in Germany, he had decided to enter the business he had learned from his father. In 1961 he acquired the bankrupt Holiday Lithograph Publishing Co. of Reading, Connecticut, and moved his operations to the new plant. A year later Holiday Greetings, Inc., went public through a stock offering at $3 per share.

In the years that followed, Holiday expanded rapidly through internal growth and acquisitions. In general, management policy was to consolidate all production operations at the Reading plant but to keep the acquired facilities and former management to facilitate distribution and to take on extra printing if necessary. Glitter Greetings of Lansing, Michigan, a firm which primarily sold "spoil-proof" acetate wrapped cards to supermarkets, became a wholly owned subsidiary in 1964 in a deal involving both cash and stock. In 1968, Holiday acquired Dorn & Co. (Long Beach, New York) for cash. Dorn was a small company which sold juvenile Valentines through a distribution system that included chain, drug, variety, and discount stores as well as wholesalers, rack jobbers, and supermarkets. Dorn was managed by one of the three brothers who had sold the company to Holiday. The brother, age 66, had spent his entire business career in the greeting card business. Still another market was opened with the acquisition of the California firm "Christmas Cheer," again by means of cash and stock. In 1969 this became "Holiday Artists" and provided the company with a convenient means of West Coast distribution as well as an operation specializing in sales of packaged personalized Christmas cards directly from the warehouse to the retailer.

Holiday operations

Unlike most small companies, Holiday manufactured a full line of greeting cards, i.e., Christmas, Valentines, Birthday, Get Well, Sympathy, Mother's Day and Father's Day, Anniversary, etc.; the 1969 line included 1,200 designs. Approximately 30% of dollar sales was accounted for by Christmas sales and 25% by Valentines, with the remainder made up by everyday and spring holiday cards. Twenty-five percent of total sales were of packaged boxes of cards which were either "title" cards (i.e., Brother's Birthday) or assortments; this helped to cut costs because the manufacturer did not have to supervise racks and reorders of individual cards in every outlet. Returns expense was low here as well, since once the package was sold to a store it was generally not returnable. In addition, the giants of the industry were not as active in packaged sales, concentrating more heavily on the sale of individual cards. At Holiday only Glitter competed heavily in this "counter" market, with 95% of this division's sales being of individual cards in 1969.

None of Holiday's designs were studio cards, which were higher fashion items. Holiday sold primarily to the over 25-year-olds. Mr. Augspach characterized a large part of his market as cost conscious and generally not college educated. He felt that most of the purchasers of his cards would not spend the time or the money in selecting *the* perfect card for each occasion, but would prefer to have the less expensive, more convenient packages at home whenever a card was needed.

Production of all cards and gift wrap was done at the 200-employee plant in Reading. The operation was fully integrated, meaning that all facets were carried out at Holiday from artwork and plate making to printing and packaging. The plant was operating at capacity but much of the printing work could be done by outside printers if necessary.

Mr. Augspach estimated that an individual card that retailed at 25 cents cost him 3½ cents to produce. The largest factors included in this cost-of-goods-sold figure were first, artwork, then envelopes, paper, and boxes.

Eighty percent of the artwork was done by individual artists connected with an independent studio in Cleveland. Besides the individual design costs of $125, color separation and plate making were extremely expensive, making it beneficial to use the design as often as possible. At Holiday the first year a design was used it was used on personalized cards sold in quality department stores; the second year it went into packages to be sold in chain, discount, or variety stores; and the third year it was reworked to be used again. In addition, it was used for gift wrap over its entire life.

Holiday's distribution method

Distribution itself was not a large expense at Holiday; the 15 company salesmen (one third of whom worked on a full commission basis) sold either directly to the central buyers for such stores as Kresge's, Woolworth's, and

Bradlee's or to rack jobbers and wholesalers. This system, however, was a prime factor in the low margins earned by Holiday, for there were often two intermediaries between the manufacturer and the ultimate customer. As a reflection of this, Mr. Augspach estimated that dollar sales of his cards at retail level were three times the sales figures in his income statement.

Operations at Holiday were closely supervised; management included two production and shipping managers, one art director, and a sales manager and an assistant to the president. Besides Mr. Augspach there were nine officers, six of whom were also directors. Mrs. Augspach held the position of secretary and director, but she was the only family member involved. The Augspachs had three daughters, but neither they nor their husbands were interested in entering the greeting card industry. Other officers included the treasurer, the controller, and an executive vice president in charge of Glitter operations.

Financial problems

According to Mr. Augspach, Holiday had never been without financial problems. The business was capital intensive, and Mr. Augspach attributed much of his success to the company's good relations with its banks and suppliers. Its line of credit with a local bank was for $1.5 million, the bank's legal lending limit, and Dorn had a line of credit with a New York bank for an additional million. The company borrowed at 2½ percentage points above the prime rate, with the prime rate being 8% in July, 1970. In addition, several of the company's suppliers extended up to six months' trade credit to the company. After the first 60 days, however, they usually charged 9½% to 10% for this service. Because of the seasonal nature of the industry, Mr. Augspach estimated that the company's peak needs for bank and trade credit, which amounted to $3.1 million in 1969, occurred in December and January. He also stated that the company's low borrowing point following each selling season recurred in April, at which point bank and trade credit was reduced to about 50% of peak needs.

Although the company had a good relationship with its banks, Mr. Augspach had been urged to seek additional equity capital. Holiday's bankers felt uneasy about the extent to which the company was depending on debt capital in financing its operations. Early in 1970 they suggested that when they went along in helping to finance the company through an enormous sales expansion in 1968, they had anticipated a period of consolidation during which sales growth would slow substantially. Under these circumstances growth in the equity account through earnings retentions would have rapidly reduced the firm's debt/equity ratio to the 1967 level, a point substantially below the lofty 5.2 to 1 reached in 1968 (Exhibit 2). Given the firm's performance in 1969 and Mr. Augspach's sales projections (Exhibits 1 and 2), however, a return to the 1967 level in Holiday's debt/equity ratio was at best still several years away. Holiday's bankers therefore insisted that the firm take some action before the 1970 peak borrowing season to make sure that the company would stay safely within two restrictions which the bankers planned to impose on future loans to Holiday.

These two restrictions, which were to become applicable as of the 1970 seasonal peak of borrowing needs, were as follows:

1. The maximum bank loans outstanding at any time could not exceed 80% of Holiday's accounts receivable.
2. Holiday's total liabilities[2] could not exceed three times the book value of the company's net worth. In the event that the company's debt[2] to equity ratio rose to a level of more than three the company's bank loans would become due on demand.

For his own planning purposes Mr. Augspach had decided that to retain some margin of safety within these restrictions he would want to hold Holiday's future debt/equity ratio to a maximum of 2.75 to 1.

DECISIONS CONFRONTING HOLIDAY GREETINGS

Mr. Kingston was familiar with this background information on the greeting card industry and on Holiday Greetings. Mr. Augspach had also referred three other questions to Mr. Kingston:

1. Should Holiday invest in equipment to enable the company to make rather than to buy its envelopes? Mr. Augspach had indicated that he believed such an investment would be profitable but he was concerned about its implications for the company's financing requirements.
2. Should Holiday Greetings acquire Humor Designs, Inc., a small midwestern manufacturer of studio cards?
3. Should Holiday go to the market to raise additional equity capital in order to relieve the pressure on its financial position?

Envelope machine proposal

The cost of envelopes was one of the largest components of total costs. As of mid-1970 Holiday was still purchasing its entire supply of envelopes. During 1969 it had spent $600,000 to purchase the 200 million envelopes used by the company in 1969. Mr. Augspach estimated that he could buy equipment for $200,000 which when operated at full capacity would enable him to manufacture all the envelopes he had used in 1969. He estimated that the envelope-making equipment would have an economic life of about eight years.

Mr. Augspach estimated that seven men would be required to run the envelope-making operation. A two-man team would be needed to operate the machine on each of three daily shifts five days per week. They would each earn $2.50 an hour. One supervisor working only one shift per day would earn $4.00 an hour. Mr. Augspach calculated that paper and glue would cost

[2] "Total liabilities" and the "debt" component of the debt/equity ratio are used here as synonymous terms.

about $1.63 per thousand for the 200 million envelopes he had purchased in 1969 for $600,000. Mr. Augspach also estimated that he would need to rent a 25,000 square foot warehouse at a yearly rental of $1.50 per square foot if he manufactured his own envelopes. From these data Mr. Kingston had calculated that the envelope machine project would generate a positive cash flow of $112,500 annually for an eight-year period, disregarding working capital and financing requirements (Exhibit 7).

The additional warehouse space would be needed since if the machine was purchased, the company would be producing envelopes at a level rate substantially in excess of shipments during the spring and summer months of the year so as to build the large inventories needed to meet year-end shipping schedules (Exhibit 8). This inventory situation troubled Mr. Augspach somewhat since he knew that paper manufacturers required payment within 60 days. Under existing arrangements with envelope suppliers Mr. Augspach ordered envelopes on an "as needed" basis, and did not pay for them until about the time he received payment from Holiday's retailers. If he started manufacturing his own envelopes, Mr. Augspach realized that his working capital requirement would be expanded by the amounts shown in Exhibit 8.

Mr. Kingston knew that Mr. Augspach expected a recommendation from him in the immediate future as to whether and when he should establish his own envelope-making capacity. Mr. Augspach wanted to know what rate of return he would make on such an investment, how his earnings would be affected, and what the implications would be for his financing requirements.

Possible acquisition of Humor Designs, Inc.

Mr. Augspach had also been investigating a possible acquisition candidate, Humor Designs, Inc. (HD), a small midwestern manufacturer of studio cards. Humor Designs was privately owned and had sales of about $2 million in 1969 (Exhibit 9). Mr. Augspach had spent considerable time over a four-month period examining the details of HD's operations. He had become convinced that under his management, HD could almost immediately reduce both its cost of goods sold and its other expenses by 5%. He estimated that if Holiday acquired HD during the summer of 1970, HD's sales would remain flat during the year of ownership change, but that beyond 1970 the company would be able to achieve sales increase at about 10% per year as it had done between 1967 and 1969 (Exhibit 9). What particularly interested Mr. Augspach about the potential acquisition was the fact HD's balance sheet (Exhibit 10) was comparatively strong. He felt HD's suppliers would be willing to go a good deal further in providing trade credit than they had in the past, and he knew that the company carried with it substantial unused bank credit lines and other debt capacity. In his discussion with the three present owners of HD, all of whom were approaching retirement age, Mr. Augspach concluded that the company could be acquired for 12 times its 1969 earnings. The principals were willing to take Holiday common stock valued at $6 a share, which would give them a total of 136,000 shares. A check with his public accounting firm convinced Mr. Augspach that the acquisition could be treated as a "pooling of interests" for accounting purposes.

Mr. Augspach had asked Mr. Kingston for a recommendation as to whether he should acquire Humor Designs on these terms. Mr. Kingston knew that he would have to consider the impact of the acquisition on the earnings position of Holiday and also the implications of the acquisition for Holiday's financial position.

Possible sale of new common stock

In order to sustain the projected rapid growth for the next several years and in view of Holiday's extremely tight financial position (Exhibits 1 and 2), Mr. Augspach was aware that he might have to raise additional equity capital. Mr. Kingston knew that Mr. Augspach would be most reluctant to accept a policy recommendation that would force him to curtail the growth in sales projected in Exhibit 1. As already indicated Mr. Augspach believed that if potential increases in orders from new or existing customers were turned down, it would be very difficult and perhaps impossible to regain these customers in subsequent years. Mr. Augspach was also concerned that restrictions on the acceptance of new orders would be demoralizing to his salesmen and perhaps would cause some of his most valuable salesmen to shift to a competing firm.

Mr. Kingston was also troubled by the fact that he knew that mid-1970 was a most difficult and expensive time for any company to raise new equity capital, and especially for a small company like Holiday with unseasoned securities.

Holiday Greetings stock was traded in the over-the-counter market. Volume was light, averaging about 1,000 shares a week. During the past several months the stock price had held at about $6, a low for the year. Earlier in the year the stock had sold as high as $11 a share. During 1968 and 1969 the price of the stock had ranged from a low of $6 to a high of $12 a share. Mr. Kingston knew that Mr. Augspach did not follow the price of his stock "too closely" and that he received relatively few telephone calls from brokers and analysts about the company. Mr. Augspach owned about 55% of the stock currently outstanding. Another 20% was owned by employees and officers of the company. About 25% of the outstanding stock was owned by the public.

Mr. Kingston knew that Mr. Augspach had recently received an offer from a group of West Coast investors who had had a long-term interest in the company. They had offered to buy 100,000 shares of Holiday's common stock at $5 a share. If this offer was accepted, Holiday would have to pay a finder's fee of $25,000, or 5,000 shares, to the individual who had brought this offer to Mr. Augspach's attention.

In considering this offer Mr. Kingston approached Tom Meservey, a friend of his and a partner in the Boston office of the investment banking firm of Stoddard, White & Driscoll, to inquire about the feasibility of a public offering of Holiday stock. Mr. Meservey was not encouraging. He commented:

Now is a tough time to raise equity money, especially for a small company like Holiday. The Dow Jones index of industrial stocks has fallen from 942 in December, 1968, to 732 right now and there's no telling what will happen tomorrow. Unemployment is now over 5% and most predictions are that it will go even higher. This is a bad time for a small company to raise money. The new issue market has badly deteriorated; in fact it has almost dried up.

I hate to say so, but I don't see how we could possibly take Holiday's stock to the market at more than $5 a share, and we could contemplate such an offering only on a "best efforts" rather than an "underwritten" basis. Frankly, I am uncertain how many shares we could sell even at a price as low as $5. In addition, you realize of course that we would have to charge a sizable commission on an offering as risky and problematical as this, and that Holiday would have to bear the legal, accounting, and other fees of preparing and registering a public issue of Holiday's stock. Moreover, it would probably take two to three months, at best, to prepare a prospectus and process it through the Securities and Exchange Commission.

This conversation confirmed Mr. Kingston's initial impression that the only realistic prospect for raising new equity capital was to accept the offer of the West Coast group. This offer would yield $500,000 for 100,000 shares. In addition there would be a finder's fee of 5,000 shares. Legal and administrative costs would be minimal since the transaction would not involve a public issue of stock.

* * * * *

With this background analysis completed, Mr. Kingston sat down to prepare his recommendations for Mr. Augspach. He knew that Mr. Augspach expected a recommendation on whether and when the envelope machine should be purchased, on whether Humor Designs should be acquired, and on whether new equity financing should be obtained. In addition to a recommended course of action Mr. Augspach expected a backup analysis explaining the superiority of Mr. Kingston's recommendations as compared with other feasible courses of action.

Exhibit 1

HOLIDAY GREETINGS, INC.
CONSOLIDATED INCOME STATEMENTS, 1967–69, AND PROJECTED INCOME STATEMENTS, 1970–72*
(Years ending December 31; dollar figures in thousands)

	Actual Data			Projected Data		
	1967	*1968*	*1969*	*1970*	*1971*	*1972*
Net sales	$3,222	$5,106†	$6,501	$7,800	$9,300	$11,200
Cost of goods sold	2,276	3,514	4,216	5,000	5,900	7,000
Gross profit on sales	$ 946	$1,592	$2,285	$2,800	$3,400	$ 4,200
Expenses:						
Selling, delivery, and warehousing	$ 406	$ 717	$ 949	$1,160	$1,390	$ 1,600
General and administrative	219	378	450	500	560	650
Total expenses	$ 625	$1,095	$1,399	$1,660	$1,950	$ 2,250
Earnings before interest and taxes	$ 321	$ 497	$ 886	$1,140	$1,450	$ 1,950
Interest	198	242	305	350§	350§	385§
Income before federal income taxes	$ 123	$ 255	$ 581	$ 790	$1,100	$ 1,565
Provision for federal income taxes	45	90	307	420	600	850
Net income	$ 78	$ 165	$ 274	$ 370	$ 500	$ 715
Earnings per share based on average shares outstanding for the period (in dollars)	$ 0.29	$ 0.60‡	$ 0.96	$ 1.28§	$ 1.72§	$ 2.47§

* Net sales and net income for 1964–66 were as follows:

	Net Sales (Millions)	*Net Income (Thousands)*
1964	$2.2	$21
1965	2.5	42
1966	2.8	59

† $600,000 of 1968 sales were from the Dorn acquisition.
‡ $0.13 was from the Dorn acquisition.
§ Based on 290,000 shares outstanding. No allowance is made for additional financing in the form of increased debt or new equity issues in these projections.
Source: Annual reports and management projections.

Exhibit 2

HOLIDAY GREETINGS, INC.

CONSOLIDATED BALANCE SHEETS, 1967–69, AND PROJECTED BALANCE SHEETS, 1970–72
(As of December 31; dollar figures in thousands)

	Actual Data			Projected Data			
	1967	1968	1969	1970	1971	1972	
ASSETS							
Cash	$ 80	$ 148	$ 96	$ 100	$ 100	$ 100	
Notes and accounts receivable	1,168	2,353	2,805	3,354	3,999	4,816	(43% of projected sales)
Inventory	1,000	1,483	2,235	2,652	3,162	3,808	(34% of projected sales)
Prepaid expenses	17	47	77	78	93	112	(1% of projected sales)
Total current assets	$2,265	$4,031	$5,213	$6,184	$7,354	$ 8,836	
Net fixed assets	361	883	973	1,000	1,000	1,000	
Investment at cost	—	40	40	40	40	40	
Goodwill	—	172	172	172	172	172	
Deferred charges and other	74	151	145	150	150	150	
Total assets	$2,700	$5,277	$6,543	$7,546	$8,716	$10,198	
LIABILITIES							
Bank loans	$ 929	$1,740	$2,428	$2,819	$3,253	$ 3,476	(PLUG)
Trade notes payable	348	630	696 }				
Accounts payable	253	469	528 }	1,482	1,767	2,128	(19% of projected sales)
Accrued expenses and payroll taxes	90	184	251	312	372	448	(4% of projected sales)
Federal income taxes	43	89	241	336	400	680	
Current portion of long-term debt	47	140	173	173	173	173	
Other	—	75	99	100	100	100	
Total current liabilities	$1,710	$3,327	$4,416	$5,222	$6,065	$ 7,005	
Long-term debt	315	1,101	983	810	637	464	(173,000 retired per yr.)
Total liabilities	$2,025	$4,428	$5,399	$6,032	$6,702	$ 7,469	
Common stock ($0.10 par value)	27	28	29	29	29	29	
Paid-in capital	290	299	319	319	319	319	
Retained earnings	358	522	796	1,166	1,666	2,381	
Total liabilities and net worth	$2,700	$5,277	$6,543	$7,546	$8,716	$10,198	
Equity	$ 675	$ 849	$1,144	$1,514	$2,014	$ 2,729	
Bank loan/receivables	0.80	0.74	0.87	0.84	0.81	0.72	
Liabilities/equity	3.0	5.2	4.7	4.0	3.3	2.7	

Exhibit 3

HOLIDAY GREETINGS, INC.
INDUSTRY PERFORMANCE—1968

Company	Sales* (in Millions)	Income after Taxes (in Millions)	Earnings per Share (in Dollars)	Price-Earnings Ratio
American Greetings	$113.1	$6.9	$1.72	23
Rust Craft	47.5	2.7	2.30	18
Hallmark	150.0	n.a.	n.a.	n.a.
Gibson	65.0	n.a.	n.a.	n.a.
Norcross	20.0	n.a.	n.a.	n.a.
Holiday	5.1	0.2	0.60	10

INDUSTRY GROWTH TRENDS

Company	Annual Percentage Increase in Sales	Annual Percentage Increase in Profits
American Greetings†	13%	13%
Rust Craft‡	7	9
Hallmark†	10–15	10–15
Gibson§	30	n.a.

* Sales include all products of these companies but they consist primarily of greeting cards.
† Annual rate over a 10-year period.
‡ Annual rate after 1962 deficit.
§ Annual rate over five-year period. Gibson's rapid increase in sales reflected a new policy of selling directly to wholesalers and of offering more favorable terms to retailers. It was believed in the industry that profits were lagging because of the high cost of the policy.
Source: "Note on the United States Greeting Card Industry," Intercollegiate Case Clearing House, Harvard Business School, 1969, ICH 14C1R(9-114-001).

Exhibit 4

HOLIDAY GREETINGS, INC.
SALES: INDUSTRY VERSUS HOLIDAY
(In millions)

Year	Industry	Holiday
1963	$332	$2.1
1964	345	2.2
1965	356	2.5
1966	370	2.8
1967	400	3.2
1968	425	5.1

Exhibit 5

HOLIDAY GREETINGS, INC.
INDUSTRY DISTRIBUTION METHODS

Company	Outlets	Salesmen
American Greetings	73,000*	1,000
Hallmark	30,000	n.a.
Rust Craft	16,000	210

* Up in five years from 11,000.

Exhibit 6

HOLIDAY GREETINGS, INC.
INDUSTRY SALES THROUGH DIFFERENT OUTLETS
(Percentage of total sales)

Type of Outlet	*Greeting Cards*	*Gift Wrap*
Variety store	25%	35%
Discount house	11	15
Department store	7	25
Drug store	16	5
Food store	5	10
Other*	36	10
Total	100%	100%

* Includes stationery and gift shops.

Exhibit 7

HOLIDAY GREETINGS, INC.
ESTIMATED ANNUAL SAVINGS IN CASH FLOW FROM OPERATION OF ENVELOPE MACHINE, YEARS 1 THROUGH 8
(In thousands)

Savings: Outlays for envelopes purchased in 1969	$600.0
Incremental expenses from manufacturing envelopes:	
Materials	$326.0
Warehouse	37.5
Labor	36.5
Depreciation*	25.0
Total expenses	$425.0
Increase in profits before taxes	$175.0
Increase in income taxes	87.5
Increase in profit after taxes	$ 87.5
Add back: Depreciation	25.0
Net increase in cash flow from operations	$112.5

* If depreciation were taken on an accelerated basis for tax purposes, as would be possible, the annual increase in cash flows would be larger in the earlier years and smaller in later years.

Exhibit 8

HOLIDAY GREETINGS, INC.

Envelope Machine Project—Working Capital Requirements Calculation*

	Feb.	Mar.	Apr.	May	June	July	Aug.	Sep.	Oct.	Nov.	Dec.	Jan.	Feb.	Mar.	Total for Final 12 Months
						(Percent of year's total unit shipments made in month)									
Shipping level per month:															
Everyday cards	2.5	2.5	2.5	2.5	2.5	2.5	2.5	2.5	2.5	2.5	2.5	2.5	2.5	2.5	30.0
Spring cards	5.0	5.0	—	—	—	—	—	—	—	—	—	5.0	5.0	5.0	15.0
Christmas cards	—	—	—	—	—	—	—	—	15.0	15.0	—	—	—	—	30.0
Valentine cards	—	—	—	—	—	—	—	—	—	—	12.5	12.5	—	—	25.0
	7.5	7.5	2.5	2.5	2.5	2.5	2.5	2.5	17.5	17.5	15.0	20.0	7.5	7.5	100.0
						(In thousands of dollars)									
Production (at cost)†	33.3	33.3	33.3	33.3	33.3	33.3	33.3	33.3	33.3	33.3	33.3	33.3	33.3	33.3	400.0‡
Usage (at cost)†	30.0	30.0	10.0	10.0	10.0	10.0	10.0	10.0	70.0	70.0	60.0	80.0	30.0	30.0	400.0
Cash out for labor	3.0	3.0	3.0	3.0	3.0	3.0	3.0	3.0	3.0	3.0	3.0	3.0	3.0	3.0	36.5‡
Cash out for warehouse	3.1	3.1	3.1	3.1	3.1	3.1	3.1	3.1	3.1	3.1	3.1	3.1	3.1	3.1	37.5‡
Cash out for material	—	—	27.2	27.2	27.2	27.2	27.2	27.2	27.2	27.2	27.2	27.2	27.2	27.2	326.0‡
Total cash out	6.1	6.1	33.3	33.3	33.3	33.3	33.3	33.3	33.3	33.3	33.3	33.3	33.3	33.3	400.0‡
Total cash collected§	—	—	30.0	30.0	10.0	10.0	10.0	10.0	10.0	10.0	70.0	70.0	60.0	80.0	400.0
Monthly cash deficit	6.1	6.1	3.3	3.3	23.3	23.3	23.3	23.3	23.3	23.3	(36.7)	(36.7)	(26.7)	(46.7)	
Working capital required¶	6.1	12.2	15.5	18.8	42.1	65.4	88.7	112.0	135.3	158.6	121.9	85.2	58.5	12.2‡	

* Cycle must begin at positive buildup point to avoid negative inventory; it continues for 14 periods to eliminate "start-up" effect on calculations.
† Cost does not include depreciation.
‡ Figures do not add because of rounding.
§ These figures do not represent anticipated sales revenue, but only that portion of revenue which represents the return of actual cash outlay for the manufacture of envelopes.
¶ *The average working capital requirement for the year beginning April 1 and ending March 31 would be $76,000.*

Exhibit 9

HOLIDAY GREETINGS, INC.
INCOME STATEMENTS FOR HUMOR DESIGNS, INC. (ACTUAL, 1967–69, AND PROJECTED, 1970–72)
(Years ended December 31; dollar figures in thousands)

	Actual Data			Projected Data		
	1967	*1968*	*1969*	*1970*	*1971*	*1972*
Net sales	$1,670	$1,830	$2,000	$2,000*	$2,200*	$2,420*
Cost of goods sold	993	1,080	1,200			
Gross profit on sales	$ 677	$ 750	$ 800			
Expenses:						
Selling, delivery, and warehousing	420	472	480			
General and administrative	112	120	140			
Total expenses	$ 532	$ 592	$ 620			
Earnings before interest and taxes	145	158	180			
Interest	30	38	40			
Income before federal income taxes	$ 115	$ 120	$ 140			
Provision for federal income taxes	58	62	72			
Net income	$ 57	$ 58	$ 68			
Dividends	32	32	38			
Retained earnings	$ 25	$ 26	$ 30			

* Projection made by Mr. Augspach.

Exhibit 10

HOLIDAY GREETINGS, INC.
BALANCE SHEETS OF HUMOR DESIGNS, INC., 1967–69
(As of December 31; dollar figures in thousands)

	1967	*1968*	*1969*
ASSETS			
Cash	$ 27	$ 23	$ 35
Notes and accounts receivable	544	613	640
Inventory	535	620	600
Prepaid expenses	13	22	25
Total current assets	$1,119	$1,278	$1,300
Net fixed assets	436	490	500
Total assets	$1,555	$1,768	$1,800
LIABILITIES			
Bank loans	$ —	$ 50	$ 100
Accounts payable	176	220	200
Current portion of long-term debt	15	20	20
Federal income taxes	50	55	65
Other	121	133	115
Total current liabilities	$ 362	$ 478	$ 500
Long-term debt	349	420	400
Total liabilities	$ 711	$ 898	$ 900
Common stock	40	40	40
Paid-in capital	120	120	120
Retained earnings	684	710	740
Total liabilities and net worth	$1,555	$1,768	$1,800
Equity	$ 844	$ 870	$ 900
Bank loan/receivables	0.00	0.08	0.16
Total liabilities/equity	0.84	1.03	1.00

Appendixes

A. TAX TABLE[1]

FEDERAL TAX RATES ON CORPORATE INCOME
AND PAYMENT DATES

Income Years	*Rate*	*Income Years*	*Rate*
1940*	24%	1954–63	52%
1941*	31	1964	50
1942–45*	40	1965–67	48
1946–49	38	1968–69†	52.8
1950	47	1970†	49.2
1951–53*	52	1971	48

*Excess profits tax also in effect for part or all of year.
†Includes special surcharge.

The 52 percent rate in effect from 1951 through 1963 consisted of a normal tax of 30 percent of taxable income and a surtax of 22 percent of taxable income in excess of $25,000. The 50 percent rate in effect in 1964 consisted of a normal tax of 22 percent and a surtax of 28 percent; and the 48 percent rate in effect from 1965 on consisted of a normal tax of 22 percent and a surtax of 26 percent.

In addition, in 1968 a special surcharge of 10 percent was imposed making the effective rate for that year 52.8 percent. This rate held for 1969, but the special surcharge was phased out gradually by quarters during 1970 so that the overall effective rate for that year was 49.2 percent and by 1971 the rate was again 48 percent.

Recent revenue acts have moved corporate income tax payments close to current payment. Beginning in 1950, payments were gradually accelerated until in 1954 they were brought entirely within the first half of the year following the tax liability. The Revenue Acts of 1954 and 1964 and the Tax Adjustment Act of 1966 set up even more accelerated schedules. Through 1967, all tax liabilities up to $100,000 were payable in equal amounts on March 15 and June 15 of the year following the tax liability. The Revenue

[1] This table has been prepared for use in connection with cases in this book. It is not a complete statement of applicable rates, and it should not be used as a reference for general purposes.

Act of 1968 provided for a gradual acceleration of tax payments for corporations with tax liabilities of less than $100,000 as well as for corporations with tax liabilities of more than $100,000. Tax liabilities over $100,000, for companies on a calendar year, were payable according to the following schedule.

	*Percentage Paid in Income Year**				*Percentage Paid in Following Year†*			
Year	*Apr. 15*	*June 15*	*Sept. 15*	*Dec. 15*	*Mar. 15*	*June 15*	*Sept. 15*	*Dec. 15*
1949	—	—	—	—	25	25	25	25
1950	—	—	—	—	30	30	20	20
1951	—	—	—	—	35	35	15	15
1952	—	—	—	—	40	40	10	10
1953	—	—	—	—	45	45	5	5
1954	—	—	—	—	50	50	—	—
1955	—	—	5	.5	45	45	—	—
1956	—	—	10	10	40	40	—	—
1957	—	—	15	15	35	35	—	—
1958	—	—	20	20	30	30	—	—
1959–1963	—	—	25	25	25	25	—	—
1964	1	1	25	25	24	24	—	—
1965	4	4	25	25	21	21	—	—
1966	12	12	25	25	13	13	—	—
1967 and subsequent years	25	25	25	25	—	—	—	—

*These are percentages of the estimated tax liability on income of the current year.
†These are percentages of the tax liability on income of the previous year.

B. NOTE ON INVESTMENT TAX CREDIT[1]

A tax credit subsidy for business purchases of capital goods was first enacted by the U.S. Congress in 1962. Its purpose was twofold. First, the United States was emerging from a small economic recession in 1961, and it was hoped that the credit would encourage business spending for new plant and equipment. While the prime goal of the credit probably was to bolster a sagging economy, it also promised a substantial secondary benefit. For a number of years trade groups from numerous basic American industries had complained that European producers with lower labor costs and more modern physical facilities were slowly exporting more and more of their production to the United States. It was hoped that a tax subsidy encouraging new investment in capital goods would allow American producers to modernize their facilities and reduce their costs enough to be more competitive in the U.S. market with European producers.

Between 1962 and 1968, the investment credit underwent several revisions. It was "permanently" repealed (there had been a temporary suspension in 1966) by the Tax Reform Act of 1969. Because of a continuing business recession and rising unemployment in 1971 the tax investment credit was re-enacted in the Revenue Act of 1971 under the name "job-development credit." As the law stands after re-enactment, a purchaser of "Sec. 38"[2] property may deduct from his federal income tax liability 7 percent of the cost of new "Sec. 38" property in the year it is purchased, so long as the property has an expected useful life of 7 years or more. For property with a life of from 5 to 7 years the credit is equal to two thirds of this 7 percent, and for property with a useful life of 3 to 5 years the credit is equal to one third of 7 percent. Property with a useful life of less than 3 years does not qualify for the credit. (Under the old investment tax credit repealed in 1969 the required lives were one year longer; i.e., the upper limit was 8 years and the lower limit was 4 years.)

---

[1] This statement has been prepared for use in connection with cases in this book. It is not a definitive statement, and it should not be used as a reference for general purposes.

[2] For purposes of the credit, "Sec. 38" property is defined as all depreciable property (not including buildings) used as an integral part of (a) manufacturing, (b) mining, (c) production, (d) furnishing of services such as transportation, energy, water, and sewage disposal.

With some exceptions the credit is not applicable to foreign-made equipment or to equipment bought for use outside the United States. Public utilities also benefit by the investment tax credit but at the lower rate of 4 percent. Subject to certain limitations, up to $50,000 of the cost of used property may be taken into account in calculating the credit for any one year.

The investment tax credit does not act to reduce the basis for depreciation of equipment; however, the same time span of useful life must be used for calculating the investment tax credit as is used for taking depreciation deductions.

The investment tax credit represents a direct credit against the total income tax liability. For a company in the 50 percent tax bracket, a tax credit of $100,000 can save as much in income taxes as a $200,000 deduction from pretax income. Taxpayers who have a total tax liability of $25,000 or less are allowed to credit up to 100 percent of the liability. For those whose liability exceeds $25,000, the limit on the credit is $25,000 plus ½ of the excess. Pre-1969 limits were the same. In both cases, calculations using a flat 50 percent will give results which are approximately correct when dealing with large corporate incomes. Any credit that cannot be used currently may be carried back for 3 years and forward for 7 years.

TAX VERSUS BOOK ACCOUNTING

Internal revenue regulations require corporations to take the investment tax credit in their tax accounting to the maximum allowable amount in the year it arises. In reports of earnings to shareholders, however, public accounting firms permit the credit to be handled by either of two methods. The entire credit can be taken in a single year, as it is for tax purposes, or it can be spread out and taken over the productive lives of the assets giving rise to the credit. The public accounting profession is somewhat divided on the issue, but most accountants favor the latter, the "deferral," approach since it causes less year-to-year distortion of after-tax income. Under the old law about 80 percent of the major U.S. corporations adopted the former, the "flow-through," treatment since it results immediately in higher reported earnings.

Exhibit 1 below shows how the accounting convention chosen can affect the after-tax income reported by a corporation to its shareholders. Exhibit 2 shows the relative importance of the investment tax credit to the reported earnings of a number of well-known U.S. corporations.

In 1967, the Accounting Principles Board (APB) of the American Institute of Certified Public Accountants proposed to eliminate the "flow-through" option allowing corporations to take the entire amount of the credit in a single year in reports of earnings to shareholders. Instead, corporations would be required to adopt the "deferral" approach and spread the tax saving over the lives of the assets giving rise to the credit. The APB argued that a corporation's after-tax profit as reported to shareholders was subject to great distortion if the entire credit was taken in a single year.

Permitting the investment credit to flow through to net income in the period when the benefit is used to reduce income taxes payable may result in increasing or decreasing reported net income solely by reason of the timing of acquisition, rather than the use, of property. The result is inconsistent with the accepted concept that income results from the use and not from the acquisition of assets. Allocation of the investment credit to those periods in which the property that gives rise to the credit is utilized associates the income effects of the credit with the use of the property, not its acquisition.[3]

In response to the proposed change, the APB was deluged with nearly 1,000 letters concerning the proposal from corporate financial officers, a large portion of whom were critical of the APB's investment tax credit proposal. The officers of those companies whose reported earnings would be affected most (for example, airlines and equipment leasing companies) were the most vocal opponents, but many other businessmen and even government representatives jumped into the fray. The Assistant Secretary for tax policy of the U.S. Treasury Department charged that the board's proposed treatment of the investment tax credit could well blunt its effectiveness as an incentive to modernization and expansion.

Again, when the investment tax credit was re-enacted in 1971, the accounting profession made an attempt to tighten the rules governing the financial reporting of the 7 percent investment tax credit. The APB had the support of the SEC for its ruling that companies would have to report tax savings in income statements over the useful life of the property involved, and the ruling would have specifically disallowed the flow-through accounting method. However, the Senate, with the formal approval of the Nixon administration, vetoed the attempt and in fact inserted into the law a provision that "no taxpayer shall be required to use for the purposes of financial reports . . . any particular method of accounting for the credit allowed by such Section 38." The taxpayer must disclose in his reports the method he uses in accounting for the credit and must use the same method in all financial reports.

Exhibit 1

ACME CORPORATION

	Tax Accounts	*Shareholder Reports*	
		1 Year Lump Sum	*Spread Over 8 Years*
Purchases of new "Sec. 38" property	$2,000,000	$2,000,000	$2,000,000
Profit before federal income tax	800,000	800,000	800,000
Federal income tax before credit	400,000	400,000	400,000
Less: investment tax credit	140,000	140,000	17,500
Federal income tax after credit	260,000	260,000	382,500
Profit after taxes	$ 540,000	$ 540,000	$ 417,500

[3] "Exposure Draft, Proposed APB Opinion: Accounting for Income Taxes," Accounting Principles Board, September 14, 1967, paragraph 58b.

Exhibit 2

CORPORATE EARNINGS AND THE INVESTMENT TAX CREDIT

	Net Income after Preferred Dividends (000's)	*1965 Investment Tax Credit (000's)*	*Investment Credit as % of Net Income*	*Net Income per Share*	*Investment Credit per Share*
Allegheny Ludlum	$ 19,474	$ 1,472	7.6%	$4.81	$ .36
American Airlines	39,571	5,330	13.5	4.61(a)	.62(a)
American Can	59,201	4,400	7.4	3.61	.27
Atchison, Topeka & Santa Fe	84,743	5,100	6.0	3.45	.21
Beaunit (j)	7,872	1,560	19.8	4.04	.80
Bethlehem Steel	150,028	20,600	13.7	3.26	.45
Bliss, E. W.	3,825	360	9.4	1.47	.14
Borden	50,912	3,700	7.3	2.03	.14
Burlington Industries	68,613	3,396	4.9	2.76	.14
Certain-Teed Products	5,630	739	13.1	1.77	.23
Champion Papers	17,865	3,693	20.7	2.81(a)	.58(a)
Cities Service	94,931	7,000	7.4	3.86(a)	.29(a)
Consolidated Edison	90,144	9,500(b)	10.5	2.42	.25
Continental Can	58,832	4,720(c)	8.0	4.81	.38
Cyclops	10,134	1,269	12.5	5.08	.64
Detroit Steel	4,692	581	12.4	1.19	.15
Douglas Aircraft (k)	14,598	806	5.5	3.15	.17
Federal Paper Board (l)	3,066	250	8.2	2.59	.21
Grace, W. R.	44,436	2,709	6.1	2.80(a)	.17(a)
Jones & Laughlin Steel	51,802	3,360	6.5	6.55	.42
Kaiser Aluminum & Chemical	32,728	2,200	6.7	2.10	.14
Kelsey-Hayes (m)	6,086	1,085	17.8	4.08	.73
McCall Corp.	5,678	560(e)	9.9	2.13	.21
Monsanto	122,967	14,199	11.5	3.89	.45
National Cash Register	24,725	1,290	5.2	2.81	.15
National Steel	87,497	5,250	6.0	5.55	.33
Norfolk & Western	89,576	9,400	10.5	9.60	1.01
Oxford Paper	3,697	292	7.9	3.57	.28
Pabst Brewing	12,439	967	7.8	2.62	.20
Pacific Gas & Electric	121,937	5,861	4.8	2.08	.10
Pittsburgh Steel	4,005	550	13.7	.97	.20
Republic Steel	77,302	8,200	10.6	4.90	.52
St. Regis Paper	35,866	2,100	5.9	2.81	.16
Scott Paper	47,001	4,610	9.8	1.63	.16
Sharon Steel	4,428	475	10.7	3.23	.35
Smith, A. O.	8,709	700(f)	8.0	4.05	.33
Southern Pacific	97,796	8,900	9.1	3.60	.33
Southern Railway	30,376	3,002	9.9	4.58	.45
Stauffer Chemical	29,740	2,990	10.1	3.13	.31
Stevens, J. P. (i)	29,414	1,935	6.6	5.63	.37
Swift & Co. (n)	16,351	1,165	7.1	2.70	.19
Union Carbide	226,917	13,531	6.0	3.76	.22
Uniroyal	32,087	2,882(g)	9.0	2.68(a)	.24(a)
United Air Lines	44,984	5,302(h)	11.8	6.69(a)	.77(a)
West Virginia Pulp & Paper (i)	19,039	1,721	9.0	3.71	.34
Weyerhaeuser	83,400	7,500	9.0	2.72	.24
Youngstown Sheet & Tube	51,587	5,167	10.0	4.85	.49

(a) Based on average number of shares outstanding; (b) including $2,200,000 representing the remaining amount available for carryback; (c) includes $1,800,000—the unamortized portion of the investment tax credit for 1962 and 1963; (e) includes adjustment to amounts reported in prior years; (f) of the total, $500,000 was carried forward from previous years; (g) includes $221,000—the amortization of 1962 and 1963 credits; (h) includes the use of $2,385,000 of a $14,200,000 available unused credit carried forward from previous years; (i) for year ended October 31, 1965; (j) for year ended March 31, 1966; (k) for year ended November 30, 1965; (l) for 52 weeks ended January 1, 1966; (m) for year ended August 31, 1965; (n) for 52 weeks ended October 30, 1965.

Source: Anna Merjos. "Generous Allowance," *Barron's*, August 1, 1966, p. 5.

C. PRESENT VALUE TABLES

Table C–1

PRESENT VALUE OF $1

Periods until Payment	1%	2%	2½%	3%	4%	5%	6%	8%	10%	12%	14%	15%	16%	18%	20%	22%	24%	25%	26%	30%	40%	50%
1	0.990	0.980	0.976	0.971	0.962	0.952	0.943	0.926	0.909	0.893	0.877	0.870	0.862	0.847	0.833	0.820	0.806	0.800	0.794	0.769	0.714	0.667
2	0.980	0.961	0.952	0.943	0.925	0.907	0.890	0.857	0.826	0.797	0.769	0.756	0.743	0.718	0.694	0.672	0.650	0.640	0.630	0.592	0.510	0.444
3	0.971	0.942	0.929	0.915	0.889	0.864	0.840	0.794	0.751	0.712	0.675	0.658	0.641	0.609	0.579	0.551	0.524	0.512	0.500	0.455	0.364	0.296
4	0.961	0.924	0.906	0.888	0.855	0.823	0.792	0.735	0.683	0.636	0.592	0.572	0.552	0.516	0.482	0.451	0.423	0.410	0.397	0.350	0.260	0.198
5	0.951	0.906	0.884	0.863	0.822	0.784	0.747	0.681	0.621	0.567	0.519	0.497	0.476	0.437	0.402	0.370	0.341	0.328	0.315	0.269	0.186	0.132
6	0.942	0.888	0.862	0.837	0.790	0.746	0.705	0.630	0.564	0.507	0.456	0.432	0.410	0.370	0.335	0.303	0.275	0.262	0.250	0.207	0.133	0.088
7	0.933	0.871	0.841	0.813	0.760	0.711	0.665	0.583	0.513	0.452	0.400	0.376	0.354	0.314	0.279	0.249	0.222	0.210	0.198	0.159	0.095	0.059
8	0.923	0.853	0.821	0.789	0.731	0.677	0.627	0.540	0.467	0.404	0.351	0.327	0.305	0.266	0.233	0.204	0.179	0.168	0.157	0.123	0.068	0.039
9	0.914	0.837	0.801	0.766	0.703	0.645	0.592	0.500	0.424	0.361	0.308	0.284	0.263	0.225	0.194	0.167	0.144	0.134	0.125	0.094	0.048	0.026
10	0.905	0.820	0.781	0.744	0.676	0.614	0.558	0.463	0.386	0.322	0.270	0.247	0.227	0.191	0.162	0.137	0.116	0.107	0.099	0.073	0.035	0.017
11	0.896	0.804	0.762	0.722	0.650	0.585	0.527	0.429	0.350	0.287	0.237	0.215	0.195	0.162	0.135	0.112	0.094	0.086	0.079	0.056	0.025	0.012
12	0.887	0.788	0.744	0.701	0.625	0.557	0.497	0.397	0.319	0.257	0.208	0.187	0.168	0.137	0.112	0.092	0.076	0.069	0.062	0.043	0.018	0.008
13	0.879	0.773	0.725	0.681	0.601	0.530	0.469	0.368	0.290	0.229	0.182	0.163	0.145	0.116	0.093	0.075	0.061	0.055	0.050	0.033	0.013	0.005
14	0.870	0.758	0.708	0.661	0.577	0.505	0.442	0.340	0.263	0.205	0.160	0.141	0.125	0.099	0.078	0.062	0.049	0.044	0.039	0.025	0.009	0.003
15	0.861	0.743	0.690	0.642	0.555	0.481	0.417	0.315	0.239	0.183	0.140	0.123	0.108	0.084	0.065	0.051	0.040	0.035	0.031	0.020	0.006	0.002
16	0.853	0.728	0.674	0.623	0.534	0.458	0.394	0.292	0.218	0.163	0.123	0.107	0.093	0.071	0.054	0.042	0.032	0.028	0.025	0.015	0.005	0.002
17	0.844	0.714	0.657	0.605	0.513	0.436	0.371	0.270	0.198	0.146	0.108	0.093	0.080	0.060	0.045	0.034	0.026	0.023	0.020	0.012	0.003	0.001
18	0.836	0.700	0.641	0.587	0.494	0.416	0.350	0.250	0.180	0.130	0.095	0.081	0.069	0.051	0.038	0.028	0.021	0.018	0.016	0.009	0.002	0.001
19	0.828	0.686	0.626	0.570	0.475	0.396	0.331	0.232	0.164	0.116	0.083	0.070	0.060	0.043	0.031	0.023	0.017	0.014	0.012	0.007	0.002	
20	0.820	0.673	0.610	0.554	0.456	0.377	0.312	0.215	0.149	0.104	0.073	0.061	0.051	0.037	0.026	0.019	0.014	0.012	0.010	0.005	0.001	
21	0.811	0.660	0.595	0.538	0.439	0.359	0.294	0.199	0.135	0.093	0.064	0.053	0.044	0.031	0.022	0.015	0.011	0.009	0.008	0.004	0.001	
22	0.803	0.647	0.581	0.522	0.422	0.342	0.278	0.184	0.123	0.083	0.056	0.046	0.038	0.026	0.018	0.013	0.009	0.007	0.006	0.003	0.001	
23	0.795	0.634	0.567	0.507	0.406	0.326	0.262	0.170	0.112	0.074	0.049	0.040	0.033	0.022	0.015	0.010	0.007	0.006	0.005	0.002		
24	0.788	0.622	0.553	0.492	0.390	0.310	0.247	0.158	0.102	0.066	0.043	0.035	0.028	0.019	0.013	0.008	0.006	0.005	0.004	0.002		
25	0.780	0.610	0.539	0.478	0.375	0.295	0.233	0.146	0.092	0.059	0.038	0.030	0.024	0.016	0.010	0.007	0.005	0.004	0.003	0.001		
26	0.772	0.598	0.526	0.464	0.361	0.281	0.220	0.135	0.084	0.053	0.033	0.026	0.021	0.014	0.009	0.006	0.004	0.003	0.002	0.001		
27	0.764	0.586	0.513	0.450	0.347	0.268	0.207	0.125	0.076	0.047	0.029	0.023	0.018	0.011	0.007	0.005	0.003	0.002	0.002	0.001		
28	0.757	0.574	0.501	0.437	0.333	0.255	0.196	0.116	0.069	0.042	0.026	0.020	0.016	0.010	0.006	0.004	0.002	0.002	0.002	0.001		
29	0.749	0.563	0.489	0.424	0.321	0.243	0.185	0.107	0.063	0.037	0.022	0.017	0.014	0.008	0.005	0.003	0.002	0.002	0.001			
30	0.742	0.552	0.477	0.412	0.308	0.231	0.174	0.099	0.057	0.033	0.020	0.015	0.012	0.007	0.004	0.003	0.002	0.001	0.001			
40	0.672	0.453	0.372	0.307	0.208	0.142	0.097	0.046	0.022	0.011	0.005	0.004	0.003	0.001	0.001							
50	0.608	0.372	0.291	0.228	0.141	0.087	0.054	0.021	0.009	0.003	0.001	0.001	0.001									

SOURCE: Jerome Bracken and Charles J. Christenson, *Tables for Use in Analyzing Business Decisions* (Homewood, Ill.: Richard D. Irwin, Inc., 1965), except for the data on 2½%, the source for which is *Mathematical Tables from Handbook of Chemistry and Physics* (6th ed.; Cleveland: Chemical Rubber Publishing Co. 1938).

Table C–2

PRESENT VALUE OF $1 RECEIVED ANNUALLY

Periods to Be Paid	1%	2%	2½%	3%	4%	5%	6%	8%	10%	12%	14%	15%	16%	18%	20%	22%	24%	25%	26%	30%	40%	50%
1	0.990	0.980	0.976	0.971	0.962	0.952	0.943	0.926	0.909	0.893	0.877	0.870	0.862	0.847	0.833	0.820	0.806	0.800	0.794	0.769	0.714	0.667
2	1.970	1.942	1.927	1.914	1.886	1.859	1.833	1.783	1.736	1.690	1.647	1.626	1.605	1.566	1.528	1.492	1.457	1.440	1.424	1.361	1.224	1.111
3	2.941	2.884	2.856	2.829	2.775	2.723	2.673	2.577	2.487	2.402	2.322	2.283	2.246	2.174	2.106	2.042	1.981	1.952	1.923	1.816	1.589	1.407
4	3.902	3.808	3.762	3.717	3.630	3.546	3.465	3.312	3.170	3.037	2.914	2.855	2.798	2.690	2.589	2.494	2.404	2.362	2.320	2.166	1.849	1.605
5	4.853	4.713	4.646	4.580	4.452	4.330	4.212	3.993	3.791	3.605	3.433	3.352	3.274	3.127	2.991	2.864	2.745	2.689	2.635	2.436	2.035	1.737
6	5.795	5.601	5.508	5.417	5.242	5.076	4.917	4.623	4.355	4.111	3.889	3.784	3.685	3.498	3.326	3.167	3.020	2.951	2.885	2.643	2.168	1.824
7	6.728	6.472	6.349	6.230	6.002	5.786	5.582	5.206	4.868	4.564	4.288	4.160	4.039	3.812	3.605	3.416	3.242	3.161	3.083	2.802	2.263	1.883
8	7.652	7.325	7.170	7.020	6.733	6.463	6.210	5.747	5.335	4.968	4.639	4.487	4.344	4.078	3.837	3.619	3.421	3.329	3.241	2.925	2.331	1.922
9	8.566	8.162	7.971	7.786	7.435	7.108	6.802	6.247	5.759	5.328	4.946	4.772	4.607	4.303	4.031	3.786	3.566	3.463	3.366	3.019	2.379	1.948
10	9.471	8.983	8.752	8.530	8.111	7.722	7.360	6.710	6.145	5.650	5.216	5.019	4.833	4.494	4.192	3.923	3.682	3.571	3.465	3.092	2.414	1.965
11	10.368	9.787	9.514	9.253	8.760	8.306	7.887	7.139	6.495	5.938	5.453	5.234	5.029	4.656	4.327	4.035	3.776	3.656	3.544	3.147	2.438	1.977
12	11.255	10.575	10.258	9.954	9.385	8.863	8.384	7.536	6.814	6.194	5.660	5.421	5.197	4.793	4.439	4.127	3.851	3.725	3.606	3.190	2.456	1.985
13	12.134	11.348	10.983	10.635	9.986	9.394	8.853	7.904	7.103	6.424	5.842	5.583	5.342	4.910	4.533	4.203	3.912	3.780	3.656	3.223	2.468	1.990
14	13.004	12.106	11.691	11.296	10.563	9.899	9.295	8.244	7.367	6.628	6.002	5.724	5.468	5.008	4.611	4.265	3.962	3.824	3.695	3.249	2.478	1.993
15	13.865	12.849	12.381	11.938	11.118	10.380	9.712	8.559	7.606	6.811	6.142	5.847	5.576	5.092	4.676	4.315	4.001	3.859	3.726	3.268	2.484	1.995
16	14.718	13.578	13.055	12.561	11.652	10.838	10.106	8.851	7.824	6.974	6.265	5.954	5.668	5.162	4.730	4.357	4.033	3.887	3.751	3.283	2.488	1.997
17	15.562	14.292	13.712	13.166	12.166	11.274	10.477	9.122	8.022	7.120	6.373	6.047	5.749	5.222	4.775	4.391	4.059	3.910	3.771	3.295	2.492	1.998
18	16.398	14.992	14.353	13.754	12.659	11.690	10.828	9.372	8.201	7.250	6.467	6.128	5.818	5.273	4.812	4.419	4.080	3.928	3.786	3.304	2.494	1.999
19	17.226	15.678	14.979	14.324	13.134	12.085	11.158	9.604	8.365	7.366	6.550	6.198	5.878	5.316	4.844	4.442	4.097	3.942	3.799	3.311	2.496	1.999
20	18.046	16.351	15.589	14.877	13.590	12.462	11.470	9.818	8.514	7.469	6.623	6.259	5.929	5.353	4.870	4.460	4.110	3.954	3.808	3.316	2.497	1.999
21	18.857	17.011	16.185	15.415	14.029	12.821	11.764	10.017	8.649	7.562	6.687	6.312	5.973	5.384	4.891	4.476	4.121	3.963	3.816	3.320	2.498	2.000
22	19.660	17.658	16.765	15.937	14.451	13.163	12.042	10.201	8.772	7.645	6.743	6.359	6.011	5.410	4.909	4.488	4.130	3.970	3.822	3.323	2.498	2.000
23	20.456	18.292	17.332	16.444	14.857	13.489	12.303	10.371	8.883	7.718	6.792	6.399	6.044	5.432	4.924	4.499	4.137	3.976	3.827	3.325	2.499	2.000
24	21.243	18.914	17.885	16.936	15.247	13.799	12.550	10.529	8.985	7.784	6.835	6.434	6.073	5.451	4.937	4.507	4.143	3.981	3.831	3.327	2.499	2.000
25	22.023	19.523	18.424	17.413	15.622	14.094	12.783	10.675	9.077	7.843	6.873	6.464	6.097	5.467	4.948	4.514	4.147	3.985	3.834	3.329	2.499	2.000
26	22.795	20.121	18.951	17.877	15.983	14.375	13.003	10.810	9.161	7.896	6.906	6.491	6.118	5.480	4.956	4.520	4.151	3.988	3.837	3.330	2.500	2.000
27	23.560	20.707	19.464	18.327	16.330	14.643	13.211	10.935	9.237	7.943	6.935	6.514	6.136	5.492	4.964	4.524	4.154	3.990	3.839	3.331	2.500	2.000
28	24.316	21.281	19.965	18.764	16.663	14.898	13.406	11.051	9.307	7.984	6.961	6.534	6.152	5.502	4.970	4.528	4.157	3.992	3.840	3.331	2.500	2.000
29	25.066	21.844	20.454	19.188	16.984	15.141	13.591	11.158	9.370	8.022	6.983	6.551	6.166	5.510	4.975	4.531	4.159	3.994	3.841	3.332	2.500	2.000
30	25.808	22.396	20.930	19.600	17.292	15.372	13.765	11.258	9.427	8.055	7.003	6.566	6.177	5.517	4.979	4.534	4.160	3.995	3.842	3.332	2.500	2.000
40	32.835	27.355	25.103	23.115	19.793	17.159	15.046	11.925	9.779	8.244	7.105	6.642	6.234	5.548	4.997	4.544	4.166	3.999	3.846	3.333	2.500	2.000
50	39.196	31.424	28.362	25.730	21.482	18.256	15.762	12.233	9.915	8.304	7.133	6.660	6.246	5.554	4.999	4.545	4.167	4.000	3.846	3.333	2.500	2.000

SOURCE: Jerome Bracken and Charles J. Christenson, *Tables for Use in Analyzing Business Decisions* (Homewood, Ill.: Richard D. Irwin, Inc., 1965), except for the data on 2½%, the source for which is *Mathematical Tables from Handbook of Chemistry and Physics* (6th ed.; Cleveland: Chemical Rubber Publishing Co., 1938).

YEAR-END ACCUMULATIONS

Table C–3 shows the year-end accumulation at various effective annual interest rates[1] of $1 received in periodic installments during the year. Observe that fractional interest rates appear at the bottom of the table.

Each period's installment is assumed to be received at the *end* of the period. For example, the entries in the column for a one-half-year period show the accumulation one year from now of two $0.50 payments the first of which is received one-half-year from now, the second one year from now.

The entries in the column for a 0 period show the year-end accumulation of $1 received "continuously" during the year. More accurately, they show the limit approached by the accumulation of $1 received in periodic installments as the period between installments approaches 0.

Example. At 10 percent effective annual interest, $1 received in installments of $0.25 each at the end of each quarter of a year will accumulate to $1.037 at the end of the year.

---

[1] If a single payment of $1 accumulates in one year to $\$(1 + i)$, the "effective annual" rate of interest is i or $100i$ percent.

Table C–3. YEAR-END ACCUMULATION OF $1

Interest Rate	Period: 1 year	½ year	¼ year	1 month	1 week	1 day	0
.01	1.000	1.002	1.004	1.005	1.005	1.005	1.005
.02	1.000	1.005	1.007	1.009	1.010	1.010	1.010
.03	1.000	1.007	1.011	1.014	1.015	1.015	1.015
.04	1.000	1.010	1.015	1.018	1.019	1.020	1.020
.05	1.000	1.012	1.019	1.023	1.024	1.025	1.025
.06	1.000	1.015	1.022	1.027	1.029	1.030	1.030
.07	1.000	1.017	1.026	1.032	1.034	1.035	1.035
.08	1.000	1.020	1.030	1.036	1.039	1.039	1.039
.09	1.000	1.022	1.033	1.041	1.043	1.044	1.044
.10	1.000	1.024	1.037	1.045	1.048	1.049	1.049
.11	1.000	1.027	1.040	1.049	1.053	1.054	1.054
.12	1.000	1.029	1.044	1.054	1.058	1.059	1.059
.13	1.000	1.032	1.048	1.058	1.062	1.063	1.064
.14	1.000	1.034	1.051	1.063	1.067	1.068	1.068
.15	1.000	1.036	1.055	1.067	1.072	1.073	1.073
.16	1.000	1.039	1.058	1.071	1.076	1.078	1.078
.17	1.000	1.041	1.062	1.076	1.081	1.083	1.083
.18	1.000	1.043	1.065	1.080	1.086	1.087	1.088
.19	1.000	1.045	1.069	1.084	1.090	1.092	1.092
.20	1.000	1.048	1.072	1.089	1.095	1.097	1.097
.21	1.000	1.050	1.076	1.093	1.100	1.101	1.102
.22	1.000	1.052	1.079	1.097	1.104	1.106	1.106
.23	1.000	1.055	1.083	1.101	1.109	1.111	1.111
.24	1.000	1.057	1.086	1.106	1.113	1.115	1.116
.25	1.000	1.059	1.089	1.110	1.118	1.120	1.120
.26	1.000	1.061	1.093	1.114	1.122	1.125	1.125
.27	1.000	1.063	1.096	1.118	1.127	1.129	1.130
.28	1.000	1.066	1.100	1.123	1.132	1.134	1.134
.29	1.000	1.068	1.103	1.127	1.136	1.138	1.139
.30	1.000	1.070	1.106	1.131	1.141	1.143	1.143
.35	1.000	1.081	1.123	1.152	1.163	1.166	1.166
.40	1.000	1.092	1.140	1.172	1.185	1.188	1.189
.45	1.000	1.102	1.156	1.192	1.207	1.210	1.211
.50	1.000	1.112	1.172	1.212	1.228	1.232	1.233
.55	1.000	1.122	1.187	1.232	1.250	1.254	1.255
.60	1.000	1.132	1.203	1.252	1.271	1.276	1.277
.70	1.000	1.152	1.234	1.290	1.312	1.318	1.319
.80	1.000	1.171	1.263	1.328	1.353	1.360	1.361
.90	1.000	1.189	1.293	1.365	1.394	1.401	1.402
1.00	1.000	1.207	1.321	1.401	1.433	1.441	1.443
.0250	1.000	1.006	1.009	1.011	1.012	1.012	1.012
.0275	1.000	1.007	1.010	1.013	1.013	1.014	1.014
.0300	1.000	1.007	1.011	1.014	1.015	1.015	1.015
.0325	1.000	1.008	1.012	1.015	1.016	1.016	1.016
.0350	1.000	1.009	1.013	1.016	1.017	1.017	1.017
.0375	1.000	1.009	1.014	1.017	1.018	1.019	1.019
.0400	1.000	1.010	1.015	1.018	1.019	1.020	1.020
.0425	1.000	1.011	1.016	1.019	1.021	1.021	1.021
.0450	1.000	1.011	1.017	1.020	1.022	1.022	1.022
.0475	1.000	1.012	1.018	1.022	1.023	1.024	1.024
.0500	1.000	1.012	1.019	1.023	1.024	1.025	1.025
.0525	1.000	1.013	1.019	1.024	1.026	1.026	1.026
.0550	1.000	1.014	1.020	1.025	1.027	1.027	1.027
.0575	1.000	1.014	1.021	1.026	1.028	1.028	1.028
.0600	1.000	1.015	1.022	1.027	1.029	1.030	1.030

Index

Index of Cases

This book has been set in 10 and 9 point Bodoni Book, leaded 2 points. Part numbers and titles are in 24 and 18 point Bodoni No. 175; case titles are in 14 point Bodoni No. 275. The size of the type page is 27 x 46½ picas.

CANISIUS COLLEGE LIBRARY
HG173 .C39 1972 c. 1
Case problems in fin
3 5084 00082 4014

MAY 5 '78
MAR 1 '78
CANISIUS
PAID
AUG 1 0 1988
PAID